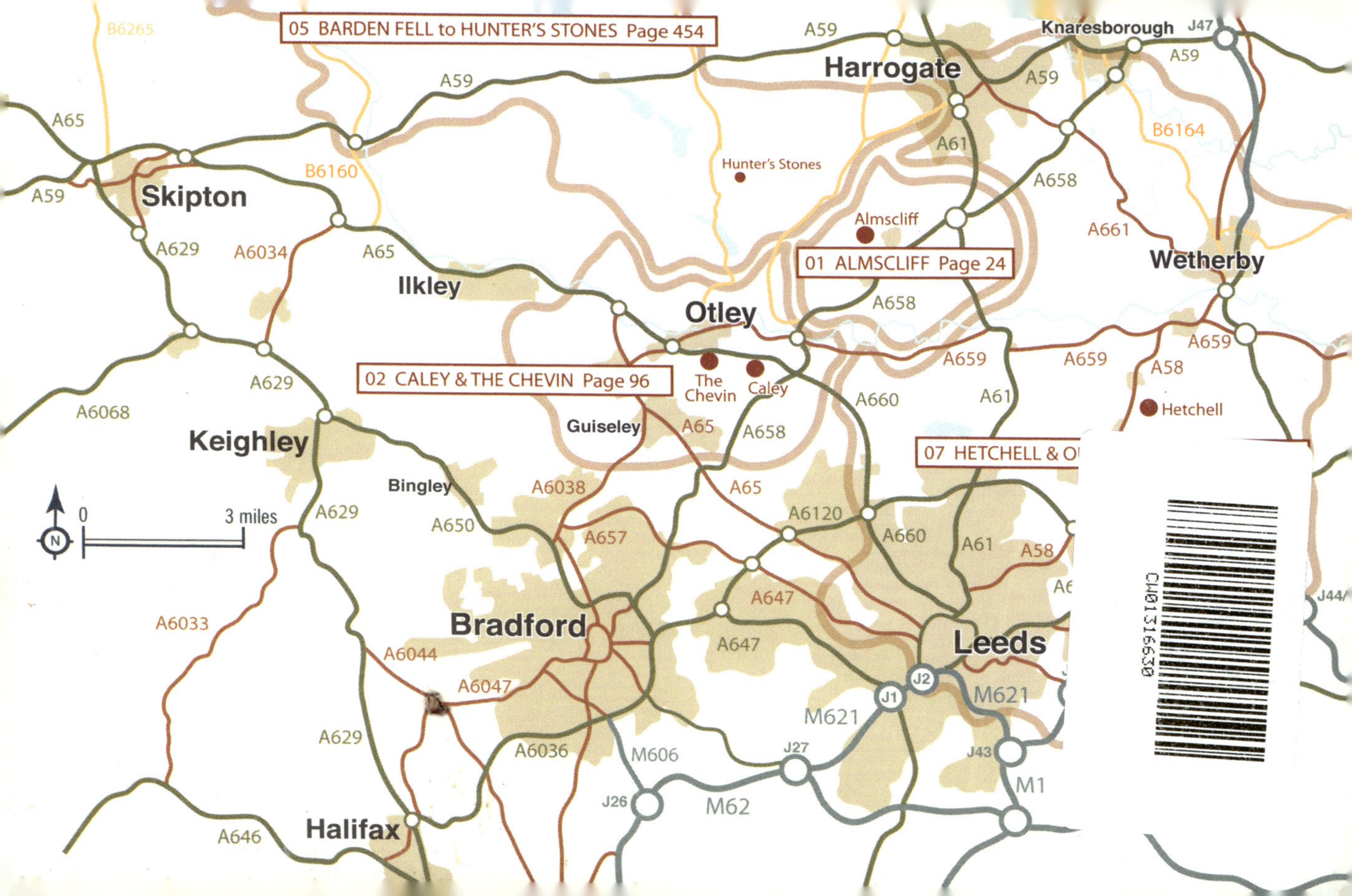
05 BARDEN FELL to HUNTER'S STONES Page 454
01 ALMSCLIFF Page 24
02 CALEY & THE CHEVIN Page 96
07 HETCHELL & O
Harrogate
Knaresborough
Wetherby
Skipton
Ilkley
Otley
Keighley
Guiseley
Bingley
Bradford
Leeds
Halifax
Hunter's Stones
Almscliff
The Chevin
Caley
Hetchell
A59
A65
A629
A6034
A6068
A6033
A646
A6044
A6047
A6036
A650
A6038
A657
A658
A660
A6120
A647
A61
A58
A659
A661
B6265
B6160
B6164
M621
M606
M62
M1
J47
J44
J43
J27
J26
J1
J2
0
3 miles
N

# Yorkshire Gritstone

## Volume 1
Almscliff to Slipstones
Yorkshire Mountaineering Club Definitive Climbing Guides

# Yorkshire Gritstone

## Volume 1: Almscliff to Slipstones

Copyright © 2012 Yorkshire Mountaineering Club, Robin Nicholson
Published by: Yorkshire Mountaineering Club (www.theymc.org.uk)
Distributed by: Cordee Ltd, Leicestershire (www.cordee.co.uk)


All rights reserved. No part of this work covered by the copyright herein may be reproduced or used in any form or by any means – graphic, electronic, or mechanised, including photocopying, recording, taping, or information storage and retrieval systems – without the written permission of the publisher.


First printed 2012
Designed and typeset by Robin Nicholson


ISBN 978-0-9515267-5-0

**Cover photo:** James Ibbertson on **The Wall of Horrors** (E3 6a) at Almscliff. Page 78. Photo: Mike Hutton.
Photo opposite: Evening light on Almscliff Crag

## Guidebook Disclaimer

This guidebook attempts to provide a definitive record of all existing climbs and is compiled by volunteers from a variety of sources. The inclusion of any route does not imply that it remains in the condition described. All climbers must rely on their own ability and experience to gauge the difficulty and seriousness of any climb.

Neither the Yorkshire Mountaineering Club nor the authors and editor of this guidebook accept any liability whatsoever for any injury or damage caused to climbers, third parties, or property arising from the use of it. While the content of the guidebook is believed to be accurate, no responsibility is accepted for any error, omission, or misstatement. Users must rely on their own judgement and are recommended to insure against injury to persons and property and third-party risks.

The Yorkshire Mountaineering Club endorses the British Mountaineering Council (BMC) participation statement that climbing, hillwalking and mountaineering are activities with a danger of personal injury or death. Participants in these activities should be aware of, and accept, these risks and be responsible for their own actions and involvement.

Produced by the Yorkshire Mountaineering Club.
Copyright © Yorkshire Mountaineering Club 2012

# Yorkshire Gritstone

**Volume 1**
Almscliff to Slipstones
Yorkshire Mountaineering Club Definitive Climbing Guides

**Editor: Robin Nicholson**
**With Adi Gill and Andy McCue**
Plus a team of guidebook volunteers

Some of the best of Brimham with Lover's Leap and Cracked Buttress in the foreground.
Photo: Robin Nicholson. Pilot: Ed Bishop

# Yorkshire Gritstone

**Volume 1**
Almscliff to Slipstones
Yorkshire Mountaineering Club Definitive Climbing Guides

Jim Davies on **Orchrist** (E5 6b) at Almscliff. Page 81
Photo: Adi Gill

# contents

| | |
|---|---|
| The Yorkshire Mountaineering Club | 8 |
| Previous Guidebooks | 9 |
| Introduction | 11 |
| Acknowledgements | 12 |
| Technical & Ethical Notes | 15 |
| Access & Conservation | 20 |
| **Mountain Rescue & First Aid** | **22** |
| Visitor's Information | 23 |
| **Chapter 1: Almscliff** | **24** |
| **Chapter 2: Caley and The Chevin** | **96** |
| Caley | 98 |
| The Chevin | 166 |
| **Chapter 3: Brimham & Outlying Crags** | **186** |
| Brimham | 190 |
| Hare's Head | 302 |
| Plantation Crack | 312 |
| Little Brimham | 318 |
| Bat Buttress | 328 |
| Crow Crag | 338 |
| **Chapter 4: Great Wolfrey to Eavestone** | **346** |
| **Great Wolfrey** | **350** |
| Wig Stones | 365 |
| Henstone Band | 366 |
| High Crag (Stump Cross) | 368 |
| **Hebden Gill** | **370** |
| Bolton Haw | 380 |
| Air Scar | 382 |
| **Guisecliff** | **384** |
| Nought Bank Boulders | 408 |
| Crocodile Crag | 412 |
| Panorama Crag | 414 |
| Whitehouses | 418 |
| **Eavestone** | **422** |
| Upper Huller Stones | 446 |
| Low Huller Stones | 449 |

**6**          **Yorkshire Gritstone**

| | | | |
|---|---|---|---|
| **Chapter 5: Barden Fell to Hunter's Stones** | **454** | Birk Gill | 596 |
| **Simon's Seat** | **459** | Roova | 600 |
| Hen Stones | 487 | **Sypeland** | **604** |
| **Lord's Seat** | **488** | Lulbeck | 619 |
| Earl's Seat | 502 | Ash Head | 620 |
| North Nab | 504 | Roundhill | 624 |
| **Brandrith** | **510** | Clint Crags | 631 |
| **Dovestones** | **518** | Arnagill | 633 |
| Cat Crags | 524 | | |
| Thruscross | 528 | **Chapter 7: Hetchell and Outlying Areas** | **636** |
| Snowden | 534 | **Hetchell** | **641** |
| Little Almscliff | 538 | Spofforth Pinnacles | 652 |
| Norwood Edge | 540 | Plompton Rocks | 660 |
| Hunter's Stones | 544 | Henry Price | 662 |
| Birk Crag (Harlow Carr) | 548 | Adel Crag | 664 |
| Calf Crag | 550 | Woolley Edge | 665 |
| | | | |
| **Chapter 6: The Slipstones Area** | **552** | History – Volume 1 | 667 |
| **Slipstones** | **556** | Graded List –the best routes and problems | 680 |
| **Brown Beck** | **586** | Index | 692 |

Almscliff to Slipstones

# the yorkshire mountaineering club

In 1941 a group of young lads from a grammar school in Wakefield got together to go hill walking and climbing on the local outcrops. They called themselves The Junior Mountaineering Club of Yorkshire. The membership expanded and eventually in the mid 1940s, a constitution was drafted and an Honorary Secretary appointed. Soon afterwards the first Honorary Treasurer was appointed, with the affairs of the Club being dealt with by the members in the absence of a President or a committee. In these early days there were many climbing expeditions to the Lake District, Wales and Scotland. Several visits to Rhum resulted in the production in 1946 of the JMCY climbing 'Guide to the Isle of Rhum'.

In 1951 climbing courses were held by the Leeds branch of the Central Council of Physical Recreation. Members of the JMYC agreed to be instructors, with the trainees being encouraged to join the Club. There followed a healthy increase in membership and at the 1952 AGM it was agreed that the Club should be renamed The Yorkshire Mountaineering Club. A President was appointed along with other Officers and a committee of five was elected. The rest, as they say, is history and many well-known and (even more) unsung club members have gone on to play an active role in the development of climbing and mountaineering in the UK, the Alps and further ranges.

In the 1960s the Club took on the role of publishing the definitive guidebooks for both Yorkshire Gritstone and Yorkshire Limestone and has continued with this commitment to the present day, producing guidebooks that have been well received and supported by the climbing community.

In 1972 the club purchased four derelict dwellings from a row of miners' cottages in Coniston in the Lake District. These were renovated by the members to become the Club's cottage. This has since given much enjoyment, not only to members but also to other clubs and organisations to whom it has been let out. In recent years the club has undertaken major refurbishment and extension works, which have resulted in a modern and well-equipped cottage.

The Club currently has a membership of around 200 and always welcomes new members who have an interest in climbing and mountain activities.

Laurie Morse, President   2012

**www.theymc.org.uk**

*The early pioneer, Charlie Salisbury, with YMC standard issue motorbike, sidecar and belayer.*

# the guidebook

## Previous Definitive Guidebooks

**1951**     **Kinder and Northern Area**
by Allan Allsop

**1957**     **West Yorkshire Area**
by Allan Allsop and Brian Evans

**1969**     **Yorkshire Gritstone (First Edition)**
by Mike Bebbington for the YMC

**1974**     **Yorkshire Gritstone (Re-print with addenda)**
by Mike Bebbington for the YMC

**1982**     **Yorkshire Gritstone (Second Edition)**
by Eddie Lesniak for the YMC

**1989**     **Yorkshire Gritstone (Third Edition)**
by Graham Desroy for the YMC

**1998**     **Yorkshire Gritstone (Fourth Edition)**
by Dave Musgrove for the YMC

**2012**     **Yorkshire Gritstone (Fifth Edition) Volume 1**
Almscliff to Slipstones: by Robin Nicholson for the YMC

*For a full guidebook bibliography all the way back to 'Climbing in the British Isles' by W P Haskett-Smith in 1894, visit the YMC website at www.theymc.org.uk.*

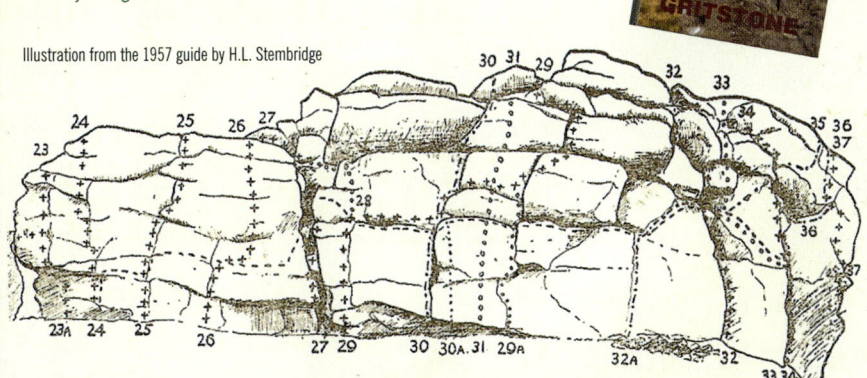

Illustration from the 1957 guide by H.L. Stembridge

S.W. FACE     ALMSCLIFF HIGH MAN     S. FACE

Robin Nicholson on **The Big Greeny** (E3 6a) at Almscliff. Page 70
Photo: Adi Gill

# introduction

I was born within a stone's throw of Caley, at a time when the Golden Age of Grit was well underway. Whilst mum was stoically refusing gas and air at Wharfedale General, the likes of Manson, Fawcett, Hammill and Syrett were pushing the climbing boundaries on my neighbouring crags.

With all these crags on my doorstep for the bulk of my formative years, I took Yorkshire Gritstone for granted. Like so many things in life, you have to leave it before you really appreciate what you had. Work took me away and thankfully brought me back again, to see the place and, more importantly, the climbing for what it is: world class.

At a chance meeting with Dave Musgrove the possibility of a new guide was discussed. It wasn't remotely on my radar at the time, but by the close of the night I had signed up. Apparently that happens a lot. He's a very persuasive man.

Taking on a guidebook to Yorkshire Gritstone has been like moving in with a friend you've known for years. Only when you live in each other's pockets for a while do you realise that you didn't really know them at all, you were only scratching the surface. Spending so much time immersed in this vast local universe of Gritstone I've found more depth and breadth to the climbing and the crags here than I ever would have imagined. There's treasure hidden in plain sight at the big hitters like Almscliff and Brimham, but elsewhere classic gems are liberally scattered that few folk know of. Once let into these secrets, you'll hold the knowledge like so many precious stones.

The decision to split the guide into two volumes was easy; Dave mentioned the heft of the last guide nearly forced them to do the same. This time it was inevitable with over 1000 new routes, a serious effort to cover bouldering and the desire to create a modern guide with photo topos and abundant action shots. The tough call was how to make the split. We wanted an equal division of major crags, number of routes and problems across the two guides and I think we got the cut about right. It won't be to everyone's taste but that's life. My wife loves Marmite and I hate it. Go figure.

Whatever's your bag, there's something for everyone in the pages that follow. From classic outcrops and remote moorland gems to the quick-hit roadside quarries. For the crack connoisseur, the slab master or the cutting-edge exploratory extreme leader or boulderer, to families and those just starting out on their journey through the Yorkshire Gritstone school of hard knocks.

It's been a privilege to be involved with the development of this, the first volume, covering the north-eastern patch of Yorkshire Gritstone. The making of it has taken me to crags I'd never been to before and areas I'd been to many times but with people I didn't know 3 years ago and whom I now call close friends. It has taught me to love the previously overlooked and be inspired to tackle routes and problems I'd only dreamed of before, particularly where I now know the climber behind the climb.

The many experiences of crags, climbs and climbers are already fond memories, a rich reward for working on this guide. I remember Ibbo's tireless metronomic climbing up and down *The Wall of Horrors* to get the cover shot, whilst we tried to pull Hutton a bit further out of the crag-face on a static line; both Sutty and Adi's infinite enthusiasm for the grit as they punched out yet another hard-extreme in 25°C summer heat; then Connors, the crag barista, blowing all our excuses out of the water as he spanked us on Brimham's *Pair in a Cubicle* - his first problem back after smashing his collar bone; that time Boggy ran to the top of the crag and stuck his leg over the top for me to grab after I'd punched above my weight on a highball; some last minute guidebook checking at The 'Cliff with Dibnah, two days before the birth of my son. As the sun went down on that winter's evening, the book was put back in the sack and we simply climbed; routes and problems so familiar, each hold remembers a thousand handshakes, old friends indeed.

I really hope this guide does the same for you. Takes you to a crag you never knew before or lets you see a place you know well with fresh eyes. To renew old friendships and make new ones, with both climb and climber.

Robin Nicholson, 2012

# acknowledgements

This guidebook was produced by a team of volunteers, over 120 strong at the last count, who added their voices to the hundreds that went before them in producing the rich tapestry within these pages and ensuring Yorkshire Gritstone definitive guidebooks live on. A huge thank you to all of them.

At the centre was a reliable engine room that kept this behemoth moving once the initial excitement of a new guide had died down and ensured the output stayed true to the old and embraced the new. This comprised the YMC Guidebook Steering Committee and the Guidebook Coordination Team. Heroes one and all.

### YMC Guidebook Steering Committee
Laurie Morse, Mike Bebbington, Alan Swithenbank, Dave Musgrove, Nigel Baker, Alexandra Homayoonpoor, Robin Nicholson, Andy McCue, Adi Gill.

### Guidebook Coordination Team
Robin Nicholson, Adi Gill, Andy McCue, Matt Troilett, Richard Connors, Stuart Lancaster. Special thanks go to the partners and families of this team for all their support: Debbie, Ethan, Shell, Lily, Arifa, Lisa, Archie, Jake, Liliya, Emma, Isabel, Louis.

### Crag Authors and all those that supported the development of the guidebook
Nigel Baker, Tony Barley, Pete Brown, Stuart Brown, Kim Buck, Will Buck, Jordan Buys, Naomi Buys, Simon Caldwell, Steve Clark, Paul Clarke, Jack Colbeck, Richard Connors, Dave Cowl, Jim Croft, Andy Crome, Jim Davies, John Dunne, Steve Dunning, Adi Gill, Adrian Hatherall, Martin Hobson, Sam Hobson, Robert Fenton, Fran Holland, John Hunt, Rachel Hunt, Will Hunt, James Ibbertson, Jenny Ibbertson, Joe Killick, Simon Kimber, Matt Kilner, Stuart Lancaster, Richard Mallinson, Al Manson, Anthony Matthews, Andy McCue, Neil McCallum, Dave Musgrove, Andrew Nicholson, Debbie Nicholson, Pauline Nicholson, Robin Nicholson, Phillipe Osborne, Tom Peckitt, Jerry Peel, Ryan Plews, Nigel Poustie, Mark Radtke, Lynn Robinson, Anna Shepherd, Chris Sowden, Emma Spink, Andy Swann, Dave Sutcliffe, Malcolm Townsley, John Wainwright, Robin Warden, Andy Wild, Bruce Woodley (and his impressive Guisecliff sketches).

### Photographers
We wanted to really go for it with the photography in this guide and have been blown away by the support from the pros and the wider climbing community. Thanks go to all those who took the time to send something in. Two folk deserve special mention. Mike Hutton (**www.mikehuttonphotography.com**) who organised dozens of crag photo-shoots for this guide, producing amazing photos, often in difficult conditions. Thanks for your awesome support Mike, you're a legend. Secondly, Ed Bishop (**www.ehbconsultancy.com**), pilot of his hand-built Sport Cruiser aircraft who generously took Robin up to the skies to photograph the crags we love from a seldom-seen view.

To all the following photographers, thank you:
Kev Avery, J. Bannister, Mike Bebbington, Marie Blake, Kim Buck, Kate Campbell, Pete Campbell, Pete Chadwick, Paul Clarke, Paul Clough, Jack Colbeck, Adam Collinge, Dave Cowl, Mark Credie, Steve Crowe, Micheal Daglish, Graham Derbyshire, Steve Dunning, Dave Gater, Adi Gill, Michelle Gill, Tim Glasby, Claire Graham, Dennis Gray, Niall Grimes, Mike Hammill, John Harwood, Alan Hinkes, Fran Holland, John Hunt, Kate Johnson, Matt Kilner, Joe Killick, Simon Kimber, Stuart Lancaster, Jude Lane, Alastair Lee, Stu Littlefair, Adam Long, Al Manson, Andy McCue, Alex Messenger, Jamie Moss, Dave Musgrove, Bernard Newman, Richard Nolan, David Ogden, Simon Panton, Becky Payne, Jon Pearson, Tom Peckitt, Jerry Peel, James Perry, Nigel Poustie, Jonathan Read, James Rowe, Keith Sharples, Dave Simmonite, Dalvinda Sodhi, Neil Stabbs, Gordon Stainforth, John Stainforth, Faye Stevens, Rob Stone, Dave Sutcliffe, Charlotte Telfer, Pippa Whitehouse. A massive thank you goes to Adi Gill for coordinating all the photo submissions.

### Proofreading
In addition to the crag authors, a core team of committed proofreaders have diligently checked and rechecked the guidebook. These include Adi Gill, Andy McCue, Richard Connors, Dave Musgrove, Niall Grimes, John Horscroft

and Mick Johnson. Steve Clark and Lynn Robinson have been the proofreading bedrock that many a BMC guidebook has been built on and we are so glad they turned their big checking guns on Yorkshire as this guide is all the better for it, particularly in terms of grade accuracy. Thanks to you both for all your support.

## ...and Others
A thank you goes to Mick Johnson (current BMC Yorkshire Gritstone Access Rep) and all those who have been involved in securing and maintaining access for climbers to the crags within this guide. Dave Musgrove has once again delivered when it comes to the climbing history of the area. Not an easy task when it involved splitting the 1998 history to account for the two volumes. A job well done. Steve Dunning and Ryan Plews of Total Climbing (**www.total-climbing.com**) have provided awesome support to the whole team in the development of the bouldering sections of this guide as has Jon Pearson and the super resource that is **www.yorkshiregrit.com**.

## Those involved in the Essays and Interviews
Allan Austin, Ben Bransby, Libby Brennan, Steve Dunning, Tom Greenwood, Mike Hammill, John Harwood, Alan Hinkes, Al Manson, Ben Moon, Dave Musgrove, Jim Perrin, Andi Turner, Ken Wood. Thanks go to Andy McCue who transcribed and edited the abundance of information that came in on the people that shaped this grit scene over the years.

Finally, this great climbing nation and specifically the climbing guidebook community owe a debt of gratitude to the legend that is Niall Grimes of the BMC. This guidebook is no exception. Grimer took the production and content of guidebooks to another level and this team can't thank him enough for his generosity of spirit, enthusiasm and advice throughout the development of this guide.

Apologies to anyone we've missed off this list.
**The YMC and Guidebook Coordination Team**

## Personal Thanks
From Adi Gill: Even with all the fantastic images provided by the photographers we still had important gaps to fill so I'd like to thank a core of guinea pigs who were prepared to be thrown on anything to get the vital shots; cheers to Dave, Richard, Jim, Neil and Andy. None of my involvement could have took place without the support of my wife Michelle and daughter Lily so my biggest thanks go to you both.

From Andy McCue: Thanks to Adi, Mike, Rich, James, Matt and everyone else who volunteered invaluable time and effort. A special thank you to my wife Arifa for her support, patience and endless cups of tea. Right, a bit of limestone anyone?...

From Robin Nicholson: I would like to acknowledge the support of Dave and Nigel for championing this new guide. To Laurie, Mike, Swiv and the YMC for the unequivocal support they have shown the team. Especial gratitude must go to Adi for all his hard work, his drive for accuracy and energy to go the extra mile; to Andy for his invaluable support and calm voice of reason throughout; to Richard for his craftsmanship on many a script and problem-solving skills when I was floundering; to Matt for his enthusiasm for the guide and cracking on with Volume 2 whilst we tried to get this one out. Finally to the kindness and patience of my wife Debbie, my son Ethan and my Lord Jesus, without whom this would not have been possible.

Ed Bishop (www.ehbconsultancy.com) and his Sport Cruiser.
Photo: Robin Nicholson

Dave Sutcliffe on his final hard addition to this volume, **The Climb The Time Forgot** (E8 6c) at Guisecliff, Page 392
Photo: Adi Gill

# technical / ethical notes

This is a climbing guidebook covering routes and boulder problems. On the photo topos and text descriptions, the routes are identified with a blue number and the boulder problems, a red one. Traverses (both for routes and problems) are given a yellow line on the photo topo.

## Ethics
**Protect the rock**. Let this be your mantra.

Despite its rough outer texture, most gritstone is covered with a relatively thin outer skin which can easily be worn through to softer rock below. Rapid erosion of the rock occurs after this point. If top roping is done to excess it can cause damage to the rock and be an inconvenience to other climbers who wish to lead the route. If you are doing it please be considerate. Use a rope protector, or equivalent, at the top of the crag.

Do not use a wire brush. Do not chip the rock or alter its appearance in any way. Avoid excessive cleaning and the interference with trees, flora and fauna at the crag.

Natural gritstone is not the place to find bolts and the placing of any is tantamount to treason. Some pegs and threads may be found on quarried grit, many left over from the 1950s and 60s when the routes were climbed by aid techniques or where modern gear can now protect. The reliability of in-situ protection can not be assured and must be treated with extreme caution.

The rapid rise in the popularity of bouldering has had, in some cases, a negative impact on the rock at several well-known venues. As a boulderer there are several measures you can take to limit the impact you have on the rock and the environment. Use a bouldering mat, this not only protects you in a fall but also limits the damage to the ground at the base of a problem. Keep the use of chalk to a minimum and consider chalkballs over loose chalk. Tick marks of chalk are unsightly so avoid using them and rely on your memory. Do not use resin. Cleaning problems, especially established ones, is unnecessary; if there is excess chalk remove it with no more than a whack with a rag. The use of blow torches or chemicals on the rock is utter lunacy and can only be described as mindless vandalism of a precious resource. If a problem is dirty then only use a soft brush, and finally before you climb clean your footwear to prevent erosion of the rock.

## Route Notes
The long-running stance on how a route should be climbed in the best style is known as 'onsight'. This means to lead or solo the climb without any falls and without prior knowledge of any of its specific attributes. Pre-practise of a route via top-rope is common for hard routes but consideration should be given to erosion if this method is employed.

## Grades
The British grading system is used in this guide, which consists of an adjective and a technical grade. Firstly it begins with an adjective grade, which takes into account what makes up the route's overall difficulty and includes factors such as seriousness, strenuousness, quality of rock and general level of difficulty. All this is on the assumption that the route is led from bottom to top with the climber having a sufficient rack of equipment to complete the task.

The **adjective grade** runs in the following order: Easy, Moderate (M), Difficult (D), Hard Difficult (HD), Very Difficult (VD), Hard Very Difficult (HVD), Severe (S), Hard Severe (HS), Mild Very Severe (MVS), Very Severe (VS), Hard Very Severe (HVS) and Extremely Severe (E). The Extremely Severe category is then sub-divided into E1, E2, E3, E4, etc.

The **technical part** of the grade gives the climber an indication of how hard the most difficult move on the route will be and runs as follows 2a, 2b, 2c, 3a, 3b, 3c, 4a, 4b, 4c, 5a, 5b, 5c, 6a, 6b, 6c, 7a, 7b...

## Symbols and Stars
Most of the routes in this guide have seen many ascents. Some venues, however, may have climbs that have not been repeated or sufficiently checked by the writer. In this case a dagger symbol (†) is added after the grade. This may also mean there is some doubt over a certain aspect of the route (e.g. exact line) but it is not intended to cast doubt over the first ascent.

# INTRODUCTION - Climbing Notes

The first ascentionists / date are added beneath each climb. Where a particular route or problem has some specific further information regarding its ascent or history there is a diamond symbol (◆) at the end. This information is at the back of each crag section.

| Route Grade - Comparison Chart |||||||
|---|---|---|---|---|---|
| UK Adj. | UK Tech. | French | US | Aus. | UIAA |
| M |  | F½ | 5.2 | 10 | I |
| D |  | F1 | 5.3 | 11 | II |
| VD | 3c | F2 | 5.4 | 12 | III |
| S | 4a | F3 | 5.5 | 13 | IV |
| HS | 4b | F4 | 5.6 | 14 | IV+ |
| VS | 4c | F4+ | 5.7 | 15 | V- |
|  |  | F5 | 5.8 | 16 | V |
| HVS | 5a | F5+ | 5.9 | 17 | V+ / VI- |
|  | 5b | F6a | 5.10a | 18 | VI |
| E1 |  | F6a+ | 5.10b | 19 | VI+ |
| E2 |  | F6b | 5.10c | 20 | VII- |
|  | 5c |  | 5.10d |  | VII |
| E3 |  | F6b+ | 5.11a | 21 | VII+ |
|  |  | F6c | 5.11b | 22 |  |
| E4 | 6a | F6c+ | 5.11c | 23 | VIII- |
|  |  | F7a | 5.11d |  | VIII |
| E5 |  | F7a+ | 5.12a | 24 | VIII+ |
|  | 6b | F7b | 5.12b | 25 | IX- |
| E6 |  | F7b+ | 5.12c | 26 |  |
|  |  | F7c | 5.12d | 27 | IX |
| E7 | 6c | F7c+ | 5.13a | 28 | IX+ |
|  |  | F8a | 5.13b | 29 | X- |
| E8 |  | F8a+ | 5.13c | 30 | X |
|  |  | F8b | 5.13d | 31 |  |
| E9 |  | F8b+ | 5.14a | 32 | X+ |
|  |  | F8c | 5.14b | 33 |  |
| E10 | 7a | F8c+ | 5.14c | 34 | XI- |
|  |  | F9a | 5.14d | 35 | XI |

Almost every single route contained in this guidebook is of a high quality. To differentiate between their specific brilliance the star system has been employed. As a general rule one star (★), being of a high quality to that crag, two star (★★), amongst the best in Yorkshire, and three star (★★★), of national significance. This system has its flaws and you can have a rewarding or horrendous experience on any route. Don't just look at the stars though; check out the descriptions as they'll often give more helpful information to the true nature and worth of the climb. A 'best of' selective graded list for routes has been added at the back of this guide.

A handful of crags have high quality routes yet the crag aspect, foliage and the lack of traffic on the climbs leave some in a perennially sorry state. In an attempt to both (a) retain the star status and (b) not betray the climber into thinking they'll be able to rock up to the crag and simply attempt a ground-up ascent of the route without (most likely) prior abseil and cleaning, a hollow star system (☆) has been adopted. The application of this is certainly an art and not a science, and any route can be dirty or out of condition, but hopefully it will save some disappointment, particularly at major crags like Guisecliff and Eavestone. Don't forget - these are high quality routes; just expect to apply some (sympathetic) TLC before climbing.

Finally, a full list of climbs (including boulder problems) in grade order feature at the end of each crag section.

## New Routes
The recording of new routes on Yorkshire Gritstone can be made at **www.leedswall.com/newroutes**.

## Climber Interviews and Essays
Profiles can be found throughout this guide on many of the individuals that shaped the climbing scene in this neck of the Yorkshire Grit woods. Notes on their training, influences, achievements are recorded along with a humourous tale or two. We hope you enjoy them and, maybe, are even inspired by them. Spare a thought for some of these stars when you're on one of their classic routes when no doubt they were running it out with runners made from stripped down engine parts and footwear more appropriate for Morris dancing.

Adi Gill feeling a tad run-out on **Love Bug** (E1 5b) at Brimham. Page 261.
Photo: Mike Hutton

# INTRODUCTION - Climbing Notes

## Bouldering Notes
### Grades
The method for grading boulder problems is the French Fontainbleau system rather than the American V system due to its accuracy in the 6a to 7a region, its flexibility in the lower grades down to Font 1 and to bring it in line with the equivalent British technical grades. The Font system runs as follows.... 1, 1+, 2, 2+, 3, 3+, 4, 4+, 5, 5+, 6a, 6a+, 6b, 6b+, 6c, 6c+, 7a, 7a+, 7b, 7b+, 7c, 7c+, 8a, 8a+, 8b, 8b+. The only exception to this is the traversing wall at Henry Price at Leeds University (Page 662) where French sport grades have been used.

### Bouldering Grades - Comparison Chart

| Font Grade | V Grade | UK Tech. Grade |
|---|---|---|
| 1 | | 3a |
| 1+ | | |
| 2 | | 3b |
| 2+ | | 3c |
| 3 | | 4a |
| 3+ | | 4b |
| 4 | V0- | 4c |
| 4+ | V0 | 5a |
| 5 | V0+ | 5b |
| 5+ | V1 | 5c |
| 6a | V2 | 6a |
| 6a+ | | |
| 6b | V3 | |
| 6b+ | V4 | |
| 6c | | 6b |
| 6c+ | V5 | |
| 7a | V6 | |
| 7a+ | V7 | |
| 7b | V8 | 6c |
| 7b+ | | |
| 7c | V9 | |
| 7c+ | V10 | |
| 8a | V11 | 7a |
| 8a+ | V12 | |
| 8b | V13 | |
| 8b+ | V14 | 7b |

### Highball Problems / Sit-down Starts
The foggy area of when a boulder problem becomes a route is known as a highball and this is identified by the equivalent route grade in brackets appearing adjacent to the Font grade. Apply some nouse though; you can get hurt on any problem. For problems with sit-down starts, although mentioned in the description text, the numbered circle for a problem will be shown at the very bottom of the topo line.

### Names and Stars
Many problems that previously were only known by numbers, e.g. Problem 1, or unnamed, have been given names by the guidebook team to improve usability for the reader. These names are to help identify the problems and are in no way an attempt to 'claim' these well-trodden lines. It saves having hundreds of unnamed problems listed in the graded list too. Due to the subjective nature of quality, stars have not been used for boulder problems. Look to the description to discern how good a problem is (or the crag introduction). A 'best of' graded list for problems has been added at the back of this guide which may (or may not!) help.

### Bouldering Circuits
A great way to get the most out of a visit to a crag is to follow a circuit of problems. It is something most of us do anyway but we've provided a helping hand with the inclusion of several circuits designed to test your mettle, reveal the quality and explore the overlooked. The major crags of Almscliff, Brimham and Caley have circuits along with the more remote Sypeland and Great Wolfrey.

### www.yorkshiregrit.com
Yorkshiregrit.com is a great resource for bouldering information on all Yorkshire crags. Problem descriptions, topos, grade debates, photo and video footage of many problems - all can be found here. Keen activists use the site and there's handy beta information to be had. It's home to the details of many new problems too. Check it out.

James Hetherington on Joker's Reach at Brimham, Page 290
Photo: Dave Simmonite

# access / conservation

The inclusion of a crag in this guidebook does not mean that any member of the public has a right to climb on it. Before climbing on any crag, refer to the access notes and maps within the crag introductions.

Some of the crags are on open access land and are covered by the Countryside Rights of Way Act (CRoW); some are on private land and others have seasonal access restrictions.

**General restrictions that apply to several crags:**
An access agreement has been established by the BMC with the estate office for **Upper and Low Huller Stones, Sypeland, Cat Crag, Dovestones and Brandrith**. The agreement states that 'climbers, walkers and members of the public are to avoid these crags from the 15th March to the 30th June. No dogs are allowed and smoking is not permitted. Observe closure notices under the CRoW Act'. There is not a legal requirement to abide by this agreement but please play your part and respect it.

**Grouse Moorland**
Several crags lie on grouse moorland. See the crag introductions for specific restrictions but as a general rule: avoid disturbance to ground-nesting birds (see below); abide by moorland closures during the shooting season. Leave dogs at home. No smoking / fires.

**Birds**
The Wildlife and Countryside Act 1981 is the primary legislation which protects birds in the UK. Harsh fines and potential imprisonment await those who cause disturbance to birds, nests or eggs. Bird restrictions apply to crags in this guide (e.g. Peregrines at Guisecliff, Tawny Owls at The Chevin). Please adhere to these. Ground-nesting birds are prevalent at many venues so keep to established paths to avoid their disturbance, especially during the nesting season which runs from March to June.

**Dogs**
Man's best friend should be kept under control at all times. They can worry livestock and disturb wildlife. Respect any notices to keep them on the lead especially at nesting and lambing time.

**Fire Risk**
During periods of drought, tinder-dry moorland is at an elevated risk of fire. In recent years this has even forced closure, so respect the landowner's wishes. Be especially careful with smoking materials to ensure they're fully extinguished and avoid campfires and disposable barbecues at all cost. If you discover a fire that is clearly not heather burning by the gamekeepers, call the fire service on 999.

**Chapter One - Almscliff**
Don't climb on the 'trouser' boulder in the field below the crag.

**Chapter Three - Brimham and Outlying Crags**
**Brimham Rocks**: The Fag Slab area has a bird ban certain times of the year (signs in place).
**Bat Buttress:** Private land. You must ask permission from the owner of Grapha House (Maud's Farm) before climbing. Always approach the crag from the main Brimham road, via the farm, and never enter the crag across the walls from the Nidderdale Way path on National Trust Land.
**Plantation Crack:** Permission needs to be sought in advance from Mr Stuart Barrett at Braisty Woods Farm (Tel: 01423 780100) in order to avoid conflict with other sporting interests, particularly shooting.

**Chapter Four - Great Wolfrey to Eavestone**
**Panorama Crag:** The eastern section is banned.
**Eavestone:** This privately owned woodland is used for fishing in the lower lake and the breeding of game birds. No issues have been encountered and the BMC Access Rep has been unable to identify the landowner but please be polite and move on if asked to do so.
**Guisecliff:** This crag is on the border of open access land. Avoid Buttress Three to Five from the 1st March to 30th June as Peregrines nest at the crag.

**Chapter Five - Barden Fell to Hunter's Stones**
**Barden Fell** (Simon's Seat, Lord's Seat, Hen Stones, Earl's Seat, North Nab): The land is part of the Duke of Devonshire's estate and is a working grouse moor. The access information boards at the entrance to the moors give shooting closure dates and these dates can also be

found by contacting the estate office on 01756 718009 or by checking the website **www.boltonabbey.com**.

### Chapter Six - Slipstones Area
All crags lie within grouse moorland so the usual restrictions apply. **Birk Gill** is a Site of Special Scientific Interest (SSSI) so approach via established paths and minimise disturbance to flora and fauna.

### Chapter Seven - Hetchell and Outlying Areas
**Spofforth:** All the boulders are situated on private farm land and access issues have been reported in the past. Cow Block and the Hell Hole Block lie on the grounds of the farm itself, are currently surrounded by electric fences, and should be considered out of bounds for the time being.
**Plompton:** Strictly no climbing. Private land. Climbing is actively discouraged by the landowners.

### Access Difficulties
Please adhere to the information outlined within each chapter regarding access in order for climbing to continue. If problems are encountered they can be reported to the local BMC access rep for Yorkshire Gritstone (see the web: **www.thebmc.co.uk/list-of-bmc-access-reps**). Alternatively, contact the BMC office on 0161 4456111. The BMC's website is a good place generally to get the most up to date information particularly if access is sensitive. The Regional Access Database (RAD) can be found at **www.thebmc.co.uk/rad.**

### Litter / Hygiene
Anything you bring to the crag, including organic matter, should return with you and not be left for others to discover. By bringing a plastic bag with you for litter collection you can do your bit and actively help to keep our crags pristine. Please don't leave any trace of your visit to the crag. Go to the toilet prior to your visit.

### GPS Coordinates
In the access notes in each crag introduction, the parking (not crag) latitude and longitude coordinates are given in bold. These can used in GPS satellite navigation systems.

**Adi Gill**

## BMC CRAG CODE
www.thebmc.co.uk

| | | | |
|---|---|---|---|
| **Access** | Check the Regional Access Database (RAD) on www.thebmc.co.uk for the latest access information | **Wildlife** | Do not disturb livestock, wildlife or cliff vegetation; respect seasonal bird nesting restrictions |
| **Parking** | Park carefully – avoid gateways and driveways | **Dogs** | Keep dogs under control at all times; don't let your dog chase sheep or disturb wildlife |
| **Footpaths** | Keep to established paths – leave gates as you find them | **Litter** | 'Leave no trace' – take all litter home with you |
| **Risk** | Climbing can be dangerous – accept the risks and be aware of other people around you | **Toilets** | Don't make a mess – bury your waste |
| **Respect** | Groups and individuals – respect the rock, local climbing ethics and other people | **Economy** | Do everything you can to support the rural economy – shop locally |

**BMC Participation Statement** — Climbing, hill walking and mountaineering are activities with a danger of personal injury or death. Participants in these activities should be aware of and accept these risks and be responsible for their own actions and involvement.

# mountain rescue / first aid

**Dial 999** and ask for:

## Police - Mountain Rescue

Stay calm and be ready to give a **CHALET** report:

**C**asualties – number, names (and, if possible, age); type of injuries, for example, lower leg, head injury, collapse, drowning etc.

**H**azards to the rescuers – for example, strong winds, avalanche, rock fall, dangerous animals.

**A**ccess – the name of area and description of the terrain. It may be appropriate to describe the approach and any distinguishing features such as an orange survival bag. Information on the weather conditions at the incident site is useful, particularly if you are in cloud or mist.

**L**ocation of the incident – a grid reference and a description is ideal. Don't forget to give the map sheet number and please say if the grid reference is from a GPS device.

**E**quipment at the scene – for example, torches, other mobile phones, group shelters, medical personnel.

**T**ype of incident – mountain, cave etc. Be prepared to give a brief description of the time and apparent cause of the incident.

**Each crag within this guide has the OS Grid Reference given at the start of the crag section.**

For over 60 years **The Upper Wharfedale Fell Rescue Association (UWFRA)** has been rescuing people and animals from the caves, mineshafts, fells and crags of Wharfedale, Nidderdale, Littondale and Mid-Airedale. Their rescue services remain free to all who need them, day or night and are financed entirely by fundraising events and donations. Donations can be made to this magnificent service at: **www.justgiving.com/uwfra**

## First Aid In Case Of Accident

1. If **spinal injuries** or **head injuries** are suspected **do not move the patient** without skilled help, except to maintain breathing and circulation.

2. **If breathing has stopped**, clear airways and commence **CPR** (cardio-pulmonary resuscitation). Do not stop until expert opinion diagnoses death.

3. **Stop bleeding** by applying direct pressure.

4. **Summon help**.

These are the basic principles of first aid. If you climb at all regularly, you should seriously consider taking a first aid course.

The **Yorkshire Air Ambulance** is an independent charity providing a life-saving rapid response emergency service to 5 million people across Yorkshire, including climbers. They fly 7 days a week, 365 days a year and need to raise £7200 per day *(in 2012)* to keep both of the helicopters maintained and in the air. Donations can be made at:
**www.yorkshireairambulance.org.uk/donate**

### A Note on Helmets

In 2012 the BMC launched a campaign and booklet to raise awareness about climbing helmets (**www.thebmc.co.uk/bmc-helmet-campaign**):

*'For more than 30 years, the BMC has studied helmets and their performance. This booklet is the distillation of that knowledge. If you are choosing a helmet, it will help you to select from the many that are now available. You'll find advice on care and maintenance, and guidance on when to retire your helmet. It contains information about how helmets work, and a brief history of climbing helmets. Finally there is a summary of helmet standards, and where to get further information'.* The BMC.

Head injuries are still common in climbing. Read the booklet, get the facts and make your choice.

# visitor's / useful information

## Accommodation
The excellent website www.yorkshirenet.co.uk has a list of all accommodation options from hotels through to camp-sites. In addition to those sites mentioned on the above website many camp-sites can be found at www.ukcampsite.co.uk and the www.yha.org.uk site has details of the nearest youth hostels to the region.

## Public Transport
The www.yorkshirenet.co.uk website has details of all the public transport links including the dales bus and the Nidderdale link.

## Public Houses and Cafés
There's nothing better after a climb than a post match analysis of your triumphant day on the rock, and where better to do it than at one of the following expertly selected public houses. There's too many to mention really, but we'll have a go: **Chapter 1 Almscliff:** *The Hunter's Inn*, Leathley, LS21 2PS, 0113 284 1090. **Chapter 2 Caley, The Chevin:** *The Old Cock*, 11-13 Crossgate, Otley LS21 1AA, 01943 464424. *The Junction Inn*, 44 Bondgate, Otley, LS21 1AD, 01943 463233. Otley is spoilt for choice with its 17 watering holes. Amongst them, *The Horse and Farrier* and *The Fleece* are worthy of inspection. **Chapter 3 Brimham:** *The Wellington Inn*, Darley, HQ3 2QQ, 01423 780362. **Chapter 4 Pateley Area:** *The Crown Hotel*, Lofthouse, 01423 755206. *The Crown Hotel*, Middlesmoor, 01423 755204. *The Bridge Inn* (next to the old watermill), Pateley Bridge, 01423 711484. **Chapter 5 Barden Fell to Hunter's Stones:** *Craven Arms*, Appletreewick, 01756 720270. *Stonehouse Inn*, Thruscross, 01943 880325. **Chapter 6 Slipstones Area**: *The Black Swan*, Fearby, 01765 689477. *Thwaite Arms*, Horsehouse, Coverdale, DL8 4TS, 01969 640206. **Chapter 7 Hetchell:** *The Duke of Wellington* or the *Old Star* (East Keswick); *New Inn* in Scarcroft or *The Half Moon*, Collingham.

There are many great cafés to visit but the following are crackers. *Dunnie's Café*, Otley, is to cycling what Pete's Eats is to climbing so you're guaranteed to get a good belly full with a pint of tea. To the north of the region, *Wildings Tea Rooms*, Pateley Bridge, is a good call - especially for cake. If you prefer to snack at the crag then Brimham Rocks has its own shack selling hot brews, cakes and ice creams.

## Outdoor Shops
*Chevin Trek*, Gay Lane, Otley, is the port of call for the south of the region and *Sypeland Outdoors* on Pateley Bridge High Street, for the north. There's a *Cotswold Outdoors* in Harrogate town centre. All have a good range of chalk products and hardware. Most of the climbing centres listed below have excellent gear shops.

## Indoor Climbing Centres
All the regions climbing centres have Yorkshire Grit climbing pedigree behind them and offer some of the country's best training facilities. For an alternative experience, try the Henry Price traversing wall in Leeds city centre (see page 662). **The Climbing Depot:** 173 Richardshaw Lane, Pudsey, Leeds, LS28 6AA. **The Leeds Wall:** 100a Gelderd Road, Leeds, LS12 6BY. **Harrogate Climbing Centre (HCC):** Hornbeam Park, Harrogate, HG2 8QT. **City Bloc:** Airdale Industrial Estate, Kitson Road, Leeds, LS10 1NT. **ROKT Climbing Gym:** Old Flour Mill, Mill Royd Street, Brighouse, HD6 1EY. **The Barn Climbing Centre:** Unit 2, Ryshworth Works, Keighley Road, Crossflatts, Bingley, BD16 2ER, **Aireborough Lesiure Centre**, The Green, Guiseley, Leeds, LS20 9BT.

## Rain and Rest Day Options
Too many in Yorkshire to mention here but here are a few for starters. Fountains Abbey, RHS Harlow Carr Gardens, Hesketh Farm Park (good for the kids), Stump Cross Caverns, Bolton Abbey, Nidderdale Pool, Harrogate Leisure Centre, Aireborough Leisure Centre, Theakstone's Brewery, Black Sheep Brewery.

## Hospitals and Medical Centres
**Wharfedale Hospital;** Otley, LS21 2LY (01943 465522). Minor Injuries but no A&E. **Harrogate Hospital:** Harrogate, HG2 7SX, (01423 885959). **Leeds General Infirmary:** Great George Street, Leeds, LS1 3EX, (0113 243 2799). **Airedale General Hospital:** Skipton Road, Steeton, BD20 6TD, (01535 652511).

# Almscliff

It doesn't get much better than this. Wonderful evening light and delightful climbing. Richard Connors on the much coveted classic of **Z Climb Eliminate** (E1 5b). Page 68
Photo: Mike Hutton

## 'Rock of Ages, cleft for me'

*From the Hymm by Augustus Montague Toplady, 1775*

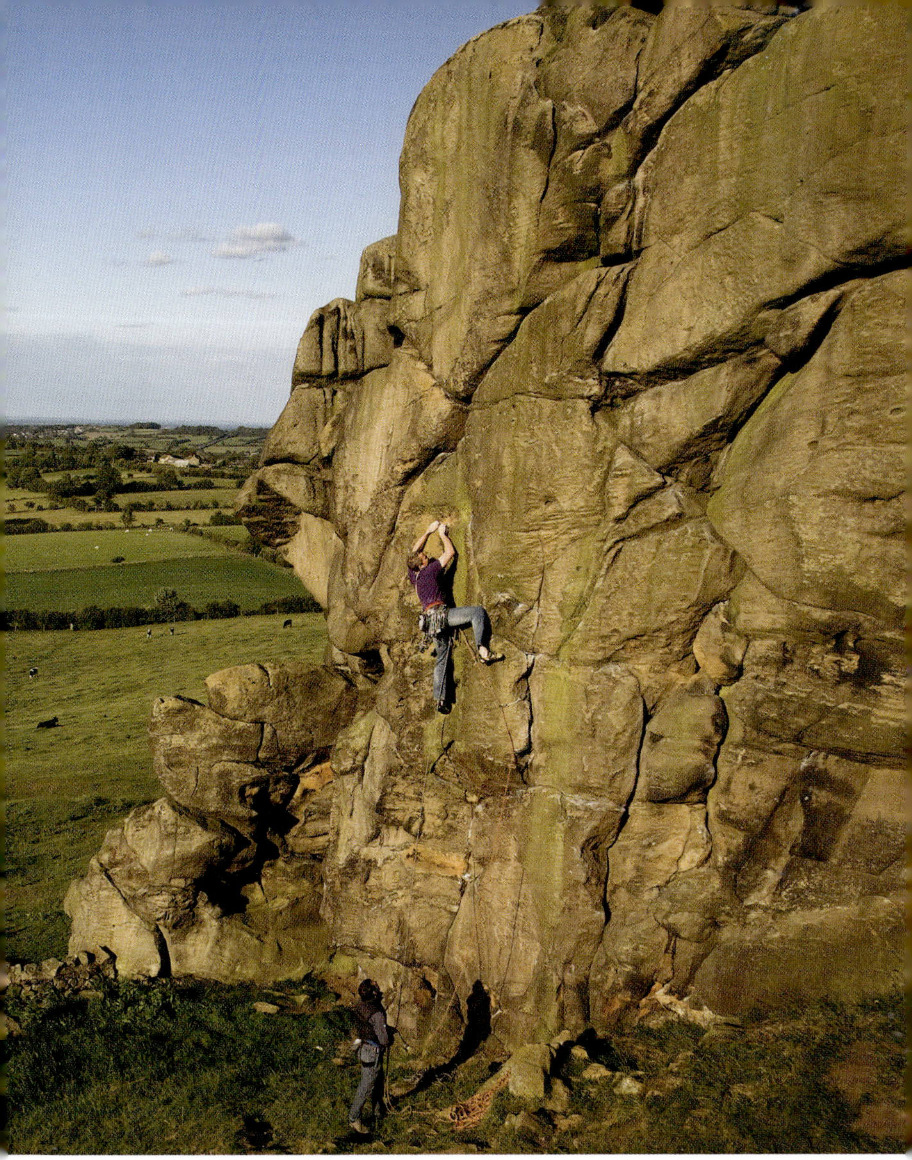

# almscliff

by **Richard Connors and James Ibbertson**

OS Ref: SE 268 490                              Altitude: 198m

The crown of Yorkshire gritstone rising out of lush green fields north of Leeds. Glorious Almscliff. Celebrated by many, loathed by some, utterly unmissable. Of spiritual significance since ancient times, 'The Cliff' continues to provide a natural altar for the ritual summoning of power. Easily accessible and quick to dry, Almscliff has attracted climbers for very many decades. The result is an incredible density of quality routes; almost every square metre of rock has been climbed, often in multiple ways. There are classic routes across the grades for the visitor and an infinity of eliminates for aficionados.

**The Climbing:** The 174 routes can be surprisingly steep, exposed and just plain knackering — even the short ones. Learn to jam, or VS can feel like E2. There's not much for the slab climber, though insecure rounded grovelling can be found if you seek to avoid the abundance of positive holds and good rock. Both safe and bold routes exist across the grade range; some of the best lines are micro routes, now usually enjoyed as highballs. The bouldering is as good as the routes, with 181 problems covering a range of styles, though the testpieces have a tendency to be powerful and crimpy on undercut blocks or buttresses. Absolute beginners may struggle with the recorded bouldering (the good stuff kicks off at Font 5) but there's entertainment to be found for all.

**Conditions and Aspect:** Great conditions exist year- round, from crisp winter friction to last light on idyllic summer evenings. The crag is totally exposed to the wind and dries very quickly. Patchy rain often blows past leaving Almscliff dry while showers sweep down Wharfedale, wetting Ilkley and Caley. On windy days shelter may be found in the boulders, on Black Wall, or in North Gully. Don't be put off by any greenness on the North West Face; it is only the routes at the very far left (beyond Cup & Saucer and in the descent gully) that can become unpleasant after wet weather. In winter the foot of Black Wall may become a foetid pool, but this can be negotiated. Greasy hair-ridden polish in odd places and widespread exuberant defecations are usually due to cows rather than feral local climbers.

**Parking and Approach:** Twelve miles north of Leeds city centre, the village of Huby sits on the A658 midway between Otley and Harrogate. If approaching from Otley, at the centre of Huby is a crossroads with Weeton signposted to the south-east, and Stainburn to the north-west. Turn toward Stainburn up Strait Lane, then left at the T-junction into Crag Lane. This road becomes Merrybank Lane and after 1 mile the crag comes into view with parking available along the roadside below the western end of the crag and in a lay-by at the corner of the road **(Parking GPS: 53.937617, -1.597424)**.

If approaching from Harrogate on the A658, turn right onto Hall Green Lane (signed to North Rigton and the Square and Compass pub). At the mini-roundabout, just past the pub, turn left onto Church Hill then second right, Crag Lane. Follow Crag Lane for 1 mile and turn right at the T-junction. The parking is on the right.

Even if it is very busy, **do not** block gates. Leave room for very big tractors to gain access to the fields. **Do not park outside Crag Farm below the crag.**

**Access:** Please stick to the described approach paths on the maps below. Do not climb 'the trousers' boulder standing alone in the field below the crag — yes, that's the one with 'keep off' painted on it.

Almscliff has a great selection of classic climbs in the VS to HVS range. Here, Becky Payne makes doubly sure all's good on the pro front before tackling the difficult top-out to **Black Wall** (VS 5b). Page 89.
Photo: Adi Gill

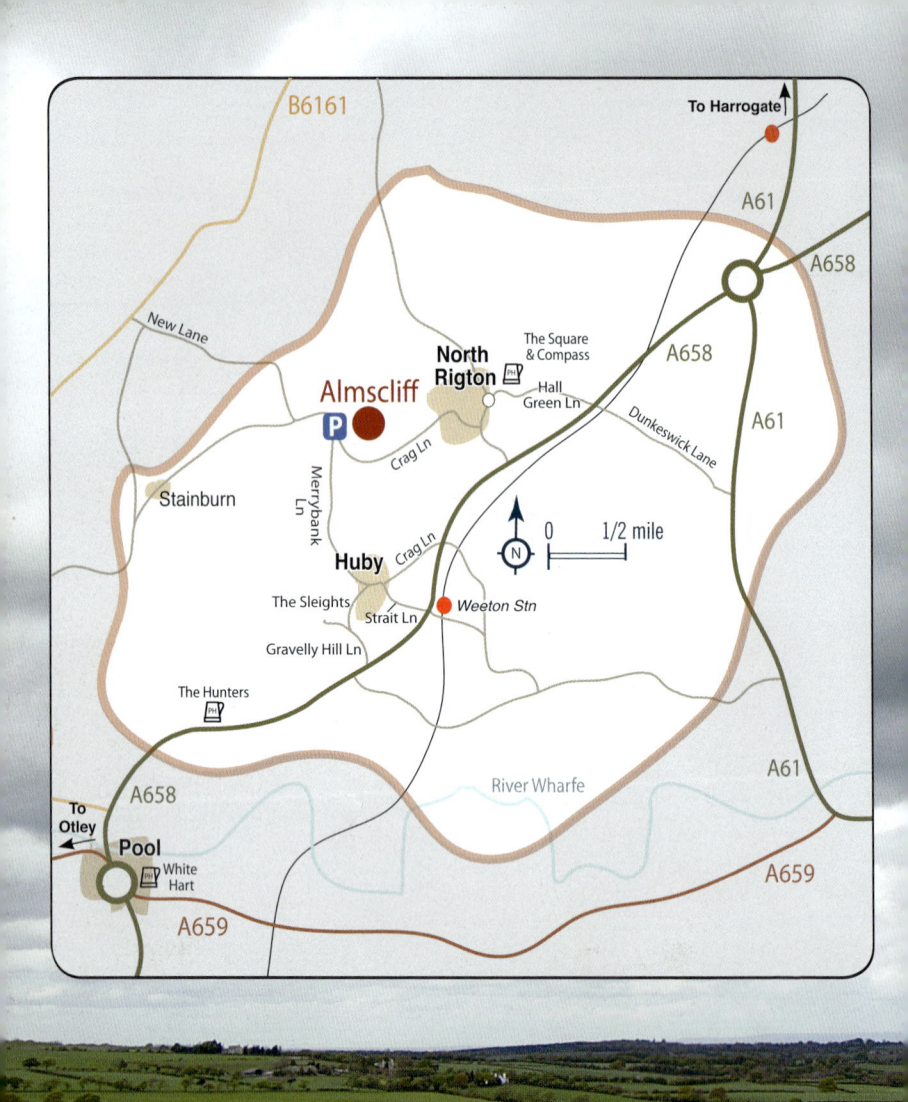

Tim Wilkinson on the **Five Star Finish** to **Great Western** (HVS 5a). Page 78.
Photo: Jamie Moss

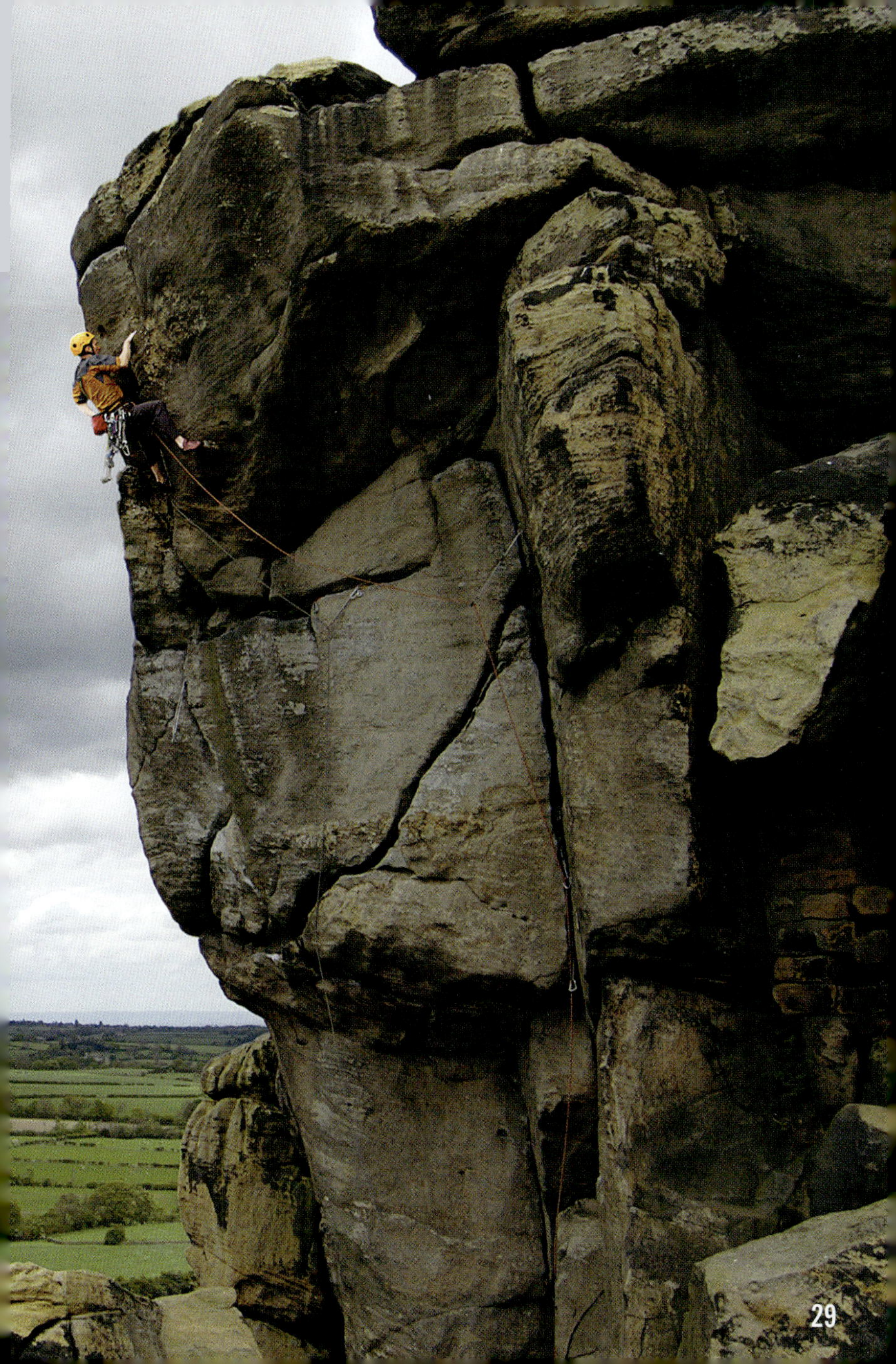

# Almscliff - Aerial Photo

Photo: Robin Nicholson. Pilot: Ed Bishop

Parking

From Huby

Aerial Photo - **ALMSCLIFF**

High Man

Low Man

South Cave

Don't Park Here

From North Rigton

31

Photo: Robin Nicholson. Pilot: Ed Bishop

# High Man

Approach From Parking

32

| 1 | End Boulder | 11 | The Matterhorn |
|---|---|---|---|
| 2 | Overhanging Nose | 12 | MK Wall |
| 3 | West Cave Group | 13 | The Wall Boulder |
| 4 | Everest Man Boulder | 14 | Pinnacle Boulder |
| 5 | The Flying Arête | 15 | The Egg |
| 6 | The Virgin | 16 | Z Climb |
| 7 | The Big Roof | 17 | Great Western |
| 8 | The Keel | 18 | Zig Zag Direct |
| 9 | Wedge Boulder | 19 | The Rift |
| 10 | Ed's Dyno | 20 | Demon Wall |

South Face / Black Wall

Low Man

To South Cave

'Trousers' Boulder - *no climbing*

# Almscliff - End Boulder

## End Boulder
On entering the main field that contains the crag, follow the wall rightwards to enter the boulder field. The large block intersected by the wall has some great problems.

### 1 Morrell's Wall Traverse  Font 7a
Low traverse from a sit-down start at the left arête via sharp pockets. Stay low through the corner (not using the huge break) to join *Morrell's Wall* at the low starting hold.

### 2 Morrell's Wall Left  Font 6a
Strenuous moves past strange jugs and a confusingly long reach bring good crimps. Avoid using the wall on the left (or use it to lower the grade).

### 3 Morrell's Wall  Font 6a
Fantastic crimping. Reaching the thin edges from the juggy sidepull may feel implausible if your feet are in the wrong place.

*Mike Drysdale  c1956* ♦

### 4 Fall In  Font 6a
Wonderfully tenuous friction that barely feels possible until you fall into it. Start off the big jug, stretch up to the rounded arête and follow it leftwards.

### 5 End Wall  Font 4
Start at the juggy nose and follow the wide crack right and up.

### 6 Slopey Traverse  Font 7c
Excellent desperate slopey slapping. Sit-down start at the jug just left of the wall and finish up *Morrell's Wall*. Purists will avoid the chipped hold that allows you to span to the arête and skip the crux undercut move.

Over the wall into the lower field is a long slabby face. Beware that the grass can hide an extremely boggy patch. Just to the left, embedded in the wall, is a small boulder. **Field Mouse** (Font 4+) traverses left-to-right, wall-to-wall (worth going back and forth to get the blood pumping); **Fledgling** (Font 4+) tackles the wall direct between the obvious pockets.

### 7 Finite Field  Font 3+
Start at the crack just right of the wall and take the easiest line to the top.

### 8 Fieldside Traverse  Font 7b
Left-to-right slopey traverse with feet in the low break all the way. Originally finished with a tricky move round the blunt arête, but possibly better to finish up it.

*Graham Desroy  pre-1993*

### 9 Field Fair  Font 5
Use the obvious sloping hold to rock up; wander easily to the top.

### 10 The High Step  Font 5+
Start on the big sidepull and climb the centre of the slab.

### 11 Swampy Arête  Font 6c+
The blunt right arête via a long reach to a shallow pocket. Can have a soggy landing.

Hop back over the wall again to find an amiable slabby face with some lovely warm-up problems. Several variations are possible.

Yorkshire Gritstone

The jug beckons. Debbie Nicholson fights her way up the uber-classic **Bird's Nest Crack** (HS 4b). Page 85.
Photo: Mike Hutton

# ALMSCLIFF - Overhanging Nose

### 12 Bungle Traverse  Font 3
Gentle left-to-right traverse, finishing up the blunt arête.

### 13 Jemima  Font 3
The middle of the wall.

### 14 Hamble's Arête  Font 3+
The blunt right arête is a short amble.

## Overhanging Nose
Just 15m right, opposite *Morrell's Wall*, is a small boulder that packs quite a punch for its diminutive size.

### 15 Overhanging Nose  Font 6a
Sit-down start. Tackle the overhanging nose using the block for your feet. Without the block is **Below The Decks** (Font 6c+).

### 16 Grape Strain  Font 7b+
From the block in front of the boulder, traverse the lip leftwards all the way around the nose, using pockets on the steep back wall, to finish on the slab over the roof.
*Simon Panton  1995*

### 17 Tumbledown  Font 5
The centre of the overhanging face from a sit-down start.

### 18 Slap and Traction  Font 6a+
Sit-down start. From the flake, go up and right to a gruesome rockover.

### 19 Lasting Satisfaction  Font 7c+
A great eliminate. Start from sitting at the flake in the centre of the face, move right to the arête and finish over the bulge. All holds are in except the deep three-pocket cluster on the lip.
*Dave Cowl  2006*

### 20 I Am a Walrus  Font 6c+
On the other side of the block, somehow enter the undercut scoop using the shallow pocket.

## West Cave Group
The craggy wall bounding the boulder field has several good problems, eliminates and a long warm up traverse.

### 21 Left Rib  Font 5
The left arête presents a peculiar problem. To the right are several polished climbs around the Font 3+ mark. **The Ear** (Font 4+) takes the arête before the next problem.

### 22 Barley Mow  Font 7a (E4 6b)
Take a deep breath and arrange your spotters for the fine highball hanging crack.
*Tony Barley  21st May 1966*  ✦

### 23 Hammill's Rib  Font 7a
The hanging arête is climbed on shallow pockets.
*Mike Hammill*

### ✓ 24 West Cave Wall  Font 3 (S 4a)
Follow the polished ramp and pull through the bulge surprisingly easily. Finish up the slab or arête.

### 25 Three Swings Traverse  Font 5+
From the centre of *Pork Chop Slab*, along the obvious break to the gully. You can stride across the gap and continue all the way to *Left Rib* (and back).

West Cave Group - **ALMSCLIFF**

### 26 The Chimney Flake  Font 5 (VS 5b)
The sharp-edged crack is secure and leads to an easy finish. The rib and wall just right is **The Blunt Edge** (Font 5+ / E1 5b), a much more taxing affair.

### 27 The Postman  Font 4 (HS 4c)
The left arête, past the deep pocket, is much easier above the ledge (or traverse off).

### 28 Hanging Rib  Font 6a
The tantalising, but decidedly awkward, blunt rib via a thin black crimp that will keep spitting you off until you figure out where to put your feet. The top-out is no give away (traverse off rightwards).

Several eliminates are possible here, both from standing and sitting. Just use your imagination.

### 29 Rib Right  Font 5+
The right edge of the wall is a good problem, especially from the sit-down start. The projecting block out right is not in.

### 30 Pork Chop Slab  Font 5+
Delicate moves up the centre of the slab lead to a committing finish if followed direct. Reach out left to good holds halfway up for an easy escape.

There is a collection of boulders up the hill, behind the West Cave Group heading towards *Great Western*. Never popular, but worthy of closer scrutiny if looking to escape the honey pots. The boulder at the top of the hill is split by an obvious wide crack; **Cold Crack** (Font 6b) takes this from a sit-down start. **Cold Shoulder** (Font 7b) is a technical teaser traversing right and uphill, starting at the downhill nose left of the crack. The tier below comprises a short wall and corner with capping roof. **Minefield** (Font 7b) starts at the left end and rocks all the way rightwards and under the roof. The wall, up rounded layaways, finishing left of the capping roof is **DMZ** (Font 6b); much better from a sit-down start via the hidden pocket (Font 7b). Other problems in this area hover around the Font 5 grade range. Just right is the distinct **Heart Slab**. The most worthwhile problem is to romp onto the slab from the downhill nose, **Heart Slab Arête** (Font 5+).

### Everest Man Boulder
Back down the hill and right of the West Cave Group the path passes between two boulders. On the left is this huge rounded block with a collection of challenging top-outs.

### 31 The North Ridge  Font 5+ (E1 5c)
Follow the wide break around right and climb up the front of the nose. The sit-down start using a pocket and a pinch is a tough proposition (Font 7b+).

Almscliff to Slipstones

37

# ALMSCLIFF - Everest Man

**32 The Hillary Step**  Font 5 (HVS 5b)
Head up to the pocket and make an awkward step to join *The Lhotse Face*.

**33 The Lhotse Face**  Font 4 (VS 4c)
Climb the short crack then follow the line leftwards.

**34 The South-West Face**  Font 6a (E2 5c)
The direct line up the crack then via the high central pocket to a rounded and scary finish.

**35 The South Col**  Font 3+ (HS 4b)
Polished holds lead up right to an awkward step onto the slabby nose and round the corner to finish.

**36 The East Face**  Font 4
Climb the back of the block trending left.

## The Flying Arêtes

On the opposite side of the path is a boulder with problems of a completely different nature.

**37 Flying Arête**  Font 6b
Packs it all in: technique, strength, courage and composure. Originally called *The Left Wing*. A direct ascent of the slab above the arête, via a rockover, is **Stallone's Stinking Banger** (Font 6c ✦). Photo on page 53.

**38 The Right Wing**  Font 6b
Starting off the boulder climb the right arête, finishing up the right side of the blunt rib. Good, but not quite as satisfying as the left side.

Arifa Chakera enjoying the stunning vistas on **Low Man Easy Way** (D). Page 51.
Photo: Mike Hutton

# ALMSCLIFF - The Virgin

## The Virgin
An enormous tilted boulder with a very overhanging front face. Worth checking out the descent before setting off.

### 39 The Lady  E4 6c  6m  ★★
The photogenic left arête makes a great highball (Font 7a). Photo on page 43.
*Ron Cowells (solo)  13th November 1985*

### 40 Jack On Fire  E4 6c  7m
The wall above the start of *The Virgin* has one tricky move, just right of the scoop. The large hole on the right takes a big cam.
*Al Manson, Martin Berzins  29th August 1988*

### 41 Jack Be Nimble  E4 6c  7m
Climb straight up the centre of the front face. Undercut the pocket and windmill an arm to latch the rounded top at the highest point on the boulder. A good crimp back from the lip aids the top-out.
*Ben Bransby  1999*

### 42 The Virgin  E3 6b  7m  ★★
From the boulder, pull into the horizontal break and slap/jam rightwards. Using a pocket on the lip, peek over the top to find blunt flutings. Pull over and finish easily.
*Pete Kitson (solo)  15th July 1973*

### 43 The Virgin Traverse  Font 6c
High intensity core stamina training. Start with all limbs on the block. Traverse the breaks rightward with a desperate move around the arête, all the way to finish in the niche.

### 44 Identity Crisis  Font 8a
Often mistakenly known as the **Gaskins' Problem**. Start bridging between the block and boulder; undercut, right hand in the groove. Gain a slopey edge and somehow lob for the break (the sitter is a project).
*Tim Clifford  2002*

40                              Yorkshire Gritstone

### 44a Cherry Falls  Font 8a+
The apotheosis of power crimping. Tick this and you're done. From the low break, gain the sharp crimp with your right hand then blast for the break. For (b) **Cherry Falls Right** (Font 8a), gain the crimp with the left hand, match, then dyno for the break.
*Tim Clifford 2002; Cherry Falls Right: John Gaskins 1994*

### 45 Crucis  Font 7b (E4 6b)   7m
A brilliant eliminate. From a sit-down start use a gnarly fingerlock in the crack to span up right to the blunt edge of the wide diagonal and hence gain the break. Drop off, or use a layaway under the roof to gain the lip, move right to the arête and finish.
*(Full route) John Paul Hotham  October 1999*

### 46 The Gypsy  Font 6b+ (E3 6a)
The super burly right arête. Powerful moves and a committing foot lock lead to the break. Move right to the sloping ledge and rock up to the top with conviction. Instead of moving right, (b) **The Fox** (E4 6b) goes directly up the arête.
*Pete Kitson 28th Apr 1973; (The Fox: Stuart Purvis Oct 2000)*

### 47 Gypus  Font 6c+ (E3 6b)
Butch underclings lead to a creaky flake. A monster move brings the ledge of *The Gypsy* within reach.
*Martin Berzins  January 1982*

### 48 Opus  E4 6b   10m   ★★
A balletic composition. Climb the widely-spaced slots to a horizontal break below a small roof. Finish with a committing move out left. At the same grade the (c) **Supo Direct Finish** climbs through the roof and up the short rib whereas (d) **Hocus Pocus** moves right under the roof to finish on the slab. Photos on pages 44 and 671.
*Mike Hammill (solo) 5th April 1975* ✦

### 49 Opeless  E7 6c   10m
Start up *Opus* and arrange protection under the mid-height roof. Move right to a good undercut and boldly pull round the roof, using a fluting, and finish up this.
*Matt Goode, John-Paul Hotham 10th November 2000*

### 50 Magnum Opus  E5 6b   10m   ★★
Gain the ramp and layback to its top. Swing left and follow the break under the roof, into the crux of *Opus*. Follow this to finish. (e) A direct boulder problem start (Font 7c+) starts at a two finger pocket on the lip of the roof and presses into the hanging groove.
*Martin Berzins, Al Manson  21st August 1988*

### 51 Hokum  E6 6c   8m   ★
A direct line above *Magnum Opus*. Start from the pocket and climb to the ramp. The bulge presents a significant obstacle, guarding the hanging groove above which you follow to the top.
*James Ibbertson  15th January 2006*

### 52 Fisher's Stride  VS 5a   10m   ★★
Make a ridiculously committing stride from The Keel boulder onto The Virgin. Fully engaged, traverse up and left to a sloping ledge. Keep going with sustained nervousness round the nose and to the top.
*Denys Fisher  1938*

### 53 Chastity  E2 5c   6m   ★
The gripping wall just right of the arête on pockets. Best not think about the landing.
*Dave Musgrove snr  c1979*

### 54 The Virgin Climb  S 4a   8m   ★
Generous pockets lead left to a huge hold on the arête. Swing round onto the slabby face and follow pockets and old chipped holds easily to the top.
*Unknown  pre-1912*

# ALMSCLIFF - The Virgin

### 55 Central Route  Font 4
The centre of the slabby face. The direct start via a rockover is a superb Font 5+ problem.

### 56 North Top Corner  Font 4
The left side of the right arête. The vague rib, 1m left, without recourse to the arête is **Thompson's Route** (Font 4+).

### 57 The Scoop  Font 5+
An engaging delicate highball up the faint scoop, without resorting to the arête.

### 58 The Full Virgin Traverse  Font 8a
Traverse the break above the roof, continue along the upper break on the front face. Reverse *The Gypsy* and join *The Virgin Traverse*. At its end, press on past the niche with a hard sequence, swapping hands in a small pocket under the roof. Wander across the north face and back to the start.
*Stuart Littlefair  1997*

### 59 Canine  Font 8a
The central line of the roof. Start from the flake at the back. Crimp, undercut, then yard out to a slopey pocket on the front face. Finish up the arête. (a) **Stretch Armstrong** (Font 7c) makes a monster reach to grab the lip from the back of the left side of the roof.
*Tom Peckitt  2005 (both problems)*

### 60 Sewer Rat Connection  Font 7b+
Sit-down start. Start on a jug under the right side of the roof, use a nasty crimp and a heel or a weird egyptian to reach the pockets round the lip. Finish at the break.
*Richard Hughes  1995*  ✦

### 61 Top Cat Traverse  Font 7b+
Traverse the line of pockets above the lip of the roof (keeping below the break) from right-to-left, then follow pockets to the top.
*Simon Panton  1995*

### 62 The Bitch  E4 6c  5m
The thin crack is short but with a nasty landing.
*Graham Desroy (solo)  24th April 1990*

### 63 The Tramp  E3 6b  6m
The wall midway between the thin crack and the arête on the north face.
*Jerry Peel (solo)  September 1985*

## The Big Roof
Behind The Virgin boulder is a long low roof with:

### 64 Snappy Roof  Font 5+
The left side of the roof on good holds with a thin wafer to start. The left wall is avoided.

### 65 Underhand  Font 7b+
The right edge of the roof starting from the block deep at the back, finishing up the arête. Or continue traversing to finish on the front face for (a) **Underhand Extension** (Font 7c) or even further for (b) **Underhand Super Extension** (Font 7c+).
*Tim Clifford 2002. Extensions added by Tom Peckitt*  ✦

### 66 Off Campus  Font 5
Up rails in the right-hand end of the roof from standing. A handy warm up. The arête can be climbed from standing **Reachy Roof** (Font 5+) above a long drop.

Matt Birch lets the climbing do the talking on **The Lady** (E4 6c). Page 40
Photo: Keith Sharples

Mark Greenbank approaching the point of no return on **Opus** (E4 6b). Page 41.
Photo: Kev Avery

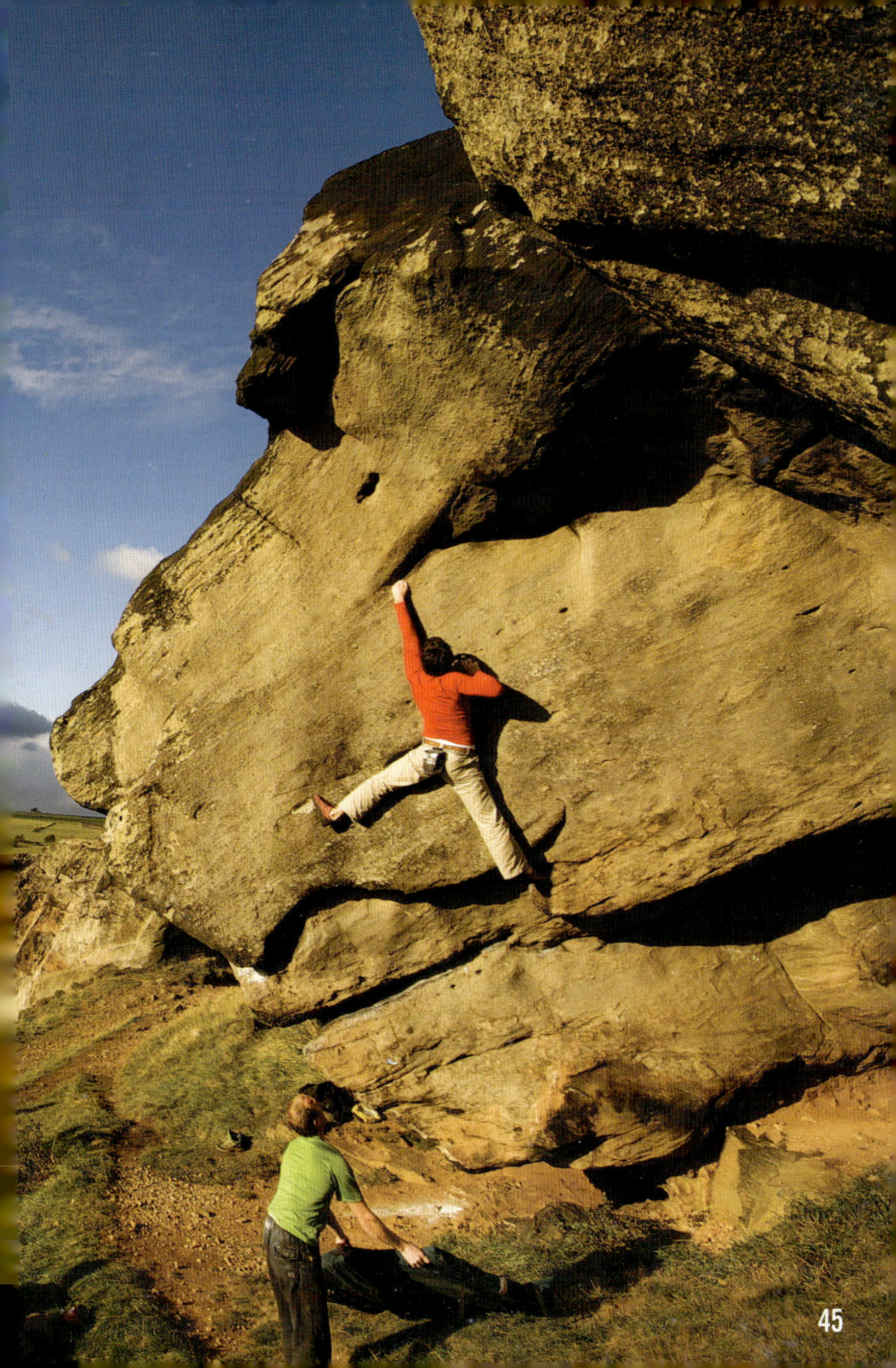

# ALMSCLIFF - The Keel

## The Keel

Dropping back down the hill, next to The Virgin boulder, is a conspicuous block with a concentration of classic hard problems and a coveted slopey traverse.

### 67 C and A Traverse  Font 7a
From the left arête, traverse right on sharp holds and finish up the crack.

### 68 In Limbo  Font 6c
A fine oddity. Limbo out on leg jams to the big hold on the lip and finish direct.

### 69 The Crack  Font 6b+
From a sit-down start under the roof. Thuggy and surprisingly technical.

> **❝ ❞**
>
> A jam will boost you when you must go, save you when you are tired, and extricate you when you are foxed. It will give you a love-bite embarrassing in its imprint.
>
> **Dave Cook in True Grit (article from *Mountain 26*, 1973 - reprinted in Ken Wilson's *The Games Climbers Play*).**

### 70 The Keel  Font 7c
The classic hard 'Cliff tick. Climb from the block at the back, cup the keel hold, stretch for the chipped edge on the lip, then unleash the power. Without the chip, **The Real Keel** gets Font 7c+ (✦).

### 71 The Bulb  Font 7c+
As for *The Keel* to the chip. Eschew the big pocket and head right via the bulb hold to a good edge.
*Andy Swann 1990s*

### 72 Bulbhaul  Font 8b+
Follow *C and A Traverse* then down-climb the crack and launch into *The Keel* (without using the block). Finish up *The Bulb* (the chip is allowed). Other finishes give **Keelhaul** (Font 8a+) and **The Real Keelhaul** (Font 8b).
*Tom Peckitt (Bh & TRK); Keelhaul Andy Swann 2004*

### 73 Sloper Patrol  Font 6c+
Start sitting on the far left at a flake and traverse rightward on slopers to finish up the right arête. Some prefer slapping downhill from the top, rocking onto the slab at the bottom.

A couple of forearm busting traverses are on offer. The **Natural Traverse** (Font 7b+), starts 3m further downhill from the flake and links into *Sloper Patrol*. The epic **All Natural** (Font 8a), starts along *C and A Traverse*, reverses the crack, traverses past the start of *The Keel*, then moves up to join and finish along *Natural Traverse*.

## Wedge Boulder
The small boulder with a slightly sandy prow.

### 74 Pocket Watch  Font 5
The left side of the arête (without using the arête). Not the best landing.

### 75 Nose Bag  Font 6a
The arête direct from a sit-down start up sandy crimps.

### 76 Pebble Frog  Font 5
Pull on to the right side of the arête by standing in the pocket. The crack just right again is a neat Font 3+ problem.

Ed's Dyno - **ALMSCLIFF**

### Ed's Dyno Boulder
Below is a small boulder with a thin horizontal crack.

**77 Charlie Sheen**  Font 5
Grab the ledge and pedal upwards.

**78 Ed's Dyno**  Font 6c+
A huge throw off the two smallest crimps; shockingly, many people opt to use the best holds instead of the correct ones.
*Ed Brown 1990s*

**79 Teflon Traverse**  Font 6c
Traverse the lower break of the boulder from right-to-left. Frustratingly polished.

**80 Scuff**  Font 5+
Up easy sloping breaks from a sit-down start.

### The Almscliff pre-1912 Challenge

Almscliff's most historic trad routes (pre-1912) can be enchained to give a grand day out and true appreciation for the mettle of the early pioneers.

Get going with a quick stroll up **Low Man Easy Way** then work across the Low Man classics **Stew Pot, Pinnacle Face Climb**, and **Fluted Columns**. Fully warmed-up you'll be ready to step up a gear for the glorious **Square Chimney & Whisky Crack**. Then finish off the tour of Low Man with the slippery **V Chimney & Traverse**. Nip over to swing around the corner and up **The Virgin Climb**, then walk up to the right-hand end of High Man. Start by padding up the run out rib of **South Face Climb**. The first of the chimneys is the fairly benign **South Chimney**. Next comes the jamming crack of **South Chimney Layback**, then **Stomach Traverse**; the desperate start up the hanging crack fits the spirit of the day! With your thrutching skills now in full flow, **Central Crack** and **Crack and Wall** follow easily with **Three Chockstones Chimney** allowing a quick descent. In the rift dash up **Tight Chimney**, then tackle some proper climbing (and grovelling) on **The Goblin** and the butch **Zig Zag Direct**. The **Zig Zag** and **Leaf Climb** provide a bit of respite, and why not quickly deal with the pulpit routes, going up **Fat Man's Misery** and down **The Easy Way**. The steep but straightforward **Cup and Saucer** then leaves the best until last. Your penultimate route is the airy **Long Chimney**, and the fitting conclusion to this monumental tour is the wonderfully outrageous **Parson's Chimney**. Sit for a minute and enjoy your place in the history of these routes, climbed for over a century, then get down The Hunters Inn for a well earned pint.

**Richard Connors**

# ALMSCLIFF - Low Man

## Low Man
Arguably one of the most recognisable chunks of Yorkshire grit with routes that never go out of fashion. At the extreme left end of the crag is a short slabby wall that provides some of the best easy problems at Almscliff.

**1 Groove On**  Font 3. A tad precarious.
**2 Hop Scotch**  Font 3
**3 Stroll**  Font 3
**4 Well Worn**  Font 3
**5 Toe Poke**  Font 4+

At the right end of the wall is a narrow entrance leading into the underworld. The wall on the right can be climbed in various ways including:

**6 Pond Life**  Font 4
Trend left via the good break and pocket to exit at the tallest point of the wall.

**7 Safe As**  S 4a  5m  ★
Follow the break out right to climb the super exposed arête on positive holds.

**8 Envy of Angels**  E1 5c  7m
The initial slab elevates you to an uncomfortable height from which to make an unnerving move off sidepulls to good holds and an easy finish. Runners are found around to the left, though the arête is out of bounds.
*Steve Bollen (solo) 15th July 1997*

**9 Angelic Upstart**  HVS 5b  7m
The rib just left of the thin crack is climbed to a good hold, then one big move off the pocket leads to an easy finish.
*Pete Brown (solo) 1997 (FRA)*

**10 Pram Pusher's Paradise**  VS 5a  14m  ★★
Reach the roof all too easily. Place stonking gear then monkey along huge holds rightwards, around the nose and up to thankfully positive finishing holds. Or, if you've not had enough, press on into and then up *Whisky Crack*, continue right along the top break above *Whisky Wall* and finish at *Fluted Crack*. (A continuation known as **Top Shelf**).
*Al Manson, Pete Kitson  June 1972*

**11 A Step in the Right Direction**  HVS 5b  10m
Delicate moves past pockets on the lower wall. Any of the finishes provide contrast.
*Adam Goulder, Mathew Collins (FRA) 22nd June 1992*

**12 Chalk Scratchings**  E2 5c  12m
The right side of the lower slab (right rib is in). Not as eliminate as it seems.
*Tony Marr, Mike Took  7th May 2000*

**13 V Chimney and Traverse**  S 4a  15m  ★★
Skate up the chimney to gain a delightful leftward traverse under the roof that's breached at its left end.
*Herbert Ingle, C.T. Dent, Thomas Gray  pre-1894*

**14 V Chimney Direct**  VS 5a  10m  ★
Eschew the traverse and mount the roof direct.
*Thought to be Arthur Dolphin, D. Varley, John Cook 29th Nov. 1942*

## Low Man - ALMSCLIFF

**15 Depth Charger & Up Periscope** E1 5b 14m ★
Follow positive holds straight up the wall right of *V Chimney*. Escapable, but with no worthwhile gear. From the large dish, going straight up is grim; at this grade you can succumb to temptation and grab positive holds out left to gain the ledge. A nice tricky move off the large ledge gains the break and the top.
*Al Manson c1977* ✦; *Dave Musgrove (solo) c1979*

**16 Trident** E2 5c 9m ★
Head right from the good crimps on *Depth Charger* past a dubious small wire to the sanctuary of the slanting break and good gear. Go up the all too short-lived rib to the ledge. Avoiding the rib by traversing right into *Piggott's Stride* is **Torpedo** (E2 5c).
*Pete Brown, Steve Turner 18th August 1994* ✦

Ever wondered where the best climbers of the '70s came from? Well, here's your answer. A rare event captured on film: **The Niche** (page 78) gives birth to Choe Brooks, Steve Bancroft and Chris Addy. Al Manson is doing his best to push them back in again. **Photo: Bernard Newman**

## ALMSCLIFF - Low Man

### The Matterhorn
The pointy boulder almost touching the crag has a clean vertical face and an arête problem which is just magic.

### 17 Fractal  Font 7b
The smooth wall with a bounce-start at the black undercut, up the thin black seam. The wall to the left is Font 6a.
*Tom Peckitt  March 2006*

### 18 Matterhorn Ridge  Font 5 (HVS 5b)
The fantastic imposing highball arête. The powerful direct sit-down start is Font 7b+, and the (a) sit-down start traversing in along the thin crack from out left is Font 7a.

The dark slabby east face of The Matterhorn has a clutch of reasonable problems, the best being the arête of *Matterhorn Ridge* taken on the right side (Font 4+).

### 19 Piggott's Stride  VS 4c  8m  ★★
An adventure. Ascend The Matterhorn boulder. Look across the gap to the blunt nose of the crag, then look down; how long are your legs? Stride across the chasm then make a frightening pull to bring all remaining limbs across. Scamper up and right to the ledge for a lie down. Finish up *Whisky Crack*.
*Claude Dean Frankland, Fred Piggott  pre-1923*

### 20 Chiasmata  Font 8a
Extreme fridge hugging directly up the blunt prow. A pad anchored to The Matterhorn is advisable.
*Steve Dunning  2003*

### 21 V Crack  HVS 6a  8m  ★★
Powerful pulls with perfect protection. Direct up the hanging crack (stepping from the ledge in the chimney is missing the point). Highball Font 6b to the break.
*Arthur Dolphin, David Varley, John Cook  29th November 1942*

### 22 Square Chimney & Whisky Crack
MVS 4b  15m  ★★★
Two healthy courses of gritstone. Cooly back-and-foot (or desperately slide and grovel) up the eponymous chimney to earn perfect jams up the finishing crack. Beware gear lifting out in the chimney.
*SC:Ingle, Dent, Gray, Calvert pre-1900; WC:Fred Botterill pre-1912*

### 23 Whisky Wall  E3 5b  15m  ★★
A wandering climb with lovely moves and just about enough protection. Climb to the big ledge. Balance up to gain pockets leading leftwards and better holds just right of *Whisky Crack* (a side-runner in the crack here is advisable, but probably only earns you E2). Step up and back right to finish up good holds.
*John Syrett, Al Manson  28th April 1973*

### 24 Whisky Wall Direct  E4 6a  15m  ★
A bold outing up the centre of the wall above the big, hittable ledge. Climb direct using the pockets and a series of long reaches. Squeezed in to the right is (b) **Wharfedale Wall** (E5 6c) which requires side-runners in *Fluted Crack*, and the ability to ignore the ledges of *Fluted Columns*.
*Unknown* ✦

### 25 Spirit Level  E2 5c  17m
From near the top of *Whisky Crack*, traverse rightward, along the second break down, to finish up *Fluted Columns*.
*Pete Brown, Pete Thistle  5th August 1997*

### 26 Fluted Crack  S 4b  14m  ★
A little route with a big feel to it. Very airy bridging made comfortable with multiple large cams to protect.

### 27 Fluted Columns  HVD  13m  ★★★
Plain lovely. Climb ledge-to-ledge to reach the columns, taking care to arrange protection as you go. Take a breath and set off over the bulge to find it's not as bad as you feared. An eliminate start can be found up the right wall of *Fluted Crack*, called **Fluted Rib** (HVS 5b). Photo page 55.
*Ingle, Dent, Gray, Calvert  pre-1900* ✦

### 28 Pinnacle Flake Climb  S 4a  12m  ★
Step up to the huge flake. An extraordinarily ungainly move left leads to a staircase of flakes. Can be started direct (c) (VS 5a); harder if you avoid straying right to grab the flake.
*Unknown  pre-1912* ✦

### 29 Pinnacle Direct  S 4a  12m
An awkward start leads to fiddly gear and a delicate finish. Only worth Severe if you avoid the flake of *LME' Way*.
*Dave Musgrove & The Almscliff All Stars  1997*

Yorkshire Gritstone

Low Man - **ALMSCLIFF**

#### 30 **Low Man Easy Way**  D  13m  ★
Follow the gully and the easiest way to the top. Its entrance is often marked with an in-situ beginner puzzling over how to start. Photo on page 39.
*William Cecil Slingsby and friends  c1870*

#### 31 **Stew Pot**  HVD  11m  ★
Struggle off the ground then climb past the 'stew pot' to finish up the incipient crack or the delicate slab. Great gear if you look for it.
*Ingle, Dent, Gray, Calvert  pre-1900*

#### 32 **Something's Cooking**  E2 6a  11m  ★
Serves up a fine technical highball/solo above a rocky landing (Font 6b). Escape right.
*Dave Musgrove jnr (FRA, solo)  1st February 1998*

#### 33 **Yorkshire Puddin'**  E2 5c  7m  ★★
The elegant groove is a serious proposition. Save plenty of gravy for the top (and don't look down).
*Al Manson, Pete Kitson  March 1973*

#### 34 **Roast Beef**  E2 6a  5m  ★
The shallow scoop leads to a long reach and insecure finish. Best to not fall off, even with the sandy cam placement. The wall just right can be climbed past a small pocket but is pointlessly escapable.
*Jerry Peel (solo)  September 1985*

#### 35 **Kiernan's Traverse & Rough Crack**  S 4a 9m ★
Follow the break leftwards on jams, then ascend the crack with a huge smile in a great position. It's all over too soon. Can be started direct (VD 3c). Belay options are underwhelming at the top.
*Leonard Kiernan (solo)  1931*

#### 36 **The Low Man Girdle**  S 4a  30m
Take the path of least resistance at this grade from *Rough Crack* to the finish of *V Chimney & Traverse* and belay on the ledge below *Whisky Crack*.

> **❝ ❞**
>
> Your climbs here are little inlaid jewels.
>
> **Legendary 1960s American Yosemite pioneer, Royal Robbins, on a visit to Almscliff and asked how the climbs compared to his local granite skyscrapers.**

51

# THE ALMSCLIFF CRANKER

Whether you're a total newbie to The 'Cliff or a local fed up with hitting the same patch of rock every time you visit the hallowed ground, this circuit of 30 problems is sure to satisfy all but the most extreme esotericist. A collection of Font 5 to 6b+ classics and rarely-trod quality blend beautifully here. Bit hard/easy for you? Not a problem; just glance to the left or right of the described circuit problem and there's most likely something in your ball park. Want crimpy face climbing? You got it. Want powerful arêtes? You got it. Want your problems slopey? You got it. Want friable rock? You've come to the wrong side of the Pennines.

Refer to the aerial photograph on **page 32** to orientate yourself. Coloured numbers after the grade refer to the problem number within the chapter.

### The Warm Up (pages 36 to 42)
Reverse **Three Swings Traverse** (Font 5+ 25), start from *Left Rib* and traverse rightwards, with a tricky move to gain the polished hanging ramp under *Barley Mow*, all the way to, and then up, **Pork Chop Slab** (Font 5+ 30). Walk to the back of The Virgin and solo **Central Route** (Font 4 55) up the centre of the slabby face. Come back around for **North Top Corner** (Font 4 56) up the (left side of the) right arête. The final warm up problem is **Snappy Roof** (Font 5+ 64) up the left side of the roof.

### The Boulders & Low Man (pages 34 to 57)
Round the back of End Boulder for **Field Fair** (Font 5 9) and **The High Step** (Font 5+ 10) then the crimpy classic **Morrell's Wall** (Font 6a 3) and the blunt nose **Fall In** (Font 6a 4) right of *Morrell's Wall*. Cross over to the best line on West Cave Wall, **Hanging Rib** (Font 6a 28), the tantalising but decidedly awkward blunt rib via a thin black crimp. Some respite from crimps on **Flying Arête** (Font 6b 37) to get shoulders engaged ready to pull onto the striking arête of The Virgin for **The Gypsy** (Font 6b+ 46) up to the break [or top-out if you're feeling heroic]. Over to The Keel for **The Crack** (Font 6b+ 69) from a sit-down start under the roof. Behind The Keel is **Nose Bag** (Font 6a 75) up the arête of the Wedge Boulder. Around Low Man (page 51), the obligatory circuit highball comes in the majestic form of **Matterhorn Ridge** (Font 5 18). Right side of MK Wall for the slabby pockets on **MK Original** (Font 5 42). Stroll down to South Cave (page 57) for the tenuous **Backhander** (Font 6a+ 3) and for a complete change of style, the surprisingly awkward **Tetrapak Crack** (Font 5 6).

### High Man (pages 65 to 89)
Up to High Man and Black Wall (to follow the sun). Start to **Black Wall Eliminate** (Font 5+ 142) traverse off right. Right side of the South Wall rib, **The Nose** (Font 5+ 133). The start to **Jacob's Ladder** (Font 5 112, descend the left arête of the wall). The wonderful balancey, **Crucifix Arête** (Font 6a+ 123), and the steady roof **Jam Pot** (Font 5+ 93). The first bulge of **Bancroft's Roof** (Font 6b+ 76) gives a good problem in its own right, continue through the high roof if you're having a good day. **The Niche** (Font 5+ 57), for the comedy value – you have to get all the way in! Start of **The Wall of Horrors** (Font 6b 55). Arête of **Pulpit Corner** (Font 6a+ 41) with sneaky toe shenanigans. Up the bald slab of North Boulder is **Out Of Pocket** (Font 5 46). Finish in the Teaspoon Cave with **Gray's Wall** (Font 6a 19) and **Teaspoon Variation** (Font 6a+ 18), the hanging layback crack.

Yet another Almscliff rite of passage: Matt Birch gains height on **Flying Arete** (Font 5b) Page 38
Photo: Keith Sharples

Joe Killick chewing the cud on the ever popular **The Crucifix** (Font 5). Page 87.
Photo: Mike Hutton

## The Egg & South Cave - ALMSCLIFF

### The Egg
The perched block next to MK Wall. Burly. Crimpy. Good.

**51 Matt's Roof**  Font 7b+
All down to the big move from the increasingly worn crimp.
*Matt Birch 1995* ✦

**52 Streaky's Traverse**  Font 7b+
Another fabulous slopey traverse. Start lying down under the roof (without using the block) and traverse the lip to finish up the groove. Continue into and up *Matt's Roof* to achieve (a) **Zen** (Font 8a). For (b) **Egg Roll** (Font 6b), from a SDS, mantel through the bulge and roll onto the slab.
*Graham Desroy pre-1993* ✦

From just right of *Matt's Roof*, gunning straight for the dish at the top without recourse to the arête is **Buffy Wants Daddy** (Font 7b); the self-explanatory **Matt Meets Buffy**, is Font 7c; **Digital Death** (Font 7c+), starts from the block under the roof to climb to the '*Buffy* finish via the mono.

**53 Silver Trout**  Font 7b
From the sit-down start you can ponder the name of this problem. With the block for feet it's about Font 6c+.

**54 Pipping Arête**  Font 6c+
A sit-down start up amazingly positive pockets leads to slopers and a slightly sandy top-out. Just left, (c) is Font 5.

**55 Cuticula**  Font 6c
From the same sit-down start pockets, reach right for more tendon hungry holes, and head up and right to good slopers and the top.

The very short wall between The Egg and South Cave, is **Steve's Wall** (Font 7a+) climbed from a sit-down start.

### South Cave
Head south for 60m where a conspicuous block is set into the wall and straddles the fence.

**1 Patta's Arête**  Font 7a
The outstanding blunt arête is very crozzly. Start from the slab below right.
*Richie Patterson 1990s*

**2 Southern Shuffle**  Font 4
Wander along the ledge and climb the wall near the arête.

**3 Backhander**  Font 6a+
The arête is tricky with a long reach needed to gain the fluting and hence the break.

**4 On the Fence**  Font 6a+
Long reaches up the wall. Bring a spotter.

**5 South Cave Traverse**  Font 7a+
Start at the crack on the right and traverse left. Finish underneath *Patta's Arête*.

**6 Tetrapak Crack**  Font 5
The crack is more awkward than you'd think.

# PROFILE

**The gangly, pale Baildon lad** with a wild, unruly blonde quiff is, arguably, one of the most significant climbers in the history of Yorkshire gritstone and, even utilising modern equipment, many of his climbs remain superb three-star tests of athleticism and technique more than half a century on.

During the post-war late 1940s and early 1950s, until his untimely death, Arthur Rhodes Dolphin rose to become one of the foremost climbers in Britain. Bill Birkett says of Dolphin: "Arthur was one of the most important and influential figures in the history of British rock climbing, spanning the social gap between the old guard and the emergence of a hungry new breed of working class climbers."

Born into a talented cricketing family, the young Dolphin, despite showing a natural skill for left-arm spin, refused a trial at Headingley and, instead, during rambles on the moors, started scrambling and climbing on the gritstone outcrops.

In his early teens Dolphin had already begun to repeat the hardest climbs at Ilkley and Almscliff and by the age of 16 he was already undisputed leader of the Almscliff group, meeting most Saturdays at the crag. The general rule was climb in 'nails' (hob-nailed boots) in the morning, a break for lunch and then climb in 'rubbers' (Woolworths plimsolls) in the afternoon. Dolphin and his climbing friends took to timing themselves on routes (solo). Nobody could touch Dolphin's times on the more daunting routes such as Traditional Climb or Pothole Direct (which he could do in around 20 seconds). At one of the Wednesday evening gatherings at the crag he was also once seen climbing up and down Frankland's Green Crack in loose-fitting wellington boots.

### ARTHUR DOLPHIN

**1925-1953**
**Grit era:** *1940s, early 1950s*
**Most famous routes:** *Birdlime Traverse, Black Wall, Crack of Doom, Demon Wall, Great Western, North-West Girdle Traverse, Overhanging Groove, Z Climb, Z Climb Eliminate at Almscliff; Angel's Wall, Little Cenotaph, Rabbit's Paw Wall at Caley; Tiger Wall at Earl Crag; Josephine Super Direct and Pebble Groove at Ilkley Cow and Calf; Beeline at Ilkley Rocky Valley; Flake Direct at Widdop; numerous in the Lake District including Communist Convert at Raven Crag, Kipling Groove at Gimmer, Deer Bield Buttress (now fallen down) and Hell's Groove on Scafell East Buttress.*
**What they say about him:** *"When you went to try one of his climbs you knew it was going to be hard."* - Joe Brown

Dolphin went on to climb in Yorkshire and the Lake District during his student years at Leeds University, where he studied metallurgy. After university Dolphin also pursued his passion for running, joining Leeds Harehills Harriers, showing an innate talent for this too. In consecutive years in the early 1950s he was in the team that finished second in the English Cross-Country Championship and Dolphin, along with Jack Bloor and Des Birch, helped establish the classic Three Peaks Race across Pen-y-Ghent, Whernside and Ingleborough. Although the first official race only took place in 1954, it was Dolphin, Bloor and Birch who made the first known running circuit of the peaks in

## PROFILE

the winter of 1948/49, completing the course in varying times from 4 hours 27 minutes to 5 hours 20 minutes.

Although he didn't look naturally sporty, all the years of running and climbing had turned Dolphin into a supreme athlete. Something of a sickly child, Dolphin exercised a lot to build his strength and used to break iron waste with a sledgehammer while working as a metallurgist in Leeds. At over six feet tall Dolphin had tiny hands and feet for his height (wearing size six shoes) but he was noted for being particularly strong in his arms and fingers. Marie Blake, Dolphin's fiancée at the time he tragically died, adds: "I don't know where they got the idea that Arthur was thin. He had a 42-inch chest. I should know, I knitted his sweaters."

The routes Dolphin put up at Almscliff are testament to this strength - Z Climb, Overhanging Groove, Crack of Doom and Great Western. In 1944, with those already under his belt, Dolphin roped in John Ball and John Cook for a famous first ascent of the North-West Girdle Traverse of the crag, taking in some of the finest terrain Almscliff has to offer and as bold an outing for the second as for the leader.

Watchers and partners say Dolphin climbed with a 'quiet ferocity', citing the calmness and ease of his climbing. In fact, partners say the most dangerous part of climbing with Dolphin was usually the motorcycle ride there and back. The astonishing black and white video footage of Dolphin climbing at Almscliff, taken by Reg Hainsworth in 1950 and 1951, shows the effortless nature of his style on routes such as Birds Nest Crack, Pothole Direct, Frankland's Green Crack and Great Western. It's easy to see how far ahead of his time Dolphin was in this footage, displaying an athletic prowess and grace to his climbing that is almost more akin to the golden era of the 1970s a couple of decades later.

But, despite being the climbing star of his era, Dolphin was unassumingly modest, some would even say shy. Out with a friend, Dolphin once met a climber on the fells who boasted about the routes he had done with Arthur, not realising who he was talking to. Arthur listened patiently and chatted away not divulging who he was nor wishing to offend the boaster.

Dolphin was also extremely generous. At the crag Dolphin was happy to pair up with beginners and less experienced climbers on routes and he also devoted a huge amount of time to checking route descriptions and lengths for the Fell and Rock Climbing Club (FRCC), of which he was a member, for their guidebooks, something which hindered his capacity for new routing.

It wasn't just about climbing, either. A member of the FRCC, the Gritstone Club and first president of the Yorkshire Mountaineering Club (YMC), Dolphin would pothole

# PROFILE

one weekend, climb the next, run and fell walk the week after. Almost every weekend, despite Saturday morning work he would be out whatever the weather.

Although Dolphin's routes in Yorkshire are hugely significant he also left his mark in the Lake District with a series of ground-breaking first ascents there, his most famous being Kipling Groove (so-named because it was 'Ruddy 'ard') in 1948 on Gimmer Crag and the now-collapsed classic Deer Bield Buttress in 1951.

The gritstone crags were actually something of a playground and training area for the bigger mountains for Dolphin, who made summer trips to the Alps in the late 1940s and early 1950s, battling through altitude sickness because the short holidays left no time for acclimatisation.

It was in the Alps that this leading light of Yorkshire and British climbing was lost to a tragic accident, leaving behind his fiancée Marie Blake. On 25 July 1953 Dolphin climbed the South Face of the Dent du Géant with Belgian mountaineer André Colard. Dolphin had free climbed most of the route despite the 25 pitons, not even using them as runners. On the descent Dolphin and Colard unroped on reaching the easier ground at the foot of the face. Although no-one witnessed the fatal slip, it appears that crossing a snow slope using footsteps of a previous party Dolphin lost his footing and fell headfirst, striking a rock sticking up from the snow slope 100ft below and continuing to the foot of the couloir, dying instantly. His grave is in Courmayeur.

Who knows what Dolphin would have gone on to achieve but in his relatively short life, he raised the standards of climbing in Britain and left a legacy of magnificent routes still much coveted by any climber today.

**Andy McCue**

*Thanks to the book* **Memories of Dolphin: The life of a climber remembered** *by Tom Greenwood (Green Woods, 2009) to which this profile of Arthur Dolphin is heavily indebted.*

Arthur Dolphin going through the motions on his majestic **Great Western, HVS 5a** (page 78)
Photo: Marie Blake Collection

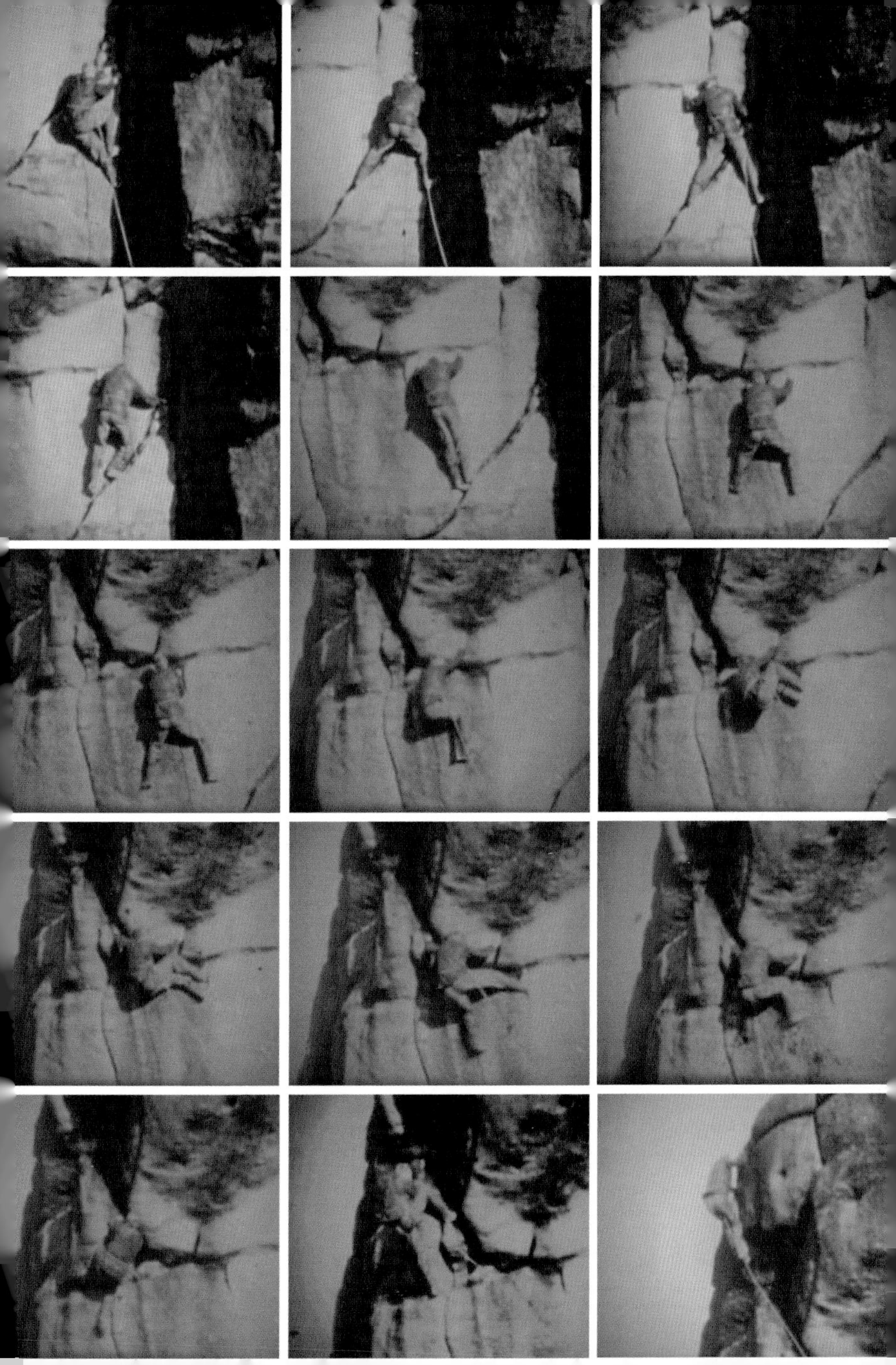

# ALMSCLIFF - North Gully

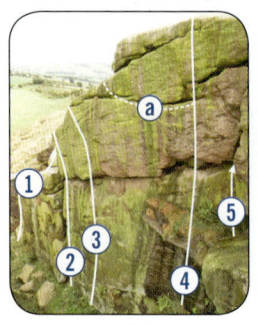

## High Man
This imperial fortress of grit is such a stronghold that scaling lines of weakness shouldn't be taken literally. A myriad of defences lie in wait, from intimidating cracklines and roguish overhangs to gutsy face climbs and adventurous traverses. The victories are hard won; many coming with a last stand that foil the presumptuous. Home to awe-inspiring climbs which finally answer the question, "What have you ever done on grit...?". Bring it on.

We begin rather inauspiciously in **North Gully** at the very far left of the crag. For the majority, this dank corridor will only be witnessed as a descent route. However, since the furtive pursuit of moist esoterica is not yet illegal, we record the following experiences.

**1 The Final Finale** HVD 5a  20m
Unique! Climb the short buttress and follow the slabby top of the crag. Beware the mauvais pas!
*Dave Musgrove & The Almscliff All Stars  Spring 1997*

**2 Green Gully Rib** VS 4c  7m
The rib and wall above.
*Pete Brown (solo) 29th July 1997*

**3 Green Gully Wall** HVS 5a  8m ☆
A worthwhile route when dry. The centre of the wall past convenient pockets. Step left to a rounded finish.
*Tony Barley, Tony Roche  May 1967*

**4 Green Wall** S 4a  8m
Climb up to the miserable seeping grassy ledge and continue up the wall above, or (a) traverse left along the break near the top (VS 4c).

**5 Corner Crack** S 4a  7m
From the same grotty ledge. Short. Surely you have better things to do?

The small buttress projecting into the head of the gully has been climbed, in half a dozen ways, from left-to-right: **Lichen Wall** (S); **Green Gully Left Arête** (S) takes the arête on its left side; **Matt's Arête** (VS 5a) takes it on the right side, right again are **Rocktalk Ruined My PhD** (HVS 5a); **Tudor Rose** (S) and in the corner **Lovat Strides** (S). The cleaner (west) wall of North-East Gully has also been climbed, mostly in descent.

Emerging from the gloomy corridor of North Gully we find the far **North-West Face**. The routes here are rarely done and hence the slabby finishes can be rather sandy, especially after heavy rain.

**6 Fisher's Traverse** HS 4b  16m
A bold climb that is sadly neglected. Marks the beginning of the full girdle of High Man. Traverse the exposed steep slab above the overhangs to a tricky pull into the scoop. Finish up easy slabs.
*Denys Fisher 1938* ✦

**7 Twelfth Night** E2 5c  15m
A thuggy route. Start in the quarried bay and traverse the top of the huge 'sardine' flake past decaying wedges to reach and follow the sloping ledge.
*Pete Kitson, Al Manson  12th July 1973*

Yorkshire Gritstone

Richard Connors gratefully receives the good hold of **Demon Wall** (HVS 5a). Page 85.
Photo Adi Gill.

# Almscliff - North-West Face

**8 The True Two Ton Sardine**  E3 6a   10m
Climb the overhanging and slightly dirty tail of the sardine flake to gain good holds in the traverse line. Finish direct.
*Martin Berzins, Bob Berzins 1979* ✦

**9 All Our Yesterdays**  E5 6a   16m
The obvious challenge, tackling the old peg traverse rightwards across some very uncompromising ground to the left side of a shallow cave. The rib above provides the crux. May need to be, quite literally, unearthed.
*Al Manson, Pete Kitson 24th July 1982*

**10 Few Tomorrows**  E6 6b   15m
A direct line up the undercut rib. Gain holds on the lip and move right, following the rib to the roof. Traverse right to the obvious foothold (runner) and struggle up left onto the ledge. Easier ground leads to the top.
*Pete Brown 31st May 2002*

**11 Exit Stage Left**  E4 6b   11m
Start just on the wide ramp. Traverse left, pasting feet along the lip of the overhang until a wild swing gains a large hold. Then up and right to easy ground.
*Martin Berzins, Al Manson 2nd June 1988*

**12 Penny Pip**  E4 6a   11m
As for the previous route, pull onto the slab and move up to an obvious pocket, follow small sharp pockets diagonally left to find runners when it's already over.
*Duncan Drake (solo) 22nd July 1995*

**13 Finale Slab**  HVS 5a   13m   ☆
An adventure out of proportion to its size. Take small gear. Place a good wire and set off across the slab. Slightly friable rock leads to dirty cracks and a short sharp finish.
*Allan Austin, Brian Evans 28th April 1957*

Yorkshire Gritstone

## North-West Face - ALMSCLIFF

### 14 Encore  E2 5c  10m  ☆
Would make a great highball if the ground didn't disappear. From the large flake, traverse the hanging wall on poor footholds to seek out a critical pocket that takes a nut. Haul over the bulge to reach a rounded boss that feels sketchy when sandy (as it often is).
*John Syrett, Al Manson, Ken Wood 1st May 1973* ✦

### 15 First Night  E3 6a  10m
Brutal. From the flake, stretch out to the lip of the roof and blindly fight in some gear. Scuttle right round the corner to stand up via aggressive jams. Originally claimed to finish up the front face, but not at this grade.
*John Syrett, Al Manson 4th May 1973*

The short sculptured wall and arête, just before the cave of *Cup and Saucer*, houses some friendly problems on clean, solid rock. They're all around the Font 3+ to Font 5 mark and a good spot to get the blood flowing.

### 16 Cup and Saucer  HVD 4a  13m  ★
A weirdly spacious outing. The obvious caves can be climbed via many variations, best on the left. Once atop the capstone, climb the left wall.
*Herbert Ingle, Thomas Gray c1891*

### 17 Teaspoon Variation Left  Font 7a
The roof left of *Teaspoon Variation* provides a great sequence, following the thin broken crack.

### 18 Teaspoon Variation  Font 6a+
The hanging layback crack. A tantalising teaser.
*Arthur Dolphin, Des Birch 25th April 1948*

### 19 Gray's Wall  Font 6a
Lovely balancey climbing up the undercut wall and rib above.

### 20 Why Climb  E3 6a  10m
Boulder up to the sloping ledge and attack the bulge above by a long lurch.
*Al Manson, Ray Conlon c1976*

### 21 X-Factor  E3 6a  13m
Climb *Gray's Wall* to the ledge. Spanning between small holds on the rib and the crack of *Z Climb*, ascend to the flaky funnel and hence the ledge. Climb the slabby wall just left of the rib above. Tough for shorties.
*Pete Brown, Dave Garner 24th June 2007* ✦

### 22 Z Climb  VS 4c  15m  ★★★
A proper grit VS that throws everything at you. Swing confidently left along the crack to a cramped rest on the sloping ledge. Gingerly stand up and mash fists into the base of the crack out right, up to the elbow as you swing into action. Slug it out up the crack to the zag where it's possible to recover a little. Follow your fate out left to the sloping ledge and a surprisingly engaging finish.
*Arthur Dolphin 1940*

Alan Hinkes going for the 15,000mm summit of **Central Climb** (VS 4c). Page 68.
Photo: Hinkes Collection.

### 23  North-West Girdle  E1 5b  65m  ★★★
A great expedition that crosses the most exciting sections of the crag. The route described here is perhaps the most satisfying, though not the original.
*Arthur Dolphin, John Cook and John (Pug) Ball 14th May 1944* ✦

**1.** (5b) Start up *Z Climb* and follow the wide diagonal crack rightwards all the way into *Central Climb*. Step down to the triangular niche and traverse right into *Overhanging Groove* and up into the cave of *Parsons' Chimney*.
**2.** (5b) From the cave, a delicate section leads upwards on the right until it is possible to swing round the corner and hand-traverse into *Frankland's Green Crack*. Move

Yorkshire Gritstone

up the crack and follow the obvious rounded break rightwards, all the way into Long Chimney.
**3.** (5b) Leaving the top of the chimney is the crux and gives plenty of food for thought, particularly for the second. Step across under the overhang and traverse airily above the top of *The Wall of Horrors* to the pinnacle of *Great Western*.
**4.** (5a) Descend *Great Western*, traverse right and finish, up *Crack of Doom*.

There are several variations all at about the same grade.
**1a.** Take the upper line on the first pitch. From the junction with *Central Climb* step up and traverse to cross *Overhanging Groove* and step down into the cave.
**2a.** The **Original Route**: from *Frankland's Green Crack* step down to belay on the Pulpit. A very long stride or a hand-traverse lead into *Long Chimney*. Ascend the chimney to belay towards the top.
**1b.** A harder variation of the first two pitches follows the very topmost break, passing high above the *Parson's Chimney* cave and much more steeply across the break under the headwall of *The Big Greeny* dropping down into *Frankland's Green Crack*.

Almscliff to Slipstones

# ALMSCLIFF - North-West Face

### 24 Microscopic Wall  E3 6b  13m
Take a literal-minded direct start through bulges to gain the black flake on *Z Climb Eliminate*. Continue direct to finish up the right-hand side of the blunt arête above.
*Pete Brown, Matthew Ramsden  18th August 1992*

### 25 Z Climb Eliminate  E1 5b  14m  ★★★
A wonderfully varied and satisfying buffet of moves stitching together some of the best climbing on this wall. The slippery start leads to a trio of crimps. Span left to reach the black flake and/or the perfect nut-eating crack. The wide crack above leads rightwards onto lovely crozzly pockets and into *Central Climb*. Up this, then right again along the thin break and up the final slim groove to a thankfully juggy finish. Photo on page 24.
*Arthur Dolphin, John Cook  23rd April 1946*

### 26 Central Eliminate  E1 5b  15m  ★
Tightly squeezed in but nonetheless, enjoyable climbing up positive holds with gear (out right) when you need it.
*Tony Marr, Alan Taylor  12th March 2000*

### 27 Central Climb  VS 4c  15m  ★★
Enjoy armfuls of gritstone on this classic excursion up huge rounded holds and sinker jams...relax and enjoy your assured grit technique, or fight all the way and get pumped out of your mind. Photo on page 65.
*Claude Frankland  pre-1923*

### 28 WASC  E1 5c  15m  ★
What A Silly Climb, but a lovely little link up. Climb directly up the steep wall from the triangular niche on *Central Climb*. Finish up the thin crack of *Z Climb Elliminate*.
*Al Manson, Ray Conlon  c1976*

### 29 Tortoises and Hares  E4 6a  14m  ★
Climb the blunt rib direct (gear in *Central Climb* reduces the grade) to the niche, traverse right a few feet and ascend the wall above with a big move to gain two obvious flutings and the break. Climb the final wall above: tricky on the left, thin on the right.
*Pete Brown, Andi Turner, Dave Garner  11th June 1998*

### 30 Overhanging Groove  HVS 5a  17m  ★★★
One of the great Almscliff HVSs, guaranteed to blow the cobwebs away. Pull into the groove using worn footholds and ascend easily. Eschew the tantalising ledge out right and stylishly bridge the groove to rest. Place perfect gear before up-and-downing a bit to decipher a tricky move into the upper groove. Now swim for the surface up spaced jugs. Exhilarating.
*Arthur Dolphin, Robert Heap  3rd May 1941*

### 31 Toad's Nose  E4 6b  15m
Start from a good hold in the chimney. Make a big move left around onto the nose and hence to the ledge. Arrange gear and tackle the increasingly bold hanging rib above. The sit-down start gives **The Dark Side of Chi** (Font 7b+).
*Pete Brown  29th October 1995* ✦

---

**❝ ❞**

It's no different than doing one...two...thr-fo-fi,' squinting one eye and following the line with his mind's eye and calculating each individual powerful move...'nine pull-ups,' he says confidently. 'You can do nine pull-ups can't you?' He says to me directly. Pete was known as 'SP', short for 'Silent Pete', not because he never said anything but perhaps more because he condensed what needed to be said to the bare facts.

This was blatant in his climbing too. To him Western Front was nothing more than a simplified exercise, silent climbing? This is how he was to persuade me up my first E3, after all I could sometimes do 11 pull-ups, especially if I pedalled my legs enough and really lifted my chin to meet the bar.

Moving left across the hand-rail I imagine the pull-ups draining from arms, the petrol gauge going down. I move up and place the crucial runner, after all, no route can be a classic without a crucial in it, can it? Back on the good hold, heel over head and I hear calmly 'Relax Andi, look out to that farm, not at the climb, 'til you've got it all back. It's in't bag this time'. He was right, Silent Pete.

**Andi Turner reflecting on the crag where he cut his teeth climbing**

North-West Face - **Almscliff**

Almscliff to Slipstones

**ALMSCLIFF** - North-West Face

### 32 Parson's Chimney   HS 4b   17m   ★★★
A brilliant adventure that is terrifyingly exposed. At one time the hardest route at The 'Cliff. Use all available appendages and unconscionable techniques to ascend the chimney. The lower half is ungainly, the upper half implausible. A belay at half-height might be required to recover and generously hand-over the lead.
*William Parsons   c1900*

### 33 Fungus the Bogeyman   E4 6a   14m   ★
A fine companion to its more famous brother. Satisfying moves above good gear to an engaging exit. An independent start can be contrived.
*Graham Desroy, Charles Cook, Paul Dawson   1980*

### 34 The Big Greeny   E3 6a   15m   ★★★
Fantastic climbing in an heroic position. Tough moves right to the very end about a thousand feet above your gear. The fall from the top is well-tested. Oh, and don't underestimate the technical start. Photo on page 10.
*John Syrett, Al Manson   1st May 1973   ✦*

### 35 Ginger Whinger   E6 7a   14m   ★
The alluring hanging scoop provides a harsh test of power and technique. Start up *Frankland's Green Crack* to reach the groove; nip across to arrange the bomber gear in *The Big Greeny*. Span in from the right to a vague sidepull, then crank up the faint groove.
*Steve Dunning   2005*

### 36 Frankland's Green Crack   VS 4c   18m   ★★★
This fine old fashioned tussle was a remarkable achievement for the time. Climb the crack until the rounded break allows a tiring rightward traverse. A bit of grunt is required to get established in the corner above, but save something for the outrageous finale. Don't let the greenness put you off, though the pigeon poo might. As an alternative to surmounting the finishing bulge, escape left along the enjoyably exposed **Eastern Exit** (VS 5a), or rightwards past in-situ pigeons on **Always Greener** (HVS 5b) to finish past flutings on the arête. Photo on page 681.
*Claude Dean Frankland   1919   ✦*

Yorkshire Gritstone

## North Boulder - ALMSCLIFF

**37 Merlin**  E3 5c   14m
A rather grotty eliminate up the crinkly green wall.
*Mark Furniss  4th September 1984*

**38 Fat Man's Misery**  HS 4b   8m
A perverse pleasure for irredeemable udgers.
Climb the cleft.
*Thomas Gray & friends (as a descent)  pre-1894*

**39 Pulpit Friction**  E2 5c   8m
Make a long move off the small pocket to grab the ledge; uninspiring gear can be arranged out right.
*Pete Brown, Mick Green, Stuart Purvis  7th June 1998*

**40 Al Says 6a**  E4 6b   8m
The direct line up The Pulpit with gear out right.
*Jerry Peel, Gil Peel  1988*

**41 Pulpit Corner**  E1 5b   18m   ★
The right arête on its left side. From atop The Pulpit, use the obvious large pocket to gain the rounded break. Traverse rightward along this to better holds and up flutings to finish. Alternatively, from the top of The Pulpit, take a deep breath, step off the rightmost corner and follow (a) **Pulpit Corner Direct** (E3 5c) straight up the rib.
*Claude Dean Frankland pre1927. P2 Allan Austin, B Evans 1956* ✦

**42 Cassock Slap**  Font 6a+
The right side of the left arête; do something clever with your right foot.

**43 Crinkle Cut**  Font 5
Easily up to the break via crozzly holds out right. Font 6c using just the crimp, without crozzles.

**44 The Easy Way**  HD 3c   8m
An introduction to thrutching. Climb the chimney facing *Long Chimney*. Now how are you going to get down?
*Thomas Gray and friends pre-1894*

### North Boulder
The large boulder with a long slabby downhill face.

**45 Chipped Slab**  Font 2
The crack on the left side that fades into chipped holds.

**46 Out of Pocket**  Font 5
Up the slab – leave the pockets and trend right.

**47 Northern Shuffle**  Font 7a
Sit-down start. Tough uphill traverse, without using the lip.

**48 Sunny Scoop**  Font 5
Sit-down start. Rock up into the scoop.

**49 Knee Biter**  Font 5+
Another rockover problem, using the big pocket.

**50 Stubby Arête**  Font 5
The short arête.

**51 Shadow Face**  Font 4
The slab using the flake and pockets, avoiding the arête.

Other variations are possible on all faces of North Boulder.

Back to the main crag we resume with the proud and historic chimney of:

**52 Long Chimney**  HVD 4a   18m   ★★
Savour your heritage with this feast of back and footing up the polished chimney. Finish with a short exposed traverse out left near the top. Character-building stuff.
*Herbert Ingle, Thomas Gray  1893*

**53 Wall of Horrors Traverse**  Font 6c+
From the chimney, descend to pass under the niche and finish on the ledge.

**54 The Horror**  Font 7a+
The bulge direct to finish at the big jug.

# PROFILE

**What about the 1920s to 1940s?**

In terms of the generation of Yorkshire climbers before me just think about Twin Cracks (HS 4b) at Ilkley. Done before the First World War. We're talking about a really hard climb. I don't care what standard you climb at. Nobody walks up that.

You'd go down south and the hardest route that any of them lot ever did was Elliott's Unconquerable at Cratcliffe (HVS 5a, 1933). It's a hand jam, on a slab but the roof comes right down. It's a hard route but then look at the (Ilkley) quarry. Bloody Botterill's Crack (HVS 5a, 1920) done years earlier. We didn't give these old boys enough credit. We climbed all these old Yorkshire routes but everywhere else we went they were a lot easier.

As for Dolphin, we all regarded him as being a gentleman. You can't say more than that; honest, straightforward. Just think, Demon Wall (HVS 5a, 1940), with no runners. There weren't even any in my day and none came I don't recall even to the day I gave up climbing. An awful lot of the people that I was climbing with had never led it. That's impressive.

**How do you feel about the climbing you see today?**

It's not for me to pass an opinion. It's not my sport. I think had I been starting afresh that the thing that would have suited me would have been something like cave diving.

**You used to climb in all weathers back then didn't you?**

Yes, we never wasted a day. I once got 100 routes in at Ilkley after tea. I got there about seven o clock and I got just under this 100 and I thought tomorrow I'll crack the hundred. So the next day I went back. It meant all the Hard VS's downwards really. That was the time I decided I wouldn't solo High Street but I did the others, Short Circuit and that sort of thing.

**What do you think is the best new route you did?**

People look at them and your reputation is limited to one or two climbs. How many routes do you think I did on grit? I did 400 new ones, plus 200 on limestone and 100 on what you'd call volcanic rock. Most people's production is like that. So when you think back out of all these routes and how many I've done that I'm really proud of, it's not that many. The best route I ever did was in Ireland in Donegal, a 550-foot HVS. Better than Centurion. Now gets three stars in the book. I made the only free ascent of White Slab, the only E4 that was climbed before 1960. Everybody else had lassooed the crucial pitch. It's E4 today that pitch. I did it in 1959.

**And what about just on Yorkshire grit?**

The big thing I aimed at because I'd looked at it for four years was The Wall of Horrors. I always hoped I might get a 10 year one. You know, one that wasn't repeated for 10 years. The Wall of Horrors was eight or nine I think. But when I think back, I think The Shelf (Crookrise) was a good one. Of course the Almscliff ones will be classics. Largely because Almscliff lines are so impressive. What else out of all those? There aren't many. Allan's Crack at Brimham? It's just an ordinary route isn't it?

**Interview by Robin Nicholson**

Neil Lowery soaking up the atmosphere having reached easy street on **Western Front** (E3 5c). Page 78.
Photo: Mike Hutton

## ALMSCLIFF - Great Western

**55 The Wall of Horrors**  E3 6a  18m  ★★★
This is what you came for; the second of the big E3s and what a corker. A powerful boulder problem start gets the juices flowing. Yard up the crack, slam cams in the deep horizontal break and get ready to pull down with everything you've got left. Bloody magic. **The Horror of Walls** uses the same start and finish but climbs the wall out left. Climbing to the dish is a must-do (Font 6b) problem in its own right. Photo on cover and page 674.
*Allan Austin (solo) 28th June 1961* ✦

**56 All Quiet**  E4 6a  25m  ★★★
The ultimate power endurance workout. Up *The Wall of Horrors* to the horizontal break, traverse rightwards under the roof across *Western Front* and up the diagonal crack into the finish of *Crack of Doom* before your forearms explode.
*Pete Livesey, Al Manson 27th June 1974*

**57 Every Man Has His Niche**  E4 6b  6m
Gain the niche, then exit by traversing out right on slopers to regain the ground, or mantelshelf with some commitment into *The Ems Telegram*. Climbing all the way into **The Niche** is worth Font 5+ in its own right. Photo on page 49.
*P. Greenland, A. Burnell, C. Sowden 1987; Pre-1912 (The Niche)*

**58 The Ems Telegram**  E5 6b  20m  ★★
Another quality pumpfest. Boldly sneak up leftwards to the obvious pocket and lay one on for the handrail. Scoot left under the overlap to the base of the bottomless curving crack. Dig deep and power up this on wilting arms to the finish of *The Wall of Horrors*. You beast!
*Mike Hammill c1977*

**59 Leaf Climb**  HVD 4a  20m
A historical oddity. Climb the crack in the crevasse back up to ground level (no bridging). Nip round the rib to the right and ascend *West Chimney* to the ledge and traverse left following jugs to the top.
*William Cecil Slingsby and friends c1870*

**60 Western Front**  E3 5c  13m  ★★★
Simply one of the best grit routes anywhere, making up the trinity of outstanding E3s. Steep but straightforward climbing leads to the Y-junction where things get ugly.

Karate chop into the crack with all your might, grit your teeth and hang on. All at once the jugs are at hand and it's in the bag. Sneaky ascents using balance and technique have been reported, but this sort of behaviour shouldn't be encouraged. Photo on previous page.
*Allan Austin (solo) 9th July 1958*

**61 Great Western**  HVS 5a  15m  ★★★
The much heralded classic of the crag and a good, honest, knackering fight. Layback up the corner to good gear and the realisation it's not a place to rest. Along the handrail the footholds end but the jugs keep coming. Gasp up into the niche for a cramped rest. Head out right in a phenomenal position along the crenulated break, using tiny footholds on the brink of the void. Sink into glorious jams and top-out with a huge grin (known as the **Five Star Finish**). Or, (a) for the **Original** exit, from the niche stand up awkwardly and finish direct up the crack. Another alternative finish is via **Pocket Variant** without use of the two cracks. Photos on pages 29 and 61.
*Arthur Dolphin, Robert Heap 19th September 1943*

**62 No Mans Land**  E2 5b  20m  ★★
If you're not tired at the end of the *Great Western* traverse, press on underneath the prow until lovely crozzly rock leads up and left to the top. Known as **Over The Top** when used as a finish to *Western Front* (a combination probably worth E4).
*Tony Marr, Mike Tooke 1st September 1991*

**63 Grand Illusion**  E3 6a  12m  ★★★
An improbable powerful line helped by a l-o-n-g reach. Excellent gear in the roof and on the traverse. Gain the obvious dish on the blunt lip and pull hard, up left to the pucker in the headwall. One more move to the finishing crack of *Great Western*. Photo on page 83.
*Charles Cook 1979*

**64 Megadoom**  E5 6b  12m  ★★★
Maximum exposure in the shortest distance. Climb up the corner-crack and straight out the widest part of the roof to a good hold on the lip. Stay calm and head directly up the rib. Finishing up the flutings out right is (b) **Impending Doom** (E4 6a, ★).
*Pete Brown, Andi Turner, Stuart Purvis 11th October 1997* ✦

Yorkshire Gritstone

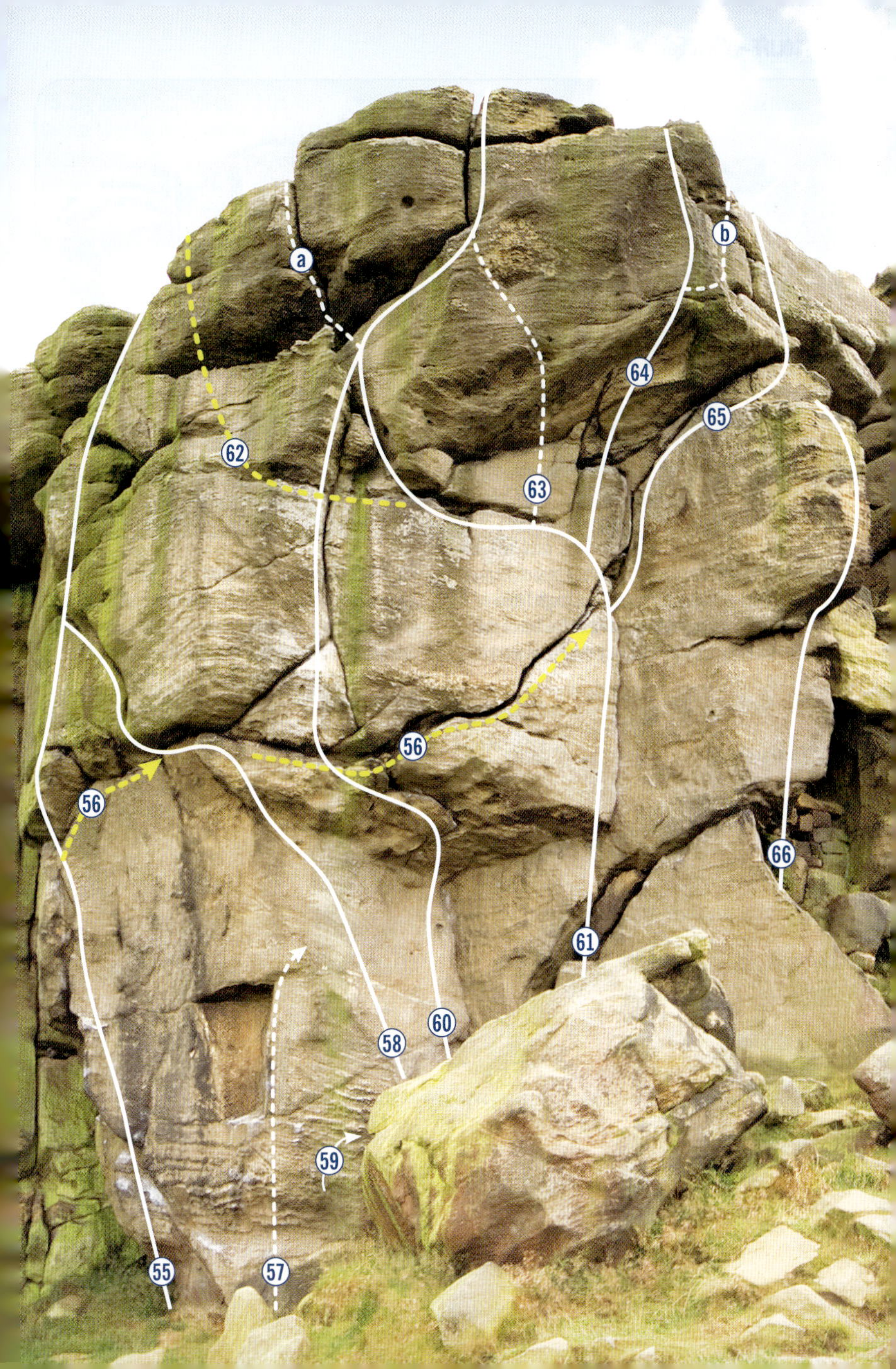
a
b
64
65
62
63
56
56
66
61
60
58
59
55
57

# ALMSCLIFF - The Rift

### 81 Si's Arête  Font 7a+
Clamp up slopers on the blunt arête from a sit-down start.
*Simon Panton* ✦

### 82 Hobgoblin  E2 5c  11m  ★★
Start as for *Clematis*. A tough leftward traverse leads to the obvious two-finger pocket in a stunning position, then sandy finishing holds.
*Andy Wild, Dave Musgrove  1st April 1983*

### 83 Clematis  E2 5c  10m  ★★
Positive holds and lovely moves lead steeply to the break. Span out left and low from the large pocket and shuffle off, or stand tall and take the (a) **Nelly-Moser Finish** (E3 6a).
Photo on previous page.
*Eric Lillie, Ian Brimrose  October 1969* ✦

### 84 Oubliette  E2 6a  8m  ★
Really packs it in. Follow generous holds left then make some hard pulls up the groove. Walk off if you've had enough (the original way) or finish as for (a) using the huge pocket for your left hand.
*Eric Lillie, Ian Brimrose  October 1969*

### 85 Daisy Chain  E3 6b  7m
Hard pulls on friable edges bring the rounded sandy ledge within reach.
*Pete Kitson (solo)  8th June 1985*

### 86 Tight Chimney  M  7m
Well named – don't take a rack! Climbed most easily deep in the bowels of the crag. Sticking to the outside and finishing left of the chockstone is worth Severe.
*William Cecil Slingsby and friends  c1870*

### 87 Constipation Crack  VS 5a  7m
A desperate pull brings the loose chockstone within reach. Exit up and right, or follow the (b) original and tougher left-hand finish through the V-notch. (c) **Suppository Wall** (Font 5+) is a serious climb above the prominent boulder.
*Unknown  pre-1969; Pete Brown  17th June 1997 (Supp' Wall)*

### 88 Rift Crack  VS 5a  7m  ★
Short and fun. At the top search around - there is a finishing hold somewhere, set well back.
*Unknown  pre-1969*

### 89 Yorkshire Relish  VS 4c  6m
Even shorter. Climb the surprisingly awkward wide crack.
*Tony Marr, Mike Tooke, Alan Taylor  22nd August 1999*

### 90 Emmaus Road  E2 5c  25m  ★
A high traverse of The Rift where butch beginnings lead to a technical finish. Start from standing on the wall and traverse left along the obvious roundedness and head for the finish of *Hobgoblin*.
*Robin Nicholson, Andy McCue  29th January 2010 (FRA)*

Yorkshire Gritstone

Stuart Lancaster wishing the pocket was nearer on **Grand Illusion** (E3 6a). Page 78.
Photo: Mike Hutton

# Almscliff - South-West Face

**The Rift Traverse** (Font 5) is an excellent excursion from the stone stile leftwards to finish in West Chimney. Over the stile, on the right-hand side, are several problems (between Font 3+ and Font 7a).

Re-emerging from The Rift onto the **South-West Face** is a compact slabby block. Variants are possible but the following problem is the best hereabouts and nicely awakens the senses to the plethora of quality climbs that abound here.

## 91 Honey Comb   Font 5+
From a sit-down start climb the undercut bulging arête and rock left onto the slabby top. The wall to the right is a tricky Font 4.

## 92 The Pothole   VD   11m
Start up the slabby boulder and traverse onto the main face high up, missing much of the climbing.
*Ingle, Dent, Gray, Calvert   pre-1900*

## 93 Jam Pot   Font 5+
Start in the low break and climb rugosities round the juggy overhang. Requires a confident approach and a good spotter. **Dots and Dabs** (Font 6c) takes the wall just right.

## 94 Pothole Direct   VS 5b   10m   ★★
A great little route. The juggy crack is protected by a desperate start. If you can't jam, you'll barely leave the ground.
*Denys Fisher   1938*

## 95 Classic Traverse   Font 4+
Traverse the easiest line from the start of *Jam Pot* to the chimney.

## 96 High Level Traverse   VS 4c   18m   ★★
Follow the top break left-to-right. Finish up *Bird's Nest Crack* or keep going to the top of *Demon Wall* (at 5a).
*Allan Austin (solo)   30th November 1957*

## 97 Traditional Eliminate   HVS 6a   10m
Put your blinkers on and climb the wall just left of the crack, deliberately avoiding it. The traditional start is by a jump to the handrail from the boulder a couple of metres out from the base of the crag.
*LUUMC Members   c1973*

## 98 The Traditional Climb   VS 4c   10m   ★★★
The obvious crack can be awkward and surprisingly tiring, or an enjoyable exhibition of your jamming finesse.
*Claude Dean Frankland   pre-1923*

Yorkshire Gritstone

## South-West Face - ALMSCLIFF

**99 Forgotten Wall** E4 6c 10m ★
A fine technical eliminate. Use the vague diagonal groove and a long reach to gain the terribly rounded break. Somehow gain a standing position and the next break, then continue with interest to the top. (a) **Remembrance Some Day** (E4 6b) allows an easier escape: from the rounded break, step left and climb just right of the crack, finishing via the large pocket.
*Rob Gawthorpe, Pete Jackson 1980* ✦

**100 Bird's Nest Crack** HS 4b 10m ★★
The polished crackline is a popular place to deposit beginners. Nigh on perfect jams allow height to be gained. Moving right is the crux where the crack is wider and more desperate than you'd think. Done it many times before? Try the old-school game of climbing without the aid of the crack. Provides much entertainment for the masses. Photo on page 35.
*Herbert Ingle, Edward Calvert pre-1900*

**101 Thompson's Traverse** HVS 5b 18m ★★
Start as for *Bird's Nest Variation*. At the top of the thin crack traverse the slopey break left with increasing difficulty to reach *Traditional Climb*. Then continue more easily all the way to *The Pothole*.
*Sydney Thompson c1934*

**102 Bird's Nest Variation** MVS 4c 10m ★★
Climb the thin crack then move left making a difficult high step. At full span the next break will just about be within reach. Step left to the juggy nose and an easier finish. An eliminate direct finish (avoiding the nose) can just about be squeezed in at E1 5b.

**103 Demon Wall** HVS 5a 10m ★★★
This little devil puts up a good fight. Move right from the top of the crack to the short flake and layback up to reach the energy sapping break. Press on before your arms fade and throw your longest possible reach over the rounded top to try and find something to hold on to. Ridiculously pumpy to lead, and definitely 5b for shorties. Photo on page 63.
*Arthur Dolphin 1940*

Almscliff to Slipstones

# ALMSCLIFF - South Face

## The South Face
Finally we come to the sun soaked south face which has a big feel about it, especially when you get above the roof.

**125 Dreamland**  Font 7a+
A slippery customer. More like a nightmare on a warm day. Trending right from the wall is **Off the Wall** (Font 5+).

**126 Shuffle Crack**  E1 5c   12m   ★
Jam up the short vertical crack and follow the corner to the roof, then shuffle left with difficulty to easy ground.
*Allan Austin, Brian Evans  1958*

**127 China Syndrome**  E6 7a   12m   ★
Extremely powerful moves round the roof. Get tired placing good gear in the flake then pull hard, rocking up using a knee bar to gain the pocket.
*Rob Gawthorpe  1980*

**128 South Chimney Layback**  S 4b   15m   ★
The Almscliff entrance exam. Stern-jamming up the vertical crack leads to a rising rightward traverse. Layback pleasantly up the flake and traverse into the chimney to an airy but easy exit.
*Unknown  pre-1912*

**129 Yellow Wall**  E2 5c   14m
A tough bold climb. Difficulties are short-lived but significant. From the chimney, traverse left under the roof. Hand holds are poor, footholds out of sight and protection difficult to place. Finish up the short crack.
*Tony Barley, Chas Hird  June 1966*

**130 Yellow Peril**  E4 6a   12m
A demanding alternative. Tackle the roof from halfway along the traverse using the pocket to reach a sandy finish.
*Mike Hammill, Mike Raine  1980*

**131 The Wall**  Font 5
The pocketed wall (no arête). A frustrating problem, **The Slab** (Font 5+), takes the polished ramp to the left.

**132 South Chimney**  VD 4a   11m   ★
Another wonderfully traditional challenge.
*William Cecil Slingsby and friends  c1870*

**133 The Nose**  Font 5+
Ascend the rib up to the break. Then try it on the right side without touching the rib via a huge reach or a slap at Font 6a+.

**134 South Face Climb**  MVS 4b   12m
Start on the right side of the rib. Climb the polished gangway, traverse left to the arête and mantel onto the tiny ledge on the nose. Now boldly pad up and left to the edge of the chimney and climb the bulges above.
*Unknown  pre-1912*

**135 South Wall Traverse**  VS 4c   14m   ★★★
An exposed adventure. Start as before and mantel onto the rib, then pad up the right edge of the slab to reach the roof and, thankfully, bomber gear. Step up and right where the short juggy break allows an airy step out onto the lip of the roof. One tough pull brings the wide break to hand. Steady moves lead to the top. From the top right corner of the slab, **South Wall Direct** (E1 5b) follows a very direct line through the rounded bulges.
*Claude Frankland  pre-1923*  ✦

**136 Kitson Did It First**  E3 6b   10m
Nice moves frustratingly close to the arête which is off limits. Finishes at the break.
*Pete Kitson  1973*

**137 Birdlime Traverse**  HVS 5b   19m   ★★★
A demanding sightseeing tour across the entire wall. Ascend the rib as for *South Wall Traverse*. On reaching the roof step down and right, following the break with a noticeable absence of good rests. At the roof's end, climb the thin crack and traverse right to exit at the notch.
*Arthur Dolphin, John Cook  18th August 1946*

**138 'Arries Left 'Ook**  E4 6c   13m   ★
A powerful route taking the toughest line through the roof. Climb straight up the wall, passing just left of the carved 'W' and arrange bomber gear under the roof. Span out to the obvious black boss and use a mono in the wall above to gain the break. Finish via the easy jamming crack.
*James Ibbertson  23rd January 2006*

South Face - **ALMSCLIFF**

**139 'Arries 'Ook** E4 6a   13m   ★★
A testing combination of committing technical wall climbing and good old fashioned thuggery. Traverse right with difficulty using undercuts to stride onto an obvious large black foothold. Keep a cool head and climb straight up (the bird lime should not affect the difficulty). Good gear in the break protects some big moves up and right to gain the top break and an easy finish.
*Pete Livesey, Ron Fawcett  1975* ✦

**140 'Arries 'Ook Direct Start** Font 7a+
Layback up the slopey ramp and press out right for the obvious black jug, or use the undercling to build your feet up and fire straight for it. Jump off, or stand up with great difficulty and continue to the top.

**141 Blackhead** E4 6c   13m   ★★
The convex wall provides an excellent highball problem (Font 7b); the rest of the route is a stroll by comparison. From the top of the flake reach high and left for a small black sidepull. Pull up to a poor sloper and then to good holds in the break. Traverse off, or continue up the thin crack and finish direct, 2m left of the notch. There is a hold over the top if you feel around a bit. Photo on next page.
*Graham Desroy, John Paul Hotham  24th April 1990*

**142 Black Wall Eliminate** E2 5c   15m   ★★★
A tremendous and exhilarating climb. A tough boulder problem start up the black flake gains the juggy break. Traverse left to the thin crack and fingery pockets. Climb up to the top break and swing boldly left onto the nose in a magnificent position. The wide crack happily swallows gear and arms, leading to the easy finishing crack.
Photo on page 91.
*Tony Barley, Chas Hird  June 1966*

**143 Blackpool Promenade** E1 5b   20m   ★★
The counter-diagonal to *Birdlime Traverse*. Start up the rib and follow the juggy break left, dropping down slightly to go under the roof. At the left end of the roof, pull up left and somehow squirm along rounded breaks to escape.
*Dave Musgrove, Mike Butler  1975*

**144 Black Wall** VS 5b   10m   ★★
A fine outing that really got the party started on this wall. Climb the right edge of the wall over an awkward bulge. Traverse left easily then finish directly through the notch above. Topping out is not always an elegant affair.
Photo on page 27.
*Arthur Dolphin, Robert Heap  24th August 1941*

Almscliff to Slipstones

ALMSCLIFF - South Face

### 145  Black Wall Direct   HVS 5b   10m
As for *Black Wall*, but stick resolutely to the right edge of the wall in order to grapple with the terribly sloping finish. The short end of the buttress has been climbed as **Stepoffable** (HVS 5b).
*Mike Hammill, S. Williams, M. Raine, S. Collins 1980* ✦

A low-level rightward traverse is possible across Black Wall starting from *South Chimney* at Font 7a. The multiple intersecting Black Wall routes offer many combinations that cover no significantly new ground. The short wall to the right is **Shothole Arête** area and houses a handful of problems between Font 2 and Font 5+, the best being the wall just right of the little arête.

### 146  Full Traverse of High Man   E2 5c   165m ★★
Mighty. The most obvious method of doing the full girdle starts with *Fisher's Traverse*, reversing *Finale Slab* to then climb across *Cup & Saucer* and join the glorious *NW Girdle*. At its end, cross easy ground above *Syrett's Roof*, then down *Zig Zag* to traverse under the *Goblin* roof, following breaks into The Rift. Skip across the wall and wander around to join *Thompson's Traverse*, then follow your nose to reverse *Shuffle Crack* so as to join *Birdlime Traverse*.
*Tony Barley   May 21st 1966 (full link-up)*

**“ ”**

First up was Encore. I watched as Syrett placed h gear, swung left and committed himself. As he da gled from the overhang he spontaneously did a hee hook, the first time I had ever seen it done. He pulle up and it was all over. Then it was straight over to Th Big Greeny. He placed the runners, leaned back an looked at the top wall, then climbed it. He made look easy, if steep. It was only when others tried to fo low that one realised that it was pretty hard. Only Ke Wood and Al Manson were good enough to second.

Although it was an historic evening, it was all take as a matter of course. Certainly in the pub afterwar there were no particular celebrations but much talk what could be done next!

John Harwood describing two of Syrett's first ascen

*Adi Gill searching for the pot of gold on **Blackhead** (E4 6c, highball to the break at Font 7b). Page 89.*
*Photo: Mike Hutton*

Lucy Creamer gearing up for the headwall of **Black Wall Eliminate** (E2 5c). Page 89.
Photo: Tim Glasby

# ALMSCLIFF - First Ascents

## Further First Ascent Information (✦)

**All Natural:** *Climbed by Andy Swann.*

**'Arries 'Ook:** *A devious solution to a long-standing problem. The name arises from the fact that Harry Mammal (Mike Hammill) had been trying the more direct line and had, it is rumoured, considered using a skyhook. Hammill and Manson did, in fact, climb the direct finish in April 1975, before the lower wall was solved.*

**Barley Mow:** *Possibly the first Font 7a problem in the UK. Allegedly Dennis Gray reckoned Royal Robbins tried & failed to climb this route during a visit in the early '60s. Tony Barley: "Dennis was quite right that Royal Robbins failed on the Barley Mow during his UK visit. He had staggered us all with his Yosemite big wall slideshow & the concept of hard climbing in stiff vibram boots - but they weren't so good on gritstone. Still he got up Morrell's Wall & Teaspoon Variation. Anyway it drew my attention to Barley Mow which, long before my time had been aided with 2 or 3 pegs. May 21st 1966 was quite a good day for me - I had made probably the 2nd ascent of Forked Lightning Crack at Heptonstall in the morning - moved on to Almscliff and made the first of my many solos of the Almscliff girdle in 40 minutes (finally I extended it reversing Finale Slab and finishing up Birdlime Traverse). Anyway, late afternoon there were a few boulderers so we did Morrell's Wall and everything and as usual Robin "sent me up" Barley Mow; "New route opposite Morrells Wall" written in my diary. Basically I got so far up I couldn't get down. It was a problem I never repeated! At that time 6a was the hardest Brit grade available."*

**The Big Greeny:** *Allan Austin made an early attempt on this unclimbed line, making it right to the sloping top-out where he failed to find good enough holds to get off, so down climbed to the ground.*

**Birdlime Traverse:** *Dolphin recorded the first descent of Overhanging Groove the same day.*

**Clematis Nelly-Moser Finish:** *Climbed by Pete Brown, Steve Turner, Dave Garner 2nd July 1992.*

**Constipation Crack Right-hand Finish:** *FRA Tony Marr, Mike Tooke 1999.*

**Cup and Saucer:** *This was the first climb attempted by the pair (Herbert Ingle, Thomas Gray), who may also have been accompanied by Edward Calvert and C.T. Dent, all of whom were among the founder members of the Yorkshire Ramblers' Club.*

**Demon Wall:** *Marked the emergence of one Arthur Rhodes Dolphin who, over the next 13 years, was to significantly increase the standard of climbing in Yorkshire.*

**Depth Charger:** *Possibly done earlier by Mike Hammill.*

**The Egg Boulder Variations:** *Buffy Wants Daddy - Ian Bitcon; Matt Meets Buffy: Tom Peckitt Nov 2005; Digital Death: Tom Peckitt March 2006.*

**Encore:** *Previously climbed by Eric Lillie with use of a hand-placed peg.*

**Fluted Rib:** *Pete Brown 19 April 1998.*

**Frankland's Green Crack:** *A major achievement for the time. The first description states "the leader can be played from the top of The Pulpit" indicating that side-runners were allowed! However, both written and photographic evidence shows that Frankland made frequent solo ascents of this climb in the 1920s.*

**Frankland's Always Greener:** *Climbed by Pete Brown, Richard Harrison 11th May 2000.*

**Frankland's Eastern Exit:** *climbed by Tony Marr, Alan Taylor 1999.*

**Great Western:** *Dolphin was apprehensive, but was spurred on by the crowd that had gathered to watch. It was an outstandingly bold ascent. Vintage film of a repeat ascent shows that Dolphin executed the traverse with both hands and feet in the horizontal crack. Dolphin led the alternative finish some time later.*

**Impending Doom:** *Climbed by Graham Desroy, Paul Dawson 1980.*

**The Keel:** *Andy Swann and John Dunne claimed this prize about the same time.*

**Matt's Roof:** *Climbed by Matt Birch. Actually christened 'Over Easy' by Matt. The crucial hold gets bigger every year...*

**Microscopic Wall:** *Originally only the top rib was climbed. The direct start was added by Pete Brown, Andi Turner 9th Sept 1997.*

**Morrell's Wall:** *Apparently, Tom Morrell had found it but couldn't do it.*

**The North-West Girdle:** *Dolphin had inspected the line before. Ball, however, was an 'Ilkley man' who joined the team at the last moment with no prior knowledge of the route and climbed it in style as last man on the rope.*

*A finish of Pitch 1b is possible up Overhanging Groove (or the rib prior to this) and is known as* **Extended Break** *(claimed by Pete Brown in 2000 but certainly climbed before).*

**Over the Top:** *Pete Brown, Dave Garner, Steve Turner 25th June 1992.*

**Pinnacle Flake Climb Direct Start:** *Climbed by Tony Marr, Mike Tooke FRA 2005.*

**Pocket Variant:** *Pete Brown, Andi Turner 2nd April 1999.*

**Pulpit Corner:** *This was the first pitch only. Frankland thought it unjustifiable and did not record it. The second pitch was added by Austin and Evans in 1956.*

**Pulpit Corner Direct:** *Climbed by Ben Bransby 1999.*

**Remembrance Someday:** *Climbed by Paul Clarke 1998.*

**Shuffle Crack:** *This was the first recorded ascent. Dolphin had top-roped the line in April 1942 and called it Crack of Apollo. There are also strong suggestions that he led the route in 1952/53 shortly*

## First Ascents - ALMSCLIFF

before his death. The route still hadn't appeared in print by 1967 when Ed Drummond had claimed it with the name The Two Ton Sardine, and he used a peg.

**Stomach Traverse**: The climb originally started up what is now Central Crack. The direct start was added later, but before 1913.

**South Face Climb**: Many of these, and other problems, were described by Benson in an article dated March 1906 in which he stated: "One meets nail marks everywhere. I should think that almost every yard of cliff and boulder has been tried at one time or another".

**South Wall Direct**: Climbed by Martin Berzins, Al Manson 1988.

**Stallone's Stinking Banger:** Named by Danny Coultrup in 2009 but a problem of 1970s vintage.

**Stepoffable:** Climbed by Pete Brown 25th Sept 1995.

**Toad's Nose:** Climbed by Pete Brown 29th October 1995. The start (to the ledge) is an old Mike Hammill boulder problem. The sit-down start was added by Tom Peckitt as The Dark Side Of Chi.

**Torpedo:** Climbed by Mike Hammill, James Mackinley 1975.

**The Wall Of Horrors**: Top-roped by Dolphin in 1944, pre-practised by Austin and even then combined tactics were needed for the problem start.

Excerpt from John Stainforth's climbing log book: "5 November 1970: John Syrett made the first sight-lead of The Wall of Horrors. Chas and I went along as support team. Chas belayed - I took photos. John climbed it with ease, making it look like any other climb. He was ten minutes arranging a Clog 1 wedge beneath the crux and climbed the whole route unhurriedly (20 mins). The weather was far from ideal - recent rain, gale-force winds, and quite cold. Abseiling down to take the runners off (neither Chas nor I could do the starting moves), the rope was whipped right out over the top of the crag by the wind." Syrett's claim to the second ascent has been disputed in Tony Howard's book, "Troll Wall", where Tony Nicholls, a member of Oldham's Rimmon Mountaineering Club, is said to have climbed it in 1965.

**The Wall of Horrors:** Start climbed by Joe Brown in the 50s – possibly UKs first Font 6b problem.

**Whisky Crack:** Fred Botterill's obituary said that "he never felt lonely until he'd runout a hundred feet of rope". However, other references and photographs from the period suggest he worked out many of the crag's boulder problems and may well have been the instigator of some of the climbs which were recorded in Laycock's 1913 guide but not credited to anyone in particular.

**Wharfedale Wall:** Climbed by Pete Brown.

**Opus Supo Direct Finish**, **Hocus Pocus**: Climbed by Pete Brown 29th June 1997.

**West Chimney Rib**: Climbed by Pete Brown 1997.

**X-Factor**: Start & finish were pre-existing.

**Zen**: Climbed by Stew Watson 2006.

High Man, Almscliff

# ALMSCLIFF - Graded List

## GRADED LIST

### ROUTES

**E7**
Right Cheeky (6c)
Opeless (6c)

**E6**
China Syndrome (7a)
Ginger Whinger (7a)
Hokum (6c)
A Few Tomorrows (6b)

**E5**
Orchrist (6b)
Wharfedale Wall (6c)
Megadoom (6b)
The Imp (6b)
The EMS Telegram (6b)
Magnum Opus (6b)
All Our Yesterdays (5c)
Retribution Rib Direct (5c)

**E4**
Blackhead (6c)
Forgotten Wall (6c)
Whisky Wall Direct (6a)
The Elf (6c)
Al Says On Fire (6c)
Jack on Fire (6c)
The Bitch (6c)
Jack Be Nimble (6c)
'Arries Left 'Ook (6c)
Hocus Pocus (6b)
Supo Direct Finish (6b)
Opus (6b)
Exit Stage Left (6b)
The Fox (6b)
Every Man Has His Niche (6b)
The Lady (6c)
Toad's Nose (6b)
All Quiet (6a)
'Arries 'Ook (6a)
Fungus the Bogeyman (6a)
Impending Doom (6a)
Remembrance Some Day (6b)
Penny Pip (6a)
Tortoises and Hares (6a)
Yellow Peril (6a)

**E3**
The Virgin (6b)
The Tramp (6b)
Rectum Rift (6b)
Grand Illusion (6a)
Daisy Chain (6b)
Kitson Did It First (6b)
Microscopic Wall (6b)
Left Cheek (6a)
X-Factor (6a)
Western Front (5c)
Why Climb (6a)
First Night (6a)
The Big Greeny (6a)
Nelly-Moser Finish (6a)
The Horror of Walls (6a)
The True Two Ton Sardine (6a)
The Wall of Horrors (6a)
Pulpit Corner Direct (5c)
Merlin (6a)
Whisky Wall (5b)

**E2**
Encore (5c)
Oubliette (6a)
Roast Beef (6a)

Full Traverse of High Man (5c)
Something's Cooking (6a)
Chalk Scratchings (5c)
Hobgoblin (5c)
Clematis (5c)
Pulpit Friction (5c)
Trident (5c)
Twelfth Night (5c)
Yellow Wall (5c)
Yorkshire Puddin' (5c)
Retribution Rib (5b)
Black Wall Eliminate (5c)
Spirit Level (5c)
Torpedo (5c)
Chastity (5c)
Emmaus Road (5c)
No Man's Land (5b)

**E1**
Acetabulum (5c)
WASC (5c)
Shuffle Crack (5c)
North West Girdle (5b)
Blackpool Promenade (5b)
Central Eliminate (5b)
Z Climb Eliminate (5b)
Pulpit Corner (5b)
Dolphinian (5b)
Depth Charger and Up Periscope (5b)
South Wall Direct (5b)
Envy Of Angels (5c)

**HVS**
Traditional Eliminate (6a)
V Crack (5a)
Fluted Rib (5b)
A Step in the Right Direction (5b)
Demon Wall (5a)
Angelic Upstart (5b)
Always Greener (5b)
West Chimney Rib (5b)
Stepoffable (5b)
Black Wall Direct (5b)
Birdlime Traverse (5b)
Finale Slab (5a)
Jacob's Ladder (5b)
Thompson's Traverse (5b)
Overhanging Groove (5b)
Great Western (5a)
Rocktalk Ruined
My PHD (5a)
Green Gully Wall (5a)

**VS**
Fence Buttress (5b)
Pothole Direct (5b)
Black Wall (5b)
Constipation Crack (5a)
Pram Pusher's Paradise (5a)
Rift Crack (5a)
Fisher's Stride (5a)
Matt's Arête (5a)
Eastern Exit (5a)
V Chimney Direct (5a)
Central Climb (5a)
Crack of Doom (5a)
Frankland's Green Crack (4c)
Green Gully Rib (4c)
High Level Traverse (4c)
Pigott's Stride (4c)
South Wall Traverse (5a)
Stomach Traverse (4c)
The Traditional Climb (4c)

Yorkshire Relish (4c)
Z Climb (4c)
Zig Zag Direct (4c)

**MVS**
Bird's Nest Variation (4c)
South Face Climb (4b)
Square Chimney and Whisky Crack (4b)

**HS**
Bird's Nest Crack (4b)
Central Crack (4b)
Crack and Wall (4b)
Fisher's Traverse (4b)
Parson's Chimney (4b)
The Goblin (4b)
The Zig Zag (4b)
Fat Man's Misery (4b)

**S**
The Virgin Climb (4a)
Safe As (4a)
South Chimney Layback (4b)
Fluted Crack (4b)
Tudor Rose
Green Gully Left Arête
Kiernan's Traverse and Rough Crack (4a)
Lovat Strides
Pinnacle Flake Climb (4a)
V Chimney and Traverse (4a)
Green Wall (4a)
Lichen Wall
Pinnacle Direct (4a)
The Low Man Girdle (4a)
Corner Crack (4a)

**HVD**
Fluted Columns
Long Chimney (4a)
Stew Pot
Cup and Saucer (4a)
Leaf Climb (4a)
The Final Finale (4a)

**VD**
The Pothole
South Chimney (4a)

**HD**
The Easy Way (3c)

**D**
Low Man Easy Way
West Chimney Variation

**M**
Tight Chimney
West Chimney
Three Chockstones Chimney

### PROBLEMS

**Font 8b+**
Bulbhead

**Font 8b**
The Real Keelhaul

**Font 8a+**
Cherry Falls
Keelhaul

**Font 8a**
The Full Virgin Traverse
Canine
Chiasmata
Identity Crisis
Cherry Falls Right
All Natural
Exorcist
Dialectics
Zen

**Font 7c+**
Lasting Satisfaction
Magnum Opus (start)
Stu's Roof
Digital Death
Underhand Super Extension
The Real Keel
The Bulb
Making Shapes

**Font 7c**
Slopey Traverse
Underhand Extension
Stretch Armstrong
The Keel
Matt Meets Buffy
Jess's Roof (E4 6c)
Demon Wall Roof
Left-Hand

**Font 7b+**
Grape Strain
Sewer Rat Connection
Top Cat Traverse
Underhand
North Ridge (SDS)
Matterhorn Ridge (SDS)
Matt's Roof
Natural Traverse
Streaky's Traverse
The Dark Side of Chi
Stu's Roof Left-Hand

**Font 7b**
Fieldside Traverse
Fractal
Buffy Wants Daddy
Cold Shoulder
Minefield
Crucis (E4 6b)
Pistol Whip
Bit of a Jerk
Silver Trout

**Font 7a+**
Steve's Wall
South Cave Traverse
The Horror
Brown's Roof (E4 6c)
Si's Arête
Demon Wall Roof
Dreamland
'Arries 'Ook Direct Start

**Font 7a**
Morrell's Wall Traverse
Barley Mow (E4 6b)
Hammill's Rib
C and A Traverse
Patta's Arête
Teaspoon Variation Left
Northern Shuffle
Crucifix Traverse
Dolphin Belly Slap
Pebble Wall (SDS)

**Font 6c+**
Swampy Arête
Below the Decks
Pebble Wall
I am a Walrus
Gypsus (E3 6b)
Sloper Patrol
Ed's Dyno
Pipping Arête
Wall of Horrors Traverse
Syrett's Roof (E3 6b)

**Font 6c**
The Virgin Traverse
Stallones Stinking Banger
In Limbo
Teflon Traverse
Cuticula

**Font 6b+**
The Gypsy (E3 6a)
The Crack
Bancrofts Roof (E2 6b)
MK Traverse
Dry Stone Wall Traverse

**Font 6b**
Cold Crack
DMZ
Flying Arête
Egg Roll
The Right Wing

**Font 6a+**
Slap and Traction
Short Arse
Que Fastidio
Backhander
On the Fence
Delphinus
Teaspoon Variation
Cassock Slap
The Crucifix Warm-up
Crucifix Arête

**Font 6a**
Morrell's Wall
Morrell's Wall Left
Fall In
Overhanging Nose
Hanging Rib
South West Face (E2 5c)
Gray's Wall
Nose Bag
JP's Problem

**Font 5+**
The High Step
Right Rib
Three Swing Traverse
Suppository Wall
The Scoop
Pork Chop Slab
Heart Slab Arête
The North Ridge (E1 5c)
Snappy Roof
The Blunt Edge (E1 5b)
Scuff
The Ladder
The Long Slab
Knee Biter
Off The Wall
Reachy Roof
The Niche
The Slab
Honey Comb
Jam Pot
The Nose (Black Wall)

**Font 5**
Field Fare
Tumbledown
Left Rib
The Chimney Flake (VS 5b)
The Hillary Step (HVS 5b)
Off Campus
Pocket Watch
Pebble Frog
Charlie Sheen
Matterhorn Ridge (HVS 5b)
MK Original
Tetrapak Crack
Crinkle Cut
Out of Pocket
Sunny Scoop
The Nose Direct (VS 5b)
The Crucifix
The Wall
Stubby Arête

**Font 4+**
Field Mouse
Fledgling
Matterhorn Ridge (right side)
Toe Poke
Askance
Thompson's Route
Leverage
Classic Traverse

**Font 4**
End Wall
North Top Corner
The Postman (HS 4c)
The Lhotse Face (VS 4c)
Central Route
The East Face
Pond Life
Cracking Yarn
Southern Shuffle
Shadow Face
The Nose (VS 4c)

**Font 3+**
Hamble's Arête
Finite Field
Puncture Repair
Pick Pocket
The South Col (HS 4b)

**Font 3**
Bungle Traverse
Jemima
West Cave Wall (S 4a)
Hop Scotch
Well Worn
Groove On
Stroll
Worn Down

**Font 2**
Chipped Slab

Yorkshire Gritstone

Stuart Lancaster enjoying magical conditions on **Syrett's Roof** (Font 6c+ / E3 6b). Page 80.
Photo: Mike Hutton

"If the rubber could have been tapped from my legs, it would have kept Goodyear in business for years"

*Al Manson on his first ascent of Adrenaline Rush*

# Caley & The Chevin

Worth three stars for the view alone. Robin Nicholson running it out on **Chevin Buttress (VS 4c)**. Page 175
Photo: Mike Hutton

Caley 98
The Chevin 166

# caley

by **Steve Dunning and Adi Gill**

OS Ref. Roadside: SE 229 445
OS Ref. Main Crag: SE 224 445

Altitude: 170m

Caley. Simply brilliant. A stellar venue that deserves all the superlatives you can throw at it, and then some. It is a crag of immaculate quality, offering a plethora of classic boulder problems and magnificent routes. Both newcomer and connoisseur will enjoy arguably the finest bouldering circuit in the UK. Almscliff may have the brutal routes and vicious boulders, but Caley is home to the finest lines on perfect rock.

The crag is split into two distinct sections; the **Roadside Boulders** and **The Main Crag**.

**Roadside Boulders:** A wonderful bracken hillside filled with brilliant boulders and behemoth blocks. Perhaps no area in the country exemplifies the development of our great game as much as Caley Roadside. Described in the 1957 guide as 'no more than a convenient practise ground for climbers of the Leeds district' it has become a modern day Mecca for the global bouldering fraternity, who make the pilgrimage for the subtlest of eliminates. How times have changed. On this spot Yorkshire's master technicians pushed the boundaries and left their mark in solid rock. Dolphin, Manson, Fawcett, Dunne, Swann, Dunning – the head boys of the Gritstone class of each era – all worked their magic here. So yes, the place has pedigree but don't be intimidated, for if nothing else, the Roadside is an everyman crag, with mint problems throughout the grades on pretty much every boulder. Perhaps Manson said it best, *'from on top of any convenient position, elevated enough to give a commanding panorama, take a good look around. Many boulders will be seen. Go forth and climb them. Do not forsake or scorn even the smallest'*. Quite.

**The Main Crag:** A different experience altogether. Described here in two sections, namely (a) the Path-side and Uphill Crag and (b) the Downhill bouldering circuit. The former is the prime area for the keen router, with the main concentration of climbing warranting a rope and a rack. The area is overlooked by the iconic and much coveted knife-edge arête of *High Noon* and has classic routes from Severe through to E8. Highball aficionados won't be disappointed, with plenty to tempt the bold and the brave, although the landings leave something to be desired in a couple of places. The downhill area is a serene wooded wonderland littered with boulders. A great area for problems throughout the grade range, with excellent landings and the added enjoyment of the treasure hunt through the forest for the next block on the circuit.

**Conditions and Aspect:** The whole crag is predominantly north facing and as a consequence is not so fast drying, nor as clean as 'Gods own crag' across the valley. Typically the crag comes into condition in spring and autumn. Summer climbing is possible but getting between the Roadside Boulders can be a real fern thrash at this time of year. The more exposed boulders stay in good nick throughout the winter months though erosion at Caley is accelerated when climbs are attempted in damp conditions.

**The Climbing:** The climbing is on perfect, natural gritstone attaining a maximum height of 15m, with plenty teetering on the highball/route threshold. All styles are catered for within the expanse of the two main areas, although it's a place tailored more to the thinking climber than the thug.

Andy McCue going for five points of contact on **Bob's Bastard** (Font 6a). Page 118
Photo: Mike Hutton

99

# CALEY - Main Map

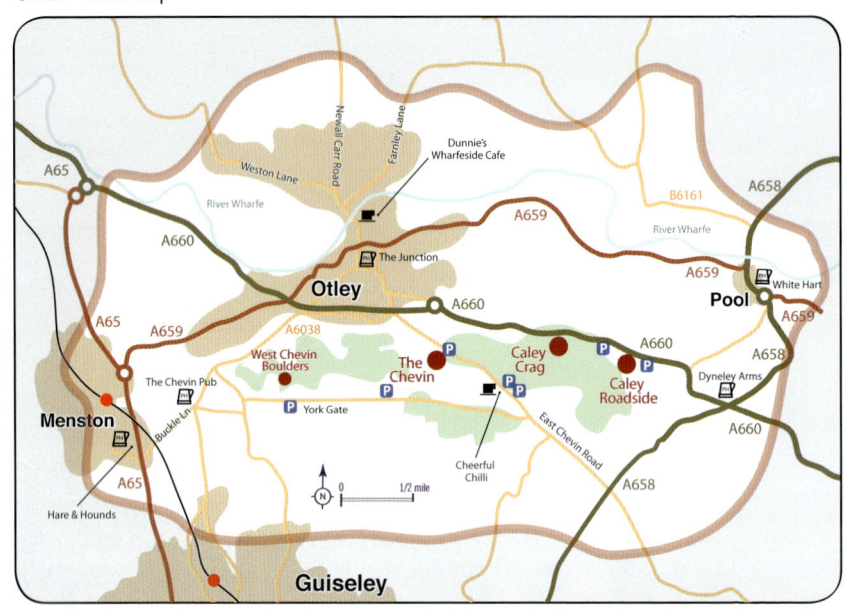

**The Roadside Boulders** predominantly offer boulder problems (over 120) though around a dozen breach the highball ceiling and are clearly routes, albeit protection-less, apart from the odd but not insignificant exception. *Rabbit's Paw Wall* (HVS 5b), *Permutation Rib* (E1 5c), *Psycho* (E5 6b), *Adrenaline Rush* (E5 6b) and *The Great Flake* (E6 6b) are the pick of the routes, with the latter two being reason enough to pop a rope in the bag. If equipped with enough mats and friends you can rely on, then *Ron's Reach* (Font 6b+), *To Be Is Not To Bolt* (Font 7b), *Terry* (Font 7c) and *High Fidelity* (Font 8b) are some of the greatest highball prizes going.

**The Main Crag** offers a greater variety, with nigh on 80 routes. Proud, bold lines sit next to well-protected Diffs. *Pedestal Wall* (S 4b), *The Scoop* (VS 4c), *Noonday Ridge* (E1 5b), offerings from Allsop, Dolphin and Austin respectively, are up there with some of Yorkshire's best at the grade. The great age of grit saw a small patch of Caley become a battleground between Peak and Pennine with the likes of Hammill, Manson, Bancroft, Allen and Fawcett leaving examples of their extreme art in *High Noon* (E4 6a), *Fred Zinnermann* (E6 6b), *Forecourt Crawler* (E4 6b) and *Quark* (E5 6a), all a must if you're operating at this level.

The *Main Crag* bouldering matches that of Roadside. Slabs of all angles, tricky arêtes and sloping lip traverses, with a liberal smattering of pebbles and mysterious chicken heads. There are 50 problems on the uphill side of the track, most are either in the higher Font grades or a bit on the high side. With over 70 problems in the wooded downhill patch and many in the Font 3 to Font 6c range, there really is something for everyone. Enjoy.

*Excessive brushing, particularly on the boulders of the Roadside area (e.g. New Jerusalem) is wrecking some problems beyond all recognition. Other problems have been attacked with chemicals. The message is simple; don't do it.*

Anna Shepherd in the zone on one of the many hard classics, **The Crystal Method** (Font 7b+). Page 123
Photo: Mike Hutton

James Ibbertson enjoying his local patch with a warm up on **Stretcher** (Font 6a+). Page 121
Photo: David Simmonite

# Roadside Map & Access - CALEY

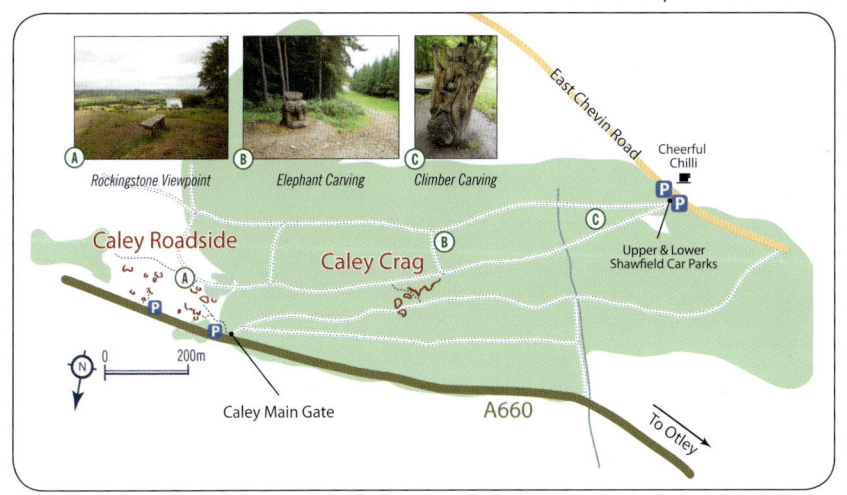

**Parking and Approach:** Two main options exist. The best approach is from the main Leeds-Otley road (A660). When approaching from Leeds, pass straight through the Dyneley Arms crossroads (junction with the A658) round the S-bend until busy roadside parking is reached on the left against the high dry stone wall (three-quarters of a mile from the crossroads). Either park at the first lay-by (**Parking GPS: 53.896653,-1.649438**), by the stile and bus stop (best for the left-hand end of the *Roadside*; the block immediately over this stile is the *Not My Stile* boulder), or go downhill for 200m to the lay-by just before the Caley Gate (**Parking GPS: 53.897364,-1.652788**). The latter is best for the right-hand end of the *Roadside* and the *Main Crag*. For the *Roadside* boulders, go through the stile just before the gate on the left and weave up faint tracks eastwards through the trees for 100m until the *Morris Wall* area is reached. For the *Main Crag*, go though the Caley gate and follow the obvious track for 450m westwards until the distinctive *Sugarloaf* is reached immediately right of the path.

When approaching uphill from Otley on the A660 don't attempt to u-turn across the road to park on the verge. The best option is to continue past the crag and turn around at the Dyneley Arms pub and then approach as if travelling from the Leeds direction.

Parking next to the stile rather than the gate makes it easier to pull out at the end of the day, either way take care as the verge is narrow and traffic passes at speed. Move quickly if getting several mats from your back seat. One last thing, please do not jump over the stone wall.

Alternatively, ample parking is available opposite the Cheerful Chilli restaurant on East Chevin Road at Lower or Upper Shawfield car parks (1 mile uphill and south-east from Otley. **Parking GPS: 53.893972,-1.671719**). Possibly a safer option if bringing the kids, albeit with a touch longer walk in. From this parking, follow the bridleway due east for half a mile (crossing a beck as you go) until the first major break in the forest on the left (wooden elephant carving at the top) allows you to drop downhill for 150m to another major track. This is the top of the right-hand end of the Main Crag. Continuing a further 100m east will bring you to the descent path on the left into the crevasse of Finger Knacker Crack area. For the Roadside boulders, stay on the bridleway from the parking until the second major clearing in the forest on the left (a further ¼ mile with a wooden grazing deer carving on the entrance) and drop down this until the next main track is reached. Go through the gate on the right and walk due east for 160m (where the trees thin out) and the top of the Rocking Stone Roof boulder is reached on the left below the viewpoint.

*Almscliff to Slipstones*

| # | Route | # | Route | # | Route |
|---|---|---|---|---|---|
| 1 | Not My Stile p106 | 5 | Hanging Nose p108 | 8 | Mini Mati p109 |
| 2 | The Money Shot p106 | 6 | Bat Cave p108 | 9 | Just the One p109 |
| 3 | Rough Rib p107 | 7 | To Be Is Not To Bolt p108 | 10 | Neat Arête p110 |
| 4 | Smooth Wall p107 | | | | |

Stile Area

Our Father's Arête

Fugee-la

Stile Area Lay-by Parking

A660 Leeds-Otley Road

# CALEY ROADSIDE BOULDERS

| # | | # | | # | |
|---|---|---|---|---|---|
| 11 | Thin Slab p112 | 17 | The Great Flake p118 | 23 | Rabbit's Paw Wall p125 |
| 12 | Blockbuster p115 | 18 | Playground p121 | 24 | Morris Crack p125 |
| 13 | Ron's Reach p116 | 19 | Otter Wall p121 | 25 | No Pebble Arête p126 |
| 14 | Rocking Stone Roof p116 | 20 | The Scoop p122 | 26 | Wall Boulder p126 |
| 15 | Pebble Wall p117 | 21 | The Crystal Method p122 | | |
| 16 | Neat Wall p117 | 22 | Adrenaline Rush p124 | | |

Viewpoint

**Adrenaline Rush Area**

Approach From Parking

# CALEY - Our Father's Arête

### Not My Stile
Just by the stile is the obvious arête which is sure to baffle.

### 4 **Stile Council**  Font 5+
The short but pleasant left arête.

### 5 **Not My Stile**  Font 6c+
The left side is a technical joy, once you know the trick.

### 6 **Free Stile**  Font 4
The arête taken on the right-hand side.

The Fugee-la boulder is situated 30m downhill from the stile, just facing the wall. Unfortunately the landing drops away rather alarmingly but the problems are worthwhile. **Fugee-la** (Font 6a) takes the left side of the wall; **Bum Fight** (Font 6c) strikes a line up the wall to the right and finally **The Mask** (Font 6a) climbs the left side of the right arête. Further right again (50m) is a boulder next to the wall and is home to **Road Kill** (Font 6c), from a sit-down start and using a flake and a pocket to finish.

### The Money Shot
Wind up the path for 50m from *Not My Stile* and you arrive at a low-slung boulder which is home to probably the hardest problem at Caley and a couple of short, classic challenges.

### 7 **Short Arête**  Font 6a
Often done footless, but only due to the lack of footholds.

### 8 **The Money Shot**  Font 6c
A diminutive gem of a problem. Hang the lip and make a dynamic move to the hidden crack. Squirm over the top.
*Andy Jack   early 2000*  ✦

### 9 **Ullola**  Font 8b
A desperate right-to-left traverse on relentless slopers. Start standing on the scoop/slab, drop down to the ledge and then keep trucking to finish up *Short Arête*.
*Steve Dunning   early 2000s*

## Caley Roadside - Stile Area
Beginning from the lay-by on the A660, immediately over the stile is the Not My Stile boulder. Go left (east) for 25m along the wall to the obvious square cut block with the 'Our Father's' writing on the roadside face. The first problem starts on the east side of the block. The circuit then unfurls itself across the hillside to the west.

### Our Father's Arête
Way-marked by the first distinctive gateway problem on the road from the big smoke to the Dales, this rectangular block is easily recognisable by the fading writing on its front face.

### 1 **Crimpy Wall**  Font 6a+
The short, crimpy wall trends leftward from a low start.

### 2 **Our Father's Arête**  Font 6a+
The short, square-cut arête.

### 3 **The Halo**  Font 6a
A fun, pumpy traverse of the top edge from right-to-left.

106  Yorkshire Gritstone

## Smooth Wall - CALEY

### The Groove/Rough Rib
20m left and further up the hill are the distinctive con-joined blocks with the soaring groove right of the corner.

**10 Low Rib** Font 5+
Make a wild contortion to mount the slab.

**11 Short Slab** Font 4+
The steady slab direct.

**12 Runnel Wall** Font 4
Follow the perfect runnels to the break and make a stretch for the top.

**13 Rough Rib** Font 5+
A Caley classic up the masterful arête. Harder on the right-hand side with a reachy finale.

**14 The Groove** Font 7a
Slink up the awkward groove. Finish rightward with much difficulty.

**15 Pocket Wall** Font 6c
Avoiding the arête tackle the wall.

**16 Steady Arête** Font 5+
The short but entertaining arête.

### Smooth Wall
Continuing uphill for 20m you come to the next block.

**17 Smooth Arête** Font 5
From a sit-down start make some shapes up the beefy, little arête.

**18 Smooth Wall Traverse** Font 6c
A finger-shredding classic with a tricky finish.

**19 Smooth Wall Dyno** Font 7b
Flying from the break is a fun trip for dynamic climbers.

**20 Smooth Wall** Font 6b
Fierce pulls passing the flake.

**21 Undercut Wall** Font 6c+
From the undercuts make a powerful slap for the top.

**22 Roadside Mantel** Font 6c
On the west face of the block, from a sit-down start, hang the big flat hold and perform a flamboyant mantel into the groove.

> **" "**
> Standards went up overnight; not because of the climbing walls, but due to the artificial advantage of chalk. Dropped everything by a grade. Maybe half a grade.
> **Allan Austin**

Steve Dunning showing the way on **To Be Is Not To Bolt** (Font 7b / E6 6c). Page 109
Photo: Mike Hutton

# Neat Arête - CALEY

## Neat Arête
40m to the west, directly above Hanging Nose and just beyond the power lines are the final three problems of this section.

### 47 Neat Crack  Font 4
The awkward steep crack.

### 48 Mantel Illness  Font 6b+
From sitting, reach for the top and finish with a desperate mantel.

### 49 Neat Arête  Font 5
Take the arête on the right-hand side.

## The Alternative Circuit

The following collection of problems are spread along the crag. They present some rewarding alternatives that perhaps go under the radar due to the neighbouring problems being a (well-worn) bigger tick. The purpose of this alternative list is to take you to new corners of the crag and to help ease the amount of traffic the traditional classics receive.

### Font 3+ to 4+
Rippled Corner  3+  (page 109)
Boneyard  4 (page 152)
The Tombstone  4 (page 152)
Horn Traverse  4 (page 157)
Yuletide Flake  4 (page 157)
Nose  4+ (page 159)

### Font 5 to 6a
Stile Council  5+ (page 106)
Steady Arête  5+ (page 107)
Gripping Groove  5+ (page 117)
Back Crack  6a (page 139)
Lippy Luvin'  5+ (page 153)
Yuletide  5+ (page 157)

### Font 6a+
The Plat Traverse  6a+ (page 112)

### Font 6b to 6b+
Flake Wall  6b (page 109)
South Wall Traverse  6b+ (page 126)
Lip Traverse  6b (page 159)
Webster's Whinge  6b (page 109)
Bob's Bastard II  6b+ (page 118)

### Font 6c to 7a+
The Money Shot  6c (page 106)
The Palm Press  6c (page 108)
Thug Arête  6c+ (page 123)
Hampered  7a+ (page 108)
Front Traverse  7a+ (page 136)
The Prow  6c (page 161)

### Font 7b to 8a
Space Ape  7b (page 108)
Ripper Arête  7b (page 116)
Mistaken Identity  8a (page 136)
The Red Squirrel  7b+ (page 161)
Otzi  7c (page 140)

## CALEY - Thin Slab

### Caley Roadside - Adrenaline Rush Area
Approximately 90m to the west, the boulders continue with Thin Slab. This whole area has a concentration of problems to rival the planet's best, where delicate slabs rub shoulders with burly arêtes on boulders high enough to make even the boldest tremble.

### Thin Slab
A fine concentration of delicate little problems requiring a cool head.

**1 Left-Hand Groove** Font 3
Short and steady.

**2 The Slab** Font 4+
Dab up the rib and slab; easier escaping right.

**3 Curver** Font 4
From the arête trend left up the sweeping groove and hand-traverse right at the top.

**4 The Thin Slab** Font 5+
A delicate little number. Starting up the arête before trending leftward to a heart fluttering finish. The arête direct is a committing affair (Font 6b+).

**5 The Arête** Font 6b+
A fine problem requiring a confident approach. Layback up the steep side of the arête.

**6 Right Wall** Font 6b+
The direct, passing the crack using hydraulic locks between distant edges. Coming in from the right (a) drops the grade to Font 5+.

Just above this is the following.

**7 Breakfest** Font 6a
Starting low on the break use brute thuggery up the hanging arête.

Facing *Thin Slab* is a low-slung roof with a nice right-to-left traverse, (b) **Beached Whale Traverse** (Font 5), starts from sitting and culminates with a tricky mantel. Down and round to the right (c) **The Plat Traverse** (Font 6a+) makes brilliant moves along the lip of the boulder. Classically tackled from right-to-left with a drop down to the break to finish. Equally good in reverse.

> Farther afield the herd of neolithic boulders called Caley Crags haunt of evenings climbing in the salmon glow of the setting fire, now sit hunched into the hill. Their brown hide, warm and rough, a rasp on the fingers and a dream on the toes is green and cold in the seeping mist.
>
> **Nick Wood, LUUMC Journal 198**

Nick Verney begins the fight on **The Rocking Groove** (Font 6c). Page 116
Photo: Stuart Littlefair

Mark Katz crushing **Blockbuster** (Font 7c). Opposite page.
Photo: Mike Hutton

# Blockbuster - CALEY

## Blockbuster
Twenty metres up the hill, above Thin Slab, sees the start of an amazing run of some of the best bouldering around and the focus of enthusiasts of the hard.

### 8  Blockbuster   Font 7c
Another class act. A problem with a number of possible starts depending on height, finger fatness and your opinions of French (jump) starts. Starting low on the pocket and flatty is worth Font 7c; jumping for the slopey rail is Font 7b. Finally from sitting on the left is (a) **Northern Soul** (Font 7c+). Photo opposite.
*Ron Fawcett 1980s; Christian Durkin  1990s (Northern Soul)*

### 9  Zoo York   Font 8a
The magnificent jutting arête has climbing to match. Perhaps the benchmark for Font 8a and a rite of passage for the aspiring bouldering wad. Has been flashed. Go from a sit-down start with two hands on the low undercut.
*Christian Durkin  2000* ✦

### 10  Guacamole   Font 7c
A real nasty little number. From good finger jugs stretch to the poor edge before making a massive spring for the unbelievably sharp lip. The sit-down start (b) **Salsa Start**, comes in from the start of *Zoo York* and bumps the grade up to Font 7c+.
*Chris Davies Nov 2004; Mark Katz Oct 2005 (sit-down start)*

### 11  Ju Ju Club   Font 7b+
Physical and involved. A rare chance to execute a 'bicycle move' on this class problem. Go from a sit-down start or as low as you can go on the sidepulls.

115

# CALEY - Ripper Wall

### Ron's Reach/Ripper Wall
A long green wall of desperate highballs and a futuristic project to the right of *Ben's Groove*.

### 12 Ripper Arête  Font 7b
The slabby left arête appears straightforward enough but soon develops into quite a struggle. Now try the sit-down start at Font 7b+.
*Tom Peckitt  Dec 2005; James Ibbertson  3rd Jan 2006 (SDS)*

### 13 Ripper Traverse/Ron's Reach  Font 6b+ (E3 6a)
The technical, rising traverse succumbs to a combination of sneaky footwork and steady nerves.
*Ron Fawcett  early 1980s*

### 14 Kindergarten Wall  Font 7b  (E5 6b)
From a couple of moves along *Ron's Reach* climb direct via a very long stretch to a pocket. The direct start just right of the arête is **Freak Technique** (Font 7b+).
*Pete Robins 20th December 1998; Direct start: James Ibbertson*

### 15 Wainright's Wobble  Font 7b+
The direct start to Fawcett's classic is a test of finger strength. Seldom repeated.
*John Wainwright  May 2000*

### 16 Ben's Groove  Font 7b
The classic problem of the wall, brilliant from both sitting and standing starts. Get established in the groove and make a 'heart in the mouth' move for the distant top. The sitter is benchmark Font 7c+. Photo on page 129.
*Ben Moon  1990; Steve Dunning  May 2001(SDS)*

### 17 Secret Seventh  Font 7b+
Massively conditions dependant arête, requiring more than a little cunning.

Continuing along the path rightwards the next block appears with its well-used boss.

### 18 The Rocking Groove  Font 6c
A fantastic little move, swinging onto the face from the groove hoping your foot doesn't slip. Photo on page 113.

### 19 The Groove  Font 5
Pad up the appealing groove.

### Rocking Stone Roof
Uphill and 20m left is the start of a long wall with the large capping block.

### 20 Rocking Stone Traverse  Font 4
Travel left-to-right under the huge stone and hope it doesn't rock.

### 21 Mini Wall  Font 3
Step off the ramp and tackle the wall.

### 22 The Rocking Stone Roof  Font 4+ (VS 5b)
A tricky start up the slab lands you beneath the roof where you can spend time summoning up the courage to top it out. Best of luck, gulp.

### 23 Rocking Arête  Font 4
Pad up the seldom clean arête-cum-slab.

# Pebble Wall - CALEY

### 24 Gripping Groove  Font 5+
Despite its brilliance a queue rarely forms below the bridging groove. A fall from the final moves would be horrendous.

### 25 Chocolate Orange  Font 7b (E5 6c)
A real beauty. The sweeping, blunt arête provides a stunning ride, with an exciting top.
*Matt Waring  13th May 2008*

### 26 Terry  Font 7c  (E5 7a)
A stunning problem. Big, bold and certainly one of Caley's best. Benchmark technical Font 7c that will test your pebble prowess and the power in your "Terrys". Photo on page 163.
*Andy Swann  23rd June 1990* ✦

On the rampline to the right is a forgotten route, **Rising More Slowly** (E2 5c) holding more than its fair share of greenness. Starting on the obvious knobbles make a series of protectionless moves across the face to the sanctuary of the break. Wrestle with the vegetation to finish.

## Pebble Wall
Across the gap to the right is a short slab with a fond classic that knocks chunks, let alone dents, out of many a boulderers pride.

### 27 Harry's Heap/The Knobbler  E1 5c  7m
Step off the block to gain the knobbles which lead to the break. Exit above or continue right along the **Knobbler Traverse** (E1 6a) all the way to *MBKC Groove*.
*Mike Hammill  April 1977; Dave Musgrove  June 1984 (Knobbler')*

### 28 Dave's Saunter  Font 7c
As hard as any slab in Yorkshire, probably unrepeated.
*Dave Abbey  1990s*

### 29 Syrett's Saunter  Font 7b+
The epitome of technical slab climbing, also known as **Pebble Wall**. Captivating and frustrating in equal measure.
*Al Manson  1970s*

### 30 MBKC Arête  Font 6c
Those who fail on the neighbouring problem can find solace up this arête.

### 31 MBKC Groove  Font 5+
The shallow groove with a finger-munching pocket. Topping out is essential.

## Neat Wall
Below and to the right are two joined blocks.

### 32 Neat  Font 6a
Sit-down start. Using the pinch then undercut progress right to the good hold or slightly easier gain the good hold out to the left and finish direct.

### 33 The Neat Wall  Font 5+
Brief but compelling - up the flake. Often done from a sitter at a shin bashing Font 6a+.

### 34 Neat Wall Arête  Font 5+
From the shelf grapple with the clean-cut arête. Climbing the wall without recourse to the arête is (a) Font 7a+.
*Tom Peckitt  April 2006 (arête eliminate)*

Almscliff to Slipstones

# CALEY - The Great Flake Boulder

### The Great Flake Boulder
Lurking right behind you is the elephant in the room. Amongst the biggest boulders in Yorkshire, this unmistakable block's north face is home to one of the country's greatest highball achievements.

### 35  Pencil's Problem   Font 7c
A classy problem. From a sitter fire up the wall to a press-hold before swinging leftward for the slopey top.
*Martin Smith; (the standing start is* Bad-Etiquette *Font 7b+)*

### 36  Monsoon Monsoon   Font 7b
Step off the block and follow the flakes rightward to a spicy finish.

### 37  Andy's Route   Font 7b
From the flat block tackle the wall above on positive but spaced holds to a committing finish. The sitter is excellent and pulls on via the sharp undercut at the back of the groove, (Font 7c).
*c1980s; SDS: Andy Brown   2001*

### 38  The Great Flake   E6 6b    8m    ★★★
One of the finest and most sustained routes on grit. Protection is marginal at the point at which you need it the most. The sitter is both burly and delicate; Font 6b to the top of the first flake.
*Craig Smith   7th April 1984*

### 39  High Fidelity   Font 8b
The magnificent arête forms a truly striking line. Powerful moves lead past the half-height undercuts. With the crux dispatched, a big move to the distant pocket remains.
Photo opposite and page 677.
*Steve Dunning   April 2003*

### 40  Nothing's Safe   Font 7c  (E6 6c)
The obstinate right arête has been transformed from a seldom-attempted route into a relatively popular highball. From the break, step left and make a series of contortions up the face to the rounded mantel finish.
*John Dunne   1988*

### 41  Bob's Bastard   Font 6a
A stern test of mantel prowess. Make use of a pocket to surmount the lip. A harder version starts in the same place before swinging left along the lip to mantel via the runnels (a) **Bob's Bastard II** (Font 6b+). Photo on page 99.

Yorkshire Gritstone

Dave Barrans making shapes on High Fidelity (Font 8b). Opposite Page
Photo: Alastair Lee

Naomi Buys cruising the Caley circuit on **Chips** (Font 4). Opposite Page.
Photo: Alastair Lee

# Otley Wall - CALEY

## Otley Wall
25m downhill is an extremely popular warm-up area and beginner's slab; the blunt left (west-facing) end of which has a much-coveted teaser.

**1 Hanging Wall** Font 7b
The wall left of the chips on mono-doigts! Yikes.

**2 Chips** Font 4
The line of chiselled holds offers a very basic problem. Photo opposite.

**3 Otley Wall** Font 6a+
A Caley classic and a fine test of clean footwork. From the start of *Chips* tip-toe along the lip to gain the hanging crack and a stiff series of pulls up the centre of the wall. Continuing the traverse to finish up the right arête is (a) a delicate Font 6b, a direct start (b) is possible with a big reach at Font 7a+ and starting from the right (c) is Font 6b.
*Dave Musgrove, Mike Butler 29th June 1975 (Otley Wall)*

**4 Calvinistic** Font 6c
The direct finish to *Otley Wall*, climbing the wall direct on pebbles from halfway along the traverse.

**5 Courser Edge** Font 5+
Paw up those slopers.

## The Playground
Round to the right of Otley Wall the rare Caley suntrap known as The Playground sees the beginning of many a visitor's circuit. Popular eliminates exist here around the Font 5 mark.

**6 Playground Traverse** Font 5
Not especially pure of line but a good way to finesse your footwork. Travel across the wall in either direction.

**7 Slab** Font 2+

**8 Chipped Slab 1** Font 3

**9 Playground Crack** Font 2

**10 Chipped Slab 2** Font 4

**11 Stretcher** Font 6a+
Big moves between the pockets with a landing to focus the mind. Photo on page 102.

**12 Chicken Heads** Font 5
Immaculate, technical climbing, also possible to eliminate the flake at Font 5+. Photo on next page.

Almscliff to Slipstones

## The Scoop

Continue 30m right (east) from *Chicken Heads* and follow a faint track for 30m downhill to The Scoop which is a fantastic boulder with a number of classic problems on first-class rock and littered with magical chicken heads. The left wall up the nobbles is Font 5.

**13  Edge Wall**  Font 6c
A frustrating fingertip shredding fun bag. Everything is in on the arête which is followed on its right-hand side. A harder eliminate without the arête goes at Font 7b.

**14  Chicken Arête**  Font 5
Enjoy the protruding features up this fat arête.

**15  The Chicken Scoop**  Font 6a
Indulge in some typical gritstone. Negotiate the scoop by palming and pebble pulling. Eliminates can be climbed to the left but this is by far the best challenge.

**16  Small Roof**  Font 6b
Round the corner is a low roof (often green). From a sit-down start, pull over this with the elongated pockets.

## The Crystal Method

Take the path up the hill for 20m towards the huge unmistakable slab of *Adrenaline Rush*. The two joined boulders at its foot begin from the left as a long forgotten vegetated slab steepens on its north face to give the following.

**17  Lip Traverse**  Font 6b+
Sit-down start. A strenuous rising traverse to the apex of the boulder.

No problem's a gimme. Steve Dunning concentrating hard on **Chicken Heads** (Font 5). Page 121
Photo: Kevin Avery

Yorkshire Gritstone

Stuart Lancaster relishing the exposure of **Permutation Rib** (E1 5c). Page 125.
Photo: Mike Hutton

# CALEY - Bouldering Circuit

# THE ROADSIDE RAMBLE

This collection of 20 Caley classics, from Font 3 to 6c, meander in a convenient anti-clockwise loop starting beneath *Rabbit's Paw Wall* with a few gentle introductions and finishing with a final sting in the tail. Many problems on this circuit are neighbours with harder challenges if you're feeling strong.

| Problem | Name | Grade | Page No. | Problem | Name | Grade | Page No. |
|---|---|---|---|---|---|---|---|
| 1 | Morris Minor | Font 3 | 125 | 11 | The Thin Slab | Font 5+ | 112 |
| 2 | Morris Crack | Font 4 | 125 | 12 | Right Wall | Font 6b+ | 112 |
| 3 | Chips | Font 4 | 121 | 13 | Breakfest | Font 6a | 112 |
| 4 | Courser Edge | Font 5+ | 121 | 14 | The Plat Traverse | Font 6a+ | 112 |
| 5 | Otley Wall | Font 6a+ | 121 | 15 | Chicken Arête | Font 5 | 122 |
| 6 | Chicken Heads | Font 5 | 121 | 16 | The Chicken Scoop | Font 6a | 122 |
| 7 | Bob's Bastard | Font 6a | 118 | 17 | Lip Traverse | Font 6b+ | 122 |
| 8 | The Neat Wall | Font 5+ | 117 | 18 | Low Pebble Wall | Font 6a | 126 |
| 9 | MBKC Arête or Groove | Font 6c/5+ | 117 | 19 | The Cruel Crack | Font 5+ | 126 |
| 10 | The Groove | Font 5 | 116 | 20 | Lightning Crack | Font 6b+ | 126 |

Antony Limbert with the compulsory gurn on **Ben's Groove** (Font 7b). Page 116
Photo: David Simmonite

Jvan Tresch showing great composure on **Marrow Bone Jelly** (E7 6b). A typical Manson route: bold, technical and brillliant. Page 124
Photo: Adam Long

# PROFILE

**The so-called golden era of Yorkshire gritstone** in the 1970s saw a rag tag bunch of competitive, talented, bold and arrogant climbers pushing both the standards and style of climbing on the grit. It was an era that saw the rise of indoor climbing walls and the application of specific training for climbing, with astonishing results that saw many of today's three-star extreme classics being claimed on a weekly basis.

Competition between the protagonists for first ascents was fierce and none were more competitive, driven or talented than the tiny, lean Al Manson who put himself through punishing training regimes, paranoid about local rivals or Peak raiders such as John Allen getting to a prize line first.

A technical wizard and rock gymnast, Manson ditched his teaching job, moved to Headingley and climbed every day, usually with Pete Kitson and later others, such as John Syrett, in that famous Leeds University Wall crowd.

Caley was Manson's canvas and probably the crag that he left his biggest mark on - check out the utterly brilliant Adrenaline Rush (originally named Psycho until Manson was told that Ron Fawcett had just put up a new route to the left by the same name), Marrowbone Jelly and High Noon for starters. And that's without mentioning his classics at Almscliff and Brimham (see box right), all of which still demand the utmost respect, even by today's standards. Manson also contributed massively to the development of bouldering as a pursuit in its own right.

## AL MANSON

Grit era: *1970s, 1980s*
Most famous climbs:
*Adrenaline Rush, Marrow Bone Jelly, High Noon, One Man And His Dogmas, Death Drop 2000, Fred Zinnerman, To Be Is Not To Bolt, Demon Wall Roof, Grit Expectations, Pathos, Sow's That, Reach for a Peach, Early Riser (Earl Crag), Lipo Suction (Wetherby).*
What they say about him:
*"One word, Legend."*
   *- Jerry Peel, Andy Swann and just about anybody who climbs in these parts.*

Founder of the climbing wall company High Noon, which he runs with Andy Swann, Manson still climbs, though nowadays preferring continental bolt clipping to the grit.

**What are your memories of the 1970s Yorkshire gritstone scene?**
There weren't many other people doing it [climbing]. There were a lot of people hanging around though and it got a bit embarrassing. I weren't into drinking at the time and they thought it'd be great to go to Almscliff with a barrel of ale. It eventually became pretty hardcore. We had groupies. People were coming to Leeds University to climb and there were just all these hangers on, these girls.

**How intense was the competition, both locally and from Peak raiders, for new routes at that time?**
We were always worried about people coming. We'd got routes that we'd planned but we thought no rush, take our time and do them. Then people started turning up at Almscliff and thinking no-one's done that, why not? People like John Allen turned up, 16-year-old lad. I was 22.

# PROFILE

**You were well-known for training hard, what kind of regime did you follow?**
I used to do a lot of rope swings. Finest exercise ever. If you think of a gymnasium, you've got your climbing ropes and then you've got them bars that go up and down that you can adjust - two parallel beams that can go up and down. You set one to quite high. Basic exercise is grab hold of the ropes, run towards the beams, cling on, pull up and kick your feet to hit the high beam and then swing back, run backwards still with the ropes and you just go backwards and forwards. You're pulling, body tension totally on the core. I developed it from that to starting totally stationary and you've got to generate the swing to get the momentum to get your feet up. Just pulling, changing your centre of gravity. I just enjoyed training. I couldn't do a one-arm pull-up but I could do loads of pull-ups and had this lock-off strength. One exercise I did was wrist curls - called child birth rolls because you'd be crying in pain. I could do 3 complete cycles. I had John Dunne round, he couldn't do one cycle of it. I could burn anybody off.

**The Leeds University wall was a focal point of the 1970s Yorkshire grit era and you and many of the other big characters of the time climbed there.**
There was a problem there I used to call the warm up. A tiny little gritstone edge you had to rock up on it, press off it and reach another for another gritstone block. Martin Berzins could never do it and that was just my warm up. There was a circuit that you just went round on smearing on the wall, just using the holds doing laps round it. We used to just smear totally then people starting using brick edges for the feet, but we didn't think it was right. Round the corner was a dance studio. I spent a lot of time in there warming up. They used to get ballet dancers and had bars for putting your leg out and stretching.

**Was the indoor wall seen as a means to an end to be able to climb harder outdoors?**
No. You'd go outside to get fit for coming indoors. But I was still doing a lot of training to be fit for climbing outdoors.

**What was it like climbing with John Syrett?**
He looked like Marc Bolan. Sometimes it would be embarrassing being with John. Glitter in his eyes and stuff. Into drugs and stuff. He had his ups and downs did John and if he was on a down he would just drink all the time and be fat. He'd just go to pot, chubby and flabby. Then when he'd start climbing hard he'd just let rip.

**Didn't you and Syrett used to have a point-scoring system when you climbed together?**
You got no points if you'd done the route before. You got one point for a VS, two points for a Hard VS, three points for an Extreme, doubled if they were new routes. And you'd try and get a 50-point day. So you had to do a lot of routes to get 30-points. Mostly soloing. And you got minus points if you did something below VS. If you did a Severe you got minus one point. And probably the VSs would now be Hard VSs. We also had a Caley bouldering system, CB 1, 2 and 3 - 1 if you could do it, 2 if it was hard and 3 if it was a new route and if it got repeated it was a 2, obviously.

**What's your memory of your first ascent of High Noon at Caley?**
Mike Hammill was holding the ropes and I think I had double 13mm, no stretch. You couldn't reverse the last few moves so I was just jumping for the runners. I jumped off a couple of times and grabbed the runners but I was always getting the rope caught round my feet and it was tipping me upside down, that's why I had a helmet on, cause I kept cracking my head. It's amazing. At one stage you are totally surrounded by space, extreme exposure. (*See page 666 for the first ascent photo of High Noon*)

# PROFILE

**What's the boldest of your routes?**
Probably the most frightening is Deathdrop 2000. Because of the landing and technically it's quite hard. It's not obvious what you've got to do. You've to do the opposite of what you want to do. You have to get an undercling and step out and you're out of balance.

**Who's the best climber you saw?**
I would probably say John Allen. Just one of the best climbers I've ever seen. I did climb quite a bit with him and Steve Bancroft. We had a little thing - right I'm going to do that route. Right you're only allowed one bit of protection and you've got to choose it now. Usually he took a Clog 1, or a half size Moac, usually get that in somewhere. John was amazing. Technique, imagination, nice lad as well.

**Did you look up to anyone?**
No. I just wanted to be the best.

**What's the thing you're most proud of climbing-wise?**
Probably doing Lipo Suction (a Font 7c monster traverse) at Wetherby 10 times without getting off. I just had to do it. I got to eight and thought I'm not stopping now.

**Adrenaline Rush at Caley is one of your classic routes. How did that come about?**
I had a dream about it and how to do it. I tried what I dreamt of and couldn't do it. Tried the moves and eventually did it but could never do it on a top rope but knew I could do it. It's different when you haven't got a top rope you just know you've got to do it. On top rope I couldn't link the moves but I knew what the moves were but knew I could do it.

**Interview by Robin Nicholson**

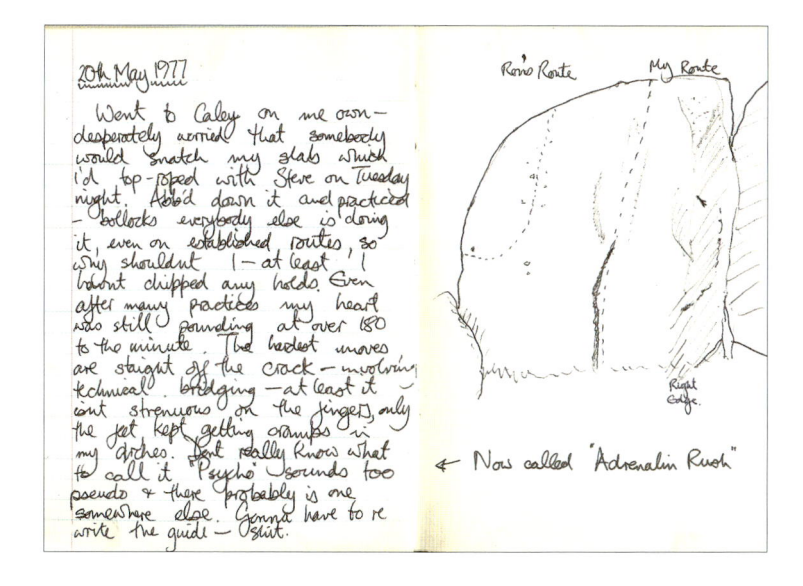

# CALEY - The Sugerloaf

## The Main Crag
This area is described for those approaching from the lower lay-by on the A660. The track is followed west from the gate for 400m with the prominent Sugarloaf boulder soon coming into view on your right and Suckers Wall boulder on your left.

## Path-side and Uphill Crag

### The Sugerloaf
A mini mountain sitting proudly amid a world of wood and grit. This path-side easy-angled slab is a great spot to get your eye in and can be climbed anywhere at around Mod (also the descent route). The entire block can be girdled at various levels. Routes start on the steep east face.

**1 Angel's Wall**  HVS 5a  7m  ★★★
The prominent front face of the boulder is a classic Caley challenge. Starting on the left make meaty moves on positive holds to gain a little respite before the final roof is tackled at its apex. The direct start is a popular Font 6a variant. Photo opposite.
*Arthur Dolphin  pre-1953*

**2 Angel's Wing**  E1 5c  7m
Eliminate, but worthwhile climbing tracking a parallel line just left of the arête. Finish as for *Angel's Wall*.
*Dave Musgrove  late 1970s*

**3 Plantation Ridge**  VS 4c  8m  ★
The arête starting with a swing from the left.
*Nancy Heron, Denys Fisher  c1944*

**4 Plantation Wall**  HVS 5b  8m  ★★
Not as popular as its visibly superior neighbours, nevertheless a superb technical trip up the face just out of reach of the left arête.
*Dave Musgrove (solo)  1975*

**5 The Can**  E2 5c  8m  ★
A rather bold proposition with a tricky move getting established above the overlap.
*Mike Hammill  1976*

**6 Central Route**  VS 5a  8m  ★★
A cracking route that takes a snaking line up the slab, just right of centre. Quite bold.

**7 Cavity**  Font 6a
The direct start to *Sweet Tooth*.

**8 Sweet Tooth**  HVS 5b  7m  ★
Starting on the boulder move up to the break before stepping left onto the slab and finishing direct.

**9 Route 3**  HS 4c  7m  ★
An awkward customer with an elusive hold. Once the rising break is reached a certain amount of cunning is required to unlock the easiest sequence. Highball Font 4.

Sean Orchard releaved to find it's a jug on **Angel's Wall** (HVS 5a). Opposite Page.
Photo: Tim Glasby

# CALEY - The Sugarloaf

**10 Route 2**  VS 5a  7m  ★★
Great climbing up the centre of the wall. Highball Font 4+.

**11 Myopia**  E1 5b  7m
A squeezed in line with little independent climbing.
*Pete Cooper 1997*

**12 Route 1**  HVS 5a  6m  ★
The short crack is a tough nut. Highball Font 5.

## Suckers Wall Boulder

Across the path from the Sugarloaf sits a fine boulder with a selection of brilliant problems. Starting from the uphill eastern arête and moving anticlockwise round the block:

**13 Chipped Edges**  Font 4+
A line of hewn holds just right of the arête.

**14 Chipped Edges 2**  Font 5+
More stone masonry up the centre of the wall.

**15 Twin Pockets**  Font 6a
Step off the boulder and tackle the wall passing a pocket.

**16 Front Traverse**  Font 7a+
An entertaining and testing journey from the arête of *Chipped Edges* all the way to finish up *Suckers Wall*.

**17 Scary Canary**  Font 7b+
A much underrated technical masterpiece that deserves to be a rite of passage. Bring strong fingers, immaculate footwork and an appetite for monos.
*Paul Greenland 1980s*

**18 Suckers Rib**  Font 5
The blunt rib on chipped holds.

**19 Suckers Wall**  Font 4
High. Another line of 'historical' chips to a reachy finish.

**20 Roll Over**  Font 7b+
Tension moves up the right-hand side of the arête allow a positive hold to be reached and a swing around the arête. Pad up the arête to finish.

**21 Mistaken Identity**  Font 8a
The steep, clean wall offers a stern test of finger strength. Start direct with a dynamic move off poor edges to gain the series of flakes and a powerful finish. A slightly easier version (a) **Ralph** comes in from the right at Font 7c+.
*Tim Clifford 2003; Christian Durkin 2000 (Ralph)*

**22 The Pinch**  Font 6c
A stretching start on the left gives access to the slopey ramp. Now hit that pinch and gun for the top. Various other variations exist, (b) a left-hand exit via a poor hold out left followed by a throw for the top weighs in at Font 7b+ or a full dyno to the top from the slopey ramp (Font 7b).

Yorkshire Gritstone

## Smear Arête - CALEY

### 23 **Tao** Font 7a+
Up the arête with your right hand on the good ear.
*Robin Warden 19th March 2010*

The uphill wall of the boulder is diminutive but hosts some micro problems right of the crack, **Short Wall** (Font 6c), **Low Traverse** (Font 7b+), **Short Wall Dyno** (Font 7b) and **Short Arête** (Font 4), despite their size all are good on excellent rock.

### Smear Arête Area
Directly behind Suckers Wall Boulder are a group of jammed blocks forming a steep roof. Slightly uphill and left of this is a long block with the following pair of problems. **Sloping Arête** (Font 4+) takes the bottom arête with a grovelling finish whilst **Sloping Rampline** (Font 6c) sits in the pit and travels up the rightward slanting feature. The next problems are on the left-most block of the steep roof.

### 24 **The Prow** Font 7b
A test of compression strength. From a sitter, clamp your way up the steep prow. Font 6b+ from standing.
*Ian Bitcon July 2001*

### 25 **Roof Layback** VS 4c  6m  ★
The monstrous corner is more fun than it looks. Just don't hang around.

### 26 **Magnetic Heels** E7 7a  6m  ★
A very modern micro route. From the slab make a series of wild contortions to get established over the roof.
*Jordan Buys March 2004*

### 27 **Smear Arête** Font 6a
The left side of the arête requires clean technique. The right side is slightly harder at Font 6a+ from standing and much tougher from sitting at Font 7a+. The slab to the left (c) is **Undercut Slab** (Font 6a).

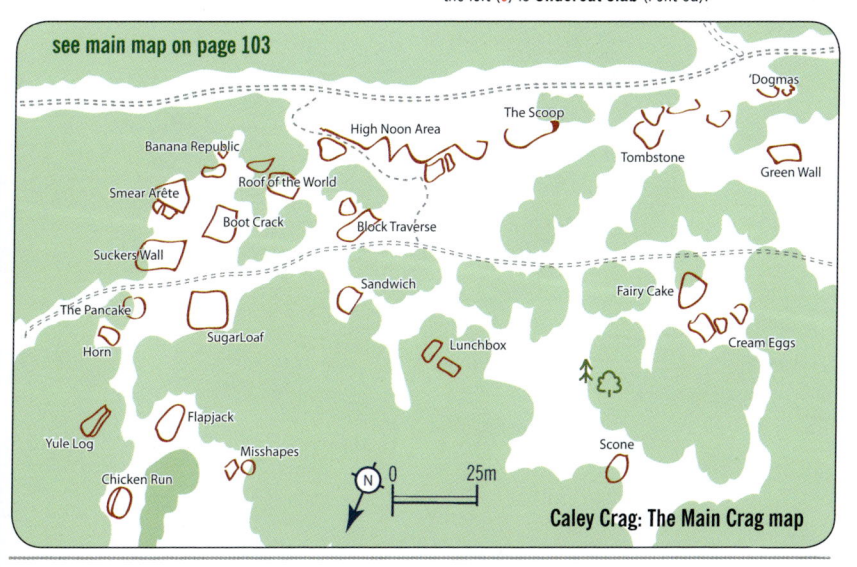

**Caley Crag: The Main Crag map**

Almscliff to Slipstones

Sean Orchard wondering if he's been thrown a sandbag on **Compulsion Crack** (VS 5a), Page 147
Photo: Tim Glasby

Boot Crack - **CALEY**

### 28 Sloper Traverse   Font 6b+
Start as low as you can and do battle with the slopers before rocking onto the slab.

Ten metres uphill from *Smear Arête* the long low roof is home to the following compact challenge. **Point Break** (Font 7b+) avoids the block and tackles the left side of the roof from sitting. Powerful stuff.

## Boot Crack
To the right of *Smear Arête* is an isolated block with a distinctive wide crack in its north face. Quality highball problems abound here, alongside the boulder's namesake - a classic that is easiest climbed in wellies...no really. Climbs start around the south-east arête (top left if facing uphill). Descent is via a down climb on the back wall (uphill) of the block.

### 29 Back Crack   Font 6a
The crack at the back from a sit-down-start in the cave.

### 30 Back Wall   Font 6a+
The wall just left of the arête and without recourse to it.

### 31 Back Stabber   Font 6a+
The left side of the arête requires control above the interesting landing. The sit-down start is **Pocket Knife** and bumps up the difficulty to Font 7a+.

### 32 Pocket Rock   Font 6b+
Quintessential Caley. The right side of the arête.

### 33 Rick's Rock   Font 6c (E3 6a)
The centre of the wall. A brilliant and committing problem.

### 34 Black Jumper   E1 5b   8m   ★
Gain the jug on the arête by either climbing or jumping from the boulder. A steady head is needed for further progress. Try to ignore the creaky flake.
*Greg Tough, Mike Dransfield   19th August 1972*

### 35 The Indirect Start   E3 6c   8m
The first half of a significant project on the front face of the block. Climb the wall direct until a lack of holds forces you left onto the sanctuary of the arête.
*Neil Carson   May 1991*

### 36 Boot Crack   VS 4b   8m   ★★
The wonderful crack. Awkward yet well protected and with plentiful jams. Photo on page 154.
*Denys Fisher   c1938*

### 37 The Glass Chipper   Font 6b
Hard, fingery moves from under the roof give access to the slab. Escape right.

Almscliff to Slipstones

# Caley - Boot Crack

**38 Shoe Shine** MVS 4b  8m  ★
Another underrated gem. Bold moves up the arête in a great position. Start from the slab on the right and follow the chips.

**39 Sneakers** HVS 5b  7m  ★
Another superb highball starting just right of the arête.

**40 Soft Shoe Shuffle** Font 6a
Shimmy up chipped holds to just below the top, then sidestep rightwards all the way around the top arête and waltz over to finish at *Back Stabber*.

**41 The Green Streak** HVS 5c  8m  ★
Engaging climbing, from the right of the wall trend up and left.

### Roof of the World - Lower Block
Twenty metres uphill and towards the main crag are two boulders; the lower one hosts orange stained *Mantel Arête*, the upper has an unmistakable juggy prow.

**42 Low Traverse** Font 6b
Starting on the eastern face of the lower block, swing leftwards along the low break before launching over the steep uphill bulge.

**43 Mantel Arête** Font 6a
The bright orange arête requires a dynamic approach.

**44 Otzi** Font 7c
On the front face. From a sitter magic your way up the wall without the arête (or with it at Font 7a+).
*Andy Swann   August 2001*

**45 Rolo** Font 6a+
Hip flexibility is a must on this tricky mantel.

**46 Low Arête** Font 6a
Tackle the knobbly arête from sitting.

---

❝ ❞

"Accomplished in nail boots in a snowstorm", Brown and Whillans on *Surplomb*. That kind of comment must be only a nostalgic memory; attached to a modern ascent it only proves the climber was not climbing a pitch worthy of his potential. No - warm windless days with climber in tee shirt and shorts will be the stage for his realisation of potential in the supergrades.

**Pete Livesey  LUUMC Journal 1974**

Lucy Creamer on **Roof of the World** (Font 5+). Page 142
Photo: Tim Glasby

# CALEY - Roof of the World

### Roof of the World - Upper Block
Doesn't quite live up to its name but nevertheless this upper block's jutting prow has a certain magnetism. The initial slab (a) is Font 4.

**47 ROTW Left Arête**  Font 6b
Swing up the left edge.

**48 Roof of the World**  Font 5+
Power for the jugs then up the steep face. The sitter (b) involves a desperate shoulder crunching press at Font 7c+. Photo on previous page.

**49 ROTW Right Arête**  Font 6b
Sticking to the steep side.

### Banana Republic
Due east (left if facing uphill), a mere 20m away, is a particularly taxing offering:

**50 Banana Republic**  Font 8a
A good intro to Font 8a climbing. From sitting use poor edges to get established on the moon shaped hold and get set for a dynamic finish. The standing start is Font 7b+.
*Tom Peckitt 2006 (SDS); JP Hotham early 2000s (standing start)*

### Finger Knacker Crack Area
Just before the main edge is reached there is a huge boulder forming a mini crevasse behind. The crevasse wall of the boulder yields several low grade problems up to Font 5 with the western arête of the block called (c) **The Gatekeeper** Font 4+. The boulder's often green front face gives rise to some tricky mantelshelf problems which when extended become the following three routes.

**51 Fried Green Tomatoes**  Font 4  (VS 4c)
More often bouldered out though gear is available. Rock up onto the ledge and get ready for a long span to the top.

**52 Hot Green Chillies**  E3 6a  8m  ★
Hard to start and terrifying to finish, but thoroughly worthwhile.

**53 The Crenellated Ridge**  HVS 5a  7m  ★
From the ramp make a tricky move to get established on the slab. Thin climbing rightward gives access to the crenellations.

The main edge is now reached and commences with an apparently featureless wall.

Yorkshire Gritstone

Finger Knacker Crack - **CALEY**

### 54  No More Mr Next Try  Font 7c+
A high quality, meaty highball with some 'old school' hard moves on bad edges. A hanging rope was used to pull through the vegetation on the first ascent.
*Steve Dunning   early 2000s*

### 55  Finger Knacker Crack  E3 6a   8m   ★★
An excellent crack climb for the aficionado/masochists amongst us. Photo on page 146.
*Ken Wood, John Syrett   6th April 1972*

### 56  The Sentry Box  HVS 5b   8m   ★
The niche is gained then exited with difficulty.

### 57  Slapstick Arête  Font 7a+
A gymnastic problem requiring a good repertoire of skills and a certain amount of nerve. The sitter is Font 7b.
*Tom Peckitt   February 2006*

### 58  Redundancy Rib  E1 5c   8m
Sketchy climbing up the rib.
*Al Manson, Pete Kitson   16th April 1973*

### 59  Storm in a Tea Cup  HVS 5b   8m
The direct line, starting left of the holly tree, onto the hanging slab and followed by a reachy move left to the sanctuary of good holds.
*J Thorpe   4th June 1988*

A climber steps off the horizon and on to **Cave and Slab** (MVS 4b) Page 148.
Photo: Mike Hutton

143

# CALEY - High Noon

## High Noon Area
A concentration of some of the best routes around from the Golden Age of Grit. Characterised by the attention grabbing flying fin of gritstone.

### 60  Holly Tree Scoop   D   11m   ★
Pass the tree and pad up the gentle scoop. The variation crack exit up and left is VD.

> To many climbers, enthusiasm for gritstone is regarded at best as the sign of a mis-spent youth, if not a poverty-stricken one. Who now, except for old men reliving past excitements over pints of Tetleys bitter, makes claims for hard gritstone that don't evoke yawns from those younger more mobile and more objective.
>
> **Dave Cook in True Grit**
> (an article from Mountain 26, 1973 - reprinted in Ken Wilson's The Games Climbers Play)

### 61  Frank Miller   E2 5b   11m
Often dirty but a good climb in its day.
*Ron Fawcett   1978*

### 62  Noonday Ridge   E1 5b   15m   ★★★
A superb and committing route that rather lives in the shadow of its more famous neighbour. Nevertheless, a rite of passage for the aspiring Extreme leader and not to be underestimated. Many will prevaricate back and forth round the prow. He who hesitates is lost my friend.
*Allan Austin   3rd October 1964*

### 63  High Noon   E4 6a   14m   ★★★
A classic frightener. The onsight is a true prize that will live long in the memory. From the depression on *Noonday Ridge* swing onto the arête and hold on for a wild ride.
Photo on page 666.
*Al Manson, Mike Hammill   20th April 1975* ✦

### 64  Gary Cooper   E3 6a   15m
The original route of this wall has lost none of its bite. Climb direct to just below the shallow depression of *Noonday Ridge*, swing round the rib and make a rising traverse rightwards to finish at the top of the large corner. *Important note: This is graded as for the original line which moved up to clip the old bolt (long gone).*
*Steve Bancroft   1977*

### 65  Fred Zinnerman   E6 6b   8m   ★★★
An audacious line up the intimidating sweep of rock. Now led without recourse to the old bolt runner by using a taped down skyhook which bumps the grade up a few notches.
Photo opposite.
*Al Manson 1977, Ben Bransby 4th April 1999* ✦

### 66  Welcome to the Neighbourhood   E1 5c  14m ★
The slab offers a good exercise in controlled technical climbing. The gear is adequate, although side-runners in the corner are possible, albeit reducing the grade a notch.
*Nigel Baker, George Pieniazek   26th April 1996*

### 67  Lad's Corner   VS 4c   14m   ★★
A stubborn lesson in gritstone climbing. The steep start is followed by an unfeasibly awkward finish.
*Arthur Dolphin, Pete Greenwood   1952*

Simon Kimber puts the marginal pro behind him on **Fred Zinnerman** (E6 6b). Page 144
Photo: Mike Hutton

Lucy Creamer digging deep into **Finger Knacker Crack** (E3 6a). Page 143
Photo: Tim Glasby

## Compulsion Crack - CALEY

**68 Block Chimney** VS 5a 14m
A stubborn lesson in gritstone climbing. A steep start followed by an unfeasibly awkward finish.
*Johnny Lees c1950*

**69 Amazing Grace** E6 6c 14m ★
Not the finest line of the crag but nevertheless a superb outing. Climb up the rib to the right of, and starting in, *Block Chimney*. The large chockstone in the chimney provides much-needed protection for the difficult moves across and up rightwards. Finish up the much easier thin upper crack.
*John Allen 17th June 1986*

**70 Saying Grace** E7 6c 14m ★★
The direct start to *Amazing Grace* is a fantastic addition with brutal and committing climbing. Climb the arête straight up from the ground.
*Gareth Parry 10th April 1999*

**71 Compulsion Crack** VS 5a 15m ★
A good introduction to the joys of gritstone crack climbing. The second wide crack right of the corner leads through a shallow chimney onto a slab and an easier finish.
Photo on page 138.
*Pete Greenwood 1952*

**72 Compulsive Viewing** HVS 5a 15m ★
A wandering line, packing in some fine climbing. Break out left, following the scoop to the break before moving left to the cracks above.
*Nigel Baker 12th April 1998* ✦

**73 Forecourt Crawler** E4 6b 15m ★
A beast of a route with a hard start and a desperate finish. Wobbly jams lead up to the roof which is passed direct, into the steep wall above.
*John Allen, Steve Bancroft 26th August 1975* ✦

**74 Forecourt Traverse** Font 7a+
Travel rightwards on crimps and 'almost pockets' to reach the slab round the corner.

**75 Indecent Postures** E2 5c 16m
A contrived route that seeks out a wide variety of climbing. Back and foot up the entrance of the cave before contorting to reach the ledge of *Pedestal Wall*. Step up and left to a direct finish up *Forecourt Crawler*.
*Nigel Baker, Andy Watts 1st October 1997*

**76 Pedestal Arête** Font 7c
From sitting, use the arête for your right hand and a small edge for your left, power up the steep arête. Strictly speaking starting with a high right heel on the ledge is out. The standing start is Font 7a.

> My hoots of derision, and ironic enquiries as to whether it would go were mere camouflage for my true fears, which were that he might actually succeed and so deprive me of all the glory.

**l Manson** speaking of his feelings when catching Mike Hammill inspecting the line of High Noon week previous to his ascent.

# CALEY - Pedestal Wall

**77 Pedestal Wall**  S 4a   18m   ★★
One of Caley's more amenable classics. A big route with a great combination of styles. Padding up the left side of the slab gives access to the stubborn short chimney before a flamboyant swing onto the steep wall brings a stroll up the final arête.
*Allan Allsop, Denys Fisher  c1938*

**78 Triple 'A'**  E2 5c   16m
A bold outing with two possible starts. Either pad up the right side of the slab or engage in a more physical tussle and layback the steep side of the arête. Either way a bold finale awaits, moving up the left front edge of the pedestal before stepping across to finish up the diagonal break.
*Dave Musgrove  1997*

**79 Cave and Slab**  MVS 4b   15m
Take the right arête of the cave's central entrance, on through the chimney and forge a line up the top slab to the left of the chipped holds. Photo on page 143.

**80 Rib and Slab**  VS 4c   14m   ★
An entertaining trip up the leaning arête on the edge of the chimney. Mounting the ledge requires a good old thrutch. Chipped holds up the slab provide a steady finish.

**81 Square Chimney**  HVD 4a   14m   ★
The connoisseur of 'back and footing' need look no further. Exit the lovely chimney and layback up the corner.

**82 Tippling Crack**  E1 5b   12m   ★★
Without recourse to any sneaky wide bridging, climb the surprisingly steep lower wall then fight your way up the glorious/appalling fist crack. Photo on page 150.
*Allan Austin, Doug Verity  26th August 1958*

**83 Dypso**  E2 5c   11m
A wandering trip but with some good positions. Starting up *Tippling Crack* gain the break and shuffle rightwards to tackle the short wall and slab just left of the arête.
*John Syrett, Andy Wild, Pete Kitson  5th April 1973*

**84 Ranieri's Reach**  Font 8a
The searing fingertip traverse is a must for aspiring beasts. Escape from the break above the far arête.
*Ben Moon  2004*

**85 Juha's Arête**  Font 7c
The brilliant right arête. A last great problem that was solved third try.
*Juha Saatsi  2002*

Yorkshire Gritstone

# Tip Off - CALEY

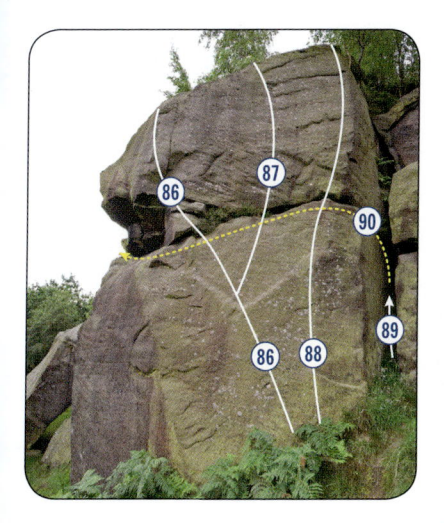

**90 I Can't Believe It's a Girdle, Girdle** E2 5c 36m
Guaranteed to raise a few eyebrows if you try to climb across a series of classics on a bank holiday Monday. Start up *Flue Crack* and follow the break to *Square Chimney*. Cross the pedestal. Traverse across *Forecourt Crawler* groove, up *Compulsion Crack* and across the scoop to near the top of *Block Chimney*. Descend this and across to finish up *Noonday Ridge*.
*Pete Kitson, Al Manson 25th May 1973*

So highball it's more of a route than a problem, **High Fidelity** (Font 8b, page 118) is a truly striking line. Steve Dunning bagged the much-coveted prize of the magnificent arête to the right of The Great Flake in April 2003, naming it after his beloved Lancia Delta Integrale Evo Club High Fidelity car.

## Tip Off Area
Just around the corner to the right is a fine slab offering butch and balancey outings.

**86 Tipster** HVS 5a 10m ★
A tough little route with punchy climbing. Moving up over the nose from the block in the break onto the slab has given more than the odd heart flutter.
*John Syrett, Ken Wood 5th April 1971*

**87 Tip Off** E2 5c 9m ★
A great little route requiring a confident approach on its technical and bold upper wall. Highball Font 5+. An alternative start, **Slip Off** (E3 6a), is possible from the lowest point of the wall to climb up to the break trending slightly left to then finish up the parent route.
*Mike Hammill 1976; B Addey, P Clough 13th May 2001 (Slip Off)*

**88 Rip Off** E3 6a 8m
Harder and with a more serious feel than its neighbours. From the break follow the right arête to its apex. Many have dived into the crack to escape.
*Mike Hammill 1976*

**89 Flue Crack** HD 8m
The stepped corner-crack has traditional values.

> High Fidelity was the standout line that grabbed my attention. At the time I reckon three or four people in the UK could have done it and I knew as soon as someone made progress the race would be on.
>
> On my first proper session it was clear that one hard move was the key to unlocking the line and for me it was a really specific press into a backhand undercut/gaston so I built a model on the board and system trained the move for six weeks, came back and nailed the move in the next session. From then on I sieged it before and after work until it came together.
>
> Without a doubt the ascent rubbed up a number of people the wrong way and certainly some climbers were rather mean-spirited over it. However, some folks had sat on their arses and talked about hard climbing whilst I put more effort in than they could dream of. Good climbers could have done it but they never really tried it with the intention of seeing it through to the end - the exception was Ben Moon and he made the first repeat. The point is that climbing Font 8b on grit can only happen when the conditions allow and how many times is that in the UK? Ten times a season maximum. So you need to be dedicated to the cause and ready, especially if you have a regular job.

**Steve Dunning**

Matt Troilett skillfully avoiding jamming on **Tippling Crack** (E1 5b). Page 148
Photo: Mike Hutton

# The Scoop Buttress

This clean, tall buttress is home to a concentration of fine and desperate lines, with a classic VS thrown in for good measure.

### 91  A Comedy Moment  E6 6a  8m
Nothing to laugh about on this brute. The steep prow left of *V Chimney* and above the slab offers bold, fierce climbing.
*Ben Bransby, Gareth Parry, Dave Musgrove (jnr)  11th April 1999*

### 92  V Chimney  HVD 4a  16m
The V chimney just left of the arête provides a tussle.

### 93  Quark Walk  HVS 5b  18m  ★
A great trip at the grade with some fine climbing. From *V Chimney* traverse rightward round the arête, along the break and take a deep breath before pulling over the steep bulge to finish.
*Dave Musgrove, Andy Wild  12th May 1982*

### 94  Quark  E5 6a  15m  ★★★
As good as it gets. Hammill left his mark with this thrilling and desperately technical masterpiece. Worth the upgrade for a clean onsight. Rip up the thin crack before making use of the arête to gain the break. Step right and finish up the wall in a serious position. (a) **Quark Quack** (E7 6b) continues up the blunt pocketed arête.
*Mike Hammill Oct 1977; Ben Bransby, Gareth Parry Apr1999 (QQ)*

### 95  Charm  E8 6c  15m  ★★★
A frightening technical offering up the leftward trending ramp, right of the crack. Originally tackled with a side-runner (E6), this style has now been superceded with a clean solo ascent.
*Graham Desroy  1988; Ben Tetler (solo)  1999*

### 96  Strangeness  E7 6c  15m  ★★
Lonely, hard slab climbing in a very serious position. A skyhook has been used as a dubious form of protection on at least one ascent. Photo on page 156.
*Steve Rhodes, Martin Berzins  1988*

### 97  The Scoop  VS 4c  15m  ★★
A last great problem from the 1940s mastered by the blonde Baildon rock wizard. Once the corner has been dealt with and the ledge gained, the upper scoop provides an outstanding delicate finish.
*Arthur Dolphin  pre-1953*  ◆

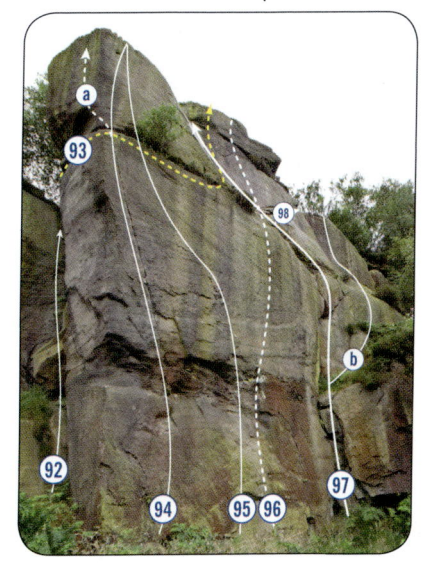

### 98  Zig-Zag  S 4b  15m  ★
A great route with varied climbing on good, positive holds and a couple of wobbly jams. A stiff corner start leads to the grass ledge. Follow the crack leftwards then rightwards on good jams to finish. Taking the scoop direct up the right-hand wall from the grass ledge is (b) **I Can't Remember** (HVS 5a, ◆).

The right-hand wall of the gully right of Scoop Buttress has been climbed at Severe whilst the micro-route on the block is **Dark Matter** (E2 6b †).

# CALEY - Double Ridge

### Crag Far End
The edge becomes steeper and more fragmented now, but amongst the jumble of blocks is the committing classic of *One Man and His Dogmas* (E5 6b) and several decent problems on the **Green Wall** block down by the path.

On the first block 25m to the right of Scoop Buttress is the block with the obvious peg-scarred crack on its left side. This crack is the very tasty **Fingers Crack** (Font 6a). The right side of the arête is the second pitch of *Double Ridge* (see below) whilst the slab to the right has several variations, the best being:

### 99 Dusk  HVS 5b   6m  ★
The centre of the wall provides a punchy little micro route. The upper bulge provides the excitement.
*Dave Musgrove, Tim Leach  21st June 1976*

The broken block directly below *Finger's Crack* is the **Tombstone**. The cool problem on the south-east corner (top left if looking uphill) is **Gravedigger** (Font 6a), which goes from a sitter and the break to tackle the clean arête on the left side. On the slabby lower face, the arête on the left side is **Boneyard** (Font 4) whilst the centre of the left-hand slab is **The Tombstone** (Font 4). The right arête is **Epitaph** (Font 4+). On the slab to the right, the left arête is the starting point for something that's just a touch different.

### 100 Double Ridge  HS 4a   15m  ★
A big fun outing at the grade, with the possibility of multi-pitch shenanigans. Romp up the ridge to the top of the block and take an optional belay. Continue up the in-cut left arête of *Finger's Crack* block.

Back down on the Tombstone, the slab and flake to the right of *Double Ridge* is **Cold Slab** (Font 4+). Continuing right for 25m is a lush green slab with a clean cut groove on its left side. The arête and crack to the left of the groove is (a) **Vegetation Arête** (Font 6a).

### 101 The High Scary Groove  HVS 5a   7m
Only scary if the slab is in full flower. Take the groove and then gibber onto and up the slab to finish.

### 102 Harum–Scarum  E3 6b   8m
From the base of the groove move right, around the rib, and across the wall to the sloping ledge. Finish up the slab left of the crack. The crack and right edge of the slab is (b) **Hello Ducky** (MVS).
*T. Marr, A. Taylor 16th Jul 2000; P. Cooper 30th May 1999 (HD)*

Scramble up the hill to the right. Sitting above the narrow path and big drop is the tall obloid block of '*Dogmas*. On a ledge 10m left of the gully is a short wall where **Pockets**

152  Yorkshire Gritstone

## One Man And His Dogmas - CALEY

or **Drop** (Font 6a) climbs the pockets and flake. Beware the gully drop behind.

**103 One Man and His Dogmas**  E5 6b  6m ★★
Manson's final addition to the crag with all his hallmarks: hard moves in a bold position and destined for modern classic status. Blast up the wall before teetering leftward to the arête, following this to the top. (c) The direct start is **Agrippa**, a brilliant proposition at Font 7c.
*Al Manson 1st Sept 1989; Andy Swann 10th June 2001 (Agrippa)*

The arête to the right is (d) **Tenet Arête** (Font 6b+) and continuing right 10m is the short sensation **Rippled Wall** (Font 5+).

**The Green Wall** block, 20m downhill to the north, is home to some good but often overlooked problems. The wall (a) avoiding any holds on the arête is **Dr Green Thumb** (Font 7a+); the left arête of the lower wall (b) **Flaky Groove** (Font 4+) grapples the groove trending slightly right of the arête; (c) the committing **Green Wall** (Font 6c) takes the centre of the wall; (d) the right arête taken on the left is **Steep Arête** (Font 6a+) whilst right of the arête is the ankle busting **Above the Slab** (Font 5). Moving around to the clean south wall there is (e) **Little Flake** (Font 5+) the small flake and mono and (f) the **Hanging Flake** (Font 6b) up the centre of the wall to the flake. The right arête is (g) **Block Arête** (Font 4).

Heading back north west (towards the Sugarloaf), after 110m there is a fine long block just to the right of the track. The path-side left arête and shelf from a sitter is (h) **Chunk Arête** (Font 5); (i) **Block Pockets** (Font 4+) yards up the wall and pockets to the right; (j) **Block and Tackle** (Font 6b) uses undercuts to climb the small wall; (k) the right-to-left **Block Traverse** (Font 6a) shimmys across just below the top edge. Just above and behind the block is a short overhung wall with the excellent (l) **Lippy Luvin'** (Font 5+) which takes a sit-start and hand jives up the arête to mantel the peak; (m) **Point n' Shoot** (Font 4+) yanks up the peak direct.

*Almscliff to Slipstones*

Lucy Creamer brings out the big guns for **Boot Crack** (VS 4b). Page 139
Photo: Mike Hutton

The Pancake - **CALEY**

## The Main Crag Downhill Circuit
Ecstatically follow the convenient loop of boulders modelled in Fontainebleau and hewn from the finest gritstone. Embark on your journey adjacent to the Sugarloaf in an anticlockwise direction from The Pancake which is 10m due east.

### The Pancake
Powerful starts merge seamlessly into a delicate slab, home to the delightful *Mr Smooth*.

**1 Pancake Scoop**   Font 6c+
Sit-down start and grapple up the scoop and faint flake.

**2 Pancake Day**   Font 7a+
Start hanging the pocket, yard up to the next and throw a mantel onto the slab.

**3 Pancake Sloper**   Font 6c
Sit-down start. Begin at the sloper, take the undercut and fathom a way of gaining the slab.

**4 Mr Smooth**   Font 6a
The best problem of the block is a class act. Subtle use of the flakes and footwork unlocks the way forward. The sit-down start notches the grade up to Font 6b.

**5 Pancake Arête**   Font 4
The right-hand side of the arête is an easy passage.

Leo Houlding eleching to rest three of his fingers for later on **Strangeness** (E7 6c), Page 151
Photo: Adam Long

## The Yule Log - CALEY

Located 5m north-east of The Pancake is a fine rising prow known as **The Horn,** offering three tricky customers.

**6 Horn Rib**   Font 7a+
Slapping up the left arête is a tad problematic.

**7 The Horn**   Font 6b
A perplexing problem up the front of the prow.

**8 Horn Dyno**   Font 6c
The right arête succumbs with a jump.

**9 Horn Traverse**   Font 4
An ascending traverse up the edge to the point of the block.

On the boulder to the west of The Horn is an excellent little challenge:

**10 Luna**   Font 6a+
Start left of the knee high cave and blaze a trail rightwards on crimps and slopers to the top.
*Robin Warden   January 2010*

Continuing on the path a large flat sloping boulder appears on your left. **Confessions of a Specimen Hunter** (Font 7a) takes a left-to-right traverse of the right-hand edge of the boulder on slopers and pockets.

45m north-north west of The Horn is a long triangular block with its steepest side facing the woodland downhill, **The Yule Log.**

**11 Yuletide**   Font 5+
On the left of the boulder's steep side is this little gem. Surmount the small roof to get onto the slab. Class.

**12 Yuletide Wall**   Font 7a
Sit-down start. Endure the pain of the smallest edges to progress up and left into the scoop.

**13 Pine Tree Arête**   Font 6c+
Sit-down start. Do not dwell on the slanting arête as the difficulties are not reached until the end. A charming line.

**14 Yule Slab 1**   Font 3
Pleasant knobbly slab padding.

**15 Yule Slab 2**   Font 3
Wade through the moss using the pocket.

**16 Yule Slab 3**   Font 2+
A nice green slab introduction.

**17 Yule Slab 4**   Font 5+
Sit-down start. Pull onto the slab from the low undercut.

**18 Yuletide Flake**   Font 4
Yard up the undercut flake.

# CALEY - The Chicken Run

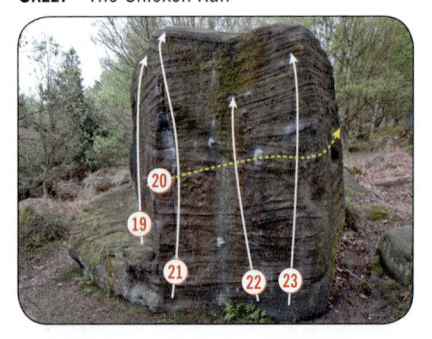

Take the low path for 20m north-west to reach **The Chicken Run** block with its rippled chicken head wall.

### 19 **Goose Bumps**  Font 6b
The wall above the plinth gives you goose bumps as a fall could be awkward.

### 20 **Chicken Run Traverse**  Font 6b+
Travel left-to-right across the block beneath the top finishing on the easy side.

### 21 **Drumstick**  Font 6a
The good flake leads the way up the arête.

### 22 **Chicken Run**  Font 7b
The Caley chicken heads throw up another perplexing challenge. Finger-lickin' good.

### 23 **Cold Turkey**  Font 5
The gobbling good arête requires a delicate approach. A sit-down start is possible at Font 6c.

Head back uphill (south) 20m towards The Sugarloaf to reach **The Flapjack** a long slabby boulder with its unmistakable traverse.

### 24 **Flapjack Traverse**  Font 7a+
Up there with Stanage Plantation's best, this Caley sideways outing won't disappoint. Start at the bottom arête truck right and finish at the end of the slab for the full tick.

### 25 **Flapjack Groove**  Font 6c+
Sit-down start at the low flake and exit the shallow scoop with a good measure of awkwardness.

### 26 **Flapjack Mantel**  Font 5
A mantel off the two crimps is a rewarding number.

### 27 **Flapjack Pockets**  Font 3
Make use of the pockets to gain the slab.

### 28 **Flapjack Slab**  Font 4
Link the miniature break and the shallow dish.

### 29 **Flapjack Scoop**  Font 5+
Plenty of choice on this one, the key being to use the right holds at the right time with very clean feet.

### 30 **Flapjack Arête**  Font 3+
The gently curving right arête.

The two poised blocks, **The Misshapes,** 15m south-west of The Flapjack are linked together with a pumpy traverse.

## The Sandwich - CALEY

**31 Lip Traverse** Font 6b
Make sure you have plenty in the tank to make a full lip traverse of both blocks. A forearm bulging bonanza.

**32 Arête** Font 5+
Hang the lip and surmount the block onto the slab.

**33 Misshape** Font 6a
Up the arête and grope over the top using the chicken heads.

**34 Mantel** Font 5+
Mantel over left of the arête.

**35 Nose** Font 4+
A sweet problem over the hanging nose.

**36 Scoop** Font 4
One move without much wonder up the scoop.

Continuing along the path for 20m (south) you encounter the slabby side of **The Sandwich**. Three worthwhile problems are on its steepest face.

**37 Sarnie** Font 6a
Slap to the top rail from the undercut break.

**38 Buttie** Font 5+
A similar problem to *Sarnie* with a sloper and pocket thrown in.

**39 Sandwich Slopers** Font 5+
An eliminate from the two big slopers to the apex of the block without using the arête.

20m west of The Sandwich are two sunken blocks known as **The Lunchbox**. Both suffer from a range of mosses and lichens.

**40 Green Traverse** Font 4+
A right-to-left lip traverse which can be coated in a bad case of green.

**41 Greener Traverse** Font 4
Another traversing cryptoganists dream.

> Another whose natural habitat can be found around boulders is about 46 years old, knows everybody and everybody knows him even if they haven't met. He knows every problem move by move, but hasn't completed any. He was there when every major problem was solved. In fact he is the universal Dennis. The guy to watch though is the skinny little gink who never stops. The one who does know every move 'cos he created them and he's the master of that patch.

*From an article by Al Manson called* **Eddie Lawson should wear Firés** *in the LUUMC Journal 1987*

159

# CALEY - The Scone

### 43 Scone Slab Left  Font 5
Slab-lovers will relish this block. Levitate up the left side at a lovely angle.

### 44 Scone Centre  Font 5+
The vague pockets up the centre provide only a shade of positivity to help the footwork.

### 45 Scone Arête  Font 3+
Turn the fat arête onto the slabbier side.

Meander back uphill for 35m (south) towards the main crag and the cluster of **Cream Eggs** are soon on your right, with arguably the best Font 7a of the circuit.

### 46 Over Easy  Font 7a+
The sit-down start of the neat undercut arête kicks off the quality of this block. Dynamic.

### 47 Scrambled Egg  Font 7b
Sit-down start as for *Over Easy* and beat a way into the *Cream Egg Eliminate*.

### 48 The Cream Egg Eliminate  Font 7a
How do you eat yours? Devour this beauty from the right arête in to the not so soft centre and top-out via the chicken head.

### 49 Cream Egg Arête  Font 6a
The smeary right arête which can end in a belly flop for some.

### 50 Arête from Sitter  Font 6a
The slanting left arête from a sit-down start.

### 51 Tricky Wall  Font 6c
Master the tricky little wall between the arêtes.

### 52 Arête Left  Font 6a
Sit-down start and slap up the left arête and mantel over at the apex.

### 53 Cracked Slab  Font 4
Follow the insignificant cracks up the slab.

Continue walking 30m to the west where you arrive at the tent shaped **Scone** and its delicate slab offerings.

### 42 The Scone  Font 6a+
Travel left-to-right with great delicacy to the fat arête. Those who require the Font 7a tick can continue along the sloping lip.

160  Yorkshire Gritstone

# The Leftovers - CALEY

Head back uphill and you reach the triangular face of the **Fairy Cake**.

### 54 Fairy Arête  Font 3
Ease up the slab side of the left arête.

### 55 Fairy Cake  Font 5+
Tackle the centre of the wall.

### 56 Fairy Slab  Font 3+
The slab is green and slippery.

The main path is found above the Fairy Cake marking the end of the circuit, well almost. If you follow a path for 90m south-west from the Scone into the woods, you reach what is known as the **Leftovers**; home to a fine selection of hidden desperates.

### 57 The Red Squirrel  Font 7b+
From the left of the block travel right into *The Drey*.
*Ben Meeks  May 2008*

### 58 The Drey  Font 7b+
From a sit-down start at the crack, power your way along the lip from right-to-left then wallop up the blunt rib. A big span or good technique may be an advantage. The extension, starting from the flake is (a) **Cuddles** (Font 7c+).
*Dave Cowl  April 2005, 2008 (Cuddles)*

### 59 Two Squirrels  Font 7b+
The original tufty challenge of the block. Start as for *The Drey* but continue to the end of the lip. The extended sit start from the flake is **Three Squirrels** (Font 7c+).
*Andy Swann 10th June 2001; Dave Cowl May 2008 (3 Squirrels)*

## The Dogside Boulders

Finally the last boulders can be unearthed by heading west along the track above the main crag until a wooden bridge is reached that crosses a small ravine. Cross the bridge and head up the hill until a faint path can be taken on your right following a low broken wall that descends downhill. The boulders come into view on your left with the first feature **The Prow** (Font 6c), which in fact takes the terrifying and awesome wall left of the big prow; **Finches Fuel** (Font 7a+) is the prow direct with a heart fluttering finish (also possible from sitting which adds a grade); **Finch Arête** (Font 6b) takes the arête to half-height then pops right onto the slab; **Finch Slab** (Font 5+) is the slab direct from a sitter.

On the next block **Twin Arêtes** (Font 6a) uses both arêtes whilst **Arête Right** (Font 6a) uses only the right one. The Long Boulder has a number of good problems starting with **Long Boulder Arête** (Font 6a) a sit-down start to the right arête of the block; **Arête Eliminate** (Font 6a) makes a long span to the top from the good hold on the right arête; **Arête to Flake** (Font 6b) goes from the pocket on the right arête leftward to reach the high flake; **Flake Standing** (Font 6a) literally gets the high flake from upright. Further down the hill is a collection of blocks with **Mono Traverse** (Font 7a) on the right-hand block, travelling right-to-left and finishing round the arête passing the useful mono.

Dave Sutcliffe on **Death Drop 2000** (Font 7a / E4 6b). Page 108
Photo: Mike Hutton

## Further Information on First Ascents (◆)

**Adrenaline Rush**: *1977 Originally called Psycho. Unbeknown to Manson, Fawcett had climbed Psycho only days earlier leaving Manson to find an alternative name. Manson tells of sticking the top on the first ascent: "If the rubber could have been tapped from my legs, it would have kept Goodyear in business for years".*
**Dark Matter**: *Climbed by John-Paul Hotham 25th May 2001.*
**Fingerknacker Crack**: *Climbed with aid in 1964 by D Cronon.*
**Dr Green Thumb**: *Tom Peckitt April 2006.*
**Forecourt Crawler**: *Direct Finish added by Ron Fawcett c1975.*
**Fred Zinnerman**: *The bolt that once existed was placed by the late Iain Edwards in order to protect this and what became High Noon. After surviving a fall, Edwards was beaten to both routes by an on-form Manson. Ben Bransby removed the bolt in 1999 and re-led the route with a taped down skyhook for protection.*
**Hanging Groove**: *Remained the truly classic sandbag for years, graded VS.*
**High Noon**: *"My hoots of derision, and ironic enquiries as to whether it would go were mere camouflage for my true fears, which were that he might actually succeed and so deprive me of all the glory. (Al Manson speaking of his feelings when catching Hammill inspecting the line a week previous to his ascent).*
**I Can't Remember**: *Climbed by Tony Burnell, 1980s.*
**Little Cenotaph**: *Recorded by Dolphin as Inverted Crack, re-named and documented by Allan Austin in 1958.*
**Permutation Rib**: *Originally called the Clinger. The direct start was added by Mike Hammill in 1977.*
**Point Break**: *Climbed by Dave Sutcliffe.*
**Rising More Slowly**: *Climbed by Dave Musgrove in 1978.*
**The Money Shot**: *Has been mistakenly known as The Hole Shot but now makes a welcomed return to its original name.*
**The Scoop**: *Was said to be the hardest climb in Wharfedale at the time.*
**Terry**: *Peak raider Ben Moon believed he had made the first ascent. However, Yorkshire bouldering legend Andy Swann had nipped in a week earlier offering the 'Old-School' E4 6c grade. The name refers to the use of your triceps (Terrys) on the powerful start.*
**Waite**: *Climbed by Andy Swann and Christian Durkin around the same time, with Matt Birch also rumoured to have got there first in the early 1990s.*
**Zoo York**: *Christian Durkin 1990s, flashed by Jvan Tresch 2002.*

James Ibbertson goes 'spatchcock' on **Terry** (Font 7c). Page 117
Photo: Dave Simmonite

# CALEY - Graded List

## Graded List

### Routes

**E8**
Charm (6c)

**E7**
Magnetic Heels (7a)
Marrow Bone Jelly (6b)
Strangeness (6c)
Saying Grace (6c)
Quark Quack (6b)

**E6**
Amazing Grace (6c)
The Green Room (6c)
The Great Flake (6b)
Fred Zinnerman (6b)
A Comedy Moment (6a)

**E5**
One Man & His Dogmas (6b)
Psycho (6b)
Adrenaline Rush (6b)
Quark (6a)

**E4**
Forecourt Crawler (6b)
High Noon (6a)
Ephedrine (6a)

**E3**
The Indirect Start (6c)
Harum-Scarum (6b)
Slip Off (6a)
Gary Cooper (6a)
Fingerknacker Crack (6a)
Rip Off (6a)
Hot Green Chillies (6a)
Hanging Groove (5c)

**E2**
Dark Matter (6b)
Frank Miller (5b)
I Can't Believe It's A Girdle, Girdle (5c)
Indecent Postures (5c)
The Can (5c)
Dypso (5c)
Rising More Slowly (5c)
Tip Off (5c)
Triple 'A' (5c)

**E1**
Knobbler Traverse (6a)
Redundancy Rib (5c)
Permutation Rib (5c)
Harry's Heap/Knobbler (5c)
Welcome To The Neighbourhood (5c)
Angel's Wing (5c)
Black Jumper (5b)
Myopia (5b)
Tippling Crack (5b)
Noonday Ridge (5b)

**HVS**
The Green Streak (5c)
Rabbit's Paw Wall (5b)
Sneakers (5b)
Quark Walk (5b)
The Sentry Box (5b)
Storm in a Tea Cup (5b)
Dusk (5b)
Sweet Tooth (5b)
Plantation Wall (5b)
The Highly Scary Groove (5b)
Route 1 (5a)
Tipster (5a)
I Can't Remember (5a)
Angel's Wall (5a)
Compulsive Viewing (5a)
The Crenellated Ridge (5a)

**VS**
Block Chimney (5a)
Compulsion Crack (5a)
Central Route (5a)
Route 2 (5a)
The Scoop (4c)
Little Cenotaph (5a)
Lad's Corner (4c)
Unfinished Crack (4c)
Rib And Slab (4c)
Plantation Ridge (4c)
Roof Layback (4c)
Boot Crack (4b)

**HS**
Route 3 (4c)
Double Ridge (4a)

**MVS**
Shoe Shine (4b)
Cave And Slab (4b)
Hello Ducky

**S**
Zig-Zag (4b)
Pedestal Wall (4a)

**HVD**
V Chimney (4a)
Square Chimney (4a)

**HD**
Flue Crack

**D**
Holly Tree Scoop

### Problems

**8b**
Ullola
High Fidelity

**8a**
Ranieri's Reach
Mistaken Identity
Vicious Streak
New Blood
Zoo York
Banana Republic

**7c+**
Feel the Noise
Three Squirrels
No More Mr Next Try
Salsa Start
Northern Soul
Cuddles
Ralph
ROTW sit-down-start
Ben's Groove sit-down-start

**7c**
Dave's Saunter
Juha's Arête
Waite
New Jerusalem sit-down-start
Terry (E5 7a)
Agrippa
Otzi
Pedestal Arête
Nothing's Safe (E6 6c)
The Rose
Guacamole
No Pebble Arête Direct finish
Pencil's Problem
Cruel Crack Right-Hand
Andy's Route sit-down-start
Blockbuster

**7b+**
Bring out the Funk (E5 6c)
The True Pebble Wall (E5 6c)
No Pebble Arête

**7b**
Mini Mati (E5 6c)
The Crystal Method
Roll Over
The Red Squirrel
The Drey
Low Traverse
Ju Ju Club
Ripper Arête sit-down-start
Bad Etiquette
Psycho Direct Start (E5 6b)
Point Break
Two Squirrels
Banana Republic Sit-Down-Start
Scary Canary
Freak Technique
Wainwright's Wobble
Secret Seventh
Syrett's Saunter

**7b**
Smooth Wall Dyno
To Be Is Not To Bolt (E6 6c)
Space Ape
Slapstick Arête sit-down-start
Scrambled Egg
Hanging Wall
Chocolate Orange (E5 6c)
The Prow
Just the One
Chicken Run
Short Wall Dyno
Monsoon Monsoon
Ripper Arête
Andy's Route
Ben's Groove
Ahab Right

**7a+**
Ahab
Front Traverse
Pocket Knife
Otley Wall Direct Start
Hampered
Slapstick Arête
Over Easy
Pancake Day
Smear Arête sit-down-start
Tao
Forecourt Traverse
The Hanging Nose
Dr Green Thumb
Finches Fuel
Flapjack Traverse
Horn Rib
Roof Traverse
Neat Wall Arête Eliminate

**7a**
Pocket Wall
Pedestal Arête Standing Start
The Cream Egg Eliminate
Nora Batty
The Groove
Mono Traverse
Yuletide Wall
New Jerusalem
Confessions of a Specimen-Hunter
Death Drop 2000 (E4 6c)

**6c+**
Jam Hard (E2 6b)
Pancake Scoop
Pine Tree Arête
Not My Stile
Undercut Wall
Flapjack Groove
Thug Arête

# Graded List - CALEY

### 6c
The Money Shot
Bum Fight
The Pinch
Fug Dup
Rick's Rock (E3 6a)
Dead Point Dyno
Edge Wall
Pancake Sloper
MBKC Arête
The Palm Press
Lightning Crack Travesre
Horn Dyno
Short Wall
Green Wall
Cold Turkey SDS
The Rocking Groove
Lightning Crack SDS
Calvinistic
Tricky Wall
Sloping Rampline
Pocket Wall
The Prow (standing start)
Smooth Wall Traverse
Roadside Mantel
The Hanging Nose
Road Kill

### 6b+
Lightning Crack
Mantel Illness
The Arête
Pocket Rock
Ripper Trav/Ron's Reach (E3 6a)
The Thin Slab Direct
Sloper Traverse
Lip Traverse
Tenet Wall
Chicken Run Traverse
South Wall Traverse
Right Wall
Bob's Bastard II

### 6b
Maurice Chevalier
The Bat
Webster's Whinge
Martin's Muff
Finch Arête
Lip Traverse
ROTW Left Arête
ROTW Right Arête
Arête To Flake
Block and Tackle
The Horn
Goose Bumps
Mr Smooth sit-down-start
The Glass Chipper
Hanging Flake
Otley Wall Right-Hand
Small Roof
Low Traverse
Otley Wall Traverse
Flake Wall
The Great Flake sit-down-start
Left Arête of Psycho
Smooth Wall

### 6a+
Stretcher
Back Wall
Rolo
Luna
Neat Wall sit-down start
The Plat Traverse
Otley Wall
Thin Slab Direct
Back Stabber
The Scone
Steep Arête
Crimpy Wall
Our Fathers Arête

### 6a
Low Pebble Wall
Cavity
The Halo
Fugee-La
South Face Arête
Twin Pockets
Smear Arête
Mr Smooth
Vegetation Arête
Long Boulder Arête
Arête Eliminate
Block Traverse
Twin Arêtes
Left Arête
Low Arête
Mantel Arête
Drumstick
Fingers Crack
Flake Standing
Soft Shoe Shuffle
Misshape
The Chicken Scoop
Picnic
Back Crack
Sarnie
Cream Egg Arête
Arête From Sitter
Pockets or Drop
The Mask
Arête Left
Arête Right
Gravedigger
Neat
Bob's Bastard
Short Arête
Breakfest
Ahab Standing
Undercut Slab

### 5+
Gripping Groove
Stile Council
Yuletide
South Face Direct
Scone Centre
Low Rib
Fairy Cake
The Neat Wall
Couser Edge
Rough Rib
ROTW
Sweet Tooth
Right Wall Right-Hand
Little Flake
Yule Slab 4
Chipped Edges 2
Rippled Wall
Lippy Luvin'
The Cruel Crack
Morris Dance (HVS 5b)
Steady Arête
The Thin Slab
Neat Wall Arête
Chicken Heads eliminate
Buttie
Arête
Mantel
Sandwich Slopers
Finch Slab
Flapjack Scoop
MBKC Groove
Flake Arête

### 5
The Groove
Beached Whale Traverse
Smooth Arête
Chicken Arête

### Chicken Heads
Above the Slab
Chunk Arête
Cold Turkey
Flapjack Mantel
Scone Slab Left
Playground Traverse
Neat Arête
Suckers Rib

### 4+
Short Slab
Chipped Edges
Sloping Arête
The Gatekeeper
Epitaph
Cold Slab
Flaky Groove
Block Pockets
Point 'n' Shoot
Nose
Green Traverse
The Slab
Short Wall
The Rocking Stone Roof (VS 5b)

### 4
Fried Green Tomatos (VS 4c)
Runnel Wall
Morris Crack (HS 4b)
Rocking Stone Traverse
Suckers Wall
Flapjack Slab
Short Arête
Curver
Boneyard
The Tombstone
Pancake Arête

### Horn Traverse
Rocking Arête
Scoop
Block Arête
Greener Traverse
Chipped Slab 2
Chips
Free Stile
Cracked Slab
Slab Right
Neat Crack
Yuletide Flake

### 3+
Rippled Corner
Scone Arête
Flapjack Arête
Fairy Slab

### 3
Slab Left
Yule Slab 1
Yule Slab 2
Chipped Slab 1
Flapjack Pockets
Morris Minor (S 3c)
Fairy Arête
Mini Wall
Slab Centre
Left-hand Groove

### 2+
Slab
Yule Slab 3

### 2
Playground Crack

Almscliff from Caley. The view across the Wharfe Valley.
Photo: Jamie Moss

# the chevin
by **Dave Sutcliffe**

Chevin Buttress & Quarry OS Ref: SE 210 445
West Chevin Boulders OS Ref: SE 195 442

Altitude: 250m

Hidden on the crest of the beautiful Chevin Forest Park lies an outstanding natural buttress, an adventurous quarry and a cult little bouldering venue. The main crag and quarry overlook the lower reaches of the Wharfe Valley to the east of the market town of Otley and are only a stone's throw away from the more popular and well-known neighbour Caley. The West Chevin Boulders are more secluded and deeper into the woods to the west.

**Routes and Bouldering:** The climbing consists of almost 100 routes and boulder problems varying both in height (8m to 23m) and style (short unprotected solos to splitter cracks that eat gear). The quality of the climbing and the rock varies from sound compact clean gritstone on the natural edges to rock of questionable quality in the quarries. They offer different and enjoyable challenges in their own right. The natural edge of Chevin Buttress is home to some classic routes; the 3-star double of the bold *Gronff* (E2 5c) and the thuggy *Waster* (E1 5b) should be on every extreme leader's tick list whilst the flagship route of *Chevin Buttress* (VS 4c) is as good as it gets at this grade. The quarry has a mixed bunch of climbs, the better of which follow near-perfect cracks and natural arêtes. The routes in here are long which give them a bit more character and feel. <u>Warning</u> - belays at the top of some of the quarried routes can be difficult to find and the top of the crag can be difficult to negotiate, so be careful! The bouldering on the main edge and West Chevin Boulders has only recently been developed and, although limited, offers good problems through the grades. The best of these tend to be in the higher echelons so if you are operating at these lofty heights then the trio of *Like a Hurricane* (Font 7c+), *Brownian Motion* (Font 7c+) and *Fluid Dynamics* (Font 8a+) should grab your attention.

**Conditions and Aspect:** Although the crag faces north, due to its aspect the natural buttress catches the wind and can be in good condition when the more sheltered quarries are damp. It is a great venue for shade on a hot day and perfect for climbing on a summer evening when the sun hits the face of the edge. The boulders are best in spring and autumn when the trees aren't in full bloom.

**Parking and Approach:** Several options are available (map on page 100). For the main edge: When approaching from Otley, from the bottom of Leeds Road (A660) take the East Chevin Road south-east and up the steep hill. Drive over the fly-over and after half a mile keep your eye out for the East Chevin Quarry car park on the right (**Parking GPS: 53.896021,-1.678661**). There is ample parking here (but be sure to leave nothing on view in the car to attract thieves). An alternative car park can be found a further 500m up the hill on the left, Lower Shawfield Car Park (**Parking GPS: 53.893972,-1.671719**), opposite the Cheerful Chilli restaurant. Walk back down the busy road to the East Chevin Car Park. From here follow the obvious path west for 150m until the quarries can be seen through the vegetation on the left. For the main buttress, continue along the path a further 150m. For the West Chevin Boulders it is best to approach from Menston. From Bradford Road (A65) turn onto Buckle Lane at the Hare and Hounds pub traffic lights and crossroads. Follow this road for half a mile and take the second right at the crossroads at the top of the hill onto Windmill Lane (opposite the Chevin pub). Turn left at the end of the road then right onto York Gate. Park in the lay-by approximately 500m up the road on the right (**Parking GPS: - 53.891868, -1.704524**). Cross the road, through the gate and walk north for 130m through the field into the woods. On entering the woods turn right and the boulders will come into view reaching *Raynman* block first.

When E1 feels like E9, Richard Mallinson feeling wasted on **The Waster** (E1 5b). Page 176
Photo: Dave Sutcliffe

# THE CHEVIN - Introduction

Alternatively if you're planning on visiting all sections of the Chevin in one trip, continue along York Gate and park in the large car park (Beacon House Car Park – busiest, but safest) which is equidistant between the venues (**Parking GPS: 53.892013, -1.690249**). Go through the stile at the top of the car park and walk west staying on the highest path to reach the West Chevin Boulders after 900m. Or go east if heading for Chevin Buttress where a flagged path drops gently downhill until after 300m where a track on the left doglegs steeply downhill for 150m to reach another main track. Go right (west) on this for a further 250m and Chevin Buttress is on the right.

**Access and Restrictions:** There are no access issues at any of the venues however the farmer's fields at the top of the quarry should not be entered. In recent years the ledge on *Central Route* on Chevin Buttress has become home to a Tawny owl. During the nesting season, signs will be in place from the Park Rangers indicating climbing restrictions.

---

Before the main crag, there are two neglected routes for the keen to seek out which lie 50m up the road from the quarry car park into the woods on the right. **Dennis the Dilapidated Pensioner** (HVS 5b), climbs the wall on the right of the buttress; **Midget Digit** (E1 6a), takes the thin crack up the middle of the wall passing the old bolt.

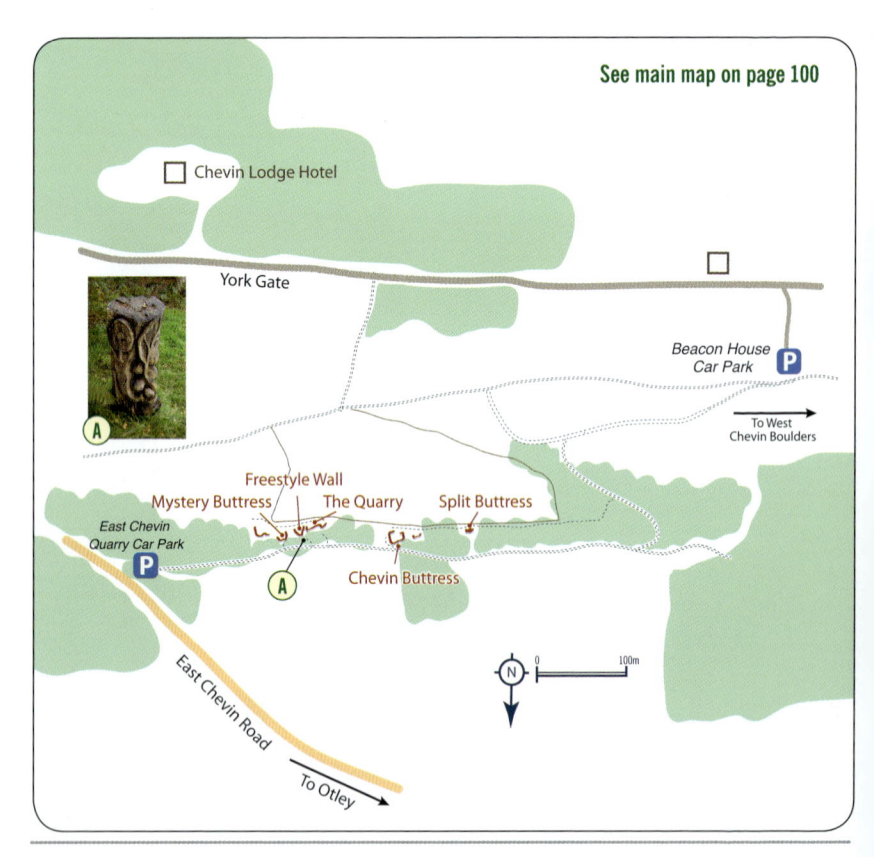

168      Yorkshire Gritstone

# Mystery Buttress - THE CHEVIN

## Mystery Buttress Area
Follow the path west and uphill from the car park. After 100m, a faint track leads through the trees on the left to the lower bay of the quarry and the *Ichthys* pinnacle, set down from the main crag. *Harvest* is located via a narrow path, up and to the left of the pinnacle. Further left is **Magic Rabbit** (E4 6a), which climbs the left side of an isolated arête.

### 1 Harvest  Font 8a
Sit-down start. Climb the sharp prow directly to a desperate finish. One of many hard problems that Dunning added to a bumper Yorkshire crop that year.
*Steve Dunning  2006*

### 2 Ichthys  E2 5b  6m  ★
Bold and fun moves up the front face of the pinnacle. Balance up the ramp to the right arête. Make a committing move to latch the left arête then make haste for the apex. Highball Font 5.
*Robin Nicholson, Adi Gill (both solo)  2nd April 2012*

### 3 Pooh Sticks  HVS 5b  10m
Start down to the left and move up a diagonal break to ledges. Step up and move right to the arête and the top.
*Andy Brown, Tim Wilkinson  c1980*

### 4 Mystery  E5 6a  10m
From the same start as *Pooh Sticks* move up to reach the edges in the centre of the face. Use these and the arête to gain the slot (gear) and climb the arête on its left-hand side to reach the top.
*Dave Sutcliffe  8th August 2002*

### 5 Solo Slab  VS 4b  8m
The left side of the slab on the left wall of the gully.
*Burns, Brown, Wilkinson  c1977*

### 6 Deception  HVS 5a  9m
Climb the crack on the right-hand side of the gully.
*Alec Burns, Andy Brown  1977*

### 7 Pipe Dreams  E4 6a  10m
Tackle the wall to the right of *Deception* on crimps up to the sloping ledge. Continue up the steep slab above.
*John Bannister, Dave Sutcliffe  June 2003*

### 8 Stonequest  E6 6b  10m  ★★
The prominent blunt overhanging arête is a bold solo with an awkward move low down. The moves above aren't exactly plain sailing either so your ability to maintain a cool head is paramount. Photo on page 177.
*Dave Sutcliffe (solo)  June 2003* ✦

### 9 Last Regret  E2 5c  10m
Round the front is a dirty chimney. Start at the foot of this then climb up the left wall trending leftwards to the top. The vegetated sandy chimney is (a) **Sand Crab** (VD).
*Richard Davies (solo)  21st June 1984*

Almscliff to Slipstones

# THE CHEVIN - Freestyle Wall

## Freestyle Wall

The next buttress to the right is the steep and impressive Freestyle Wall with its shades of orange, red and green. It can be accessed via a small track (at the entrance to which is a wooden carving of leaves and a clock) leading through the trees to the base of the steep undercut wall.

### 10 The Thin Crack  HVS 5a  10m
The steep thin crack directly up to the left of the main wall to easier ground near the top.
*Alec Burns, Andy Brown 1977*

### 11 Freestyle  HVS 5a  20m  ★
The main event of this buttress presents a fine challenge for the grade. Launch up the crack to a broken ledge then head straight up the wall, trending right at the top to finish. Other variations exist, including climbing the easier broken line just to the left from the ledge or a harder and bolder link up into *Cool for Cats* at E3 6a.
*Tim & Andy Wilkinson 1977*

### 12 Cool for Cats  E5 6b  20m
Start up the crack as for *Freestyle* to just below the overhangs. Move up and right to a pocket then boldly climb directly up the wall above, placing a runner in *Freestyle* at half-height as you go.
*Darren Hawkins, Carol Mossop 1992*

### 13 Jenny Tulls  E5 6b  20m  ★
At the time of the first ascent this was the hardest challenge at the Chevin and still sees few repeats. Start in the centre of the wall and climb the overhang directly with difficulty to the creaky flakes above. Finish up the thin peg-scarred crack, topping out at the small tree growing out of the top ledge.
*Don Barr, Brian Lockett, G. Watson 1983* ✦

### 14 From the Shadow  E7 6c  23m  ★
Mighty, mighty, mighty! A real outing with plenty of everything. Climb the right corner for 2m then rock left onto the scooped slab. Stretch out and clip the peg then attack the wall above via cunning footwork to gain crimps and then the ledge. Mantel this and balance right to join *Revision Revolt*. Follow this to the top. The Chevin's hardest offering.
*Dave Sutcliffe 26th March 2012*

### 15 Revision Revolt  E3 6a  23m
Climb the broken gully on the right of the wall until a move left takes you to a ledge on the wall. Finish up the centre of the wall above, passing the obvious slot.
*Adam Wainwright, Simon Franks 24th April 1988*

## The Quarry

The next routes start at a higher level and are accessed via a path through the woods on the left of the path.

First up is **Graunch** (*Awful*), climbed sometime in the dark ages and included here only for historic reference and not the quality of the climbing; unless you are into this kind of thing, in which case crack on. Start up the short wet overhanging corner at the far left of the bay and continue up a mixture of grass, mud and loose rock.

### 16 Clarence Tenthumbs  E7 6b  12m  ★
Only the bold, strong and dynamic need apply for an assault on this blunt arête. Climb from the grassy ledge up the arête and wall. Place a side-runner out right from the only good hold at half-height; this will stop you hitting the floor but not the ledge.
*Dave Sutcliffe 29th August 2003* ✦

Yorkshire Gritstone

The Quarry - **THE CHEVIN**

**17 Max Wall** MVS 4b   12m
The crack to the ledge then the cracks in the wall above.
*Dennis Gray c1956*

**18 Bellow** VS 4c   14m
The rightward trending crackline just left of the corner.
*P. Cole, S. Ringrose 28th June 1984*

**19 Ladder Climb** S 4a   14m   ★
Climb the shallow corner up the ladder of nicely spaced ledges. (a) **Ladder Climb Direct** (HVS 5b) tackles the crack to the right directly to join the parent route at half-height.
*Dave Musgrove, Bob Knapton 11th April 1971* ✦

**20 Primate** E6 6b   15m   ★★
A ferocious challenge and only for those with a strong disposition. Ride up the arching line of sidepulls and undercuts which trend left to join *Ladder Climb* at half-height. Breathe deep, then either climb the left side of the arête above, or harder (and better), move up to the jug on the arête and swing back round onto the front face and power up the arête on its right-hand side. Scary. Photo on page 173.
*Dave Sutcliffe (solo) 9th Aug 2003; right finish 8th Mar 2011* ✦

**21 Weasel** HVS 5b   15m   ★★
A stemming delight which is more about using your legs than arms. The prominent corner in the centre of the bay provides a good lesson in technical bridging.
*John Ramsden, Dennis Gray c1956*

**22 Rampant Hippo** VS 4c   15m   ★
A pleasurable trip which romps up the sandy steep crack to a finish that requires care. (b) **Lindsey, Lindsey** (E1 5b) is a variation start that climbs the wall to the right of *Weasel* on broken edges to gain the break, then climbs across to join *Rampant Hippo*.
*Dave Musgrove, Bob Knapton 4th April 1971* ✦

**23 No Prisoners** E1 5b   16m   ★★
A contender for the best line in the quarry. Start as for *Rampant Hippo* then swing right via a tricky move to the thin crack just right of the arête. Gain some composure and cool your way up the crack and breaks to top-out at the large tree. A great route with a big feel.
*Alec Burns, Andy Brown 8th April 1978*

Almscliff to Slipstones

# THE CHEVIN - Pygmy Buttress

### 24 **Layback Corner**  HVS 4c   16m
Climb the diagonal crack up and right to the corner system. Finish up the loose dry stone wall at the top - eeek! The short blank corner can be climbed direct to join this route for **The Inmate** (E2 5c).
*Burns, Brown, Wilkinson c1977* ✦

The excellent slab problem to the right is **LSG** (Font 6b+). It starts up chipped holds in the centre of the slab to make tenuous moves up to reach, and rock around, the right arête. The horrific chimney in the right-hand corner of the bay is **Smokey Joes Last Freakout** (Vile)...go on I dare ya! The right wall of the bay contains three short cracks. Climb the central one, **Porno Crack** (HVS 5c), as it's the cleanest and best.

### Mortal Wall
Further along the path is the start of the natural buttresses. The first problems of note are on the small walls just past the end of the quarry, up on the hillside.

### 25 **Mortal Wall**  Font 5+
Climb the wall making use of the impressive feature. The right finish is harder.

### 26 **Straight Crack**  Font 5+
The obvious straight crack to the right.
*Allan Austin (solo) 11th May 1965*

The challenge to the right is still 'work in progress' for some lanky beast! Step off the block and use the pathetic crimp and some dynamic skills to levitate up the thin wall.

### Pygmy Buttress
The next block to the right has several highball boulder problems; all harder than they first appear.

### 27 **Little People**  Font 6b
Climb the arête on its left-hand side. Climbing the arête on its right-hand side is the same grade. (aka **Alter Ego**).

### 28 **Pygmy Wall**  Font 6b+
Sit-down-start. The steep wall on good pockets.

### 29 **Rawhead Rex**  Font 7c (E3 6c)
Leap to the obvious pocket and make a desperate slap right to the shallow crack. A further airy move gains better holds.
*John-Paul Hotham 16th February 2001*

### 30 **Pygmy Traverse**  Font 6b
Start as for *Little People*, then traverse rightwards above the overhang to finish up *Porky* (aka **Alter Ego Traverse**). **Obstinacy** (Font 5+) traverses under the roof to the foot of *Porky*.

### 31 **Porky**  Font 6b+
Climb the pocketed wall direct.

### 32 **Twin Cracks**  HVS 5b   6m
The rightward-slanting double crackline round to the right.
*Allan Austin (solo) 11th May 1965*

**Primate Right-Finish** (E6 6b) takes its toll on Dave Sutcliffe. Page 171
Photo: Mark Credie

Mark Credie beginning the adventure on **Gronff** (E2 5c). Page 176
Photo: Dave Sutcliffe

Chevin Buttress - **THE CHEVIN**

**36 Chevin Buttress**  VS 4c   16m   ★★★
Eponymous for the crag, an imposing onsight and only yields its charms to an honest approach. Tackle the steep crack until it fades out then depart right to the arête where the exposure increases to a fitting climax. A direct finish straight above the crack is only slightly harder and almost as good. Photo on page 96.
*Brian Evans, Rick Horner 7th January 1957*

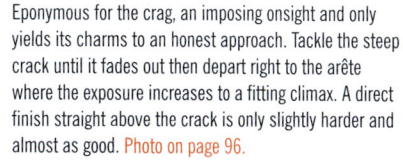

**Gronff** (described on the next page) was climbed by Ken Wood and named after the noise made by Boot, the sheepdog from The Perishers comic strip and cartoon, when eating sausages.

Of Ken Wood, Allan Austin said:

❝ ❞

I climbed at the same time as Ken and he was what I would call a great climber. In other words, you get out onto somewhere and you've done your pitch and you look up and you think, 'Heck, it's wet and it's a bit loose,' but you're relaxed because Ken's at the next pitch you see. Some guys that you climb with are so good that you decide eventually that they're perhaps the best in the country. Well, Ken Wood was at one point.

The next time you're on Gronff, ponder this little gem from Dave Musgrove:

❝ ❞

I would solo Gronff all the time. Admittedly it became a little trickier after I lost my fingers but an enjoyable outing nonetheless.

## Chevin Buttress

As you leave the trees the fine gritstone promontory of Chevin Buttress comes into view. A high proportion of quality routes are to be found, all on superb rock with the best being as good as any in Yorkshire. If this is your first visit to the Chevin this buttress is a must.

**33 Rear Entry**  E1 5c   6m
Start high up the bank on the left side of the buttress below the bulge. Climb the overhang and the wall above.
*Mike Hammill, Mike Raine 1981*

**34 Leech's Wall**  VS 4c   8m   ★
Bold. Follow the faint groove in the centre of the wall until the overhang. Step right and escape up the short corner.
*Rod Leech c1958*

**35 Visual Deception**  E2 5b   12m
An eliminate squeezed between *Leech's Wall* and *Chevin Buttress*. Climb directly up the slab just before the crack. Side-runners are not allowed at this grade.
*Mike Hammill, Mike Raine 1981*

# THE CHEVIN - Chevin Buttress

### 37 **Gronff Left-Hand** E4 6a  16m  ★
Up the arête, starting at the overhanging crack. The crux is a huge move from the crack to the next break. Some may find it easier to dyno! Others may bypass the move by making a step right then back left to the break but this reduces the grade down to E3 5c. Doesn't pack to the same quality as its neighbours but nevertheless an intriguing route.

*Mike Hammill, Al Manson  13th April 1975*

### 38 **Gronff** E2 5c  16m  ★★★
One of the best routes at the crag which provides an exhilarating adventure up the front of the buttress. Gain the diagonal sloping ledge then, using the two undercuts, make a long reach up left to better holds. Continue up the thin wall above. High in the grade with the gear above the crux.
Photo on page 174.

*Ken Wood, John Harwood  12th April 1973* ✦

### 39 **The Waster** E1 5b  16m  ★★★
The archetypal Austin classic; a natural line with brilliant climbing throughout. Commit to the technically interesting groove and flake in the centre of the buttress. The final pull over the bulge before the finishing slab proves a pumpy move too far for many suitors so dig deep for glory.
Photos on pages 167 and 178.

*Allan Austin (solo)  11th May 1965* ✦

### 40 **Waster Wall** E5 6c  16m  ★
A bold, technical offering which climbs the centre of the wall to the right on sloping holds and fingernail edges. The side-runner in *The Waster* can reduce the grade to E3 depending on how high you place it.

*James Ibbertson  2011* ✦

### 41 **Vampire's Ledge** HVS 4c  18m  ★
A wandering line that's not without interest. From a

176  Yorkshire Gritstone

## Chevin Buttress - THE CHEVIN

taxing start, head rightwards up the slanting cracks to the groove of *Central Route*. Progress up and left onto the upper slab and teeter tentatively across this with a series of delicate moves to finish out left.
*Johnny Lees c1950*

**42 Central Route** S 4b  15m  ★★
A pleasant excursion up the central line of weakness to a tough finale. Start below the overhangs and ascend into the niche which leads to an awkward exit via the cracks above.
*Johnny Lees c1950*

**43 Central Route Direct** VS 4b  14m  ★★
A worthwhile direct line which adds a little meat to the previous route. Wander up the groove until the overhang is reached, then delve into the prominent crack above via some hand-swallowing sinker jams.
*Dennis Gray, Doug Verity 1957*

**44 Slide In** E1 5b  14m
Climb the wall just to the right of *Central Route* and just left of the small overhang.
*S. Ringrose, T. Valley 1985*

The short shallow corner is (a) **Slide Back** (HVS 5c) and passes the small overhang on its left via some bold, reachy moves to the easier upper wall. True independence from *Slide In* is hard to maintain.

**45 The Backslider** E2 5c  13m  ★
Take the same shallow corner as *Slide Back* to the overhang and engage a hard move up the groove to the right to reach the break. A direct line up the wall above completes the difficulties.
*John Syrett, John Lupton 14th April 1971*

**46 Growler** VS 5a  12m
From the slab, move right to a crack and climb this to finish directly up the arête. A better finish, is to move left and climb the blunt arête in the centre of the upper slab.
*Paul Clough, Karl Zientek 4th November 1995*

**47 The Girdle Traverse** VS 4c, 5a  36m  ★★
The right-to-left traverse of the entire buttress. A glorious outing which takes in some interesting ground and tests your rope skills to the full, especially on the second pitch.
**1.** Start on the terrace at the right-hand end of the crag next to the tree. Gain the horizontal break and traverse this leftwards then cross the slab to gain the jamming crack. Swing down this, under the bulge, to belay on the ledges out left.
**2.** Follow the hand-traverse across *The Waster* to reach the arête. Climb round the corner and continue to *Leech's Wall*. Follow the crack below the bulge to the end of the buttress.
*Allen Austin, Brian Evans, Eric Metcalf 23rd June 1960*

To the right of the main buttress are several smaller buttresses providing numerous short routes and boulder problems. Most climbs in this area have poor landings and a pad and good spotter are recommended - either that or a comprehensive life insurance policy.

Just right is a buttress with a collection of short offerings. **Blunt Nose** (HS 4b) takes the left arête; the groove in the centre of the buttress via the blind flake is **Groovy** (Font 4) and the blind crack just right is **Two Foot Tumbler** (Font 5).

Dave Sutcliffe on **Stonequest** (E6 6b). Page 169
Photo: J. Bannister

Some gifts just keep on giving. Jenny Ibbertson playing to the crowds on **The Waster (E1 5b)**. Page 176
Photo: Mike Hutton

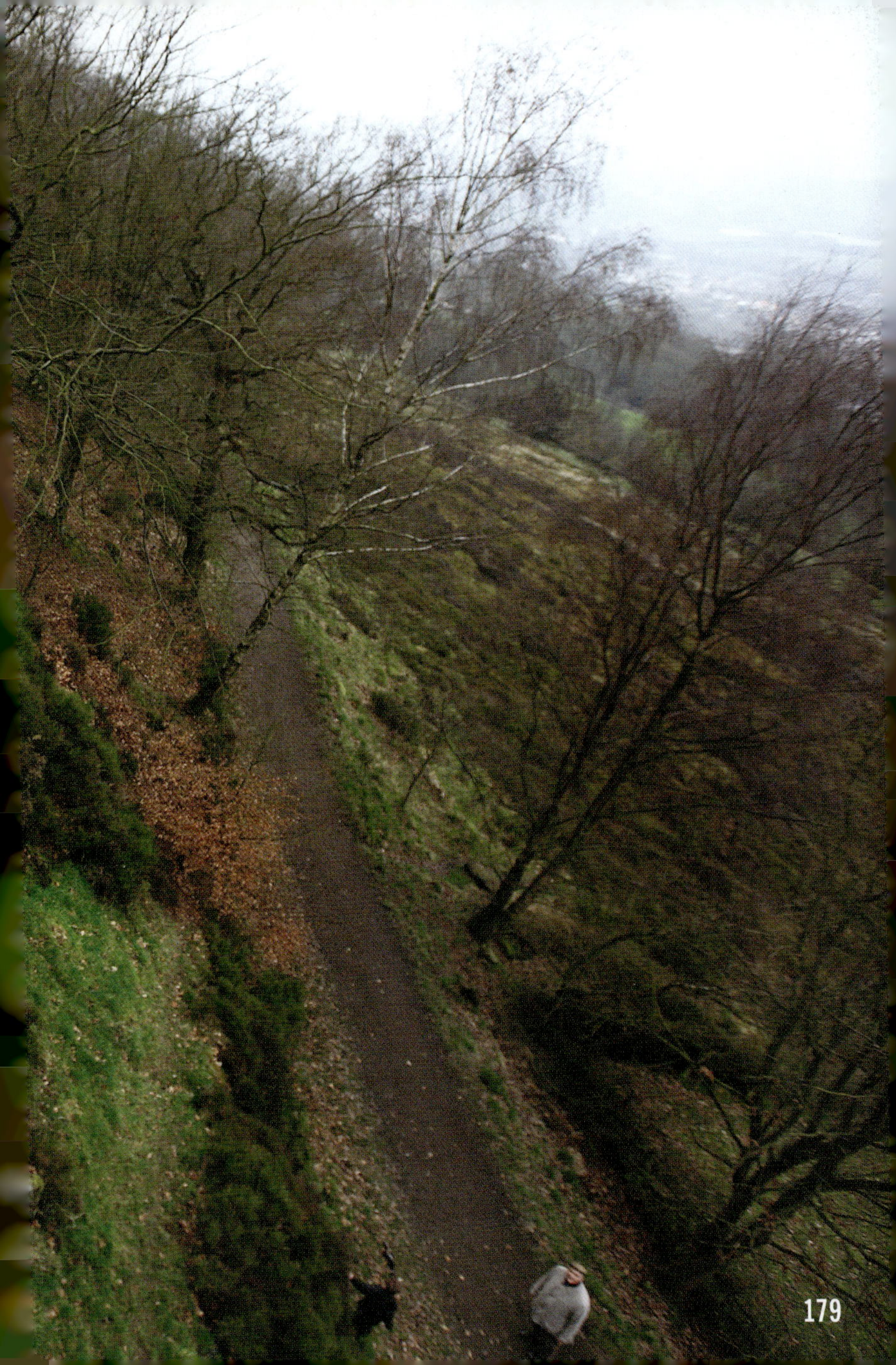

# THE CHEVIN - Split Buttress

## Split Buttress
Follow the path westwards for 70m. Up on the hillside to the left is a smashing buttress containing short problems with a big fall potential; tread carefully. The crack on the left wall is (a) **Split Buttress Crack** (Font 5+).

### 48 Split Second  Font 6a (E1 5c)
The wall right of the crack, with a tricky move in the middle.
*John-Paul Hotham  16th February 2001*

### 49 Omega  Font 8a
This heavyweight has a finish that really packs a punch. From a sit-down start at the back of the roof climb out to the lip then tackle the hanging arête on its left-hand side.
*Steve Dunning  2006*

### 50 Like a Hurricane  Font 7c+
From the same start as *Omega* climb out to the far arête and make a hard move to latch the jug just over the lip. Finish here or, for the full tick, make a committing rock-over onto the jug and finish precariously up the groove. Probably worth E5 if you go the whole hog as the ground dips away and you would take a big ride if you dropped it from the upper arête!
*Andy Earl (to the jug) Steve Dunning (top-out)  2006*

### 51 Splitting Heirs  E2 5b  6m
From the ledge, climb the wall using the seam and the edge of the groove. The drop off the ledge is nearly as long as the route.
*John-Paul Hotham  16th February 2001*

### 52 Split Ends  E1 5c  6m
Awkwardly mantelshelf the narrow ledge to reach the sidepull and the ledge out left.
*Tony Burnell, Mark Spreadborough  1985*

Another 50m to the right is a small compact buttress with an oak tree growing off the ledge in its centre. All the problems step off the ledge and have a big feel. Routes or highballs? You decide! All are the work of *Tony Burnell* who soloed them in 1985 and are as follows: **Sweet And Sour** (Font 5+) the short crack in the left wall; **Done But Not Dusted** (Font 5) the left arête of the buttress; **Slape** (Font 4+), just to the right of the tree gain the left-hand ramp and continue direct; **Short and Sweet** (Font 4) the right-hand rampline; **Fossil Groove** (Font 4+) the centre of the wall climbed direct; **Done and Dusted** (Font 5+) the centre of the slabby wall to the right; **Nine Foot Crack** (Font 4) the short crack to the right.

Continuing a further 100m along the path you encounter a small dirty quarried bay which pays host to the following three routes: **Another Deception** (HVS 5b) climbs the vertical crack in the cleanest wall; **Layaway** (E1 5c) follows the thin crack to the break then heads out right to the arête; **Give-away** (E4 6b) climbs the arête direct with great difficulty.

The gate and approach to the West Chevin Boulders from York Ga

## West Chevin Boulders - THE CHEVIN

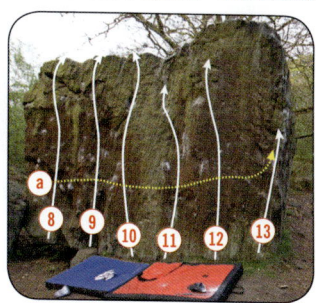

### West Chevin Boulders
This small collection of boulders can be found in the far corner of the woods. Although north-facing and green for most of the year, this area does offer some worthwhile bouldering and is home to the classics *Fluid Dynamics*, *Brownian Motion* and *Time After Time*.

**1 Eat the Light** Font 7a+
From crimps in the centre of the wall climb left on small edges to the jug. The sit-down start has been climbed at a crimpy Font 7b+.

**2 Avatar** Font 6b+
Starting on the crimps move up and right.

The next block is 100m right and split by various cracks.

**3 Twin Finish** Font 5+
The left-hand crack.

**4 Defence System** Font 6a+
The thin central crack.

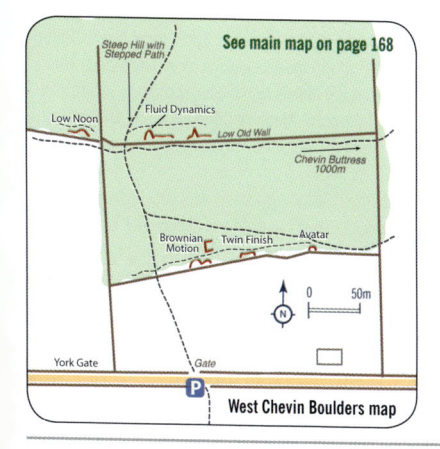

**5 Exorcist Green** Font 6a
The left arête.

**6 Walking the Plank** Font 6c+
The centre of the wall without the arête.

**7 Homeland** Font 6a+
The arête up to the ledge.

The wall just left of the arête is **Supergreen** (Font 6a). The crack on the right is **How Green Was My Valley** (Font 4+).

**8 Ground Up** Font 6a+
Crimp your way up the scooped wall. Trending left to the arête is a shade easier.

**9 Blobby** Font 6a
The wall passing the strange blobby hold.

**10 Super Central** Font 5+
The centre of the wall passing the slot is definitely central and quite possibly super.

**11 Sideliner** Font 6a
The wall on sidepulls, just right of the centre.

**12 Unit of Power** Font 6a
The wall just left of the arête (which is out of bounds).

**13 The Barn Door** Font 5
Climb the big arête – steady, steady - watch that barn door now. A traverse of the face can be made at a low-level; this is (a) **West Face Traverse** (Font 6b) and can be climbed in either direction.

Almscliff to Slipstones

# THE CHEVIN - West Chevin Boulders

## 14 Particle Collision  Font 7b
The highball left arête, old school E4/5!

## 15 Brownian Motion  Font 7c+
The centre of the wall is a modern classic and one for the strong to seek out. Use undercuts to reach the poor crimp. The left arête was used on the first ascent via a monster reach to toe-hook the arête. The problem without the arête has now been climbed direct by Martin Smith at a whopping grade of Font 8a+.
*Andy Brown, Martin Smith 3rd November 2010* ✦

## 16 Time After Time  Font 6a (E1 6a)
Juggy pockets and good heelwork lead up the steep side of the arête until a rockover round to the left enables an easy summit bid. Escaping left after the rockover is **Time**; half the problem, half the name, still the same grade.
*Andy Watts  April 1990*

## 17 Green Wing  Font 6b+
A varied low traverse from right-to-left. Finishing up *Time After Time* is **Missing Time** (Font 6c).

## 18 Raynman  Font 6a (E2 6a)
The central line of the wall through the break requires tons of commitment. The choice of brushed holds are more hindrance than help.
*Andy Watts  April 1990*

## 19 Third Friend Lucky  Font 6a (E2 5c)
Meander up the right side of the wall to the break and courageously reach for the top via poor edges.
*Matt Hannah  8th Sept 2001*

## The Lower Edges
Follow the path down the hill for 200m and as it steepens the following mini buttresses are revealed. Firstly 15m to the left of the path (looking down), over a low wall, are the following: **Low Noon** (MVS 4b), climbs the crack on the left of the secluded buttress, followed by the left arête climbed on its right; **Smooth and Groovy** (VS 4c ★) is just to the right and climbs up the middle of the wall using two breaks, finishing up the 'smooth' groove; just right again, **Twin Cracks** (D) climbs the twin cracks.

Back to the main path and 15m to the right (east) side is a mini-edge with the prominent block containing *Prows That*, *Perfect Jam* and the mighty *Fluid Dynamics*, clearly visible bounding its right-hand end. About 35m further left is a steep high rib and cracked wall; **Kit-Kat** (HVS 5b), takes the buttress with three prominent breaks in it and is climbed from its lowest point using the right arête and the handy horizontals.

Down to the right of this at a slightly lower level is **Plum Prow** (Font 6b) the cool looking prow from sitting; **Thin Cut** (Font 6a) makes nice balancey climbing up the wall right of the prow; **Medium Cut** (Font 6b) is the wall just right using the vague rib.

The buttress to the right starts with dirty problems but steadily increases in height and quality. **The Sad Traverse** (Font 4) hand-traverses left-to-right across to the nose to the same finish as *The Crease*; **The Crease** (Font 5) takes the blunt nose with a vertical crease up its left side; **Up She Rises** (Font 5+) is a rising traverse right-to-left finishing at the trees above the blunt rib; **Flight Path** (Font 5 (HVS 5a)) takes a tricky rockover to gain the ramp left of *Disinfection* and where a precarious step up gains better

Yorkshire Gritstone

holds and the top; **Disinfection** (VS 4c) gardens its way up the wall just before the corner using the obvious cracks: **Aimless** (VD) takes the obvious and rather dirty corner; **Composure** (E2 6a) is the narrow slab without crack or arête and does indeed require composure especially as the hardest move is at the top whilst **Foot in Mouth** (VS 4c ★) takes the sweeping arête and appears to be a handful but is actually relatively straightforward.

### 20 Prows That  E3 6b  5m  ★
The front of the buttress is a stiff challenge and one where falling off is not recommended.
*Dave Musgrove (solo) 4th August 2001*

The prow-clamping sit-start to *Prows That* is known as **Low Pressure** (Font 7a+/b) and when combined with the finish gives a problem to be reckoned with.

### 21 Perfect Jam  HVS 5a  6m  ★
This brilliant exercise in steep hand-jamming would be a sought after classic on Burbage North.
*Nigel Baker (solo) April 1990*

### 22 Fluid Dynamics  Font 8a+
The awesome arête is a fingery hard testpiece so bring your steel fingers for this one. Start squatting, pulling on two crimpy undercuts, throw the heel out wide and crimp your way to join the stand up (Font 8a in its own right).
Photo on page 185.
*Tom Peckitt  March 2011*

By following the path back east above these problems you eventually reach the Chevin Buttress and the quarries after 1km. After 800m however, you pass above a small quarry with: **Feeling Lucky** (E1 5b), which takes the slab with a small crack and crimps to the left of the quarry and **Where's Lucky?** (HS 4c), the easier crack system to the right of the previous route.

*The Chevin Cross - erected every Easter by volunteers and clearly visible from Otley and the surrounding area. The current cross is constructed from salvaged wood from the Manchester bombing of June 1996.*

# THE CHEVIN - First Ascent Information

## Further First Ascent Information (✦)

**Another Deception:** *Climbed by Tony Burnell 1985.*
**Blunt Nose:** *Climbed by Tony Burnell (solo) 1985.*
**Clarence Tenthumbs:** *Named after Sherman Lofthouse, whose fingers were that thick he looked like he had 10 thumbs. Handy on a route like this!*
**Dennis the Dilapidated Pensioner** and **Midget Digit:** *Climbed by Simon Howley and Duncan Swarbrick 1985.*
**Feeling Lucky** and **Where's Lucky?:** *Climbed by Matt Hannah, Rob Dickinson 8th September 2001.*
**Give-away:** *Climbed by Chris Sowden, Tony Burnell June 1985.*
**Gronff:** *This was the noise made by Boot, the sheepdog from The Perishers comic strip and cartoon, when eating sausages!*
**(The) Inmate:** *By Damiam Tolon, J. Boggiano 4th June 1983.*
**Jenny Tulls:** *B. Woodley had reached the upper section previously by a traverse from Freestyle and Alec Burns climbed the lower roof only to be deposited back on the ground when a flake snapped. The flake in question landed on him and knocked him out for good measure. Don Barr was killed later the same year by a freak lightning strike in the Verdon Gorge; such a tragedy given Don's unrecognised talent on the rock.*
**Ladder Climb Direct:** *Climbed by Nigel Scarth, Chris Wentworth 15th May 1992.*
**Layaway:** *Climbed by Mark Spreadborough 1985.*
**Like a Hurricane:** *Andy Earl originally climbed the problem but only as far as the jug on the lip. Steve Dunning pushed on through later the same year to finish the problem off.*
**Lindsey** *By Peter Sissons, Robert Addey 10th June 1997.*
**LSG:** *Climbed by Adi Gill, 2nd April 2012.*
**Magic Rabbit:** *Climbed by Alec Burns, Andy Brown 25th September 1980.*
**Porno Crack:** *Climbed by Alec Burns, Andy Brown c1980.*
**Primate:** *Climbed solo in the summer of 2003 without any cleaning on the upper part of the route! Re-climbed with the better right finish in 2011 but only after a couple of ground falls from the damp lower wall - eek!*
**Rampant Hippo:** *A sling was required at the top to exit up a loose wall of collapsing earth climbed free, July 1971, by Frank Wilkinson and Allan Austin.*
**Sand Crab:** *Climbed by Burns, Brown, Wilkinson c1977.*
**Smokey Joes Last Freakout:** *Climbed by Peter Brown (aged 10) 1977.*
**Stonequest:** *Climbed in less than perfect conditions in true summer grit style! No friction, no ropes, no brains!*
**The Waster:** *Allan Austin (solo) The original route finished by moving left. The direct finish for the route description was soloed by Al Manson in the mid 1970s. Rumour has it that a mould was taken of the flake to fashion the one on the top pitch of Cratcliffe's Suicide Wall as the Peak climbers had nothing like it down there...*
**Waster Wall:** *A coveted line that fell in damp conditions. The direct start, from the top of the initial 'The Waster' crack, was attempted but crucial foot pebbles had gone from the lower wall.*
**Visual Deception & Rear Entry:** *Mike Hammill, Mike Raine 1981 Hammill considered both the routes unworthy variants and didn't claim them at the time. The names were given by Simon Howley and Tony Burnell respectively when they re-discovered the climbs in 1985. Tony Burnell went on to solo and be the first to document the majority of the easier problems to the right of Chevin Buttress in the same year.*

## West Chevin Boulder Problems

*Many of the un-credited low grade lines in the West Chevin Boulders are the work of Andy Watts and Nigel Baker back in the early 1990s although these rocks were first known to be explored by Brian Evans way back in the 1950s and undoubtedly by others in between. Dave Musgrove collated the known problems for a Leeds Wall web-download in 2002 and Paul Clarke updated the known problems in the upper section for www.yorkshiregrit.com around 2004 and probably added some new variations of his own. In recent years several of the harder problems have had more first ascent claims than you could shake a stick at, but it is undisputed that Andy Brown first climbed* **Brownian Motion***, and Martin Smith later climbed it direct. Dave Musgrove climbed* **Prows That** *in 2001 and, most recently, in 2011, Tom Peckitt added* **Fluid Dynamics***. The rest, unfortunately, is a little unclear.*

**Flight Path, Sad Traverse, The Crease** and **Up She Rises** *were all recorded by Nigel Baker and Dave Musgrove in August 2001.*
**Low Noon, Smooth and Groovy, Twin Cracks, Disinfection, Aimless, Composure** and **Foot in Mouth** *were all climbed by Matt Hannah and Steve Micklethwaite in June 2001.*

## GRADED LIST

### ROUTES

**E7**
From The Shadow (6c)
Clarence
  Tenthumbs (6b)

**E6**
Stonequest (6b)
Primate (6b)

**E5**
Waster Wall (6c)
Cool For Cats (6b)
Jenny Tulls (6b)
Mystery (6a)

**E4**
Give-away (6b)
Magic Rabbit (6a)
Pipe Dreams (6a)
Gronff Left-Hand (6a)

**E3**
Revision Revolt (6a)
Prows That (6b)

**E2**
Composure (6a)
Last Regret (5c)
The Inmate (5c)
Gronff (5c)

The Backslider (5c)
Splitting Heirs (5b)
Ichthys (5b)
Visual Deception (5b)

**E1**
Midget Digit (6a)
Layaway (5c)
Rear Entry (5c)
Slide In (5b)
No Prisoners (5b)
Split Ends (5c)
Lindsey, Lindsey (5b)
The Waster (5b)
Feeling Lucky (5b)

**HVS**
Slide Back (5c)
Dennis the Dilapidated
  Pensioner (5b)
Weasel (5b)
Kit-Kat (5b)
Another Deception (5b)
Pooh Sticks (5b)
Porno Crack (5c)
Ladder Climb
  Direct (5b)
Twin Cracks (5b)
Deception (5a)
Freestyle (5a)
Perfect Jam (5a)
The Thin Crack (5a)
Vampire's Ledge (4c)
Layback Corner (4c)

**VS**
Growler (5a)
The Girdle
  Traverse (4c,5a)
Bellow (4c)
Disinfection (4c)
Rampant Hippo (4c)
Smooth and Groovy (4c)
Leech's Wall (4c)
Chevin Buttress (4c)
Foot in Mouth (4c)
Central Route Direct (4b)
Solo Slab (4c)

**MVS**
Max Wall (4b)
Low Noon (4b)

**HS**
Where's Lucky? (4c)
Blunt Nose (4b)

**S**
Central Route (4b)
Ladder Climb (4a)

**VD**
Aimless
Sand Crab

**D**
Twin Cracks

### PROBLEMS

**Font 8a+**
Fluid Dynamics
Brownian Motion direct

**Font 8a**
Harvest
Omega

**Font 7c+**
Like a Hurricane
Brownian Motion

**Font 7c**
Rawhead Rex (E3 6c)

**Font 7b**
Particle Collision
Low Pressure

**Font 7a+**
Eat the Light

**Font 6c+**
Walking the Plank

**Font 6c**
Missing Time

**Font 6b+**
Avatar
LSG
Pygmy Wall

Porky
Green Wing

**Font 6b**
Plum Prow
Medium Cut
Pygmy Traverse
Little People
West Face Traverse

**Font 6a+**
Defence System
Homeland
Ground Up

**Font 6a**
Exorcist Green
Raynman (E2 6a)
Split Second (E1 5c)
Time After Time (E1 6a)
Third Lucky
  Friend - (E2 5c)
Time
Supergreen
Blobby
Sideliner
Unit of Power
Thin Cut

**Font 5+**
Twin Finish
Super Central
Obstinancy
Up She Rises

Split Buttress Crack
Done and Dusted
Mortal Wall
Straight Crack
Sweet and Sour

**Font 5**
The Barn Door
The Crease
Two Foot Tumbler
Flight Path (HVS 5a)
Done But Not Dusted

**Font 4+**
How Green Was My
  Valley
Slape
Fossil Groove

**Font 4**
The Sad Traverse
Short and Sweet
Nine Foot Crack
Groovy

Tom Peckitt clamping hard on his **Fluid Dynamics (Font 8a+)**. Page 183
Photo: David Gater

# Brimham
## & Outlying Crags

Castle Rock, awash with classics through the grade range and most punctuated with taxing finishes. The frustrating offwidth of Desperation Crack (HVS) is left of centre and Jabberwock (VS) cuts through the centre of the wall into and out of the cave. **Picnic** (E2 5c) completes the sweet set with Robin Nicholson here on the easier ground before things get lively. Page 219.
Photo: Mike Hutton

"Beware the Jabberwock, my son! The jaws that bite, the claws that catch!
Beware the Jubjub bird, and shun, the frumious Bandersnatch!"

*From Jabberwocky, Lewis Carroll, 1872*

| | |
|---|---|
| **Brimham** 190 | Little Brimham 318 |
| Hare's Head 302 | Bat Buttress 328 |
| Plantation Crack 312 | Crow Crag 338 |

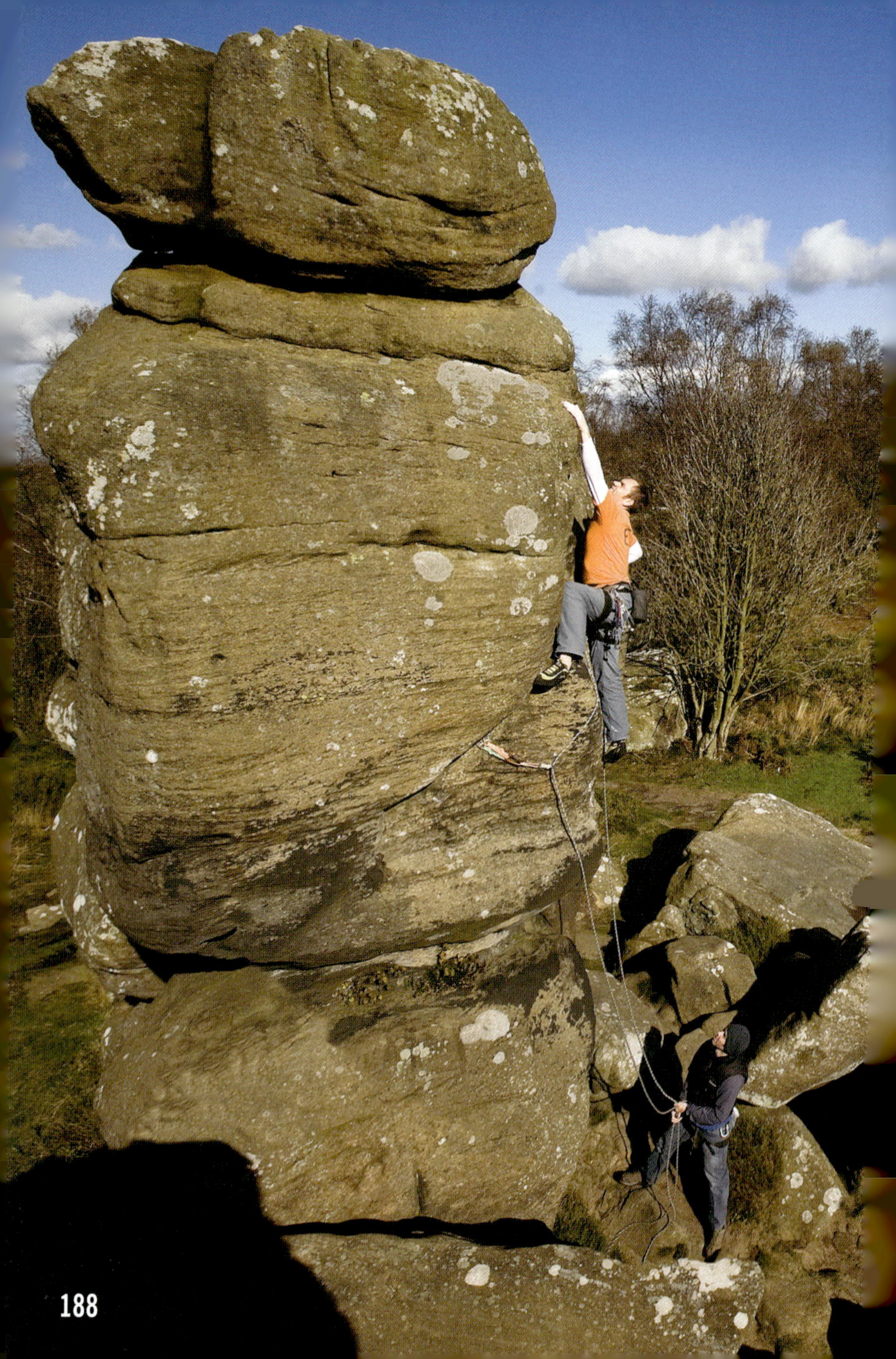

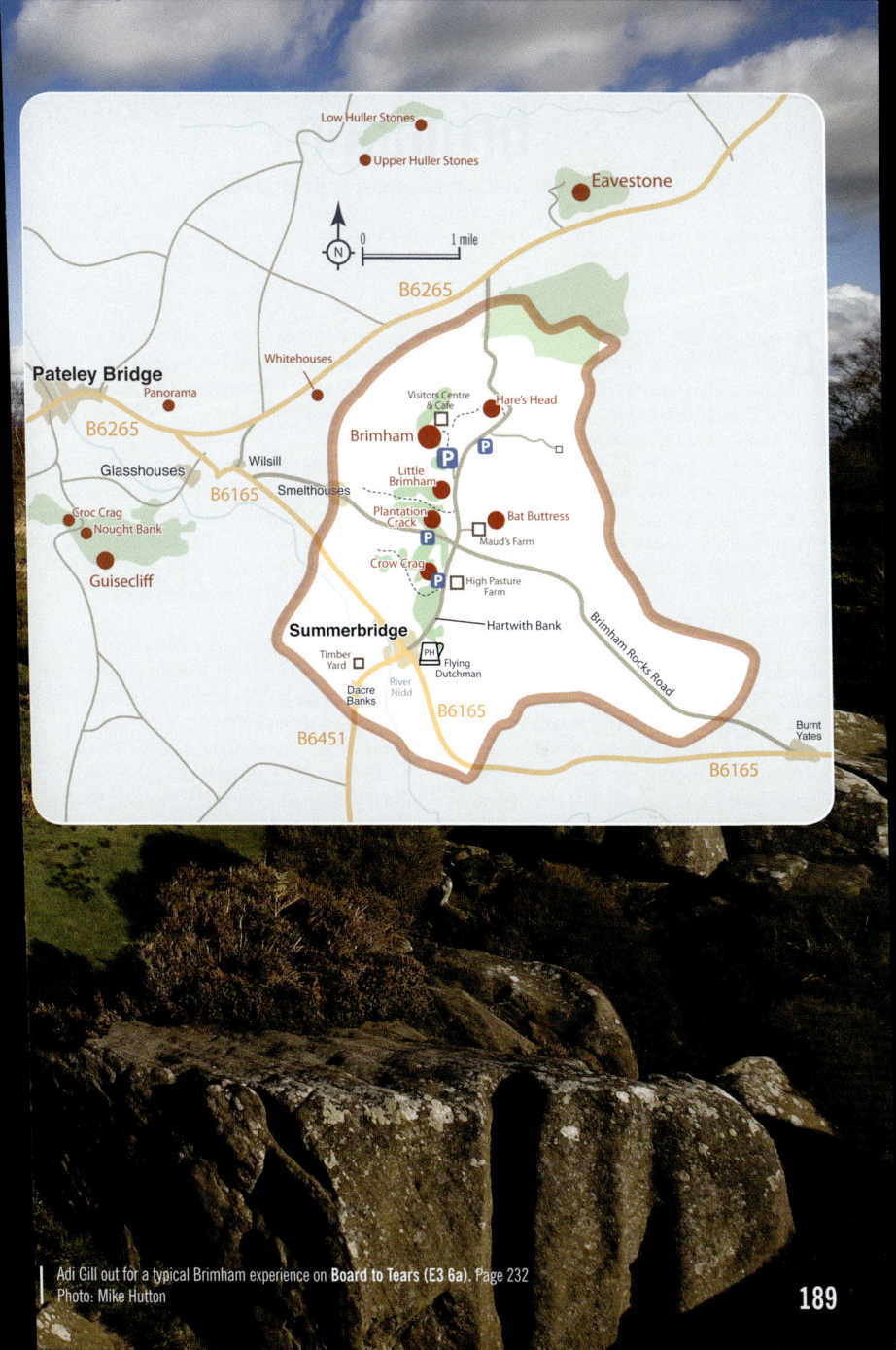

Adi Gill out for a typical Brimham experience on **Board to Tears** (E3 6a). Page 232
Photo: Mike Hutton

189

# brimham

by **Jim Croft** with bouldering by **Dave Cowl**

OS Ref: SE 209 647                                      Altitude: 295m

A huge theme park of a crag; an inspirational land filled with everything a climber needs to graduate in the school of hard knocks that is the Gritstone Academy. Delicate slabs, bold walls, irksome offwidths and a profusion of steep, hand jamming cracks all add to the spice of the climbing here. Excellent VDiffs rub shoulders with some of the boldest sloping horror show E7s on the planet. Technical nail-biting highballs mingle with gentle padding problems in a beautiful moorland setting high above the Nidderdale valley.

Nature has sculpted the rock formations of Brimham into a maze of weird and intriguing shapes; the many pinnacles and the secluded, yet extensive edge offers a lifetime's worth of climbing to cater for all abilities and tastes. Many of the rocks have their own character with names to match such as The Druid's Writing Desk, Cannon Rock, The Dancing Bear and 'The Frozen Boulderer' (typically found around the Hare's Head area). It's easy to get overwhelmed by the vastness of Brimham and navigating between the climbs can be challenging, especially if visiting for the first time. Study the maps, diagrams and photos in the following pages to ease the mind-blowing enormity of it all. Often things are closer than they seem.

Brimham is run by The National Trust (NT) and is popular with tourists. In fact, the place can be swarming with day-trippers on sunny summer weekends. Expect some rubber necking if you opt to climb on the obvious pinnacles between the car parks and the house. In return you'll likely get to enjoy the sight of an over-testosteroned teenage lad stranded atop one of the towers. The lower edge is the place to head for on days like this if you prefer some peace and quiet. The NT also runs a café (open 11-5pm weekends and sometimes mid-week during holidays) next to the house, which provides drinks and snacks to keep sugar levels up.

**The Climbing:** With almost 500 routes and more bouldering than you can poke a toothbrush on a stick at (over 350 problems recorded here but the list is endless), there is something for everybody at Brimham; bold or safe, easy or hard, technical or strenuous. Beware the Brimham mantelshelf finish, it catches many off guard.

In the history of the game, whilst the big players in the grit scene, the Almscliff's and the Ilkley's, shouted their prowess from the hill tops, Brimham just got on with it. A proving ground, and a place of bold innovators who pushed gritstone development to its limits. Austin's *Frensis Direct* (E1), Syrett's *Picnic* (E2) and *Joker's Wall* (E4), Hammill's *Left Wall* (E5), Peel's *Gigglin' Crack* (E6), Dixon's *Tender Homecoming* (E8), all testify to the pedigree of the place and stand as milestones on a grit climber's progress through the ranks. Yet, cometh the hour, cometh the boulderer; significant developments over the past decade have propelled Brimham into the mainstream when it comes to bouldering, in a sense that it's only the beginning. Scattered far and wide amongst the monuments of Brimham's historic gritstone routes are a proliferation of problems, from Font 2 to Font 8a at the last count. Classics abound throughout the grades and the bouldering royalty have left some significant calling cards. *Pommel, Fantasy League, Titfield Thunderbolt, Pair in a Cubicle* – grief! The list is endless. It's time to get ticking.

Mike Hutton on the wrong side of the lens, unable to resist the stunning **Cubic Corner** (MVS 4b). Page 286
Photo: Mike Hutton (Mike Hutton collection)

Glory, Glory, Hallelujah. Richard Connors about to have an out-of-body experience on the classic, **Frensis Direct (E1 5b)**, Page 198.
Photo: Mike Hutton

## Introduction - BRIMHAM

**Conditions and Aspect:** Climbing is possible all year, especially on the quick drying pinnacles (all aspects). The lower edge (faces mainly west) sits in the trees and is prone to greening up over winter, but gets plenty of shade in mid summer when the greener routes yield their charms. Climbs north of Allan's Crack are often green even in summer. The Joker's Wall side of Cubic Block is an all-weather bouldering venue due to the steepness of the overhanging wall. Brimham was originally believed to be formed by druidic climbers overeager with their chipping hammers, the reality turned out to be boring old weathering. The rock is generally sound, rough gritstone that's rather well rounded in places. Some areas are very soft and fragile, and particular care should be taken to preserve them for future generations. Brimham is well known for having wonderful viewpoints to watch the sun go down, the Pinky area being just one of them. Watching the pinnacles set alight at sunset is a sight not to be missed.

**Approach and Parking:** The best approach is from Summerbridge on the B6165 (Knaresborough to Pateley Bridge road). From the crossroads at its centre (where the Flying Dutchman pub sits on the corner) take Hartwith Bank that heads steeply up the hill heading north-east. The entrance to Brimham is 0.5 miles past the crossroads at the top of this road on the left-hand side **(Parking GPS: 54.075561,-1.681783)**. Approaching via Burnt Yates is also popular and signposted (following Brimham Rocks Road to the same crossroads above Summerbridge). The rocks are managed by The National Trust (Tel: 01423 780688). The slow-changing stonefaced formations in the car park are National Trust volunteers, happy to slap you with a parking ticket (they're actually pretty friendly). Parking charge for the main car park is £5 for the day and free to NT members. The car park is locked at night, so be careful not to spend too long on the crux of your last climb (gate closing times are given at the entrance – typically 8am until dusk – but it's always best to check). The nearest climbs are reached in less than a minute just west of the car park: routes on Cubic Block and boulder problems in the Pommel Area. There is a layby for around 7 cars approximately 0.4 miles past the main Brimham entrance on the right-hand side **(Parking GPS: 54.079973,-1.676488)**. This is a good option if heading to the Hare's Head area but ensure no valuables are visible in your vehicle.

**Restrictions:** There is occasionally a bird ban around the Fag Slab and Pig Traverse Area and fire restrictions occur during the summer. Bouldering on The Druid's Idol (Indian's Turban Area) is not permitted.

---

**Navigating Brimham:** To the first-timer (and even those who've been many times before), Brimham can prove confusing. Therefore the climbing in this guide has been split into four areas to help simplify things:

**1. The Pinnacles:** Located between the car parks and Pinky bouldering area at the far northern end of the grounds (approximately 900m via the main track, extending north of the house).

**2. The Northern Edges:** Keeper Crack working back west to Lover's Leap and then south to Cleft Buttress (750m along the tracks).

**3. The Southern Edges:** Notice Board Wall back south to Cubic Block (300m of wooded paths).

**4. Roadside & Hare's Head Area:** Further up the road (0.7 miles) from Brimham proper are a handful of small pinnacles, popular with boulderers.

If you want to get a quick fix, for routes try Cannon Rock, Castle Rock, Allan's Crack Area, Lover's Leap, Cracked Buttress and the Cubic Block. For bouldering, you can't go wrong with the Pommel Area, Joker's Wall, The Niche, Cleft Buttress and the Pinky Area. If you want to escape the crowds, there are plenty of hidden away areas where you can enjoy a bit of peace.

All the pinnacle routes are described anti-clockwise (i.e. left-to-right from the first climb) and the lower edge is described left-to-right from the far east of the northern end. As you drive into the first car park the pinnacles are straight ahead and the edge runs off to the left of the main walking track, often hidden in the trees.

Almscliff to Slipstones  **193**

## Keeper's Crack Area

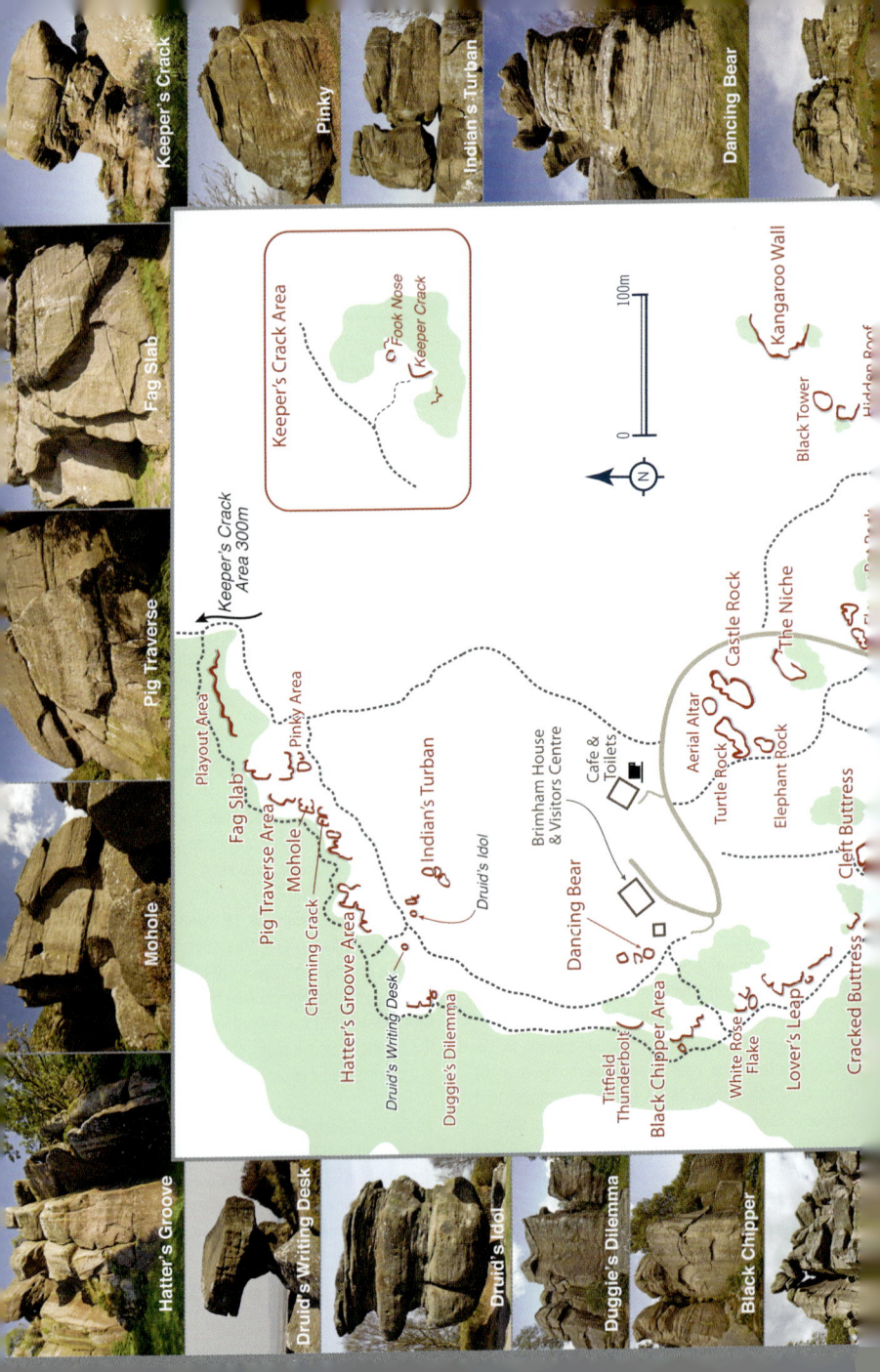

**Photos (top, left to right):** Keeper's Crack, Pinky, Indian's Turban, Dancing Bear

**Photos (left side):** Fag Slab, Pig Traverse, Mohole, Hatter's Groove

**Photos (bottom):** Druid's Writing Desk, Druid's Idol, Duggie's Dilemma, Black Chipper

### Map labels

- Keeper's Crack Area 300m
- Fook Nose
- Keeper Crack
- 100m
- N
- Kangaroo Wall
- Black Tower
- Hidden Roof
- Playout Area
- Fag Slab
- Pinky Area
- Pig Traverse Area
- Mohole
- Charming Crack
- Hatter's Groove Area
- Indian's Turban
- Druid's Writing Desk
- Druid's Idol
- Duggie's Dilemma
- Brimham House & Visitors Centre
- Cafe & Toilets
- Dancing Bear
- Aerial Altar
- Castle Rock
- Turtle Rock
- The Niche
- Elephant Rock
- Cleft Buttress
- Titfield Thunderbolt
- Black Chipper Area
- White Rose Flake
- Lover's Leap
- Cracked Buttress

## Map

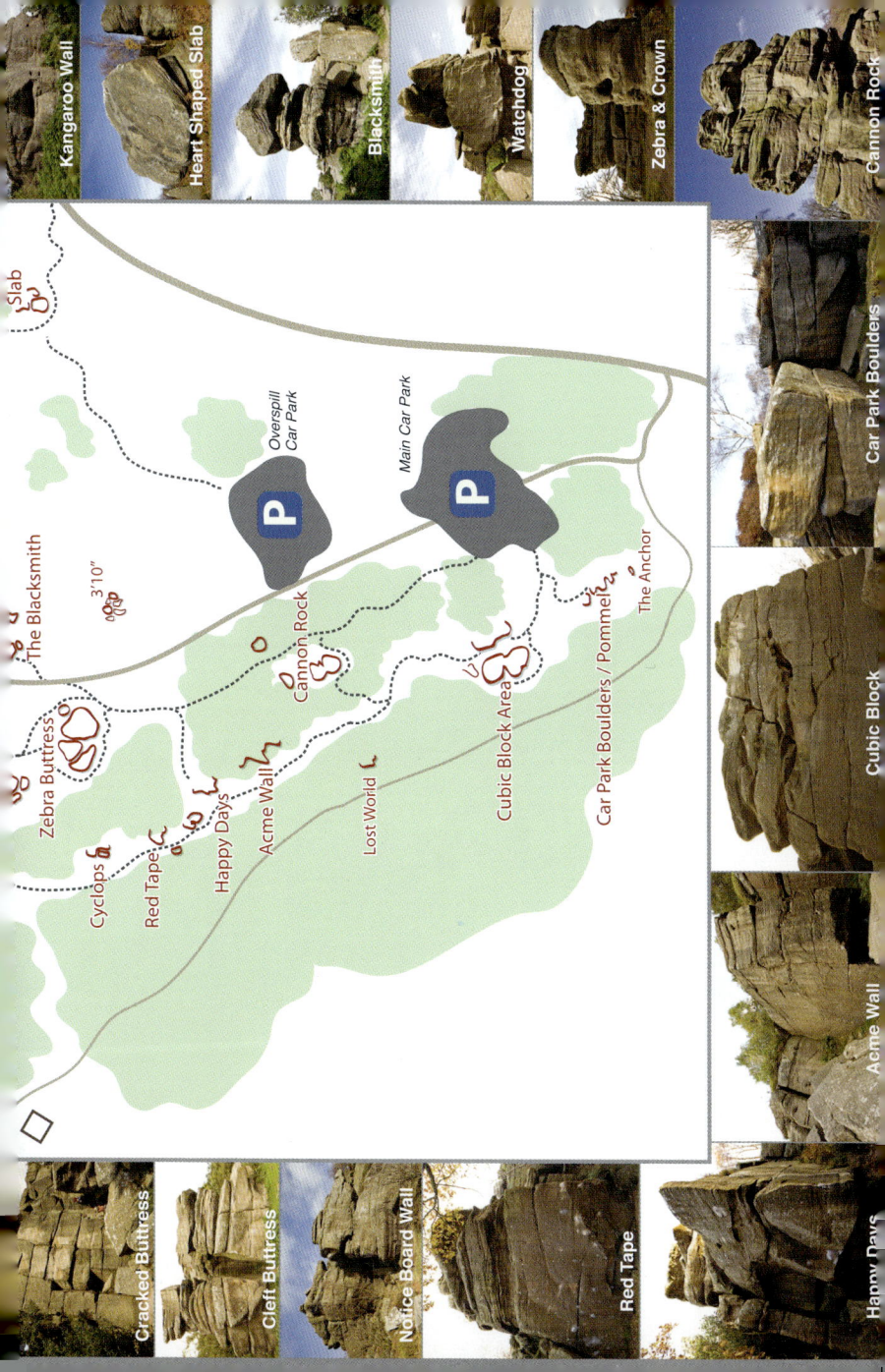

**Top photos (left to right):** Kangaroo Wall, Heart Shaped Slab, Blacksmith, Watchdog, Zebra & Crown, Cannon Rock

**Right side photos (top to bottom):** Car Park Boulders, Cubic Block, Acme Wall

**Bottom photos (left to right):** Cracked Buttress, Cleft Buttress, Notice Board Wall, Red Tape, Happy Days

### Map labels

- Slab
- Overspill Car Park
- Main Car Park
- The Blacksmith
- 3'10"
- Zebra Buttress
- Cannon Rock
- Acme Wall
- Cyclops
- Red Tape
- Happy Days
- Lost World
- Cubic Block Area
- Car Park Boulders / Pommel
- The Anchor

**BRIMHAM** - Aerial Photo

# Brimham - Looking East

House
Cafe and Toilets

To Hatter's Groove & the rest of the Northern Edges

## Northern Edges

| # | Name | # | Name | # | Name |
|---|---|---|---|---|---|
| 1 | Black Chipper p253 | 4 | White Rose p256 | 7 | Cracked Buttress p268 |
| 2 | Tender Homecoming p230 | 5 | Lover's Leap p260 | 8 | Rachael's Box p270 |
| 3 | Dancing Bear p229 | 6 | Double Back p263 | 9 | Cleft Buttress p272 |

Aerial Photo - **BRIMHAM**

| 16 | Turtle Rock p226 | 20 | The Watchdog p204 | 24 | Hidden Roof p207 |
| 17 | Elephant Rock p227 | 21 | The Niche p215 | 25 | Black Tower p209 |
| 18 | Aerial Altar p220 | 22 | Zebra Buttress p201 | 26 | Kangaroo Wall p210 |
| 19 | Castle Rock p218 | 23 | The Blacksmith p206 | | |

**The Outback**

**The Pinnacles**

Approach From Parking

**Southern Edges**

To Cubic Block

| 10 | Notice Board Wall p275 | 12 | Red Tape p279 | 14 | Happy Days p280 |
| 11 | Cyclops p277 | 13 | No Problem Wall p280 | 15 | Acme Wall p282 |

**BRIMHAM** - Cannon Rock

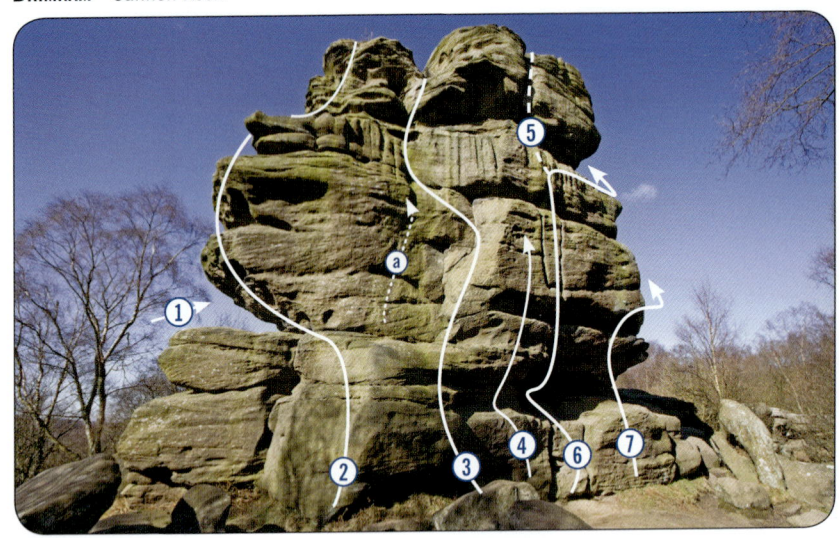

## The Pinnacles
Between the car parks and the far end of the grounds are a multitude of rock towers and jumbled boulder formations that make this destination popular with climbers and sightseers alike. The main track to the house is a good reference point and most of the pinnacle routes are not too far from this.

### The Southern Pinnacles

### Cannon Rock
Easy access and containing some quality routes, this pinnacle should be in your sights. From the main car park, walk north up the main track for 100m, to the overflow parking, and look left (west). Cannon Rock is clearly visible 50m through the trees. Try to find the cannon hole through the rock. The obvious twin cracks of *Frensis* face the track.

**1 Go Joe**  HVS 5a  9m
Commence battle from the right-hand end of the platform by jamming through the crack in the roof and struggling past this to the top.
*Joe Brown  1958*

**2 Mons Meg**  VS 5a  9m
The undercut nose on the end of the pinnacle is all rather rounded and looks scary! Large ammo in the form of a cam at 4m can be placed with a long reach.
*Dave Musgrove, Jim Worthington  12th March 1974*  ✦

**3 Maloja**  VS 4c  11m  ★★
A great crowd pleaser with some good climbing and is deservedly popular. Climb the groove and waft past the ribs to the sanctuary of decent holds. Finish up and left past the cannon hole. Stick with it; difficulties are short lived. (a) **Maloja Direct** (HVS 5c) starts from the ledge to then join the original finish.
*Pre-1957*  ✦

**4 Goof Aydee and the Mango**  E2 5c  10m
Inch up the pocketed wall and sneak out left over the roof.
*Dean Bradley  17th November 1990*

**5 Frensis Direct**  E1 5b  11m  ★★★
One of the best routes at Brimham and a good candidate for your first E1? March up the fantastic twin cracks of *Frensis* to the overhang. Move left into the wide upper crack for an enjoyable short-lived tussle. Photo on page 192.
*Allan Austin  14th April 1957*  ✦

Yorkshire Gritstone

The Flying Saucer - **BRIMHAM**

**6 Frensis** VS 5a  10m ★
Start up the twin cracks as for *Frensis Direct* to the overhang to finish via an airy traverse right and a tricky mantel onto the ledge.
*Harold Drasdo 1956* ✦

**7 Cannon Fodder** E2 6a  8m ★
Make a perplexing move to get established in the break, then make a precarious step right, around the arête, to holds on the slab. Follow this to the large ledge.
*Nigel Baker, Dave Musgrove (both led)  11th March 2000*

**8 Point Blank** HVS 5b  6m
Somehow overcome the roof and follow the short crack, escaping via a mantelshelf.
*Tony Marr, Mike Tooke, Peter Shawcross  14th October 1990*

**9 Whiz-Bang** S 4a  6m
From the boulder climb the reachy corner groove to the roof, move left to a good hold and pull onto the ledge. **Whiz-Bang Direct Start** without the boulder is 5a. The corner-crack (b) just right is HD 3b and a possible alternative descent to *Cannon Route*.
*Tony Marr, Mike Tooke (FRA)  29th September 2005* ✦

**10 Cannon Route** D 3a  9m ★
Start from the boulder left of *Go Joe*, but aim left under the roof and follow your nose to the top, passing the hole along the way. Often used as a descent route by the competent.
*Pre-1957* ✦

### The Flying Saucer
Walk down from the north end of Cannon Rock and head north for 20m to an undercut plinth with a huge roof on its downhill side. Not a great area for routes but home to a couple of problems that are well worth seeking out. The first starts from under the north-east arête, closest to the track.

**11 Gamma Goblins** Font 6b+
With gravity working against you, traverse the break rightwards to finish up *Alien Nation*. Extra-terrestrial effort required to hang on in there.

**12 Alien Nation** Font 6a+
The slopey north-west arête from a sit-down start.

Dropping down the hill and around to the right (east) of the huge roof are five short routes: **Back Bower** (M 2c) takes the traverse ledge and chimney facing the roof. **Legover** (HVS 5a) takes the front of the tower to a tough finish. **Bower Route 1** (VD 4a) and **Bower Route 2** (D 3b) are the two chimneys to the right of *Legover*. **Neon** (VD 3c) climbs the fun luminous corner-crack on the boulder opposite *Legover*.

Back up to the track and 60m north. On the right is the **Eccles Cake** (aka Threaded Block). There's a couple of scrappy unlisted highballs here, and a handful of routes.

**13 Hats Off to Andy** S 4b  7m
Start at the left-hand end of the rock platform on the south side. A tough start gets you to the first break, pull onto the second ledge and up.
*Jim Croft, Stuart Holmes  12th July 2009*

# BRIMHAM - Crown Rock

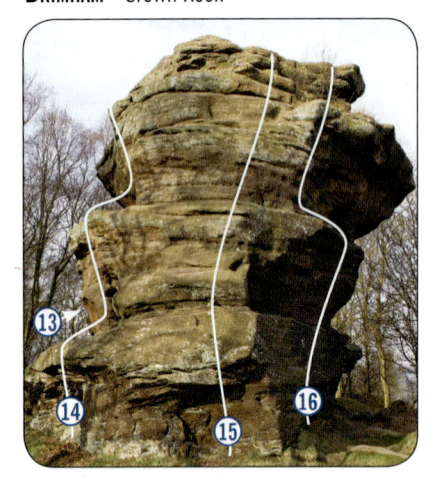

### 14 One Flew Over the Eccles Cake  VS 4b   7m
From the undercut, gain the sloping ledge and make a tricky mantel to gain the second ledge.
*Stuart Holmes, Jim Croft   12th July 2009*

### 15 East Ridge of the Eccles Cake  HVD 4a   8m  ★
Make an awkward rounded boulder problem start to the ridge and finish direct.
*Stuart Holmes, Jim Croft   24th March 2009*

### 16 Icing on the Cake  HVS 5a   10m  ★
Climb to the large thread on the right side of the north face. Traverse out left to two small threads. Make a long move up to a good hold and then the top.
*Stuart Holmes, Jim Croft (both led)   5th June 2009*

## Crown Rock and Zebra Buttress
Follow the track north for 70m. This is probably the most complex area at Brimham which in the past has caused people to give it a miss. Take time to get orientated and give these climbs some deserved attention. The first three routes are on the pinnacle next to the track.

### 17 King Cobra  E3 6b   8m
Climb directly up the bulge to a good sidepull pocket. Make a hard move up and trend right past a second pocket to the break and a direct finish.
*Alan Taylor, Tony Marr   18th July 1999*

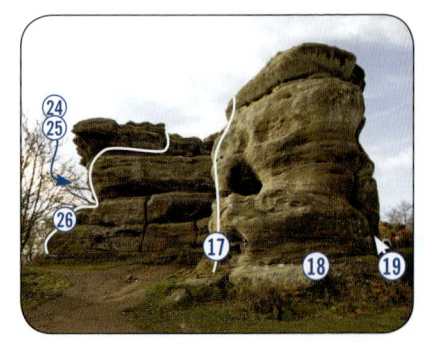

### 18 Morose Mongoose  E4 6b   8m  ★
Desperately gurn over the scary bulges between *King Cobra* and *Roadside Crack*.
*John Allen   September 1988*

### 19 Roadside Crack  E1 5b   8m
Hitch your way up the wide crack. The boulder at the top of the crack wobbles. It used to be HS when it had chockstones.
*Pre-1957* ✦

## Crown Rock
The largest buttress in this group is next to the track. From the trackside pinnacle walk around the north side into an open gully. *Roaring Boys* starts on the west face just right of the central Moderate descent chimney.

### 20 Roaring Boys  E1 5b   6m
The wall, using a finger pocket to gain a recess and the crack to exit.
*Tony Marr, Mike Tooke (FRA)   17th August 2005*

### 21 Left-Hand Bias  VS 4c   7m
Start on the nose and trend left across the slabby wall to a flake. Pull over the bulge to a ledge and finish up the chimney.
*Tony Barley, Robert Kinnear   3rd September 1972*

### 22 Top Dead Centre  HS 4b   6m
The wide crack - it's hard to know if avoiding the tree is harder than the climb.
*Tony Barley, Robert Kinnear   3rd September 1972*

Yorkshire Gritstone

## Zebra Buttress - BRIMHAM

### 23 Two Tier Crack  HS 5a   11m
10m right, take the wide crack to a ledge and then step left to the wide slanting crack. A bold direct start can be made on the wall to the left at VS 4c.
*Tony Marr, Mike Tooke (FRA)   17th August 2005*

### 24 Oak Tree Crack  S 4c   11m
Start up a short crack under the oak and climb the brutal corner behind. The overall grade can be reduced to HD 3c if the tree is used.
*Tony Marr, Mike Tooke (FRA)   17th August 2005*

### 25 Keyhole Cops  VS 4c   8m   ★
Unusual! From the same start bridge up right through the hanging slot above the tree.
*Gaz Parry, Ben Bransby (both solo)   27th March 1999*

### 26 Right-Hand Bias  HVS 4c   13m
Scrape up the broad rib right of the tree with help from a fluting, to below the large roof. Now stomach traverse right to escape. The much harder **Right-Hand Bias Direct** (E4 6b) takes a direct finish over the roof to the right of the nose.
*Tony Barley, Robert Kinnear   3rd September 1972* ✦

## Zebra Buttress
Across the open gully from Crown Rock are three large free-standing boulders close together. The boulder on the south-west of the group consists of three blocks stacked on top of each other with a slab below an overhang on its south side. The *Vamoose* chimney is just left of this slab, but continue leftwards to the low roof for the first route, *Gwyneth*. Descend by jumping the gap to the north-west block and taking the corner ramp on its east side.

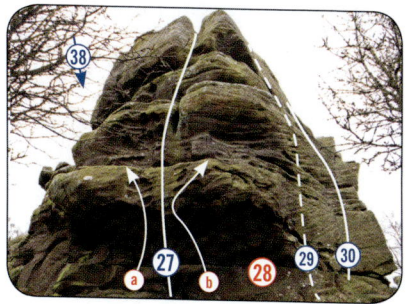

### 27 Gwyneth  E4 6a   12m   ★
Struggle onto the ledge above the overhang, teeter up to the deep hold-less groove (crux) and tremble to the top. An alternative start gains the ledge from the right then traverses left (5b) - but the finish is still the real crux. There are two good value problems with sit-down starts, (a) **Gwyneth Left** (Font 6a+) uses the left-hand scoop to the ledge, (b) **Gwyneth Right** (Font 6a) the right-hand scoop.
*Al Manson   1977*

### 28 Ethel  Font 5+
From a sit-down start, romp over the roof to the ledge.

The boulder with a leaning roof downhill and south of the *Gwyneth* roof has a smattering of tough problems. They're on poor rock though and there are plenty of other things to be going on with.

### 29 Peekabu  E2 6a   10m
Head up the wall left of the crack to an awful mantelshelf to finish up *Jackabu*.
*Steve Rhodes (solo)   8th August 1988*

### 30 Jackabu  E1 5b   11m   ★
Cruise up the delightful layback corner to a nasty mantel onto a ledge. The wall above and to the left presents a challenge; bold and with the last hold hard to find. Can be climbed by starting up the arête on the right, passing a small thread (5c).
*Pete Hindle, George Steele   1st February 1959* ✦

### 31 Vamoose  HD 3b   8m   ★
The impressive chimney, with a slightly awkward start. The north end is easier but less fun.

Almscliff to Slipstones   **201**

# BRIMHAM - Zebra Buttress

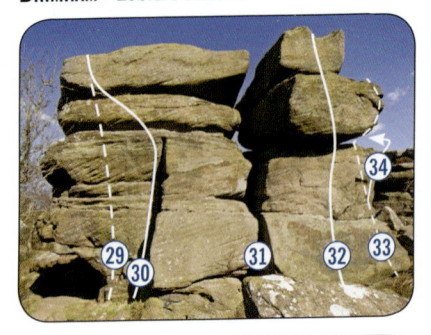

### 32 Vam  E3 6b   8m
Scuttle up the centre of the slab to the overhang where a thread can be arranged. Above lies a large hold which can be used to propel oneself to the top.
*Martin Berzins  1977*

### 33 Steady VS Arête  E3 6a   8m
Tiptoe up the right side of the slab to the roof, and continue up the arête with difficulty.
*Steve Rhodes, Alec Burns, Justin Volger  8th August 1988*

### 34 The Mantelshelf  HVS 5a   12m  ★
As for 'Steady' to the roof. Pull right around the arête and continue until it is possible to mantel up, then follow the scoop to finish.
*Tony Barley  1st October 1972*

Routes on the middle buttress start in the left side of the gully. *Closet Crack* is right of the slit leading through to *Vamoose*.

### 35 Closet Crack  VS 4c   8m  ★
Struggle up the crack, passing a hole to a deep horizontal break. For the full experience, historical correctness and the star, stomach traverse off leftwards. Alternatively step over to the ledge opposite.
*Pete Hindle, George Steele  1st February 1959*

### 36 Tube Break  E3 6a   8m  ★
As for *Closet Crack* to the ledge, then sidle right to below a wide crack. Ignore common sense and jam up it or take the harder option and layback it at 6b.
*John Syrett  pre-1980*

### 37 Tube Break Direct Start  HVS 5b   6m
The vague groove right of *Closet Crack* into *Tube Break's* cave. Slope off right or finish up *Tube Break*.
*Tony Marr, Mike Tooke  5th September 1993*

### 38 Felicity  E2 5b   12m
The deep discontinuous crack left of *Gwyneth* is no pushover. The difficult overhanging finish provides a good challenge.
*Dennis Gray, Eric Beard  1962*

202 Yorkshire Gritstone

Zebra Buttress - **BRIMHAM**

For routes on the final buttress, start on the west side, looking back into the narrow gully left of *Felicity*. The first route is on the left.

### 39  House Points Tomorrow  E2 5c   8m
Start from the top of the large boulder left of the gully. Power through the bulges to a gently rising break, then scamper right with difficulty to a good jam and pull over for a gold star.

*Greg Rimmer, Steve Rhodes   10th June 1988*

### 40  Don't Step Back Crack  E1 5b   9m
Start from the bottom of the crack just inside the gully. No bridging allowed!

*Steve Rhodes, Greg Rimmer   10th June 1988*

### 41  Lay Back and Think  E1 5c   6m
Continuing into the bay another crack is reached. Follow this to a wild layback and a sting in the tail finish. The chimney to the right with an awkward exit is (a) **Grumble and Grunt** (S 4b).

*Steve Rhodes, Nic Kidd   1st August 1988*

Shaun Duke cutting loose in the popular Car Park Boulders. Page 298.
Photo: Daglish Photography

# BRIMHAM - The Watchdog

## The Watchdog

This conspicuous guardian of the lower edges contains a collection of good hard routes above less than ideal landings. A great spot to hang out on a summer's evening as it catches the breeze while the wooded areas are overrun with midges. Continue 50m north-west along the track from Zebra Buttress to reach this area. It is a collection of boulders but the main boulder (Watchdog) is clearly identified by being severely undercut with a prominent prow. Just before this, to the south, is a smaller boulder with a couple of routes, the first starting on the south face: **Puddle Jumper**, (VS 4c), climbs the wall using a sidepull and moves left to a harrowing finish left of the arête; **I'd Rather be at Dalby** (VS 5a) tackles the green overhangs to an awkward step onto the ledge before moving left to the obvious protrusion and an exciting mantel finish (◆).

### 42 **Ratbag**  HS 4b   8m
Scurry up the undercut and jagged wide crack. Pull over into a large basin in the top of the rock.
*Pete Hindle, George Steele  1st February 1959*

### 43 **Rattler**  E1 5c   18m
A girdle of the buttress. Start as for *Ratbag* and traverse into *Rat Arsed*, step up to the break and continue past *Rat Trap* to finish easily.
*Martin Berzins, Al Manson   April 1988*

### 44 **Rat Arsed**  E4 6c   8m   ★★
Precariously steep climbing from a punishing start. Struggle up the rippled undercut wall and from the cave flit left and pass the overhang on good holds.
*Martin Berzins, Nic Kidd  27th March 1988*

### 45 **Rat Trap**  HVS 5a   8m   ★
Faith-leaping fun. Carefully climb onto the top of the boulder and lean across to climb the exposed rib. Finish up the crack on the left. A direct from the ground is worth 5c.
*Tony Barley, Tony Roache  30th April 1972*

### 46 **Ratfink**  E3 6a   9m
Courageous climbing up the wall well right of *Rat Trap* with use of the pocket.
*Martin Berzins, Al Manson   April 1988*

### 47 **Rat Catcher**  HS 4b   6m
The awkward bulging crack to the right.
*Tony Marr, Mike Tooke  20th August 2000*

Yorkshire Gritstone

Descent from the Watchdog is possible via a scramble just to the right. The two short cracks on the east side have been climbed. **Dirty Rat** (HS 4b) takes the crack on the left. **Rat Pack** (E1 5b) is the hanging fault to a moss covered ending.

Back in the gully and opposite *Ratfink* is a large, often green boulder with four routes.

**48 Ratlin'** HS 4b  6m
The offwidth crack, broken by deep ledges, on the south side of the block.
*Jem Tuck, Phil Harris  19th June 2001*

**49 Doberman Pincher** Font 6c+
The terrifying arête. Mats 'to the power of ten' very handy.

**50 Rataonee** E2 5c  7m
Start within the gully and from just left of the right-hand arête. Climb to a good break and then scuttle left to a wide horizontal break and a testing last move.
*Steve Rhodes, Nic Kidd, Al Manson, M. Berzins  27th July 1988*

**51 Ratatwoee** HVS 5b  6m
Follow the arête direct.
*Martin Berzins, Al Manson  April 1988*

**52 Rattlesnake** E1 5c  8m
Slither leftward up the wall to a mantel finish.
*Jim Croft, Stuart Holmes  5th June 2009*

## THE DIRTY DOZEN

Put your thrutching, chicken wings, armbars and fist stacking skills to the test on this selection of some of Brimham's best offwidth climbs from Severe to E6.

1. **Inside Out**  S 4a (Page 305)

2. **Crackaroo**  S 4b (Page 210)

3. **Top Dead Centre**  HS 4b (Page 200)

4. **Constrictor Chimney**  VS 4c (Page 247)

5. **Harry's Crack**  VS 4c (Page 232)

6. **Closet Crack**  VS 4c (Page 202)

7. **Central Crack**  VS 5a (Page 268)

8. **Desperation Crack**  HVS 5b (Page 218)

9. **Bog Crack**  E1 5b (Page 215)

10. **Roadside Crack**  E1 5b (Page 200)

11. **Tube Break**  E3 6a (Page 202)

12. **Gigglin' Crack**  E6 6c (Page 242)

**Jim Croft**

# BRIMHAM - The Blacksmith

## The Blacksmith
To locate the next routes, return to the track at Crown Rock (100m due east) and locate the pinnacle to the right of the track (if facing towards the house). This anvil shaped rock and the area immediately behind it is home to a handful of problems, two of them absolute corkers, and a rollercoaster of a route up the steep wall.

### 53  Cocoa Club Board Meeting  E5 6b    8m
Climber – know your limits. Savour the boulder start and drop at the break (Font 6a) or max up the terror factor and crank on up to the top passing the old bolts of the long-gone notice board. Originally the board provided protection and handholds, so it may now be impossible.
*Steve Rhodes, Martin Berzins  5th May 1988* ✦

### 54  Cocoa Runnel  Font 6a
Get into the groove baby! The left arête on the short block to the right is (a) **Tempered Steel** (Font 4+).

### 55  Swing Arête  Font 6c
Balancey moves up the arête. Just as good from a sitter at Font 7a+.

On the back of The Blacksmith (east side, away from the track) is a frightening little number.

### 56  Bare Back Side  HVS 5c    6m
Mildly scary. The Blacksmith pinnacle is summited via a short crack and insecure mantel.
*Steve Rhodes, Martin Berzins  5th May 1988*

Behind the Blacksmith, 15m east, is a perched slabby block with three of the best problems going.

### 57  Fantasy League  Font 7a+
A great problem and well worth the rash! A crouching start on the block allows you to get a leg jam and 'on trust' lean out to gain and match the ramp. Follow this to latch the big hold on the arête. Squeeze to top-out. The big hold on the arête has deteriorated due to traffic and justifies the new grade.
*Jim Baxter 1990s*

### 58  Striding Edge  Font 6a+
Mint. Step from the boulder and coolly tackle the arête to the summit.

Yorkshire Gritstone

# Hidden Roof - BRIMHAM

**59 Dreamcast** Font 7b
Slopey strength-sapping shenanigans. From a sit-down start move up from the block, past the slopey dish and up the arête.

**60 Lookout Wall** Font 5+
Ripples, reach and rockovers.

Due south, 60m away, is a group of innocuous boulders, most no taller than waist height. In this group is a small round undercut boulder, with a blunt arête and obvious starting slot.

**61 3'10** Font 7c+
Brutal! Sit down and pull the slot to gain the rounded top of the boulder. Pull up and mantel.
*Dave Cowl*

**62 Jim's Mantel** Font 7a
Pull for all you're worth onto the left end of the block from a sitter (aka: **Hillbilly Loving**).

**63 Andy's Traverse** Font 7b
Sit-down start. Traverse the lip using a heel all the way. Follow this right around and finish with a mantel.
*Dave Cowl* ✦

## The Outback

Just visible 160m to the north-east is the remote area of Brimham known as The Outback. A collection of buttresses and towers containing good climbing for both the adventurous router and keen boulderer on nice compact gritstone. Take a bearing on the distant Black Tower (due north-east) and follow the myriad of weaving paths that land you in the area.

### Hidden Roof

First up, and masked by trees on the west side, is a neat low roof with a couple of worthwhile problems and a taxing traverse.

**1 Hidden Roof Traverse** Font 7a+
Sharp and pumpy movement from left-to-right.

Almscliff to Slipstones    **207**

Dave Cowl making an ascent of **Pommel** (Font 6c+) look graceful. Page 298
Photo: Mike Hutton

Black Tower - **BRIMHAM**

**2 Hidden Crack**  Font 4+
Nice crack finishing on sloping ledges.

**3 Hidden Wall**  Font 6a+
Neat wall via the flake and features.

## Black Tower

Immediately north is a lonely pinnacle with three routes. The belay is by looping under the undercut tops of the arêtes. Take care with the descent, which is to exit the right dish (west) and to move left and reverse *North-West Arête* for a few moves then escape right; or abseil.

**4 Black Tower Face**  HVS 5a   10m
At the north corner facing *Kangaroo Wall*, climb to a ledge (possible walk off). Move up to the undercut flake and use this to gain a good hold on top.
*Tony Barley, Robin Brown   May 1973*

**5 North-West Arête**  HS 4a   8m   ★
From the lowest point of the arête, climb straight up. Best finished in the left notch, protectable if a touch reachy. The finish in the right dish is trivial and the overall grade is HVD 3c.
*Andy Wild   24th June 1997*

**6 The Periwocky**  E1 5b   8m
Named after a mythical beast that haunts Brimham! Climb the undercut start to the break, head right then up and left to a smaller break (a difficult to place cam is possible out right) and pull up to the top.
*Stuart Holmes, Jim Croft (both led)   2nd July 2009*

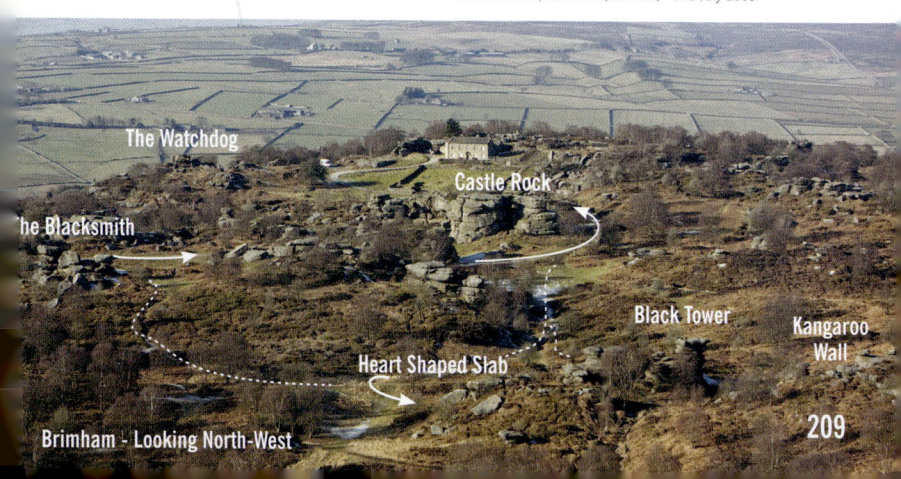

209

# BRIMHAM - Kangaroo Wall

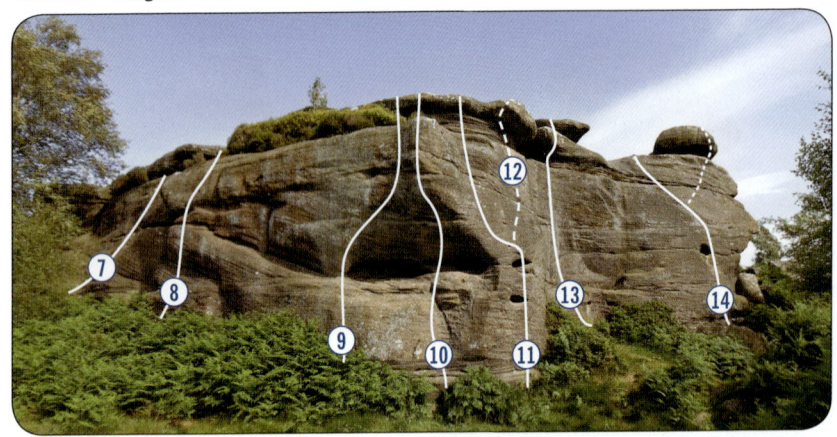

## Kanagroo Wall
Across the clearing, 30m to the east, is the smooth façade and jutting prow of Kangaroo Wall. An often-overlooked area but well worth exploring. The routes are short, but not generally well-protected, and some venture into highball bouldering territory.

**7 Concave Slab** VS 4c  6m  ☆
Scoot up and right to a tiny ledge, teeter up to the hole and finish direct.
*Tony Marr, Frank Fitzgerald, Mike Tooke  29th May 1995*

**8 Crackaroo** S 4b  6m
Grapple with the wide crack.
*M.Tooke, F. Fitzgerald, T. Marr, Pam & P. Shawcross 4th June 1995*

**9 Walleroo** E2 5c  7m
From the shallow scoop left of the cave, wander up and slightly right to two pockets.
*Tony Marr, Mike Tooke, Peter Shawcross  1st August 1993*

**10 The Road Rage Experience** E6 6c  6m
Attain the cave and with telescopic arms find small sandy edges above. With help from the edge of the shallow groove, launch up left to a large hold on the nose.
*Tony Simpson  1996* ◆

**11 Dame Edna** E4 6b  6m
Follow the left-hand side of the wall past a pocket and swing left into the shallow groove to a precarious finish.
*Pete Kitson (solo)  July 1988* ◆

**12 Botany Bay** E1 5c  6m  ★
Start as for *Dame Edna,* but step right to a difficult mantel onto the ledge.
*Andy Wild, Al Manson  1977*

**13 Sir Les** E3 6b  6m
The centre of the wall using two rounded layaways in a green scoop.
*Al Manson (solo)  July 1988*

**14 Kangaroo Wall** VS 4c  6m  ★
Heart-in-the-mouth movement up the wall where your chance of success is proportional to reach. Pretty much a solo unless you can get an 8ft thread to work for you! Tackle the right end of the wall and step left to the deep

Yorkshire Gritstone

# Heart Shaped Slab - BRIMHAM

hole. Make a wobbly mantel onto the ramp above and finish easily left or, better, up the arête on the right. HVS for shorties.

*Pre-1970* ✦

## Heart Shaped Slab

Located 125m south is a colossal undercut leaning pancake of rock. This venue offers a selection of rash-inducing rounded problems with the classic being *Heart Shaped Slab Arête*. This huge boulder is clearly visible 150m north-east from the overflow car park, and the road. Good if you're looking for a quick hit and a change of scene from the Pommel area, though the problems' starts can hammer the vertically challenged.

### 15 Flatline  Font 6b
A class act that punishes poor footwork. From a sit-down start, with both hands in the rounded slot, use the crimpy ripples to traverse left and continue around the arête. Move upward to finish on the obvious juggy break.

### 16 Bilberry Groove  HS 4b  10m  ☆
Haul up into the leaning groove and continue to the higher slab. A good line with good moves but dirty at the crux and now a bit vegetated above.

*Tony Marr, Mike Tooke, Peter Shawcross  17th October 1993*

### 17 Love Scoop  Font 6a+
Grit rash time. From standing, press your way up the beautiful rounded scoop. Brave the top-out or choose to escape. From a sitter is **Vision On** (Font 6c+).

### 18 Pulse Rate  Font 5
The undercut slab is harder than it looks. Climb direct using the dishes.

### 19 Just Do It  Font 6b+
Another tricky customer with a hard start. Mantel onto the slab with the use of the layaway.

### 20 Dead Man Walking  Font 7c+
From sitting, using heels and ripples underneath, climb the full length of the arête. Brutal. The line avoids the plinth.

*Andy Swann*

### 21 Heart Shaped Slab Arête  Font 6c+
A tough cookie but well worth the effort. From standing, use the undercut to gain the rounded arête, then thug, hug and udge your way onto the slab and the top. Quality stuff.

The east wall of the boulder can be grovelled up via the diagonal ramp at D 3a and in reverse provides a descent route.

Hare's Head Area
23 24 25
Dolphin's Nose
Twin Towers
Crimpy Roof
Cyclops
Fag Slab
Pinky Area
13 14 15 16
Hatter's Groove Area
Druid's Writing Desk
12
Indian's Turban
Druid's Idol
Dancing Bear
Cafe & Toilets
Brimham House
Titfield Thunderbolt
Black Chipper Area
0
100m
N
Castle Rock
17 18
The Niche
Kangaroo Wall
Lover's Leap
Cracked Buttress
Cleft Buttress
11
Notice Board Wall
The Watchdog
19
The Blacksmith
Heart Shaped Slab
20 21 22
Zebra Buttress
10
Cyclops
Red Tape
9
8
Happy Days
7
6
Acme Wall
Cannon Rock
P
Overspill Car Park
To Hare's Head 600 metres
Lost World
Main Car Park
P
Cubic Block Area
5
4
Car Park Boulders
1 2 3

# THE SACRIFICIAL IDOL BOULDERING CIRCUIT

This is a 25-problem circuit and a blend of some of the classics and unsung gems in the Font 3+ to Font 6c+ range. Designed for both enjoyment and inspiration. Try to follow it in order as it will shorten the distances you need to cover, and it also takes warming up into account. Enjoy the spaces between the problems as much as the climbing. Do this and you'll have got the Brimham philosophy cracked. Once you have completed this circuit you're ready for the hard circuit. Well, once you've recovered...

| Problem | Name | Grade | Area | Page No. |
| --- | --- | --- | --- | --- |
| 1 | Sunshine | Font 3+ | Car Park Boulders | 297 |
| 2 | Sunbeam | Font 4 | Car Park Boulders | 297 |
| 3 | Trench | Font 5+ | Car Park Boulders | 298 |
| 4 | Cubic | Font 6a+ | Cubic Block (slab side) | 285 |
| 5 | Joker's Reach | Font 6b | Joker's Wall | 290 |
| 6 | Gamma Goblins | Font 6b+ | The Flying Saucer | 199 |
| 7 | Happy Days' Start | Font 6b+ | Happy Days | 281 |
| 8 | Green Roof | Font 6a+ | Red Tape | 279 |
| 9 | Red Face | Font 5 | Red Tape | 279 |
| 10 | Learn n' Groove | Font 6a+ | Cyclops | 276 |
| 11 | Murky Rib | Font 6c | Cleft Buttress | 274 |
| 12 | Capsize | Font 6a | Boat Rock/Indian's Turban | 231 |
| 13 | Perky | Font 6b+ | Pinky Area | 233 |
| 14 | Minidigit | Font 6a | Pinky Area | 234 |
| 15 | Piglet Wall | Font 4 | Pinky Area | 233 |
| 16 | Ripple Traverse | Font 5 | Pinky Area | 234 |
| 17 | Niche Arête | Font 6c | The Niche | 215 |
| 18 | Niche Roof | Font 6b | The Niche | 215 |
| 19 | Striding Edge | Font 6a+ | The Blacksmith | 206 |
| 20 | Flatline | Font 6b | Heart Shaped Slab | 211 |
| 21 | Love Scoop | Font 6a+ | Heart Shaped Slab | 211 |
| 22 | Heart Shaped Slab Arête | Font 6c+ | Heart Shaped Slab | 211 |

Phew. Huge effort so far but have you got it in you to finish? Slap the pad on the back and trek out to the wilderness of Hare's Head where the last three problems of the circuit remain. Bring it on.

| 23 | Fisherman's Friend | Font 5+ | Hare's Head (Dolphin Roof) | 306 |
| --- | --- | --- | --- | --- |
| 24 | Flipper | Font 6b | Hare's Head (Dolphin Roof) | 306 |
| 25 | Sharkbait | Font 6a | Hare's Head (Dolphin Roof) | 306 |

# BRIMHAM - Flower Pot Rock

## The Central Pinnacles

### Flower Pot Rock Area

200m west, back to the main track and just north of The Blacksmith (towards the house) sits a collection of unusual low boulders.

**1 Bill & Ben**  Font 6c
The technical wall on great features. It is often a bit damp, otherwise it would be a classic.
*Mike Gray*

**2 Flobbalobba**  Font 6a
Technical and fun up the fissure and face.

**3 Hussefelt**  Font 7c+
The smooth undercut arête from a sitter on tiny features and with a lot of squeezing.
*Andy Swann*

**4 Guy's Traverse**  Font 6a+
Hitchhike the break rightwards.

**5 Caveman**  Font 6c
From a sitter, escape from the depths.

Tom Lee on **The Grouch** (Font 7b). Page 231
Photo: Daglish Photography

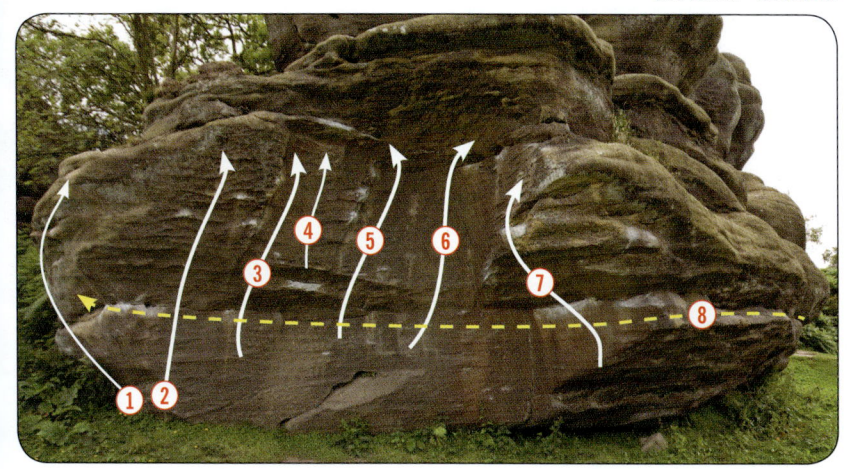

The Niche - **BRIMHAM**

### Castle Rock Area
Up the track towards the house (north) for 80m, on the left, is one of the crag's major areas, and quite rightly so. Quintessential Brimham; a showground jam-packed with routes and stars from Diff to E7. Quick to dry and near the cafe - what more could you want?

On the buttress opposite the south face of Castle Rock is **The Niche** an area popular with the bouldering fraternity. Home to a great concentration of problems in a sheltered spot with the potential for some DWS action if there's been a downpour. The route on the buttress is one for the crack connoisseurs.

**1 Niche Arête** Font 6c
From a sitter tackle the blunt prow on slopers.

**2 Niche Wall** Font 7a+
The steep wall from a sit-down start.

**3 Left Flake** Font 6a
The frangible flake.

**4 Jumper's Dyno** Font 7c
Pneumatic moves with big air time. Graded for the jump from jug to break but can you go again? Aka: **Niche Dyno**.

**5 Right Flake** Font 6a
Very tasty indeed. A delightful problem up the right flake.

**6 Niche Corner** Font 6b+
Technical but rewarding. The left wall of the corner.

**7 Niche Roof** Font 6b
Start from under the roof. Bodypop up left then right to glory.

**8 The Long Haul** Font 7b
Quality big jug wanderings; head leftwards to finish up *Niche Arête*.

**9 Bog Crack** E1 5b 9m ★
Graunch up the wide crack (long thread runner at half-height) and finish with an insecure thrutch. Take a big cam for near the top. Good offwidth fun.
*Tony Barley, Robin Barley 1963*

Almscliff to Slipstones

215

The sting in the tail beckons on **Desperation Crack** (HVS 5b). Lucinder Whittaker prepares for the fight. Page 218
Photo: David Simmonite

217

# BRIMHAM - Castle Rock

The imposing bulk of **Castle Rock** is opposite *Bog Crack*. Descent is via a steep corner on the north side or via a chimney from the start of this descent through to the east.

### 10 Bottom's Up  HVS 5b  6m
Start at the 'elephant's bum'. Surmount the centre of the bulge using the break/flake, then more easily to a good ledge. Walk off.
*Tony Marr, Mike Tooke  20th August 2000*

### 11 Moat Rib  Font 5
Pleasurable pocket pulling up the rib.

### 12 Castle Traverse  Font 6a+
Crack-to-gully rightward traverse. Now run across to *The Long Haul* and repeat ten times for the max burn.

### 13 Castle Corner  D 3b  8m  ★
Short but sweet. Up the corner, pull hard onto the ledge on the left and finish up ledges. The polish at the top means this is a 'trad' ascent.
*Tony Marr, Mike Tooke  2nd March 1997*

### 14 Hawk Traverse  HS 4b  24m  ★★
A delightful journey capturing the fine positions of the buttress while avoiding the harshness of the 'up' routes. Follow *Castle Corner* and traverse into *Desperation Crack*. Yomp up this, making a further traverse under the roof, finishing up the chimney of *Jabberwok*. High in the grade; a competent second is a must.
*Brian Evans  April 1959*

### 15 Michael Michael Superman  E3 5c  12m  ★
Bold solitude in a crowded spot. Climb up and out of the niche, trend right and pull over the bulge (just left of the crack). Make lonely moves up the steep slab to finish.
*Martin Berzins, Nic Kidd, Steve Rhodes  27th March 1988* ✦

### 16 Desperation Crack  HVS 5b  12m  ★★★
The name says it all. You must do it once, but you'll probably never want to do it again. Things are easy enough until near the top, where your wide crack skills are put to the test. Dive into the jaws of the monster fissure and swim for the surface. Many will be chewed up and spat out. Most will weep. A variation start to the right of the original is 5c and needs care with protection. Photo on page 216.
*Pre-1957* ✦

218  Yorkshire Gritstone

## Castle Rock - BRIMHAM

**17 Swan Arcade** E4 5c   12m   ★
Head carefully up the wall and traverse right to below the widest part of the roof. Now float out on broken flakes to a spike on the lip for your first good pro. A difficult pull is all that remains.
*Mike Hammill, Mark Clark, Tony Barley  1976* ✦

**18 Jabberwok** VS 4b   12m   ★
The classic path up Castle Rock is no pushover. Very bold beginnings on good but spaced holds lead to a right squirmish in the bulging chimney.
*c1950* ✦

**19 Jabberwok Variation** VS 4c   12m   ★★
More popular and certainly worthy of a description in its own right. The climbing is even better and safer on the slanting crack which leads to the finish of the original route.
*c1950* ✦

**20 Picnic Variation** HVS 5a   12m   ★
Cracking. Follow *Picnic* to the top of the hanging corner and then tread delicately leftwards on tiny holds until it is possible to escape up the chimney of *Jabberwok*.
*Allan Austin, Brian Evans, Jennifer Ruffe  1956* ✦

**21 Picnic** E2 5c   12m   ★★★
An essential E2 tick that provides much food for thought. The steady climbing turns mean above the cave where only brave soldiers will find fortune. Climb the thin crack and short hanging corner to its end where a step right leads to the deep hole. The fantastic final moves over the flutings are both elusive and awkward. Photo on page 186.
*John Syrett, Geoff Hankinson, Pete Kitson  7th June 1973* ✦

**22 Picnic Alternative Start** E3 6b   12m   ★
A full-bodied cruncher that dispenses with the gentle introduction for something much more unforgiving. Tackle the lower wall on the right, past a large pocket, to gain a ledge. Move left to the deep hole and finish straight up, as for *Picnic*.
*John Syrett  20th January 1974*

**23 Kneewrecker** E1 5b   12m
Climb a short wall to a recess. Gain a short hanging crack and follow it to a large ledge before tackling the leaning, undercut crack (crux). Escapable, but worthwhile.
*Tony Marr, Frank Fitzgerald, Pam & Peter Shawcross 8th Oct 1995*

**24 Windy Day Flop** E2 5b   10m
Climb the groove in the left end of the wall to finish up the smooth runnel. Steady start, tough finish. Small protection is available; placing it is another matter.
*Mick Johnson, Dick Tong (both led)  9th May 2003*

**25 Windy Miller** E3 5c   11m   ★
Climb the groove to a good ledge. Trend up and right to an insecure rockover to a good foothold. Finish with a reachy, rounded topout.
*Dave Musgrove (jnr) and Dave Musgrove (snr)  9th April 1999*

**26 Cakewalk** VS 5a   10m
Tackle the short crack left of the tree and the difficult wall above with the hole. Move up to a ledge and traverse rightwards to walk off on a larger ledge.
*Allan Austin, Brian Evans, Jennifer Ruffe  1956*

**27 Rainy Day** HVS 5c   14m   ★
Up the wall behind the tree stump with difficulty to reach better holds. Move left to the ledge on *Cakewalk* and finish straight up the tower above.
*Jeff Appleyard, Frank Wilkinson, M. Bebbington  17th Oct 1971* ✦

**28 Perfect Day** E2 6a   9m
Up the short crack, direct to holds in the left side of the cave and gear. Make a long move to finish at the ledge.
*Andy Moss (un-seconded)  16th January 2000*

Walk around the buttress, until the north side of Castle Rock is reached. The routes here are often dirty.

### ❝ ❞

No climb, however short, is agreed to have value and importance unless it satisfies certain uncodified but stringent aesthetic criteria - it must be difficult, it must be separate, it must be unique, it must not change, it must not incorporate the irrelevant.

Harold Drasdo in Climbing as Art (article from Ascent, 1974 - reprinted in Ken Wilson's The Games Climbers Play).

# BRIMHAM - Aerial Altar

#### 29 Rod's Roof  E7 6b   6m  ☆
Alarmingly hard full-stretch moves under the dark foreboding roof. From directly beneath the tree, left of the runnel, cross the roof at its widest part trending right to finish via a slight flake.
*Ben Bransby   28th March 1999*

#### 30 Castle Crack  HS 4b   6m
The obvious crack with the chockstone.
*Tony Marr, Mike Tooke   2nd June 1995*

#### 31 Pick and Nick  E5 6b   7m  ★
Funky movement with an out-there feel. Cramped moves lead rightwards, below the roof, to a hard move to pull over. Friends and tricams to protect.
*Gaz Parry   27th March 1999*

#### 32 Squeeze Crack  HS 4b   6m
The right-hand crack isn't too big a squeeze – as long as you don't get sucked in.
*Tony Marr, Mike Tooke   2nd March 1997*

#### 33 Sculptured Wall  VS 5a   6m  ★
Climb the unusual pocketed wall to a cave, step right and climb direct to a sloping finish. Small gear.
*Tony Marr, Mike Tooke   20th August 2000*

The **Aerial Altar**, a huge puff-pastry tower of grit, is 20m north from the back of Castle Rock. The first route is on the side facing the house. Come midweek or expect to have an audience. Descent is awkwardly down the trackside, or carefully by abseil from the wide horn of rock right of the top of *Back Breaker*.

#### 34 Mumbojumbo  E1 5b   13m
An enjoyable route. Take the flared crack to a ledge on the right. An undercut and a long reach gains a pocket and the next ledge. Climb to a pocket on the lip on the right and pull over (or bottle out).
*Tony Barley, Tony Roache   15th May 1971*

#### 35 Back Breaker  VS 5a   13m
The twisting and broken wide crack. Start by traversing in on ledges from the right, with a thoughtful move close to the top. *Topo line also shown on page 227.*
*Tony Barley   1972*

West across the gully from Turtle Rocks is a dirty wall with a small collection of routes. **Excursion** (HS 4b) is opposite *Back Breaker* and is a filthy former VDiff sandbag which, after the tricky crack, wanders right up ledges to a dirty finish. A direct finish from the second ledge above the crack, finishing through the groove in the bulge is **Excursion Direct** (E3 6b).

#### 36 Kiosk Crack  VS 5a   8m
Climb the awkward crack in the nose of the buttress to the overhang, move right and finish up the short chimney. The ancient chipped dog-leg crack system right again is D 3a.
*Tony Marr, Mike Tooke (FRA)   7th September 2005*

#### 37 Turtleneck Crack  HS 4b   6m
Shimmy up the interesting leaning corner-crack with help from some good holds.
*Tony Marr, Mike Tooke (FRA)   31st August 2005*

Adi Gill putting his semaphore skills to good use on **Grit Expectations** (E4 6a). Page 250. This stands for 'send help'.
Photo: Mike Hutton

# PROFILE

Yorkshire born **Ben Bransby** is one of Britain's top all-round climbers with many classic first ascents from boulder problems, the grit and sea cliffs at home to the Alps, Yosemite and Patagonian big walls. But it all began on Yorkshire grit, born in 1979 a stone's throw from Almscliff where he did his first lead. He won the first ever Junior British Indoor Climbing competition and has done first ascents up to E9 but, big numbers aside, it is his talent and quest for adventure that shine through his achievements across the globe.

### How did you first get into climbing?

My mum and dad were climbers so I was born into it, almost literally - my mum was bouldering around at Almscliff only a few hours before I was born (on a little slab just left of Morrell's Wall) and I was born at home later that evening. We lived in North Rigton and I ended up learning to walk up at the crag. My dad (and mum) were in the Harrogate Mountaineering Club so I hung out with those guys. Did my first multi-pitch climb aged 5 and first lead aged 11.

### When you were at university you shared a house in Headlingley in the early 2000s with John Wainwright, Sam Whittaker and Adam Long, plus all the passing climbers like Leo Houlding who crashed there. It sounds like it was a particularly fun, crazy and productive (in climbing terms) time. What are some of your best memories of that period?

Definitely not that productive in terms of my degree! It was a great time with a bunch of like-minded people. We weren't competitive with each other but just through climbing with other good and bold climbers our standards rose and we didn't let the reputation of routes put us off. It was during this time that we started to make the breakthrough into onsighting E7 a little bit more regularly. Leo was particularly impressive as he would just drop into the scene and be operating at the top straight away - we were all climbing on the grit week in week out but for him it was just flying visits. He was (and obviously is still) a really great technical climber but he was supremely confident in his ability - this was before he had a few bad falls and he was pretty good at bouncing.

### What were the more significant ascents you and that gang did during that time?

I can't really remember! Onsight/ground-ups of things like Strangeness, Deathwatch, Snap Decision, Marrowbone Jelly...

### During that time John Wainwright remembers you climbing Eternal, then down climbing on lead and taking the gear out, and then you flashing Carmen Picasso, the two classic Dunne routes at Gorple. Do you remember that day?

It just felt like a normal day out for us. A crowd of us headed up to Gorple and I think

**BEN BRANSBY**

*Grit era: Late 1990s/2000s*

*Top grit ascents: A famously productive spree whilst at Leeds University in 1999 saw a host of hard extreme first ascents including The Chisel (E7 6c), Rod's Roof (E7 6b) and King of the Snakes (E4 6b) at Brimham; Right Cheeky (E7 6b) and Jack be Nimble (E4 6c) at Almscliff; and Quark Quack (E7 6b) and A Comedy Moment (E6 6a) at Caley, plus others at the likes of Ilkley and flashing Carmen Picasso (E8 6c) at Gorple in 2000. Later on Bransby returned to Rylstone in 2009 and bagged the prize boulder problem Lanny Bassham (Font 8a+).*

about five or six of us flashed Eternal (E7 at that time). When I did it I didn't fancy getting my boots wet walking down so reversed it. Dave MacLeod was down trying Carmen. He had been down a few weeks earlier and was getting ready for the headpoint. He climbed up to the lip and placed a little micro wire and down climbed. I asked if it would be ok to have a little look. I was a little concerned about putting Dave off so said I would leave his wire in and just be quick. I then flashed it. Don't remember much about it really. I think it was one of those times when you fully focus on the climbing and the fear/fall don't even enter your head. Once I set off I was just thinking about the climbing not about doing the route, whether to commit, what the gear was like etc. After I had done it I felt a bit dodgy about the pre-placed wire so I re-lead up to that point and placed the wire and down climbed - so I felt happy that I could have done this before I lead it.

**What was the prevailing ethic on Yorkshire grit at that time?**
For us it was ground-up/onsight. Adam felt pretty strongly about this - he said 'top roping is cheating' and after top roping one route as a teenager he never top roped on grit again. For the rest of us it was less of on issue - sure we thought it was a better style but we were happy to headpoint too. It was more an issue of us being a bit lazy - lots less effort/smaller rucksacks needed to flash or solo things. Bouldering pads were also starting to appear which opened up a lot of the shorter solos to becoming quite safe and even if only in your head made bigger routes that bit safer.

**What's your favourite Yorkshire grit crag?**
Almscliff as it is so full of memories for me - both my time as a youth getting into climbing and the excitement of it all but also from when I moved back to Leeds for uni and was part of the vibrant Yorkshire grit scene of the late 90s/early 00s. I also enjoy the more remote places - Rylstone, Simon's Seat, etc it feels like a completely different place, so much less travelled and quieter and some real gems of routes hidden up there.

**How would you describe Almscliff climbing to the first-time visitor?**
'Arms cliff', great rough rock, steep and thuggy but don't be too much of a brute as there is often a bit of cunning to make things easier - don't worry a local will be along soon to show you the knack. Many classic problems and routes and even more eliminates. A good bet when the weather is a little poor.

**Favourite routes or problems at Almscliff?**
All of them! A bit of a boring choice but Great Western was a pretty special moment for me. I led it when I was 11 and it was one of my first HVS's. I remember being really keyed up for it - I knew some of the beta from talking about it with my dad and his mates. I think my dad first lead it when it was climbed with just a sling over the spike and no gear on the traverse. I pretty much worked my way up through the grades at Almscliff so I ended up doing most of the classics when they were close to my limit so all pretty memorable. Z Climb, Black Wall, Demon Wall, etc were all done in my first summer of leading.

Ben Bransby elegantly poised on **Halcyon Daze** (E2 5c). Page 226
Photo: David Simmonite

# PROFILE

**The majority of classic hard new lines on Yorkshire grit have been climbed. How do you see the Yorkshire grit scene in the future - is it bigger numbers or more going to be about doing existing stuff in a more pure style?**
For me the ground-up/highball approach seems the obvious direction. As you say, there are far fewer new lines to do so the emphasis should be on improving style and the most obvious improvement is to do without the top rope inspection.

**You claimed the prize of Lanny Bassham at Rylstone in 2009. What drew you to that project and was anyone else trying it at the time?**
I had the line in my head ever since I did Cocoa Team back in 2000 or so. I had been bouldering a lot in 2007/08 (largely due to young daughter so less time for routes) but by 2009 had a bit more time and energy and felt I needed a big project. This fitted the bill. I didn't think it was possible the first time up looking at it but gave it another visit and did most of the top but still felt a bit unsure about the bottom. I had about eight sessions on it before the ascent. Slowly it all pieced together but in the two or three weeks leading up to the ascent I was really busy and didn't get to go up or even climb locally but by this point I was completely obsessed by it, so all I could do was diet! Then did it first go next time up.

**What are the moves like?**
Classic compression moves (squeezing) up a rounded prow. Lots of slopey sidepulls on either side of the prow with just a couple of better pockets on it. Quite high - it is nice to have a few mats.

**Why did you call it Lanny Bassham?**
I was reading Jerry Moffatt's book Revelations at the time and reading about his diets (hence me having one) and some of his mental training. Jerry read a book called 'With Winning in Mind' about mental preparation and as all I could do in the weeks before the climb was visualise it. I called it after the guy who wrote the book.

**You've obviously climbed far and wide across the globe from outcrops to big walls and the Alps. Do you have any future things you'd like to still do on Yorkshire grit?**
A few classics I would love to repeat - New Statesman and Reservoir Dogs. Have had lead attempts on both. Fell off near the start of New Statesman and right at the end of Reservoir Dogs. Need to finish them off.

**Interview by Andy McCue**

# BRIMHAM - Turtle Rock

A few metres further west is the rocky tower, **Turtle Rock**, with perched boulders on top; a tipped block forms a chimney cleft with the previous buttress. Those who think climbing isn't a spectator sport have never climbed *Halcyon Daze* on a bank holiday.

**38 The Turtle Rocks Chimney** VD 3c  9m  ★
Uber offwidth action to exit the narrowing chimney. Don't be alarmed if you find an over confident day-tripping teenager wedged in there (take a big sling to make the most of this in situ gear). If you've eaten too many pies, head out under the roof to the ledge for an alternate finish. The widening chimney on the opposite side of the tilting block gives a nice climb and a lovely beginners line at the entrance (**Halcyon Chimney** M 2c ★). The scrambling descent loops further inside.

**39 Cantilever Pinnacle** E1 5c  9m
From the front face of the boulder make thin, bold moves up and leftwards to the obvious thread (this can be pre-placed by squirming through a hole from behind). Pass this to the ledge, and totter up the groove to the top.
*Tony Barley  1965*

**40 Halcyon Daze** E2 5c  9m  ★
'The' route for playing to the crowds at the picnic tables. Bold, technical and good fun. Float up the sculpted wall below the precariously stacked boulders. Photo on page 224.
*Al Manson (solo)  July 1988*

Moving around to the south side of Turtle Rocks is a collection of weird and wonderful routes; many are recent additions and some of the hardest at the crag.

**41 Runnel Trilogy No 1** E3 6c  9m  ★
Almscliff's *Rectum Rift* comes to Brimham. Elephant proctologists will be in their element. The hanging cleft to the right of *Halcyon Daze* is very hard to enter and not easy to leave. It can however be well protected with a little 'jiggery-pokery'.
*Ben Bransby  27th March 1999*

**42 Keystone Chimney** HS 4b  8m  ★★
An overlooked Brimham gem and one for the gymnasts. From inside the south end of the chimney climb up to the chockstone and arrange some gear. Now move down and bridge out in style to pull over it.
*Tony Marr, Mike Tooke  15th December 1996*

**43 King of the Snakes** E4 6b  6m  ★
Short sharp shock treatment. Gain the twin-pocketed feature right of *Keystone Chimney* and leave it on the left to an insecure and rounded finish.
*Ben Bransby  14th March 1999*

**44 King Snake** E3 6b  5m  ★
Tackle the twin-pocketed feature direct (wire in left pocket) to a venomous finish.
*Ben Bransby, Gaz Parry, Chris Savage  14th March 1999*

Yorkshire Gritstone

# Elephant Rock - BRIMHAM

The bold wall to the right has been climbed - **King Worm** at Font 6a with a nasty landing.

To the right is a tricky chipped scrambling descent. Moving right again to the cave are several short routes with a big feel. Hard as nails too.

**45 Jimmy's Crack**  E5 6c   7m   ☆
A frustrating test requiring a bit of gumption. The obvious undercut groove just right of the blank wall is gained with considerable difficulty.
*Gaz Parry 14th March 1999*

**46 The Chisel**  E7 6c   8m   ☆☆
Outrageous roundedness in a perilous position conspire to give a route requiring superhuman speed and ability. Make hard moves on ripples up the blunt arête to a sloper. Finish slightly right.
*Ben Bransby 27th March 1999*

**47 The Green Giant**  E7 6c   8m   ☆
More cold press levitation action on nothingness. A bulging start leads to two odd humps. Mantel these precariously and finish direct.
*Chris Savage, Ben Bransby  14th March 1999*

**48 Crack of Bof**  E1 5c   8m   ☆
Dig deep baby! The hideous green crack. After an easy start the continuation is safe, hard and painful. Fun.
*Ben Bransby  14th March 1999*

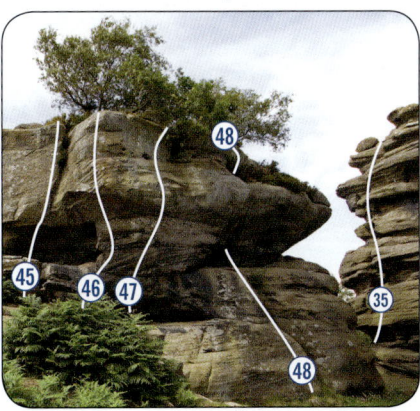

### Elephant Rock
Returning back west to the track, 15m south of Halcyon Daze/Turtle Rock (i.e. away from the house) is one of the last pieces of rock at Brimham to receive its first recorded climbs having never been included in a guidebook before. The block has a 'trunk' like feature at its north-east corner. Routes start on the west side and the descent is down the northern cleft.

**49 Jumbo Jam**  S 4a   8m   ★
The delightful bouldery crack facing the footpath.
*Tony Marr, Alan Taylor, Mike Tooke, F. Fitzgerald  23rd May 1999*

**50 Footprints in the Butter**  E1 5a   8m
To the right, gain the two small pockets in the overhang and surmount the lip slightly to the left for an easier finish.
*James Sample  25th August 2001*

Almscliff to Slipstones

Neil Kershaw reaching the punch-line on **Joker's Flake** (Font 6c+), E2 5c. Page 291
Photo: Simon Panton

Dancing Bear - **BRIMHAM**

## The Northern Pinnacles

### Dancing Bear Area

Most famous for its shape, the climbs are trickier than they look. Descent is by abseil or by following the polish back down. Quietly lurking in this cul-de-sac, just north of The Dancing Bear, is one of the hardest routes on grit.

**1 Dancing Bear**  VD 3b   7m   ★★
Oddly delicate to start and rather thuggish to finish. Waltz up the polish on the west face to belay off a handy horn on the east face. A lovely pinnacle tick.

**2 Zig-Zag Bear**  S 4a   8m
Saunter up to the horizontal break using the pockets. Traverse left and pull up using sloping holds to a large ledge. Now over the top on large jugs.
*Adrian Dye, Paul Avenell  27th May 2004*

**3 Dancing Bear Variant**  HVD 4a   7m   ★
This interesting route takes the awkward crack and shallow corner, finishing rightwards.
*Unknown  1996*

Immediately north of the Dancing Bear is a modern day problem up the east-facing undercut prow.

**4 Take a Bough**  Font 7b
A classic problem up the prow (the tree has now gone). Start just to the right of the nose and continue to a committing top move at the peak.
*Tom Peckitt  Nov 2010*

North again, just across from the prow, pay homage to Brimham's hardest offering.

**51 Mammoth**  E2 6a   8m
Climb the short flake under a roof, which is gained using either a cunning technique or a 'mammoth' reach. Pull over (hole on the left takes a cam) and continue over the next bulge on flutings.
*Tony Marr (un-seconded)  13th June 1999*

**52 Tusk Chimney**  S 4b   8m
The interesting chimney to the right. Finish up the crack.
*Mike Tooke, Frank Fitzgerald, Alan Taylor, T. Marr 23rd May 1999*

**53 Mastodon**  E2 6a   6m
From the rock shelf at the right end of the sculpted wall, climb up via a teardrop-shaped fault and two holes to the break. A bit thin. Escape rightwards.
*Alan Taylor, Tony Marr  11th July 1999*

From the main track to the west of Elephant Rock, head north towards the house. As the track joins the road that runs in front of the walled enclosure in front of the house, go left (west) and follow the road behind the garage built into the rock. Here squats the Dancing Bear buttress.

Almscliff to Slipstones

# BRIMHAM - Tender Homecoming

**5 Eyes Left**  HVS 5b   6m
The short arête right of the descent.
*Nic Kidd   March 1988*

**6 Tender Homecoming**  E8 7a   9m   ★★
The thriller up the pillar. An unrelenting, desperate journey up the technical arête. An amazing lead for the day; all the more impressive since Dixon broke his heel on the first go, only to return and claim Brimham's hardest route to date. Originally started on the left then climbed on the right-hand side. A hold has broken and it has now been climbed on the left-hand side by Tom De Gay. A good cam in a pocket at half-height helps, for a while anyway. Surely now a candidate for the highball cognoscenti to step forward and give it some serious attention.
*Nick Dixon   7th April 1990* ✦

**7 Eyes Right**  HVS 5c   6m
The arête to the right is bold with a landing that doesn't bear thinking about.
*Steve Rhodes   March 1988*

Hidden in the trees 40m west, across the path, down the slope, and just above the prominent pinnacles of *Black Chipper*, is a chipped east facing slab and a handful of green chimney-cum-crack climbs (Slanting Chimney Buttress). The highball left edge of the slab is **Essence of Cool** (Font 4) whilst the slab centre is **Dark Deed** (Font 3). 6m east is **Slanting Chimney** (S 4a). Variations exist here both within and to either side of the chimney at Severe and VS. The dirty corner-crack and rounded wall to the right is **Mr & Mrs Hemmingway** (HVS 5b).

### Indian's Turban

From the main track west of the Dancing Bear, head north for 200m to an outcrop of small buttresses on the right-hand side of the path. Often overlooked in favour of other areas at Brimham, the Indian's Turban is a great area for climbers operating in the Severe to VS grade. A little imagination is required in escaping the top of the boulders. Belays are fine for the south-west pinnacle but the routes finishing from the north-west need care with the belay (there is a thin flake but, if unsure, it's best to traverse to the gap). Descent is a bugger of a slither down the cleft or, more sensibly, by abseil.

The implausibly perched boulder next to the path is *The Druid's Idol*, a useful landmark for this area. Climbing on this unique feature is banned. An unusual pair of blocks known as **Boat Rock** and the **Yoke of Oxen**, sit immediately behind the Idol and contain a couple of fun technical traverses and a reachy arête.

Indian's Turban - **BRIMHAM**

**1 Barnacle Bill** Font 3+
A surprise package and one of the best problems around for the grade. Not so short but sweeeeet.

**2 Capsize** Font 6a
From sitting, traverse the low break from right-to-left concentrating on your footwork all the way. Finish up the arête on its right-hand side. Committing and good. The arête (**Boat Arête**, Font 6a) alone is worth a go if you're not too hot on sideways movement.

**3 The Yoke of Oxen** Font 5+
Traverse the boulder at mid-height from right-to-left. Enjoy those features all the way. Delicate footwork and a bit of cunning is required unless you have a monster span.

Just 15m south-east are the main routes on the unusual pinnacles. The first climb starts on the north end nose.

**4 The Grouch** Font 7b
The left prow from a sitter. Use the block to get established and travel via slopers and a seam to mantel it on the left.
Photo on page 214.
*Dave Cowl*

**5 Indian's Arête** VS 5b   8m   ★
The well-positioned northern arête is accessed by an appalling struggle up the cleft (Font 5+ to the ledge). Follow the arête to finish on magnificent flutings. Starting on the left is a nice protectable S 4a ★ (care required to protect the second though) and more in keeping with the climb. If you want a greater challenge, the sit-down start to the ledge is **Born Again** (Font 7a+).
*Tony Barley, Robin Barley 1962; BA: Andy Swann* ✦

**6 Pounce** Font 7c
The next overhanging prow to the right, again tackled from a sitter. From the break climb direct via a dynamic move to the rail, then finish by throwing as much of yourself over the top as possible. Escape by crawling left to find the easy descent.
*Andy Swann 2005*

**7 Ponce** Font 7c+
Sit-down start. Traversing left on poor holds to connect into *Pounce*. Mega.
*Andy Swann*

**8 Indian's Turban West** VS 4b   8m   ★
Follow the scoops to a vague corner up high. Good gear low down, bold higher up and reach dependent. The direct start gives a 5a variation.
*Pre-1957* ✦

**9 The Jewel in the Crown** E2 5c   8m
From the obvious hole, tackle the wall direct. The crux is a long reach for the rounded edge of the final break.
*Andy Moss   April 1998*

Almscliff to Slipstones

# BRIMHAM - Indian's Turban

### 10 **West Indian's Turban Route** S 4a  8m  ★
Climb the chimney crack between the pinnacles on the west side. Easier than the original way on the eastern side. Take a big cam or throw caution to the wind, go light and earn HS.
*Tony Marr, Mike Tooke  22nd September 1996*

### 11 **Fist Fight**  Font 4+
On the next block right, the green and problematic flake crack. There's a clue in the name.
*Tony Marr, Mike Tooke  31st July 2007*

### 12 **Argy Bargy**  HVD 4a  5m  ★
The enjoyable crack on the left side of the wall. If only it was longer.

### 13 **Jibber**  HS 4b  6m  ★
No need for jibber jabber on this steady wall, fool. Take the pleasant flakes and pockets up the right side.

### 14 **Harry's Crack**  VS 4c  6m
Pull up into the steep overhanging corner to a rest below the difficulties. Arrange some gear and get stuck in.
*1970* ✦

The highball problem with a bad landing is (a) **Raj** (Font 5)

that ascends the shallow corner, steps left and follows the rising break to finish.

### 15 **Board to Tears**  E3 6a  8m  ★
A unique experience. On the east side of the main pinnacle use the obvious flake to gain height. This was originally climbed using yet another long-gone notice board on the right, which provided a crucial hold. The remnant bolts can be used for protection, if you trust them. Photo on page 188.
*Steve Rhodes, Nic Kidd, Mick Ryan, Ed Douglas 12th June 1988* ✦

### 16 **Indian's Turban Route**  HS 4a  8m
A puzzling route, but the difficulties are short lived. Take the opposite side of the chimney crack between the boulders.
*Pre-1957* ✦

Yorkshire Gritstone

## 17 **Zero Option**  E2 5c   7m
Take the centre of the steep east wall direct to the small black hole in the break below the top and step up to finish on a small flake.
*Tony Marr, Mike Tooke, Peter Shawcross  22nd September 1996*

## Pinky Area
The Pinky boulder, a slumbering sloping giant block, can be found 110m north-east at the top end of the track on the left. Much fun can be had on this boulder and the easier problems surrounding it. Wonderful views and a great place to watch the sun go down.

## 1 **Pinky**  Font 7a+
Now we're talkin'. Start on the sloping break and climb the groove direct. Come on! (Font 8a from a sitter).
*Andy Swann 2001*

## 2 **Pinky Traverse Flake Finish**  Font 7b
Start as for *Pinky* and tenuously follow the sloping break rightwards. Don't go around the arête, aim for the high rounded flake just before it, and use this to top-out. Continuing around the arête to finish up and right ((a) **Pinky Full Traverse**) is Font 7c+.
*Andy Swann*

## 3 **Perky**  Font 6b+
From a sit-down start gain the massive flake and go right, to finish up the right-hand side of the arête.

In an alcove behind the boulder is a clutch of compact problems.

## 4 **Mike's Problem**  Font 7c+
The hanging arête for have-a-go heroes.

## 5 **Piglet Wall**  Font 4
Savour the neat little wall.

*Al Manson on **True Grit** (E4 6b). Page 241*
*Photo: Manson Collection*

# BRIMHAM - Pinky Area

**8 Ripple Traverse** Font 5
Traverse the many ripples from left-to-right to earn the grade.

**9 Raspberry Ripple** Font 4
Straight up the featured wall.

Looking east across the moor is the obvious **Mushroom Throne**, approximately 500m away. A pleasant walk across the moor (can be boggy in places). Several climbs exist here, none exceeding 5m. Standing downhill from these with the obvious fin to the right, the first route starts in the gully of the small buttress with the blunt prow on the left. **Sideline** (Font 4+) climbs the wall just right of a short crack/hole. **Cold Play** (HVS 5a) starts beneath the curving ramp and follows this to the top. **Jamboree** (VD) takes the filthy crack in the next gully. **Scallywag** (VS 5a) tackles the hanging groove in the gully, left of the right fin. (*All routes Tony Marr (solo) 26th February 2003*)

**6 Piglet Arête** Font 5
The arête is best from a sit-down start.

**7 Minidigit** Font 6a
Climb the middle of the wall on super rock.

Just east along the track on the left is a wonderfully featured short wall.

## The Northern Edges

A different animal altogether from the fun loving tourist trap of the pinnacles. A premier venue concealed from the masses. There's not a wealth of bouldering 'up top end' but what it lacks in problems is more than made up for in routes. Individual buttresses dominated by fine cracklines, soaring arêtes and sumptuous slabs, are

Keeper's Crack Area

From Playout & Fag Slab

# Keeper Crack - BRIMHAM

interspersed with short pleasant wooded walks that are useful for getting ones breath back if opting for a day on crack(s). Enough starred routes to keep you returning for years to come, or for at least the time it takes most to climb to the top of *Charming Crack*.

The first two areas, the far end of Keeper Crack and Playout, are not representative of the climbing in this section of Brimham. The bracken can become a jungle in summer and these areas are best visited early in the year. Some spots are particularly vegetated and are best climbed on…well, never. Although we'd never admit it, things get an awful lot better the further south you go.

## Keeper Crack Area

From the Pinky area, go due east 50m to the end of the main track. Go north-east here, downhill on a faint track that bends round to the east as it flattens out (250m). Up the hill 30m to the right is a small collection of buttresses, home to a traditional VS crack that's worth the walk (though in midsummer it's a fern jungle).

**1 The Brute**  E1 5c  5m
From the gully at the rear of the *Fook Nose* buttress tackle the short hanging offwidth crack with the chockstone.
*Tony Marr, Mike Tooke  4th April 2007*

**2 Detour**  HVD 4a  14m
Monkey up the short easy crack to the terrace and walk along left, finishing up the wide corner-crack.
*Pre-1970* ✦

**3 Fook Nose**  E3 5c  8m
Unpleasant climbing up to the unfinished crack. The crack stops a metre from the top – you shouldn't (but bet you do).
*Paul Ingham, Nick Dixon  1982*

**4 Look No Hands**  E2 6a  7m
Mantel onto the thin break and 'go-big' for the ledge above. A friend went in the crack on the first ascent.
*Andy Moss, Mike Boyd  June 1999*

**5 Keeper Crack**  VS 4c  8m  ★
The cliff-splitting crack passing the chockstone is a tough customer. A right-hand finish is 5a.
*Allan Austin, Brian Evans  1956*

**6 Dennis the Menace**  E2 6a  7m
Go around the buttress nose to the hanging crack on the wall. Hard to get into, hard to get out of and hard to protect.
*Steve Brown, Paul Ingham  1982*

On a small buttress 10m right and uphill are some short climbs. **Pantomime** (Font 4+) is the entertaining left-hand crack, **Right Pantomime** (Font 6a) the right crack and **Capped Corner** (Font 4).

# BRIMHAM - Playout Area

### Playout Area (♦).

If approaching from Keeper's Crack area, head back south-west towards the Pinky area but keep an eye out for a faint track that leads west into the woods before the path steepens (170m). Over a ruined dry stone wall on the left is the start of the Playout Area. If approaching from the Pinky Area, drop down the hill as if heading for Keeper's Crack, but after 70m, go west into the woods on the faint track mentioned above.

Sadly this area is heavily wooded, faces north and only with a heavy dose of napalm is ever to become attractive to climbers. This track ultimately leads to Fag Slab Area which, after passing this lot, will feel like the world's best climbing spot. With all that said, it is worth checking out *Britt* (E1 5b), a bold challenge and usually clean.

(a) **Crackology** (HVS 5a) the awkward wide crack. (b) **Brown's Crack** (HVS 5a) the vegetated hanging crack just right. (c) **Bratt** (E2 6a) the short crack, a monster span to a pocket and a final rockover.

### 1 Chinese Crack  VS 4c    8m  ★
The corner-crack is a challenge. Cut right to finish.
*Allan Austin, Brian Evans  24th April 1958*

### 2 Britt  E1 5b    9m  ★
A good bold route. Climb the rib on the left of the narrow buttress until a knob can be reached to pull into the groove.
*Tony Barley (solo)  1963*

### 3 Britt Right-Hand  E1 5b    8m
Climb the buttress immediately right of *Britt* on good holds to a big sidepull/undercut. Move left to finish up *Britt*.
*Paul Clough (solo)  November 2000*

(d) **Blind's Crack** (E2 5b) the nasty crack right of the prow. (e) **The Grunch** (E1 5c) the leaning offwidth cleft at the back-left of the gully. The chimney to the right has been climbed. (f) **Playout** ('Filthy') The low angled prow, from the left. (g) **Fallout** (VS 4c) The scoopy slabs, far right of the prow. (h) **Wayout** (MVS 4c) Layback or chimney to the block and move left to finish on top of it. The two cracks in the hidden bay are Severes. (i) **Flake Out** (VS 4c) The flakes to a ledge and then up the cracks above. (j) **Half Crown Corner** (VS 5a) up the groove. (k) **Lilo** (HVS 5a) up the broken cracks below the capping roof then traverse left under the overhang. (l) **Deep Chimney** (S). (m) **Cubicle Crack** (VD) the wide crack and corner. (n) **Chicane** (E3 6a) up the short corner in the right side of the bay to reach a handrail. Follow this right under the prow into a scoop and finish with a very nasty mantelshelf. (o) **Fat Belly Gut Bucket** (HVS 5c) a direct line through *Chicane*. Climb the arête left of the prow to the break, step left and head direct to the top. (p) **Control Your Inappropriate Actions** (E3 6b) the technical slab using the left arête. Make a long reach from the break to finish. (q) **For Pete's Sake** (E2 6a) The slab and pocket behind the tree. 20m right across the wide gully is: (r)

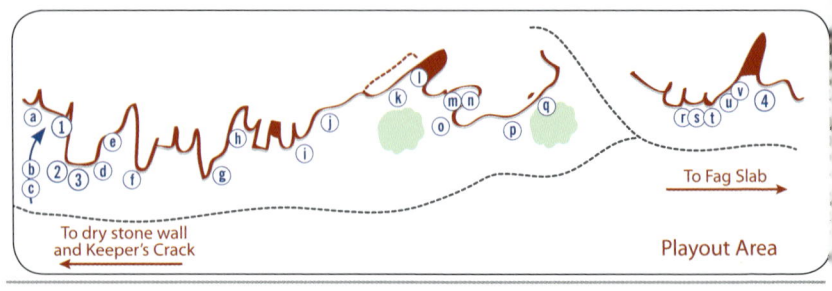

Bellyporker's Progress - **BRIMHAM**

**Wilt** (VS 5a) the crack splitting the overhang. (s) **Tilt** (HVS 5c) the hanging groove. (t) **Dyson** (VD) the wide crack in the arête. (u) **Vax** (VD) The flake and groove (v) **Hoover** (VS 4b) the thin flake to the right. The chimney at the back can be climbed at about HVS.

### 4 Mae West's Rib  E4 6b   10m   ☆
The rib and crack gives an interesting problem with good protection.
*Steve Rhodes, Greg Rimmer   10th June 1988*

### 5 Hourglass Chimney  VS 5a   11m
The chimney to the right.
*Brian Evans, Allan Austin, Brian Fuller, Doug Verity  1956*

### 6 Bellyporker's Progress  E7 6c   10m   ☆
A harrowingly steep offering, which is sadly green and doesn't see the attention it warrants. Climb the left side of the steep prow to the break and onward to the top. An early escape at the break gives an excellent Font 7b+ problem in its own right.
*Nick Dixon, Andy Popp  19th May 1990*  ✦

William Welsh on **The Titfield Thunderbolt** (Font 7b+). Page 253.
Photo: Daglish Photography

Richard Connors emerges from the shadows for some welcomed warmth on **The Hattery** (HVS 5a). Page 248
Photo: Mike Hutton

239

# BRIMHAM - Fag Slab

### Fag Slab Area
Around the prow and into daylight is a superb area with several popular climbs in the Severe to HVS range. It's worth the walk just for the classics of *Allan's Crack, Fag Slab* and *Fag Slab Variant*. A great place to end the day.

**7  Allan's Crack Direct**  HVS 5b   11m   ★
An enjoyable route with much food for thought. Balance up the slab using polished holds to a foothold on the left arête, then climb direct.
*Les Brown, Tony Marr  1967*

**8  Allan's Crack**  VS 4c   12m   ★★★
Pure gritstone class. An absorbing natural line, good protection and strenuous technicality, beautifully blended together. A hard start (getting harder with polish) gains the left slanting corner-crack. Commit to pumpy laybacks until it is possible to truck right and finish up the wall. Make haste. (a) **Sally Would** (E2 5c) starts on the slab, climbs directly through the overhang to finish direct. (b) **Allan's Crack Right-Hand** (VS 5a, ★) takes *Allan's Crack* to the first break and trends up and right to finish at the top right corner of the final wall.
*Allan Austin, Brian Evans, Doug Verity, Brian Fuller  1955* ✦

**9  Little Funnel**  VS 5a   8m   ★
The narrowing chimney is bridged to rattly jams that improve with height. Well-protected. The inside of the chimney has been climbed to escape between the chockstones, **Funnelology** (S 4a).
*c1955* ✦

**10  Fag Slab**  S 4a   8m   ★★
This popular classic groove is tough and well-protected to start then bold but steady above (if you keep your head together). **Nicorette** (HVS 5c) is a blinkered eliminate which goes directly up the wall between *Fag Slab* and *Woodbine*.
*c1955/56* ✦

A scrambling descent is available to the right.

**11  Woodbine**  HVS 5b   8m   ★
Delightfully delicate and bold climbing up the technical slab. Increasingly bouldered out, but by no means an easy ride.
Photo on page 246.
*Duncan Drake  22nd August 1980*

**12  Fag Slab Variant**  VS 4c   8m   ★★
An excellent pitch that teeters up the left-leaning groove.

# Gigglin' Crack - BRIMHAM

Can be the scene of much wobbling. Small gear is available but is awkward to place.
*Brian Evans (solo) January 1956*

### 13 Silkcut  E3 6c  8m  ★
Make a very hard move up right, over the overlap, to stand in the break. Step left and smear up to a higher break, then pockets, to a sapling.
*Paul Clarke  23rd April 1984*  ✦

### 14 Fag End  S 4a  8m  ★
Spicy. Start at the recess and follow the crack. When that peters out, inhale deeply and make bold moves on the chipped slab above to the break and beyond.
*Harold Barraclough  1959*  ✦

### 15 Smoke Ring  HVS 5a  27m
A bit of a drag. Guaranteed to see you stoned if you attempt it on a busy bank holiday (and not in the happy way). A leftward horizontal outing from the upper break of *Fag End* to join *Allan's Crack*. Follow this into the top of *Hourglass Chimney*.
*Tony Barley  3rd August 1975*

### 16 Capstan Full Strength  E3 5c  8m  ★
Good climbing with a bold start. Step up left from the foot of the arête and climb slopers to below the overhanging top block. Surmount this by use of a pocket. Low in the grade. (Aka: **Senior Service**).
*Francis Holland & Peter Budd  1993*  ✦

### 17 Filter Tip  E2 5c  7m
The green arête offers a bold micro route. From the ledge in the gully make a couple of tricky moves low down.
*Derek Hargreaves, Lianne Jay  c1981*

To reach the next two climbs, walk through the cave of *Little Funnel* and turn left into the gully behind Fag Slab. The left-hand crack with an awkward step at mid-height is **Finders Keepers** (VS 5a) and the right-hand corner-crack is **Hyde and Seek** (VS 4c).

## Gigglin' Crack Area
Around the corner from *Filter Tip* is an area that holds two crack testpieces within metres of one another: *True Grit* and *Gigglin' Crack*. Two strong natural line, yet very different customers. Routes that give Brimham a tough reputation. It's taken 320 million years of geological movement to shape Brimham so you'll be waiting a long time before the width of *Gigglin' Crack* changes to something more friendly. Just go for it.

### 18 The Shootist  E3 6a  6m
Scramble over boulders on the left until below a green and slimy wall. Pull up to a small overlap, step over this and commit to the top. (a) **Squat Rocket** (E4 6b) climbs the wall just right to a slot in the overlap. Gain the jug and the undercut pocket out right and use these with imagination to make the huge reach to the edge above. Finish out right.
*Al Manson 1978 (Shootist); Dave Sutcliffe 28th Oct 2011 ('Squat)*

### 19 Narrowing Chimney  VS 5a  8m
The block-filled chimney is climbed until forced out at a constricting finish. Originally climbed inside at VD by a very small person. Good luck trying...
*Pre-1970*  ✦

### 20 True Grit  E4 6b  11m  ★★
A wild west ride that'll test the mettle of the young gunslingers and old roosters alike. The thin crack is a real finger-mangler and is particularly tough to start. If you are lucky enough to reach the ledge, step left and finish up the wider left-hand crack. (b) **True Grit - Direct Start** (E4 6c) tackles the technical hanging rib to the left of the original crack. Photo on page 233.
*Ken Wood, Mike Mortimer  18th June 1970*  ✦

Almscliff to Slipstones

# BRIMHAM - Pig Traverse

### 21 The Snuffer   HVS 5b   11m
Good value. Start well inside the deep chimney and back-and-foot out to gain a jam and ledge on the left. A direct start is possible that starts at, and skirts, the jaws of the chimney at E1 5c.
*Baz Ingle, Hugh Banner, Alan Clarke  1961*  ✦

### 22 Gigglin' Crack   E6 6c   10m   ★★★
Brimham's best hard offwidth will bring tears to the eyes, of both laughter and pain! Commit to full-body udging up the obvious overhanging crack. Not much hilarity involved but facing left and opting for a straddling / humping combo up the arête may somehow make it possible to squirm into the depths of the crack higher up. The ones giggling will be the onlookers. Enjoy with friends.
Photo below.
*Jerry Peel, Gill Peel  1976*  ✦

## Pig Traverse Area
Immediately right of *Gigglin' Crack* and onto the slab side of the buttress are a number of popular routes, well worth seeking out. Classic technical slab routes abound, for both the mortal and the powerful pad masters. *Pig Traverse* (HS) is the route of the buttress and good value for all comers. Heed the bird restrictions if in place. Often it's home to nesting Tawny Owls that love adding climbers eyeballs to the diet of their young.

### 23 Pig Traverse   HS 4b   12m   ★★
A wonderful rising traverse to a show-stopping step out of the corner under the overlap. Grunt up the broken cracks to the roof and follow your snout right along the fault to the arête. Finish easily on the right or boldly on the left.
*c1956*  ✦

### 24 Reach for the Sty   E5 6b   9m   ★
A real frightener of a route that requires a huge span to reach safety. Follow *Pig Traverse* to the overhang and step up left to the finger pocket. Crank hard on this to reach the larger pocket out left (crucial 1 slider, placed blind) and make a big move for the top.
*Martin Berzins, Craig Smith, Al Manson  17th April 1988*

### 25 Sow's That   E5 6b   9m   ★★
Another nerve jangler. Follow *Reach for the Sty* to the finger pocket in the overlap where powerful moves gain the slab. Trend up and rightwards to make a hard rockover to safety before anxiety levels go off the dial.
*Al Manson, Martin Berzins  19th April 1988*

### 26 Pig Slip Cow Punk   E6 6b   9m
Unbelievably bold and delicate movement up the slab and wall, crossing *Pig Traverse* to finish just right of *Sow's That*.
*Nick Dixon, A. Mclean, Alan Taylor  1st April 1990*

### 27 Pig's Ear   HVS 5b   9m
The right arête of the slab.
*Steve Rhodes (solo)  17th April 1988*

### 28 Long Funnel   HVD 3c   10m   ★
The chimney formed by the leaning block is bold to start. The stepped crack just left (D 3a) gives a possible descent.
*Brian Evans (solo)  14th April 1957*

Jerry Peel on the first ascent of **Gigglin' Crack** (E6 6c).
Photo: Jerry Peel collection

Pig Traverse - **BRIMHAM**

**29 Pathos** E3 6a 8m ★★
A brilliant route with good protection where you need it.
A good contender for your first E3? Follow the corner to
the break, move right and tackle the left-hand crack to a
reachy finish. Photo on next page.
*Al Manson 1980*

**30 Si's Cheese Slice** E4 6c 10m ★
An eliminate that climbs the direct start to *Lithos*, then
climbs the wall between the cracks with gear in *Pathos*.
*Danny Coultrup 9th July 2008*

**31 Lithos** HVS 5b 9m ★★
Wonderfully delicate climbing with committing moves and
big swing potential if you have a wobble at the critical moment.
As for *Pathos*, but continue to traverse right to below
the right-hand crack and use this and the arête to finish.
*Mike Hammill or Al Manson 1976*

**32 Lithos Direct Start** E1 6b 8m
Desperately thin climbing leads to the bottom of the
crack and up.
*Al Manson pre-1976*

**33 Jelly Baby Wall** E4 6a 6m
Starts on the wall over on the right. Wobble up the wall via
a faint crack and step right to a good break to finish. Don't
bite off more than you can chew.
*Nic Kidd, Steve Rhodes 17th September 1989*

Between the *Lithos* wall and the *Mohole* buttress, set
back and behind two trees, is **Rush Hour** (HD 3b),
bridging the shallow chimney between flakes, and **Cosy
Corner** (VD 3c), the short corner just right.

**66 99**

I used a massive hex wedged in as high as
it would fit. I threaded the rope over the hex
and this was my only runner. I remember at
the time everyone climbed in Helly Hanson
fleece pants and a baggy fleece top which
would really stick to the rock. Them pants
made the difference!

Jerry Peel on the FA of **Gigglin' Crack**

243

# BRIMHAM - The Mohole

## The Mohole
Set back from the path and 15m on from *Lithos*, lies a short slabby wall of grit with an obvious hole (the Mohole) and a distinct groove on the front face. Worth stopping off for the committing *Mohole Arête* if nothing else.

### 34 Three Trees Crack  VS 4c   7m
Layback the crack. Needs very large gear to protect.
*Allan Austin, Brian Evans  1957*

### 35 Mohole  HVS 4c   9m   ★
Climb the crack until it is possible to hand-traverse right to the arête. Swing round this and then up to the hole. Finish direct.
*Robin Barley, Tony Barley  1963*

### 36 Mohole Arête  E1 5b   9m   ★
Good climbing with a real 'out-there' feel. Step up and right to gain the obvious foothold on the arête. Make a tenuous move around the arête and continue in an impressive position on its right-hand side. Not easy to protect and with a nasty landing.
*Tony Marr, Mike Tooke  18th June 2000*

### 37 Mohole Direct  E3 6b   7m
A very difficult entry can be made into the Mohole via a series of tiny edges leading up and left. Finish direct.
*Tony Marr, Mike Tooke  15th July 1992*

### 38 Hanging Groove  E1 5b   7m   ★
Follow the groove to a break and step left to the top.
*Mike Hammill  1976*

### 39 Flibbetigibbet  E3 6b   6m   ★
The wall and arête just right of *Hanging Groove*.
*Andy Watts, Nigel Baker  10th April 1999*

In the left wall of the next chimney (up the gully) is a flake with a vegetated finish **Hanging Flake** (HVS 5a, *Tony Barley pre-1970*).

## Charming Crack Area
Here it is. Lurking in the front of the corner just right of The Mohole is the tough crack that sees off most suitors. A testimony to the skill of 'The Master' and forever the subject of debate on the correct grade. A climb that epitomises the saying 'there's only two grades in climbing: those routes you can do, and those that you can't'.

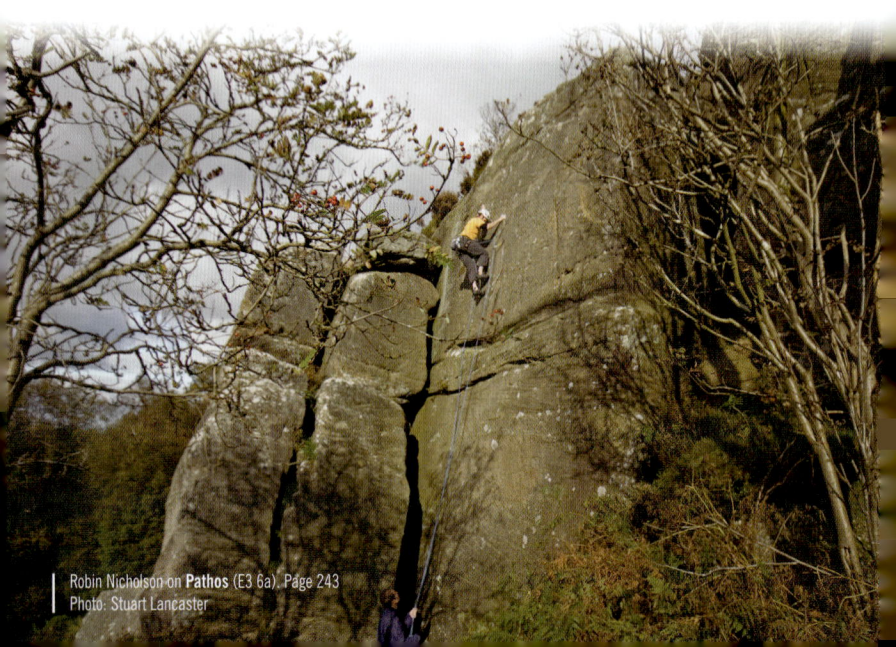

Robin Nicholson on **Pathos** (E3 6a), Page 243
Photo: Stuart Lancaster

Charming Crack - **BRIMHAM**

**40 Charming Chimney** HVS 4c 8m
The wide chimney, start inside and work outwards.
*Tony Barley 1972*

**41 Brutaliser** E3 5c 9m ☆
Always the bridesmaid, never the bride. A harder and often overlooked alternative to its adjacent sibling. The name says it all. Gut-busting climbing up the wide overhanging chimney.
*John Syrett 4th November 1970* ✦

**42 Charming Crack** E1 5c 9m ★★
Crack open the can of whoop ass! The teeth-gnashing, hand-mangling, pride-wrecking crack of the crag. Winner of the prize for 'spanking-per-inch-of-upward-movement', and yet a fond favourite. Tackle the overhanging bulging crack with gusto.
*Joe Brown 1958*

**43 White Wash** E3 5c 9m ☆
The steep gritty slab right of *Charming Crack* past a pocket to a break. Pull up on pebbles to a bold and reachy finish.
*Martin Berzins, Chris Sowden 1976* ✦

**44 Mantelshelf Corner** VS 4b 8m ☆
Alternating between the arête and the rounded ledges, boldly climb the right-hand side of the steep slab.
*Allan Austin, Brian Evans, D. Verity, B. Fuller, Jennifer Ruffe 1957*

The corner-crack in the wide cleft to the right of *Mantelshelf Corner* has been climbed using old-school techniques, called **Jam and Blast** (S 4a). Across the gully on a tree-hidden lonely pinnacle is a neat excursion.

**45 Green Prioress** E1 5b 9m ★
Climb the crack in the front of the buttress to a large pocket on the right (possible 10m thread runner). Move up left to a ledge which is then relinquished with a degree of boldness.
*Ron Kenyon, D. Bowers 1978*

### Corner Crack Area

Across the way (6m right (west) from *Green Prioress*) is a wall with three huge pockets. Following this round to the right is a small area with routes that climb out of a pit.

**46 Classic Bagger** E1 5b 6m ★
Follow the three holes to the arête. Alternatively the top can be reached from the second hole (but this only warrants two-thirds of a tick).
*Chris Hamper, Nick Hallam 1974*

**47 Lichen Wall** E3 5c 6m
A nasty little climb, originally graded HVS 5b! From a ledge up and left of *Corner Crack* climb the wall trending left to a horror mantelshelf.
*Nick Dixon, Paul Ingham 1982* ✦

Jon Pearson on **Woodbine** (HVS 5b). Page 240.
Photo: Fran Holland

Wedge Crack - **BRIMHAM**

### 48 Corner Crack  S 4a   9m  ★
Climb up the corner-crack moving round an overhang at half-height. The arête and crack above the overhang, finishing in *Corner Crack,* is **Here Be Dragons** (VS 5a).
*c1955/56* ✦

### 49 Games with the Nephfesch  E1 5c   7m
The arête is followed to the break, then make a long reach to rounded holds and the top.
*Steve Parker (un-seconded)   20th June 1994*

## Wedge Crack Area
Going west for a further 20m is another quiet backwater with an overpowering bulbous prow. A spot that would benefit from more attention to stop it from greening up.

### 50 Connoisseurs Corner  S 4b   8m
Climb (or bypass) the awkward short corner and from the ledge continue up the hanging corner-crack with interest.
*Tony Marr, Mike Tooke (FRA)   27th July 2005*

### 51 Charlie's Dilemma  E5 6a   9m  ☆
An under-appreciated, and extremely taxing offering from one of Yorkshire Grit's unsung heroes. The gnarly groove to the left of the impressive prow. Chimney up the groove to the first of two pockets. Climb to the second and step right onto a rounded ledge. Continue direct to a difficult finish.
*Iain Edwards, Tim Riley   29th July 1981*

### 52 Constrictor Chimney  VS 4c   12m
The top section of the chimney right of the large prow is a bit of a squeeze and can spit larger types out (S 4b if you escape right to various dirty exits).
*c1955/56* ✦

### 53 Boa Cracks  HVS 5b   11m
Undercut the arête and jam the crack, or is it the other way around? The groove to the right is similar and possibly slightly more pleasant.
*Robin Barley   1962*

### 54 Viper  HS 4b   8m
The V-groove looks harder than it is. Is better than it looks.
*Ken Jackson, Tony Marr, Ken Austin   18th March 1971*

### 55 Choked Chimney  HVD 4a   9m
Follow the corner to fight the chockstone, cleaning as you go.
*Brian Evans, Aileen Evans   1st January 1960*

### 56 Wedge Crack  E1 5b   8m
The narrow chimney requires a high expenditure of energy. Udging and grunting seem to help, so this is not a route to attempt in shorts and t-shirt.
*Jim Fullalove (aka Dan Boone)   mid-1960s*

The filthy bullet prow to the right contains (a) **Mad Hatter** (E1 5b). Start below the prow, step up right and then back left to gain and ascend the evergreen slab.

Walking west around the prow and in front of the *Hattery Arête* is a moss covered slab. The front face and right side have been climbed all over between VS and HVS.

Almscliff to Slipstones

**247**

# BRIMHAM - The Hattery

## The Hattery Area
A quality area, particularly in the HVS range, with top-notch routes for both slab enthusiast and crack muncher. The harder offerings are up there with the best too, *Grit Expectations* leading the charge. Being slightly more open to the sun than its neighbours, the better climbs here stay reasonably clean.

The stepped ridge moving left to a crux exit is **Old Hat**, HD 3b. Just right, the corner of the slab gives a descent.

### 57 The Hattery  HVS 5a  9m  ★★
A fine line with varied climbing and airy padding high up. Climb the arête to the break, step left and climb the bold wall above on pockets and layaways. Two variations exist: **The Hattery Direct** (E1 5c) takes the lower wall without the arête and **Hat Stand** (E2 5c) follows the *Direct* to the break then goes left to a pocket and straight up to finish right of the step. Photo on page 238.
*Tony Barley, Robin Barley  1966* ✦

### 58 The Hattery Arête  HVS 4c  9m  ★★
Another classic outing with exposed and balancey climbing directly up the arête. Start as for *The Hattery*. Continue straight up, passing the horizontal break and follow the arête to the top.
*George Broadhead  10th June 1973*

### 59 The Hattery Chimney  HS 4b  8m
The fine corner chimney immediately behind *The Hattery Arête*, passing behind the enormous chockstone; don't be fooled by appearances.
*Tony Marr, Mike Tooke (FRA)  27th July 2005*

### 60 Hat Trick  HVS 5b  8m
The steep central arête passing behind the enormous chockstone succumbs to old fashioned gritstone technique.
*Tony Marr, Mike Tooke (FRA)  3rd August 2005*

### 61 Running on Red  E2 6a  7m  ★
The wall left of the arête provides good climbing when clean. A difficult start leads left to a hole then steep, but easier, climbing to the top.
*Steve Rhodes, Al Manson  22nd June 1988*

### 62 Walk in Silence  E7 6c  10m  ★★
A classic natural line and a real character builder. Make quick frightening moves up the engrossing arête on its

248  Yorkshire Gritstone

## The Hattery - BRIMHAM

left side. Move around the arête at the top to finish. An unrelenting solo above a less than ideal drop zone.
*Matt Troilett (solo), Mick Johnston, Neil Herbert  19th March 2000*

### 63  Close to the Hedge   E4 6a   8m   ☆
A fine, scary and technical climb up the imposing arête. Climb to the hole (small wire thread). Step left on to the arête and make for the top.
*Al Manson  1977*

### 64  Hedgeup   E4 6a   7m   ☆
Quite a buzz. Take a direct line up the taxing wall. The hole (also used for *Close to the Hedge*) provides a good small wire thread. The continuation up the wall used a hand-placed peg and a poor nut in pockets to provide some solace on the first ascent.
*Dick Tong, Mick Johnson (both led)  2nd October 1997*

### 65  Last Crack   VS 4b   8m   ☆
The corner-crack provides a traditional test, especially in the second half.
*c1955/56* ✦

The crag drops back to form a recessed ledge known as **The Pulpit**.

### 66  Cracked Rib   VS 5a   8m
Swing onto the rib from the left side of *The Pulpit* and follow the crack. The rib can be gained direct from the ground at 5c.
*Brian Evans, Allan Austin, Jennifer Ruffe  6th October 1957*

### 67  Brief Crack   VS 4b   6m
Satisfying. The left-hand crack.
*c1955/56* ✦

### 68  Graft Crack   VS 4c   6m
Starting in *The Pulpit*, the right-hand crack. Often dirty.
*c1955/56* ✦

### 69  Serendipity   E3 5c   12m
Climb the short scruffy crack into *The Pulpit*. Gain the wall on the left from the right-hand side. Cross the notch and make a difficult move to reach the top of the sloping nose. Trend leftwards to escape right beneath the capstone.
*Tony Marr, Mike Tooke  27th August 1995*

### 70  Slippery Crack   VS 4b   12m   ★
Appearances can be deceptive. Heed the name and the grade. Huff and puff up the friendly sized fissure. Perseverance is key.
*c1955/56* ✦

# BRIMHAM - Hatter's Groove

**71 Grit Expectations** E4 6a  12m  ★★★
What larks! A bold but straightforward introduction leads into the short and subtle groove that will challenge your expectations. Begin at two head-height pockets and go up to the groove and its almost blind high wire placement. Use the groove and holds on the right to gain the break. A pocket above enables the top to be reached. Step right into *Hatter's Groove*. Photo on page 221.
*Al Manson  1975* ✦

**72 Troilett Wall** E5 6b  12m  ★
The sustained and intimidating left wall of *Hatter's Groove* provides an elegant, committing test. Climb the wall to a sloping hold just above mid-height. Make a tough move right to a pocket where you get the first protection (RP3 and Tricam 2). Commit to another hard move up, then eventually finish on the last moves of *Hatter's Groove*.
*Matt Troilett  4th April 2007*

**73 Hatter's Groove** HVS 5a  12m  ★★★
Trouser splitting, hand shredding, head banging of the highest order. A tough classic that will leave you with either fond memories or serious emotional scars. Make gymnastic moves up the green corner until forced left below the top block to an awkward exit. A good thread protects the finish but isn't easy to place. The ill-named (a) **Easy Exit** (VS 5a) follows the groove until a couple of metres below the top where it is possible to traverse onto *Right-Hand Arête*. An even harder finish is (b) **Hard Hat** (E1 5c) which shuffles right under the final capstone to a difficult mantelshelf escape.
*Allan Austin, Brian Evans, Ron Tyler (some aid) 22nd Jan 1956* ✦

**74 Grit Escape** HVS 5b  13m
Follow *Hatter's Groove* then go along the thin crack to the notch in the right arête. Tackle the short wall using the arête to join *Easy Exit*. Finish up the chimney on the right.
*Tony Marr, Mike Tooke  31st October 1993*

**75 Right-Hand Arête** HVS 5a  8m
Follow the arête until forced right.
*Ken Tilford  1981* ✦

The large crack to the right of *Hatter's Groove* is (c) **Lichen Chimney** (HVD 4a).

Yorkshire Gritstone

## Duggie's Dilemma - BRIMHAM

### Duggie's Dilemma Area
Follow the path for 50m west through the trees to two short faces with a distinct corner. This area can also be accessed easily from the upper path (i.e. the track that runs north between the Dancing Bear and Pinky Area) by walking down to the lower edge via a small gully located just before The Druids Writing Desk (the obvious rock feature standing alone on top of the edge).

The short wall to the ledge, continuing on the left side of the arête throughout is (**a**) **Gnome's Revenge** (HS 4b).

### 76 Gnome's Arête  HVS 5a  10m  ★
A popular outing with bold movement in a good position. Start up the centre of wall (chipped holds) until awkward moves left allow the second ledge to be gained. Step back right onto the wall and climb to the cave and possible runners. Climbing directly up the wall to the cave is E2 5b.
*Pre-1970* ✦

### 77 Grit Corner  HVD 4a  10m  ★
Pull energetically up the groove to a rest and finish up the fine flakes to the left. The original finished right and is inferior.
*Pre-1957* ✦

### 78 Lunatic Rib  VS 4c  8m
Climb the short overhanging groove and pull round the roof onto ledges below a poorly-protected and often green slab.
*Ken Tilford  1981* ✦

### 79 Grit Bit  HVS 5c  8m
Start as for *Lunatic Rib*, but swing up right onto the wall with a couple more bold moves to gain the arête. Easier ground leads to the top.
*Tony Barley  1966*

### 80 Pebbledash  E2 5c  8m
Make delicate moves up the wall to the tree via the thin crack splitting the overlap. Finish up the crack and corner above. The block behind is out at this grade.
*Tony Marr, Alan Taylor, Peter Shawcross  15th July 1990*

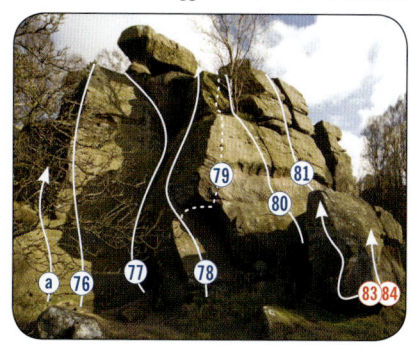

### 81 Overlapping Wall  HS 4b  7m  ★
Turn the awkward overlap at its centre and finish via the easy chimney or, better still, by the wall to the left.
*Tony Marr, Mike Tooke, Frank Fitzgerald (FRA)  29th May 2005*

### 82 Gully Arête  HS 4b  7m  ★
The interesting arête, taken on the left, has a bold start and a fine finish. Starting on the right-hand side (without the aid of the gully block) is HVS 5b.
*Tony Barley  13th August 1972*

**Micro Arête** (Font 4) takes the edge of a slim triangular pillar in the gully, finishing up the short crack. Immediately right **Still Tight Chimney**, M 2c, climbs the entrance and the continuation crack.

### 83 Ten Bears  Font 6c+
Pull up from a lying-down start using the flake, and move left on pockets by heel hooking the lip. Don't touch the ground when you swing! Finish up the arête.
*Dave Cowl*

### 84 Grizzly  Font 6a
Start as for *Ten Bears*. Rock up from a sitter to the slab.

### 85 No Doubt  HVS 5b  7m
Take a direct line to the left of the overhang and make a reachy move to finish. (**a**) A variation, **Duggie's Doubt** (VS 4c) cuts out right to the ledge and back left up the narrow wall.
*Tony Barley  13th August 1972*

Almscliff to Slipstones

# BRIMHAM - Duggie's Dilemma

**87 Spare Rib** E2 5c  7m
The impressive right arête. Start from the right, but shift left just below the top for a reachy last move.
*c1955/56* ✦

**88 Spring Roll** E4 6a  7m ★
The brilliant arête and wall right of *Spare Rib*, with a helpful pocket and friendly drop zone.
*Matt Troilett, Neil Herbert (FRA) 18th March 2000*

**89 Tight Chimney** D 3b  7m ★
The slot gives a good fight just inside.
*Pre-1957* ✦

**90 Ram Jam** VS 5a  6m
Climb the vertical crack and turn the capstone on the left, then finish up the arête.
*Tony Marr, Mike Tooke (FRA) 22nd June 2005*

50m right, above the track in woodland, is a pleasant compact buttress with a crack in the right-hand side. **Arête and Pockets** (Font 4+) takes the left arête to good pockets, **Soft Touch** (Font 5) takes the rough wall to the left of the crack. The right arête, formed by the crack, gives a good Font 3+ warm up.

## Black Chipper Area

Approximately 150m from *Duggie's Dilemma*, south through the trees, is one of Brimham's finest climbs: *The Black Chipper*. Great moves, spaced gear, but can you trust the thread? Good bouldering with excellent rib and arête highballs make this a place of pilgrimage for all climbers. The area can be reached by descending west from The Dancing Bear, but the path is not easy to follow. It's also an easy walk north from Lover's Leap (around 60m). Just before the main crag is a short, red and green streaked wall with a collection of the best problems going in the Font 7 range.

**91 Whisky Galore** Font 7a
A technical testpiece and must do problem. Climb the corner by smearing, palming and balancing your way to glory.

**92 Pussy Galore** Font 7a
Pebble pull up the blunt arête.

**86 Duggie's Dilemma** VS 4c  7m ★
How bold are you feeling? Cool moves from an unprotected and steep first half, finishing with a balancey mantelshelf to easier ground.
*c1955/56* ✦

Yorkshire Gritstone

## The Black Chipper - BRIMHAM

### 93 The Titfield Thunderbolt  Font 7b+
A popular favourite. Use the ramp line and high crease to pop for the top. No chip! Classic. Sit-down start is Font 7c. Photo on page 237.
*Dave Cowl (sit-down start Mike Gray/Tom Peckitt)* ✦

### 94 Chicken  Font 7c
Tough, but top quality. Start on the crimp and the chip to gain a poor sloper and use it to power to the top.
*Andy Swann*

Just south of this is the main event. The chimney on the left is M 2c and walking through this gives access to the *Black Cleft* lines.

### 95 Natural Grit  E3 5c  12m  ★
A demanding and thrilling ride up the left wall. Climb direct to reach the left end of the ledge. Tread carefully right to the thread on *Black Chipper* from where bold and precise climbing leads left up the scoop.
*Jerry Peel, Tony Barley  1975* ✦

### 96 Chipper Traverse  Font 7a+
The lactic acid burning, character building, monster traverse. From the middle of the *Black Chipper* wall, head right all the way round to step off at *Rogue Trader*.

### 97 The Black Chipper  E2 5b  12m  ★★★
A classic route where there's never a dull moment. A boulder start, thoughtful middle and committing final move in a great position combine to give a real belter. Start at two large pockets and climb the wall left of the arête to a good edge (possible runner). Scoops up the steepening wall above lead to the sanctuary of a crucial tiny thread runner with a rather worrying hairline crack that you don't want to test – eek! Move up and right to the top and commence blind piano playing in a desperate search for the chipped hold. Those that find it have a somewhat less stressful bid for the summit. For those that don't, make a committing bathtub exit as your life flashes before your eyes (tough at 5c). Photo on page 255.
*Tony Barley, Chas Hird  August 1966*

### 98 Deepfry  Font 6b
Arête taken on the left side.

In front of the buttress is a tent like boulder with a low roof.

### 99 Black Chipper Arête  Font 7a+
A bouldering battleground where a victory is hard won. From a sit-down start, match the sloping pinch. Crimp the crease low on the arête and hence catch the bottom of the hanging arête. Campus up to the jug and top-out. Grade is method-dependent, but it goes at Font 7a+ and is a classic. Photo on page 259.

Almscliff to Slipstones

# BRIMHAM - Ritornal

Between *Black Chipper* and *The Arch*, deep within the bowels of the dark cleft, lie several multi-pitch variations where no hold has been left unfondled in the search for a way out. They are accessed by the awkward, dirty, 4m VD 4a corner or by walking through from the mod chimney on the left. These include: the chimney on the left above the corner chimney, **Black Leg** (VD 3c); the next crack just right, bridged to start, **Black Cleft Left-side** (D 3a); and best of all, bridging up the corner-crack at the back is **Black Cleft** (VD 3c), where from the top you can spiral easily clockwise to a pinnacle summit.

### 100 The Arch   E2 6a   7m   ★
A fine route with a technical start and a finish that can give a bit o' bother. Make bouldery moves onto the sloping ledge below the arch and truck up and over the crown to a rounded finale. Good gear where you need it.
*Ken Wood   c1974*

### 101 For Crying Out Loud   E2 6b   7m   ★
Move up to pockets from the right side of the arch, where harder moves then lead up the wall.
*Ian Dunn, George Haydon, Nick Dixon   1982*

### 102 Rotifer   E3 6a   8m   ★★
A faint heart never a true love knows. Spicy times up the arête with the unforgiving top moves being the hardest. Class. Linking *Rotifer* to *Dogleg Crack* via the good holds is (a) **One Quick Look** (E1 5c).
*Bob Berzins   1977*

### 103 Dogleg Crack   E1 5c   12m   ★
A neat two pitch crack combo. Most folk savour the first course and make a dog's dinner of the second.
**1.** 5a. The corner-crack and left to the continuation (7m).
**2.** 5c. Now up the hanging offwidth (5m).
A good variation to the first pitch takes the thin blind crack above the corner-crack (b) **Straight Leg** (E1 5c).
*Des Hadlum, Dennis Gray   c1960* ✦

The short corner to the right is **Rogue Trader** (VD 3c), harder and better as a blinkered layback.

### 104 Ritornal   E1 5b   6m   ★★
The brilliant arête that cries out to be climbed. Enigmatic moves, but once you've cracked the code the left side is an excellent trip, despite delicate final moves. Highball Font 5 over a particularly nasty landing.
*Bob Berzins   c1980* ✦

Yorkshire Gritstone

Stuart Lancaster tinkling the ivories in search of the elusive chipped hold on **The Black Chipper** (E2 5b). Page 253.
Photo: Mike Hutton

# BRIMHAM - White Rose Flake

### 105 What a State  E4 6b   6m   ★
Sustained and extremely technical. Climb the arête of *Ritornal* on its right side and traverse right below the top, on pebbles and small edges, to finish using the flat hold of *Successor State*. The direct finish is the same grade. Highball Font 6c+.
*James Ibbertson (solo)16th Oct 2005 (direct finish 11th Dec 2005)*

### 106 Inner State  E5 6c   6m   ★★
A technical highball that sends the senses into overdrive. Forsake both arêtes and levitate up the wall direct. An impressive characteristic onsight from Ibbertson. Highball Font 7a+.
*James Ibbertson (solo)  16th October 2005* ✦

## ALAN HINKES - The Yorkshire Mountaineer

A proud Northallerton-born Tyke who became the first British climber to summit all 14 of the 8,000m peaks including K2, Everest, Kanchenjunga and Nanga Parbat. He's probably more proud, however, of his Yorkshireman of the year award in 2011...

"I got into climbing at Northallerton Grammar School. My first grit experiences were at Slipstones, Brimham and Almscliff, where I quickly learnt to jam. I had a few early scary experiences; Birch Tree Wall with no runners, balancing up and expecting to slip and fall off. I probably had walking boots on with Vibram soles. I remember a struggle with Notice Board Crack, learning to jam. I honed my rock skills on Yorkshire grit, which helped in the Greater Ranges, but I definitely also appreciated the grit when I returned. Great Western at Almscliff and Birch Tree Wall at Brimham are two of my favourite routes and crags. Yorkshire grit packs interest and excitement into every move. What it lacks in length it makes up for in quality, with both technical and thuggy routes."

### 107 Successor State  E4 6b   7m   ★
Delicate and brilliant climbing up the highball arête above a less than encouraging landing. Highball Font 7a.
Photo on page 278.
*Richard Davies  19th March 1986*

### 108 A Sign for the Dynosaurs  E2 6b   6m
The overhanging crack and groove above the first pitch of *Combination Cracks*.
*Al Manson (solo)  July 1988*

### 109 Combination Cracks  VS 5a   14m   ★
More cracking shenanigans that weaves a line up the blocks.
1. 4c. Bridge and jam up the crack in the left-hand corner of the bay, with tricky moves where it narrows (7m).
2 5a. Walk up and left to locate a fierce looking offwidth. All it requires is the right combination of moves (7m).

### 110 Alcove Wall  VS 4c   6m   ★
Scale the sustained and tricky featured wall at the back of the recess. Side-runners in the crack at this grade, or highballed at Font 4+. (a) **Straddle** (Font 4+) bridges the right-hand corner whilst (b) **Flaky Wall** (Font 5) takes the hanging wall on flaky ledges.
*Ken Jackson, Tony Marr  1966*

### White Rose Flake Area
Heading south for a further 40m is a neat wall with a crack that stops a couple of metres short of the top. Just right and slightly uphill is the lone anvil-shaped pinnacle which is home to the second pitch of *George II* on its northern flank.

### 111 White Flag  HVS 5a   6m
The worrying rib. A side-runner in *White Rose Flake* might stop the nerves surrendering but reduces the grade to VS.
*Dave Musgrove (solo)  1st December 1990*

### 112 White Rose Flake  VS 5a   7m   ★
The Villain's only recorded route at Brimham and a punchy little number. Haul away on great holds and jams, only cutting right to the ledge when the crack disappears. Over far too soon.
*Don Whillans  late-1950s*

### 113 Arthur  Font 6c+
Royal 'high'-ness. A top notch problem using slopers to reach the undercut and pull for the top.

### 114 George II  HVS 5a   12m   ☆
A game of two halves with many bouldering out the enjoyable first pitch (Font 4+) and avoiding the demoralising second. Serious forethought is required to get back to terra firma from the top. Abseil descent is possible by pre-arranging a rope over the top of the upper pinnacle (good cams in the gully on the south side). Alternatively, a two-person counter-balance abseil is possible by the competent.
**1**. 4c. Climb the wall using flakes to a dodgy pull on to the ledge using a hollow hold (6m).
**2**. 5a. Walk left to below a short, usually dirty, runnel on the north side. A small wire in the crack higher up protects a desperate heel hook to gain the top (6m).
*Tony Barley, Robin Barley  1963* ✦

### 115 E.S.P.  Font 7b+
A committing, top quality, recent addition to the prominent prow above the George II pinnacle. Glom up extreme slopers from a sit-down start. Awful landing. Font 7a+ from standing. (c) **One Love** (Font 7b+) steps off the boulder to grab the huge flake under the roof and moves up the left wall using the arête and poor slopers on the face to a scary final move.
*Nigel Poustie  30th October 2010; (O.L. Tom Peckitt March 2012)*

Mary Birkett on **Red or Dead** (Font 7a+). Page 279.
Photo: Neil Stabbs

# BRIMHAM - Lover's Leap Area

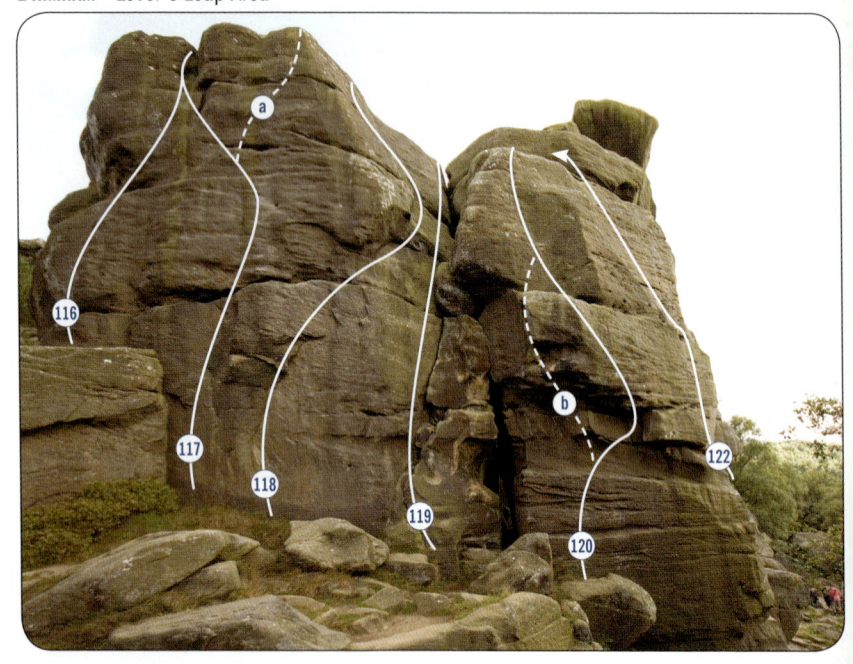

## Lover's Leap Area

One of the most recognisable climbing areas of Brimham. The first routes start 15m south on a wall on the north-west face, running down the hill side. Around the corner and the area opens up into the popular amphitheatre of Lover's Leap. Legend has it that two lovers, Edwin and Julia, were chased here by her father. They leapt off to spend eternity together in the afterlife, but instead survived and were allowed to marry. Lover's Leap Chimney is recognisable by a metal bar fastened across its top. There's plenty to love about this area with starred climbs across the grades. If approaching from the house, drop down the hillside as for *Cleft Buttress* and take the path west into the trees. The area is 60m further on, past *Cracked Buttress*, on the right.

### 116 Friends and Enemies  E4 5c   10m
From the top of the pedestal, move directly up the wall to the rounded break. Step right to finish up the final cleft of *Who Needs Friends*.
*Dave Slater, Andrew Simon  July 1994*

### 117 Who Needs Friends  E3 5c   9m   ★★
A brilliant solution to the wall and one that doesn't see the attention it deserves. Start just right of the boulder (on to which it is possible to jump from the crux if it all goes pear shaped!). Climb to the first horizontal break and push on to the second. Now step left to finish up the short jam crack.
(a) **Arête Finish** (E3 5c) steps right at the second break to finish up the blunt arête. Photo on page 269.
*Mike Hammill, J. M. Hammill  1980*

### 118 Black Bob  VS 4c   9m
Climb the flakes left of *Difficult Crack*, making a rightwards-rising traverse into that route. Finish leftwards up the slab.
*Rob Everett  1981*

### 119 Difficult Crack  VD 3c   7m   ★★
A great climb with plenty going on. Steady climbing leads to a wedged boulder, protection and a couple of ungainly moves around it. Sometimes the top-out can be green.
*Pre-1957* ♦

Anna Shepherd locked in for the finish of **Black Chipper Arête (Font 7a+)**, Page 253
Photo: Mike Hutton

# BRIMHAM - Lover's Leap Area

### 120 Enigma  E1 5b   12m   ★★
A humdinger with a taxing finish for those who can't think with their feet. Climb up to the mid-height overhang and then right to the block. Commit to the wall, stepping left onto the ledge for a breather. Delicate padding up the shallow groove leads to safety. For the one-star (b) **Enigma Variation** (E1 5b) gain the ledge below the groove by a long reach for a jam crack.
*Ken Wood, M. Biden, Mike Mortimer  16th October 1971* ✦

### 121 Birch Tree Wall Eliminate  E1 5c   15m
A harder, blinkered variation on the original. Climb to the overhang and trend right into the groove. Move up and left to the foot of a second groove. Either cut right to the harder variation finish of *Birch Tree Wall*, or track left up the wall to a blunt tapering rib.
*Tony Marr, Mike Tooke, Peter Shawcross  9th May 2004*

### 122 Birch Tree Wall  VS 4c   15m   ★★★
A justifiably well-trodden classic in a wonderful position. The top section is difficult to protect but it can be savoured if you keep cucumber cool. Claw your way up the shallow corner to the ledge on the nose. Canny exploration will reap rewards on the pro. Move left and tiptoe up the slanting groove to a choice of exits. Either continue up the groove or (slightly harder) step right (a) and enjoy the exposed rib with a tricky mantelshelf finish. For the one-star **Birch Tree Wall Direct Start** (E1 6b) take the wall below the scoop via an obvious pocket. Imagination helps.
*Brian Evans, Allan Austin 20th Mar 1955; (DS: Al Manson 1978)* ✦

### 123 Left-Wall Girdle  HVS 5a   20m
Follow *Love Bug* to the arête and take the easiest line left across *Birch Tree Wall* to finish up *Black Bob*.
*Mike Hammill, Paul Craven (alt)  January 1981*

## Lover's Leap Area - **Brimham**

**124 Love Bug** E1 5b  15m ★
An absorbing journey that can become a terror trip if both leader and second can't cope at this grade. Climb to the top of the crack in the left wall. Make tenuous moves on rounded holds left to the arête, which is boldly followed all the way on good holds to an exciting finish. For **Love Bug Variation Start** (HVS 5a) leave the crack almost immediately for a delicate traverse left to the arête at a lower level. For **Love Bug Direct Start** (E1 5b) take the right-hand side of the arête. Photo on page 17.
*Tony Barley, Tony Roache  8th August 1970*

**125 Left Wall** E5 6a  15m ★★★
One of the best E5s in Yorkshire. A high octane fuelled joyride up the wall. Good pro early doors leads the unwitting into a false sense of security. Hold on tight cowboy, the upper wall can be a rough ride. After a steady start up the crack, step left to the thinner crack. Move up right to good holds and, with the strength sapping from the arms, push for the top. Awesome moves with a slapping finale. Photos on pages 265 and 267.
*Mike Hammill, Al Manson  September 1977* ✦

**126 Resurrection** E6 6b  15m ★
A mind and body workout up the wall to the right. From the top of the boulder follow twisting grooves up the wall leftwards to join and finish as for the tough final move of *Left Wall*. Small wires and friends are available.
*Dave Pegg  10th August 1989*

**127 ResErection** E6 6c  15m ★
An independent direct line on *Resurrection*. From the boulder, hard climbing up and slightly rightwards leads to a small cam slot. Step slightly left and tackle the wall straight up to gear before finishing over the rounded bulge above.
*Danny Coultrup  September 2008*

**128 Lover's Leap Chimney** S 4a  14m ★★
Full of character. Attack the polished crack and monkey over to the cave on the right (crux). A belay can be arranged here before continuing via the left-hand chimney. A possible scramble through the bowels of the cliff runs from the left side of the belay cave right through to near *Secret Crack* and is good for kids (with supervision).
*Sidney Thompson  pre-1937* ✦

**129 Lover's Leap Chimney Right-Hand Variation HS 4b**  14m ★★
A better and harder variant. Start as for the previous route but from the belay tackle the wide right-hand chimney and finish up out right. Taking the alternative S 4b start up the right of the boulder is independent and balances the climb nicely.

Caving up the twisting chimney deep within the right-hand cleft is **Lover's Rift** (Mod).

**130 Close to Critical** E3 5c  18m ★
Mopping up the gaps with some bold moves. Climb the left side of the boulder to enter the cave. Take the outside of the left chimney for about 4m to a good finger slot in the left wall. Traverse the wall on the break above *Love Bug* to finish up the arête of that route, or the ramp of *Birch Tree Wall*. An intermediate belay in the cave may reduce rope drag.
*Tony Marr, Alan Taylor  26th March 2000*

**131 Ménage a Trois** E3 6a  14m ★
A good climb with a bold final step. From the cave of *Lover's Leap Chimney* take the overhanging wall and arête, past difficult to place wires, between the more usual finishes of the parent route.
*Phillipe Osborne (unseconded)  9th September 2001*

**132 Leap Frog** E5 6a  12m
The left arête of the right wall. Climb the wall past a pocket to a ledge. The arête on the left provides serious technical climbing. Finish over the boulders above.
*Jerry Peel, Dave Hollows, Tony Barley  1976*

**133 Ambidexter** HVS 5a  12m
A contrived route that visits most of the crag. Grapple past the right side of the boulder at the back of the chimney and make a delicate traverse to the crack on *Right Wall*. Move up to the roof and traverse left to a belay (essential to reduce rope drag). Crawl up, out between the boulders and traverse left to the top of the climbs on the left wall for an unusual, exposed and spectacular finish.
*Tony Barley, Robin Brown  April 1973*

## BRIMHAM - Lover's Leap Area

### 134 Right Wall  VS 4c  14m  ★★
Ticks all the boxes and a great route to see how your jamming's coming along. Go easily up the short crack to a ledge, step up and move left to secure jamming up the left-hand hanging crack above a hole. Follow the groove above finishing right of the overhang.
*Dennis Gray, Joe Smith  1957*

### 135 Bilberry Jam  E3 6a  15m
A linked series of problems starting up the right arête to the ledge (a Font 5+ problem) and then the right-hand of the two short hanging cracks. Finish as for *Right Wall*. The **Arête Finish** (HVS 5b) goes to the right of the final groove of *Right Wall* via a large foothold on the arête.
*Mick Ryan, Steve Rhodes, Alec Burns  21st August 1988*

### 136 Orange Crush  Font 5
Grapple the hanging crack.

### 137 Anniversary Arête  Font 6b+
The right arête of the crack is worth doing every year.

### 138 Nameless Chimney  HS 4b  14m  ★
Appearances can be deceptive. Despite looking far too wide to climb easily, the chimney is well furnished with holds and runner placements. Finishing over the jammed block at the top can be a struggle for gritstone newcomers.
*Pre-1957* ✦

### 139 Stepped Buttress  E1 6a  14m
A worthwhile extension to a popular boulder problem. Climb the centre of the steep slab to a big ledge (Font 5+). Climb the front or, more easily, the right arête of the blocks above and then tackle the interesting final bulge (crux) by way of the flake on the rounded top.
*Tony Marr, Mike Tooke  14th June 1996*

### 140 Love Handle  Font 6a
Arête taken on the left-hand side.

### 141 Monostate  Font 6b
The right side of the arête past the pocket.

### 142 President's Progress  HVD 4a-5a  12m  ★★
A traditional test, especially so for the short. Somehow hoist yourself into the undercut corner and celebrate on the perfect cracks above. The short cleft below is a Font 4 for chimney specialists, if you take the hint.
*Harry Stembridge, D.McKelvie, Yorkshire Ramblers' Club 1955* ✦

### 143 Love Bite  E2 5c  10m
Contrived, but with some interesting climbing in the bay up the hill from the last route.
**1.** 4a. Climb the corner beneath the prow of rock to the top of the block on the right (4m) or at 5b, take the hanging crack just left of the corner to gain the block.
**2.** 5c. From the top of the block pull up into a cave via flutings and move out left to the nose to escape (6m).
*Tony Marr, Mike Tooke, Peter Shawcross  9th February 1997*

### 144 Secret Crack  HVD 3c  6m
The left-facing corner-crack on the ledge right of *Presidents Progress* (care is required with protection). There's an optional S 4a chimney thrutch above.
*Pre-1997*

### 145 Lost Corner  HD 3b  6m
The pleasant corner at the back of the next cleft round the block to the right.
*Pre-1997*

### 146 Forgotten Buttress  HVS 5b  7m
Tackle the crack in the nose of the three-tier buttress to the ledge. Move left to gain the ledge on the nose. Finish up the awkward V in the final block.
*Tony Marr, Mike Tooke (FRA)  21st September 2005*

### 147 Left Edge  VS 4b  10m  ★
Climb the left of the slab to a flake then move up to a crack and hidden hold just left of the arête, take a deep breath and pull up over the bulge. The enjoyable top slab can be adjusted to taste. Originally weaved more at HS.
*Pre-1997*

### 148 Lichen Slab  HVD 3b  8m  ★
Popular with climbers and abseilers alike, this chipped slab needs a steady leader as the crucial runner is near the top and after the crux; VD with a big cam in the variation, which strictly takes the slab's (a) **Right Edge** (S 4a)
*Pre-1957* ✦

Double Back - **BRIMHAM**

## Double Back Area
To the right and uphill of *Lichen Slab* is a secluded area among the trees that contains some good, overlooked routes. A touch green though.

### 149 Alcove Chimney  D 3a  5m
Climb the inside of the chimney to a tight exit. Two variations have been added both traversing out of the chimney using the horizontal breaks for the hands. Facing the large overhang the grade is HS 4b, facing the slab is S. Finish over the rocking chockstone or the short crack on the left.
*Pre-1997*

### 150 Rigsby  VS 5a  5m
At the alcove entrance, use holds on the overhang to gain the sloping ledge on the arête. Finish up the chimney or the short crack on the left.
*Tony Marr, Mike Tooke  11th September 2007*

From the birch tree, the traverse left to the chimney and up the short final crack to the left is **Rising Damp** (VS 4c).

### 151 Thriller  E2 6a  9m
Start behind the mature birch and climb the wall, following a shallow curving scoop. From the ledge, step right and finish up the wide crack of *Birch Climb* (extremely bold without a high runner in the tree). Having a long reach is a distinct advantage.
*Tony Marr, Mike Tooke  21st July 2005*

### 152 Crossover  VS 4c  9m
Crosses *Birch Climb*. The overhanging crack right of *Thriller* leads to the tree on the ledge. Now step right to gain a thin crack.
*Allan Austin, Brian Evans, Jennifer Ruffe  6th October 1957*

### 153 Birch Climb  S 4b  9m
Safer now with monster cams though getting harder as the tree loses more branches. Climb the back of the groove, step up left to the birch tree and launch yourself into the offwidth.
*Pre-1957* ✦

### 154 Double Back  MS 4a  8m  ★
Climb the back of the groove or bridge further out, step right under the overlap, and finish up the big crack.
**Double Back - Direct Start** (Font 5) presses the ledge and thin crack to the right.
*Ken Jackson, Tony & Eric Marr  10th January 1971*

### 155 Druid's Chimney  HS 4b  9m  ★
A hidden gem. The chimney is climbed with a very useful crack in the left wall to a crux landing on the ledge. Finish direct or escape through the gap.
*Pre-1970* ✦

### 156 In Retrospect  HVS 5a  10m
Between the chimney and the right arête is a vegetated hanging crack, reached by climbing the wall just right of the chimney. The direct start is 5c.
*Bob Larkin (solo)  15th October 1972*

### 157 Chox Away  E3 5c  10m
The arête and rounded breaks behind the tree give a bold climb with the main difficulties in the middle.
*Tony Burnell, Mick Ryan, Ed Douglas  12th June 1988*

# PROFILE

**A**lthough he never really attracted as many headlines and plaudits as some of his contemporaries, Bradford lad Mike Hammill was one of the climbers from that golden era of Yorkshire grit in the 1970s who, with improvements in equipment combined with dedicated training, pushed the boundaries of what was thought possible, picking off plum extreme lines and leaving a legacy of historic first ascents that remain some of the county's most coveted ticks for any aspiring cutting edge climber or boulderer.

A regular at Almscliff, Brimham, Ilkley and Shipley Glen in particular, Hammill climbed with some of the best to ever grace Yorkshire grit - Al Manson was a regular partner, but also John Syrett, Ken Wood, Dennis Grey and Ron Fawcett (nearly killing Ron on a couple of occasions - one falling off high on Gordale Right Wing and pulling the belay peg out and on a separate occasion dropping a loose limestone block to the area that Ron had just moved to avoid the rock). Despite climbing at the same time as the great Pete Livesey, Hammill never actually even met him. Hammill's power and strength were key characteristics of his climbing style and can be seen in some of his finest routes and boulder problems, such as Opus at Almscliff, Quark at Caley and Red Baron at Shipley Glen. Still climbing and working as a senior structural geologist in Leeds, a job that has sent him far and wide to Sicily, Chile, Peru, Bolivia, Argentina, Mozambique, Sudan, Yemen and Uganda on fieldwork trips, something that he says accounts for his "erratic" climbing career over the years.

### MIKE HAMMILL

*Born: 16 May 1950*
*Grit Era: Late 1960s - late 1970s*
*Best known for: First ascents of Opus at Almscliff, Quark at Caley and Red Baron at Shipley Glen. Climbed regularly with Al Manson and Pete Kitson.*
*Climbing Style: Fast, strong, powerful and sometimes bold. Did onsight solos of Opus and Psycho.*
*10 best routes/problems: Left Wall, Thirty Seconds Over Winterland, The Ems Telegram, Quark, Sour Grapes, Swan Arcade, Opus, Hammill's Horror, Wolf at the Door, Red Baron, The Gnome.*

**How did you get into climbing?**
I started climbing in 1963 with some people I met at school and while helping at the Thornton's camping shop in Bradford. I saw the Guns of Navarone when I was 12 and thought that was what it was all about. I didn't like team sports and was attracted by the heroic pointlessness of it all (see Bonatti's autobiography – the man was a giant).

**How different was the Yorkshire grit scene back then in the 1970s?**
It was the golden age of grit. You could just go out to a crag and find things that hadn't been done and just climb them – generally ground-up till the late 1970s. It was possible to do this from the late 1960s through to the late 1970s by which time most of the 'easy pickings' were gone. There were hardly any people at the crags. I seemed to be the only person climbing at the Glen for years. Ilkley was very popular but Rocky Valley was usu-

# PROFILE

ally empty. The higher edges were generally empty but, paradoxically, a lot cleaner than nowadays. Great days and great people to be on the crags with.

### What were the accepted ethics at that time?
Ground up! But there were dirty routes that needed cleaning (look above Teaspoon Variation (Almscliff) on the right side: there is a nice blank wall that provided two good routes after a big clean – but they got dirty again and no-one did them – they vanished!)

### What was your approach to new routes?
Just spotting gaps in the course of a day's climbing and giving then a go. Sometimes it worked and sometimes it didn't. Sometimes I would persist and other times not. For example, I did solo onsight three-quarters of the way up Equilibrium (now graded E10 7a) at Burbage in the late 1970s, doing Yogurt (E3 6b) on the way, several years before that was actually claimed. Never went back though – the upper arête looked terminal. My ascents were always spontaneous and hardly ever planned as I hate feeling enslaved by a line.

### Which of your routes are you most proud of?
Opus (E4 6b) at Almscliff. After several years of casual encounters I got serious, moving the boulders from underneath and practicing baling out. It took about six months after that. Until the first ascent I had absolutely no idea that there was a jug under the top roof (don't tell anyone)!

Mike Hammill on the first ascent of **Left Wall** (E5 6a). Page 261
Photo: Mike Hammill collection

# PROFILE

**Al Manson was a regular partner of yours. What was it like climbing with him?**
Al and I had rooms in the same house in Headingley and used to climb regularly on the grit together. We generally did our own things – I liked the power stuff and he did the pebble pulling. He took things very seriously, originally wanting to be the best in the world, then UK, then Yorkshire, Almscliff and finally settled on Wetherby. I used to like watching him climb and then trying to see what he was supported by – close up it usually looked like air and lichen scraps!

**How did you train for climbing?**
I just climbed a lot and did a lot of traversing for stamina and still do. Retrospectively I seemed to be able to do harder things than the others in the late 1960s and also again in the mid-late 1970s. I never took it too seriously though - Al Manson didn't like me clowning about at all! I still climb a lot and train so I guess I am still pretty keen. Back in the 1970s I must have been damn near insufferable!

**Which climbers inspired or mentored you?**
Eric Lilley of Almscliff is an unsung hero and one of his problems is down at Font 7b in a recent guidebook. He showed me what was possible on the Virgin boulder in the late 1960s and was years ahead of his time. Allan Austin showed me the benefits of power, technique and tenacity. Ken Wood taught me common sense and technique.

**Which are the biggest lobs you've taken on the grit?**
Full-height fall in the Ilkely Quarry (thank you Derek Cummings). Ditto at Almscliff off some slush into a snow drift. Also off the top of Psycho at Caley after doing the second ascent onsight - after the last move I leapt for the top out of sheer high spirits – you get a marvellous view of Wharfedale!

**What do you make of the current Yorkshire grit scene?**
There hasn't really been that much progress considering the advances in equipment, particularly shoes and protection. That said, some of the head point ascents on grit are very impressive. Sport climbing ethics are zero. Today's first ascents would only have been regarded as sub-red points (pink points?). I find Yorkshire grit a bit worn out and crowded these days and it can be very depressing. The Glen has been allowed to get overgrown for instance. The high moorland crags are still wonderful though.

**Are you still climbing today?**
I'm keen but not enslaved by it. At 60+ it is important to keep trying to advance your fitness. Attempting to remain stable is a mistake as there are too many things going on physically and you end up crashing frequently. You have to keep trying to get stronger – maintain an even strain.

**Interview by Adi Gill**

Mark Credie on **Left Wall** (E5 6a), Page 261
Photo: Adi Gill

# BRIMHAM - Cracked Buttress

## Cracked Buttress Area
A splendid little area with top quality grit. The name says it all; for quality jamming action, this is the place.

### 158 Parallel Cracks  VS 4c   11m   ★★
Brilliant, well protected, reachy and taking no prisoners. The pleasant twin cracks with a hard finish, which is softened by a hidden hold but will you find it in time? Each crack can also be climbed independently at HVS. The left-hand finish is pleasant but leads to a desperate crux exit; the right-hand is nicely sustained, again to a crux exit. Both finishes are rarely done elegantly.
*Allan Austin, Brian Evans   1956*

A technical contrived eliminate, **The Feel Good Hit of the Summer** (†) has been recorded between *Parallel Cracks* and *Central Crack*, which involves placing gear blind in either of these routes. The grade varies between E3 5c and E5 6b depending on the usage of the cracks.

### 159 Central Crack  VS 5a   12m   ★★★
Another corker with an infamously strenuous and insecure finish. Wonderful material for the great Yorkshire sandbag debate! The central crack is followed past a small overhang to a good crack, which widens and leads to the hard fought finish. An escape left or right below the final crack reduces the grade to HS 4b.
*Pre-1957* ✦

### 160 Grit Attack  HVS 5b   12m   ★
A pumpy and reachy climb that shoots the gap between *Central Crack* and *Right-Hand Crack* up the series of horizontal breaks. The gear is good if you can hang on long enough. Finish up either of the adjacent routes from the last ledge. **Grit Attack – Direct Finish** (HVS 5c) with a side-runner is also possible.
*Ron Kenyon   23rd September 1988* ✦

### 161 Right-Hand Crack  VS 4b   12m   ★★★
Dazzling moves up the easiest of the three VS cracks and a good route for cutting your jamming teeth. Romp up the crack direct to a finish that's a darn sight more friendly than its crack-brothers to the left.
*c1950* ✦

Rising traverse lines (both left-to-right and right-to-left at HVS) have been added on Cracked Buttress by *Tony Marr, Mike Tooke and Pete Shawcross (20th March 2005)*.

### 162 Frost in the Shadows  E2 6a   12m
An interesting eliminate between *Right-Hand Crack* and *Cracked Corner*. The start and finish require long reaches.
*Terry Holmes (solo)   10th December 1989*

### 163 Cracked Corner  VD 3c   9m   ★
A short sparkling gem and a popular choice for a first outdoor lead. The right-hand corner of the buttress from the boulder. Purists will make it harder (up to Font 3+) by wearing blinkers at the start.
*Pre-1957* ✦

To the right of cracked buttress is an awkward short corner-crack, **Little Cracker** (Font 3); right again the slab corner-crack gives a lovely basic lead, **Modulus** (M 2c), and 10m further right is a fun, steep **Slanting Groove** (S 4a), left of an arête.

In front of Cracked Buttress, towards the main track, are two boulders with two very different natures. One, the **Trackside Boulder**, a fun and friendly spot for padding enthusiasts. The other, **Rachael's Box** boulder, a strength test for those that like to sit comfortably before they begin.

**268**   Yorkshire Gritstone

Matt Troilett answering the question with a definite "me" on **Who Needs Friends** (E3 5c). Page 258
Photo: Mike Hutton

# BRIMHAM - Trackside Boulder

**164 Sidestep**  Font 5
From the ledge, cruise up and left.

**165 Darkside**  Font 5+
Cool moves from the ledge and up the arête.

**166 Trackside Arête**  Font 6a
Straight up!

**167 Trackside Left**  Font 4+
Mint slab padding.

**168 Trackside Right**  Font 5
More of the same but a touch harder.

**169 Heart Arête**  Font 5

**170 The Archer**  Font 7c
From a sit-down start, take the lip to end via the same finish as *Rachael's Box*.
*Ian Bitcon 2001*

**171 Triangular Roof**  Font 6c+
Sit-down start as for *Rachael's Box* but cut left and up past the pocket.

**172 Rachael's Box Variation**  Font 7a+
From a sit-down start use the undercling and follow the obvious flake feature on small holds to top the arête on its left-hand side. Remaining pure to the roof adds a lot.

**173 Rachael's Box**  Font 7a+
Sit-down start. From the cling, crimp your way along the flake to top the arête on the right. Classic.

**174 Longbow**  Font 7a+
From sitting, climb the undercut arête on the other side of the block. Scary but quality.
*Tom Peckitt January 2011*

## Cleft Buttress

An unique landmark that separates the Northern and Southern Edges. Sat on the edge of a clearing 150m down a prominent path south of the house, this mini fortress of rock has more than enough to keep any climber going for hours. Once the domain of the router alone but now the boulderers reign, especially those that like their classic problems slopey. Many of the original routes are now problems in their own right and typically finish on early ledges. If this is the case, the Font grade will be given at the end of the route description.

Orientation: Cleft Buttress is actually three independent free-standing pinnacles. Three gullies (entrances at the north-west, east and south faces) lead to the centre, and the corking line of *Lancet Crack*. Each pinnacle is described independently in an anti-clockwise (left-to-right) direction. The first route starts on the centre of the north pinnacle (facing the house). Descent from North Pinnacle is by abseil or a tricky down-climb on the south-east side

Fran Holland sticks the sloper on **Murky Rib** (Font 6c), Page 274
Photo: Jon Pearson

# BRIMHAM - Cleft Buttress

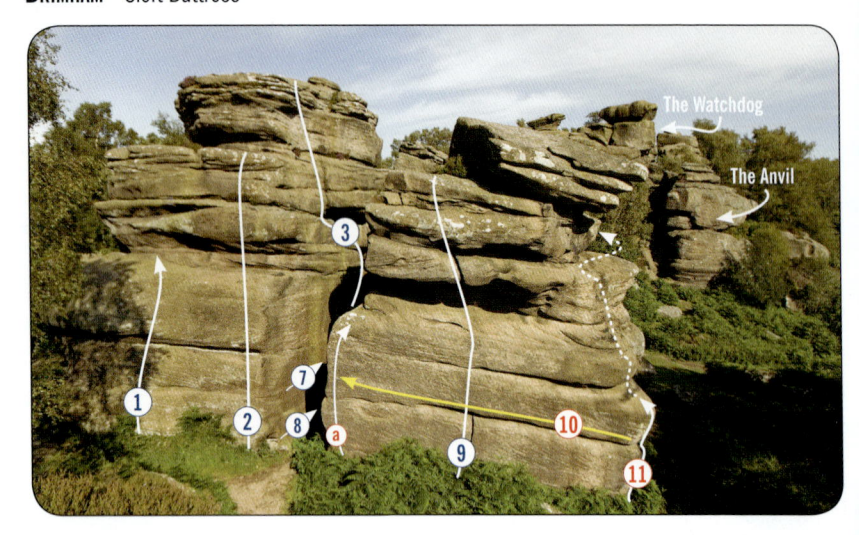

## The North Pinnacle

**1 Gordon's Wall** E1 6a  12m
Climb the rounded bulges with a very long reach for the most appallingly sloping holds. (Font 6a+ to the scoop).
*M. Berzins, B. Berzins, Gordon Higginson, J. Syrett 16th Oct 1976*

**2 Syrett's Rib** E1 5b  12m ★
The blunt and rounded arête is followed in its entirety. (Font 6a to the ledge).
*John Syrett 16th October 1976*

Walk into the gully to the distinct crack on the left.

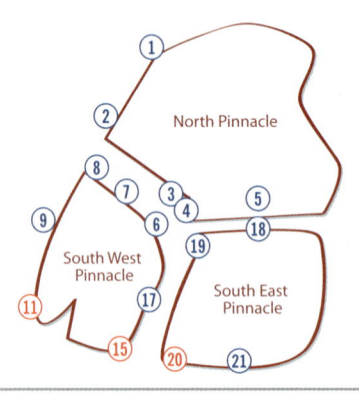

**3 Lancet Crack** VS 5a  12m ★★
A spectacular climb that keeps on coming. A yardstick tough Yorky VS, which can see the nonchalant getting plenty of air time. At the gully intersection, follow the corner-crack up and over the roof. Chimney specialists will outwit roof climbers every time.
*Allan Austin, Brian Evans 24th April 1958* ◆

**4 Stone Age Reveller** E4 6b  12m ★★
The rib is climbed precariously on the right to good holds. A contorted pirouette onto the projecting nose may then just enable slopers to be reached at the top of the scoop above. Finish up right as for *Druids Reality*. If you're athletic enough, a hands-off bat hang can be executed on the nose for a breather...
*Nigel Baker 22nd July 1997*

Follow the gully toward the east exit (first exit if *Lancet Crack* is on the left). The following climb is in the centre of the face beneath the roof.

**5 Druid's Reality** HVS 5b  16m ★
The steep wall below the rock bridge is climbed to the roof. Traverse left in a ludicrous position to a short groove. Finish easily.
*Alec Burns pre--1987* ◆

272  Yorkshire Gritstone

Cleft Buttress - **BRIMHAM**

## South-West Pinnacle

Return to the gully crossroads and start at the innermost arête (opposite *Lancet Crack*) and move round anti-clockwise. Belays are tricky for the easier routes: it's best to sling the undercut south-west nose (the obvious flake crack expands). Descent is also tricky, either roped or by down-climbing *Max Crax*.

**6 Cleft Pinnacle** HS 4b   12m   ★
Using the arête and a couple of high steps, climb the left edge of the green slab to a rounded landing on the ledge. Trend left with interest up ledges to a mantel finish.
*Pre-1957* ✦

**7 Max Crax** HS 4b   10m
Climb the crack in the centre of the wall to a useful pebble and a thin step to good holds. Finish more easily up a short crack in the top bulge on the right.
*Dave Musgrove, Nigel Baker (FRA)   19th July 1997*

**8 Cleft Arête** VS 5a   10m
The arête climbed on the left. The outside edge (a) **Cleft Butty** gives a good Font 5+ problem.
*Gordon Higginson, Martin Berzins   16th October 1976*

**9 Womb with a View** E1 5c   11m
Take the short crack in the centre of the west face. Continue to another short crack leading over the bulges.
*G. Milner, D. Fitt   5th April 1988*

**10 Mirky Way Kid** Font 6b+
Pumpy sloping traverse which links the arêtes.

**11 Clingon** Font 6c
Climb the arête to reach the sloping ledge. The original route (E1 6b) continued up the line of the arête finishing right at the top.
*Alan Taylor, Tony Marr   18th September 2005*

**12 Jumper's Traverse** Font 7a
A sloping traverse around the arête to finish at the far arête deep within the gully.

**13 Murky Crack** MVS 4c   10m
The overhanging crack is followed until it is possible to traverse right. (Font 4+ and also known as *Mirky Way*)
*Allan Austin (solo)   2nd February 1958*

**14 Cleft Dyno** Font 7a
Big moves. Savour the roundedness.

Almscliff to Slipstones    **273**

## BRIMHAM - Cleft Buttress

**15 Murky Rib**  Font 6c
The arête climbed on it's left and escaping at the break. Much better from sitting at Font 7a. Photo on page 271.

**16 Murky Rib Right**  Font 5+
The right side of the arête. The route continues at HVS 5b.

**17 Mantelshelf Blues**  E1 6a   6m
Climb the wall right of the arête using a thin pull and a high step up. (Font 6b to the ledge) *Mistakenly called High Steppa in the 1989 YMC guide*. The centre of the wall, starting at a deep pocket, is **Tin Can Alley** (Font 7b+).
*John Mackenzie, G. Corner 1982; TCA: Tom Peckitt April 2009*

### South-East Pinnacle
On the opposite side of the gully from *Druid's Reality* and just right of the arête at the east exit is the next route. This is the start of the climbs on the South-East Pinnacle. Follow these left-to-right, out of the south gully to the south face. Descent is by down-climbing *Cleft Buttress*.

**18 Cleft Buttress**  HVD 3c   12m   ★
Start opposite *Druid's Reality* on the north face of the south-east pinnacle. Follow slippery holds, to a tricky unprotected mantel, move up and right to the arête (or go up through the cave) and gain the ledge to the right of the roof. Either stomach slither back left across the chasm to an easy finish or try to find the hidden elegant solution to the undercut wall on the right (S 4b).
*Pre-1957* ♦

**19 High Steppa**  HVS 5c   6m
Let the real High Steppa steppa forward. Start to the right, around the corner. Take the short, slabby, pocketed wall above the boulder. Finish up or down *Cleft Buttress*. *See Mantelshelf Blues above*.
*John Mackenzie, G. Corner  1982*

Follow the wall out of the southern exit. The next problem is to the right of the arête when facing the south face.

**20 Green Arête**  Font 5+
A frustrating tussle up the arête on its right.

**21 Perverted Crack**  VS 5a   6m   ★
A good old-fashioned testpiece that tackles the rounded bulging crack on the front face of the right-hand block. Nowadays a popular Font 4+ problem to the ledge.
*c1958*

**22 Pair in A Cubicle**  Font 7a
A Brimham rite of passage. Avoiding the crack to the left, use the pocket undercling to find the seam at the back of the first break. Top out where the top curves slightly. Hard and sloping all the way. Mega. Photo on page 296.

**23 Governor**  Font 7a+
Want more of the same? Undercut's and up.

**24 Jim's Problem**  Font 7c+
Prove you've mastered the Brimham top-out. Sit-down start. Climb the bulging nose via the dish undercling. Shuffling right a bit when topping out supposedly helps. Not often repeated.
*Jim Baxter 1990s*

**25 Pair in a Cubicle Traverse**  Font 7b
A taxing right-to-left traverse along the low rounded break to finish up *Pair in a Cubicle*.

**26 Thelma**  Font 7b+
The bulge squeezed between *Jim's* and *Pablo*.
*Andy Swann June 2005*

**27 Pablo**  Font 7a+
Climb the blunt arête from low down. Keep a look out for the sidepull.
*Andy Swann*

On a boggy faint track leading east towards the *Watchdog* is one of Brimham's hidden delights and fun for all the family. The 'Smartie Tube' is a short tunnel through a small buttress just left of the track. Not for the claustrophobic or large of girth. Good squirm value.

Notice Board Wall - **BRIMHAM**

## The Southern Edges
So begins the labyrinthine trail back towards the car park. Expect to see the tweed clad skeletal remains of climbers from the 1920s who entered and never found a way out. A great place to climb in the shade on a hot summer day providing the midges are snoozing.

This section starts at *Notice Board Wall* and runs south along the edge to *Cubic Block* and the *Pommel* area by the main car park.

### Notice Board Wall
The most obvious features on *Notice Board Wall* are the crack and the two old bolt heads, all which remains of an old notice that banned climbing. An open aspect means it's out of character from the rest of the wooded southern edge but that only adds to the appeal. Home to a clutch of fine routes, the best with 'Notice' somewhere in their title. This area is located 170m south from the house, and can be clearly seen on the left as for the approach to *Cleft Buttress*.

On the left of *Notice Board Wall*, (a) **The Tube (**VS 5a) goes directly up the filthy wall to finish up the tube at the top.

**1 Notice Board Wall**  E2 5b  8m  ★
Not for dunces. Engage brain and tackle the left-hand crack until its termination halfway up the wall. Make thoughtful moves leftwards to climb boldly into and out of the scoop above. Awaits a direct finish. (b) **Short Notice** (HVS 5b) links the top of the crack with the finish of *Notice Board Crack* via the sloping horizontal break.
*Mike Raine, Mike Hammill  1981*

**2 Take No Notice**  E4 6b  9m  ★
A cruel mistress. Wonderful features carry you calmly to the bolts. Regroup here, for Mother Nature has sanded anything positive away from the upper wall other than a distant pocket. The outcome is by no means certain.
*Steve Rhodes, Rona Ryan  2nd June 1988*

**3 Notice Board Crack**  VS 4b  9m  ★★★
A classic gritstone crack – claimed to be Brimham's oldest VS and a bit of a frightener if you've not brought big cams. Squirm up the rounded crack to the right of the old notice board bolts.
*Sidney Thompson  pre-1937* ✦

**4 Buena Ventura**  E2 6a  10m
Tackle the bulging greenness just right of the crack. A desperate boulder problem start soon leads to easier climbing.
*Mike Hammill  1980*

**5 Gluon**  E2 5b  10m  ★
In the gully, step from a sharp boulder onto the dirty wall and gain a slot. Move left and pull out onto a big ledge. A mantel leads to the exit up a shallow fault in the final bulge.
*M. Tooke, F. Fitzgerald, T.Marr, Pam & P. Shawcross 4th June 1995*

Almscliff to Slipstones

# BRIMHAM - The Anvil

To the right of, and slightly below Notice Board Wall is a large two-tier block known as **The Anvil.**

### 6 Tensile Strength   E1 5b   10m
From the foot of the gully to the left gain a rounded ledge then step left and slot yourself into the break below the arête. Attempt to stand up then climb the flake to good finishing holds.
*Dave Musgrove, Nigel Baker, Paul Clarke   17th July 1998*

### 7 Mild Steel   S 3b   6m
Climb *Tensile Strength* to the ledge and then move right until it is possible to step up and mantelshelf onto the big ledge. Traverse off easily to the right.
*Dave Musgrove (solo)   22nd July 1997*

### 8 Spring Steal   E1 5c   10m   ★
The awkward slanting depression in the slab is followed to a ledge. A delicate move is required to surmount the top block just left of centre.
*Tony Marr   28th March 1992*

Moving around the back of the block and to the right of The Anvil 'nose' are two climbs that are usually dirty.
(c) **Boc No Hero** (E2 5c) takes the steep pocketed wall without bridging on the back wall. (d) **The Flue** (VD 4a) is the corner chimney to the right which requires respect but rewards with impressive situations.

Just on entering the woods, 10m uphill of the path is a small solitary block under an oak tree – **The Snout Boulder**. On the south side it sports a huge undercut pocket and a wonderfully sculptured snout.

### 9 Learn 'n' Groove   Font 6a+
Ace. From a sit-down start, move from undercuts in the huge hole to crimps and then a pop for the top. A funky heel-toe out left may help.

Other problems exist here, all sadly very green, including a very technical blunt prow just to the right.

Photo: Jamie Moss

Cyclops - **BRIMHAM**

## Cyclops Area
Diving deep into the woods after 70m is a clean grit oasis in a sea of greenery. A great area to introduce your friends to climbing and enough to keep the more experienced happy.

**10 Long John's Rib** S 4a 6m ★
The left arête is a gem, albeit with fiddly protection. Add a grade if tackled on its left.
*Pre-1989*

**11 Acme Error** HVS 5a 6m
The wall left of the arête past a pocket to a delicate finish. A squeezed independent line (a) goes to the left via a small horizontal nut slot and rounded breaks.
*Ken Tilford, Gordon Russell 1981*

**12 Gordon's Proffer** VS 5a 6m ★
A fine line to a grasping top-out. The undercut left side of the arête, from a boulder problem start (which can be bypassed by starting on the right). HVS 5a if finishing direct, as is the bold right side of the arête throughout.
*Ken Tilford, Gordon Russell 1981*

The scary arête left of *Cyclops* is (b) an unfriendly Font 6a, **Soobitie.**

**13 Cyclops** HVD 3c 6m ★
Unique. A short but fun route up the wall past the hole.
*Unknown pre-1997*

**14 Centre Point** M 2c 6m
The slab starting at the crack is ideal for beginners and has a number of harder variations.
*Unknown pre-1997*

**15 Slab Arête** VD 3c 6m ★
An enjoyable climb with a well positioned crux bulge. Finishing on the right, under the nose, is a reachy HS 4b.
*Unknown pre-1997*

Around to the right are two low grade highball problems. **Sideline** (Font 4+) starts at the right side of the narrow wall then climbs direct to finish up the left edge of the wall. **Wall Bar Buttress** (Font 3) tackles the reachy and steep narrow pillar to the right.

Almscliff to Slipstones

The essence of Brimham captured on camera; wonderful climbing that's rarely without an audience. Adi Gill becomes the tourist attraction on **Successor State** (E4 6b). Page 256.
Photo: Mike Hutton

Red Tape - **BRIMHAM**

### Red Tape Area
Tucked away in the trees, 40m right and slightly uphill, is a brilliant wall. Home to a classic E2 and some tasty bouldering. This area is good in autumn when the leaves have fallen and the climbs are (hopefully) clean.

### 16 **Bureaucrat**  VS 5a   11m  ★
Enjoyable varied climbing. Climb the corner or the slabby arête on the left to the ledge. The blunt arête is then taken direct via a little niche. Pull up and step left to finish over the bulge.
*Tony Marr, Mike Tooke, Alan Taylor  23rd May 1999*

### 17 **Red Tape Traverse**  Font 7b
Classic low break left-to-right traverse. Keep on going to finish on the right of the arête.

### 18 **Red Tape**  E2 5b   11m  ★★
A great find by the Keegan-permed grit prodigy. Rounded breaks lead directly up the centre of the wall with a long reach at mid-height and a mantelshelf finish. The gear is good but hard won. Vegetation often comes to the aid of those who struggle getting their leg over the final hurdle. It is possible to traverse right to the arête. This is less difficult, less protected and also less sensible.
*John Syrett  15th April 1971*  ✦

### 19 **Red Face**  Font 5
A bit of a nerve-jangler but still class. Tackle the perfect wall direct and shift right to escape at the break.

### 20 **Red Roof**  Font 6c+
Tough cookie. From a sit-down start, under the roof, hitch up to finish right of the arête.

For an excellent rockover problem, give (a) **Red or Dead** (Font 7a+) a go. From a sit-down start, gain the positive crimp on the lip of the roof and rock left. Photo on page 257.

The next two climbs are set well back and up to the right of Red Tape Buttress. A large oak sits immediately in front of the right flank. **Quercus** (Font 5) struggles past the vertical fault in the wall to finish up the flake crack of the next route. **Acorn Antics** (E2 6a) goes from behind the tree to a small shelf. Trend left around the corner to the short crack.

Just round the corner is the **Green Roof Boulder**, a tent-like block buried just below the main edge. There are some neat problems on its east side if clean and dry, the best being:

### 21 **Green Roof**  Font 6a+
Really good fun, and very different. From sitting, get around the lip and take on the slab.

### 22 **Moss Arête**  Font 6b+
The arête taken on the right from a sit-down start. Cool, but often green.

Almscliff to Slipstones   **279**

# BRIMHAM - No Problem Wall

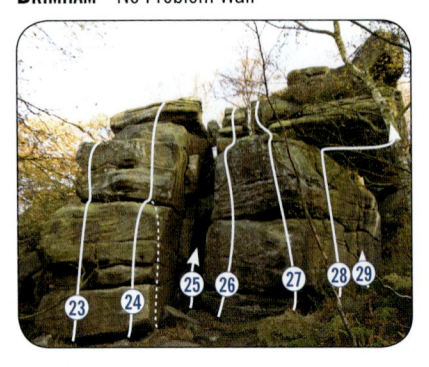

## No Problem Wall Area
Approximately 20m right again is an area that never seems to get much traffic, but worth a visit. Characterised by the large rift and huge chockstone.

Five short problems exist (between Font 4+ and 5+) at the top of the slope on the left flank of the buttress. **Zero Hour** (left arête); **No Prisoners** (From *Zero Hour* trend right into the niche); **No Prisoners Direct** (straight up to the niche); **Nonplus** (up the diagonal crack behind the overgrown bush) and finally **No-problem Wall** (straight past the undercut in the break to a difficult finish).

### 23 Merlon  VS 5a  8m
The problematic wall over the bulge to the ledge.
*Tony Marr, Mike Tooke  26th June 2007*

### 24 Merle  VD 4a  8m
A good climb up the front of the buttress with a crux start then a romp up the easier steps. A nice juggy variation start takes the right of the arête at VD 3c.
*Ernie Shepherd, Jack Wilson  c1965*

### 25 Chockstone Chimney  HD 3b  8m  ★★
Now we're talking. Good ol' back scratching action at its best. Back and foot the chimney staying right of the flake until you can land safely on the chockstone.
*Pre-1957*

### 26 Hanging Crack  E1 5c  5m  ★
An interesting problem up the hanging crack.

### 27 Hanging Arête  E2 6a  5m
The arête to a dirty escape.

### 28 Powered By Gaz  E6 6c  5m  ★
Fierce climbing up and over the roof. Make huge moves which involve a jam, a friable flake, a sloper and a far-away pocket.
*Gaz Parry  2nd April 1999*

### 29 Unfinished Crack  HVS 5c  5m
The short wall and flake crack under the roof.

## Happy Days Area
Hidden away in the trees 20m to the right, is a compact buttress with a prominent undercut prow. Popular for its easier routes and tougher problems.

### 30 H.K.T.  S 4a  7m
Climb the diagonal crack then the arête on the left to escape left above.
*Ken Tilford  1965*

### 31 Stretching Hekate  VS 5a  8m
Climb the crack of *H.K.T.* to the top and then make a delicate move up to the next break. From here three mantels lead to the top.
*Steve Parker, Gill Kirk  8th June 1994*

### 32 R.P.T.  HS 4a  13m  ★
The bold arête feels precarious, especially so for the short. Step left at the top to climb over the bulge and, depending on jangled nerves hand or stomach-traverse off left, or finish direct with a worrying rounded mantel at VS.
*Ken Tilford (FRA)  1965/1989*

### 33 The Belfry  S 4a  13m  ★★
A brilliant climb despite the wandering line. Take the compressed chimney to the top and gain the ledge on the right as elegantly as you can. Move right and delicately climb the bulges at the convenient natural thread. A variation (VS 4c) hand-traverses the break out right to join the finish of *Happy Days*.
*Pre-1970*

Happy Days - **BRIMHAM**

#### 34 Ian's Traverse  Font 7b
Traverse the lip to finish in the niche of *Happy Days*.
*Ian Bitcon  2001*

#### 35 Mr. C  Font 8a+
Super cool. Continue *Ian's Traverse* into *The Fonze*.
*Andy Swann*

#### 36 Happy Days  E3 6b  7m ★
A fond favourite as a Font 6b+ problem in its own right. From a big hold on the lip of the roof make awkward and desperate moves to gain the niche. The bulging wall and pocket above prove perplexing. Mortal climbers may have to traverse in from the left. Bouldering in from a sit-down start under the roof is Font 7b.
*Chris Hamper  1978*

#### 37 The Fonze  Font 8a
Heyyy! Traverse right from the niche using micro pockets to gain and finish up the arête. Exactamundo!
*Andy Swann 2001*

#### 38 Bilge Pump  E3 6b  7m ★
All hands to the…Step onto the prow with difficulty and follow it with even more difficulty. Another popular problem from a sitter at Font 6c+.
*c1988*

#### 39 Bilge Crack  E2 6a  7m
The chunderous hanging crack.
*Al Manson  1980*  ✦

#### 40 Layback Crack  HVD 3c  7m
The wide layaway crack on the right-hand side wall to an awkward exit. It's a good Font 3 problem in its own right if you drop or reverse after 4m.
*Ken Tilford  1965*  ✦

### Acme Wall Area
Approximately 40m to the south is a 6m prow with a long left-facing wall. A compact little area with some quality micro routes. *Acme Wall* provides a stiff little testpiece.

On the slab just north of Acme Wall is a series of fun problems.

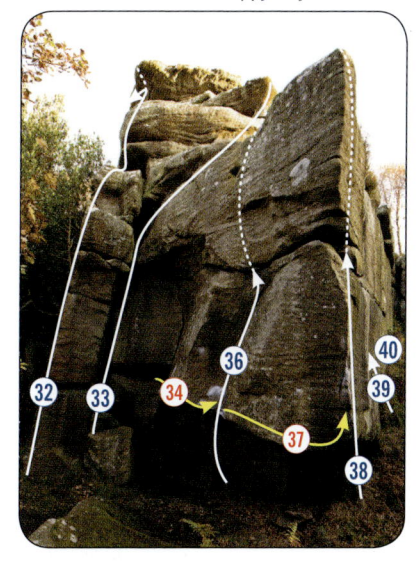

#### 41 Donald  Font 6b+
The short steep arête taken on the left from a sitter.

#### 42 Huey  Font 5

#### 43 Luey  Font 4

#### 44 Duey  Font 4

#### 45 Not So Army Barmy  HS 5a  6m
Up the wall with a hard start (Font 4+) and a rounded mantel at the top. The crack just left (M 2c) gained by bridging is also a useful descent.
*Paul Smith, Steve Rigby, Will Steed  23rd June 2000*

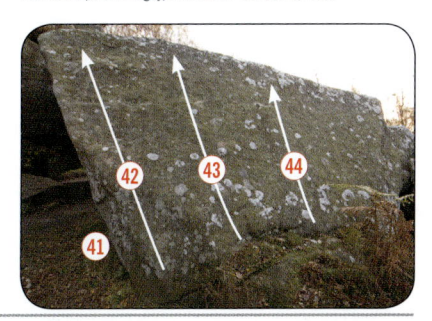

Almscliff to Slipstones

**281**

# BRIMHAM - Acme Wall

### 46 Block Chimney  VD 4a   5m
The enjoyable clean chimney (Font 3).
*Tony Marr, Mike Tooke (FRA)   21st September 2005*

### 47 Chimney Arête  VS 4c   5m
The blunt right arête of the chimney direct is well worth doing (Font 4). To the right it's best to avoid the nasty corner (VD 3b).
*Tony Marr, Mike Tooke (FRA)   21st September 2005*

### 48 Acme Wall Lower Traverse  Font 6b
Excellent technical climbing across the delicate wall, using the obvious hole, to finish up the right arête.

### 49 Acme Wall Traverse  HVS 5a   18m
Traverse the upper break right. Usually dirty. **Acme End** (VS 5a) goes from the same start and moves diagonally right up to the tree.
*Mike Hammill   1980*

### 50 Acme Wall  E3 5c   7m   ★★
A short strength-sapping classic. Positive crimps and a pocket lead to committing moves high up. Go on, give it just one more try. Highball Font 6a. Photo below.
*Mike Hammill   1980*

### 51 Appiewand  HS 4b   6m   ★
A technical gem that is both hard to start and finish. Use the short crack to gain a ledge at two-thirds height and mantelshelf to finish. An alternative start up the wall to the left is possible (Font 4+).
*Jeff Appleyard   pre-1970*

Joe Killick pushing the limits on **Acme Wall** (E3 5c). Described above.
Photo: Pete Campbell

## Lost World - BRIMHAM

### 52 Peerless  S 4b   5m ★
The prow is a delight once you get going. Worth doing twice: on the left and right. The central start is also good (Font 4+).
*Ernie Shepherd, Jack Wilson  c1965*

### 53 Forever Man  Font 5 (HVS 5b)
The small wall to the right of the arête is done without using the left edge.
*R. Allen, M. James  1985*

### 54 The Rack  Font 7a+
Reach as far as you possibly can…then go another half-inch! Span huge up the wall (break-to-break).

On the right wall of the descent cleft round to the right is:

### 55 Hideaway  Font 6b+
An overlooked gem. Go from the big ledge to the break via the good pocket. Ascent via the boulders on the left is Font 3.

Deep in the trees between Acme Wall and the Lost World is the **Green Nose Boulder**, home to pumpy problems on amazing features. (a) **Green Nose** (Font 7b) Sit-down start. Pull up using a pinch/sloper on the left arête and a sharp cling. Body roll into the crimp then heel-hook up the arête. (b) **The Ripple Effect** (Font 7c). From far right, start in the jug and using a small cling lift up, jam a leg and roll along the lip to join and finish as for *Green Nose* *(Dave Cowl Aug 2011)*. (c) **Brothers** (Font 6c). Start as for *The Ripple Effect* then jam a leg and make a long pull from the jug to the sloping break. Rockover on the jug to gain the top and a mantel finish *(Dave Cowl Aug 2011)*.

### Lost World
Buried deep in the undergrowth 80m south and downhill from Acme Wall area is this small roof with a couple of worthwhile excursions. Don't expect a queue for the problems.

### 56 Lost World  Font 6c
From under the roof, 'go big' for the hole and up. Most bail at the hole due to the filthy ledge.

### 57 Boomerang Traverse  Font 6c+
Go left under the roof, reach up and then head back right along the ledge.

### 58 Stretch  Font 6a
Make big moves past the pocket.

Almscliff to Slipstones

# BRIMHAM - Cubic Block

## Cubic Block Area

Continue south and slightly uphill for 70m through the woods until stopped by this slumbering giant of rock. This area, popular due to its proximity to the car park, offers everything - cracks, arêtes, slabs, overhangs and across the grades from Moderate to E7, bold and safe. You are unlikely to be alone, however. *Rough Wall, Minion's Way* and *Joker's Wall* are well renowned and there's plenty of bouldering too, providing you can operate above Font 6a. Descend off the south end with a tricky exposed step across the void. Nervous beginners may be better belayed across it, to avoid a slip down *Cave Chimney*.

The first three routes, all less than 10m in length, lie on a large filthy boulder opposite the north face of the Cubic Block. **Moss Alley** (HVS 5a ☆) takes the north side of the slabby boulder with a flake. A difficult pull gains this. Trend left to finish. **Northern Rock** (VS 4c) starts at the right edge of the slab, climbs a short wall then pads up the smooth slab using the arête. **Moss Lane** (HS 4a) Overgrown at present. Step off a boulder opposite *Moss Side* (on Cubic Block). Climb the large flake and follow the diagonal faults rightwards, using the top edge as and when necessary.

The first climbs start on the most southerly end of Cubic Block in an alcove just south of the slab.

### 1 The Fridge   Font 7c+
A super hard eliminate avoiding all of the breaks/cracks on the block.
*Dave Cowl*

### 2 Pocket Drop Traverse   Font 7a+
Mega classic rightwards traverse. From the break gain the arête. Crafty feet allow you to drop into the pocket. Stay low to round the arête and then pass the juggy flake to traverse the lip.

### 3 Cubic Left   Font 6c
A sit-down start to tackle the arête using the pocket.

**Brimham - Looking North-East**

## Cubic Block - **Brimham**

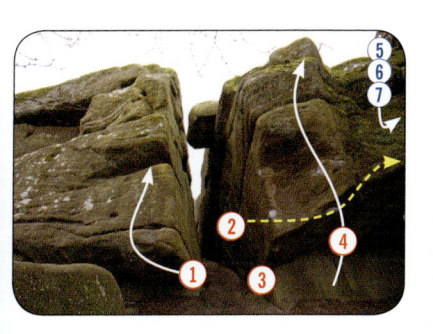

**6 Collyhirst** E3 6b  10m ★
Start as for *Ugly*, but climb direct up through the overhanging bulges via big reaches. Good gear, but can you miss the ledge?
*Ben Hirst  13th October 2010*

**7 Cutie** E1 5c  11m
Climb the easy corner then follow the highest diagonal break leading rightwards to the arête. Finish easily.
*Tony Marr, Mike Tooke  26th September 2006*

**4 Cubic** Font 6a+
Great. From a standing start on perfect jugs pull upward and top-out. A confident rock-over leads the way.
Photo on page 691.

**8 Old Corner** S 4a  9m ★
Reachy and rounded, so tough for shorties. Take some big gear. Follow the left arête of the east face to a short crack up this and the ledges above.
*Pre-1957* ✦

**5 Ugly** HVS 5c  11m
It is possible, just, to follow the diagonal crack leading rightwards to gain the arête, which leads easily to the top.
*Mike Hammill, Mike Raine  1980*

**9 Shorty's Dilemma** S 4c  9m ★
A worthwhile variation with a hard start. Use the shallow hole to gain a shelf and pull over the overlap. Finish direct.
*Tony Marr, Mike Tooke, Frank Fitzgerald  1988*

# BRIMHAM - Cubic Block

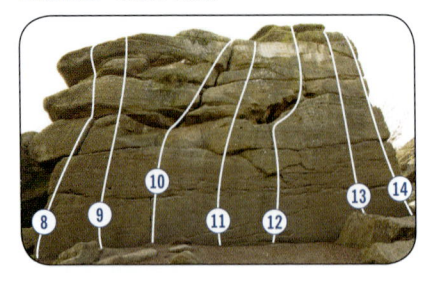

### 10 Heather Wall  S 4b  11m  ★
The pleasant crack gives an entrance examination in polish. Gain the ledge and follow the crack rightwards to the top.
*Pre-1957* ✦

### 11 Heather Wall Variant  HS 4c  10m
The direct variation. Start beneath the final crack on *Heather Wall* and climb straight up the wall towards it via a bulge. Step right, avoiding the crack, and climb to the top.
*Tony Marr  1976*

### 12 Great Slab  HVD 4a  11m  ★
Another hard start to reach the nice climbing above. Reach the cave and then follow it to the base of a crack on the right that leads to the top.
*Pre-1957* ✦

### 13 Square Root  HS 4b  11m  ★
A hard but protectable start leads to an easy but bold climax. Start just right of a pointed boulder and take a direct line up the slab using small holds and breaks.
*Tony Barley  September 1964*

### 14 Cubic Corner  MVS 4b  11m  ★★
Impressive climbing up a strong line. Pretty soft at MVS but bold and with worn cam placements. Photo on page 191.
*Pre-1937* ✦

### 15 Thin Line  HVS 5a  11m  ★
A route which feels bold but it's all there. The left edge is considered out of bounds. Pull onto the wall from a stack of boulders and make a series of moves past the breaks.
*Tony Barley, Robin Barley  1963*

### 16 Stone Wall  E1 5b  12m  ★★
Engaging moves are made up and right until you are left of the arched overlap. The final section feels even bolder, even with secure protection below you.
*Tony Barley  13th May 1974*

### 17 Rough Stuff  HVS 5b  13m  ★
From the short vertical crack climb direct to the short curving corner. Turn the overlap direct just right of this corner.
*Tony Barley  20th May 1989*

### 18 Rough Wall  VS 5a  13m  ★★★
This is what you came for! Brilliant climbing with a sting in the tail. Breeze up the slabby wall to the thin crack on the right. Tiptoe over to the left crack and make technical and committing moves to surmount the overlap and grab the top edge. Now go back around and do it again. Photo on opposite page.
*Allan Austin, Brian Evans, Jennifer Ruffe  6th October 1957*

### 19 Rough Neck  HVS 5a  12m  ★
Climb direct to the overlap and reach right over it to a twin pocket, then finish up the wall.
*Tony Barley  20th May 1989*

### 20 Moss Side  VS 4c  13m  ★★
Quality moves with a fun finale. Trend rightwards to a sloping ledge high on the right arête. Move left to good jams and then make a precarious step up to gain the top.
*Joe Smith, Dennis Gray  April 1958*

Yorkshire Gritstone

Julia Harker on the Brimham classic, **Rough Wall** (VS 5a). Opposite page.
Photo: Dave Ogden

# PROFILE

**They come once in a while like meteors**, and like meteors, sometimes they hit an atmosphere and just burn out, though the bright trail remains vivid to all who witnessed it. Another of the modern Yorkshire greats, Pete Livesey, wrote of John Syrett's "blue-eyed god-like expression", and then, presciently, of him as "the reincarnation of JME" – John Menlove Edwards, maybe the greatest of those tragic heroes with whom the history of climbing abounds.

Syrett was a friend of mine, a near-contemporary. In some strange and indefinable way he was one of the most impressive human beings I ever met - in the sense that he left an impression on all who knew him, and he lives on in their memories. For me, this isn't to do with his way of dying – a despairing, drunken leap from the top of Malham Cove in 1985 after a time when his life seemed to be spiralling down out of control and his unhappiness was manifest. His impressiveness was to do with the way he lived, the way he was. In a short space of years at the beginning of the 1970s, in the dog-days before Livesey re-invented rock-climbing in all its globe-trotting and athletic, bright and liberated modernity, John was the man. Search out his record in this guidebook: Joker's Wall, The Brutaliser, Propeller Wall, Earl Buttress, Encore, Brown Sugar, Thunderclap, Midnight Cowboy, Syrett's Roof, The Big Greeny and the rest – most of us would be dining out for decades on just one or two from that list. John shrugged them off with a quick, darting, dismissive glance, went his way to other things.

Given that pure and exceptional ability, he should have done so much more, the Jeremiahs complain – ignoring the fact that he did, and was, a great deal more than any mere list can comprehend. Uniquely among pioneers of his time, no hint of dubious tactics ever attached to his climbing, which had a majestic quality I have occasionally seen matched but never surpassed. I never saw a climber better to watch than John at his peak – the languourous drift; the elegant right power of his moves; the exquisite sense of physical pleasure his style on rock expressed. He was beautiful too – the body slim and strong and a miracle of proportion; dark, curling ringlets and a fine, high bone-structure; those quick, dark eyes that could never bear to look straight at you, but would hold your gaze for a quizzical second and then with a half-smile flicker away. He was fabulous company, testing, excitable, mettlesome – and wild! Sometimes he would dance out his frenzy – a man to spur you on, drag you in, encourage you along. Days climbing with him were like that. Often they were orgies of soloing and bouldering, for he often seemed to look on a rope only as a form of restraint. "Come on," he'd say, "You're doing well. What's next..?"

A southerner of all things, he turned up at the old Leeds University Wall as a second-year student of Applied Mineral Sciences in 1970. On a cold and blustery autumn day that year announced his presence by a faultless sight-lead – thought at the time to be the first – of Almscliff's mega-classic, The Wall of Horrors. A myth of invincibility was shattered and a new era set in train.

I wish he had been around for longer, that his time had been easier. So often the beautiful suffer too much. There was a ridiculous accident opening a party-can of beer when his finger-tendons were cut. The women, savage with desire, gave him a hard time. He worked offshore on brutal rigs. For those who knew him, he is still there at Brimham or Almscliff as when we were in our young 20s – the flared jeans trailing in the peat, raven curls blowing about his face, and just as you catch his gaze, his eyes flickering away to direct you at some new and more desperate creation.

**Jim Perrin**

## JOHN SYRETT

*Grit era: 1970-73*
*Best known for: Making what at the time was thought to be the fir repeat of Allan Austin's benchma grit route The Wall of Horrors on a gale force November day at Almscliff in 1970*
*Climbing Style: Bold, visionary, gymnastic, graceful, honest*
*10 of his best: Joker's Wall, The Brutaliser, Propeller Wall, Earl Buttress, Encore, Brown Sugar, Thunderclap, Midnight Cowboy, Syrett's Roof, The Big Greeny.*

John Syrett on the first ascent of **Joker's Wall** (E4 6a). Page 290. Photo: John Stainforth
Small inset photo: John Harwood

# BRIMHAM - Joker's Wall

### 21 **Rubic**   E1 5b   14m   ★
Start at the foot of the arête and climb the edge of the wall to a sloping ledge and the junction with *Moss Side*, then continue to the final horizontal crack and step right onto the arête. Pull straight over the final bulge to an interesting sloping finish (crux).
*Tony Marr, Mike Tooke   14th September 2003*

### 22 **Joker's Wall Traverse**   Font 7a+
A true classic. Start as far left as possible and moving right, traverse the break via pockets and the large flake. Finish up the wall using the huge undercut and ledges (using the *Minion's Way* central crack drops the grade to Font 6c+).

### 23 **Joker's Wall Left**   Font 6a+
Big moves to the right of the arête. Bail at the second break.

### 24 **Joker's Wall Arête**   E3 6a   14m   ★
A few long and imaginative moves up the pocketed overhanging wall right of the arête bring a sloping ledge into reach. Use a good undercut pocket to gain the ledge and cracks above for a direct finish.
*Hank Pasquill   c1974*

### 25 **Joker's Wall**   E4 6a   14m   ★★
An epoch defining route from one of the period's major protagonists. From the large pockets move up to the first significant break at 4m, then make a strength-sapping traverse right to a large ledge. Step up and left to the next break and follow this strenuously back to the sloping ledge on the arête. Gain a standing position on it and move up right to finish. Gymnastic and powerful climbing. (The problem start to the jugs past the hole is Font 6a).
Photo on page 289.
*John Syrett   17th April 1971*   ✦

### 26 **Joker's Wall Crack**   E4 6b   12m   ★
The direct finish is to be underestimated at your peril. Serious steepness and a nightmare for the short. From the larger ledge, step up and climb the flared bottomless crack above. An independent start can be made up the wall just left of *Minion's Way*.
*Ron Fawcett   c1975*

### 27 **Joker's Reach**   Font 6b
A pumpy little number on amazing features. From a sitter and holding the giant flake, trend up and right to make a committing final move that gains the ledge. The *Minion's* crack out right is avoided. Photo on page 19.

### 28 **Slapstick**   Font 8a
One of the better problems of its kind anywhere. Desperate slopey moves from a sitter up the wall.
*Mike Gray*

Yorkshire Gritstone

## Joker's Wall - BRIMHAM

#### 29 Minion's Way   HVS 5b   11m   ★★★
A real mauler that makes grown men weep. Many won't get off the ground and will go and do something more nourishing for the soul instead. The steep overhanging crack in the centre of the wall has a nasty habit of making a mess of unsuspecting hands. Tackle this direct to the ledge and an opportunity to regain some composure. The layback crack above is much easier. Taping the hands is recommended.
*Allan Austin, Brian Fuller   26th October 1957* ✦

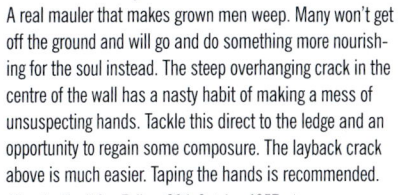

An unusual variation finish, **Wisecrack** (HVS 5b ★), climbs *Minion's Way* to near the top and then swings left to traverse the high horizontal break to the top of *Joker's Wall Crack* before stepping up and continuing left.

#### 30 Wasted Years   E6 6c   10m   ★
Gadzooks! A heinously hard offering from the silver fox. Hunker down for a pumpy ride up the wall and bulge between *Joker's Wall Crack* and *Minion's Way* via a blind flake to a hideously sloping finish.
*Jerry Peel, Dave Barton   14th September 1998*

#### 31 No Way Out   E3 6a   10m
From the top of the first crack on *Minion's Way* step right to a thread and then make difficult moves up the arête to a sloping finish just right of the top corner.
*Nigel Baker, Paul Clarke, Andy Kassyk   17th July 1998*

#### 32 Joker's Flake   Font 6c+
Flake to slopers. Sit-down start is Font 7a+.
Photo on page 228.

#### 33 The Bottom Line   E7 6c   12m   ★★
The big daddy of bum roundedness succumbs to plenty of heel action and much squeezing. Start from the flake on the right and thrash through the leering breaks to one hell of a slopey finish. The insitu thread is no more.
*Dave Pegg   26th November 1989*

#### 34 Beatnik   E3 5c   12m   ★
From the hanging crack on the yellow wall inside the cave, gain a thinner crack and pull over the bulges to rounded ledges. Traverse left to a sloping ledge from where you can scramble off up the easier upper slabs.
*Robin Barley, Tony Barley   August 1963* ✦

#### 35 Ironside   Font 8a+
Monster right-to-left traverse requiring funky moves to keep your feet up. Photo on page 293.
*Andy Swann*

#### 36 Cave Chimney   S 4a   11m   ★
Better than it looks. Either bridge or use the diagonal cracks with continuous interest until you reach daylight.
*Pre-1970* ✦

## 10 MUST-DO BRIMHAM VS'

The VS climber is spoilt for choice at Brimham although, like many Yorkshire Grit crags, it's a grade that can be humbling even for the extreme leader if not treated with respect. Here's a selection of some of the best two and three-star VS' to put on your Brimham ticklist.

1. **Allan's Crack**   VS 4c (Page 240)
2. **Birch Tree Wall**   VS 4c (Page 260)
3. **Central Crack**   VS 5a (Page 268)
4. **Jabberwok Variation**   VS 4c (Page 219)
5. **Lancet Crack**   VS 5a (Page 272)
6. **Maloja**   VS 4c (Page 198)
7. **Parallel Cracks**   VS 4c (Page 268)
8. **Right Wall**   VS 4c (Page 262)
9. **Right-Hand Crack**   VS 4b (Page 268)
10. **Rough Wall**   VS 5a (Page 286)

**Jim Croft**

# BRIMHAM - The Cubic Slab

## The Cubic Slab
To the right is a brilliant clean slab that plays host to some of the best easier graded padding challenges around. The left ramp and cleft on the sidewall is (a) D 4b (crux start).

### 37  Slab Central   HD 2c   8m   ★★
The excellent main central line, on just good enough scoops is brilliant. Easy climbing with no protection. Start from the block with crux smears at 3m and finish on the right of the blind flake. The same start and left side of the slab to the cleft is (b) D 2c. Padding the middle right of the slab (c) is Font 4 with a crux start.
*Traditional*

### 38  Slab Right   HS 4a   8m   ★
The right arête is a delightfully sustained climb (highball Font 3).

Opposite the east face of the Cubic Block is a jumble of small walls with many route variations and a unique boulder problem.

### 39  Idle Slabs   M 2b   6m
The easy-angled slab gives a good beginners lead.
*Pre-1997*

### 40  The U Tube   Font 7c
This has not had the attention it deserves, or the grade. Put first impressions aside and climb in under the smooth dished lip halfway up the wall. Start clinging the back of the block. Get the huge press to gain and pinch both holds that form the arch and then gain the break. Make sure you have a reliable spotter standing on the ledge.
*Andy Swann*

To the right **Idle Slabs Arête** (HVD 3c) takes the reachy right arête past the hole whilst **Little Corner** (D 3b), just right, is quite awkward. **Helter-Skelter** (HS 4b) climbs past the obvious large hole, trending diagonally right to the ledge. Finish over the bulge just left of the holly tree.

### 41  Green Crack   VD 4a   6m
Good moves up the short crack 5m right and behind the tree. Finish up either the crack on the left, or the awkward overlap behind the holly.
*Tony Marr   16th March 1997*

### 42  Problem Wall   VD 3b   8m   ★
Delightfully airy and a little bold and reachy. A foot traverse that starts behind the tree and leads right until it is possible to escape up the ramp onto the right-hand arête.
*Pre-1957*

### 43  Old Pals   HVS 5a   8m
Mantelshelf onto the wall and up to the holly. Step right and finish direct.
*Tony Marr, Mike Tooke, Alan Taylor, F. Fitzgerald 11th Nov 2007*

Yorkshire Gritstone

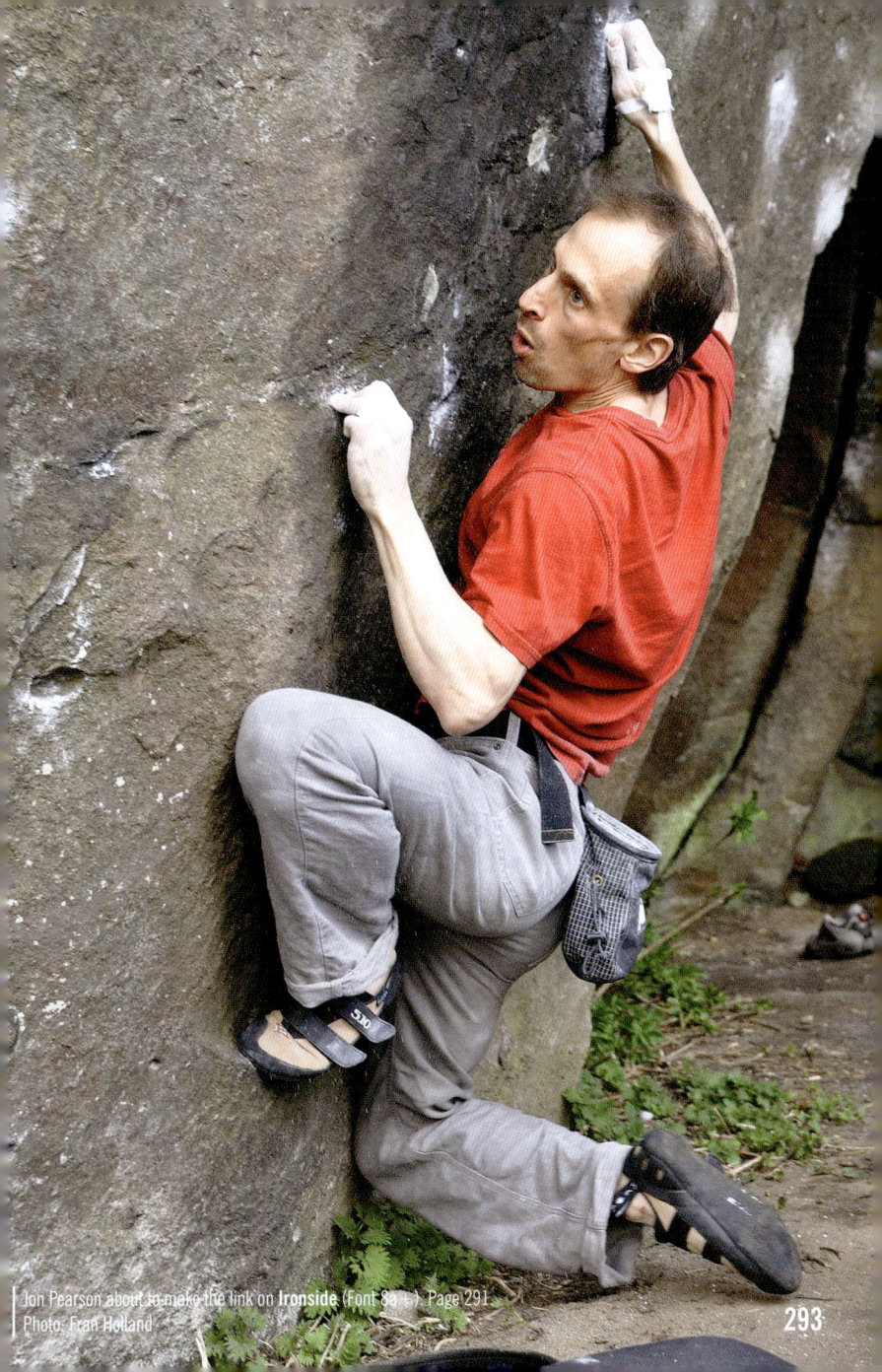

Jon Pearson about to make the link on **Ironside** (Font 8a+). Page 291.
Photo: Fran Holland

# Brimham Rocks Map

- Fag Slab
- Pinky Area ⑱ ⑲
- Hatter's Groove Area
- *Druid's Writing Desk*
- Indian's Turban
- *Druid's Idol*
- Dancing Bear
- Brimham House
- Cafe & Toilets
- Titfield Thunderbolt ⑭ ⑮ ⑯
- Black Chipper Area ⑰
- Castle Rock
- The Niche
- Kangaroo Wall
- Lover's Leap
- Cracked Buttress
- Cleft Buttress ⑬
- ⑪ ⑫
- Notice Board Wall
- The Watchdog
- Heart Shaped Slab
- Zebra Buttress
- The Blacksmith ⑳
- Cyclops
- Red Tape
- Happy Days
- Acme Wall
- Cannon Rock
- Overspill Car Park
- Lost World
- Main Car Park
- Cubic Block Area
- ⑩
- ① ② ③ ④
- ⑤ ⑥ ⑦ ⑨   ⑧   Car Park Boulders
- N
- 0   100m
- *To Hare's Head 600 metres*

# THE ALTAR EGO BOULDERING CIRCUIT

Were you bottle fed Iron Bru from the age of 6 months? Have you been cloned from the DNA of Fatima Whitbread and Geoff Capes? If so, then this circuit could be right up your street. Just as for the mid-grade circuit, this takes into account warming up and the wise boulderer will really make sure the blood's flowing before going large. Just check-out the list once you hit Font 6c+! A mighty collection. May the force be with you.

| Problem | Name | Grade | Area | Page No. |
|---|---|---|---|---|
| 1 | Sunshine | Font 3+ | Car Park Boulders | 297 |
| 2 | Sunbeam | Font 4 | Car Park Boulders | 297 |
| 3 | Sunstroke | Font 4 | Car Park Boulders | 297 |
| 4 | Trench | Font 5+ | Car Park Boulders | 298 |
| 5 | Trench Left | Font 6b+ | Car Park Boulders | 298 |
| 6 | Dugout | Font 6b | Car Park Boulders | 298 |
| 7 | Pommel | Font 6c+ | Car Park Boulders | 298 |
| 8 | The Anchor | Font 7a+ | Car Park Boulders | 300 |
| 9 | Benchmark | Font 7b | Car Park Boulders | 298 |
| 10 | Joker's Wall Traverse | Font 7a+ | Joker's Wall | 290 |
| 11 | Pair in a Cubicle | Font 7a | Cleft Buttress | 274 |
| 12 | Murky Rib *(SDS)* | Font 7a | Cleft Buttress | 274 |
| 13 | Rachael's Box Variation | Font 7a+ | Rachael's Box/Cracked Buttress | 270 |
| 14 | The Titfield Thunderbolt | Font 7b+ | Titfield Thunderbolt | 253 |
| 15 | Chicken | Font 7c | Titfield Thunderbolt | 253 |
| 16 | Whisky Galore | Font 7a | Titfield Thunderbolt | 253 |
| 17 | Black Chipper Arête | Font 7a+ | Black Chipper | 253 |
| 18 | Pinky | Font 7a+ | Pinky Area | 233 |
| 19 | Pinky Traverse *Flake Finish* | Font 7b | Pinky Area | 233 |
| 20 | Fantasy League | Font 7a+ | Blacksmith | 206 |

Photo: Jamie Moss

# BRIMHAM - Car Park Boulders

### 44 Problem Wall Direct  HS 4c  8m
Mantel onto the incut ledge of the normal route (crux), then step up right to finish using the short vertical right-hand crack. The **Left-Hand Finish** (VS 5a) goes straight up the wall to finish using the short vertical left-hand crack at the same grade.
*Pre-1997*

### 45 Problem Wall Arête  VS 5a  6m  ★
The slanting crack and the tricky arête provide a fine test.
*Pre-1997*

Round to the right from *Problem Wall Arête* a cleft leads inside the rock to a D 3a exit. Right again, the next cleft forms a right-angle through-route with a fun traverse at Font 3.

Neil Sugden making the span on **Pair in a Cubicle** (Font 7a). Page 274.
Photo: Adi Gill

Car Park Boulders - **BRIMHAM**

### Car Park Boulders / Pommel Area
A small collection of boulders 40m south of the Cubic Block and 50m south-west of the car park. One of the best areas of Brimham for bouldering, with excellent rock, brilliant problems throughout the grades not to mention the quintessential Brimham sloping top-outs to get you in the mood.

### Warm Up Block
A great starting point. Many variations are possible on this block including a Font 3 traverse along the entire break.

**1 Sunbeam**  Font 4
Tackle the wall and 'beach whale' over the edge a little to the left where the top curves in (Font 4+ direct). The left arête to the same finish is pleasant (Font 3+).

**2 Sunstroke**  Font 4
Link *Sunshine* with *Sunbeam* by traversing left. It's a good idea to do this a few of times to get the blood flowing.

**3 Sunshine**  Font 3+
Quality rock. Climb the perfect narrow face between the arêtes. The arête on the right is also good (Font 3+).

### Small Roof
Back towards the car park is a 'big' little roof with some problems having a committing feel. A good rainstorm shelter too. Many eliminates are possible.

**4 Bellyflop**  Font 6b+
The left side of the roof using the hole to reach an inelegant finish.

**5 Overdo**  Font 6b+
Up the right side of the roof finishing up *Fright Arête*.

**6 Fright Arête**  Font 6b
Name says it all. Trend up left from *Façade* to finish by the flake on the arête.

**7 Façade**  Font 5
Straight up the wall just right of the roof.

**8 Wally**  Font 3+
Funky little wall to the right.

There are problems on the boulder to the right but they're not the best and you'd be wiser to save your energy for the next block along. However, the most worthwhile outing in this area is the right-to-left traverse (Font 3+) finishing in the corner. The obvious 'up' problems are around the Font 4+ mark.

# BRIMHAM - Pommel

## Pommel
The best collection of problems in this area with a bit of everything, including rounded top-outs.

### 9  Black Dog Arête  Font 6c
Compulsory. Launch up the arête on its right-hand side. The fun starts at the end.

### 10  Flake Ache  Font 7a+
From a sit-down start and the sloping break, lay one on for the flake. Great climbing. (a) **Flake Right** has a testing finish (Font 4+).

### 11  Pommel  Font 6c+
Originally topped out as if sitting on a pommel horse. Funny to watch and a good barometer to let you know how the rest of the day is going to be. Benchmark problem for Font 6c+ grade.
*Andy Swann*

### 12  Sirpicco  Font 7b
Gain the sloper and move left via a crafty foot lock in the low break. Get the small hold in the groove and use it to get the top of *Pommel*. Finish with the same top-out.
*Andy Swann*

### 13  Benchmark  Font 7b
There are a number of methods, all good, and all lead to a difficult top-out. But, if you want to take the strength test then start with the right hand in the break, left pulling the flake undercling. Use this only to gain the sloper with the right hand and bounce this to get the top.
*Andy Swann* ✦

The arête (b) is taken from the right-hand side to a very juicy top-out (Font 6b+) whilst the pocketed wall right again goes at Font 6a.

Move right and into **The Pit**. This bay tends to be a suntrap, so if you are struggling to get warm it's worth spending extra time here.

### 14  Trench Left  Font 6b+
Drop into The Pit and start by sitting at the very left of the juggy break. Use the chip and slopey crimp out left to cruise to the top.

### 15  Trench  Font 5+
From a sit-down start, thug your way up the centre of the slightly overhanging wall using the juggy breaks. Much more satisfying to top-out left. An eliminate, **Dugout** (Font 6b) starts as for *Trench* but goes left to the chip before making a big move up right to the sloping rail and a pop for the top. Photo on opposite page.

### 16  Trench Foot  Font 5+
Sit-down start. Up the wall from the sloping ledge.

**298**

Adi Gill on **Dugout** (Font 6b). Opposite page.
Photo: Mike Hutton

# BRIMHAM - The Anchor

### The Anchor
You need to travel over the wall on the right from The Pit to find the next one. You will find a lone squat boulder with a low overhang and rounded top. Named The Anchor because of the small anchor carved in the boulder.

### 17  Pieces of Eight   Font 7b+
Start as for *The Anchor* but avoid the big pocket, the pocket, and the huge flake sidepull. Instead climb through sloping underclings to gain the anchor chip, and then pull for the top and mantel. Grrrrr.
*James Ibbertson 2005*

### 18  The Anchor   Font 7a+
One of the most coveted problems at Brimham. Start on the shelf at the back and span out to the huge pocket on the lip. Use the pocket and large ear to top-out. Class.
Photo opposite.

Dave Cowl showing how it's done on **The Anchor** (Font 7a+). Opposite page
Photo: Mike Hutton

# BRIMHAM - Roadside & Hare's Head

## Roadside & Hare's Head

OS Ref: SE 214 653

A somewhat detached, yet condensed version of Brimham that will satisfy the adventurous type. An excellent bouldering area but certainly not an all season venue. In the summer, the ferns go above head height and you'd be bonkers to trek in here with a pad on your back. Each to their own though.

The routes here have not had many ascents so beware the odd loose hold. There's a wealth of problems in these outposts of Brimham, most documented in previous guides. The best and most solid are listed here.

**Approach:** The most straightforward approach is to walk north up the road. The best parking is a lay-by on the right and 600m up the road (north) from the entrance to the main car park. There is room for 6-8 cars but ensure no valuables are left on view here. From here, walk

Brimham Hare's Head - Looking South-West

## Roadside & Hare's Head - BRIMHAM

200m further up the road and the first outcrop of boulders (Low Roof and Roadside Roof) are clearly visible on the left. Follow faint tracks to reach these. If your destination is the Hare's Head area (Cyclops, Crimpy Roof, Dolphin's Nose, etc), continue along the road for a further 300m. The puff pastry pillars can be seen on the left just up from the road. Follow faint tracks that bring you out to the right of the outcrop.

If parked in the main car park, the corner can be cut to reach the road by taking the path which leads to the Brimham house but only as far as the overflow car park on the right. Go to the far right-hand corner (north-east) of the overspill car park and take the obvious track to Heart Shaped Slab that is clearly visible to the north-east. From the slab, take the track due east to the road. Take this north and follow the directions as for the lay-by approach mentioned above.

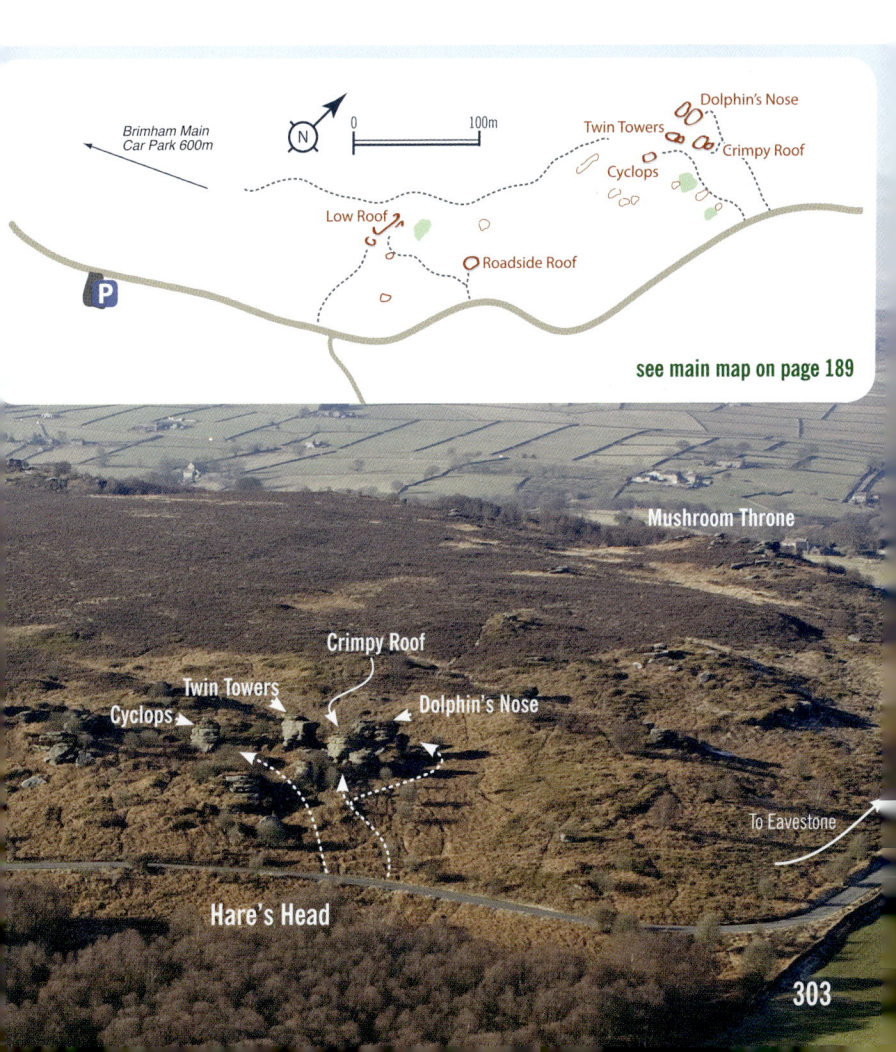

**see main map on page 189**

# **BRIMHAM** - Cyclops

The **Low Roof** closest to the lay-by parking on the road. A smattering of problems, all quite hard and often damp.

**1 Roofer**  Font 6a *(Sit-down start).*

**2 Born Slopey**  Font 7c
Sit-down start. Sloper horror show from *Roofer* to the arête.

**3 Elwood P. Dowd**  Font 7a
Reachy. Go from sitting, straight up the wall.

**Roadside Roof**
**4 True Brit**  E2 6a   7m  † ★
Climb the short wall to the roof. Monkey round on the hanging ledge and make a scary pull on to the top.
*John-Paul Hotham   June 1999*

**5 Restless Natives**  E1 5c   6m  †
Climb to the break and make a long reach to a sandy finish.
*John-Paul Hotham   June 1999*

Return to the road and head north for 300m (or follow faint paths north through lots of unlisted bouldering). **The Hare's Head** pinnacles are clearly visible on the left. Faint tracks lead to this collection with the pinnacle furthest left (south) being the **Cyclops Buttress**.

**6 Lobo**  Font 8a
Start in the pit and go up right via a pocket, avoiding the plinth all the way. Connect to traverse right along the fading break until the crux on very poor holds. Battle past these to finish once established on the shelf.
*Dave Cowl*

**7 Harobics**  HVS 5b   7m
Start next to the cave and make stiff pulls out onto the wall. A tough start from the pit is also possible.
*John-Paul Hotham   June 1999*

**8 Taggart**  Font 7b
From the same start as *Lobo* finish up *Cyclops*.
*Andy Swann.*

**9 Cyclops**  Font 6a+
Straight up the wall past the hole.

**Yorkshire Gritstone**

Crimpy Roof - **BRIMHAM**

### 10 Ten Traverse  Font 7c+
Reversing *Lobo* to finish at the obvious jug above the pit. Meeting the hard moves earlier and finishing on bigger holds creates an easier traverse.
*Dave Cowl*

### 11 5p 10p  Font 7c
Same start as *Ten Traverse* to finish up *Cyclops*.
*Dave Cowl*

## Twin Towers
Ten metres north is the distinct feature of the Twin Towers with an obvious chimney. All routes require a roped descent or the ability to down-climb *Inside Out* at Severe.

### 12 Stone Cold  VS 5a  7m  ★
The shallow corner on the west face leads to an interesting exit.
*Tony Marr, Mike Tooke  3rd April 1994*

### 13 Knobbly Wall  VS 4b  6m
The centre of the south wall on knobbly edges.
*Tony Marr, Mike Tooke, P. Shawcross, F. Fitzgerald 20th Feb 1994*

### 14 Little Wonder  VS 4c  6m
Gain the sloping ledge direct and continue via the diagonal crack.
*Tony Marr, Mike Tooke, Peter Shawcross  9th May 1994*

### 15 Inside Out  S 4a  5m
Up the chimney, mainly on the outside of the southern end. You've started, now go back 100 pages.
*Tony Marr, Mike Tooke, Peter Shawcross  9th May 1994*

### 16 For My Next Trick  E2 5c  6m
The arête via a tricky mid-height mantelshelf and an even trickier finish using two good pockets.
*Andy Moss, Mike Boyd  13th February 2000*

## Crimpy Roof
Ten metres to the right (east) is a mini-mecca for boulderers. There's enough going on for the crack climber to pay the spot a visit too. Descent from this block is tricky. Abseil is best but reversing the west slabs is possible (watch for gritty and loose rock).

### 17 Crimpy Roof  Font 7b
Start from lying down deep under the roof with a heel on the large spur. Climb through the short roof to crimps on the lip. Now power for the juggy break.

### 18 To Me To You  Font 7c+
From the same start as *Crimpy Roof*, traverse the lip on small holds to gain the poor sloper with your right hand and go for the juggy break.
*Dave Cowl 2005*

### 19 To You Too  Font 8a
An extension of *To Me to You* exists, finishing fully around the arête. A final powerful move, with your left hand on the poor sloper, to get the notch at the end of the break. This can be linked back along the break to drop down into the jug in the roof, and finish up *Crimpy Roof*. A contrived link, but good for training. Font 8a+. Photo on page 307.
*Andy Swann (link: Dave Cowl)*

Almscliff to Slipstones  **305**

# BRIMHAM - Dolphin's Nose

### 20 **Claret** Font 7b
Starting with the crimp on the arête and the blade in the roof, traverse the lip left to finish as for *Crimpy Roof.*
*Andy Swann*

### 21 **Leveretation** E1 6a   7m
Start in the cave and gain the break. Follow the arête direct and move right to the crack to finish.
*John-Paul Hotham   June 1999*

### 22 **Forced Entry** HVS 6b   8m
Start below and to the left of the hanging crack by the cave. Pull up and hand-traverse into the crack (crux). Finish easily up this.
*Tony Marr   8th April 1994*

### 23 **Hare's Head Crack** VS 5a   8m
One of the better routes 'hare'abouts. Start below the hanging crack using the corner to a ledge on the right. From the ledge, step back left and finish direct up a dirty exit. It is possible to traverse left (a) around to the exit of *Forced Entry* at the same grade, but it is bolder and has suspect rock at the finish.
*Tony Marr, Mike Tooke   17th April 1994* ✦

### 24 **Homefront** E1 5c   6m
A tough little number. Wrestle the bulging crack on the east side of the subsidiary block.
*Tony Marr, Mike Tooke   17th April 1994*

The west slabby side of the block has (b) **Emerald Eye** (S 4a) a poor route which climbs directly into, and out of, the hole to a dirty exit on suspect rock; while the direct line to the right is the highball (c) **Sloper Groper** (Font 4+).

## Dolphin's Nose
Twenty metres north-west is another popular haunt for boulderers; a heather topped block with the unusual feature of a dolphin's face (the mammal, not 'A. Dolphin' the legendary 40s Yorkshire climber) on the north side.

### 25 **Pod Wall** Font 5

### 26 **Fisherman's Friend** Font 5+
Start by holding the huge vertical thread. Gain the big sloper and use this to rock up to the two slopers in the seam. Escape here.

### 27 **Flipper** Font 6b
From the thread, traverse right past the big pocket and two crimps to slap to the big ledge. From here use sharp holds to make a long pull to the lip and finish.

### 28 **Dolphin's Nose** Font 7a
From sitting, use the big pockets to swim up past crimps to the nose of the dolphin.

### 29 **Sharkbait** Font 6a
From the big ledge used in *Flipper,* with fun in your heart, double-hand dyno to the lip. Wow!

To the right from the *Dolphin's Nose* wall is a subsidiary block with two short cracks on its southwest side. Descent is down the east face (Mod).

### 30 **Zakely Syndrome** VS 5a   7m
The central groove leads to, and through, the crack in the roof. **Zakely Right-Hand** (Font 3) takes the crack on the right, escaping right under the top block.
*Tony Marr, Mike Tooke, P. Shawcross, F. Fitzgerald 10th April 1994*

## Hare's Head Area - BRIMHAM

It is possible to take tracks north-north-west for 400m to reach the Mushroom Throne boulders. From here, faint tracks on the top can be followed due west for 300m to reach the Britt/Pinky area and the start of Brimham's main Northern Edges. If heading for Keeper's Crack area then it's best to follow paths westwards under the edge.

Dave Cowl powering through the tough moves on **To You Too** (Font 8a), Page 305. Photo: Dave Cowl collection

# BRIMHAM - First Ascent Information

### Further Information on Brimham First Ascents (✦)

**Allan's Crack**: *The first contribution from a team which was to dominate development for the next few years. The Slab start was added by Austin in 1958 and the direct finish by Les Brown and Tony Marr in 1967.*

**(The) Anchor**: *Named "The Anchor" because of the small anchor carved in the boulder, you will know it when you find it. The first ascent could be any of the following... Andy Swann, Ian Bitcon, Steve Rhodes or Little Jim Baxter, all Brimham pioneers.*

**Andy's Traverse**: *Called Andy's Traverse as it was Andy Chapman's project.*

**Beatnik**: *An important addition, for many years considered the hardest climb at Brimham.*

**Bellyporker's Progress**: *Allegedly climbed before by Andy Bowman.*

**Benchmark**: *Swann called it "Benchmark" because it was a personal strength test.*

**Bilge Crack**: *Unlikely ever to be done again.*

**Birch Tree Wall**: *There was evidence of earlier traffic before 1955.*

**Board to Tears**: *FRA ascent without the notice board - Adi Gill 2011.*

**Boc No Hero**: *Variation by Alan Firth, Roy Healy 1995.*

**Brutalizer**: *The first 'first' from a young rising star who graded it HVS. "F\*\*\*ing impossible, but only just. A pitch to delight the connoisseur"- Bernard Newman's comment in L.U.C.C. logbook.*

**Capstan Full Strength**: *Retro claimed in July 1997 as Senior Service by Mick Johnson and Dick Tong.*

**(The) Chisel**: *Top-roped prior. Protection was a tied off cold chisel placed from the right by climbing up the first few moves of The Green Giant.*

**Dame Edna**: *In a pair of "Streaky" re-soled trainers.*

**Dogleg Crack**: *The top pitch was climbed first.*

**Druid's Reality**: *Tony Barley climbed a route, Dingo, on this wall in 1975.*

**Enigma**: *The groove finish was led by Tony Barley the following day. Variation start by Tony Barley and Tony Roache 30th April 1972.*

**Excursion/Excursion Direct**: *Tony Barley, Tony Roache 15th May 1971; Excursion Direct Ben Bransby 1999*

**Fag End**: *Later spoiled by chipped holds.*

**The Feel Good Hit of the Summer**: *Jon Jewitt, Darly Cavanagh*

**Frensis**: *One of the hardest leads on the crag at that time. For years accredited to Allan Austin and Doug Verity but Austin categorically denied this when interviewed in 2010 and stated it was Drasdo's climb.*

**Frensis Direct**: *The crag's first extreme.*

**George II**: *A peg for aid was required. It was climbed free by George Broadhead and Bob Metcalfe in 1974, hence the name.*

**Gigglin' Crack**: *Absolute monster. Named after a fit of hysterics which brought about Joe Brown's failure from close to the top in 1958.*

**(The) Green Giant**: *Top-roped first.*

**Grit Attack**: *Believed to have been climbed before.*

**Grit Expectations**: *A new boldness reaches Brimham. The groove used to have a grass sod in it. A test of manhood was to pull on this. Steve Webster pulled too hard!*

**Half-Crown Corner**: *The finishing hold was scooped out by Nat Allen using a coin. (The forerunner of the wire brush).*

**Hare's Head Crack**: *The original finish traverses left to join the finish of Forced Entry at the same grade. Marr & Tooke 10th April 1994.*

**Hat Stand**: *Variation by Mick Johnson, Dick Tong, Steve Wilkinson, Steve Martin.*

**Hatter's Groove**: *Combined tactics and a peg for aid were required. Led free in April, 1958, by Joe 'Morty' Smith, Joe Brown and Dennis Gray.*

**(The) Hattery**: *Rediscovered in 1973 by George Broadhead who climbed a variation finish.*

**The Hattery Direct**: *Direct by Mick Johnson, solo.*

**Here Be Dragons**: *climbed by Steve Parker, G. Kirk.*

**Indian's Arête**: *An insignificant climb, but it marked the emergence of two young brothers who were to take over, and dominate, the crag's development throughout the 1960s.*

**Indian's Turban West (Direct Start)**: *Variation by Toby Speight, Paul Eakins, Andy Buckley.*

**Inner State**: *Onsight above pads.*

**Jackabu**: *The top section of Jackabu was added later.*

**Jackdaw Wall**: *Variation by James Karran.*

**Jimmy's Crack**: *Top-roped prior.*

**Joker's Wall**: *Another major step forward. It climbed the line of the bogusly-claimed Lecher's Wall and became 'the route to do' at Brimham during the 1970s. Even Syrett took several falls before the successful ascent.*

**King of the Snakes**: *Onsight with mat.*

**Legover**: *Recorded by Tony Barley.*

**Left Wall**: *Well-rehearsed, but a brilliant and bold ascent. As hard as anything on grit in Derbyshire at this time.*

**Lichen Wall**: *A similar line on this wall had been climbed much earlier by Tony Barley.*

**Mad Hatter**: *Originally climbed by Tony Barley.*

**Maloja Direct**: *Variation by Karl Zientek, Paul Clough.*

Yorkshire Gritstone

# First Ascent Information - BRIMHAM

**Michael Michael Superman:** *Done in bits previously, Mike Hammill (bottom), Jerry Peel (top).*
**Minion's Way:** *A controversial climb. Did Austin really stand on his second's shoulders? Dennis Gray led the climb the same day but the crux had, in fact, been worked out the week before by Brian Evans.*
**Mohole Arête**: *Side-runner was placed in Three Trees Crack on the first ascent to protect the start.*
**Mons Meg:** *The Rock & Ice return to put a big gun on Cannon Rock.*
**Moss Lane:** *Recorded by Tony Barley, Robin Barley.*
**Mr & Mrs Hemmingway:** *Variation by Karl Zientek, Phil Hemingway.*
**Natural Grit:** *The intended line of Black Chipper.*
**Old Corner, Heather Wall, Great Slab, Problem Wall, Cleft Buttress & Pinnacle, Cracked Corner, Lichen Slab, Nameless Chimney, Difficult Crack, Tight Chimney, Grit Corner, Indian's Turban Route, Indian's Turban West, The Chimney, Maloja, Birch Climb, Cannon Route, Roadside Crack, Desperation Crack, Central Crack:** *All these problems were recorded in the 1957 guide or the 1957 Y.R.C. Journal. Some were obviously long established judging by the depth of nail scratches. The East Yorkshire M.C. is probably responsible for many, but its records are no longer traceable. Birch Tree Wall and Maloja were originally credited to Johnny Lees but he categorically disowns them. Any claimants?*
**Picnic Variation:** *Fine climb, pushing up the standards.*
**Powered By Gaz:** *Solo after practise with mats and spotters.*
**Puddle Jumper/I'd Rather Be at Dalby:** *Recorded by Jim Croft and Stuart Holmes.*
**R.P.T., K.P.T Layback Crack:** *Possibly climbed before.*
**Red Tape:** *Easier variant had been climbed by Ken Tilford in the mid 1960s.*
**Resurrection:** *Solo after top rope practise.*
**Right-Hand Arête, Lunatic Rib:** *These routes were named and recorded for the 1982 guide but were old problems probably first climbed in the 1950s.*
**Right-Hand Bias Direct:** *Direct finish by Ben Bransby.*
**Ritornal:** *Probably done before 1980.*
**Rod's Roof:** *Solo after top-rope practise.*
**Rogue Trader:** *Climbed by Adam Collinge 5th June 1999*
**Runnel Trilogy No 1:** *Flashed after abseil inspection.*
**Sally Would:** *Variation by James Thompson, Mark Selby.*
**Silk Cut:** *Top-roped first.*
**Si's Cheese Slice:** *Ground up.*
**Slanting Chimney:** *Previously unrecorded.*

**Sloper Groper**: *Recorded by Andy Moss, Mike Boyd.*
**(The) Snuffer:** *A raiding party from the Alpha Club snatch an obvious, but intimidating, line.*
**Soobitie:** *Problem by Karl Zientek, Paul Clough.*
**Swan Arcade:** *The start had been climbed before 1976.*
**Tender Homecoming:** *Solo after headpoint. The crag's first E8. FA/repeat information taken from www.gritlist.wetpaint.com.*
**The Belfry, Druid's Chimney, Gnome's Arête, Cave Chimney, Kangaroo Wall, Narrowing Chimney, Detour, Harry's Crack:** *All these routes were first recorded in the 1969 guide. The section writer was Jeff Appleyard who presumably climbed them at or around this time, but some may well be of greater antiquity.*
**(The) Titfield Thunderbolt:** *Previous guides have shown the chip to the right of the line being used but this was not used for the first ascent or as part of the problem.*
**Troilett Wall:** *Protection pre-placed by abseil.*
**True Grit:** *A finger crack of the highest calibre and difficulty marked the start of a new wave of development.*
**True Grit - Direct Start:** *Direct start by Ian Vickers, Ben Bransby,*
**The Tube:** *Recorded by Stephen Reid, C. King.*
**White Wash:** *This is the first recorded ascent but it was believed that Joe Brown climbed a similar line in 1958.*

### Playout Area First Ascents

**Crackology** Tony Marr, Mike Tooke 9th August 2007
**Brown's Crack** Steve Brown, Paul Ingham 1982
**Bratt** Andy Moss, Mike Boyd 1998
**Chinese Crack** Allan Austin, Brian Evans 24th April 1958
**Blind's Crack** Tony Barley 1965
**The Grunch** Tony Marr, Mike Tooke 29th August 2007
**Playout** Tony Barley, Mike Mortimer 24th July 1972
**Fallout** Tony Barley 1965
**Wayout** Tony Barley, Mike Mortimer 24th July 1972
**Flake Out** Tony Barley 1965
**Half Crown Corner** Des Hadlum, Dennis Gray 1961
**Lilo** Brian Evans, Allan Austin, Jennifer Ruffe 6th October 1957
**Deep Chimney** Tony Barley, Mike Mortimer 24th July 1972
**Cubicle Crack** Tony Marr, Mike Tooke 22nd August 2007
**Chicane** Tony Barley, Mike Mortimer 24th July 1972
**Fat Belly Gut Bucket** Greg Rimmer, Steve Rhodes 6th May 1988
**Control Your Inappropriate Actions** Andy Moss, Mike Boyd March 2000
**For Pete's Sake** Steve Webster pre-1980
**Wilt, (T) Tilt, (U) Dyson, (V) Vax** - all Tony Marr, pre-1997
**Hoover** Roger & Graham Mackintosh Spring 1964

# BRIMHAM - Graded List

In a long running campaign of nigh on 20 years, perhaps no group has recorded more of the untrodden rock at Brimham than the collective team of Tony Marr, Mike Tooke, Frank Fitzgerald, Alan Taylor and Peter Shawcross. In addition to the routes within the text, the following impressive list, including variations, has been added by this group. Acme End, Acorn Antics, Alcove Chimney Variations, Allan's Crack Right-Hand, Arête Finish, Bilberry Jam Arête Finish, Black Leg, Black Cleft Left-side, Black Cleft, Bower Route 1, Bower Route 2, Capped Corner, Cosy Corner, Dark Deed, Duggie's Doubt, Emerald Eye, Essence of Cool, Gnome's Revenge, Grit Attack - Direct Finish, Grumble and Grunt, Gully Arête – Right Side, Hard Hat, Helter-Skelter, Idle

## GRADED LIST

### ROUTES

**E8**
Tender Homecoming (7a)

**E7**
Walk in Silence (6c)
The Bottom Line (6c)
The Chisel (6c)
The Green Giant (6c)
Bellyporker's Progress (6c)
Rod's Roof (6b)

**E6**
ResErection (6c)
Powered by Gaz (6c)
The Road Rage Experience (6c)
Wasted Years (6c)
Gigglin' Crack (6c)
Pig Slip Cow Punk (6b)
Resurrection (6b)

**E5**
Jimmy's Crack (6c)
Inner State (6c)
Sow's That (6b)
Reach for the Sty (6b)
Troilett Wall (6b)
Cocoa Club Board Meeting (6b)
Pick and Nick (6b)
Leap Frog (6a)
Left Wall (6a)
Charlie's Dilemma (6a)

**E4**
Rat Arsed (6c)
Si's Cheese Slice (6c)
True Grit Direct Start (6c)
True Grit (6b)
Mae West's Rib (6b)
Dame Edna (6b)
Successor State (6b)
Stone Age Reveller (6b)
Squat Rocket (6b)
Joker's Wall Crack (6b)
Take No Notice (6b)
What a State (6b)
Morose Mongoose (6b)
King of Snakes (6b)
Right-Hand Bias Direct (6b)
Close to the Hedge (6a)
Grit Expectations (6a)
Jelly Baby Wall (6a)
Hedge Up (6a)
Spring Roll (6a)
Gwyneth (6a)
Joker's Wall (6a)
Friends and Enemies (5c)
Swan Arcade (5c)

**E3**
Silkcut (6c)
Runnel Trilogy No. 1 (6c)
Picnic Alternative Start (6b)
King Cobra (6b)
King Snake (6b)
Bilge Pump (6b)
Happy Days (6b)
Vam (6b)
Mohole Direct (6b)
Collyhirst (6b)
Flibbetigibbet (6b)
Control Your Inappropriate - Actions (6b)
Excursion Direct (6b)
Sir Les (6b)
Chicane (6a)
Joker's Wall Arête (6a)
The Shootist (6a)
Tube Break (6a)
No Way Out (6a)
Ratfink (6a)
Ménage à Trois (6a)
Rotifer (6a)
Bilberry Jam (6a)
Pathos (6a)
Steady VS Arête (6a)
Board to Tears (6a)
Acme Wall (5c)
Lichen Wall (5c)
Close to Critical (5c)
White Wash (5c)
Michael Michael Superman (5c)
Serendipity (5c)
Who Needs Friends (5c)
Who Needs Friends Arête (5c)
Natural Grit (5c)
Brutaliser (5c)
Windy Miller (5c)
Arête Finish (5c)
Beatnik (5c)
Capstan Full Strength / Senior Service (5c)
Fook Nose (5c)
Chox Away (5c)

**E2**
A Sign for the Dynosaurs (6b)
For Crying Out Loud (6b)
Peekabu (6a)
Buena Ventura (6a)
Bratt (6a)
Bilge Crack (6a)
Running on Red (6a)
Acorn Antics (6a)
Pebbledash (6a)
Cannon Fodder (6a)
Perfect Day (6a)
Frost in the Shadows (6a)
Hanging Arête (6a)
Mammoth (6a)
Mastodon (6a)
Dennis the Menace (6a)
For Pete's Sake (6a)
True Brit (6a)
Look No Hands (6a)
The Arch (6a)
Thriller (6a)
Filter Tip (5c)
The Jewel in the Crown (5c)
Ratoonee (5c)
For My Next Trick (5c)
Halcyon Daze (5c)
Boc No Hero (5c)
Picnic (5c)
Hat Stand (5c)
Love Bite (5c)
Walleroo (5c)
House Points Tomorrow (5c)
Spare Rib (5c)
Sally Would (5c)
Zero Option (5c)
Goof Aydee and the Mango (5c)
The Black Chipper (5c)
Gluon (5b)
Felicity (5b)
Notice Board Wall (5b)
Windy Day Flop (5b)
Red Tape (5b)
Blind's Crack (5b)

**E1**
Lithos Direct Start (6b)
Stepped Buttress (6a)
Gordon's Wall (6a)
Leveretation (6a)
Mantelshelf Blues (6a)
Charming Crack (5c)
Spring Steal (5c)
The Snuffer-Direct Start (5c)
Botany Bay (5c)
The Brute (5c)
Cutie (5c)
The Grunch (5c)
Straight Leg (5c)
One Quick Look (5c)
Lay Back and Think (5c)
Rattlesnake (5c)
Cantilever Pinnacle (5c)
Restless Natives (5c)
Rattler (5c)
Crack of Bof (5c)
The Hattery Direct (5c)
Womb with a View (5c)
Birch Tree Wall Eliminate (5c)
Hard Hat (5c)
Home Front (5c)
Games with the Nephfesch (5c)
Hanging Crack (5c)
Love Bug Direct Start (5b)
Birch Tree Wall Direct (5b)
Britt Right-Hand (5b)
Syrett's Rib (5b)
Britt (5b)
Mohole Arête (5b)
Rat Pack (5b)
Roaring Boys (5b)
Classic Bagger (5b)
Wedge Crack (5b)
Bog Crack (5b)
Dogleg Crack (5b)
Stone Wall (5b)
Rubic (5b)
Green Prioress (5b)
Mumbojumbo (5b)
Lovebug (5b)
Kneewrecker (5b)
Mad Hatter (5b)
Ritornal (5b)
Jackabu (5b)
Enigma (5b)
Enigma Variation (5b)
Hanging Groove (5b)
Tensile Strength (5b)
Mad Hatter (5b)
The Periwocky (5b)
Don't Step Back Crack (5b)
Frensis Direct (5b)
Roadside Crack (5b)
Footprints in the Butter (5a)

**HVS**
Forced Entry (6b)
Bare Back Side (5c)
Maloja direct (5c)
Ugly (5c)
Rainy Day (5c)
Unfinished Crack (5c)
Eyes Right (5c)
Tilt (5c)
Fat Belly Gut Bucket (5c)
Grit Attack Direct Finish (5c)
Nicorette (5c)
Grit Bit (5c)
High Steppa (5c)
Bottom's Up (5b)
Hat Trick (5b)
No Doubt (5b)
Harobics (5b)
Short Notice (5b)
Druid's Reality (5b)
Mr & Mrs Hemmingway (5b)
Desperation Crack (5b)
Grit Escape (5b)
Gully Arête - Right Side (5b)
Pig's Ear (5b)
Boa Cracks (5b)
Allan's Crack Direct (5b)
Tube Break Direct Start (5b)
Point Blank (5b)
Ratatwooee (5b)
Rough Stuff (5b)
Lithos (5b)
The Snuffer (5b)
Eyes Left (5b)
Grit Attack (5b)
Minion's Way (5b)
Wisecrack (5b)
Druid's Reality (5b)
Woodbine (5b)

Forgotten Buttress (5b)
Bilberry Jam- Arête Finish (5b)
Forever Man (5b)
Lilo (5a)
George II (5a)
Left Wall Girdle (5a)
Love Bug Variant (5a)
In Retrospect (5a)
The Hattery (5a)
Rat Trap (5a)
Black Tower Face (5a)
Go Joe (5a)
Old Pals (5a)
Picnic Variation (5a)
Legover (5a)
Coldplay (5a)
The Mantelshelf (5a)
Gnome's Arête (5a)
Acme Error (5a)
Right-Hand Arête (5a)
Acme Wall Traverse (5a)
Smoke Ring (5a)
Hanging Flake (5a)
Ambidexter (5a)
Brown's Crack (5a)
Crackology (5a)
Moss Alley (5a)
White Flag (5a)
Hatter's Groove (5a)
Thin Line (5a)
Rough Neck (5a)
Icing on the Cake (5a)
Right-Hand Bias (4c)
Charming Chimney (4c)
The Hattery Arête (4c)
Mohole (4c)

**VS**
Indian's Arête (5b)
Hourglass Chimney (5a)
Cakewalk (5a)
Finders Keepers (5a)
Rigsby (5a)
Zakely Syndrome (5a)
Lancet Crack (5a)
Allan's Crack Right-Hand (5a)
Central Crack (5a)
Ram Jam (5a)
Stone Cold (5a)
Bureaucrat (5a)
The Tube (5a)
Perverted Crack (5a)
Frensis (5a)
Merlon (5a)
Wilt (5a)
Hare's Head Crack (5a)
Sculptured Wall (5a)
Half Crown Corner (5a)
Cracked Rib (5a)
Gordon's Proffer (5a)
Cleft Arête (5a)
Acme End (5a)
Easy Exit (5a)
Back Breaker (5a)
Cakewalk (5a)
Mons Meg (5a)
Rough Wall (5a)

Scallywag (5a)
Little Funnel (5a)
I'd Rather be at Dalby (5a)
Narrowing Chimney Outside Finish (5a)
Combination Cracks (5a)
White Rose Flake (5a)
Stretching Hekate (5a)
Problem Wall Arête (5a)
Kiosk Crack (5a)
Here Be Dragons (5a)
Puddle Jumper (4c)
Kangaroo Wall (4c)
Keyhole Cops (4c)
Rising Damp (4c)
Jabberwok Variantion (4c)
Allan's Crack (4c)
Chimney Arête (4c)
Concave Slab (4c)
Northern Rock (4c)
Duggie's Dilemma (4c)
Closet Crack (4c)
Three Trees Crack (4c)
Fag Slab Variant (4c)
Graft Crack (4c)
Dougie's Doubt (4c)
Chinese Crack (4c)
Fall Out (4c)
Flakeout (4c)
Alcove Wall (4c)
Parallel Cracks (4c)
Maloja (4c)
Hyde and Seek (4c)
Crossover (4c)
Right Wall (4c)
Keeper Crack (4c)
Birch Tree Wall (4c)
Black Bob (4c)
Little Wonder (4c)
Moss Side (4c)
Harry's Crack (4c)
Lunatic Rib (4c)
Left-Hand Bias (4c)
Constrictor Chimney (4c)
Mantelshelf Corner (4b)
Indian's Turban West (4b)
Hoover (4b)
Notice Board Crack (4b)
Right-Hand Crack (4b)
Slippery Crack (4b)
Jabberwok (4b)
Left Edge (4b)
Last Crack (4b)
Knobbly Wall (4b)
Brief Crack (4b)
One Flew Over the Eccles Cake (4a)

**MVS**
Murky Crack (4c)
Way Out (4c)
Cubic Corner (4b)

# Graded List - **BRIMHAM**

*Slabs Arête, Jam and Blast, Lichen Slab Right Edge, Little Corner, Love Bug Direct Start, Love Bug Variation Start, Lover's Rift, Micro Arête, Neon, Nicorette, Narrowing Chimney - Outside Finish, No Prisoners Direct, No Prisoners, No-problem Wall, Nonplus, Northern Rock, One Quick Look, Pantomime, Problem Wall Left-Hand Finish, Quercus, Raj, Right Pantomime, Rising Damp, Rush Hour, Short Notice, Sideline, Soft Touch, Still Tight Chimney, Straight Leg, The Flue, The Snuffer Direct Start, Thriller, Wall Bar Buttress, Whiz-Bang Direct Start, Wisecrack, Zero Hour, (4 routes on the moss slab by The Hattery - Leftovers, Top Dog, Absent Friends, Old Hat).*

## HS
Not So Barmy Army (5a)
Two Tier Crack (5a)
Problem Wall Direct (4c)
Heather Wall Variant (4c)
Pig Traverse (4b)
Viper (4b)
Helter Skelter (4b)
Druid's Chimney (4b)
Jibber (4b)
Keystone Chimney (4b)
Appiewand (4b)
Nameless Chimney (4b)
Dirty Rat (4b)
Excursion (4b)
Squeeze Crack (4b)
Lover's Leap Chimney RH – Variation (4b)
Castle Crack (4b)
Gully Arête (4b)
Bilberry Groove (4b)
Hawk Traverse (4b)
Turtleneck Crack (4b)
Max Crax (4b)
Rat Catcher (4b)
Ratlin' (4b)
Ratbag (4b)
Overlapping Wall (4b)
Gnome's Revenge (4b)
Top Dead Centre (4b)
The Hattery Chimney (4b)
Cleft Pinnacle (4b)
North West Arête (4a)
R.P.T. (4a)
Indian's Turban Route (4a)
Cubic Slab Right (4a)
Square Root (4a)
Moss Lane (4a)
Slab Right (4a)

## S
Shorty's Dilemma (4c)
Oak Tree Crack (4c)
Grumble and Grunt (4b)
Tusk Chimney (4b)
Crackaroo (4b)
Heather Wall (4b)
Hats Off to Andy (4b)
Birch Climb (4b)
Connoisseur's Corner (4b)
Peerless (4b)
The Belfry (4a)
Fag Slab (4a)
Slanting Groove (4a)
Corner Crack (4a)
Right Edge (4a)
Long John's Rib (4a)
Fag End (4a)
West Indian's Turban Route (4a)
Funnelology (4a)
Emerald Eye (4a)
Jam and Blast (4a)
Slanting Chimney (4a)
Inside Out (4a)
Jumbo Jam (4a)

H.K.T. (4a)
Zig-Zag Bear (4a)
Old Corner (4a)
Cave Chimney (4a)
Whiz-Bang (4a)
Lover's Leap Chimney (4a)
Mild Steel (3b)
Deep Chimney

## MS
Double Back

## HVD
President's Progress (4a-5a)
Argy Bargy (4a)
Chocked Chimney (4a)
Great Slab (4a)
Lichen Chimney (4a)
Detour (4a)
Dancing Bear Variant (4a)
Grit Corner (4a)
East Ridge of the Eccles Cake (4a)
Idle Slabs Arête (3c)
Cleft Buttress (3c)
Long Funnel (3c)
Layback Crack (3c)
Secret Crack (3c)
Cyclops (3c)
Lichen Slab (3b)

## VD
Green Crack (4a)
The Flue (4a)
Bower Route 1 (4a)
Merle (4a)
Block Chimney (4a)
Black Leg (3c)
Black Cleft (3c)
The Turtle Rocks Chimney (3c)
Cosy Corner (3c)
Slab Arête (3c)
Rogue Trader (3c)
Difficult Crack (3c)
Cracked Corner (3c)
Problem Wall (3b)
Dyson
Dancing Bear
Neon
Jambouree
Cubicle Crack
Vax

## HD
The Flue (4a)
Vamoose (3b)
Rush Hour (3b)
Chockstone Chimney (3b)
Lost Corner (3b)
Slab Central (2c)
Old Hat

## D
Tight Chimney (3b)
Bower Route 2 (3b)
Castle Corner
Cannon Route
Little Corner (3b)
Black Cleft Left Side (3a)
Alcove Chimney (3a)

## M
Centre Point (2c)
Still Tight Chimney (2b)
Back Bower (2b)
Halcyon Chimney (2b)
Modulus (2b)
Idle Slabs (2b)
Lover's Rift

## PROBLEMS
### 8a+
Mr C
Ironside

### 8a
The Fonze
Slapstick
Lobo
To You Too

### 7c+
Jim's Problem
The Fridge
Ten Traverse
Pinky Full Traverse
To Me to You
Mike's Problem
Ponce
Hussefelt
Dead Man Walking
3'10

### 7c
Chicken
The Archer
The Ripple Effect
The U-Tube
Born Slopey
5p 10p
Pounce
Jumper's Dyno

### 7b+
The Titfield Thunderbolt
E.S.P.
One Love
Tin Can Alley
Thelma
Pieces of Eight

### 7b
Pair in a Cubicle Traverse
Red Tape Traverse
Ian's Traverse
Sirpicco
Green Nose
Benchmark
Taggart

Crimpy Roof
Claret
Pinky Traverse Flake Finish
The Grouch
Take a Bough
The Long Haul
Andy's Traverse
Dreamcast

### 7a+
Chipper Traverse
Black Chipper Arête
Rachael's Box Variation
Rachael's Box
Longbow
Swing Arête (SDS)
Governor
Pablo
Red or Dead
The Rack
Pocket Drop Traverse
Joker's Wall Traverse
Flake Ache
The Anchor
Pinky
Born Again
Niche Wall
Hidden Roof Traverse
Fantasy League

### 7a
Whisky Galore
Pussy Galore
Jumper's Traverse
Cleft Chimney
Murky Rib (SDS)
Pair in a Cubicle
Elwood P Dowd
Dolphin's Nose
Jim's Mantel

### 6c+
Arthur
Triangular Roof
Red Roof
Vision on
Boomerang Traverse
Joker's Flake
Pommel
Ten Bears
Heart Shaped Slab Arête
Doberman Pincher

### 6c
Clingon
Murky Rib
Cubic Left
Lost World
Mirky Rib Left-Hand Brothers
Black Dog Arête
Niche Arête
Caveman
Bill and Ben
Swing Arête

### 6b+
Anniversary Arête
Mirky Way Kid
Moss Arête
Overdo
Donold
Happy Days Start
Hideaway
Trench Left
Bellyflop
Perky
Niche Corner
Just Do It
Gamma Goblins

### 6b
Deepfry
Moonstate
Acme Wall Lower Traverse
Joker's Reach
Fright Arête
Dugout
Flipper
Niche Roof
Flatline

### 6a+
Green Roof
Alien Nation
Cyclops
Cubic
Joker's Wall Left
Castle Traverse
Guy's Traverse
Love Scoop
Hidden Wall
Striding Edge
Gwyneth Left
Learn n' Groove

### 6a
Grizzly
Love Handle
Trackside Arête
Soobitie
Stretch
Roofer
Sharkbait
Right Pantomime
Minidigit
Boat Arête
Capsize
King Worm
Right Flake
Left Flake
Flobbalobba
Cocoa Runnel
Gwyneth Right
Soobitie

### 5+
Darkside
Cleft Butty
Murky Rib Right
Green Arête
Trench Foot
Trench
Fisherman's Friend

Yoke of Oxen
Lookout Wall
Ethel

### 5
Soft Touch
Flaky Wall
Orange Crush
Double Back Direct Start
Sidestep
Trackside Right
Red Face
Quercus
Raj
Huey
Forever Man
Facade
Pod Wall
Ripple Traverse
Piglet Arête
Moat Rib
Pulse Rate

### 4+
Arête and Pockets
Straddle
Trackside Left
Sideline
Flake Right
Tempered Steel
Sideline
Sloper Groper
Fist Fight
Pantomine
Hidden Crack

### 4
Micro Arête
Heart Arête
Luey
Duey
Sunbeam
Sunstroke
Capped Corner
Raspberry Ripple
Piglet Wall
Essence of Cool

### 3+
Sunshine
Wally
Barnacle Bill

### 3
Wall Bar Buttress
Zakley Right-Hand
Little Cracker
Dark Deed

**311**

# BRIMHAM OUTLYING CRAGS - Aerial Photo

Aerial Photo - **BRIMHAM OUTLYING CRAGS**

Bat Buttress

To Crow Crag & Summerbridge →

Plantation Crack

**Brimham Outlying Crags - Looking North**

# plantation crack
by **Dave Musgrove**

OS Ref: SE 206 638
Altitude: 200m

A broken edge once shrouded in trees, though felled and re-planted in 2010. It is one of the least popular areas of Brimham but, with one particularly good buttress, limited bouldering and some potential for new development, it is worth at least one visit in your gritstone career - if only for the superb HVS of *Plantation Crack*.

**The Climbing:** 16 routes and a handful of boulder problems. The main buttress has a fine steep wall split by a wide crack. There are some reasonably clean boulders high up to the right of here and to the left a series of smaller but generally vegetated buttresses which could provide more sport if cleaned up. Most climbers will approach this crag from below or from the right. The most obvious landmark (at least before the new trees grow up) is the clean wide face of Plantation Crack Buttress. This currently offers by far the best climbing on the crag, including the two-star route mentioned above.

**Conditions and Aspect:** South-west facing and currently, whilst the new trees are small, fairly open and quick-drying. Moving about between the buttresses is quite arduous due to jumbled mossy boulders and dead tree trunks.

**Parking and Approach:** The crag lies at the edge of Braisty Woods. If approaching from Summerbridge, before you reach the main Brimham National Trust car park, turn left (west) at the crossroads onto Brimham Rocks Road. Park in a lay-by on the right about 400m down this road. (**GPS 54.0689, -1.6874**). Go through the gate and follow the track that leads up through the new young plantation past a portacabin/shooting box directly towards the most obvious large buttress. The crag and approach are on private land.

**Access Issues:** This edge is outside the National Trust Boundary and occasionally now used by a shooting club and other sporting interests. Access for climbing was rarely questioned in the past as the rocks were shrouded in trees and hidden from view. However, since the recent felling operations climbers can be seen and some have been asked to leave in recent years. Permission now needs to be sought in advance from Mr Stuart Barrett at Braisty Woods Farm, (Tel: 01423 780100) in order to avoid conflict with other sporting interests, particularly shooting, which occurs below the crag. No big groups.

---

The first climbs are situated about 100m left of *Plantation Crack*, where a dirty low prow provides a good landmark. **Deception** (S 4a) takes the roof-capped corner to the left of the prow, avoiding the steep stuff by cutting left at the roof and onto the slab. **Bracken Crack** (VS 4c) however, bravely faces the massive challenge of overcoming the huge roof crack. **The Prow** (HS 4b) takes the arête on its left-hand side via the hanging crack. A further 30m right and slightly higher is a broken, slabby buttress. Higher still on the left side of this are the following routes.

**1  Overhung Buttress**  HVS 5a   6m   ★
The left arête of the undercut prow is climbed gymnastically on its left side.
*Greg Tough  25th July 1972*

**2  Left-Hand Arête**  S 4a   12m
Confusingly named, this is the right arête of the buttress but left arête of the gully. It has a scrappy lower half followed by a better finish.
*Greg Tough  25th July 1972*

**3  Easter Egg Ridge**  E2 5c   7m   ★
The blunt arête provides a hard problem. A long reach may gain the ledge above the arête. The slab above is not much easier and the ground is even further away.
*Greg Tough  25th July 1972*

**4  Easter Egg Crack**  HS 4b   6m
Climb the crack behind the first tree to a birch stump, step right and up to a heathery finish.
*Tony Barley, Robin Barley  1961*

# PLANTATION CRACK

**5 Salubrious Navaho Indians** E1 5c  10m  ★
The wall right of *Easter Egg Crack* starting just right of the tree where a long reach gains the big break. Use slopers to reach the notch in the left arête and climb it to the top.
*Luke Dow (solo)  8th May 1993*

Another 50m right is **Plantation Crack Buttress**.

**6 Greenfingers**  VS 4c  9m  ★
Climb the cracks below the left arête to the ledge on *Side Track*, which is followed to the top.
*Jeff Appleyard, John Ellis  1969*

**7 Southern Belle**  E3 6a  10m  ★
Start beneath a blind flake. Use the flake to gain the horizontal break then take the thin crack on the right to reach another break before a big move to the top.
*John Henderson, Paul Carling  12th April 1992*

**8 State of the Union**  E2 5c  14m  ★
Follow *Southern Belle* to the top break then traverse right to *Plantation Crack*. Move up and right again to finish as for *Yankie Beau*.
*Paul Carling, John Henderson  12th April 1992*

**9 Side Track**  HVS 5a  16m
From the base of the wide crack on *Plantation Crack* continue traversing to the ledge on the left of the arête. Move up and round to finish up the slabby rib above.
*Tony Barley, Tony Roach  18th March 1972*

**10 Plantation Crack**  HVS 5a  10m  ★★
The route of the crag and worth dropping by for this alone. Traverse into and ascend the wide crack splitting the buttress. Finish direct for optimum enjoyment.
*Dennis Gray, Des Hadlum  1960*

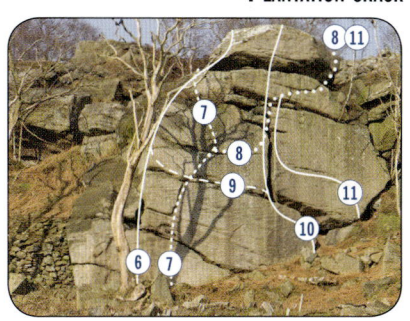

**11 Yankie Beau**  E3 5c  10m  ★
Start 4m right of *Plantation Crack* and traverse left with difficulty to the edge of the crack. Layback this to a small break and protection in *Plantation Crack*. Move back right to a final break and thence the top.
*Paul Carling (unseconded)  12th April 1992*

Another 30m right is a wide moss-covered buttress.

**12 Abrasion**  E3 5c  12m
Climb the stepped arête on the right of the bay. The wide horizontal crack crossing the headwall facilitates a short, sharp and difficult finish.
*Tony Barley, Ken Wood  2nd Oct 1971*

**13 Evergreen Cracks**  HS 4b  8m
Bridge the wide crack 6m right of *Abrasion* and finish up the cleaner, hanging crack above.
*Tony Barley, Robin Barley  1961*

At a higher level, starting at the back of the top block of *Abrasion*, is a collection of boulders of good quality rock.

Almscliff to Slipstones    315

## PLANTATION CRACK

### 14 I'm Chief Kamanawanalaya  Font 7b
From a sit-down start below the low break on the left, move rightwards on a thin seam to gain the vertical crack and a slopey finish.

### 15 Big Fish  Font 7c+
The blunt arête from a sit-down start. Font 6c from standing.

### 16 Minnow  Font 6b+
Climb flakes from sitting with a long reach to a sloper on top.

### 17 Jaws  Font 7b+
Traverse right-to-left on the thin break under the small overlap to a finish above the roof.

The central arête can be climbed on either side as (a) **Pyramid Ridge** (Font 5+), and the right-hand arête. (b) **Ridgeback** (Font 6b+), is climbed on the left from a sit-down start.

### Further Information on First Ascents
*Tony and Robin Barley climbed The Prow, Bracken Crack and Deception in 1961.*

### GRADED LIST

**ROUTES**
E3
Southern Belle (6a)
Abrasion (5c)
Yankie Beau (5c)

E2
Easter Egg Ridge (5c)
State of the Union (5c)

E1
Salubrious Navaho Indians (5c)

**HVS**
Overhung Buttress (5a)
Plantation Crack (5a)
Side Track (5a)

**VS**
Bracken Crack (4c)
Greenfingers (4c)

**HS**
Easter Egg Crack (4b)
Evergreen Cracks (4b)
The Prow (4b)

**S**
Deception (4a)
Left-Hand Arête (4a)

**PROBLEMS**
7c+
Big Fish

7b+
Jaws

7b
I'm Chief K.......

6b+
Minnow
Ridgeback

5+
Pyramid Ridge

---

'**World famous in Yorkshire**' is the affectionate description given to Nidderdale-born Tony Barley who, from the 1960s onwards, was a significant and prolific pioneer of hard new routes on both Yorkshire grit and limestone.

The son of a Summerbridge mill owner, Tony and his brother Robin began climbing together in their teens at nearby Brimham, initially ropeless and in gym shoes until their father spun them a hemp rope of their own. It was at Brimham and the neighbouring towering walls of Guisecliff that the brothers first started to make their mark in the early 1960s, their most prolific period on the grit. Robin often had the eye for the line but Tony was often the one thrown into the lead when things got tough.

A remarkable weekend in 1965 saw Tony, aged just 17, lead three of the hardest routes in Yorkshire at the time, all onsight — Don Whillans' Forked Lightning Crack at Heptonstall (possibly the second ascent) on the Saturday morning, the first ascent of Creation at Guisecliff that afternoon, and the first ascent of Carnage at Malham. Tony also had a long-standing love-affair with Almscliff where he was probably the first (and possibly still the only person)

### TONY BARLEY

*1947-2009*
*Yorkshire grit era: 1960s onwards*
*Climbing style: No-nonsense gnarly hardman, bold and tough.*
*Top Yorkshire grit first ascents: North Buttress Direct, Guisecliff, Beatnik (Brimham), Creation (Guisecliff), Mastermind (Guisecliff), Black Wall Eliminate (Almscliff - photo above), Yellow Wall (Almscliff), Barley Mow (Almscliff).*

# PROFILE

to solo the full crag girdle. More famously his Black Wall Eliminate and Yellow Wall are still important testpieces and his 1966 boulder problem Barley Mow was years ahead of its time and likely the first highball Font 7a in the country.

After graduating as an engineer in 1967 Tony left the UK for South Africa, joined a year later by Robin and together they transformed climbing there, adding over 50 new routes in the Transvaal in the late 1960s. After fracturing his skull in an accident, Tony returned to the UK in the early 70s, forging a productive partnership with then rising grit star Jerry Peel and ticking the extreme classics of the day in England and Wales. Tony's hard climbing days weren't quite over yet and he added another bold testpiece, Mastermind at Guisecliff.

By the late 1970s Tony moved back to his beloved Yorkshire, scouring remote moorland outcrops cleaning and recording new boulder problems. Tony documented well over 100 problems on Sypeland during constant running battles with the local gamekeeper and led similar solo campaigns on many other private grouse-moors eventually producing his Wild Bouldering in Yorkshire guide in 1997, which introduced us to the esoteric delights of venues such as Thruscross, High and Low Huller Stones, and Little Brimham.

For a period of three years in the early 1990s Tony also partnered Dave Musgrove to unearth (often quite literally) the unique Eavestone, using a murderous machete blade to hack a 30-metre tunnel through the rhododendrons to gain access to The Fort Buttress.

Although he continued to boulder almost right up to the end, Tony sadly died after heart problems in 2009, leaving behind a legacy of gnarly hard climbs and bouldering across Yorkshire grit from the big crags to remote esoteric moorland outcrops.

**Dave Musgrove**

Steve Webster, Tony Barley, Bob and Martin Berzins. Photo: Ken Wood

# little brimham
by **Paul Clarke**

---

OS Ref: SE 205 641
Altitude: 272 m

---

Little Brimham - not generally a good place if you're a bit of a wuss. The crag comprises three areas; The Edge, which lurks in a wood that feels ancient and a bit Lord of the Ringsy; Bovine Buttress, with a more open location like its big neighbour, and finally Adam's Ale Block, an obscure overhanging block close to the woodland stream. Each area has high quality routes and problems, though some do attract natures detritus. Overall it's well worth a visit for the accomplished highballer and the solitude seeking boulderer.

**The Climbing:** The discontinuous edge is an intimidating spot where the rocky landings make mats hard to place and where the height is often of that "Is this a route?" variety. All manner of grit features are on offer here including many a baffling arête such as *Boris or Bust (Font 6c)* and *So Pussy (Font 7b)*. Bovine Buttress is different and has generally flat landings yet still with splat potential (of more than one kind). If you like ribs then there are plenty to go at here with a couple amongst the best micro routes in Yorkshire; *Cowboy Daze (Font 6c)* being a particular highlight. The use of a rope may be sensible for some 'problems' on first acquaintance, particularly around the Bay of Pigs and Adam's Ale areas.

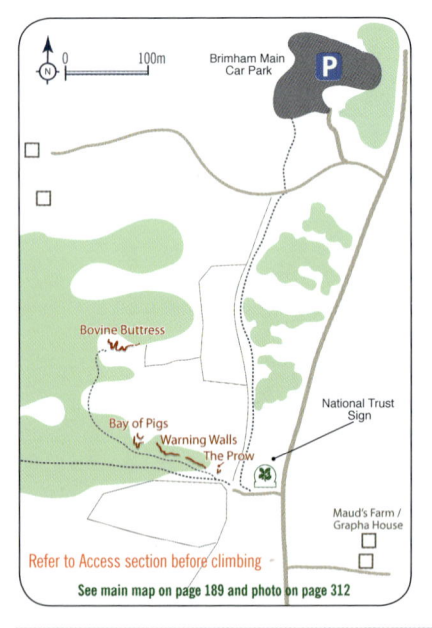

**Routes and Bouldering:** A total of 87 boulder problems/highballs ranging from Easy to Font 7c and three routes (two at HVS and one at E6 that deserves some traffic), but this doesn't by any means ensure your safety. If in doubt bring your rope.

**Conditions and Aspect:** Facing south-west, the rocks on the edge would get plenty of sun if it wasn't for the trees. As it is, the shade is welcome in summer but the rocks can remain damp in places after prolonged rain. Bovine Buttress is less shady, catches the afternoon and evening sun and dries quickly. It's a popular haunt for both climbers and cows.

**Parking and Approach:** From the main Brimham car park (page 189) return to the entry gate by the old pay box and take the track on the right signposted to Druid's Cave Farm. After 50m, at a right-hand bend, take a path on the left that follows the wall above the fields for about 400m. You will see Bovine Buttress across the field on the right but **please don't approach over the walls** as this is very likely to give rise to access problems. Keep on the path until it drops to a grassy track at the right-hand end of the Little Brimham edge and from where the first rocks (but the last described) are obvious. This point is also easily approached from the road by Maud's Farm, but please don't park here.

**Access Issues:** There are no access issues at present but as this is private land please keep a low profile at Bovine Buttress so as not to annoy local residents, either of bovine or human kind.

# Bovine Buttress - LITTLE BRIMHAM

## Bovine Buttress
Some very worthwhile and quite highball problems. The finishes can be dirty and scary and may need to be inspected beforehand. Worth a visit, especially to sample the rib-roaring delights of *Cowboy Daze*. To reach the buttress you can easily skirt around the edge bottom but need to carefully cross a wall/fence and climb up to the boulders; about 200m past the last rocks of the edge. The first four problems (including two ace Font 7a's) are on a block directly below Bovine Buttress.

### 1 Rodeo Rider   Font 7a
Cling on to the direct line on ripples through the roof.
*Neil McCallum   December 2008*

### 2 Bucking Broncos   Font 7a
A thin, left-hand rib finish to *Wielding the Branding Iron*.
*Neil McCallum   December 2008*

### 3 Wielding the Branding Iron   Font 5
A problem that leaves a lasting impression. Romp the crack above the right-hand side of the roof.
*Tony Barley   June 1995*

### 4 Tan Your Hide   Font 5+
The fine wall and upper arête.
*Tony Barley   June 1995*

Returning to the main buttress, to the left of the main walls is a niche and easy corner (Font 2) with two highball problems to its left.

### 5 Rawhide   Font 6a
Climb onto the ledge and continue, by the skin of your teeth, over the prow at the short crack.
*Tony Barley   1966*

### 6 Home on the Range   Font 5
The steep wall on good holds.
*Robin Barley   1962*

### 7 Hang 'em Low   Font 6b+
A left-to-right traverse from the corner, dropping low and finishing around the arête … and keep your feet up!
*Nigel Baker, Andy Watts   1997*

### 8 Just Grazing   Font 4+
From the left side of the long wall, climb past the hole to breaks and up to a spicy finish.
*Tony Barley   1964*

### 9 Riding Bareback   Font 6a
A nice problem just to the right. Make a hard start up the faint ramp trending leftwards to a good finish.
*Tony Barley   1996*

### 10 Beef Crisis   Font 5+
From the base of the faint ramp move up right to the highest point. Undercut the pocket and muscle up to the break or (harder at Font 6b) use a crimp up and right and rock on. Both ways are good. **Pot Black** (Font 7c) is a huge dyno between the two breaks avoiding the holds on *Beef Crisis* – could have been called Potted Beef Crisis.
*Nigel Baker, Andy Watts 1997; David Mason Apr 2006 (Pot Black)*

# LITTLE BRIMHAM - Bovine Buttress

### 11  Saddle Sore   Font 5+
From the left side of the break climb the wall passing the big pocket and step round the arête.
*Tony Barley   1962*

### 12  Pony Express   Font 6a+
Grovel over the bulge and past the hole.
*Nigel Baker, Andy Watts   1997*

Around the rib and on the left side of the gully are a series of adjacent groovelines.

### 13  Trailblazer   Font 5
The left-hand, hanging groove and the edge of the rib.
*Tony Barley   1962*

The following three grooves, **Cleft Hoof** (Font 5), **Side Saddle** (Font 3+) and **Load of Bull** (Font 3), suffer from a good layer of verdure and have lost their appeal somewhat. *(All by Tony Barley, June 1995)*

### 14  Chewing the Cud   Font 4
Stonking. On the right, at the back of gully, the green flake crack is well worth grazing on but take care with the awkward exit.
*Nigel Baker, 1997*

### 15  The Watering Hole   Font 5
On the left of the next rib is a scoop and pocket. Gain the ledge and upper break via these features and finish boldly right to the 'watering hole' on top. Less bold but still with interest, up left, is really a separate problem; Font 5.
*Tony Barley   June 1995*

### 16  Think Pink   Font 7a
Dyno between the breaks on the wall left of the *Cowboy Daze* prow and just right of the hole.
*Jim Purchon   July 2006*

### 17  Cowboy Daze   Font 6c (E3 6b)
The most prominent undercut arête is a real attention grabber. It can be protected, but the solo is much more satisfying (despite, or in spite of, the rounded finish). Takes runners if you have a rope. Photo opposite.
*Nigel Baker, Andy Watts, Mike Stacey   1996*

### 18  Yipycaye   Font 6a
The nose just right with a problematic finish.
*Paul Clarke   May 2000*

### 19  Rustler   Font 2
The wide corner/crack. The left-hand finish is Font 3.
*Tony Barley   August 1995*

Past the jutting nose is a useful descent.

### 20  Shake, Cattle and Roll   Font 6a
The left rib.
*Paul Clarke   May 2000*

### 21  Braised Steak   Font 5
Step off the boulder and climb the right side of the nose. A better variation goes from a sit-down start and out along the break (Font 6b).
*Tony Barley   August 1995*

### 22  Lariat   Font 3
A fun rib starting from its right.
*Tony Barley   August 1995*

Charlotte Telfer commits to **Cowboy Daze** (Font 6c / E3 6b). Opposite page
Photo: Tom Peckitt

Charlotte Telfer showing her hand on **Boris or Bust** (Font 6c) . Page 324
Photo: Tom Peckitt

### 23  Stirk   Font 5
Sit-down start . Tackle the undercut wall using the arête and thin crack.
*Tony Barley   August 1995*

### 24  Steer   Font 5
Sit-down start . The undercut wall on the right using the crack. Variations are (a) **Steer to the Left** (Font 5+) left of the clean crack with feet on the back wall and no arêtes and (b) **Steer to the Right** (Font 5) goes right of the crack with feet on the back wall.
*Tony Barley   August 1995, Nigel Baker   1997*

### 25  Buffalo   Font 3+
The enjoyable wall to a rounded finish.
*Tony Barley   August 1995*

Located about 200m south south-west the next area of climbs continue.

## The Little Brimham Edge
Near the left-hand end of the edge is a very impressive smooth wall and imposing arête. Above these is a higher tier of rocks known as The Aiguille de Premier Alert which is actually a series of detached pinnacles with some good and quite exposed lines on the main block. Most are hard/impossible to mat, require a confident approach and you may very well consider some to be routes.

### 26  Eastern Block   Font 4+   *Tony Barley  1962*
### 27  Missile Crisis   Font 4+ (HVS 5a)   *T. Barley  1962*

### 28  Bomber Command   Font 5 (HVS 5b)
Bold and superb. *Tony Barley  1962*

## Bay of Pigs - LITTLE BRIMHAM

**29 Heat Seeker**  Font 4+ (HVS 5a)
A good exposed line. *Tony Barley 1962)*

**30 Fallout**  Font 4+ (HVS 5a)  *Tony Barley 1962*

**31 Red Alert**  Font 5 (HVS 5b)
A contrived start up the awkward undercut groove gives access to the headwall on the left before moving right to the edge of the rib.
*Tony Barley 15th June 1996*

**32 Missile Attack**  Font 4+ (HVS 5a)
The overhanging prow direct, above a big drop. Good holds seem to materialise from nowhere as do runner placements for those with a rope.
*Tony Barley 15th June 1996*

There are problems on the back of the block, on the slab behind and the blocks to the right *(all done first by Tony Barley in 1962)*. The green chimney left of *Eastern Block* has several green slab and wall problems from Font 3. Right of *Missile Attack*, the cracked groove is Font 2; the nice exposed hanging flake on the prow is Font 3+; the prow front finishing right is a scary Font 5; the right trending slab is a pleasant Font 1+; the slab arête via the overlap is an exposed Font 4 with easier variations just left.

### Bay of Pigs
Returning to the lower tier. To the right is the major feature of this part of Little Brimham, an immaculate steep wall and the fine hanging arête taken by *Ancient*.

**33 First Strike**  Font 5
The hanging arête over to the left of the big wall.
*Tony Barley 15th June 1996*

**34 Cuban Blockade**  Font 5
The shallow groove on the left of the big wall is most easily climbed using the edge on the left. Climbed direct it is a good and tough Font 6b+.
*Tony Barley April 1996; direct Paul Clarke May 2000*

**35 The Good News**  Font 7b (E6 6c)
Technically high in the grade(s). The good news is the steep blank wall is immaculate and is achieved via three powerful yet tenuous moves to a finishing dyno. The bad news is that unfortunately it gets green through lack of traffic and a tumble would be unthinkable. Be sure to make the headlines for the right reason.
*Mike Gray 1st May 2003*

**36 Ancient**  E6 6b   7m   ☆☆
The big arête is excellent and fully E6 due to the intimidating landing. The hanging nose is climbed front-on using both edges and a powerful series of slaps.
*Paul Clarke May 2000*

**37 Kruschev's Chimney**  Font 2+
Classic stuff.
*Tony Barley 1964*

**38 Western Alliance**  Font 6b+
Sit-down start. Ingenious moves on huecos gain the fine groove above the roof. Needs lots of mats. Bridging from the boulder is Font 5+.
*Tony Barley 1972*

**39 Supreme Soviet**  Font 5
Make a precarious pull up onto the right rib then trend left to finish.
*Tony Barley 15th June 1996*

To the right is a handful of poor problems but the arête is a nice Font 4+ (watch the wobbling top block). A further 20m right is a block with a scoop near the top.

# LITTLE BRIMHAM - The Warning Walls

### 40 Curving Overlap  Font 6a
Climb past two pebbles. Always green.

### 41 Whitehall  Font 5
Gain the front of the block and scoop without recourse to the chimney.
*Tony Barley  6th July 1996*

### 42 Red Square  Font 4
The little triangular groove.
*Tony Barley  1972*

## The Warning Walls
A collection of fins and bold arêtes with one of Yorkshire's star problems up the sharpest of these.

### 43 Miss Monypenny  Font 3
The green crack/groove to the left of the first arête.
*Tony Barley  1964*

### 44 Bold Finger  Font 6a
The rib from the left - rockover right. **Pussy Galore** (Font 5+) climbs the rib from the right to a rockover left.
*Tony Barley  1992*

### 45 License to Thrill  Font 6b (E3 6a)
A Barley classic. The big clean wall is a superb micro-route on ripples, pebbles and with a reachy finish. Pads have reduced the impact but a proper onsight solo is worth E3.
*Tony Barley  6th July 1996*

The wall left of the fine arête has three squeezed-in problems:

### 46 Unwanted Gift  Font 5
The flake and bulge just to the right of the corner.
*Nigel Baker  3rd August 1996*

### 47 The Spy Who Loved Me  Font 3+
The sustained line via a scoop and pocket on the left wall.
*Tony Barley  1964*

### 48 Natasha's Just Desserts  Font 5+
Climb the left side of the prow.
*Tony Barley  2nd July 1996*

### 49 Boris or Bust  Font 6c
One of the best problems around these parts. Grapple with the right edge of the sharp overhanging arête. Sometimes described as a harder but smaller *High Noon* but climbed very differently. Photo on page 322.
*Nigel Baker, Tony Barley, Dave Musgrove  3rd August 1996*

### 50 Back in the U.S.S.R.  Font 6a
The blunt rib just right of the arête – avoid the flake on the right if you can/dare. **For Your Arms Only** (Font 5) has been recorded to the right.
*Tony Barley  6th July 1996*

Yorkshire Gritstone

## The Prow - LITTLE BRIMHAM

The grassy shallow corner on the right is **From Russia with Love** (Font 2+). On the nose to the right of a big twin-stemmed tree are five problems that get progressively more serious and harder to mat:

### 51 Coldfinger  Font 4
Up pockets to the hanging crack, trending left.
*Tony Barley  1962*

### 52 On Her Majesty's Secret Service  Font 4+
Nice moves on the left side of the prow into the scoop.
*Tony Barley  1972*

### 53 For Queen and Country  Font 6a
An honourary highball. The hanging fin direct.
*Tony Barley  14th June 1996*

### 54 Shaken Not Stirred  Font 6a
You might be both. The right-hand side of the arête to a small flake. Bad landing.
*Tony Barley  1972*

### 55 M  Font 6a+
The right-most line on the wall is green and tricky.
*Tony Barley  15th June 1996*

The next block contains **Goldfinger** (Font 3) up the middle, with the technical **Q** (Font 5) just to the right. Right again and lower down is **Stepped Rib** (Font 2); **Live and Let Die** (Font 3) is the dirty rib just to the right again; **Tonic** (Font 2) climbs the obvious square corner in the next block.

Right again is a distinct tower with:

### 56 You Only Live Twice  Font 6a+
Or once if you fall. If you don't – that's one life used up. Make a full-frontal assault on the highball tower. Drop the grade a notch if taken on the right.
*Tony Barley  24th March 1996*

### 57 Man With the Golden Gun  Font 6b
The centre of the prominent tooth, following the crack. Highball with a nasty landing.
*Tony Barley  2nd June 1996*

To the right are the following poor problems, **Lemon Twist** (Font 1+), **Vodka** (Font 3) and **Smirnoff** (Easy).

### The Prow
The last climbs are on a fine pointed prow 40m to the right.

### 58 Licence to Kill  Font 6a
The rib by leaping from the boulder – yes really!
*Tony Barley  1972*

### 59 So Pussy  Font 007b
Sit-down start . The classy prow climbed direct. A very good problem.

### 60 Thunderball  Font 4+
The wall past the shallow runnel.
*Tony Barley  1996*

# LITTLE BRIMHAM - Adam's Ale Block

## Adam's Ale Block (SE 204 643)

An isolated overhanging block can be found near the footpath and above the eponymous spring. It is best approached down the track that leads to Druids Cave Farm. Follow it for 200m turning to the left at the junction to descend to a farm. Turn left and then go through the gates past the farm buildings, over the stile bending right towards the wood. A stony path descends then bends left deeper into the wood passing the Adam's Ale springs. Alternatively go through the woods northwards from Little Brimham.

### 61 Adam's Ale  HVS 5b  6m  ☆
A classic thrutch. Climb the chimney that splits the block.
*Tony Barley, Robin Barley  1966*

### 62 Adam's Apple  HVS 5a  6m
The overhanging crack to the right of the chimney is well protected to a rounded finish.
*Dave Musgrove, Tony Barley  20th April 2005*

---

**GRADED LIST**
**ROUTES**

**E6**
Ancient

**HVS**
Adam's Ale
Adam's Apple

**PROBLEMS**
**Font 7c**
Pot Black

**Font 7b**
The Good News
So Pussy

**Font 7a**
Think Pink
Rodeo Rider
Bucking Broncos

**Font 6c**
Boris or Bust
Cowboy Daze

**Font 6b+**
Western Alliance
Hang 'em Low

**Font 6b**
License to Thrill
Man With the Golden Gun

**Font 6a+**
You Only Live Twice
Pony Express
M

**Font 6a**
Curving Overlap
Rawhide

For Queen and Country
Shaken Not Stirred
Back In The U.S.S.R.
Riding Bareback
Licence to Kill
Yipycaye
Shake, Cattle and Roll
Bold Finger

**Font 5+**
Tan Your Hide
Beef Crisis
Pussy Galore
Natasha's Just Desserts
Saddle Sore
Steer to the Left

**Font 5**
Steer to the Right
Bomber Command
Red Alert

Wielding the Branding Iron
Trailblazer
The Watering Hole
Supreme Soviet
First Strike
Home on the Range
Cuban Blockade
Whitehall
Unwanted Gift
Q
Cleft Hoof
Braised Steak
Steer
Stirk

**Font 4+**
Heat Seeker
Fallout
Missile Crisis
Missile Attack

Eastern Block
Thunderball
Just Grazing
On Her Majesty's Secret Service

**Font 4**
Chewing the Cud
Coldfinger
Red Square

**Font 3+**
Side Saddle
Ban the Bomb
Buffalo
The Spy Who Loved Me

**Font 3**
Miss Monypenny
Live and Let Die
Goldfinger

Lariat
Vodka

**Font 2+**
From Russia with Lov
Kruschev's Chimney

**Font 2**
Stepped Rib
Tonic
Rustler

**Font 1+**
Lemon Twist

**Easy**
Smirnoff

---

**One of the top climbers** from the 1970s Leeds University golden era on Yorkshire grit, Ken Wood first started climbing in the Lake District (born in Leeds he had moved there as a youngster), doing his first climb in 1959 on Raven Crag, Langdale. Within a year of working his way through the graded list in the old Langdale guidebook with partner Pat Callaghan he had got up to doing the likes of Kipling Groove. In the Lakes Wood met Yorkshire grit legend Allan Austin, who introduced him to God's own grit. The rest, as they say, is history and Woods left his mark, most notably at Brimham, with the likes of True Grit and Batman, which remain much-coveted classic extreme routes today.

**What was your introduction to Yorkshire grit?**
I remember one of the first routes Allan Austin pointed me at was Bald Pate at Ilkley. I found that hard and very scary for a VS and it took me a while to get used to jamming cracks as well but I survived and passed his tests and the rest I suppose is history.

**When did you get involved in the Yorkshire scene?**
I came to Leeds to do a food science MSc in 1969 and that's when I met the rest

### KEN WOOD

*Yorkshire grit era: 1970s*
*Top Yorkshire grit first ascents:*
*True Grit (Brimham), Gronff (Chevin), Batman (Bat Buttress), Walter's Rib (Great Wolfrey), Fire Knacker Crack (Caley).*
*What they said of him: "He was great climber. Maybe the best in country at the time." Allan Aust*

# PROFILE

of the uni team like John Syrett, Al Manson, John Harwood and Bernard Newman. I climbed quite a bit originally with Mike Mortimer who was a bit older than the rest and more my age.

**Did you do any specific training for climbing?**
Not really. We didn't think of it as training but I did use the old Leeds uni wall and bouldered a lot at Almscliff and Shipley Glen.

**Two of your hardest new grit routes were True Grit at Brimham in 1970, which still rates as E4 6b today, and Batman at E3 6a. What were your motivations for these two lines?**
A few of us had been trying the start to True Grit and after several attempts I was first to crack it. I could rest at the halfway break and someone threw me up a rope and some runners and I managed to battle my way up the final offwidth. I think it was a similar thing with Batman but once I cracked the crux traverse I just carried on soloing.

**What are your personal favourites amongst your own new routes?**
It's hard to say. Walter's Rib at Great Wolfrey was memorable as were some of the routes at Earl like Trite Rib and Hatchet Crack. Finger Knacker at Caley took a bit of doing. That was another that John Syrett and I just kept nibbling away at until I eventually was first to the top. Gronff on the Chevin was good as well and there is a shorter route, Vim at Shipley, that I don't think I've been previously credited with. I was pretty pleased with that and am sure it hadn't been done before.

**Who did you enjoy climbing with the most and who was the best of your contemporaries?**
In the early days it was more a matter of who was available and/or who had transport. Al Manson was probably the best when it came to technique and finesse but John Syrett was probably stronger and had more 'get up and go'. Al was probably the best boulderer I've ever seen, especially his ability to perch almost casually in the most precarious positions. Then Mike Hammill and Ron Fawcett, of course, came along and they were also very impressive to watch.

**What was the Yorkshire scene like at that time?**
Lively. Parties and piss-ups in Leeds and we once dragged a half-full barrel of beer out to Almscliff and continued a party that had started at my house the night before, out on the crag.

**Did you witness any major first ascents of that era?**
I was around for most of the big ascents at Almscliff in the early 70s and was involved in some like Encore and The Big Greeny with Syrett and Manson. If I wasn't on the first ascent I repeated most of these routes within a few days, things like Twelfth Night, First Night, and Yorkshire Pudding – that was exciting with no gear and an atrocious landing!

**You seemed to drop out of the regular climbing scene after the 70s. Why was that?**
I got hooked on cave exploration through the Gritstone Club. Digging out new passages soon began to mean more to me than doing new rock climbs so that sort of took over. I also had a passion for hard mountain walking and got engrossed in ticking off Munros and then Corbetts in Scotland.

**Interview by Dave Musgrove**

# bat buttress

by **Dave Musgrove** with bouldering by **Dave Cowl**

OS Ref: SE 211 639
Altitude: 247 m

One big, tall buttress, lots of good blocks and two short but interesting edges scatter the hillside behind the farm before the entrance to Brimham Rocks. The crag provides plenty of good year-round bouldering and is worthy of at least a couple of visits by the keen router.

**The Climbing:** There are around 25 routes and more than 50 boulder problems at Bat Buttress. A handful of the longer routes are worth seeking out, such as the superb layback flakes of *Trio Wall* (HVS), the wandering easy ramble of *Bat Buttress Original* (Diff) or the puzzling challenge of *The Riddler* (E3 6a). The area is undoubtedly best for bouldering. There's lots to go at in the lower Font grades with a few harder, more modern classics, such as *Turn Me Loose* (Font 7b+) and *Vogue* (Font 8a) for the wads. Sit-starts and low-level traverses abound on the Oak Tree Walls area and there is still plenty of scope for new lines.

**Conditions and Aspect:** South-facing, and generally quick drying. Good all year round but the bracken can be a bit intrusive around the first blocks and the main buttress in summer. The Oak Tree Walls area is pleasant and sheltered with good flat landings.

**Parking and Approach:** These rocks are just outside the National Trust Boundary and on private land. To avoid any potential access issues it is best to park in the main Brimham Rocks National Trust car park (page 189, **GPS: 54.075561,-1.681783**) and walk back down the lane. The farm is clearly seen on the right beyond the crossroads, when approaching from Summerbridge, and about 300m short of the main entrance to Brimham Rocks. Always enter on foot via the farm driveway and, after asking

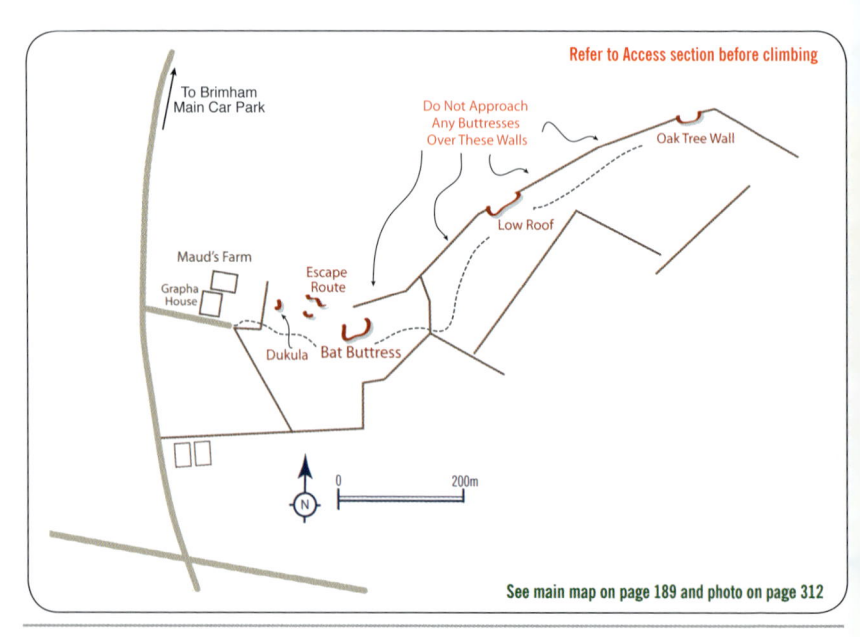

Refer to Access section before climbing

See main map on page 189 and photo on page 312

**Yorkshire Gritstone**

## Introduction - Bat buttress

permission (see below) continue through the bottom gate to the boulder field and main buttress. To get to the Oak Tree Walls walk down slightly from the main buttress and climb over the old metal gate into the open fields from where the first Oak Tree Wall can clearly be seen.

**Access Issues:** The area of land covered by these rocks is owned by two different farmers. Mr. Barker owns the first field behind the farm (historically known as Maud's Farm and shown as such on the OS Maps) and now lives in the newly converted Grapha House which is the first one passed on the walk in. **Always ask his permission before climbing.** It is rarely refused. The fields containing Oak Tree Walls are owned by Mr. David Smith of Shepherd's Lodge Farm. He has granted a general permission to climb on the understanding that he accepts no responsibility for accident or injury. He does sometimes have cows in these fields, which shouldn't cause any problems but use your own judgement if they are present. **Never enter either section of the crag across the walls from the Nidderdale Way path on National Trust Land.**

The routes and all significant problems are described from left-to-right starting with the first collection of small boulders up near the wall and fence surrounding the back garden of the farmhouse. Please keep the noise levels down in this vicinity.

Fine conditions for Neil Sugden on **Trio Wall** (HVS 5a). Page 332
Photo: Adi Gill

# BAT BUTTRESS - Count Duckula

### 1 Count Duckula  Font 7a+
A fun but hard problem. Crouch low and climb the over-hanging triangular wall with aid of the left arête.
*Ben Meeks  2004*

### 2 Vlad Von Carsen  Font 7c
Crouch low and dyno the centre of the wall. The block is used for feet. The full sit-down start without the block goes at a monster Font 8a.
*Ben Meeks  29th May 2004 (sit-start by Mark Katz 2010)*

To the right and at a higher level is a jumble of blocks and craglets with scope for many problems and micro routes. Moving around this area in the summer is a problem due to lush bracken, hidden gaps and deep holes. Two named problems exist, **Kitchen Sync** (Font 5+), a low-level traverse and **Jiggle of the Sphinx** (Font 6a), an undercut arête through the middle of the traverse which can be found on the back wall near some faded 'Keep Out' graffiti.

At a lower level the lone block is split by a diagonal crack.

### 3 Pipestrelle  Font 5+
The wall left of the crack.
*Dave Musgrove, Alan Spurrett  2006 (FRA)*

### 4 Bat Crack  Font 5
The crack has an awkward finish.

### 5 Daubenton's Wall  Font 4
The wall past the hole to the top of the crack.
*Alan Spurrett, Dave Musgrove  2006 (FRA)*

## Escape Route Buttress
Up and right, a more continuous tier of short, featured walls provide more bouldering opportunities and the starts to three longer routes which finish on the upper tier.

### 6 Break Out  Font 3
A shallow crack has a heathery exit.

### 7 Colditz  Font 4
The flake and hanging prow.

### 8 The Cooler King  HVS 5a  15m
The short rib and slab above leads through the heathery terrace to a pocketed wall on the left of the upper tower. Climb this (bold) and improvise rightwards on the top ledge to finish up the final rib. A sit-down start to the rib of *The Cooler King* is **The Tunnel King** (Font 5+) which escapes left at the heather.
*Paul Farrish (solo)  11th June 2011 (FRA)*

### 9 Escape Route  MVS 4b  14m  ★
Gain a shallow groove on the right-hand side of the lower wall and climb to a heathery ledge. Climb up under the overhang and swing right to a narrow ledge finishing up the top wall on slopers and the edge of a shallow crack.
*Jeff Appleyard  January 1969*

### 10 Free and Breezy  HS 4b  15m  ★
Just right of the gully is a rib. Climb this on the right-side then swing left to layback the edge of the short crack (optional belay on the birch tree). Continue up the right-hand side of the upper tower from a high stepping move by the short crack. The upper slab is easier and very pleasant.
*Dave Musgrove, John Hunt  11th June 2011 (FRA)*

# Bat Buttress

**11 The Great Escape** Font 5+ (E1 5c)
Bridge up under the triangular roof and escape boldly right via the scoop. (a) The scoop can be gained more easily from the right at HVS 5a.

**12 Tom** Font 3 (S 4b)
Up through the cut-away hole to a rounded finish with or without the aid of the tree.

**13 Dick** Font 4+ (E1 5b)
The central line on the slab to a bold bilberry exit.
*Paul Farrish 11th June 2011*

**14 Harry** Font 5 (E1 5c)
The right-hand line up the slab – just how strong are bilberry roots?
*Paul Farrish 11th June 2011*

## Bat Buttress

The highest buttress here has a lower tier just about within bouldering height. Several of the older routes link to pitches on the upper walls. The slightly unnerving descent from the top is across to the pinnacle behind, across a big drop.

**15 Vampire Rib** Font 5+
The short arête climbed on its left is a bit 'necky'.

**16 Yo-Yo Direct** HVS 5b 10m
Climb to the heart-shaped hole and up the flake above. Traverse off or tackle the bulging nose above the ledge.
*John Hunt, Dave Musgrove 11th June 2011* ✦

**17 Yo-Yo** HVS 5a 14m ★
Probably best in two pitches. From the heart-shaped hole move right along the ledge to cracks which allow an exit onto the large ledge above (VS 4c to here). Finish up the tricky scoop in the upper wall (crux).
*Pre-1957*

**18 Diablo** Font 5
Variation Start to *Yo-Yo* just left of the low undercut cave.

**19 Whip and Top** Font 5+
A cracking problem. Direct to finishing crack of lower wall of *Yo-Yo*, starting 2m left of the arête.

**20 Fingers Rib** Font 6a
The arête on its left-hand side is a classic. Previously erroneously named *Fiddlesticks*.
*Andy Wild 31st March 1971*

**21 Fiddlesticks** Font 6b+
The arête on its right is a harder and higher classic.
(Erroneously named *The Riddler* in the old bouldering guide).

# BAT BUTTRESS

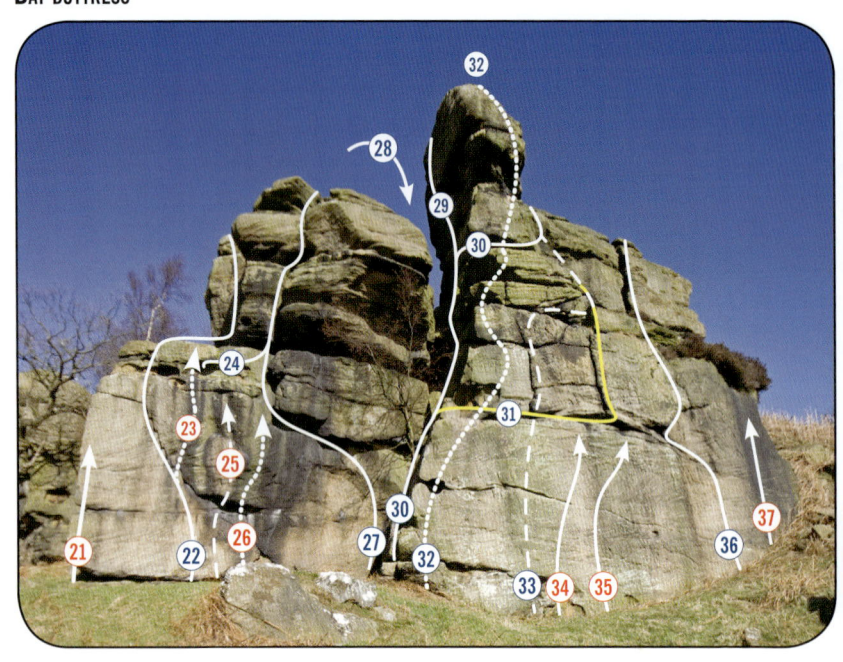

## 22 Trio Wall  HVS 5a   11m   ★★
A superb little route. Layback up the flakes at the left end of the front face. Finish up the scoop above as for *Yo-Yo*.
Photo on page 329.
*George Dale, Allan Austin  1955*

## 23 The Buns of Navarone  Font 5+
Straight up the thin flake to a reachy finish.
*Allan Austin, George Dale, Brian Fuller  1955*  ✦

## 24 Buns to Batman  E2 5c   12m
A hybrid starting up *Buns of Navarone* followed by a hand-traverse right on the lower ledge to join and finish up the offwidth chimney of *Batman*. Traditionalists (or is that masochists?) will love this.
*Paul Farrish, Dave Musgrove  11th June 2011*

## 25 All Buns Blazing  Font 6a
A super problem. Use the undercling to stretch for the jugs then keep your cool and blast straight up for the top.
Photo on page 337.

## 26 Man with a Golden Bun  Font 6c+
Climb from undercut to a hold on the nose then move right and up on slopers.

The **Bat-Bun Project** is an, as yet, unclimbed problem directly below the traverse of *Batman*.

## 27 Batman  E3 6a   14m
The evil-looking overhanging offwidth is gained by a very strenuous traverse from the right using holds both under and over the overlap.
*Ken Wood  16th September 1971*  ✦

## 28 Caped Crack  VS 4c   12m
Climb the corner and slab as for *Bat Buttress Original* but then bridge out onto the east-facing wall to gain and climb the left-hand hanging crack.
*Phillipe Osborne  3rd November 1996*  ✦

## 29 Grotto Wall  E1 5b   20m   ★
Gain the centre of the west-facing wall of the upper gully

from *Bat Buttress Original* (or more easily from the back of the crag) and use an undercut and long reach to gain a higher handrail and good thread on the left. Swing further left and reach blindly around the arête for a good hold. Pull round and up the rib and shallow corner to the top.
*Phillipe Osborne   3rd November 1996* ✦

**30  Bat Buttress Original**  HD 3b   22m   ★
A jolly pleasant ramble with some good variations possible. Climb the slab and corner, up to the big ledge on the right (possible belay) and finish up the corner-crack and slab on the right of the nose.
*pre-1957*

**31  Robin**  HS 4b   22m   ★
A flighty little number. Start up the slab arête and traverse the lower ledge to climb the crack (belay possible). From the big ledge take the corner-crack of *Bat Buttress Original* for 2m and pull right onto the slab.
*Steve Clark, Lynn Robinson   29th August 2011 (FRA)*

**32  The Riddler**  E3 6a   20m   ★★
Low in the grade but still takes a bit of puzzling out. Climb the right side of the arête, just right of the slab of *Bat Buttress*, and then the steep cracked wall above. Pull onto the big, sloping ledge on the left and move right under the nose. Climb up and move slightly left to the 'nostril' of the nose and arrange protection (beware of rope drag). Use pockets to pull up and right (thread) then compose yourself for the final moves onto the exposed arête to good finishing holds – eventually.
*Phillipe Osborne, Tim Harbour   2nd November 1996*

**33  Bat Buttress Direct**  E1 6a   14m   ★
Make a desperate rockover to a ledge using a spike (or, more easily, a big span right from the hole at the start of *The Riddler)*. Continue up the flake and wall or, better, traverse right to a crack which leads to the ledge. The lower wall is **Bun Fight at the OK Corral** (Font 6a).
*Robin Barley, Tony Barley   August 1963* ✦

**34  Wongy**  Font 7a+
Get established with an undercut and lots of body tension. Span the blank wall direct via a dyno or monster reach.
*Matthew Wong   May 2011*

**35  Vogue**  Font 8a
Style and cool your way up the wall from the scoop and break. Leave these behind and move right on small holds trusting your feet all the way. Finish at the break.
*Andy Swann   2008*

**36  Dragnet**  HVS 6a   15m   ★
Start left of the right-hand side of the buttress and gain a break with difficulty, particularly so for the short. Climb the undercut flake and wall above to the ledge. Finish up the easy wide crack beyond. The lower half is **The Bunforgiven** (Font 6a).
*Jeff Appleyard   1969*

**37  Turn Me Loose**  Font 7b+
Hard and highball. Climb the black wall direct on pebbles.
*Andy Swann   2005*

### The Oak Tree Walls
About 150m right, through a gate and into a pleasant flat field, the edge re-emerges as a series of shorter walls, most of which sprout large projecting oaks. The first section – below and left of the first big oak - is the **Little Acorns** sector.

**38  Annie Oakley**  Font 4
Climb the left edge of the sidewall via a vague rib.
*Dave Musgrove   1st June 2011 (FRA)*

**39  Little Acorns Grow**  Font 3
The central line is pleasant if a little reachy.
*Nigel Baker   1st June 2011 (FRA)*

**40  Oak A Arête**  Font 3+   (S 4b)
The rib can be led and protected if necessary. Slightly harder if you start underneath at around Font 4+.

**41  Crack Attack**  Font 5 (HVS 5b)
The left-hand crack has a tricky top-out.
*Dave Musgrove, Nigel Baker   1st June 2011 (FRA)*

**42  Wooden Heart**  Font 4   (VS 4c)
The right-hand crack is more conventional.
*Dave Musgrove, Nigel Baker   1st June 2011 (FRA)*

# BAT BUTTRESS - Low Roof

### The Low Roof Sector (by Paul Clarke)
Very different in character to the rest of the rocks here is the obvious long, low roof of black grit. Power pulls, throws and much grunting are the order of the day. Sit-down starts are obligatory, though all could be done without at much easier grades. Some problems can be continued beyond the obvious break but no-one seems to bother. The undercut soft band that has caused the roof to be formed does seep so choose a dry period to visit.

### 43 Low Loader  Font 6c
Swing out leftwards from the first scoop to small slopers on a vague arête.

### 44 Lowlander  Font 6a
The easier line just to the right.

### 45 Lowlife  Font 6a+
Sit-down start. From the stone and up the vague groove.

### 46 Low Spirits  Font 6a+
The low flake and then the vertical flakes provide the line. Taking the shallow groove on the right instead is **Lowbrow** (Font 6a+).

### 47 Lowercase  Font 6b
The slopers and faint flake.

### 48 Lowest Common Denominator  Font 6b+
Start at the lighter coloured rock. From the pinch, udge up using the flat holds on the wall.

### 49 Low-tech  Font 6c+
The hole and crack. A bit painful.

### 50 Low and Mighty  Font 7a
Use the jug in the cave and dyno for the obvious hold. A variation is **Low Impact** (Font 7a+), and takes the same start and climbs direct using the unhelpful groove. Linking *Low and Mighty* into *Lowest Common Denominator*, keeping feet above the plinth, is **Low Season** (Font 7a+).

### 51 The Lowdown  Font 6c
Go from the flat hold to the shot gun blast and the break.

### 52 Low Tide  Font 6c
Using the same flat hold, swing up right to another (and over the roof if keen).

### 53 Low IQ  Font 5
The groove on the right from a tricky start. A bit harder (but not much) if you miss the holds further right.

There are good traverses hereabouts. The obvious mid-height break is **Swing Low** (Font 5+). Starting from *Low Season* and going low and left with feet on the plinth is **Long Good Friday** (Font 6c+). The latter can be extended from the far right for **Just Another Saturday** (Font 7b) and is mighty fingery.

A further 100m to the right is the original **Oak Tree Wall** containing another huge tree. A slightly higher sector with routes rather than problems, although several are amenable solos above good landings. Before all that though, the short flake, right of the prominent nose on the wall set back left from the main buttress is **Quercus** (Font 4).

### 54 The Mighty Oak  E3 6a  6m  ★★
The standard bearer of the buttress. Steep juggy flakes on

# Oak Tree Wall - BAT BUTTRESS

the left side of the buttress lead to a tricky and committing finish via the small flake on the rounded headwall.

The lower-left wall has two short sit-down start problems, **Roots** (Font 6c) in the centre and **Stumpy** (Font 6a), on the right. Both start from the same obvious slot using different hands. Micro variants are possible.

### 55 **The Wood Cutter** HVS 5a  6m  ★
The main arête with a step right to a reachy finish on hidden flutes.

### 56 **A-Corner** S 4a  12m
Start just left of the left arête. Go up and round onto the front face and traverse into *Oak Tree Crack* to finish.
*Jeff Appleyard  January 1969*

### 57 **Heart of Oak** HS 4b  7m
Climb the thin, diagonal crack and finish a bit further right to good holds on top.
*Jeff Appleyard  January 1969*

### 58 **Sparrow Wall** Font 5 (HVS 5c)
The short, fingery wall between *Heart of Oak* and *Oak Tree Crack*. Finish easily through the upper breaks.
*Dan Duxberry  1994*

### 59 **Oak Tree Crack** HVD 4a  7m  ★
Climb the crack passing right of the tree.
*Jeff Appleyard  January 1969*

### 60 **Thin Veneer** S 4a  7m  ★
Very nice indeed. Boldly climb the thin flake to a jug on the right and then finish trending left.
*Bob Larkin  25th July 1991*

### 61 **Easy Way** D  7m
The far right, trending left to the tree.
*Jeff Appleyard  January 1969*

### 62 **Branch Line** S 4a  15m  ★
A lovely traverse from right-to-left starting up the slanting crack. Steam along the juggy break and finish up *Heart of Oak* (protectable) or, at the same grade but better soloed or done as a Font 3 highball, continue puffing around the arête to finish on the buffers (the big block) at the back of the buttress. You'll feel quite chuffed.
*Dave Musgrove (solo)  8th June 2011 (FRA)*

A traverse of the lower, less positive break starting around on the left wall and continuing to a step down onto the block on the far right is **Call of the Wild** (Font 4).

---

### Further Information on First Ascents (✦)

**Bat Buttress Direct**: *One point of aid was used. Dennis Gray and Allan Austin both claim to have made the first free ascent a short while later - quite impressive for the time. Whether they climbed it direct or by the slightly easier left-hand variant is not known.*
**Batman**: *Only the evil, overhanging, lower traverse was new. The macho upper chimney had been climbed in 1955 by Austin, Dale and Fuller as an alternative to Trio Wall and continuation of what is now known as the Buns of Navarone.*
**(The) Buns of Navarone:** *This was first climbed as a variation start to Trio Wall continuing up the evil upper chimney of what later became Batman. The 'Buns' naming theme came from the 2000 Rockfax guide.*
**Call of the Wild**: *First recorded by Andy Wild on 8th June 2011.*
**Caped Crack:** *Osborne was wearing his blinkers at the time and avoided bridging. He gained the crack via a rounded hand-traverse and thought it HVS 5b.*
**Grotto Wall:** *Osborne soloed the first ascent after thoroughly cleaning it but he climbed more directly via small pockets to the thread at E1 5c. Not sure many subsequent ascents have avoided the big useful undercut further right.*
**Quercus:** *Was first recorded by Paul Farrish on 8th June 2011.*
**Sparrow Wall**: *The lower, crux, wall was soloed by Bob Larkin in 1991, but he traversed off.*
**Yo-Yo Direct:** *The whole route may have been climbed before but the top half was previously un-described.*

# Bat Buttress - Graded List

*All unaccredited routes and problems either first appeared in the 1998 YMC guide (and were probably all climbed by Phillipe Osborne who checked the crag for that volume) or Alan Cameron Duff's Rockfax bouldering guide published in 2000 (and were presumably climbed by him around that time). Many will undoubtedly have been climbed much earlier by others.*

## GRADED LIST

### ROUTES

**E3**
Batman (6a)
The Mighty Oak (6a)
The Riddler (6a)

**E2**
Buns to Batman (5c)

**E1**
Bat Buttress Direct (6a)
Grotto Wall (5b)

**HVS**
Dragnet (6a)
The Cooler King (5a)
Yo-Yo Direct (5b)
Yo-Yo (5a)
Trio Wall (5a)
Great Escape (Right-Hand) (5a)
The Wood Cutter (5a)

**VS**
Yo-Yo (pitch 1) (4c)
Caped Crack (4c)

**MVS**
Escape Route (4b)

**HS**
Heart of Oak (4b)
Free and Breezy (4b)
Robin (4b)

**S**
Thin Veneer (4a)
Branch Line (4a)
A Corner (4a)

**HVD**
Oak Tree Crack (4a)

**HD**
Bat Buttress Original (3b)

**D**
Easy Way

### PROBLEMS

**8a**
Vogue
Vlad Von Carson (SDS)

**7c**
Vlad Von Carson

**7b+**
Turn Me Loose

**7b**
Just Another Saturday

**7a+**
Wongy
Low Season
Count Duckula
Low Impact

**7a**
Low and Mighty

**6c+**
Man with a Golden Bun
Long Good Friday
Low Tech

**6c**
Low Tide
Low Loader
The Lowdown
Roots

**6b+**
Fiddlesticks
Lowest Common Denominator

**6b**
Lower Case

**6a+**
Low Life
Low Spirits
Lowbrow

**6a**
Jiggle of the Sphinx
Fingers Rib
All Buns Blazing
Bun Fight at the OK Coral
The Bunforgiven Lowlander
Stumpy

**5+**
Whip and Top
The Great Escape
The Buns of Navaronne
Vampire Rib
Kitchen Sync
The Tunnel King
Pipestrelle
Swing Low

**5**
Harry
Diablo
Crack Attack
Sparrow Wall
Bat Crack
Low IQ

**4+**
Dick

**4**
Daubenton's Wall
Colditz
Wooden Heart
Quercus
Call of the Wild
Annie Oakley

**3+**
Oak A Arête

**3**
Branch Line extension
Break Out
Tom
Little Acorns Grow

## leaps of faith

Take a pad (or two), a good spotter, fasten your seatbelt and enjoy the flight for this selection of som of the best dynos Yorkshire grit has to offer from the crags in this volume.

- **Famous 45** (Font 6b) Guisecliff

- **Big Dyno** (Font 6b) Lord's Seat

- **Ed's Dyno** (Font 6c+) Almscliff

- **Think Pink** (Font 7a) Little Brimham

- **Sprite** (Font 7a) Guisecliff

- **Jumping Jack Flash** (Font 7a+) Great Wolfrey

- **Arries Ook Direct Start** (Font 7a+) Almscliff

- **The Titfield Thunderbolt** (Font 7b+) Brimham

- **Pot Black** (Font 7c) Little Brimham

- **Fluide** (Font 7c) Crow Crag

- **Big Kicks** (Font 7c) Lord's Seat

- **New Blood** (Font 8a) Caley Roadside

- **Super Furry Animal** (Font 8b) Slipstone

**Compiled by Adi**

Neil Sudgen with **All Buns Blazing** (Font 6a). Page 332
Photo: Adi Gill

# crow crag

by **Phillipe Osborne** with bouldering by **Dave Cowl**

OS Ref: SE 205 636
Altitude: 220m

A wooded grit wonderland that's gone under the radar of the masses due to its sprawling big brother up the road. Bold slabs, stonking cracks and some modern testpieces lie hidden from view in this secluded and peaceful crag. It is a fine spot with half a dozen independent buttresses tucked away among the trees.

**The Climbing:** Just shy of 30 routes on similar if not (dare we say it) more solid rock than Brimham Major; less scrittly at least on the cleaner sectors. Good climbing can be had throughout the grades but if you're operating in the extreme range then there's more to go at. The enigmatic crack of *Corkscrew* (E2 5c) and the classic recent addition of *Stone the Crows* (E5 6b) are up there with some of the best. If you're a pad-master, don't miss out on the Upper Tier, the cleanest buttress at the crag with some wonderfully delicate offerings. Bouldering wise, well it's all about quality rather than quantity. Seven recorded problems though there's evidence of more here. The supremely technical *Fluide* (Font 7c) warrants the trip in itself.

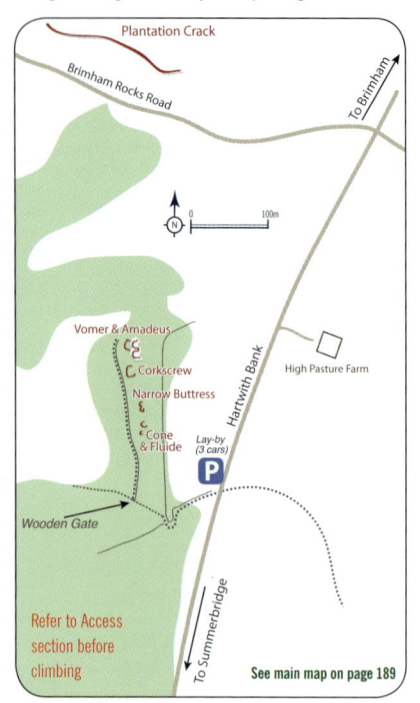

**Conditions and Aspect:** Sheltered climbing can be had all year-round. The crag faces west and although it sits within woodland, all buttresses except Vomer tend to stay clean in the winter months. The upper tier climbs (*Amadeus* area) and the climbs above the ledge on Corkscrew Buttress are above the tree line and will be a good bet in all but the worst weather.

**Parking and Approach:** The crag is called Needham's Crag on OS maps and approach is as for Brimham. From the Summerbridge crossroads follow the road (Hartwith bank) steeply up the hill heading north-east for just over half a mile. There is room for three cars on a grass lay-by (**GPS: 54.063651,-1.685863**) just on the left by the stile and public footpath sign (at the edge of the wood). Park considerately here or alternatively, continue to the Brimham main car park and walk back.

Cross the stile and follow the path as it runs alongside the wall, doglegs and reaches a stone stile on the right. Go through this. The path drops downhill to a wooden gate. Go through this and immediately leave this main track and follow a faint path on the right. This runs alongside a 2-strand barbed wire fence and the crag comes clearly into view through the trees up the hill on the right. The Cone Buttress appears first (also the area for bouldering). Keep walking for 250m until the far left of the crag is reached with Vomer Buttress closest to the path and clearly visible on the right. Carefully cross the wire fence. The first route is on the left of this lower tier.

**Access Issues:** The crag is on private land. There have been no reported problems climbing here but keep a low profile, don't damage the fences or walls and avoid visiting in large groups.

The gap yawns for Adi Gill on the first ascent of **Jericho Falls** (E4 6b). Page 341.
Photo: Dave Sutcliffe

# CROW CRAG - Vomer Buttress

## Vomer Buttress

A two-tiered area with contrasting experiences. The lower crag is perennially green but home to some committing offerings on and around the arête. The Upper Tier is always clean, has excellent slab climbing and a spicy fall potential of twice the route length.

The first climb is at the left end of the crag. **Holly Tree Climb** (HS 4b) tackles the dirty groove below the holly tree.

### 1 Strongbow  VS 5b  10m
Hard moves gain the green gangway on the wall to the right. A traverse left leads to a bow-shaped crack which is climbed to the tree followed by a short crack above.
*Tony Barley, Robin Barley  8th September 1961*

### 2 Owl Chimney  VS 5a  12m  ☆
The wide corner chimney is taken to the overhang. Step left and finish up the twin cracks.
*Allan Austin, Brian Evans, Jennifer Ruffe, Brian Fuller  1956*

The next three routes share a common start on the arête to the right.

### 3 Virtual Reality  E4 6b  12m  ☆
Climb the arête to the second break and hand-traverse left below the overhanging wall. Thin and strenuous moves up a blind crack lead to good holds and a finish up the groove above.
*John Henderson, Paul Carling  30th May 1995*

### 4 Vomit  E3 5c  16m  ☆
Up the arête to the second break. Savour an exquisite move up the overhanging arête before an urgent hand-traverse left to finish up the twin cracks of *Owl Chimney*.
*Phillipe Osborne, James Brooke  23rd September 1997*

### 5 Vomer  E3 5c  13m  ☆
Make a tough bouldery start around the arête to gain the front face of the slab to the sapling. Surmount the overhang and boldly climb the wall to the ledge. Finish up the groove on the left. A direct start is possible at the same grade.
*D. Gray, H Harrison May 1962; A. Austin (direct start)  1965*

A combination is possible, **Vomerite** (E3 5c, ☆). Halfway across the *Vomit* hand-traverse, convulse into *Vomer* upper corner thereby avoiding the full 'chunder' into *Owl Chimney*. No new climbing but a fine 'diced carrot' combo.

### 6 Grasshopper  VS 4c  13m
Start up the corner of the right-hand side of the slab. Move right and climb the crack to the ledge then trend left to the terrace.
*Allan Austin, Brian Evans, Jennifer Ruffe, Brian Fuller  1956*

### The Upper Tier

To access the upper tier, go up the hill to the right then double back onto the wide ledge. Take care here (belayers and falling climbers alike) as the ledge is just above the west face of Vomer Buttress. Descent from the top of these climbs is via faint tracks which lead left (facing in) to well past Vomer Buttress or right, to the right side of Corkscrew Buttress. The first routes are on the left side of the slab, past the obvious dead tree, and are characterised by heinous mantel top-outs (*it's worth examining the cleanliness at the top before having a go*).

### 7 Salieri  E4 5c  10m  ★
Tantalisingly tentative climbing on small holds up the wall just right of the arête. A poor wire and big Friend (hard to place) protects the taxing final moves. Steady E3 if you've a No. 6 Friend.
*John Henderson, Paul Carling  31st April 1993*

### 8 Sola Fide  E4 6a  10m  ★
The centre of the technical slab is balancey and low on

Yorkshire Gritstone

# The Upper Tier - CROW CRAG

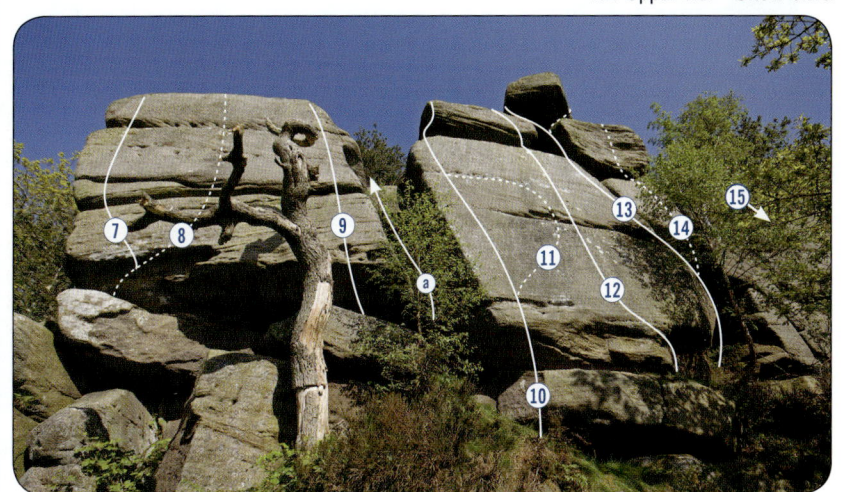

pro where you need it the most. Move up and right to the middle of the wall where sideways pocket pulling allows the final break to be reached. A long reach and a worrying mantelshelf finish is all that remains.
*Robin Nicholson, Adi Gill   15th October 2011*

**9  Captive Conscience**  E1 5b   10m   ★

The easier introduction to these slabby buttresses is still no pushover. The arête, taken on the left-hand side, to a committing move high up. E2 without small narrow cams.
*Robin Nicholson   5th June 2012*

The prickly (a) **View From The Hill** (VD) goes from the gully up the slabby right side of the arête to a holly bush exit.

**10  Tetelestai**  E4 6a   10m   ★★

Technical movement from the word go. From the bold, bouldery start on the undercut wall, climb the arête via a committing sequence. A crucial wire/slider in the pocket protects the balancey layback to the big ledge. Pull over the bulge above to finish. Photo on next page.
*Robin Nicholson, Dave Sutcliffe   29th May 2012*

**11  Amadeus**  E4 6a   13m   ★★

A real sizzler where no move is a gimme. Trend up and right to stand in the horizontal break. Traverse left on fingerpockets to the arête and the crucial wire/slider placement. Finish as for *Tetelestai*. An alternate direct finish is possible from the mid-height break up *Jericho Falls* at 6b.
*Paul Carling, John Henderson Apr 1993* ✦

**12  Jericho Falls**  E4 6b   10m   ★★

Super reachy and extremely technical. Using a vital pebble, make a heinous rockover onto the slab. Mantel the mid-height break and wonder how on earth you're going to get to the ledge. Finish over the bulge. Photo on page 339.
*Adi Gill   5th June 2012*

**13  Curious Motion**  HVS 5b   10m   ★

From the small shallow cave, climb the crack to the ledge then move left to an exposed mantel finish over the steep block. Alternatively, crawl right from the ledge to a mantel onto the final block.
*Luke Dow, Rob Liddle   6th March 1993* ✦

**14  Stop Motion**  E1 5b   10m   ★

Where *Curious Motion* moves left, go direct to a thread on the right arête. Pad up this and mantel the centre of the steep block above.
*Robin Warden, Rob Weston, Paul Tanton   April 2011*

**15  Sameness**  S 4b   8m

The obvious crack to the right.
*Luke Dow (solo)   7th March 1993*

Almscliff to Slipstones

**341**

The best things come to those who wait. Robin Nicholson balances his way up the finish to **Tetelestai** (E4 6a). Page 341.
Photo: Dave Sutcliffe

Corkscrew Buttress - **CROW CRAG**

## Corkscrew Buttress

The upper tier now blends into the top of the next buttress, a hulking great block with a huge ledge at two-thirds height. *Summer Dreams* and *End Slab* are short routes which start from the ledge but are best done as part of a link-up with a route from the lower section. It is possible to scramble off the left side of the ledge if only climbing the lower routes. The first route is **Crack And Chimney** (VD) which takes the green crack behind the tree on the left end of the lower buttress. Climb this to traverse up the grass gangway and the diabolical chimney above.

### 16 Nonawin   HVS 5b   13m
Climb a scoop in the lower wall to gain a short slab leading to the halfway ledge. Finish up a shallow corner just right of the trees or better the groove of *Summer Dreams*.
*Tony Barley, Robin Barley   1961*

### 17 Corkscrew   E2 5c, 5a   15m   ☆
A plum line and a historic sandbag. Originally given HVS and now settled at a much more suitable grade.
**1.** The fierce crack in the front of the buttress is climbed until a traverse can be made to the wider crack. Imaginatively climb this to the broad ledge above (10m).
**2.** Stretch or jump for a hold below the sapling on the left-hand edge of the slab and finish up the crack above (5m).
*Allan Austin, Brian Evans, Jennifer Ruffe   14th April 1957*

### 18 Corkage   E3 6a   14m   ☆
Boulder out the centre of the wall to the break and move right to the intimidating bulge above. A hard, but well-protected, move gains the oft-dirty ledge. Move right and climb the arête to the right of *End Slab*.
*John Henderson, Paul Carling   30th May 1995*

### 19 Spoiler   VS 4b   12m
Start at the right-hand end of the front face and climb to the wide ledge. Can be combined with *Summer Dreams* or *End Slab* to top out.
*Allan Austin, Brian Evans, Malcolm Lomas   23rd Nov 1958*

The next two climbs go from the ledge at two-thirds height.

### 20 Summer Dreams   VS 5b   6m
Bold; 6m of climbing with 18m of drop if you muff the last move. Climb the delicate groove behind the tree.
*Luke Dow, Rob Liddle   6th March 1993*

### 21 End Slab   HVS 5b   5m   ★
More boldness. Hard moves lead up the scoops at the right-hand end of the slab.
*Allan Austin, Brian Evans, Jennifer Ruffe, Brian Fuller   1956*

Almscliff to Slipstones

# CROW CRAG - Narrow Buttress

Halfway up the right-hand side of the buttress is a wide crack (*Lost Crack*) above a small cave.

### 22  Intreegued  VS 5a    7m
Make a hard move left from *Lost Crack* to gain the flake which is followed to the top.
*Nic Kidd, Alec Burns   25th September 1988*

### 23  Lost Crack  VS 4c    6m    ★
Guess what? Climb it.
*Tony Barley, Robin Barley   1961*

An alternative experience is **Armed, Dangerous and Off Medication** (Grade 11…). Go through the cave and squeeze up through a hole into a smooth protectionless chimney. This is climbed direct to an exit between boulders.

## Narrow Buttress
About 150m right is a tall narrow buttress; home to two hard-extreme gems.

### 24  Staircase Chimney  VD    9m
The block-filled chimney on the left is pleasant enough.
*Luke Dow (solo)   27th March 1993*

### 25  Stone the Crows  E5 6b    14m    ★★★
A magnificent line and the route of the crag. Start at the lowest point and climb easily to the ledge on the right. Step up left and move around the arête. A hard pull gains the small ledge, tree stump and good Friends. Swing onto the left side of the upper arête and layback the finger-crack. When this runs out, long reaches may gain the juggy top.
*Neil McCallum, Matt Troilett (both led)   31st December 2008*

### 26  Scarecrow  E4 6a    14m    ★★
Another superb, tough route. Climb as for *Stone the Crows* to the small ledge and tree stump. Continue up the left-hand leaning block using both its arêtes.
*Matt Troilett, Neil McCallum (both led)   31st December 2008*

### 27  The Outer Passage  E1 5c    14m    ★
The alternative finish to *Narrow Buttress Chimney* is likely to get the heart rate well over 100bpm. Go up the chimney but precariously exit its front. Extremely taxing without big guns. Scuttling left to finish in the V of the two rock fingers drops the grade to Severe.
*Bruce Woodley, Amanda Phillips   9th March 2011*

### 28  Narrow Buttress Chimney  VS 4c    11m
Open climbing leading to a cavernous climax. Climb to the ledge on the right and onward up the chimney, exiting from the back.
*Tony Barley, Robin Barley   1961*

### 29  Six Inch Stare  E2 5c    13m    ★
Pad up the short wall and bravely climb the thin crack using the left arête to a difficult and bold finish.
*Rob Liddle, Luke Dow   7th May 1993*

Yorkshire Gritstone

## Fluide - CROW CRAG

### Cone Buttress
It is possible to bushwhack rightward at the same elevation for 40m to reach the next conical shaped buttress and the crag's bouldering, although it's probably best to drop down the hill, circumnavigate the brush and head back up again.

On the filthy slab left of the crack is **(a) Passing Strangers** (E2 5c) which most likely requires Agent Orange before ever being climbable again.

**30 Horizontal Memories** E2 5c 11m ★
A delicate little outing up the flared crack with an awkward move to leave the halfway ledge.
*Rob Liddle, Luke Dow 7th May 1993*

**31 Rubicon** Font 7a
Very bold. The highball arête, taken on the right-hand side.

**32 Counting Crows** Font 6c
The committing slab to a reachy final move.

**33 Half A Drainpipe** Font 7b
The tasty curving arête is climbed on the right side.

**34 After Thought** Font 6b+
Teeter up the little slab.

Just in front of Cone Buttress is a small block with a smooth square wall on its west side. The two arêtes are very good but the showpiece problem, and much coveted bouldering prize, takes the centre of the wall.

**35 Corvus Arête** Font 6a+
Get the sequence right and it's smiles all round.

**36 Fluide** Font 7c
Simply awesome. From the crack gain the under-cling and build your feet to make a lunge for the top.
*Jim Purchon 2006*

**37 Raven Arête** Font 6a
More delicate moves up the right arête.

### Further First Ascent Information (✦)
**Amadeus:** *Alternate finish climbed by Adi Gill, 22nd May 2012*
**A View from the Hill:** *Climbed by Luke Dow, Rob Liddle 6th Mar 1993*
**Armed, Dangerous and Off Medication:** *Climbed by Nic Kidd (solo) 25th September 1988.*
**Curious Motion**: *LH finish climbed by James Brooke, Phillipe Osborne 7th March 1997.*
**Holly Tree Climb** and **Crack and Chimney**: *Climbed Pre-1957.*
**Passing Strangers**: *Climbed by Luke Dow (solo) 27th Mar 1993.*
**Vomerite:** *Climbed by Robin Warden, Bruce Woodley and Paul Tanton on the 19th April 2011.*
*Luke Dow remembers climbing* **Rubicon** *and* **Counting Crows** *in 1998 but made no claim to being the first ascensionist.*

### GRADED LIST
**E5**
Stone the Crows (6b)

**E4**
Virtual Reality (6b)
Jericho Falls 6b
Scarecrow (6a)
Tetelestai (6a)
Amadeus (6a)
Sola Fide (6a)
Salieri (5c)

**E3**
Vomit (5c)
Vomer (5c)
Vomerite (5c)
Corkage (6a)

**E2**
Corkscrew (5c, 5a)
Six Inch Stare (5c)
Passing Strangers (5c)
Horizontal Memories (5c)

**E1**
The Outer Passage (5c)
Stop Motion (5b)
Captive Conscience (5b)

**HVS**
Curious Motion (5b)
Nonawin (5b)
End Slab (5b)

**VS**
Strongbow (5b)
Summer Dreams (5b)

Owl Chimney (5a)
Intreegued (5a)
Grasshopper (4c)
Lost Crack (4c)
Narrow Buttress Chimney (4c)
Spoiler (4b)

**HS**
Holly Tree Climb (4b)

**S**
Sameness (4b)

**VD**
View From The Hill
Crack And Chimney
Staircase Chimney

**Problems**
Fluide Font 7c
Half A Drainpipe Font 7b
Rubicon Font 7a
Counting Crows Font 6c
After Thought Font 6b+
Corvus Arête Font 6a+
Raven Arête Font 6a

Pippa Whitehouse dwarfed on the huge block whilst sampling the delights of **The Flakes** (Font 6a) at Great Wolfrey. Page 36
Photo: Jamie Moss

"Only a mountain has lived long enough to listen
objectively to the howl of a wolf."

*Aldo Leopold*

# Great Wolfrey to Eavestone

| | | |
|---|---|---|
| **Great Wolfrey** 350 | Bolton Haw 380 | Panorama 414 |
| Wig Stones 365 | Air Scar 382 | Whitehouses 418 |
| Henstone Band 366 | **Guisecliff** 384 | **Eavestone** 422 |
| High Crag 368 | Nought Bank 408 | Upper Huller Stones 446 |
| Hebden Gill 370 | Crocodile Crag 412 | Low Huller Stones 449 |

# Map

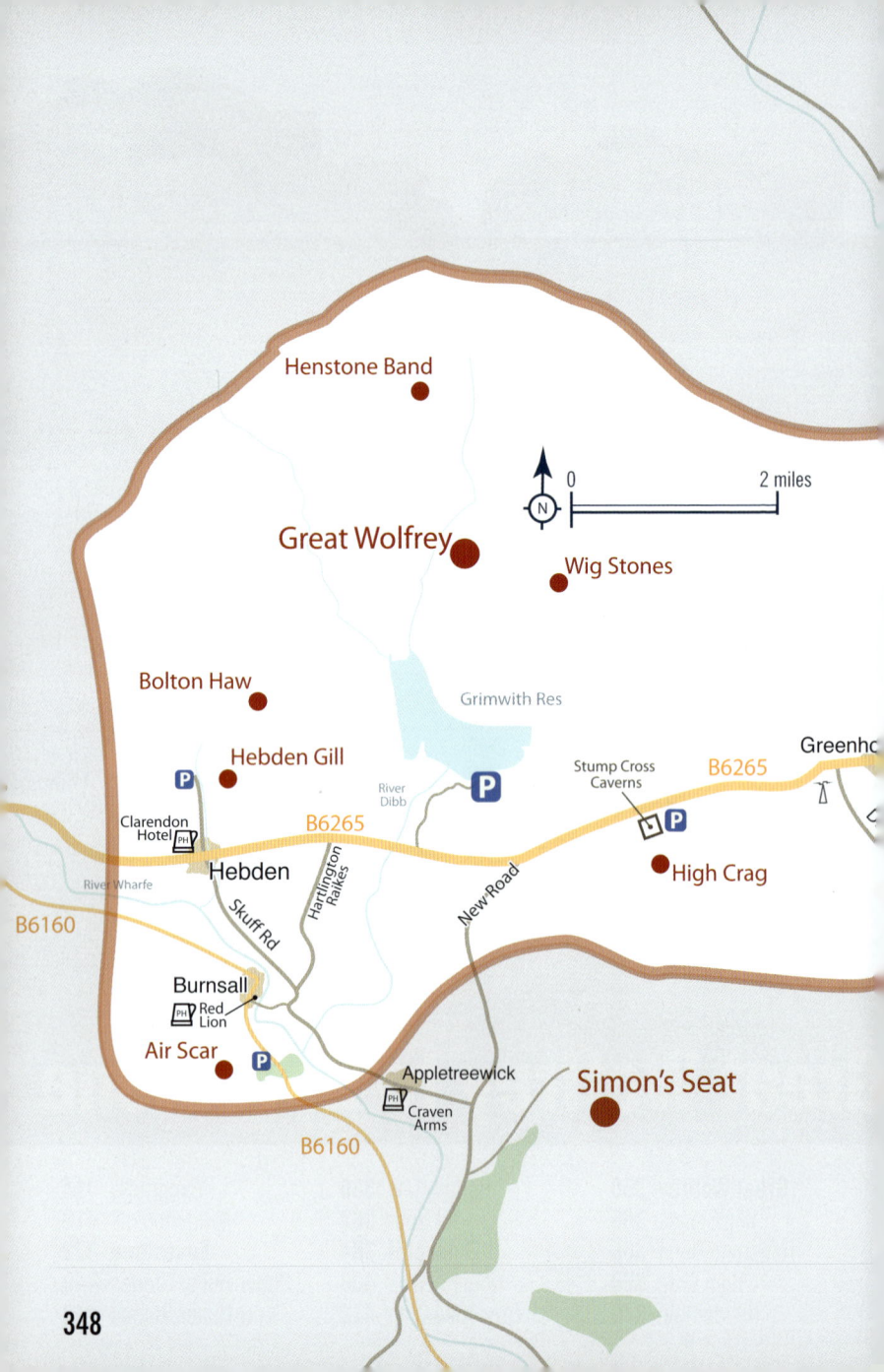

- Henstone Band
- Great Wolfrey
- Wig Stones
- Bolton Haw
- Grimwith Res
- Hebden Gill
- River Dibb
- Stump Cross Caverns
- B6265
- Greenh...
- Clarendon Hotel
- Hebden
- River Wharfe
- Skuff Rd
- Hartlington Raikes
- New Road
- High Crag
- B6160
- Burnsall
- Red Lion
- Air Scar
- Appletreewick
- Craven Arms
- Simon's Seat
- B6160

0 — 2 miles

# Pateley Bridge

- Gouthwaite Res
- High Grantley
- Low Huller Stones
- Upper Huller Stones
- Eavestone
- B6265
- River Nidd
- Half Moon
- Old Church Ln
- Royal Oak
- Panorama
- Whitehouses
- Brimham
- B6265
- Peat Ln
- Glasshouses
- Wilsill
- Croc Crag
- Nought Bank
- Yorke's Folly Ruin (Twin Pillars)
- Nought Moor Rd
- Guisecliff
- B6165
- Summerbridge
- Flying Dutchman
- Brimham Rocks Road
- Foldshaw Ln
- Dike Ln
- Dacre Banks
- B6165
- B6451
- B6165
- scross Res

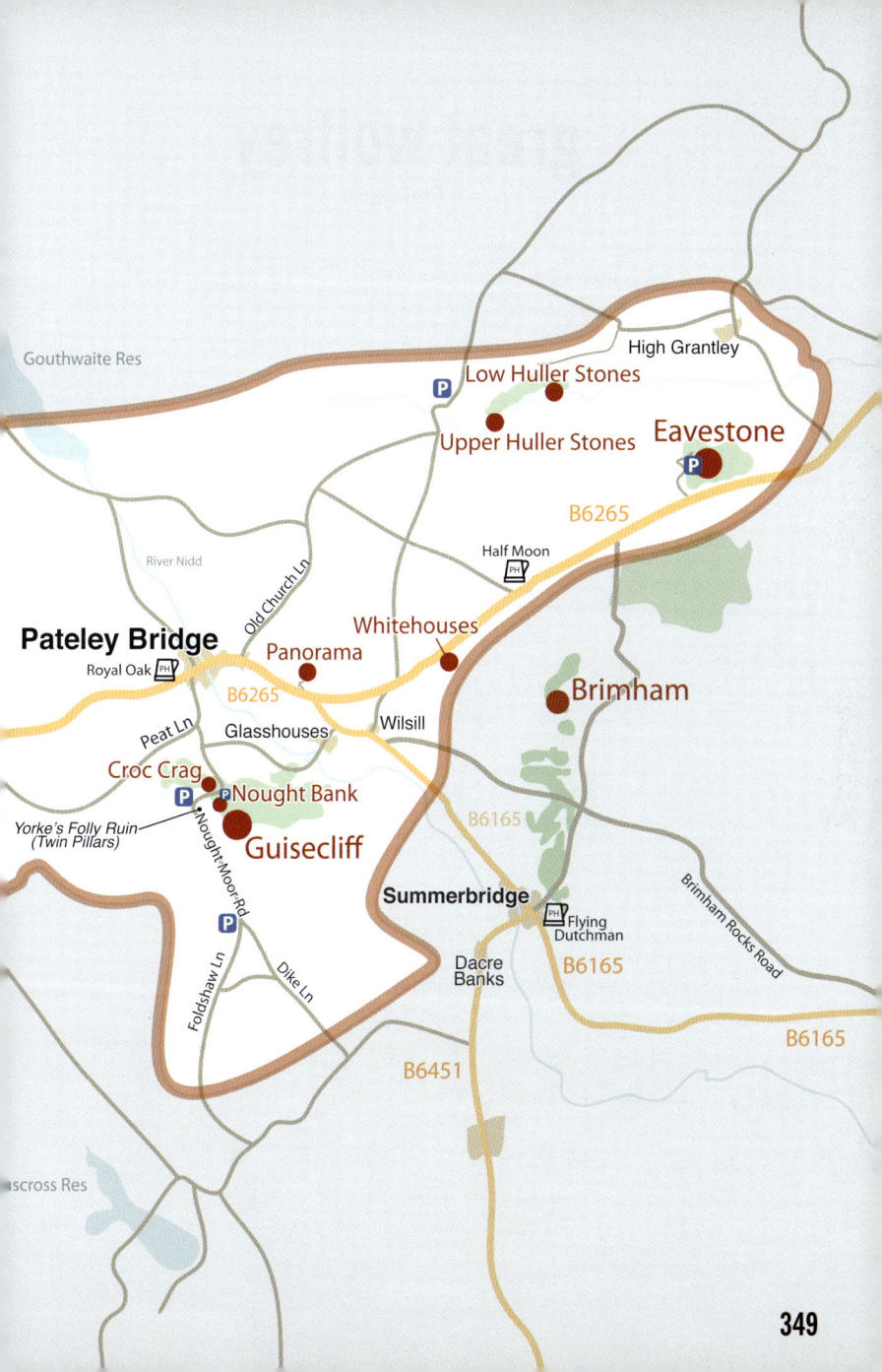

349

# great wolfrey
## by Paul Clarke

OS Ref: SE 063 674              Altitude: 450m

Great Wolfrey is a great place to escape the hordes and hearten the soul. It is perhaps *the* 'out there' crag in Yorkshire; a place reserved for the true Gritstoner. The rock is excellent; a silvery gritstone, similar in feel to that at Slipstones. Although the approach is long, it is not steep or altogether unpleasant if the correct line is followed. Great Wolfrey varies in height from six to fifteen metres and the ground in front of the crag is speckled with boulders, providing good fun for those who are mad for the pad. Grassy swards and stunning views make lounging at the foot of the crag all too enjoyable.

**The Climbing:** There are 65 superb routes and more than 30 problems across a broad range of grades. Their rarity value make them real collector's items. The Martin Berzins three-star E6 duo of *Little Red Riding Hood* and *A Company of Wolves* are the crag testpieces, both requiring a good deal of skill and nerve. The superb arêtes of *Walter's Rib (E2)* and *Werewolf (E4)* are the venue's standout lines and make the crag worth a visit for these alone. Many of the routes are bold to start, which lends to a feeling of commitment, so think about how you will get back to the car before throwing abandon to the wind. A mat will be found useful, as will a good range of gear, so a team sharing the load works well.

**Conditions and Aspect:** Despite the crag's elevated situation, most of the faces are quick drying. Unsurprisingly, it can be a windy spot (unless the wind is from the north and blows over the top), but its southerly aspect means it is often too warm in summer. Calm, clear days in spring or autumn are ideal.

**Parking and Approach:** Ample free parking, toilets, picnic tables and incredulous looks (as you hoist your pack, rope and mat and set off into the wilderness) are available at Grimwith Reservoir car park. This is approached from the B6256 Grassington to Pateley Bridge road just under two miles to the east of Hebden where you take the signposted Yorkshire Water Grimwith Reservoir access road. The crag you can see across the reservoir from here doesn't look too far away but is actually The Wig Stones. Great Wolfrey hides under a veil of secrecy only revealing its delights as one approaches, usually via the right-hand of the two obvious valleys you will see at the far left corner of the reservoir.

From the car park, cross the long grassy dam and head north-north-west, following the good track clockwise around the reservoir for 2.3km to the second bridge (crossing Gate-Up Gill). Climb the wooden gate on the left and follow the track up the valley to the old mine workings and the 'four second' shaft. Continue through the gap in the grouse pens and zigzag up the green track to pass through a narrow gate in a stone wall. At this point there are two options for getting to the crag, both about 1km from the gate. For the first, just after the gate, leave paths behind and cross the little stream to climb steeply out of the valley up a bracken and heather slope. Once the angle eases, follow the moor northwards until the crag comes into view. Or, for the second approach, from the gate follow the beck and broken dry stone wall at an amenable gradient (passing a barn ruin along the way) until the crag comes into view on the right. Whilst the first approach offers a full moor-top gale force experience, the second is somewhat more scenic but can be boggy with a few hidden ditches; the choice is yours. The whole approach from the car park takes around an hour. If you visit Great Wolfrey you will definitely have earned a post-climb pint. Either of the pubs in Appletreewick (see chapter map on page 348) are well worth a visit. The nearest café is just up the B6256 at Stump Cross Caverns.

**Access Issues:** There have been problems in the past but the crag is undoubtedly on access land. All guards, barbed-wire fences and gun turrets have now been removed. The route described is via the only permitted access point to this part of the moor. Check the BMC's Regional Access Database and the car park notice board for periodic access restrictions. No dogs.

The major features of the crag are the three towers: Left Tower, Central Tower and the free standing, North Pinnacle. To the left of the towers the buttresses get smaller and eventually degenerate altogether after 100m before rising again at Little Wolfrey. There are two huge blocks in front of the crag. The left-hand block is situated just in front of the Left Tower, this is the North Boulder. Approximately 100m right is the second block; South Boulder. Behind South Boulder is a fine buttress split on its left by two cracks. This is Great Wolfrey Buttress. Right again is a slim pinnacle, South Pinnacle, which is attached to the main crag by a jammed boulder that forms a natural arch.

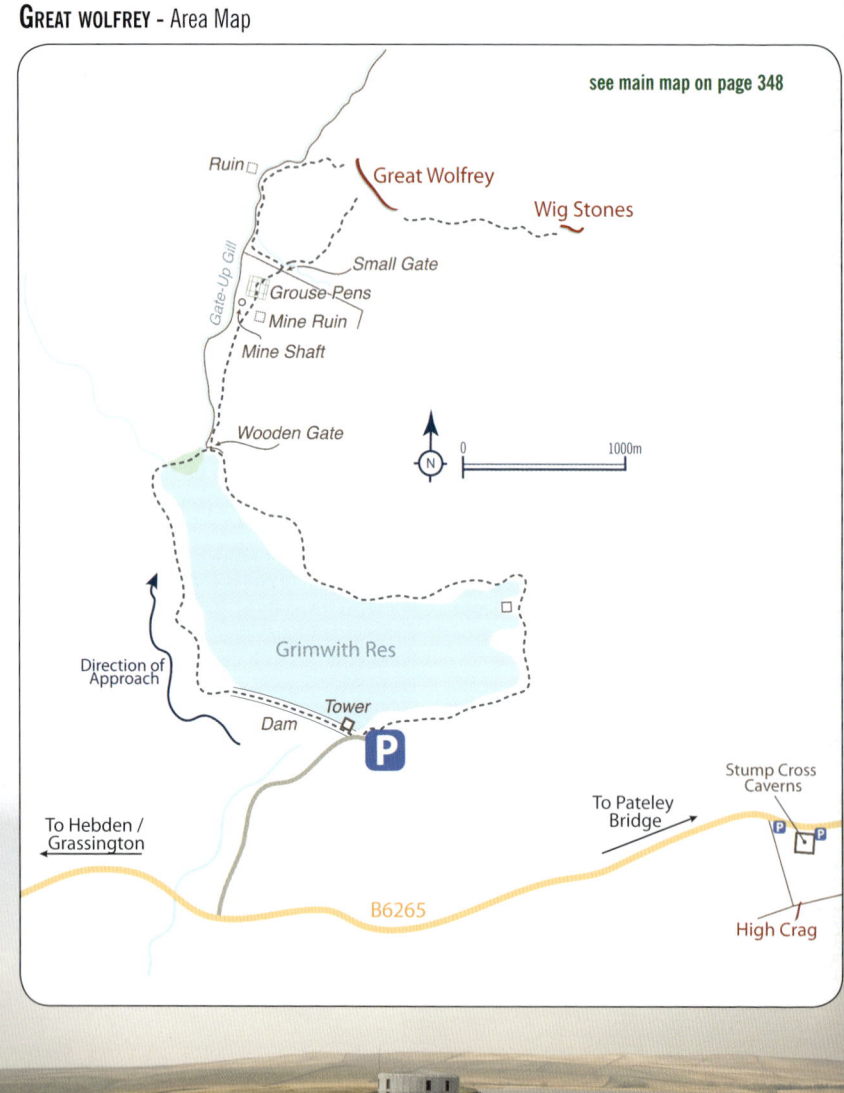

# Great Wolfrey - Area Map

see main map on page 348

Ruin

Great Wolfrey

Wig Stones

Gate-Up Gill

Small Gate

Grouse Pens

Mine Ruin

Mine Shaft

Wooden Gate

N

0    1000m

Grimwith Res

Direction of Approach

Dam  Tower

P

To Hebden / Grassington

To Pateley Bridge

Stump Cross Caverns

B6265

High Crag

352

## Approach - GREAT WOLFREY

Gate-Up Gill, the second bridge on the path and the wooden gate to the track up the valley.

Approach Option 1
Across the moor

Approach Option 2
Following the beck

Small gate after the grouse pens

Almscliff to Slipstones

353

# GREAT WOLFREY - Leapfrog Buttress

## Little Wolfrey
A small outcrop 100m left of the main edge. There are several easy walls and arêtes here and one described problem, **Loup Garou** (Font 5+). This highball takes the centre of a smooth wall in a bay in the middle of the edge.

## Leapfrog Buttress
A small buttress at the left end of the crag.

**1 Bluster Arse Vessel**  E2 6b   6m   ★
The obstinate wall left of *Autumn Gold* by a series of technical and then bold moves to the top. Highball Font 6c.
*Rob Weston, Stuart Lancaster (both solo)   16th September 2000*

**2 Autumn Gold**  VS 4c   6m   ★
The delicious and highly enjoyable crack.
*Glen Gorner, John Mackenzie   23rd October 1985*

**3 Auternative Arête**  HVS 5a   6m   ★★
The compelling arête on its left side by some subtle moves.
*Glen Gorner, John Mackenzie   23rd October 1985*

**4 Moon Madness**  E1 6b   6m   ★
Climb the same arête on its right side using thin flakes on the wall. Finish up the short groove.
*Paul Clarke   24th July 2010*

**5 Leapfrogger**  VD 3a   6m   ★
The widening crack in the right wall of the buttress. The main snag is leapfrogging over the chockstone at half-height.
*Jim Walton, Brian Smith and Ed Thackeray   c1950*

**6 Groove Time**  D   5m   ★
Climb the shallow groove in the right wall.
*Jim Walton, Brian Smith and Ed Thackeray   c1950*

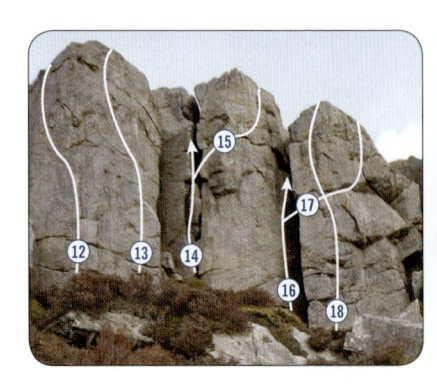

A steep block in the jumble to the right provides three lines.

**7 Tea-Cake Wall**  VS 5a   5m
The left wall is no piece of cake.
*John Mackenzie, Rik Weld   6th November 1988* ✦

**8 Winter of Discontent**  VS 4c   6m   ★
Tackle the steep arête utilising flakes on its left side.
*Unknown but possibly John Mackenzie, Rik Weld   1988*

**9 Summer of 76**  HVS 5b   6m
The wall immediately right of *Winter of Discontent*. Start on the right and trend left to finish just left of the arête on a thin flake.
*Malcolm Townsley (solo)   29th October 1995*

## Rocking Stone Buttress
The next two routes are below the obvious rocking stone.

**10 Rock 'n' Roll**  M   6m
Climb the corner below and left of the rocking stone.
*Dave Musgrove Jnr (solo)   19th June 1996*

**11 The Duke**  HVS 5b   6m   ★
The arête directly below the rocking stone.
*Dave Musgrove Jnr   19th June 1996*

## Pedestal Area
Just to the right is a wall with a pedestal at two metres.

**12 Pedestal Arête**  VS 5a   5m   ★
Step onto the pedestal (no medal yet) and then climb up

Yorkshire Gritstone

and left to the arête before reaching the top.
*Probably Glen Gorner, John Mackenzie  23rd October 1985*

### 13 Alternative Arête  HS 4a  6m  ★★
Lovely moves tackling the surprisingly amenable right-hand arête.
*Glen Gorner, John Mackenzie  23rd October 1985*

The open gully is a useful means of descent.

### 14 Chockstone Crack  M  5m  ★
The crack, chock full of stones in the right wall of the gully.
*Brian Evans, Phillip Leese  1952*

### 15 Chockstone Wall  VS 4b  6m  ★
The narrow wall. Gained from 3m up *Chockstone Crack* at this grade.

### 16 North Chimney  S 4a  7m  ★
An interesting exercise in chimney technique – or not!
*Brian Evans, Phillip Leese  1952*

### 17 North/South Divide  E2 5b  15m  ★
Climb *North Chimney* for about 4m and swing boldly rightwards round the arête onto the face. Stenuously follow the break on good holds to then pull over the small roof using more good holds and finish using even more of the same.
*Unknown but possibly John Mackenzie, Glen Gorner  1985*

### 18 Crock Around the Block  E2 6a  7m  ★★
A superb sequence. The lower wall is surmounted with difficulty to reach better holds and a runner at the handrail before you blast straight up to the top.
*Tony Burnell, Chris Sowden, Martin Berzins  17th Oct 1987*  ✦

In the corner is **Open Chimney** (Mod). It can be climbed via the steps and exited through the cave to the right or by squeezing up the narrow chimney to the left.

## Left Tower
### 19 Wolfschmidt  E3 6a  9m  ★
Leave the ground with difficulty and move up and right to gain poor breaks. Continue up to a very shallow V-feature then move rightwards to the top.
*Chris Sowden, Tony Burnell, Martin Berzins  17th October 1987*

## last great problems

A list of some of the last great problems around these parts of the Yorkshire grit woods.

Are some of these even possible?

- Wall right of *Wolfschmidt* (Great Wolfrey).
- Left side of arête of *Bad Company* (Great Wolfrey).
- Wall/arête left of *Left Wolfrey Crack* (Great Wolfrey).
- Wall right of *Wall of Horrors* (Almscliff).
- Walls left and right of *Great Flake* (Caley).
- Wall right of *Marrow Bone Jelly* (Caley).
- Wall left of *Gigglin' Crack* (Brimham).
- Nose right of pitch 2 of *George II* (Brimham).
- Arête to the right of *Ancient* (Little Brimham).
- Overhanging wall and arête left of *Salieri* (Crow Crag).
- Direct finish above the start to *Life Begins at Forty* (Eavestone).
- The 'ship's prow' to the right of *Question of Balance* (Simon's Seat).
- Walls left and right of *Womb with a View* (Earl's Seat).
- Wall right of *Cypher* (Slipstones).
- Left wall, left arête and main wall of All Black Buttress (Arnagill).

The extremely fine wall to the right awaits a direct ascent.

### 20 Troubled with Lycans  E5 6b  11m  ★★
The bold direct arête start to *Werewolf* leads intrepidly to the small roof at half-height. Launch left up the diagonal line to the sanctuary of the flakes. Move rightwards to finish.
*Paul Clarke  12th April 2007*  ✦

Almscliff to Slipstones     **355**

# GREAT WOLFREY - Left & Central Tower

### 21  Werewolf  E4 6a  9m  ★★★
Bold, beautiful and 'airy; a superb arête climb. Start up the flake to the roof then move left to the arête. Go round the arête and up the wall moving back right to gain the arête below a fin. Layback the fin to finish. Can be climbed direct at E5 6b.
*John Eastham, Geoff Myers, John Myers  27th Sept 1980* ♦

### 22  Wolf at the Door  E5 6a  9m  ★★
A sheep in wolf's clothing? A one-move wonder? Some say it's low in the grade but we'll let you decide. A brilliant line up the middle of the face and through the big roof at the top of the wall. Start up the flake as for *Werewolf* to the small roof before heading up right for the main event of the upper roof and crucial, though hard to place and therefore not totally reliable, opposing runners. Power round the roof (crux) on sloping holds to reach the top.
*Mike Hamill, John Yates  16th May 1986*

### 23  Huff-Puff Chimney  M  8m
Take a deep breath, then climb up the chimney.
*Dave Musgrove Jnr and Snr (both solo)  30th Dec 1993* ♦

### 24  Hangover Crack  HS 4b  9m
The green crack in the corner provides a tortuous struggle.
*Brian Evans, Phillip Leese  1952*

### 25  Hangover Chimney  M  9m  ★
To the right is another chimney-cum-crack. Lovely.
*Brian Evans, Phillip Leese  1952*

## Central Tower
To the right of *Hangover Chimney* is a pale green wall and on its right, above the plaque, the fine arête of *Walter's Rib*.

### 26  Shades of Green  E2 5c  9m
Harder than it looks. The use of the crack, and often dirty holds, enable the ledge to be gained. Finish up the short wall above.
*John Mackenzie, Norman Hitch  pre-1985*

### 27  A Wolf in the Wild  E3 6b  10m  ★
Climb directly up the left side of *Walter's Rib* until a hungry move left gains the flake on the wall. A stiff pull gains the better holds on *Shades of Green* and the break. Move right and finish up the wide crack.
*Paul Clarke  16th May 2006*

Yorkshire Gritstone

## North Pinnacle - GREAT WOLFREY

**28 Walter's Rib** E2 5c 9m ★★★
An elegant feature providing a climb that rarely fails to please. Start by using holds and the groove on the right, then climb the superb arête stepping right at the top. Also known as **Brown's Rib**. Photo on page 361.
*Ken Wood, Charles Dracup 17th June 1975*

**29 Angua** E3 6a 10m ★
A desperate and vicious mutation continuing the starting groove of *Walter's Rib*. Finish direct.
*Neil Herbert, Robin Ellis 18th April 1999* ✦

**30 In Memoriam** E5 6a 9m ★★
A lonely solo that could make a lasting impression. Climb the centre of the wall using edges and layaways to gain the wide horizontal break. Finish up the crack on the left.
*Martin Berzins (solo) 16th October 1987*

**31 Arvel Chimney** D 9m ★
A good old-fashioned line. Climb over the jammed blocks into the chimney. Now thrutch up and over the chockstones.
*Brian Evans, Phillip Leese 1952*

**32 Grand Defiance** E2 5b 12m ★
Sustained and quite serious. The constricted groove just right of *Arvel Chimney* is a quality route when clean.
*John Mackenzie, Rik Weld 6th November 1988*

### North Pinnacle

To the right is a huge detached block. The slight arête at the junction of the gullies provides the easiest way off the top – or why not jump the gap!

**33 Cowell's Rib** E3 5c 9m ★★
Steep and technical climbing makes this a fine excursion. Climb the left arête of the front face of the pinnacle moving right at the break to gain the flakes.
*Ashley Cowell 1983*

**34 The Wilderness Years** E4 6a 11m ★★
Bold to start and tricky to finish. Follow the line of inverted edges to gain the break. Step right along this and go up the rippled wall directly above the thin crack of *Little Red Riding Hood*.
*Paul Clarke, Alan Cross 12th April 2007*

**35 Little Red Riding Hood** E6 6b 9m ★★★
What small holds you have...The wall and ever-so-thin crack next to the ever-so-green streak. Edge slowly up the face using the crack, hope and whatever else comes to hand to gain a flat hold. More hard moves and/or a Berzinian leap lead to a fairytale ending on the right (or the chop).
*Martin Berzins, Chris Sowden 24th October 1987*

**36 A Company of Wolves** E6 6b 9m ★★★
The compelling and overhanging rib at the right-hand end of the face takes the title of a gothic fantasy-horror. Progress is with increasing technical difficulty until the move to the break provides a test of strength and nerve.
*Martin Berzins (solo) 24th October 1987*

**37 Bad Company** E1 5b 9m ★★
Excellent rock (and roll). Start on the block at the entrance to the wide gully behind North Buttress. Climb confidently up the right side of the arête using thin edges and knobbles to gain the horizontal break, swing around left in a fine position and finish up the vertical crack splitting the top centre of the block.
*Martin Berzins, Chris Sowden, Tony Burnell 17th October 1987*

# GREAT WOLFREY - Loyalty Wall

### 38 Limited Company   VS 4c   9m
Offers a few good moves on green ripples before finishing up the wide crack.
*Bob Larkin (solo)   23rd June 1991*

### Loyalty Wall
The broad wall to the right, split by the wide *Loyalty Crack*.

### 39 Good Friends   HVS 5b   8m   ★
The thin crack in the gully is a pleasant and safe route when clean.
*John Mackenzie, Rik Weld   6th November 1988*

### 40 Lipstick Wall   HVS 5c   10m   ★
From the ledge, take the wall via a friendly stone 'mouth'. Exit up the middle one of three cracks.
*Rik Weld, John Mackenzie   6th November 1988*

### 41 Deception   VS 4c   6m
Climb the flake and wall to a ledge on the left. Climb the left-hand crack to finish.
*Brian Evans, Allan Austin, Ashley Petts, E. Shepherd Nov 1955*

### 42 Loyalty Crack   S 4b   8m   ★
Climb the wide crack in the centre of the buttress. **Loyalty Crack Continuation** is a nice extension up the short wall on the left at the top of the crack at the same grade.
*Brian Evans, Phillip Leese 1952; (Cont'n: Ben Barnard Jun 2005)*

### 43 Sheep's Clothing   E3 6a/b   8m   ★
Insecure. Negotiate the wall on mediocre holds to somehow gain a small recess. Move up and right to a blind crack and mantelshelf to finish.
*Tony Burnell, Chris Sowden, Martin Berzins   17th October 1987*

To the right is a sharp block known as **The Recess**.

### 44 The Fang   Font 5
The front of the sharp block to an obvious fang. Font 5+ from a sit-down start.
*Paul Clarke   2006*

### 45 Recess Arête   S 4a   7m
The arête in the bay above *The Fang*. It ends in a scoop.
*Malcolm Townsley (solo)   29th October 1995*

### 46 Perfectly Gasless   E1 6a   7m
The left edge of the block. A slap to a flat hold leads to the crux and eventually a wobbly top-out onto a glacis that can be scrittly.
*John Hunt, Paul Clarke (both solo)   8th October 2006*

The next three routes are on the left wall of the large bay behind South Boulder.

### 47 Flow Arête   E1 6a   8m   ★
Start using two poor sidepulls (no standing on the boulder) and follow the arête to the niche. Escape is possible by several lines.
*Malcolm Townsley (solo)   29th October 1995*

Yorkshire Gritstone

Great Wolfrey Buttress - **GREAT WOLFREY**

**48 Foxy** VS 4c  8m  ★
Climb the thin crack then step right to a ledge to finish.
*Bob Larkin (solo) 23rd June 1991*

**49 Got It in One** E1 5b  7m
Climb the wall using a poor horizontal edge to gain a good break. Continue up blind vertical cracks to finish.

### Great Wolfrey Buttress
A fine piece of rock hidden behind the South Boulder.

**50 Left Wolfrey Crack** VS 4c  10m
The left-hand of the two cracks making limited use of the right one.
*John Hunt, Paul Clarke  8th October 2006*

**51 Wolfrey Crack Indirect** S 4a  10m  ★
Climb the right-hand crack until an obvious short traverse leads into the left-hand one. Climb this to the top.
*Brian Evans, Phillip Leese  1952*

**52 Wolfrey Crack Direct** VS 5a  10m
Finish direct instead of stepping left.
*Paul Clarke (solo)  April 2006*

**53 Great Wolfrey Buttress** VS 4c  11m  ★★
A great value route for the grade with plenty of protection in the lower half, if you have the strength to place it. From just right of the cracks follow a diagonal line up through the two horizontal breaks to a mantelshelf onto the ledge and a wonderfully airy finish up the crack in the wall above.
*Brian Evans, Phillip Leese  1952*

**54 Wolverine** E4 6b  11m  ★★
A fine, tenuous and varied route. Climb the wall slightly leftwards, passing the two horizontal breaks until a tricky step up gains the left rib and brings the crack in reach. Take the upper wall using a rounded edge out right. A much easier finish is up the crack (E3 6a).
*Paul Clarke  16th May 2006*

**55 Holly Tree Hover** E1 5b  9m  ★★
The bold, tricky and blunt arête leads to the ledge. Head left up the exposed rib to a fluttery finish.
*John Mackenzie, Glen Gorner  23rd October 1985*

**56 Above Average Age** MVS 4b  8m
The wall right of *Holly Tree Hover,* finishing up a flake crack right of *Great Wolfrey Buttress*.
*Robin Ellis, Neil Herbert  18th April 1999*

### Holly Bush Area
**57 Holly Bush Crack** D  7m  ★
Climb the wide crack that no longer has a holly bush growing near its base. Finish on the right.
*Brian Evans, Phillip Leese  1952*

## GREAT WOLFREY - Holly Bush Area

#### 58 Heather Groove  VD   7m  ★★
One of the best lower grade routes at the crag offers wonderful climbing up the shallow bottom groove and the slabby top wall. Use some flakes to finish.
*Brian Evans, Phillip Leese  1952*

#### 59 Devious Dave's Dubious Direct  HVS 5a   7m
Take the wall to the ledge. Alternatives get progressively more difficult the further right one strays.
*Paul Clarke, Bob Larkin, Dave Musgrove  24th July 2010*

#### 60 The Loser  MVS 4b   9m
Climb up the groove to the overhanging block and then move right to climb the crack formed by its right-hand side. Walk off or finish easily up the short wall behind.
*Ben Barnard  23rd June 2005*

### South Pinnacle
The pinnacle is attached to the main crag by a jammed boulder forming an arch. It provides some great little routes.

#### 61 Somnolent Jack  HVS 5a   6m  ★
The arête is climbed direct on breaks.
*Neil Herbert, Robin Ellis  18th April 1999*

#### 62 West Face  MVS 4b   6m  ★★
A cracking little route that takes the centre of the attractive west face of the buttress, easily at first, using horizontal breaks. A difficult move left allows the crack and good finishing holds to be gained.
*Brian Evans, Phillip Leese  1952*

#### 63 West Face Variant  VS 4c   6m  ★
Climbing the right arête throughout is a good route in its own right.
*Brian Evans, Phillip Leese  1952*

#### 64 Corner and Traverse  D   6m
Take the eastern arête of the pinnacle for a few feet, then move left and climb the groove to the top.
*Brian Evans, Phillip Leese  1952*

#### 65 Arête Direct  VD   6m
Start as for *Corner and Traverse* but instead of moving left, continue up the right side of the arête.
*Ben Barnard  23rd June 2005*

The sizable block below South Pinnacle sports a fine flake. There are three lines; the left (a)**Edge**, the (b) **Flake** and the (c) **Slab**. All are Font 3+ and all are good.

360   Yorkshire Gritstone

Jamie Moss bravely tackling one of the crag classics, **Walter's Rib** (E2 5c). Page 357.
Photo: Pippa Whitehouse

## GREAT WOLFREY - The Bouldering

### The Boulders
Bouldering has always been part of the attraction of a day at this crag. A circuit is the best way to approach them, starting at The Twin Boulders found on the left, below *Autumn Gold*. The main problems are described here but there are also many more awaiting rediscovery.

### Twin Boulders
The two crinkly boulders, side-by-side and below *Autumn Gold* at the left end of the main crag. There are a number of short warm-up problems but the best are:

1 **Romulus** Font 5+. Left arête (sit-down start).
2 **Remus** Font 5. Right arête (sit-down start)

### Heather Top
Down to the right is a heather-topped boulder with a fine south face. Altogether there are around 10 problems here with excellent soft landings.

3 **Ling Arête** Font 4+
4 **Erica** Font 4. Wall just to the right.
5 **Calluna** Font 5. Just right again and left of the crack.
6 **Heather Crack** Font 3+
7 **Cassiope** Font 6a+. (No using the crack).
8 **Little Red-Haired Girl** Font 5. Thin crack & arête.
9 **Green-Eyed Monster** Font 5. Right side of arête.
10 **Hurricane Heather** Font 5

### The Slab
About 30m right is a large, slabby boulder with two cracks. **Cracking Left 11, Cracking Right 12** and **Slab Edge 13**, are all fun Font 2. **14 Ladders** (Font 5+) takes the ladders right of the left crack to an interesting finish.

### Flat Top
15 **Flattened** Font 5. The right edge of the scoop.
16 **Flaky** Font 5. The thin flake.
17 **Flat Top** Font 5+. The middle arête.
18 **Ripples** Font 5+. Just right, with a semi sit-start.
19 **Calm** Font 6a

### Cooper's Boulder
To the right, and slightly further down the hill, this boulder has a nice big slab with a good landing.

20 **Cooper's Crack** Font 3. Crack on left.
21 **Over the Barrel** Font 4+. Left side of the arête.
22 **Gun Barrel** Font 3. The front arête and slab.
23 **Cask** Font 4+. The slab just right again.

### Pinnacle Boulder
About 20m right of South Boulder is this boulder. There is one worthwhile problem here. 24 **Pinnacle Arête** (Font 5+) which takes the arête and the flakes out right.

### South Boulder
Returning leftwards and below Great Wolfrey Buttress is the east facing big slab with several easy problems.

25 **Mantel** Font 5+. A mantel to the left.
26 **Scoopy Doo** Font 4+. The obvious scoop.
27 **Silver Machine** Font 5. Trend up to *Silver Surfer*.
28 **Slapstick Slab** Font 5+. Highball. The slab direct.
29 **Silver Surfer** Font 4. The right arête.

### North Boulder
You can pick up a few problems on the way back along the edge, including *The Fang*, but there is little worth doing amongst the small blocks until all that changes at the North Boulder. It has an impressive, overhanging west face.

30 **Lichen Grope** Font 6c (E4 6b)
Highball and excellent. The line of flakes and edges left of *Wolfsbane*, finishing at a worryingly creaky flake.
31 **Wolfsbane** Font 6a. The cracked groove.
32 **Around the Corner** Font 5+. The arête's RHS.
33 **Shallow Hal** Font 6b+. Shallow cracks and flakes to the top.
34 **Jumpin' Jack Flash** Font 7a+
A wild dyno from the rail to the top. One of the best leaps in Yorkshire and rarely flashed.
35 **Millionaire** Font 7b
Excellent. Trend up rightwards via the rail and crimps.
36 **The Flakes** Font 6a. Climb flakes from a SDS.
Photo on page 346.
37 **Baby Sitter** Font 6b+. Right arête from a SDS.

The Bouldering - **GREAT WOLFREY**

> ❝ ❞
>
> The first mat I saw was one Chris Sowden brought to the crag and was part of an old settee covered in plastic and tape. How we laughed (until its use became evident).

Paul Clarke

363

# GREAT WOLFREY - First Ascent Information & Graded List

## Further First Ascent Information (✦)

There are a number of climbs with unknown first ascents. It is likely they are the work of the small number of protagonists who have recorded routes here.

**1940s:** *Sidney Waterfall and friends climbed on the crag.*
**Circa 1950:** *Several cracks and chimneys climbed by Jim Walton, Brian Smith and Ed Thackeray.*
**Huff-Puff Chimney:** *Undoubtedly done before.*
**Troubled with Lycans:** *The direct start to Werewolf had been done before (see below).*
**Crock Around the Block:** *Also recorded as Bone People by Dave Musgrove Jnr (solo) 1996.*
**Tea-Cake Wall:** *The advent of the 80s saw a scramble for rock in Yorkshire and in relative terms the crag became popular with regular forays by John McKenzie who on one of his visits made the unfortunate mistake of letting go, the penalty was a slow and painful retreat.*
**Werewolf:** *A brilliant find (one of many on remote crags by this team around this time) that was mistakenly called 'What You Like' for some years. The first ascentionist allegedly said "Call it what you like". The necky direct ascent of the lower arête was first climbed by Paul Clarke whilst doing the first ascent of Trouble with Lycans.*

### Boulder Problem First Ascents

The problems were first documented by Paul Clough in 2005 and Paul Clarke in 2006 though many will have been done before.

**Around the Corner,** Paul Clough, 2005
**Baby Sitter,** Paul Clarke, 2007
**Calluna ,** Paul Clough, 2005
**Calm,** Not known
**Cask,** Paul Clough, 2005
**Cassiope,** Paul Clarke, 2006
**Cooper's Crack,** Not known
**Edge,** Not known
**Erica,** Paul Clough, 2005
**Fang The,** Paul Clarke 2006
**Flake,** Not known
**Flakes The,** Paul Clough, 2005
**Flaky,** Not known
**Flat Top,** Paul Clough, 2005
**Flattened,** Not known
**Green-Eyed Monster,** Paul Clough, 2005
**Gun Barrel,** Not known
**Heather Crack,** Paul Clough, 2005
**Hurricane Heather,** Paul Clough, 2005
**Jumpin Jack Flash,** Jim Purchon, 2006
**Ladders,** Paul Clough, 2005
**Lichen Grope,** Mike Grey, Oct 2005
**Ling Arête,** Paul Clough, 2005
**Little Red-Haired Girl,** Paul Clough 2005
**Loup Garou,** Paul Clough, 2005
**Mantel,** Paul Clough, 2005
**Millionaire,** Mike Grey, Oct 2005
**Over the Barrel,** Paul Clough, 2005
**Pinnacle Arête,** Paul Clough, 2005
**Remus,** Paul Clough, 2005
**Ripples,** Not known
**Romulus,** Paul Clough, 2005
**Scoopy Doo,** Paul Clarke, 2007
**Shallow Hal,** Paul Clarke, 2006
**Slab,** Not known
**Silver Machine,** Bob Larkin 2010
**Silver Surfer,** Paul Clarke, 2007

## GRADED LIST

### ROUTES

**E6**
Little Red Riding Hood
A Company of Wolves

**E5**
Trouble with Lycans
Wolf at the Door
In Memoriam

**E4**
Wolverine
The Wilderness Years
Werewolf

**E3**
Angua
Sheep's Clothing
A Wolf in the Wild
Cowell's Rib
Wolfschmidt

**E2**
Bluster Arse Vessel
Crock Around the Block
Grand Defiance
Walter's Rib
Shades of Green
North/South Divide

**E1**
Moon Madness
Perfectly Gasless
Bad Company
Got It in One
Flow Arête
Holly Tree Hover

**HVS**
Good Friends
The Duke
Summer of 76
Lipstick Wall
Devious Dave's - Dubious Direct
Somnolent Jack
Auternative Arête

**VS**
Great Wolfrey Buttress
Wolfrey Crack Direct
Tea-Cake Wall
Pedestal Arête
Limited Company
Autumn Gold
Left Wolfrey Crack
Foxy
Deception
Winter of Discontent
Chockstone Wall

**MVS**
West Face
The Loser
Above Average Age

**HS**
Alternative Arête
Hangover Crack

**S**
Loyalty Crack
Recess Arête
Wolfrey Crack Indirect
North Chimney

**VD**
Arête Direct
Leapfrogger
Heather Groove

**D**
Corner and Traverse
Holly Bush Crack
Groove Time
Arvel Chimney

**M**
Huff-Puff Chimney
Hangover Chimney
Rock 'n' Roll
Open Chimney
Chockstone Crack

# wig stones

by **Paul Clarke**

OS Ref: SE 076 672
Altitude: 450 m

An out of the way group of boulders and blocks on Wig Stones Allotment that has provided succour for those wishing to get away from it all for many a year. **The Climbing**: A small collection of pleasant (if clean), short climbs that cater for those operating in the sub-extreme low-middle grades. **Conditions and Aspect:** Faces south-west and is fairly quick drying, though exposed to any weather that is going. The rock is compact and solid but rarely used and so may feel sandy. **Parking and Approach**: As for Great Wolfrey. One permitted access is via Great Wolfrey and then eastwards across the moor, 1 hr 15 mins. Alternatively, use one of several approaches from the east via Burnt Hill.

There are boulder problems on the short walls to the left but the first substantial lines are on the square pinnacle. The first two routes gain the bilberry ledge on the left arête.

**1 No Rest for the Whippet** HS 4b   7m
Gain the ledge using another on the left. The left edge of the scoop above is taken to the top.

**2 Life and How to Live It** MVS 4b   7m   ★
A small flake on the face allows holds in the groove on the arête to be reached. The arête is then followed to the ledge. The right side of the scoop above leads to the top.

**3 The Afghan Whigs** HS 4a   7m   ★
The ear-shaped flake is used to reach the break, followed by a direct finish using right-hand holds on the arête.

**4 The Anthill Mob** VD   7m
Follow the left side of the next wall easily to a ledge. The moves above can be done either by bridging to the pinnacle or by stepping right onto the face (better). Watch out for the ants nest below the belay boulders.

**5 Life in the Old Dog Yet** MS 4a   6m   ★
The corner to the left of a large overhang. Excellent holds and lots of gear.

The thin crack in the wall leading up to the roof is **Let Sleeping Dogs Lie** (VS 4c). The roof is highly suspect and extreme caution should be exercised when moving direct through it. Slightly safer with a move left.

**6 Gardening at Night** HVD   10m
A left-slanting line is taken from the rightmost corner of the wall to finish just right of the overhang.

**7 Grimwith Bridge** M   6m
From the left-hand side of the square cut cave, bridge easily, but pleasantly, up left to the large jammed boulder.

On the right is a bulge with a rather fine Font 4 problem.

**8 Some Holds are Bigger than Others** S 4a   7m
The undercut wall is taken direct on good holds.

**9 Feeling Gravity's Pull** D   7m
The wall left of the right arête on rounded ledges.

**10 Wigged Out** D   7m
The right arête is taken direct from a small triangular niche with a slightly awkward move to start.

**11 All Bark and No Bite** VD   8m
At the far right-hand side of the crag, prior to *Chin's Prow*, is a small buttress split by a large horizontal crack. Start at the boulder that is detached from the buttress, climb this to one big move onto the corner of the crag proper. Some of the best jug holds in Yorkshire await.

**12 Chin's Prow** VD   4m
At the right end of the crag is a short but dramatic overhanging prow and rippled wall. The prow is taken just on its left side with foot holds on the arête. The arête itself is a fine problem but a bit steeper.

### First Ascent Information

*All recorded routes are the work of Martin Holland and Mick Darfield between June and September 2005.*

# henstone band

### by Paul Clarke

OS Ref: SE 057 695
Altitude: 540 m

This noteworthy little bouldering edge is a collector's item since it must be the most remote in Yorkshire. A reward for the long walk is a collection of pleasing problems including the excellent rib problem, *Shadows of Forgotten Ancestors*.

**The Climbing:** 20 problems. Flat grassy landings and immaculate rock that runs to good incut holds. The long approach means this is a place that will be enjoyed by those that like to walk the wide open spaces.

**Conditions and Aspect:** Facing south, these rocks get plenty of sun and are clean and quick drying. They are in a high and exposed moorland position so choose your day carefully.

**Parking and Approach:** Drive through Grassington and park at Yarnbury. Follow Old Cote Moor Lane and keep going out onto Grassington Moor crossing the Blea Beck/ Deep Cut stream at a wooden bridge. Pass to the right of the sheep fold, where a faint quad track leads to another sheep fold alongside the wall/fence that can be followed, rising up to the ridge on top of the moor. A further 750m along the ridge leads to the rocks, 7km in total. This will take around 90 minutes. A mountain bike would speed access to the bridge, after which, spongy ground means that dry conditions or a good pair of boots are required.
**Access:** There are no known issues.

The first two problems, both from sit-down starts, are on a low block. **Nature Calls** (Font 4) takes the left side of the first wall and **The Wild Bilberries** (Font 4) takes the right side. Also on the same block:

1 **Wild Bunch** Font 5. Sit-down start. The front rib.
2 **Where the Wild Things Are** Font 6a+. A traverse of the block starts on the left and goes around the rib and into the chimney.
3 **Born Survivor** Font 4. Sit-down start. The front of the next little pinnacle, past a glacis and on to the top.

There are easy problems on the right and then a thin fin.

4 **Remote Control** Font 4. Sit-down start. The fin.
5 **Outer Limits** Font 3+. The left rib.
6 **Above and Beyond** Font 3. The easy crack.

Paul Clarke on **Shadow's of Forgotten Ancestors** (Font 6a). Opposite Page.
Photo: Paul Clarke

# HENSTONE BAND

**7 Reap the Wild Wind**  Font 3. The wall past a big square hold.

Over to the right is a fine protruding rib. The wall left of the rib is **Room to Grow** (Font 4+).

**8 Shadows of Forgotten Ancestors**  Font 6a. The rib from the back is very satisfying. A sit-down start adds a grade. Photo on opposite page.

**9 King of the Wild Frontier**  Font 5+. The wall right of the rib stepping off the block. Without the block is Font 6b. The crack to the right is Font 2.

Next comes a nice recessed wall.

**10 Caged**  Font 4. Left side past a flake.
**11 Diamond in the Rough**  Font 4+. Wall and crack.
**12 Combat de Fauves**  Font 4. The right rib.
**13 The Long Walk**  Font 2. Wall around to the right.
**14 Spread-eagled**  Font 2. The rib. A good line.
**15 Long, Long Ago, Far, Far Away**  Font 2. The crack in the next block.

There are further problems on the right. Most start from sitting and a few are quite tough. One kilometre back along the edge is Ragstaff Crag. The obvious sit-down start nose is **Rags to Riches**; a good Font 6a problem but there is little else.

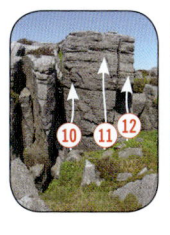

### First Ascent Information

*All problems climbed by Paul Clarke 2nd May 2011.*

Almscliff to Slipstones

# high crag (stump cross)

by **Malcolm Townsley**

OS Ref: SE 090 627
Altitude: 410 m

The crag is located half a mile south of Stump Cross Caverns on top of Craven Moor with lovely views across Appletreewick Moor and Simon's Seat. A quiet backwater offering generally short routes and bouldering that will provide an afternoons entertainment for the low and mid-grade climber. Most of the lines provide friendly solos and although the place receives limited traffic the rough grit is generally clean.

**The Climbing:** 11 lines that may just reach route height and 20+ boulder problems that generally have good landings.

**Conditions and Aspect:** The crag faces north-west and so is a bit damp and green in a normal winter although pleasant in dry weather at other times of the year. It gets sun in the afternoon but is exposed in windy weather.

**Parking, Approach and Access:** The crag is visible from the main B6265 Grassington-to-Pateley Bridge road (5 miles west of Pateley Bridge). Limited parking is available on the road with the best point being close to a gate a couple of hundred metres west of Stump Cross Caverns (**GPS: 54.068123, -1.869323**). Walk south over CRoW access land directly to the crag avoiding several holes on the way. The approach takes approximately 20 minutes and the crag itself is also on CRoW land. See maps on page 348 and 352.

At the left end of the crag, to the right of two small boulders (housing several short easy problems), is a large clean pointed boulder, the north-west face of which gives four worthwhile problems that are in the Font 4 and 5 grade range (with sit-down starts). To the right is a pleasant square buttress giving five short lines.

**1 Route A**  S 4a  6m
The left arête of the buttress.

**2 Route B**  S 4a  6m
The slab and thin crack right of the arête.

**3 Route C**  VS 5a  6m  ★
An eliminate up the pleasant and absorbing slab without using the cracks to either the left or the right.

**4 Route D**  MVS 4b  6m
The slab and thin crack direct to finish up the prominent short twin cracks.

**5 Route E**  D  6m
More fun for spectators than the climber. The wider crack splitting the right side of the buttress with the grass overhang (crux).

The next buttress, **Camel and Fish Buttress**, contains an obvious corner and capping stone at its left-hand side and provides the most interesting climbing on the crag.

**6 Slab and Wall**  D  6m
The easy slab and wall to the left of the corner.

**7 Camel's Crack**  S 4b  6m
Better than it looks although an ascent in damp weather is the best way to fully appreciate this route. The crack in the back of the obvious corner, exiting beneath the capstone in either direction.

A hand-traverse from *Camel's Crack* along the lip, around the overhanging arête and finishing up *End Slab* is **The Hump** (Font 5+).

## HIGH CRAG

**8 The Prayers of a Fish**  E1 6a   6m   ★
By far the most serious route on the crag with a bad landing. The hanging arête to the right of the corner is climbed direct, finishing on its right side.

**9 The Breath of a Camel**  VS 4b   6m   ★
The most enjoyable outing on the crag. Start up *End Slab* then traverse left to the arête, feet above the lip and finish up the arête on its right-hand side.

**10 Camel and Fish Slab**  HVS 5b   6m
The centre of the slab using the big square hold low down to rock over to the big slot.

**11 End Slab**  S 4b   6m
The right side of the slab.

To the right of Camel and Fish Buttress is a two-tier buttress split by a large ledge, the bottom half of which provides an undercut square boulder with the best problems on the crag.

**12 Ship of the Desert**  Font 3
The left arête then up and over the boulder above.

**13 The Doomed Dromedary**  Font 6a+
The nice wall from a sit-down start with a powerful move to begin.

**14 The Lost Llama**  Font 5
The crack/groove in the middle of the boulder from a sit-down start can be continued up the crack on the upper part of buttress.

**15 Two Feet Dyno**  Font 6a
From a sit-down start with feet on the block, tackle the rounded right arête on its left-hand side.

To the right and immediately left of a dry stone wall is a smaller boulder giving four short problems.

**16 Stone Fish**  Font 4+
The jugs and thin crack from a sit-down start.

**17 Angel Fish**  Font 5
The crack in the centre of the boulder from a sit-down start.

**18 A Fish Called Wanda**  Font 5+
Sit-down start. Tussle with the cool wall to the right of the crack using a small spike.

**19 Billy the Fish**  Font 6a
The insecure right arête of the boulder from a sit-down start.

To the right of the dry stone wall are a further three boulders giving several further problems in the Font 3 to 5 range including some nice crack problems.

### First Ascent Information

*No historical information is available for the crag. All the recorded routes and boulder problems were climbed by Malcolm Townsley between 1994 and 2009.*

# hebden gill
by **John Hunt**

---

OS Ref: SE 026 641
Altitude: 250 m

---

A big old rambling crag on the hillside overlooking Hebden Beck. The main buttress is steep and gives routes up to 21 metres long. The climbing continues into smaller walls then the very steep Crevasse Area. The rest of the crag consists of other buttresses up the valley overlooking the beck. This was a favourite with YMC teams in the 1950s and has continued to be developed since.

**The Climbing:** There are just over 50 climbs in total with a real mixture of 1950s old school classics and 'new cool' offerings between E3 and E6. There are also a good spread of climbs from HS to E1. The routes are often long by gritstone standards and belaying atop the main crag has an almost Lakeland feel to it.

**Conditions and Aspect:** The main crag dominates an extensive, but disappointing, boulder field whilst the valley crags overlook the beck. West-facing and best avoided on windy days, though sheltered spots can usually be found. Classics such as *Wall & Nose* (HVD), *Right of Way* (VS) and *Prosecutor* (HVS) on the main crag can look a livid greenish white but don't be put off; it's a special form of climbable lichen and the routes are real belters. Some of the routes in the Crevasse Area have very insecure rock on them (where this is obvious it has been highlighted in the route description) but reasonable caution and good judgement are sensible companions.

**Parking and Approach:** Hebden village is located on the B6265, a couple of miles east of Grassington. At the crossroads in the centre of the village, head north up High Green Lane for just over half a mile to Hole Bottom (Jerry & Bens B&B). Park courteously here or well off the road on the grass banking back towards the village (do not block driveways or road access). Walk over the bridge to the opposite side of Hebden Beck. Follow the track north northeast for 300m to the left end of the valley buttresses, Roof Buttress being the furthest out and up on the hillside to the right. If heading for the main crag, turn right as soon as the little bridge is crossed and bushwhack and boulder hop for 200m south-east up the hill; beware ankle snapping boulders lurking under the bracken. There is also a pleasant footpath on the east bank of the beck leading directly to the top of the Crevasse Area of the main crag.
**Access:** No issues, on access land.

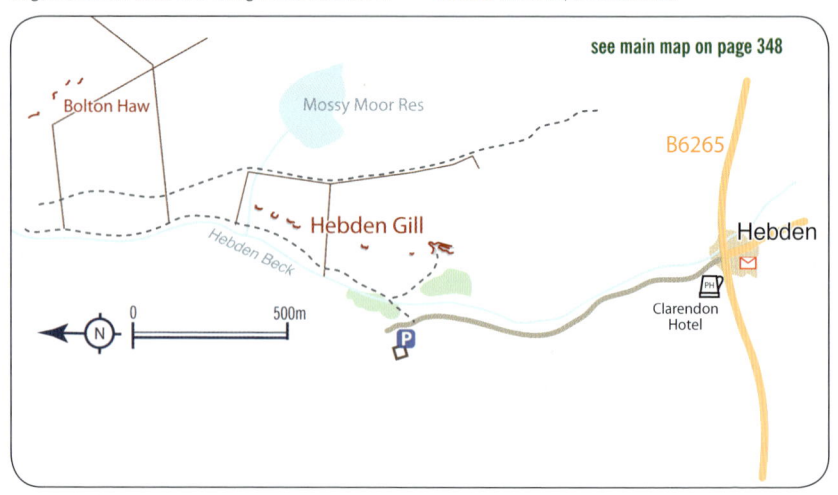

Yorkshire Gritstone

Roof Buttress - **HEBDEN GILL**

### The Tower Beyond the Tunnel
Past the gated tunnel, 350m up the valley, is a prominent tower feature. The rock requires care, but some old mining gear on top provides one of the best belays on gritstone. **The Tower** (MVS 4b) climbs the underlying crozzly sandstone-like wall to the ledge then takes the front face of the tower as directly as possible. An equally good HS 4b climbs the right face.

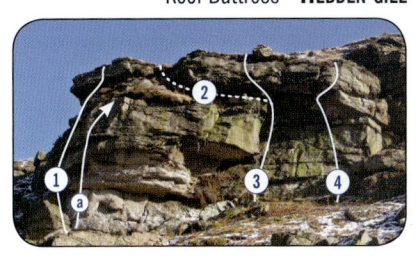

### Roof Buttress
Prominent overhangs mark it out. Some of the lower bands of rock are more akin to sandstone and are suspect in places.

On the left side of the buttress **Conscript** (D) takes the left side of the little bay to gain the large flat ledge then uses the big crack to reach the top. **Unorthodox** (HVD) laybacks the corner-crack to an awkward exit onto the ledge before a step left to finish up the upper wall. A direct finish goes straight over the roof at VS 4c.

### 1 **Saunter** HS 4b   10m
A short ramp leads to a ledge. Continue up the wall above, crossing an easy overlap to a second ledge, and finish up a short crack. An alternative VD finish moves right, omitting the crack. (a) **Kestrel on a String** (E3 5c, ★) leaves the base of the ramp early to climb the wall via good holds, before reaching over the overlap for a large flat hold right of the rib (to finish up this). Marginal gear is available but is way below in dubious rock.
*Mike Bebbington (solo)   19th June 1996*  ✦

### 2 **Adamant** HS 4b   10m
Climb the obvious corner to the roof. Traverse left to ledges and then the top.
*Adam Wainwright   29th June 1988*  ✦

### 3 **The Unpaid Chauffeur** E1 5a   9m   ★
Takes the challenge *Adamant* avoids. From the corner pull wildly over the roof on good holds.
*Fraser Hardie, Adam Wainwright   29th June 1988*

### 4 **What!!!** HVS 5a   9m
Climb the middle of the slab to gain the crack which runs round the roof at its right-hand end. Pull over on good holds to finish on vertical grass.
*Fraser Hardie, M. Perry, S. Franks, A. Wainwright   26th June 1988*

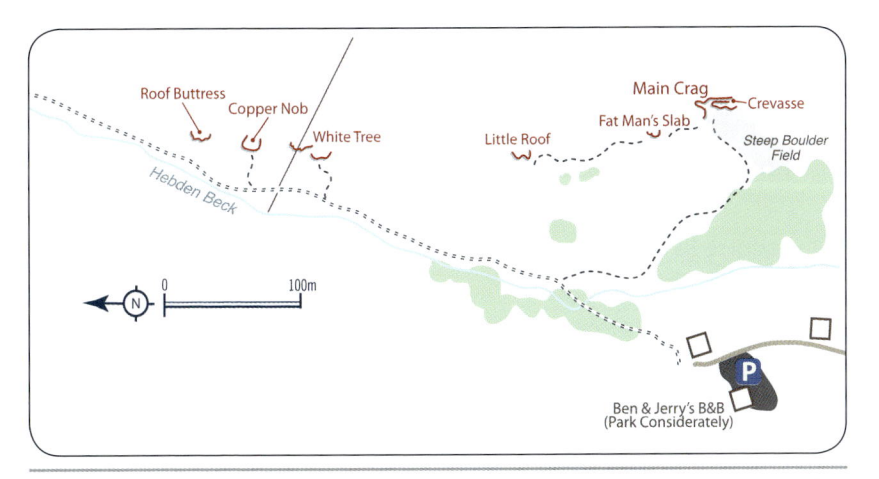

Almscliff to Slipstones

# HEBDEN GILL - Copper Nob Buttress

## Copper Nob Buttress
Heading south for 40m is a mighty buttress with good belays on top.

**5 Shed Ahoy!** HS 4b  10m
The big corner. Step right onto a ledge and up to the top.
*Simon Franks  29th June 1988*

**6 Silent Memory** E4 6b  10m
The centre of the wall. Use the letterbox hold to gain the break, step right to place gear then climb the wall direct via a long reach and a small crimp out left.
*Dave Sutcliffe  July 2002*

**7 Dead Man's Crankshaft** E2 6a  11m ★
The cracked wall beside the arête. Make a difficult start to gain a break and continue up the unhelpful incipient crack and breaks above.
*John Paul Hotham  17th August 1988* ✦

**8 Tall Man in the Bidet** VS 5a  10m ☆
The arête is climbed on the right-hand side, with a hard move low down. A little overgrown, but still enjoyable.
*Adam Wainwright  29th June 1988*

**9 Hieronymouse** HS 4b  10m
The central line of the wall with some bushwhacking.
*Fraser Hardie  29th June 1988*

**10 Bisexual Bratwurst** VD  10m ★
A classic, good-natured route. The blunt right arête of the slabby wall is climbed on flakes and horizontal breaks.
*Simon Franks  29th June 1988*

On the track directly below Copper Nob Buttress is a jutting roofed boulder. Three Font 4-5 problems are available, all from sit-down starts with feet on the underlying boulder.

## White Tree Buttress
The one with the big white tree on top a further 30m south, parallel with the wall crossing the path.

**11 YMC Revisited** S 4a  6m
Climb the ledges and the big crack.
*David Campbell, John Hunt  22nd September 2010*

**12 Promises More** E1 6a  6m
Climb the left side of the face. Escapable and easy, until a stopper move through the headwall to the ledge.
*John Hunt, Dave Campbell  22nd September 2010*

**13 Hole In The Sky** E1 5c  6m ★
The right-hand side of the unprotected slab moving left past a flat hold to finish left of the tree.
*Dave Sutcliffe  July 2002*

## Little Roof Buttress
Contour the hillside southwards for 180m to the easily identifiable buttress with the overhanging arête and roofs.

**14 Parallel Universe** E5 6b  5m ★
Make a difficult move over the steep overlap to gain the bottom of the obvious ramp. Grab the higher holds just right and make a massive stretch to the break (threads or huge cams here). Finish over the small roof beside the arête. The angle, fall potential and brittle nature of some of the holds make this a serious route.
*Dave Sutcliffe  July 2002*

Yorkshire Gritstone

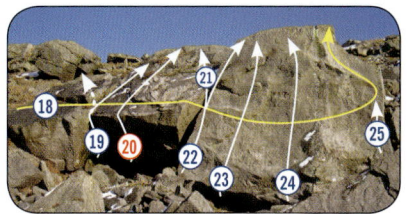

## Fat Man's Slab - HEBDEN GILL

**15 The Fourth Dimension** E6 6b  6m  ★★
An audacious modern problem. Use the prominent sloper on the lower arête to gain the break. Reach to the central rib which is used with difficulty to gain the hanging arête. Once established on the arête, climb directly to the top.
*Dave Sutcliffe (solo)  7th July 2002*

**16 Wind Rider** VS 4c  6m  ★
Start as for *The Wishing Chair,* but make an exposed traverse out and up to the arête.
*John Hunt, Bob Larkin  3rd November 2010*

**17 The Wishing Chair** VS 4c  5m
From a hard start, climb the arête of the chimney until the big chockstone can be embraced.
*John Hunt (solo)  23rd February 2004*

Just right is a Mod, then a Diff which climbs into a cave.

### Fat Man's Slab

The huge clean slab, visible from the parking, with two neighbouring slabs. Brave boulderers and highball warriors will be drawn to this one, though the main slab routes are also good technical exercises on a rope.

**18 Red & White Traverse** HVS 5a  20m  ★
Traverse the three slabs in turn. Cross the first two slabs to a step across to a small ledge on the main slab. Use small finger-holds to step down, then balance across the blankness and finish up the right-hand rib.
*Bob Larkin (solo)  6th August 2000*  ✦

**19 Bacchus** VS 4c  6m
Start at the junction of the first two slabs. Pull strenuously through the bulge then follow the slab just right of the crack or climb diagonally leftwards up the slab to finish over the hanging nose of rock.
*Bob Larkin (solo)  6th August 2000*

**20 Humper** Font 5+ (VS 5c)
Forget being elegant. Mantel, heel hook and hump your way onto the centre of the slab. Finish gracefully up the upper slab.
*John Hunt (solo)  3rd November 2010*  ✦

**21 Fruit Of The Vine** MVS 4a  6m
Take the left rib of the main slab for a metre or so, then step left, across the crack, onto a good foothold. Climb boldly up the slab above.
*Bob Larkin (solo)  6th August 2000*

**22 Lardies Route** S 4a  6m
The left-hand rib of the main slab. Limit yourself to one chip-butty per ascent.
*Dave Musgrove  22nd February 1998*

**23 Fat Man's Slab** E3 5c  6m  ★
The left-hand line of undercut flakes leads to a crux above the tiny overlap at the top. Any mat will look like a postage stamp from the top.
*Ian Renshaw  24th June 1988*

**24 Diethard, Slim With a Vengence** E4 6a  6m  ★
A bold, direct line up the centre of the triangular slab. Stay off the flakes to the left and the arête to the right.
*Jason Lister (solo)  1st June 1996*  ✦

**25 Do or Diet** HVS 5a  6m
The right-hand line, stepping off the boulder and using the right arête near the top. Beware the underlying boulder.
*John Paul Hotham  24th June 1988*

# HEBDEN GILL - The Main Crag

### The Main Crag
The main event, where half the challenge is trekking up to the amphitheatre before girding the loins for battle. In the first bay, just before the huge buttress, is a short, cracked slab below a split block.

### 26 Jerry and Ben  HVS 5a   10m
Climb the crack in the slab then move right to battle up the crack in the block above.
*Harold Barraclough  c1957*

### 27 Tigga, the Bagpipe Dog  S 4a   17m
Boulder up the slab to some steep grass. Move right to the wall and climb this to a large sloping ledge. Step back left to some exciting mantelshelves to finish. The initial slab, avoiding the crack and the block on the right, is a good Font 4+ problem.
*Luke Dow, Kate Turner  3rd May 1993*

### 28 Wall And Nose  HVD   20m   ★★
A magisterial route of quality and length. Climb the right wall of the corner to a tree. Finish up the corner above or make a spectacular traverse right to the nose.
*YMC members  c1957*

### 29 The Mutant Midge  HVS 5a   20m   ★
The fierce finger crack quashes any hopes of a gentle start. Suitably engaged, climb the wall to a short curving crack and triangular overhang. Pull right to finish easily.
*Adam Wainwright  24th June 1988  ✦*

### 30 The Way  E1 5b   21m   ★
A demanding assault on the blunt nose. Start on the platform below the nose. Climb the groove to the overhang and duck left to a small ledge. Move up and right to a thin crack which allows access to an easier finish left of the prow.
*Tony Barley, Robin Barley  1964*

### 31 Midway  E3 6a   18m   ★★
The wall left of the corner via some brilliant and bold moves. Climb the twin cracks in the slab to the first overhang; the bold crux involves reaching up to a small flake and using this to win the horizontal break. Step left to finish up a chimney right of the prow.
*Chris Sowden, Tony Burnell  19th July 1980*

### 32 Prosecutor  HVS 5a   16m   ★★
Butch as hell, but brilliant. Climb the overhanging corner. An antique peg runner on the left can be clipped for historical interest. Photo on page 377.
*Dave Berry  1964*

### 33 Right of Way  VS 4c   18m   ★
The original YMC route of the crag and a good one. Start as for *Prosecutor* then climb the thin cracks on the right to an overlap. Traverse right at the second break, pull onto a ledge and finish up a huge flake.
*Harold Barraclough  1957  ✦*

### 34 Forgotten Rib  E3 5c   19m   ★
Start as for the two previous routes, but traverse right at the first break to difficult moves up the rib. From here, move up and swing right onto the upper slab.
*Paul Farish, John Hunt  7th November 2010*

### 35 Dan Dare  HVS 5b   16m
From the slope climb up the thin crack and pull over the overhang. Finish leftwards up the slab.
*John Paul Hotham  24th June 1988*

Right again are two right-angled corners. The lower rock on these routes is mostly excellent, while the finishes are creaky so take care.

### 36 Fat Crack  D   9m
The obvious chimney on the left is okay, but loose on top.
*Bill Todd  c1957*

### 37 Thin Crack  VS 4b   9m
The honest crack in the centre of the wall.
*Charlie Salisbury  c1957*

### 38 Tree Climb  HS 4b   9m
The corner on the right with a tree has a strenuous start.
*c1939  ✦*

### 39 French Fancy  E1 5c   6m   ★
The *chic*, lime green arête is bold. The thin bough of the tree can be lassoed, but will it take your weight? Move left at the top.
*John Paul Hotham  17th August 1988*

# The Main Crag - HEBDEN GILL

The next corner, **The Layback** (VS 4c), has some loose blocks and is not recommended.

### 40 Innominate   HVS 5b   9m   ★
The lower crack in the wall right of the corner is superb. At the ledge, the original went right, but take your pick.
*YMC members   c1957*

Manteling the ramp to the right before drifting left to small pockets and finishing as for *Innominate* is **Rediscovery** (HS 4b). The wall just right has three little problems, all of which can be finished at "dangerous Diff" standard over the creaky upper bands. **Scamper** (Font 5) takes the flat hold in the centre of the wall to reach up and scamper for the good hold on the left and the shelf: **Little Rowan** (Font 3) follows the shallow ramp to the little rowan; **One 5b** (Font 4) bookends the block to reach the shelf.

Next there are two descent gullies, both of which require care. The next routes are on the left end of the wall leading towards the **Crevasse Area**.

### 41 Fun with Friends   VS 4b   7m
The strenuous left-hand wide crack.
*Adam Wainwright, Glyn Appleyard   8th May 1988*

### 42 Funny Friends   Font 6a+  (HVS 6a)
Climb the highball wall dynamically.

### 43 Friendly Fun   HVS 5a   8m   ☆
The right-hand diagonal crack. May need a prune.
*Glyn Appleyard, Adam Wainwright   8th May 1988*

### 44 Twin Cracks   VS 4c   10m
Start up the right-hand crack; finish up the left-hand one.
*YMC members   c1957*

### 45 The Buneater   E1 5b   12m
From the crevasse entrance, climb to a break then step right into a shallow groove. Climb this until a thin crack can be followed leftwards. WARNING: the traverse uses a captive block which looks dangerous. Finish up the wall above.
*John Paul Hotham, Adam Wainwright   17th July 1988*

Almscliff to Slipstones

# Hebden Gill - Crevasse Area

### 46 Wacko Saco  E3 5b  13m
Climb *The Buneater* to the break. Now move right to the arête, which is climbed boldly on both sides.
*John Paul Hotham  17th August 1988*

The next routes are on the impressive **Crevasse Wall**. Belays are a long way back and care needs to be taken with some of the tops – **a preplaced belay rope is strongly recommended**.

In the ugly corner at the left end of the wall is **The Crag, The Climber, His Girl and Her Dog** (HVS 5a). This route is **not recommended** due to the potential for falling rock. It gains a large block then uses the corner-crack to reach holds under a loose block before traversing left and manteling up amongst much avalanche potential. **Comeuppance** (E2 5b) is a left-to-right traverse following a rising break between the overhangs of the upper wall. The crux involves a well-protected move on a pocket just after a halfway resting ledge.

### 47 Laid to Rest  HVS 5b  16m
Start just left of *Crevasse Wall* and climb straight up to, then follow, the sustained corner-crack. Finish leftwards. Take care with the scramble off.
*Phillipe Osborne, Andy Gudgeon  6th September 1997*

### 48 Crevasse Wall  E2 5b  18m  ★
An exciting, bold route on perfect rock. Climb a short groove line to a horizontal break. Hand-traverse right and move up rightwards on good ledges. Step left to finish.
*Chris Sowden, Tony Burnell, Gordan Higginson  31st July 1980*

### 49 Performance Management  E4 6a  20m  ★
A hard start to *Crevasse Wall*. From the fallen blocks, teeter onto the ledge below the left side of the overhang. Gain the first break and step right to pockets below a square-cut corner which is laybacked to the next break. Small holds and an undercut lead to a third break. Take the same line on features and flat holds to the good ledge near the top of *Crevasse Wall*. Finish up this.
*Andy Moss (unseconded)  11th June 2000*

### 50 Three Day Rave  E5 6b  17m  ★
Start as for *Performance Management*, then climb to the base of the rightwards sloping ramp which is followed until it runs out. Take a direct finish on crimps. Rave on!
*Dave Sutcliffe  September 2002*

Another dangerous and **not recommended** route is (a) **Climbing by Runners** (E1 5b). It climbs up cracks to the overhang in the centre of the wall, steps left and pulls over a dangerous block to continue up the capped chimneys to the top. Suicidal.

You try it in thick jumper and big boots! Allan Austin on **Prosecutor** (HVS 5a), Page 374
Photo: Mike Bebbington.

# Hebden Gill - First Ascent Information & Graded List

## 51 Magnificrack  E3 6a   20m   ★
Start below the hanging crack in the upper wall. Climb the initial wall (crux) to gain a thin, leftward-slanting crack which is used to reach two pockets. These should allow entry to the overhanging crack which is followed to the top.
*Chris Sowden, Tony Burnell, Gordan Higginson   31st July 1980*

### Focal Point Boulder
The chaotic boulder-field below the main crag has options for the modern boulderer. The problems are on the obvious big boulder, which fell from the crag and stuck where it landed; the climbs are mostly up what would have been the flat top of part of the crag. **Chaos Roof** (Font 5), is the huge roof in the bay up and left of the main face. Start at the top of the underlying slab, reach around the roof using three sharp pockets and the edge of the overlap. Balance up the slab above. On the main lichen and pebble covered wall there are three unusual highballs. Carefully test each hold. **Gunga Din** (Font 4 / E1 4c), goes from a sit-down start below the left arête before taking the face on mostly big holds. **Siren Song** (Font 4+ / E1 5a), climbs dead centre. **Brittle Crack** (Font 4 / HVS 4c), take the right edge and brittle crack around the arête. The back of the boulder is more conventional. **Pocked Arête** (Font 4+), the wall and arête; **Pocked Back Wall** (Font 6a), goes from a sit-down start, eliminating the arête; **Ash Bulge** (Font 3), behind the rowan from a low start. Snappy holds.

---

### Further First Ascent Information (✦)
**Adamant, Tall Man in the Bide:** *These routes had possibly been done before; the 1957 guide makes reference to climbs on Copper Nob Buttress.*
**Climbing by Runners:** *climbed by Gordan Higginson, Tony Burnell, Chris Sowden   31st July 1980*
**Comeuppance:** *climbed by Luke Dow (unseconded) 3rd May 1993*
**Conscript:** *John Hunt, Tara Hunt   27th April 2011*
**Diethard, Slim With Avengence:** *Originally graded E1 5b; at least one subsequent ascentionist thought it might be worth E5.*
**Dead Man's Crankshaft:** *In the 1998 guide: "A route that requires a stiff pull."*
**Friction, Jerry Wall:** *A 60ft VS and an 80ft V.Diff were recorded by Ron Hirst and J Greaves respectively (possibly the original versions of Right of Way and Wall and Nose).*
**Kestrel on a String:** *John Hunt, Paul Clarke, 16th April 2011 Climbed the same day as rescuing a kestrel caught on Hieronymouse by abseil.*
**Rediscovery:** *John Hunt 4th May 2011*
**The Crag, The Climber, His Girl and Her Dog:** *climbed by Luke Dow, Kate Turner   3rd May 1993*
**The Mutant Midge:** *Solved onsight. Described in the 1998 guide as "essentially the old variation start to **The Way**" – it is clearly a classic route in its own right.*
**Tree Climb:** *Believed to have been climbed by a local farm boy.*
**The Tower:** *First recorded by John Hunt   27th April 2011*
**Unorthodox:** *John Hunt, Tara Hunt   27th April 2011*

*All the bouldering on the Focal Point Boulder, the problems to the right of Innominate and those below Copper Nob Buttress, are the work of John Hunt.*

### GRADED LIST

**E6**
The Fourth Dimension (6b)

**E5**
Three Day Rave (6b)
Parallel Universe (6b)

**E4**
Silent Memory (6b)
Performance Management (6a)
Diethard, Slim With A Vengence (6a)

**E3**
Magnificrack (6a)
Midway (6a)
Wacko Saco (5b)
Forgotten Rib (5c)
Fat Man's Slab (5c)
Kestrel on a String (5c)

**E2**
Dead Man's Crankshaft (6a)
Comeuppance (5b)
Crevasse Wall (5b)

**E1**
The Way (5b)
Climbing by Runners (5b)
Promises More (6a)
Hole In The Sky (5c)
The Unpaid Chauffeur (5a)
The Buneater (5b)
French Fancy (5c)

**HVS**
Prosecutor (5a)
Jerry and Ben (5a)
The Mutant Midge (5a)
Laid to Rest (5b)
Innominate (5b)
Dan Dare (5b)
Friendly Fun (5a)
What!!! (5a)
Red & White Traverse (5a)
Do or Diet (5a)
The Crag etc (5a)

**VS**
Right of Way (4c)
The Layback (4c)
Tall Man in the Bidet (5a)
Wind Rider (4c)
The Wishing Chair (4c)
Twin Cracks (4c)
Unorthodox Direct (4c)
Fun with Friends (4b)
Bacchus (4c)
Thin Crack (4b)

**MVS**
The Tower (4b)
Fruit Of The Vine (4a)

**HS**
Shed Ahoy! (4b)
Adamant (4b)
Tree Climb (4b)
Rediscovery (4b)
Saunter (4b)
Hieronymouse (4b)

**S**
Tigga' (4a)
Lardies Route (4a)
YMC Revisited (4a)

**HVD**
Wall And Nose
Unorthodox

**VD**
Bisexual Bratwurst

**D**
Conscript
Fat Crack

**Font 6a+**
Funny Friends (HVS 6a)

**Font 5+**
Humper (VS 5c)

Yorkshire Gritstone

Josh Robinson gratefully emerges unscathed from the bowels of **Hook Route** (E1 5b) at Guisecliff. Page 393
Photo: Adi Gill

# bolton haw

by **Robert Fenton**

OS Ref: SE 031 651
Altitude: 350m

The Bolton Haw (aka Temple of the Winds) boulders can easily be ticked by a solo adventurer in a couple of hours, but are best savoured at a leisurely pace with family and friends. Bring along a picnic blanket and take time out to appreciate the magical views of the Yorkshire Dales.

**The Climbing:** Problems tend to be clean and generally consist of soft grassy landings. The rock quality is excellent throughout. Younger and less experienced climbers may benefit from bringing along a bouldering mat.

**Conditions and Aspect:** This bouldering crag faces south-west and is a great place to climb on a sunny summer or winter afternoon. Be warned - out of season, the crag is deserving of its nickname!

**Parking and Approach:** Follow the parking and approach for Hebden Gill (page 370) to the quaint bridge. The bridleway continues northwards for a further kilometre until an open area containing a few ruined buildings. After a final gate the path splits and it winds steeply up the hillside in an easterly direction towards the photogenic spires. The boulders are found 100m south of these. Approach time is 30 mins, but allow an extra 15 mins or so for the final steep climb if you are bringing small children.

**Access:** The crag lies on open access land.

### First Boulder
**1 Almanac** Font 6a. The leaning arête is taken on its left-hand side to a sloping top. For those with long arms, it is also possible to bull-work your way up both arêtes from a sit-down start at a similar grade.
**2 Gun Crime** Font 5. The vague flake up the wall.
**3 Fighter** Font 5. Sit down start. Crimp your way up.
**4 Four Winds** Font 5+. A worthwhile eliminate with a sit-down start from low holds (avoid holds utilised on the adjoining problems).
**5 Main Corner** Font 4+.
**6 Call Social Services** Font 3. Start on the small boulder.
**7 Straight Up** Font 3. The arête left of the crack.

### The Wolf Boulder
**8 The Wolf** Font 5+. Sit-down start. Use good jams then big holds to climb the roof.

Just around the bay is a well-featured, overhanging, knobbly boulder. Various eliminates are possible but the star turn is **Recorder** (Font 5) which tackles the overhanging face direct. Font 6a+ from a sit-down start.

### Big Sloping Boulder
**9 Mountaineer** Font 4. Follow the vague runnel into cracks above the heather.
**10 South Face** Font 5. Rock onto a small dimple and on up to the apex of the boulder.
**11 Ramp** Font 4+. Fun climbing from a tricky start.
**12 Shallow Flakes** Font 5+. Sit-down start up to a layaway pinch and on to easier ground.
**13 Traddo** Font 3. Avoid the right-hand arête.

# BOLTON HAW

### Lookout Boulder
**19 Footstool** Font 3. The left arête to a mantel finish.
**20 Wrinkly Wall** Font 3. The weathered wall.
**21 Long Haul** Font 3. Sit-down start on the right-hand arête and traverse leftwards as far as you can with hands on top of the boulder.
**22 Slabby Back** Font 2. Great for small kids. Many variations are possible.

### Bounce Boulder
**23 Bounce** Font 5+. Using the left-hand two-finger pinch and right-hand sloper, pull on and wonder how you are going to reach the top.

### First Ascent Information
*Credit should be given to John and Tara Hunt and Paul, Ben and Holly Clarke for their initial efforts in documenting the crag in 2008. Robert Fenton added the bull-worker variation to* **Almanac***;* **The Wolf, Bounce** *and* **Mystical Powers** *on FA Cup Final Day 2009. It was reported to be 100 degrees at pitch-side.*

### Arête Boulder
**14 Scythe** Font 4. The left side of the arête starting from a shelf. A heel-hook proves useful.
**15 Chariot** Font 4+. Right side of the arête.
**16 Triumph** Font 4+. The middle of the wall.

A pyramidal boulder tucked away 30m to the right contains **Ben's Boff** (Font 5). Gain the top from a sit-down start using both hands and a heel-hook on the ledge. The slab just to the right of the arête can be climbed at Font 4.

### Roof Boulder
Moving along for 20m are three boulders. Roof Boulder is at the same level as the rest of the crag but the other two (Lookout and Bounce) are positioned slightly lower.

**17 Mystical Powers** Font 7b. Use lateral thinking to negotiate the roof from a sit-down start.
**18 Burn Out** Font 3. Start on the arête and once established, trend leftwards along the slab. The right-hand side of the arête can be climbed at the same grade. The pleasant slab just right is **(a) Big Slab** (Font 2), and is useful for introducing the newcomer to the art of gritstone smearing.

Just behind this boulder is a small enclave containing a Font 4 wall starting from a prominent foothold. A few additional problems exist approximately 100m further on. These are left for a young pioneer to discover and climb.

# air scar
by **John Hunt**

OS Ref: SE 031 603
Altitude: 320m

An impressive outcrop, prominent above the Burnsall to Bolton Abbey road. Spectacular views can be had over Burnsall and one of the most picturesque valleys in the Dales. The routes on the main buttress mostly face north-east while the roof climbs in the hidden crevasse face west. Climbing is possible at most times of the year; especially in the hidden crevasse which offers shelter from the wind.

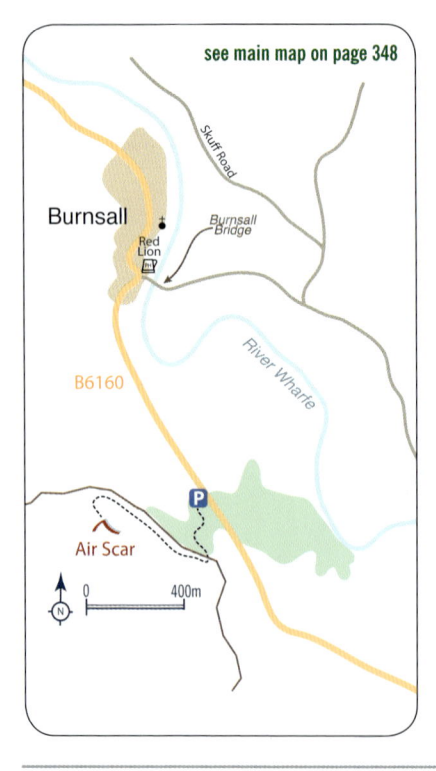

**The Climbing:** A handful of short routes on top notch, clean moorland grit. There is also lower grade bouldering in the chaos of rocks and bilberries behind the main crag (not recorded here).

**Parking and Approach:** From Burnsall go south on the B6160. Pass the Burnsall bridge on the left and after a further half a mile, parking is reached on the edge of the wood in the lay-by on the right by the moorland access sign. Follow the footpath, up through the woods, and follow the wall until just beyond the crag, before flogging up the hillside. Takes 15 minutes and is good for you. **Access:** On access land; the sign by the parking displays any shooting closures. No dogs.

### The Main Buttresss

**1 Burnsall Sports** E3 5c   6m
Step off a projecting rock to a big handhold high on the steep left face. The original finish moves right onto the upper slab; going straight up is slightly easier.
*Tony Barley   19th July 1994*

The next two routes start in the same place and climb the main arête (on different sides). They also cross each other.

**2 Thick As Thieves** E1 5b   10m   ★
Start under the roof before pulling onto the face. Follow the handrail below the overlap to the arête. Cross this with difficultly and climb the fine slab beyond it.
*Tony Barley   19th July 1994*

**3 Bag End** E5 6a   10m
Probably unrepeated. Start on fragile holds under the roof. Stay under this until the lip can be turned to join the arête, which is climbed on the right.
*Tony Simpson   1990s*

**4 In Cahoots** HVS 5a   9m
Gain the thin diagonal crack from an undercut start. Make technical moves leftwards to finish up the upper part of the arête.
*Tony Barley   19th July 1994*

**5 Fell Race** S 4a   8m
The wide crack with a wedge shaped chockstone.

## AIR SCAR

**6 Sack Race**  S 4a  7m  ★
Fantastic. The right side of the main face between the two obvious cracklines.

Up and left of the main buttress is a cleft leading into an open gritstone chamber. The routes all climb the impressive roof.

**7 Burnsall Ham**  E3 5c  5m
Climb into the scoop on the left and go for the top.
*Tony Barley  19th July 1994*

**8 Disreali Gears**  E2 5b  5m  ★
The nose direct. Make a long reach from a brittle flake under the roof to a good slot just left of the rib. Slap and scrabble up.
*John Hunt  12th February 2008*

**9 Fryer's Front**  E3 5c  5m  ★
The line of the bay, tackling the widest part of the roof. From the brittle flake under the roof use the right face of the rib and its arête to reach a good break.
*Tim Fryer  31st March 2008*

**10 The Greasy Pole**  E1 5b  5m  ★
Fairly wild. The lesser overhang and steep fingery wall.
*Tony Barley  19th July 1994*

Opposite the last routes, and behind the main buttress, is a deep crevasse about 6m high and about a metre apart for most of its length. Tony Simpson climbed a number of routes here. His thin leaning rib might be worth re-examination at a suggested grade of Font 7b+/7c (or E6 6c).

There is a variety of bouldering and short routes in the boulder field behind the main crag. To the south, there is an obvious overhanging corner, **Lunchtime** (HS 4b). For more bouldering options, follow your nose.

### Further First Ascent Information
**Fell Race:** *The gully has been explored and climbed in from the earliest times judging by the nail scratches, but no one thought it worth recording until Tony Barley, and then Tony Simpson, made separate visits in the 1990s and started naming climbs.*
**Lunchtime**: *John Hunt, Rachel Hunt 19th December 2004*

# guisecliff
## by Bruce Woodley

OS Ref: SE 165 633     Altitude: 290m

One of the Shire's most sizeable chunks of grit. Guisecliff's sylvan seclusion and north-east aspect combine to give the edge a serious atmosphere more akin to a mountain or sea cliff crag; indeed a spare abseil rope and prusiks can be useful to avoid the jungle beneath. Crag foot exploration has provided entertaining tales of bizarre rashes, bee stings, twisted ankles, hidden chasms and malarial midges.

**The Climbing:** In visits spread over 20 years the crag author has seen chalk once, evidence of cleaning twice and other climbers, never. With well over a hundred routes, and some of the tallest on grit, every visit provides a splendid adventure irrespective of your grade, or indeed even if you end up taking your gear for a walk. The best lines are numbered and should require little cleaning; note that large cams will be dearly appreciated on many of these. Those drawn to the thrill of taking on the more vegetated routes must be ready for anything from vicious holly to mud and moss clawing finishes. *A word of caution: many of the long standing sub-HVS routes were reclimbed and upgraded in the checking of this crag (Autobahn, a former VS, now weighs in at E2). This may be the last stand for the Yorkshire sandbag but keep alert for some 'top-end' potential on the 1950s routes.*

**Conditions and Aspect:** Sheltered from prevailing westerlies and open to some early and late sun, encroaching vegetation has rendered many routes unclimbable. Several routes will need sensitive cleaning and inspection first and are graded for when in climbable condition. The best buttresses with the numbered lines remain relatively free of 'adventure layers' and dry reasonably quickly. A dry, early spring will provide optimum conditions. In the rare event of a scorching summer there's welcome shade or dry autumn leaf peeping can also work.

**Access Issues:** This crag is on the border of Open Access land and woodland. Avoid Buttress Three to Five from the 1st March to 30th June as peregrines nest at the crag.

**Approaches:** The crag overlooks Glasshouses and Pateley Bridge and is about 20-45 minutes walk from the car, depending on your choice of route.

North lay-by parking (**GPS: 54.069125,-1.763467**) is best for North Buttress and North Buttress Block. Head to the south lay-by (**GPS: 54.055757,-1.7536**) for Buttresses One to Five (*Pulpit, Creation, Comet Wall* areas).

Arriving from the north, cross the bridge in Pateley Bridge heading south on the B6265. Turn left at the Royal Oak pub and along Bridgehouse Gate, through Bewerley village, over a second bridge and right up Nought Bank Road, whereupon you can see the crag. After 1.5 miles from Pateley Bridge you arrive at North Crag lay-by on the sharp bend. Cross the road and follow a footpath up to the clearly visible stone towers of Yorke's Folly marking the start of the northern edge.

From the south, 3.6 miles north of Blubberhouses on the Pateley Bridge road, turn right into Braithwaite Lane. After a little under a mile turn left (north) at another T- junction, (signposted Pateley Bridge) onto Foldshaw Lane. Continue past Fouldshaw Farm to the hilltop, where a lay-by on the left provides parking opposite the end of Dike Lane: South Crag lay-by. North lay-by is half a mile further on at a sharp right-hand bend before the descent to Pateley Bridge.

A hundred metres further up the road from South Crag lay-by, a footpath trends right (east) past a trig point to a telecoms mast, marking the southern end of the edge. Please study the detailed crag maps on the following pages.

Aqil Gill attempting to stay **On The Edge** (E6 6b). Page 392.
Photo: Dave Sutcliffe

# GUISECLIFF - Area Map

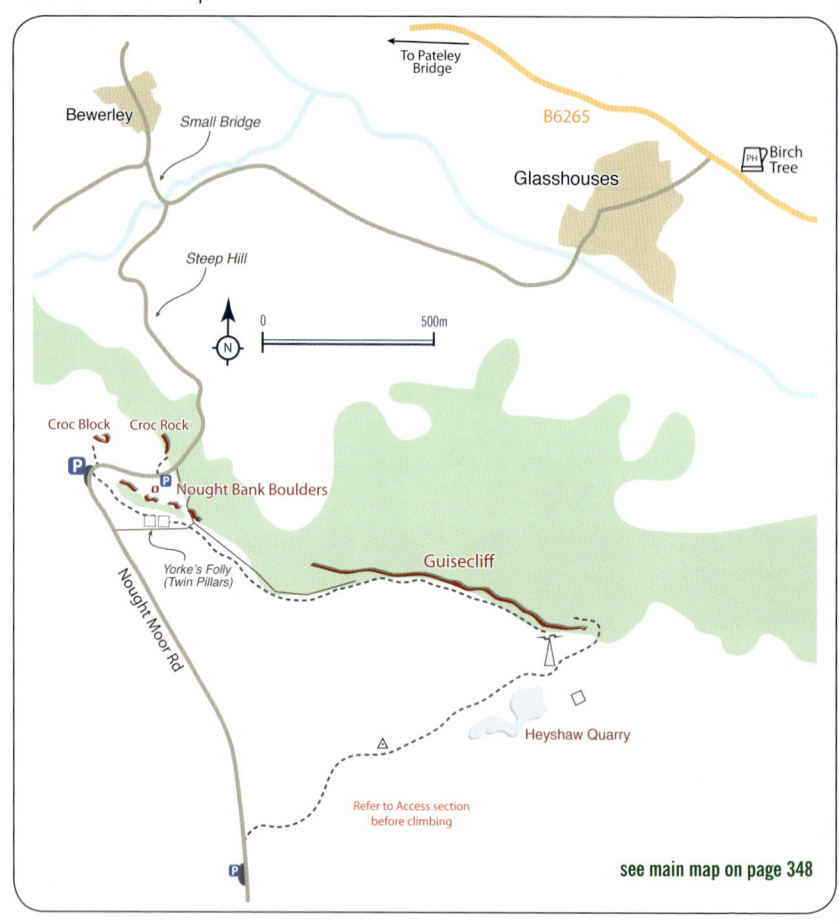

Access to the crag base is tricky and a full on epic can be assured for those taking a laissez faire attitude to the approach. Or, maybe that's what you're looking for, in which case ignore the above.

**Suggested Game Plan:** For a first visit and orientation the most accessible range of routes are found on Comet Buttress (300m north-west of the telecom mast). Abseiling in from a big platform adjacent to the crag top footpath (silver birch tree/iron stake anchors) is easiest. Alternatively the classic E2 hand crack, *The Creation,* and HVS warm-up, *Magnificat,* can be walked into via vague paths that contour left (west north-west) along an old quarried slope, starting about 300m downhill (east north-east) from the mast. On North Buttress Block, *Double Top*, an oft dry classic (top-end HVS), is just off the footpath. North Buttress itself is a natural gritstone crag attaining a height of 24m. It has excellent rock with striking lines in the Severe to HVS range, all with a big feel to them. This section is best kept for quality dry conditions.

386　　　　　　　　　　　　Yorkshire Gritstone

Richard Mallinson on the first ascent of **Nipscrew** (E5 6b). Page 398.
Photo: Dave Sutcliffe

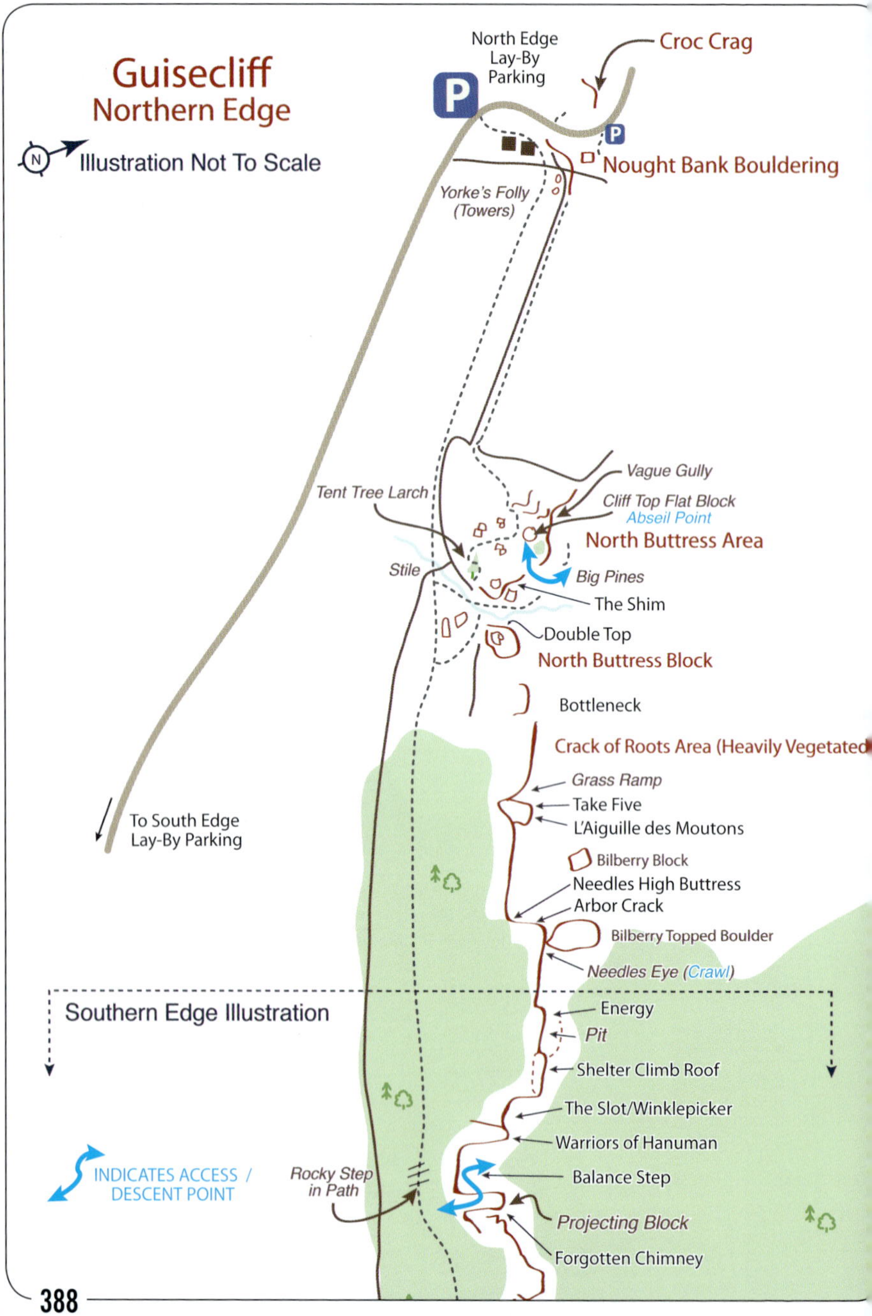

Guisecliff
Northern Edge
N
Illustration Not To Scale
North Edge
Lay-By
Parking
P
Croc Crag
P
Nought Bank Bouldering
Yorke's Folly
(Towers)
Vague Gully
Cliff Top Flat Block
Abseil Point
Tent Tree Larch
North Buttress Area
Stile
Big Pines
The Shim
Double Top
North Buttress Block
Bottleneck
Crack of Roots Area (Heavily Vegetated
Grass Ramp
Take Five
L'Aiguille des Moutons
To South Edge
Lay-By Parking
Bilberry Block
Needles High Buttress
Arbor Crack
Bilberry Topped Boulder
Needles Eye (Crawl)
Southern Edge Illustration
Energy
Pit
Shelter Climb Roof
The Slot/Winklepicker
Warriors of Hanuman
INDICATES ACCESS /
DESCENT POINT
Rocky Step
in Path
Balance Step
Projecting Block
Forgotten Chimney

# Guisecliff
## Southern Edge

*Illustration Not To Scale*

N

Northern Edge Illustration

To North Edge Lay-By Parking

P

South Edge Lay-By Parking

*Bouldering*

**Heyshaw Quarry**

Cottage

Straight Rift

Twisting Rift

Flat Slab

Oaks

3 Crag Top Boulders

Small Quarry Bouldering

Rocky Step in Path

*Pit*
- Shelter Climb Roof
- The Slot/Winklepicker
- Warriors of Hanuman
- Balance Step
- *Projecting Block*
- Forgotten Chimney
- *Large Roof*
- Ryvoan/Haberdashery
- The Long Step (Mod 3c)
- Humus (Large Oak)
- Mastermind
- *Large Platform*
- **Comet Wall**
- KOYLI
- *Projecting Roof*
- Autobahn
- Coyote
- Tombstone
- Agrippa Area
- **No.5 Buttress**
- Ruscator
- Roc's Nest Chimney
- **No.4 Buttress**
- Foreign Bodies
- **No.3 Buttress**
- **No.2 Buttress**
- Creation / On the Edge
- Post Office Wall
- **No.1 Buttress**

Metal Spike

Area Free From Birch Scrub

*Cliff Top Silver Birch*

Access Restrictions Apply

INDICATES ACCESS / DESCENT POINT

**389**

# GUISECLIFF - Number One Buttress

## Number One Buttress
A compact buttress located 150m north north-west of the mast and down broken ground. An easier alternative is to walk in via vague paths which contour left (west north-west) along an old quarried slope, starting about 300m downhill (east north-east) from the mast.

### 1 The Verger  E1 5c  14m
Climb a thin twisting crack and pull over an overhang to gain a small ledge. The unhelpful corner above is the crux.
(a) **Lectern Chimney** (MS), is the chimney just right
*Tony Barley, Robin Barley  2nd July 1966*

### 2 The Belfry  HVS 5a  16m
Easier than it looks but a bit of udge is required. Climb the shattered crack into a recess and exit via the overhanging crack. The right-hand **Bat Finish** (E1 5c), takes the hanging groove.
*Tony Barley, John Williams  13th July 1966* ✦

For (b) **Curate's Crack** (S), head into the crack, exiting onto a large ledge. Now take the corner-crack on the left, initially by a layback, then using holds on the left wall. (c) **Pulpit Steps** (VD), tackles the series of ledges to the top of 'The Pulpit'. Climb up a short crack on the right then traverse off right along an unpleasant sandy ledge. Not recommended.

### 3 Pulpit Chimney  VD  15m
Romp up the square chimney to 'The Pulpit'. Either of the two cracks above and a loose gully leads to the top.
*Yorkshire Ramblers Club/Royal Engineers CC  pre-1954* ✦

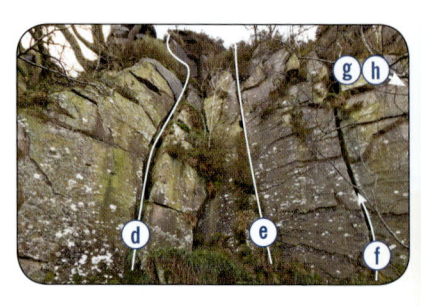

### 4 Magnificat  HVS 5a  15m  ★★
Show the strength of your arm. Climb up to the large yellow flake and up its left side. Pull over the overhang strenuously and finish up the twin cracks above.
*Tony Barley, Robin Barley  September 1964*

Next comes a fan of vegetation and broken rock, then Number Two Buttress begins above the left of the two mine entrances.

## Number Two Buttress
An intimidating quarried buttress offering a number of hard extremes. On the left-hand end of this buttress is **Post Office Wall**. Further right the crag becomes higher and very impressive in the form of a superb corner and to its right a buttress presenting an imposing front: this is why you came! The best descent is to the left (east, facing the crag) of Post Office Wall.

The Post Office Wall climbs are currently in great need of gardening. (d) **Letterbox Climb** (D), climbs the chimney to a ledge, bridges up the outside of a cave and exits left onto a large ledge, climbs the recess behind a tall tree and through the letterbox slot to the moor. (e) **Microcrack** (HVS 5a) takes the thin crack with difficulty until it widens. (f) **Postman's Crack** (VS 4c) climbs the strenuous boot-wide crack. (g) for **Bold John** (HVS 5a), climb up the thin crack, left of the blunt right arête, until a horizontal break leads rightwards to a good ledge. Follow the improbable-looking arête above using layaways. (h) for **Scalped** (VS 4c), tackle the offwidth past a hollow flake. Undercut left, round the overlap, and jam up the top crack just right of the arête of **Bold John**. Just right, **Sprog** (VS 4c), climbs the steep jamming crack and the groove above exiting left at the overhang. Right of the

390  Yorkshire Gritstone

## Number Two Buttress - GUISECLIFF

recess is a steep chimney leading to a large block roof full of doubtful blocks. Right of this are a couple of routes. **Cretin's Crack** (VS 5a), takes the crack behind the tall tree. Easy to start, but matures into strenuous wedging, leading to an awkward exit onto a grass ledge. Traverse left and up the corner to finish. The scary looking flake crack just to the right is **Drum Crack** (VS 4c). Climb the friable flake to a grass ledge. Traverse right in an exposed position and up a loose corner to the moor.

Dave Sutcliffe realises the **Doomed Oasis** (E6 6b). Page 392.
Photo: Adi Gill

# GUISECLIFF - Number Two Buttress

To the right the crag completely changes character and takes the form of a huge clean corner, with a mine entrance at its foot.

**5 The Creation** E2 5c  23m ☆☆☆
A classic line on loan from Millstone. Climb the fierce crack to a block. Enter the upper section by a precarious pull on fist jams and continue strenuously to the ledge. The loose corner above leads to the moor.
*Tony Barley, Robin Barley  22nd May 1965*  ✦

**6 Barleycorn** E3 5b  23m
Battle up the neck of the formidable overhanging chimney to a capstone, then easily up the ramp above. Protection can be found deep within.
*Gordon 'speedy' Smith, John Midgley  10th June 1973*  ✦

**7 On the Edge** E6 6b  23m ☆☆☆
The magnificent beguiling arête. Protected by reasonable cams in the low break, with two good pegs finally arriving near the top. Photo on page 385.
*Paul Jenkinson, Steve Earnshaw  June 1990*  ✦

**8 The Climb That Time Forgot** E8 6c  23m ☆☆
One of Yorkshire's greatest prizes falling into rock-steady hands. Climb the amazing wall boldly on crimps and small pockets to the break (peg/gear). Make a hard, long, deadpoint to the tiny edge above then match and crimp your way rightwards to join *On the Edge* at its highest peg. Photo on page 14.
*Dave Sutcliffe  12th May 2012*

**9 Illusion** HS  22m
Ascend the cleft passing behind the first chockstone and finishing by an awkward move either left or right, over the bulging chockstone, near the top. Scramble up the easy gully to a cave. The square flue at the back leads to the top.
*Frank Spence, Lynne Noble, M Sanderson  c1960*

**10 Doomed Oasis** E6 6b  22m ☆☆
The direct finish to *Aftermath*. From the block, step onto the sloping ledge and climb directly and boldly up the right side of the arête to gain the big ledge. Mantel this and step right to finish up the ramp system in the centre of the wall. A brilliant outing when clean. Photo on page 391.
*Dave Sutcliffe, Adi Gill  23rd March 2012*

## Number Two Buttress - GUISECLIFF

**11 Aftermath** E5 5c  23m  ☆
A fine route (originally E3!) with bold climbing. Climb to the first chockstone and step right with difficulty into a shallow scoop. Traverse delicately to the rib and reach round to a dubious peg. Move up just left of the rib (crux). A hand-traverse left and a mantelshelf lead to a ramp which is taken to a short, steep corner and the top. It is also possible to continue directly up the rib and left into the corner.
*Tony Barley, Chas Hird   March 1973* ✦

**12 Lowdowns** E6 6b  23m  ☆
Start in the groove then bust out right below the bulge. Climb through the centre of the overlap via difficult and balancey moves to gain a standing position on the ledge. Small gear provides just enough protection to attack the wall above, left of the small groove, on edges and pockets (crux) to yet another mantel. Finish as for *Aftermath*.
*Richard Mallinson  12th May 2012*

**13 Wild Abandon** E5 6b  23m  ☆☆
The arm sapping ride up the fat arête is a newly unearthed treasure. Boulder up to the ledge above "No.2". Place a high wire then lovingly hug your way up to reach welcome jugs and the peg of *Aftermath*. Keep it together for the final slab up to the summit of *Hook Route*.
*Adi Gill, Adam Collinge   25th May 2012*

**14 Hook Route** E1 5b  22m  ☆☆
A grand exit from Neverland. In the nose of the buttress, tackle the square-cut chimney. An iron hook, a hidden pocket and good layaways lead you on. Through the roof, scrunch back left into and up the crack. Photo on page 379.
*Yorkshire Mountaineering Club   pre-1957*

**15 Crocodile** E5 6a (A0)  24m
Tick tock: how long until it's freed? Climb the thin crack to a block. Undercut left and use a wire to clear the roof before following the crack to the top.
*Bruce Woodley, Ritchie Allen, Denis Gleeson   13th July 2000*

**16 Dingbat** E3 6a  20m
Up the impressive, clean-cut, overhanging corner, which is sustained and very strenuous. Move left to the prow and then straight up the steep front of the buttress.
*Tony Barley, Robin Barley  2nd July 1966* ✦

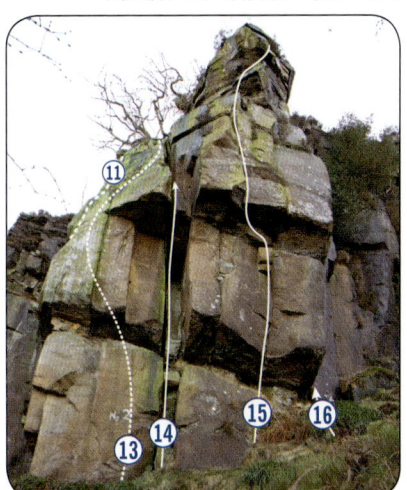

The prickly horror show to the right is **Holly Grooves** (MVS).

### Number Three Buttress
The left-hand and central parts of this buttress are broken and mossy. The best descent is via a tricky scramble down to the west (right, facing in). On the extreme left, and near the top of the grassy slope, is a smooth lichenous wall. **Right-Hand Wall** (VS 4c), is essentially a solo. Start on good holds, which dwindle, and mantelshelf onto a small ledge. Traverse left for 2m then climb the wall rightwards to a pocket. Make an awkward move up to the top from here.

**Short Chimney** (S), takes the chimney for 8m to the trees. Step left and up twin cracks to the top. For **Mantelshelfman** (HVS 5c), from the bottom of *Short Chimney*, move right and up into an oak tree. Ascend the thin crack behind the tree until a hard mantel gains the narrow ledge above. Climb the slab, move right and up the wall and shallow groove, using the arête, to the overhang. Step left and up the arête to finish. **Tree Cracks** (S) follows the cracks towards an oak tree then through the overhang above, stepping right to finish.

**17 Buttress Route** VD  24m  ☆
An expedition for all seasons. Climb to a grass ledge below and left of the pinnacle. Go up the pinnacle and

# GUISECLIFF - Number Three Buttress

step off the top into the crack on the left. Follow this and the chimneys above, finishing over a tree.
*Yorkshire Ramblers Club/Royal Engineers CC  pre-1954* ✦

**18 Clodhopper**  HS   24m
Start at the lowest point of the buttress and climb up the left-hand crack to reach the right side of the pinnacle. Step right and move up into an overhung bay. Climb the overhang moving rightwards and continue to the top.
*Tony Barley, Martin Jones, Gwyn Evans  24th February 1974*

**19 Footpatter**  VS 4c   24m                     ☆
Start at the lowest point of the arête and climb past grassy ledges. Follow the crack until a fine traverse right below the overhang leads to a delicate and exposed crack. Up this via a small ledge to the top.
*Robin Barley, Tony Barley  1964*

**20 Pendulum**  E1 5b   20m
Strenuous moves on dubious holds. Climb up the groove just left of the most prominent crack to a loose block. Make a difficult swing left onto the arête and follow this (*Footpatter*) to finish. Calls for strong nerves.
*Robin Barley, Dennis Gray, Tony Barley  June 1964*

**21 Foreign Bodies**  E2 5c   15m
Climb *Pendulum* to the loose block and layback into an awkward hanging groove above (peg runner). Follow the groove to the top.
*Robin Barley, Nick Barley  June 1989*

**22 Stretcher**  E1 5b   20m
Tackle the prominent crack, with some difficulty, to a small cave. Pull round the overhang into the chimney and make a long reach for a good hold. Continue steeply.
*Robin Barley, Dennis Gray, Tony Barley  June 1964* ✦

**Ruminant** (S), is the shallow chimney-groove further right. An awkward start leads to a small tree and grass ledge on the left. Continue up, using tree roots, to surmount the final overhang.

## Number Four Buttress
Identified by a fine clean-cut chimney splitting the nose of the buttress. Access is as for Number Three Buttress. The left wall is rapidly reverting back to nature because of tree-cover. At the extreme left end is the first route: **Overhanging Groove** (VS 4c), the double-tiered groove just left of the large oak tree. **Nippem** (S), takes the line of a deep V-groove with a crack in the back just right of the large tree. **Rootless Groove** (S), is the broken jamming crack right of the large oak. **Chockstone Chimney** (M), is the chimney just to the right, leading to large ledges. **Kandahar Groove** (S), is the open groove directly above the lower of the two tall holly trees.

**23 Roc's Nest Chimney**  HS 4b   24m          ☆☆
A character building traditional classic. Enter the chimney from the right by an awkward move. Climb strenuously inside the chimney and exit right at the top. Continue up the gully and over blocks on the right wall. Scrambling remains.
*Arthur Birtwhistle, Heywood, Pearson  1937*

(a) **Dhobi** (MVS 4b) is the deep V-groove to the right. Be warned – the route name derives from army slang meaning dirty washing! Follow the deep V-groove, past a cave, over a bulge and to a large chockstone. Surmount this with care, then move left to a tree and finish up the gully. (b) **Stigma** (VS 4c), starts up the narrow groove then steps right to follow a larger groove with increasing

394   Yorkshire Gritstone

difficulty to a ledge and tree belay; the crack leads to the final overhang, traverse left to finish.

### 24  Ruscator  E2 5c  27m  ☆☆
An engrossing expedition up the nose of buttress. Gain the hanging square-cut chimney from the arête on the right. Climb into and up a groove. Traverse left to finish. The less wise may move right to a poor belay, wide crack and scary vegetated finish (5a). The unclimbed thin headwall crack suggests a hard variation.
*Robin Barley, Tony Barley  16th July 1966* ✦

### Number Five Buttress
A large expanse of rock extending 150m or so. The left-hand section is a high and rather vegetated wall with some large overhangs just right of Shoulder Gully. After 80m is the lowest point of the buttress and the crag becomes broken by chimneys and gullies. The best descent is by abseil, by descending *Scissors* or by *The Long Step* (page 399), 40m further right (if looking in – west). Starting at the extreme left-hand end of the left wall of Number Five Buttress is the steep gully separating it from Number Four Buttress. 30m right of this is the first climb of note, the overgrown **Hawk Slab** (S): start from a terrace just above the base of the crag and climb a steep cracked wall to a tree belay below a large corner; move right along the base of the slab and ascend into a small cave, traverse left and up a short overhanging corner. Four other routes have been done hereabouts but are heavily vegetated. 15m to the right is **Shoulder Gully** (VD) a very dirty and poor climb: start a few metres right of the gully and climb a short wall below large overhangs to a terrace, walk left to the foot of a chimney (sometimes a waterfall) – 'nuff said! Just right of *Shoulder Gully* is an area of large overhangs, sadly now overtaken by the Nidd's finest flora. **Nice 'n' Sleazy** (E3 5c), found its way through the left-hand side of the overhangs. **Agrippa** (E1 5b), took the right-hand side of the large overhangs. **Agrippina** (HVS 5a), finished up the wall further right. **Daniel** (VS 4c), finished up the deep V-groove between **Shoulder Gully** and the nose of the buttress to the right.

### 25  Tombstone  E2 5c  18m  ☆
Like all the best Westerns this has a tough opening sequence and an all guns blazing finish. Follows a steep and strenuous crackline, 10m right of *Daniel*, finishing right of the obvious jutting prow. Scramble up into a heathery bay and boulder up into a short V-groove capped by a triangular overhang. Undercutting gains the crack on the right, which leads via a niche to a ledge. Truck back right and up with difficulty into an overhanging groove. Climb up this and exit left.
*Tony Barley, Robin Barley  13th September 1970*

**Coyote Wall** (HS 4b), starts 4m right of *Tombstone* along the ledge. Climb to an oak at 3m, then the steep cracks behind. The middle section is the most difficult. **Coyotillo** (E2 5c), is a left-hand finish to *Coyote Wall*: sling the oak sapling then traverse down left to a recess before attacking the top crack with gusto. Just round to the right is a small bay overhung by oaks with a chimney on the right and a crack in the left corner. The latter marks the start of the next climb.

### 26  Jezebel  HS 4b  36m  ☆☆
An interesting climb with a fine, airy finish.
**1.** Start at a corner capped by overhangs. Climb the steepening corner until a traverse to the left arête can be made. Step round this and up into a fist-wide crack. From the birch tree traverse right to a good stance below a square chimney.

Almscliff to Slipstones  **395**

# GUISECLIFF - Number Five Buttress

**2.** Up the square chimney to the overhang, then step out right in a splendid position onto the rib. Finish rightwards around the roofs. Steep but juggy.
*Tony Barley, Robin Barley (alt leads)  1961*

**27 By-Pass**  S  4a   ☆
Starts as for *Jezebel*. Climb the corner to a ledge then traverse right across the slab passing trees to finish in *Boundary Chimney*. Scramble off rightwards across ledges.
*Tony Barley, Robin Barley  1961*

**28 Jehu's Chariot**  E2 5c   26m   ☆☆
Drives up the flake crack between *Jezebel* and *Autobahn*, crossing *By-Pass* and cranking into the square-cut squeeze. Finish directly up the wall or, better, step right for the top pitch of *Jezebel* or its harder neighbour.
*Bruce Woodley, Paul Tanton  5th July 2009*

**29 Autobahn**  E2 5c   24m   ☆☆☆
Only Yorkshire and Scots 1950s Tigers need apply. A former VS that gets its comeuppance.
**1.** Layback the crack then climb the groove, moving left at the overhang. Traverse right beneath the prow to a large ledge and belay (5a).
**2.** Climb to the large overhangs. Swing left across the smooth wall (peg) to reach the nose, then easily to the top (5c).
*Tony Barley, John Williams  9th September 1966*

**30 Boundary Chimney**  HVD   12m
Climb the obvious chimney passing a large block, with care, to ledges and a tree belay on the right. Either scramble off (**a**) to the right, or take (**b**) the **Direct Finish** (HS) up the large V-groove above, with some loose rock on the way.
*Yorkshire Ramblers Club/Royal Engineers CC  pre-1954*  ✦

**❝ ❞**

If doused in defoliant and swivelled through 180 degrees it'd be better than Brimham!

Dave Gilyeat

**31 The Kraken**  HVS 5a   17m
Follows a deep undercut groove reached by scrambling left along ledges from the foot of *Apparition*. Enter the groove with difficulty and climb past a holly until a traverse right to a narrow ledge can be made. Above is a wall split by a thin crack, which provides a difficult finish.
*Robin Barley, Tony Barley  November 1962*

**32 The Rifles**  E4 6b   17m
The thin roof crack and shallow groove direct lead to *The Kraken* finish.
*Bruce Woodley, Ritchie Allen, Denis Gleeson  2011*

**33 KOYLI**  HVS 5a   18m   ☆
A satisfying sortie up the steep slab. Climb up to an overlap and move awkwardly into the cracks above. Finish steeply up the hanging crack left of the arête. (**c**) The **Variation Start** (E1 5b), takes the thin curving finger crack out left.
*Ronnie Hields, J. Eastwood  1955*  ✦

**34 Apparition**  VD   18m
An interesting dark and damp route.
*Yorkshire Ramblers Club/Royal Engineers CC  pre-1954*  ✦

To the right of the black gully of *Apparition* is an oak-filled chimney capped by overhangs.

**35 Synchromesh**  HVS 5a   35m
A diagonal route across the buttress commanding some exposed positions. Start in a shallow corner and climb up a crack in the right wall, round the rib and up the chimney. Traverse right to gain the face of *Skyjacker*. Descend a little to swing across and up to the stance. Climb *Comet Wall* to the top of the crack then move right up the arête, moving rightwards.
*Tony Barley, Tony Roche  1971*

**36 Phillipa's Ridge**  VS 4c   23m
Climb the chimney to an oak tree. Move left to the arête. Follow this to an earthy ledge and tree belay below a chimney-crack. Climb the crack to the top.
*Brian Hields, Ronnie Hields  1954*

## Comet Buttress - GUISECLIFF

### 37 Brian's Climb  VS 4c   23m
The chimney direct. Ascend the shallow chimney into the deeper one and continue up, mostly on the right wall, until a step left onto a block can be made. Climb up the roof and, using good jams, move out right to finish up the rib.
*Brian Hields, Ronnie Hields  1954*

### Comet Buttress
Right of *Brian's Climb* the buttress stands forward presenting an imposing front and some of the best routes on the crag. These are below the rock platform with a metal stake described in the introduction. Access by abseil down the routes is straightforward enough and allows some inspection. Alternatively, descend *The Long Step* (page 399).

### 38 North Wall Eliminate  HVS 5a   23m   ☆☆
Climbs the arête of the buttress in a splendidly exposed position. Ascend the chimney of *Brian's Climb* then tangle your way through the oak, traversing right out to the rib. Follow this, grinning all the way to the top.
*Robin Barley, Tony Barley  August 1963* ✦

For the fine routes around *Comet Wall*, if the lower wall is wet, abseil in and establish a belay to access the upper sections.

### 39 Skyjacker  E2 5c   21m   ☆☆
An intricate route with a grand finale on the headwall. Start beneath a peg in the black wall. Awkward moves up and left gain the front of the buttress. Continue left (good hidden peg) and ascend the crack. Make an awkward traverse left and tackle the exposed front of the buttress via thin cracks. An alternative start takes a direct line from the roofed recess in the centre of the buttress.
*Tony Barley, Robin Barley  13th September 1970* ✦

### 40 Mastermind  E4 5c   26m   ☆☆
A tremendous line crossing uncompromising territory. Gain the front of the buttress and climb the difficult blunt rib to the small ledge on *Comet Wall*. Move up right to gain the horizontal break. A sensational traverse leads to a hanging groove (runner). Climb the wall slightly rightwards on spaced holds. Bold climbing requiring careful ropework. The (often damp) lower pitch can be avoided.
*Tony Barley, Robin Brown  5th May 1975* ✦

## GUISECLIFF - Comet Buttress

hand-traverse left to a good foothold. Bold moves up left now to finish. Needs a clean.
*Tony Barley, Tony Roche   1970*

**Scissors** (D), is the gully on the right. A useful means of ascent but scary in descent! **Jaywalk** (HVS 5a), is a nine pitch high-level girdle of Number Five Buttress but is unlikely to ever catch on. See the Yorkshire guide archives if you're that keen.

### The Long Wall
The wall that starts right of *Scissors* consists of about 250m of more-or-less continuous rock. Much of it is heavily vegetated, but several good buttresses can be found.
**Millroy's Climb** (VD), is the obvious V-groove just right of *Scissors*. Very slimy.

### 44  Savage Sentence   E1 5b   15m
Garden the thorn if you dare. The clean-cut green corner with a projecting spike. Finish up the open corner above.
*Andy Wild, Dave Musgrove   1st June 1985*

Further right of *Scissors* is a square bay between two undercut and overhanging arêtes. The fine hanging flake on the left wall provides a hard route.

### 45  Guillotine   E3 6a   14m   ☆
An aptly-named climb awaiting the chop. The flake crack requires a horizontal approach with strenuous climbing to achieve the vertical section. Finish more easily.
*John Syrett   7th May 1973*  ✦

### 41  The Scryking   E5 6a   20m   ☆☆☆
Grapples with the obvious challenge posed by the wildly exposed arête. Slightly contrived in its lower section. Start as for *Mastermind*, but move up awkwardly to clip a peg in the wall. Delicately balance leftwards around the arête and climb to the ledge with difficulty. Traverse right, past good gear in the break and blast straight up the arête, making a committing move to gain the break just below the top.
*Mark Radtke, Dave Barton   May 1997*

### 42  Comet Wall   HVS 5a   20m   ☆☆☆
Everything a great HVS should be; burly and atmospheric. Climb the corner to the cave, then cross the left wall to perch on a small ledge. Tackle the flake crack with enough gusto to carry you up the steep groove above. The marginally harder (**a**) **Left-Hand Finish** (HVS 5a), offers bridging then wide jams to the top. The slimy initial corner start can be avoided by (**b**) scrambling up to the cave and traversing .
*Ron Hields, Vince Murphy   1957*  ✦

### 46  Angle Crack   HS   10m
In the left corner of the bay is a crack. Climb it, starting from the right.
*Unknown   pre-1969*

Next comes a black tree-covered wall, which ends after 30m at a projecting buttress with a huge oak.

### 47  Humus   E3 5c   15m
The shallow groove just left of the oak, moving right through the overhang to a nasty pull out on the moor. Will need cleaning.
*John Eastham, Geoff Myers   24th September 1988*

### 43  Side-show   HVS 5a   14m
Climb the crack and groove left of the gully to the top of a pedestal. Move up to a good horizontal break and semi-

Yorkshire Gritstone

## The Warriors of Hanuman - GUISECLIFF

**48 Nipscrew** E5 6b  12m  ☆
A bold outing as the broken gully provides a rather suspect landing. Step across the gap and make awkward moves to get established at the base of the *Humus* oak tree. Climb firstly up to, then onto, the obvious spike using holds in the groove out left. From here make devious moves out right to gain holds on the face, climb this boldly to the top. A short route that packs a punch. Photo on page 387.
*Richard Mallinson, Dave Sutcliffe 2nd April 2012*

To the right of *Humus*, some 40m right of Comet Buttress, is an easy but exposed ascent/descent route in the form of a short chimney with ledges on the left (known as **The Long Step** (Mod 3c), see map on page 388) and an easy-angled gully at the top. 20m right the steep little buttress provides two interesting climbs. The first being **Ryvoan Crack** (MS), An imposing chimney-crack. where big cams are required. Just left:

**49 Haberdashery** E2 6a  14m  ☆
A fine little route of considerable technical difficulty and a hidden gem, but only if clean and dry. A thin layback crack leads to a standing position on a sloping ledge. Move up and make a hard move or long reach to gain holds beneath the overhang. A short steep traverse right to the arête leads to easier climbing.
*Tony Barley  1974* ✦

Fifteen metres down to the right is an overhanging crack with an arête finish, started by scrambling up to belay beneath a holly.

**50 Barney Rubbles Bookcase** E3 5c  15m
Fight the crack to a break then up the arête. Bridging into the holly may be required. A preplaced 4m cord around the final oak protects the otherwise worrying finish.
*Paul Tanton, Bruce Woodley, Robin Warden  April 2011*

Fifteen metres further down, through an eye, is a large roof that has been climbed with 3pts of aid (**When the Bough Broke**). **The Sapling Bends** (E2, 5b,5b) takes steep cracks in the left wall of *Tanton's Tunnel* to a traverse leftwards into a hanging groove and birch tree belay. It then traverses the line above the roof of *When the Bough Broke* until tricky moves, with low footholds,

allow a long step onto a sapling (possible belay) and the groove above to finish. **Tanton's Tunnel** (D), is the chimney to the right. Lower down to the right is a heavily overgrown buttress. Rounding the foot of this and ascending 10m we come to **Forgotten Chimney** (VD), easily up to the last metre or so and then a short back-and-knees section to finish. At the top of the slope is short but exposed ascent/descent, the Balance Step (see map on page 388), identified by the protruding block with the flat top. To the right is the **Slot Buttress**. (c) **Careful Crack** (VS 4c), is the obvious crack in the left wall; climb the cracked wall trending rightwards to below the crack proper. Pull over friable rock to enter it, then on to the top.

**51 The Warriors of Hanuman** E5 6b 15m ★★★
The outrageous flying arête. Climb the lower arête (peg) to the large ledge below the roof. Clip two pegs then make a series of wild gymnastic moves through the roof and up the wall using the flying arête on the right. Superb.
*Mark Radtke, Jerry Peel  June 1997*

Almscliff to Slipstones    **399**

# GUISECLIFF - Needles High Buttress

Right again, (a) **The Slot** (S 4a), follows the chimney, passing behind the chockstone or, less securely, over it and climb to the overhang; step right and follow the 'slot' above to finish. (b) **Little Something** (VS 4c), surmounts the initial overhang with difficulty and up to a groove which leads to a tree; take the left ledge of the slab above, moving left at the overhang. (c) The sustained **Winklepicker** (HVS 5a), moves awkwardly up to a small pinnacle, then continues with difficulty to a final overhanging layback.

On the right is a mossy slab and round the corner is a cracked wall capped by a large roof. For (d) **Barracuda** (VS 4c), the blunt arête just right of an oak at the left end of the wall is climbed delicately to an earthy ledge. A short, wide crack above is awkward to start and strenuous to finish. For (e) **Shelter Climb** (D), go up the left side of the cracked wall to a ledge under the overhang, traverse right round the corner, using large holds, to a small ledge; a gully leads to the moor. (f) **Energy** (HVS 5c), pulls over the initial overhang and then strenuously up the crack. For (g) **Rhino** (VS 4c), climb the groove with increasing difficulty to an overhang; awkwardly gain jammed blocks below the final overhang, move onto the left rib to a good foothold, then up.

### Needle's High Buttress

20m on from the hollow, a huge bilberry-topped boulder stands against the crag forming the Needle's Eye. Starting from the eye is a steep undercut cracked groove. (h) **Offspring** (VS 4c) is interesting: climb the groove, gained from the left, and the wall above, passing the tree and finishing up the jam crack. (i) **Arbor Crack** (Cordite Start) (E1 5c), (was originally VS!) climb the difficult rib to gain the chimney crack, continue strenuously past the tree and blast up the chimney above. (j) **Ledge and Crack** (D), is the steep cracked gangway climbed on good holds; finish over a bulging block. (k) **Oak Wall** (HS): pull up to the tree, traverse left and up to an oak. Belay. A steep wall above is climbed on good holds to a rather awkward finish. **Oak Wall Direct** (HVS 5b) gains the large oak direct via strenuous moves past a jammed block. (l) **Wafer Crack** (VS 5a): just right of the dirty corner is a straight narrow crack starting at half-height. Climb easily to the crack then by strenuous jams to the top.

Another 20m to the right, around the foot of a vegetated buttress, is a cave. High above this on the right is a pinnacle - the Aiguille des Moutons. **Intestine** (M), is the cave: climb the loose subterranean chimney, emerging through a hole onto a grass ledge; the gully on the right leads to a large ledge behind the pinnacle. **Aiguille des Moutons** (VD), starts from the finishing point of the previous route, which may also be gained by scrambling up a leftward-slanting grass rake 20m right of *Intestine*. Ascend directly to the top. Reverse to descend, which

## North Buttress Block - GUISECLIFF

may be awkward if wet. Easy access is available to or from the moor from behind the *Aiguille des Moutons* through the cave. **Take Five** (VS 5a), is a more direct way of reaching the Aiguille, starting up the right-hand side of the slab right of *Intestine*; hard-ish climbing up the slab and groove on the right and up to the summit block by a tree; right to finish. Overgrown. To the right of the Aiguille is a high wall. The first feature is a steep vegetated crack containing a stout oak. **Crack of Roots** (VS 4c), climbs a shallow groove, then the crack on good jams to the tree, continue easily to the overhangs; the chimney above is awkward to enter and leave but holds seem safe.

Several routes have been climbed up the next section of wall but are heavily vegetated. Rounding the foot of the buttress and ascending a short way there is a cutaway, and a few metres higher up is the end of the Long Wall. The last feature is a cave which narrows to a crack. **Bottleneck** (VS 4c), is a worthwhile little route on typical rounded grit. Climb the cave until the walls converge, then pull out round the overhang into a short crack above. This gives out onto a heathery ledge. Continue up the short awkward crack, then under the summit boulder to finish through the cave.

### North Buttress Block

The next climbs are found by traversing 50m along the hillside to an isolated buttress of rounded gritstone. A superb natural outcrop, sporting some gymnastic roof climbing. **The Chimney** (HVD 4b), takes the obvious fissure at the left end of the block with a hard start. **Hotrod** (VS 4c), starts up the thin crack splitting the initial overhang and moves right to a bulging crack which leads to a small ledge. Traverse left for a metre then make a direct ascent up the wall by delicate balance moves

### 52 Speedway   VS 4c   13m
Just right are two thin cracks 3m apart. Ascend either one, then the bulging crack above. Move left and finish up the awkward bulging green crack to the top.
*Tony Barley, Robin Barley   29th August 1965*

### 53 Cutting the Cord   E4 5c   15m   ★★
A jaw-dropping traverse right on the brink. Take the left-hand start to *Speedway* and aim direct through the bulging pocketed wall to the roof. Make a long reach to gain gear in the horizontal break at the lip. Ape excitingly rightwards until an awkward move enables a standing position to be attained above the roof.
*Mark Radtke, Greg Rimmer   May 1997*

### 54 Double Top   HVS 5a   10m   ★★
An impressive line up the steep clean wall. Climb to the ceiling and traverse the break leftward. A short incipient crack in the bulge above provides a way up. Surmount the bulge with increasing strenuousity (E1 5b some say). **Ringway** (VS, 43m) is a left-to-right girdle of the block finishing up *Double Top*.
*Allan Austin, Brian Evans   26th April 1958*

Almscliff to Slipstones

## GUISECLIFF - North Buttress

### 55 Over the Top  E4 6a  10m  ★★
A fearless line through the roof. Follow *Double Top* to the ceiling and good holds just below the roof. Take a deep breath and in an unfaltering frame of mind, turn the roof using slopers and a heel hook.
*Dave Barton, Mark Radtke  May 1997*

Across the small stream and down the footpath (40m rightwards) is a detached block.

### 56 The Shim  E1 6a  8m
From the down-slope end of its chimney, bridge across the gap and climb the wall rightwards. Named after she-nanigans with grit slat packing to help a cam fit. The tiny groove at the start would yield a fine (Font 6c) problem.
*Bruce Woodley, Denis Gleeson  21st June 2006*

For the next climbs, follow the footpath downhill to the right for 150m until a high buttress can be seen (or follow the path up onto the moor at the stile/or if intending to abseil into North Buttress go through the stone wall and under the lovely larch - the rap being some 60m further on by a flat rock).

### North Buttress
A fine crag about 25m high at its maximum, the main feature being a great corner just left of centre. At the left end is a subsidiary buttress which is in fact a pinnacle. The front of this left-hand section is split by a cracked recess and a wide clean-cut crack. **Pinnacle Face** (VS 4c): ascend the awkward cracked recess to an overhang. Traverse right, then up, to the foot of a slab. Climb this, and the blocks above, to the top of the pinnacle. **Thin Man's Delight** (S) is the clean wide crack just to the right that overhangs at the start. A bulge at 3m provides difficulty. The easier-angled crack above leads to a ledge and block. Surmount the block and continue to the overhang. Traverse right to top the pinnacle. **Pinnacle Ordinary Route** (D), starts at the mossy slab. Make a high step up then left into the grassy chimney. This leads to a cave. A crack in the left wall leads to the top. 15m to the right is the large corner of *North Buttress Crack*. 7m left of this is a prominent rib with an overhang at 2m. This marks the start of:

### 57 Midsummer Night's Dream  HVS 5b  36m  ☆
Rather devious, but of much technical interest. Climb the rib by difficult layback moves, then easily to the overhang. Make a sensational hand-traverse to the blunt arête, and continue to the corner (belay). Move up, then delicately left, to reach a good hold atop the flake. A tough pull gains a ledge, then climb the blunt rib to the top.
*Tony Barley, Robin Brown  21st June 1972*

### 58 Caveman's Corner  S  14m
Sneak left along and up the sloping rock ledge to a semi-hand-traverse left onto the rib of *Midsummer Night's Dream*. Climb up this for a metre then follow an awkward heathery break leftwards onto bilberry ledges.
*c1958*

### 59 North Buttress Crack  HS  17m  ☆☆
The great corner and crack. Climb to a good spike runner and layback up the wide crack (often green). Pull round a jammed block into a recess, then go through a constriction onto easier-angled rock. Follow this and scramble left to a tree belay.
*Allan Austin, Brian Evans  26th April 1958*

### 60 North Buttress Ordinary  S  20m
A convenient means of avoiding the crux of *North Buttress Crack* but still providing worthwhile climbing. From the spike runner, traverse right and mantelshelf on to a small ledge below an obvious flake crack. Follow the flake up and left and pull onto the ledge above. Tree belay. Traverse left back into the crack and finish up this.
*Bill Todd, John Johnson  29th October 1958*

### 61 North Buttress Direct  HVS 5a  24m  ☆
Tackle the pea-pod-shaped crack to the overhang. Pull over this (crux) to a tree belay. The short steep corner above leads to large terraces. Gain a narrow ledge and traverse left under the overhang to the nose of the buttress. Move up and right to the top.
*Tony Barley, Robin Barley (alt leads)  1961*

### 62 Spring Fever  VS 4c  30m
Start as for *North Buttress Direct*. At the overhang traverse right across the face. Mantelshelf up right and continue to the arête. Gain the ledge and tree belay. Climb

# North Buttress - GUISECLIFF

the short steep corner to the terrace. Pull up into a short slanting crack, move up right then leftwards to finish.
*Tony Barley, Tony Roche 29th April 1972*

### 63 Campanile HVS 5a  28m
Climb the rib and slab boldly, trending slightly leftwards, and continue up the centre to the ledge. Move left and follow the short steep corner to the terrace (belay). Go left under the roof and traverse the exposed tower face to reach a good pocket. Climb directly up the cracked face to the top. The (**a**) **Campanile Direct** (E3 6a) start takes thin cracks up the centre of the slab.
*Tony Barley, Joe Tasker 27th May 1972* ✦

**The Cleavage** (S), is the deep V-groove right of *North Buttress Crack*. For **The Right Rib** (VS 4c), layback up the sharp crack in the right wall of *The Cleavage* and continue right to gain the front face. Finish awkwardly up the arête moving left (often damp). **Gossamer** (HVS 5a): climb the slab to the horizontal break, delicately reach the small overhang above, then go rightwards into the centre of the face; follow the cracks, finishing right. **Albatross** (HVS 5b), follows *Gossamer* to the small overhang, moves left and climbs adjacent to the arête finishing on the right rib. About 10m right of *The Cleavage* is another deep cleft – The Catacomb. There are twin niches set in the overhangs both left and right of this. **Nobutjust** (HVS 5b): start below the short undercut niche on the left of the cleft. Traverse left to a blunt nose and mantelshelf up onto the horizontal rail. Move right and delicately into the groove. Bridge up this to a good ledge. Traverse left and climb the cracks finishing rightwards. A direct start is also possible by climbing the overhang on the left and pulling right into the base of the groove. **Crystal Dance** (E1 5c): follow *Nobutjust* to the horizontal rail. Climb the slab above next to the thin curved crack (runner) using a small crystal hold. Move left to finish up the cracks. **The Catacomb** (VD), starts steeply up the deep cleft and has a loose sub-terranean exit. **Shindig** (E2 5c), starts left of a holly and climbs up to the roof. Gain the groove above with difficulty, then up left to an awkward exit. Ascend the wall and arête above to finish. **The Fairway** (Massively Vegetated Slab!)

Almscliff to Slipstones **403**

## GUISECLIFF - Heyshaw Quarry

starts to the right, above the holly, at the right-hand side of an undercut slab. A girdle traverse (**Voortrek**, VS 4c) of the North Buttress area says it all. Leave well alone.

**The Peeler** (VS 4c): lies on an isolated buttress 20m to the right of the holly below *Shindig*. There is a thin bulging crack in the centre. At the top, traverse right and mantelshelf to finish. Further right there are problems but no routes of any length. There is a square block close to the road at the far end of the edge, behind which you might find a little buttress containing **The Raggy Arsed Frog** (E4 6a, †).

### Heyshaw Quarry (see map on page 386)
OS Ref: SE 170 630

If the brooding 'Nordwand' of Guisecliff main edge is not in nick you could try this sheltered suntrap of occasionally soft rock. Good gear, splitter cracks and a sunny aspect give a flavour of American desert rock without the expense of the flights. Approaching from the south end parking spot this small quarry lays to the right of the footpath a few hundred metres before the big telecom mast. Scramble down wherever looks good. The most fun can be had on the Black Roof Buttress which stands above a 4m fin sticking up from the quarry floor scree. Cliff top belay options are as follows: **1**: (the easiest) sit well braced, well back; **2**: pre-place/pull through a rope and hunt for a suitable block; **3**: Pack a stake and hammer. Don't be tempted to over clean the top-outs as: (a) It can increase erosion; (b) well-rooted heather can be more useful for a pull over than sand and dirt.

**Black Roof Buttress**: **Stretchin'** (HVS 5a), takes the line up to, and then left of, the black roof via a wide layback crack. Hand-traverse leftwards and jam/layaway the flake. **Sketchin'** (E2 5c) climbs the wide layback and thin crack through the right-hand side of the roof. **Crankin'** (E1 5b) takes the wide groove, small recess and cracks to the top. Well protected but strenuous. **Stemmin'** (E1 5b) is good and steep. It takes the wide groove just right. Stemming and laybacking up the slim groove / chimney.

**Titanic Buttress:** The black wall with a slim groove in its right-hand side and tree to its right, about 60m left (west) of the quarry floor fin and Black Roof area. All cleaned and climbed on the centenary of the sinking of the Titanic. All the top-outs require care. Routes described *right to left*:

**Clinging to the Wreckage** (E1 5c) swings in from the left (crux) to climb the thin central cracks. **White Star Line** (E1 5c): a bouldery rockover or easier traverse in from the right (runner in tree) accesses the slim black groove. **That Sinking Feeling** (E1 5b) takes the hanging corner and left-hand roof crack 10m right of *White Star Line*.

### Bouldering

For the uber-keen, 'Nam-trained jungle boulderer, many problems can be discovered deep within the woodland of the Guisecliff massif. Boulders are found, lost and found again all the way from the quarry antennae at the east end, down to the tarn and back out again at Yorke's Folly to the west, These problems are covered extensively by *Yorkshire Gritstone Bouldering Guide - Volume 2 by Steve Dunning & Ryan Plews (Total Climbing, 2011)* and if you're going to deep-dive into the woods take this book and make sure all your affairs are in order beforehand. For the less adventurous, Yorke's Prow, Folly Prow and the Mop Top Bloc offer excellent problems and are located south-east of the Folly. The roadside Nought Bank boulders and Crocodile Crag are covered within this guide (see pages 408 and 412).

### Rowantree Crags
OS Ref: SE 153 626   Altitude: 335m

A quaint moorland venue that warrants a visit if you fancy a spot of solitude. Predominantly south-facing and split into two areas, (Incredible Boulders Part 1 & 2), the crag has boulder problems in the Font 3-5 range as well as a couple of harder offerings. Full details are available from www.yorkshiregrit.com. **Parking and Approach:** Park as for the Guisecliff south crag lay-by (page 388). Walk north up the road, past the footpath to the antenna and Guisecliff on the right, until a gated track appears on the left. Follow this track as it leads to the boulders after around 20 mins. The Rowantree Crags marked on the OS map are actually before the boulders described here.

---

### Further First Ascent Information (✦)

**Aftermath**: *1pt aid. FFA Jerry Peel, Tony Barley 27th October 1974.*
**Agrippa :** *Robin Barley, Tony Barley August 1964.*
**Agrippina :** *Tony Barley, Robin Brown 22nd September 1971.*
**Aiguille Des Moutons, Apparition, Boundary Chimney, Buttress Albatross:** *Colin Tee, Paul Dearlove 18th May 1987.*
**Route, Intestine, Pulpit Chimney, Right-Hand Wall, Scissors,**

# First Ascent Information - GUISECLIFF

**Shoulder Gully, The Chimney:** *Geoff Scovell recorded these routes in 'Climbs on Guisecliffe' YRC Journal 1955.*

**Arbor Crack (Cordite Start):** *Tony Barley, Robin Barley 1961.*

**Barleycorn:** *The Right Eliminate of Guisecliffe snatched by the Rock and Ice under the nose of local experts.*

**Barney Rubbles Bookcase, Coyotillo;** *Paul Tanton, Bruce Woodley, Robin Warden April 2011.*

**Bold John, Microcrack:** *Robin Barley, Tony Barley, John Williams 16th July 1966* (**Bold John**: *Start added later by Tony Barley*).

**Campanile:** *Alt. variation by Colin Tee, P. Dearlove 12th May 1987.*

**Campanile Direct:** *By Bruce Woodley, Neil Game, Denis Gleeson, Simon Charge 3rd May 2007.*

**Careful Crack, Coyote Wall, Crack of Roots:** *Tony Barley, Robin Barley 1965.*

**The Catacomb, The Cleavage, The Right Rib:** *Tony Barley 1972.*

**Comet Wall**: *A major addition to the crag at the time although some aid (pegs still in situ) were necessary to avoid the flake crack. FFA Tony and Robin Barley in July 1963.*

**The Creation**: *Climbed after a morning ascent of Forked Lightning Crack at Heptonstall. Considered harder and, with only token protection, one of the hardest routes in Yorkshire at the time.*

**Crystal Dance:** *Colin Tee, S Cook 21st May 1987.*

**Curate's Crack, Pulpit Steps**: *T. Barley, J Williams 13th July 1966.*

**Cretin's Crack, Dhobi, Rhino, Stigma:** *Frank Spence, Lynne Noble, M Sanderson c1960.*

**Dingbat:** *Climbed with 2pt aid. FFA John Syrett, Al Manson 1973.*

**Drum Crack:** *Robin Barley, Tony Barley March 1963.*

**Energy**: *Tony Barley, Robin Barley 10th July 1966.*

**The Fairway:** *Tony Barley, Howard Walker 1972.*

**Forgotten Chimney**: *Ashley Petts, Mrs Petts, B. Evans May 1954.*

**Gossamer:** *Tony Barley, Tony Roche 27th May 1972.*

**Guillotine:** *Previously called Stingo, with two points of aid by Tony Barley on 1st June 1971.*

**Haberdashery:** *One aid point on first ascent.*

**Hawk Slab:** *Allan Austin, Eric Metcalfe 24th July 1960.*

**Holly Grooves:** *Allan Austin, Dave Roberts 30th April 1960.*

**Hotrod**: *Tony Barley, Chas Hird 1966.*

**Jaywalk:** *Tony Barley, Ken Wood 3rd October 1971.*

**Kandahar Groove:** *Robin Barley, Tony Barley February 1961.*

**KOYLI – Variation Start:** *by John Eastham, Geoff Meyers 1969.*

**Lectern Chimney:** *Robin Barley, Tony Barley 1964.*

**Ledge and Crack, Thin Man's Delight:** *Arthur Birtwhistle, Haywood, Pearson 1937.*

**Letterbox Climb, Shelter Climb:** *Harry Stembridge, Fred Stembridge pre-1950.*

**Little Something, Oak Wall, Postman's Crack, The Slot, Tree Cracks**: *YMC pre-1957.*

**Mantelshelfman:** *Tony Barley, Martin Jones, Robin Brown 1974.*

**Mastermind:** *A new advance in difficulty at the time and possibly Barley's hardest lead. Peg used on the damp first pitch. FFA Peter Short, Alan Towse 7th July 1984.*

**Millroy's Climb:** *Millroy and party pre-1954.*

**Nice 'n' Sleazy:** *A free ascent of an old peg route (Bastion) through a large overhang. Martin Berzins, Bob Berzins 1st September 1978.*

**Nippem, Rootless Crack, Barracuda:** *Harold Barraclough, Ron Tyler, H. Tyler, C. Salisbury, B. Todd 1960.*

**Nobutjust:** *Tony Barley, Robin Brown 16th April 1972.*

**North Wall Eliminate**: *Immortalised in a magazine article by Dennis Gray in 1968 as one of 'The 10 best climbs on Gritstone'.*

**Oak Wall Direct**: *By Paul Tanton, Bruce Woodley April 2011.*

**Offspring:** *Tony Barley, Tim Barley 11th March 1989.*

**On the Edge:** *The crag's first E6.*

**Overhanging Groove:** *Tony Barley, Robin Barley November 1962.*

**The Peeler:** *Robin Barley, Tony Barley September 1963.*

**Pinnacle Face:** *Tony Barley, Robin Barley September 1963.*

**The Raggy Arsed Frog:** *Adrian Ledgeway, M. Radtke, D. Barton 1999*

**Ruminant:** *Brian Evans, Robin Barley, Tony Barley 29th Oct 1961.*

**Ruscator**; *Originally with an aid peg but later FFA by same party.*

**Ryvoan Crack:** *Tony Barley, Robin Barley March 1961.*

**The Sapling Bends:** *Paul Tanton, B. Woodley (Alt. leads) May 2011.*

**Scalped**: *Dave Brown, Rob Glendunning 25th July 2006.*

**Shindig:** *Tony Barley 4th April 1971 Sling used for aid at the roof. FFA Ken Wood, John Harwood on 11th July 1972.*

**Skyjacker**: *First pitch with 2 pegs. FFA Peter Short, Alan Towse 7th July 1984.*

**Sprog**; *Climbed by Frank Spence, L. Noble, M Sanderson c1960*

**Stretcher:** *Direct start by Tony Barley in 1965.*

**Take Five:** *Robin Barley, Tony Barley 1961 Five aid pegs. Practicing for Kilnsey. FFA 1965.*

**Tanton's Tunnel:** *Paul Tanton April 2011.*

**The Belfry Bat Finish:** *By Bruce Woodley, P. Tanton 7th May 2011.*

**Wafer Crack:** *Robin Barley, Tony Barley 12th March 1966.*

**When the Bough Broke**: *By Bruce Woodley, Robin Warden April 2011. Given a grade of E1 5c with 3pts of aid. The large roof came within a centimetre of being climbed free via the groove on its right-hand side. That was until the essential oak broke. May free up at E6 6c or just require a 20-year wait until the bough regrows.*

**Winklepicker:** *Robin Barley, Tony Barley 18th June 1966.*

*All routes in* **Heyshaw Quarry** *were climbed by Paul Tanton, Bruce Woodley, Chris Wiles April 2012.*

# Guisecliff - Graded List

## GRADED LIST

### E8
The Climb That Time Forgot (6c)

### E6
On the Edge (6b)
Doomed Oasis (6b)
Lowdowns (6b)

### E5
The Warriors of Hanuman (6b)
Wild Abandon (6b)
Nipscrew (6b)
The Scryking (6a)
Crocodile (6a) (A0)
Aftermath (5c)

### E4
The Rifles (6b)
Over the Top (6a)
The Raggy Arsed Frog (6a)
Mastermind (5c)
Cutting the Cord (5c)

### E3
Guillotine (6a)
Dingbat (6a)
Campanile Direct (6a)
Bat Finish (5c)
Nice 'n' Sleazy (5c)
Humus (5c)
Barney Rubble's Bookcase (5c)
Barleycorn (5b)

### E2
Haberdashery (6a)
The Shim (6a)
Shindig (5c)
The Creation (5c)
Skyjacker (5c)
Stretchin' (5c)
Coyotillo (5c)
Jehu's Chariot (5c)
Autobahn (5a, 5c)
Arbor Crack (Cordite Start) (5c)
Ruscator (5c)
Foreign Bodies (5c)
Variation Start (5b)
The Sapling Bends (5b,5b)
Tombstone (5b)

### E1
The Shim (6a)
Crystal Dance (5c)
Crankin' (5c)
The Verger (5c)
Arbor Crack (5c)
Savage Sentence (5b)
Agrippa (5b)
Hook Route (5b)
Pendulum (5b)
Stretcher (5b)

### HVS
Mantelshelfman (5c)
Energy (5c)
Midsummer Night's Dream (5b)
Albatross (5b)
Nobutjust (5b)
Oak Wall Direct (5b)
Magnificat (5a)
Side-show (5a)
North Buttress Direct (5a)
Double Top (5a)
Aggrippina (5a)
Campanile (5a)
Crossover (5a)
The Belfry (5a)
The Kraken (5a)
Comet Wall (5a)
KOYLI (5a)
Left-Hand Finish (5a)
Gossamer (5a)
Synchromesh (5a)
Bold John (5a)
Winklepicker (5a)
Jaywalk (5a)
North Wall Eliminate (5a)
Microcrack (5a)

### VS
Cretin's Chimney (5a)
Take five (5a)
Wafer Crack (5a)
Spring Fever (4c)
Postman's Crack (4c)
Scalped (4c)
Sprog (4c)
Drum Crack (4c)
Right-hand Wall (4c)
Footpatter (4c)
Overhanging Groove (4c)
Stigma (4c)
Daniel (4c)
Phillipa's Ridge (4c)
Brian's Climb (4c)
Pinnacle Face (4c)
Careful Crack (4c)
Little Something (4c)
Barracuda (4c)
Rhino (4c)
Offspring (4c)
Crack of Roots (4c)
Bottleneck (4c)
Hotrod (4c)
Speedway (4c)
The Right Rib (4c)
Voortrek (4c)
The Peeler (4c)

### MVS
Dhobi (4b)
Holly Grooves
The Fairway

### HS
Roc's Nest Chimney (4b)
Coyote Wall (4b)
Jezebel (4b)
Illusion
Clodhopper
Angle Crack
Oak Wall
North buttress Crack

### S
Curate's Crack
Short Chimney
Tree Cracks
Ruminant
Nippem
Rootless Crack
Kandahar Groove
Hawk Slab
By-pass
The Slot
Thin Man's Delight
Caveman's Corner
North Buttress Ordinary
The Cleavage

### MS
Lectern Chimney
Ryvoan Crack

### HVD
The Chimney (4b)
Boundary Chimney

### VD
Pulpit Steps
Pulpit Chimney
Buttress Route
Shoulder Gully
Apparition
Millroy's Climb
Forgotton Chimney
Aiguille de Moutons
The Catacomb

### D
Letterbox Climb
Scissors
Tanton's Tunnel
Shelter Climb
Ledge and Crack
Pinnacle Ordinary Route

### M
Chockstone Chimney

Yorke's Folly.

Tom Peckitt putting faith in friction on the aptly named **Trust** (Font 7b). Page 409
Photo: Charlotte Telfer

# nought bank boulders

by **Nigel Poustie**

OS Ref: SE 157 637
Altitude: 290 m

A fine collection of angular gritstone boulders scattered conveniently near the Guisecliff northern car park. Plenty of easy warm ups that might ready you for the clutch of outstanding highball walls and arêtes. Some of the best problems require commitment; otherwise known as multiple pads and a diligent spotter.

**Conditions and Aspect:** The majority of the boulders on the circuit face north and are just below the treeline. Spring or late Autumn are the best times to visit when the rock is clean and the short walk between blocks is far easier as the bracken's subsided.

**Parking and Approach:** See approach and parking as for Guisecliff crag (page 386). Parking is either at the northern lay-by on the sharp right-hand bend before the descent to Pateley Bridge or 200m further down on the right after the boulders (room for two cars). Two minute walk to the first boulders. No access issues.

## Glass Alley

This is the small boulder below the Nought Bank Boulder. It is useful for warming up, and for kids. (a) **Green Glass** (Font 3) is the left-hand scoop, moving right. (b) **Tumbler** (Font 3) takes the wide rib. Bridge up the middle scoop and finish direct for (c) **Marbles** (Font 3). (d) **Alley Rib** (Font 3) is the right arête, finishing on the right.

## The Nought Bank Boulder

This is the large cubic block nearest the road and an obvious starting point. The shorter problems were all done in the early sixties by the Barley brothers and the tall north face waited until 2007 for an ascent. All problems are excellent, some are up there with the best. Descent is by down-climbing *Happy Wall*.

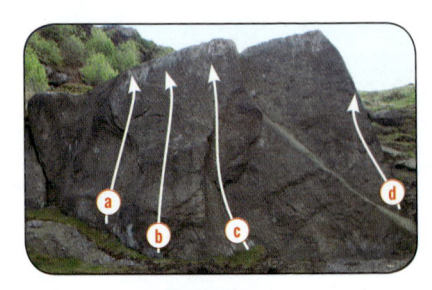

**1 All or Bust**   Font 4. Exciting climbing up the left-hand side of the arête.
**2 By The Fin**   Font 4. A beautiful warm up. The left side of the face, utilising a great pinch. Finish direct or with the arête.

**Yorkshire Gritstone**

# Bonjoy's Wall - NOUGHT BANK BOULDERS

**3 Happy Wall** Font 3
**4 Happy Landing** Font 3
**5 Nought Corner** Font 4. Tricky but good.
**6 All or Nothing** Font 4. The arête just right of the corner. (e) **Nothing Or All** (Font 4) takes the arête on the right-hand side.
**7 Ryvita** Font 6a. Always feels like an onsight. The centre of the wall on disguised holds. A good introduction to what follows. *Paul Clough 2006*
**8 Saffner Arête** Font 6b+. The left-hand side of the arête. A technical crux start and a committing finish. *Paul Clough 2007*
**9 Slideshow** Font 7a. The superb right arête. Several mats are useful to prop up the one you're going to land on along with a 'third man' to keep them in place. Serious. *Nigel Poustie 2007* Photo on page 417.
**10 Toboggan Wall** Font 7b. The centre of the wall to a dynamic crux finish. One of the best highball walls in Yorkshire. *Nigel Poustie 2007*
**11 Cool Runnings** Font 6b. The right arête on the left-hand side with a reachy finish. Mats and spotters won't help with this one. More like a route due to the sharp boulder you'd land on. *Paul Clough 2007*

The **Eclipse Pinnacle** is 20m south-west. Useful for warming up, with two interesting easy problems. (f) **Full Eclipse** (Font 4) takes the ramp to the top of the pinnacle. The wall right of the rib is (g) **Cornish Corona** (Font 5).

## Pok-A-Tok Block
To the right is a boulder which is home to an excellent problem and an amazing looking wall. Shame it has no holds.

**12 Pok-A-Tok** Font 7a. The right arête on its left-hand side. A fingery start leads to a dynamic finish. *Andy Crome 2007*

## Bonjoy's Wall
Head eastwards for 100m to the dry stone wall. This block can be found straddling the wall higher up on the hillside.

**13 Hump Bump** Font 6c. The proud central wall on great crimps with an exciting finish. *Jim Purchon*
**14 Bonjoy's Wall** Font 6c+. Sit-down start. From the good undercut, reach for the small sidepull and then again for the break. Traverse leftwards and finish as for *Hump Bump*.
**15 Salvador** Font 7c. From a sit-start, climb the left side of the arête using a foot lock, a tiny crimp and a campus move to the sloping top. *Nigel Poustie 2008*
**16 Dali** Font 6b+. From a sit-down start, the right side of the arête uses an unique hold. Traverse around to finish on the left. Suffers from seepage. *Nigel Poustie 2008*

Dropping downhill and between Bonjoy's Wall and the Trust Block is the Gardeners World cave. **Down Under** (Font 7b) starts on the block at the back of the cave and climbs out to the light whilst **Around the World** (Font 7a) starts with the block on the right and traverses the lip to finish as for *Down Under*. *Both problems by Nigel Poustie 2010*

## Trust Block
Superb quality gritstone. This is home to the stunning line of *Trust* in a lovely setting. At the left end, the groove and arête is **Kid** (Font 3), with (a) **Grown-Up** (Font 4) taking the left arête in its entirety.

**17 Grow-Up** Font 7b. The centre of the slab to finish at the left arête. *Tom Peckitt 2008*
**18 Trust** Font 7b. A beautiful line up the left side of the arête is both technical and strangely powerful. Photo on page 407. The arête on its right (b) **Little Faith** (Font 5+) is harder than it looks. *Nigel Poustie 2008*

# Nought Bank Boulders - Trust Block

**19 Famous 45** Font 6b. From the hole dyno to the top. *Jim Purchon*

## Oak Ridge

Contour westward now and after a short walk the small crooked ridge with a twisted oak on its left-hand side comes into view.

**20 Spirit of Oak** Font 4. Take the knife blade ridge but sneak left avoiding the bulge at the top.
**21 Hellbent** Font 6a. The right side of the arête all the way.
**22 Twisted Oak** Font 4. The slab to the right.

410          Yorkshire Gritstone

# Inca Wall - NOUGHT BANK BOULDERS

## Nought Bank Pinnacle
The tallest pinnacle at Nought Bank has four good problems, all finishing at the obvious break. With a bit of gear in the break, topping out would justify full route status.

**23 Grimace** Font 6c. Good technical climbing up the thin side wall. *Tom Peckitt 2006*
**24 Transmission** Font 7a. The square cut arête on the left-hand side. *Tom Peckitt 2006*
**25 Eclipse** Font 7b+. The other side of the arête. *Tom Peckitt 2006*
**26 Tuition** Font 6a. The right arête on its left-hand side. *Tom Peckitt 2006*

## Checkers
The buttress highest on the hill.

**27 Noughts** Font 5. A tricky start using the arête. *Tony Barley 1997*
**28 Suckerpunch** Font 7a. A quality line. The steep technical arête starting on the right, finishing on the left. Morpho. *Tom Peckitt 2006*

**Super G aka Pinch Perfect** (Font 7c+) is a steep rampline to the right of *Sucker Punch* and Nought Bank's hardest offering. It goes from the lowest possible holds and avoids the ledge out right. *Nigel Poustie April 2011*

## Green Fingers
An excellent rock formation which is home to another great Guisecliff arête.

**29 Crosses** Font 4. *Tony Barley 2000*
**30 Audit** Font 4. *Tony Barley 2000*
**31 Green Fingers** Font 6c+. The bulging right side of the arête has a font-like quality. *Nigel Poustie 2008*
**32 Sprite** Font 7a. Dyno from low holds to the break then drop off. *Tom Peckitt 2006*

## Moon Shadow Blocks
Continuing rightwards a couple of boulders can be found on two different levels.

**33 Full Moon** Font 5. The left arête and scoop.
**34 Moonshadow** Font 4. The rounded arête on its left-hand side with the aid of little ledges.
**35 Glitterbug** Font 6b. High and mighty. Up the crack and wall.

Amongst the heather on the boulder above this block is (c) **Moonshadow Rib** (Font 5+) which tackles the steep right arête on its right-hand side.

## Inca Wall
This boulder is on the right, high on the bank. Problems are on good rock and have a route feel to them. The wall and ramp with the **Green Hole** is Font 4+.

**36 Sacrifice** Font 4. *Tony Barley 2000*
**37 Trail of the Incas** Font 5+. *Tony Barley 2000*
**38 Traverse of the Incas** Font 5+. Finish up *Sacrifice*. *Tony Barley 1999*

# crocodile crag
by **John Hunt**

OS Ref: SE 158 638
Altitude: 250 m

Crocodile crag is in woodland at the extreme end of the mighty Guisecliff escarpment. The prominent boulder of Crocodile Rock sits alone on the hillside above it and combined with Nought Bank boulders they offer a fine day out.

**The Climbing:** The 20 or so routes and boulder problems provide worthwhile outings, especially in the VS to E3 range. The crag divides into the areas of Croc Block, Tail Swipe Buttress and Shark Slab. There is some good bouldering on the main edge as well as four problems up on Crocodile Rock.

**Conditions and Aspect:** The crag receives good morning sun and is well sheltered. It is a good bet early in the year. Shark Slab can be a bit dirty early in the season, but most of the routes stay fairly clean.

**Parking and Approach:** Park as for Nought Bank in the little lay-by on the right-hand side of the road (facing downhill). For Crocodile Crag, cross the road and follow the wall up the hill until a makeshift gate is reached. Cross this, then trend up the hill towards the crag. For Crocodile Rock, from the road strike up along the wall to the brow of the hill, where the boulder comes into view. Alternatively walk up from Crocodile Crag. Paradoxically, it offers nice sheltered bouldering if the main crag is wet.

**Access:** No access issues to date.

The first boulder problems are just before the prominent tower of Croc Block. **Toothpegs** (Font 4) climbs the left arête of the first block over the wall; the corner-crack below the oak is **Croak** (Font 4); **Freerider** (Font 6c+) climbs the roof and hanging prow from a low start. From standing it is **Snout** (Font 4+).

## Croc Block
The tall pinnacle with climbs that bite.

**1 The Tear Jerker Finish**  HVS 5a   10m
A proper jamming crack; some will cry. Savour the crack then climb the hanging cleft on the left.
*Dave Musgrove, Tim Fryer  2nd April 2008*

**2 Thick Skin**  HVS 5b   10m
The overhang direct from the same crack.
*Tony Barley (solo)  20th February 2000*

**3 Tears**  VS 5a   10m   ★
The original crack route and the best of the trilogy. Traverse right and climb the rib over the ledges.
*Nick Barley, Tony Barley  December 1999*

**4 Croc Bloc**  E3 5c   10m   ★★
The line of the crag. Climb the fine face by bull-working both arêtes.
*John Hunt, Dave Musgrove, Tim Fryer  2nd April 2008*

**5 Muck & Brass**  Font 5+ (E1 5c)
The arête and wall to a sloping ledge. *Paul Clough  2008*

The next routes are on the wall above the shallow sandy cave.

**6 Tail Swipe**  E3 6a   8m
From the supporting boulder, climb the rib to the overhang. Arrange interesting protection before fully committing to strenuous pull-ups to reach the top.
*Dave Musgrove, Tony Barley  11th September 2002* ✦

**7 Crocodile Gully**  D   6m
Start on the mucky slab in the recess and use both sides of the gully.
*John Hunt, Tara Hunt  20th April 2008*

## Shark Slab
The biggest chunk of rock on the edge.

**8 Shark Nose**  VD   10m
Climb the left side of the rib. Move left under the roof into

**Yorkshire Gritstone**

# CROCODILE CRAG

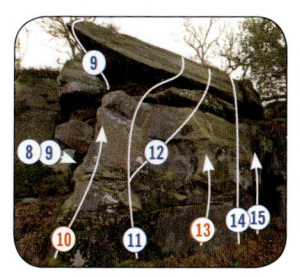

the gully, then boldly onto the nose for an airy finish.
*Tony Barley   20th February 2000*

**9 Shark Attack**  E2 5b   10m   ★
The jutting prow. Follow *Shark Nose* to the ledge. Pull into the roof and gain a good hold on the left. Span right to another hold near the point of the prow. Use the rib and a bit of umph to finish.
*John Hunt, Tim Fryer   2nd April 2008*

**10 Octopus**  Font 5. The right side of the rib.
*John Hunt   2008*

The next routes climb the main face. *Predator, Scales and Jaws* began life as boulder problems which finished at the break and can still be enjoyed in that style.

**11 Predator**  E2 5b   10m   ★
Climb the scoop to the sloping ledge. Gain the good hold and then the break. Pull onto the slab and climb direct.
*Tony Barley   27th October 2000*

**12 Scales**  E2 5c   10m   ★
Bridge right from the scoop to gain the break below the central nose. Traverse right to the highest point of the top break and climb the slab.
*Tony Barley   1st July 2000*

**13 Hippo**  Font 6c+. Tough moves to join and climb the right rib of *Scales*. *Nigel Poustie   2008*

**14 Jaws**  E1 5b   10m   ★
Muscle up the wall left of the chimney. Make committing moves onto and past the upper slab.
*Tony Barley   23rd August 2000*

**15 Tradnasty**  S 4a   8m
The awful, dirty vice-like trad-fest. Three finishes await: skulk off right, bridge up or go caving.
*John Hunt   20th April 2008*

### Crocodile Rock
Said by some to look like a crocodile. It is clearly visible from the Nought Bank Boulders across the road.

**16 Mick Dundee**  Font 5. Gain and share on a good hold on the lip, then make a long reach for the break. Take care with the fragile flakes under the roof and don't fall off.

**17 Romancing the Stone**  Font 6a

**18 Captain Hook**  Font 6a. Climb the right arête from a sitter. Guess how? Alternatively traverse the break left, (a) **Tick-Tock** (Font 6a+), to finish up *Romancing the Stone*.

### Further First Ascent Information
*Any uncredited boulder problems are the work of Tony Barley.* **Free Rider** *was climbed by Nigel Poustie in 2008. For* **Tail Swipe***, Musgrove was drafted in to make the lead just after Barley's open heart surgery. The problems on Crocodile Rock were recorded by Scott Walker and John Hunt in 2008.*

# panorama crag
## by Francis Holland

OS Ref: SE 162 654
Altitude: 200 m

Panorama Crag lies less than a mile to the south east of Pateley Bridge in the heart of Nidderdale. It commands a fine view of Guisecliff and provides a popular viewing area for locals and tourists alike. The crag is divided in two by an obvious wall, with access to the eastern section being 'difficult' (The landowner does not permit access at the moment). However, the western section offers an excellent sheltered section for dry winter days and plenty of shade for summer afternoons.

**The Climbing:** 20 climbs in total. The routes reach a maximum of 11m with many offering tricky overhanging starts. The crag is mainly a venue for trad climbing with a little easy bouldering thrown in and one very hard testpiece problem that has repelled some of the best. The crag is mainly natural with evidence of some quarrying. The main buttress has limited runner placements and provides bold climbing that will test the mettle of the best of climbers. Overall the routes are excellent, high in the grade and deserve more popularity. All in all, worth driving those extra few miles past Brimham, even if it's only for an afternoon.

**Conditions and Aspect:** South-west facing and quick drying are the key aspects of this esoteric venue. Year-round climbing can be had but it's particularly good on a spring or autumn afternoon. The trees can cause the main buttress to become a little green in the damper months though it's never as bad as it looks.

**Parking and Approach:** The crag is best approached from Pateley Bridge up the steep B6265 Pateley Bridge-to-Harrogate road. After just over half a mile, (and only a hundred yards past the national speed limit signs) turn left onto Panorama Way. Continue up this and park on the right, opposite the Catholic church, and below the houses **(Parking GPS: 54.083351, -1.753596)**. From here continue up the road to the cemetery and turn right up the narrow lane. Continue until you reach the viewing platform via a gate. A second (often locked) gate to the left leads down some narrow steps. Turn left to reach the western section and the first boulder problem in an obvious bay with a steep blank slab.

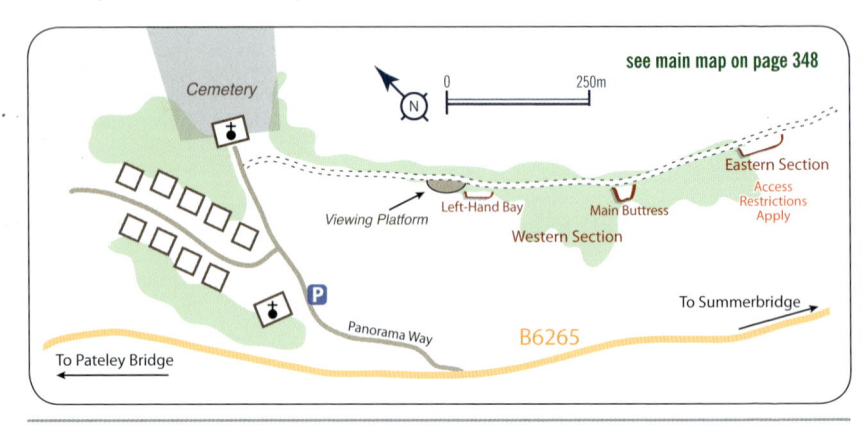

414     Yorkshire Gritstone

# The Main Buttress - PANORAMA CRAG

The eastern section is best reached by continuing along the lane past the gate. After another 100m the broken wall and fence can easily be crossed and the crag reached down the steep bank, through the beech trees.

**Access Issues:** The land owner of the western section at this time is quite happy for considerate climbers to use the crag providing there is no damage and no littering. The owners of the eastern section will ask you to leave as climbing is banned here.

### The Western Section
### Left-Hand Bay

A few metres to the left of the bottom of the steps. Landings are generally very good with the first problem being the hardest of the crag.

**1  Phoenix Wall**  Font 7b+
Probably one of the best hard problems in the dale. A relatively easy start onto the centre of the slab leads quickly to small spaced holds and high steps.
*Andy Crome   October 2004*

**2  Gecko Arête**  Font 4+
The left-hand side of the arête without the use of the flake.
*Francis Holland   28th July 2007*

**3  Goanna Arête**  Font 5+
The same arête on its right-hand side.
*Francis Holland   28th July 2007*

**4  Lizard Wall**  Font 5
The centre of the wall using an obvious step.
*Francis Holland   1st May 2002*

### Main Buttress

The way to the main buttress is via rougher terrain with one big step down. Reaching an impressive 11m in height and overhanging at its base, this block has some formidable climbing.

**5  Dispatches**   E4 6a    10m
Starting as for *No News Is Good News*, climb the centre of the left side of the buttress. Trend left from the pockets, on crimps, to a thought provoking reach to the break and gear. From here it is possible to traverse off. Alternatively, make moves up through the notch in the roof to the delights of a slopey top-out (5c), or attempt to go direct via a pocket (hard).
*Dave Warburton, Huw Goodall, Rosie Cole  6th May 2012*

**6  No News is Good News**   E5 6b    11m
The hardest route on the main buttress is intimidating but the tree directly behind saw the first ascentionist using it as a swift bale out. Start on the left wall of the buttress, just to the left of the overhang, and gain the pocket up to the right (poor runners). Make a tough move to stand in the pocket, (another poor runner), then make a tenuous move up to the right to finally reach reasonable holds just left of the arête.
*Chris Sowden, Tony Burnell   1988*

**7  World in Action**   E4 6a    11m     ★
A tough route on the front of the main buttress. Climb into the niche above the roof with difficulty, step left to the arête and commit to delicate layaways to a ledge. Finish more easily in a fine position.
*Tony Burnell, Chris Sowden 1988*

Almscliff to Slipstones          **415**

# Panorama Crag - The Eastern Section

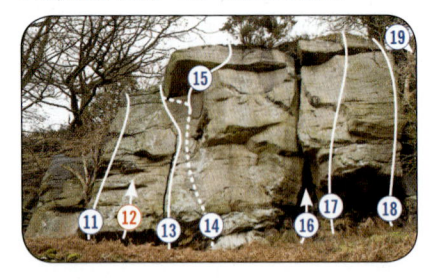

## 8 Panorama  E3 5b   11m  ★
Gain the niche as for *World in Action*, and climb to the large hole up to the right. Push on straight up the wall above. Commitment is the key.
*Tony Burnell, Chris Sowden  1988*

## 9 Yesterday's News  E2 5b   10m  ★
The original line on the buttress and a fine example of a Barley brothers route; brilliant climbing and low on gear. Start at the right arête, trend left across the front face and finish at the top of *World in Action*.
*Robin and Tony Barley  Easter 1963*

## 10 News Night  E1 5b   11m  ★
A good line. Start from the obvious block and climb the arête on its left side, in a bold position, to a rounded finish.
*Chris Sowden, Tony Burnell  1988*

### The Eastern Section
An area which sports some excellent mid-grade routes on good quality gritstone. Shame it's off limits at the moment.

## 11 Pateley Show  HVS 5c   7m
A boulder problem start leads over the awkward bulge and up the slab and left arête.
*Tony Barley (solo)  April 1983*

## 12 The Now Show  Font 6b+
Make a very hard pull onto, and up, the undercut slab.
*John Hunt  29th March 2005*

## 13 Glasshouse Groove  MVS 4b   7m  ★
The initial bulge leads to pleasant climbing via the crack and shallow flake. Step left into the short groove to finish.
*Robin and Tony Barley  Easter 1963*

## 14 Nidderdale Wall  S 4a   8m
An easier variation of *Glasshouse Groove*. Gain the ledge and surmount the bulge to reach the scoop below the roof. Step left and finish as for *Glasshouse Groove*.
*Robin and Tony Barley  Easter 1963*

## 15 Not the Nine O'clock News  E3 6a  8m  ★★
An excellent, yet testing, route for the grade. Follow *Nidderdale Wall* to the scoop below the roof and small wires. Boldly step right and summon the courage to overcome the overlap.
*Chris Sowden, Tony Burnell  1988*

## 16 Dimbleby's Crack  HVS 5b   7m
The obvious offwidth crack. If that's your bag - enjoy.
*Robin and Tony Barley  Easter 1963*

## 17 Power Pull  E1 5c   6m  ★
A tricky boulder problem start leads to easier ground. Be prepared for a tricky top-out.
*Robin and Tony Barley  Easter 1963*

## 18 Padded Arête  HVS 5c   6m
Good value. Climb the left arête of the chimney with interest maintained throughout.
*Malcolm Townsley (solo)  20th Sept 1994*

Venture into the chimney at your peril for a Diff tick. The crack to the right is also Diff.

## 19 Ripley Bank  VD   7m
Gain the undercut rib from the crack and then continue to the top.

Further right are a series of easy slabs that eventually lead to a small steep and juggy roof known as **Rob Wood 1827** (Font 4+). Variations exist.

Nigel Poustie squeezing hard on his own **Slideshow** (Font 7a) at Nought Bank, Guisecliff. Page 409.
Photo: Paul Clough

# whitehouses

by **Andy Crome**

OS Ref: SE 185 651
Altitude: 230 m

Whitehouses lies nestled on the rim of the Nidderdale valley, enjoying far reaching views towards Brimham and Guisecliff and across to the golfballs of RAF Menwith Hill. It offers perhaps the greatest concentration of hard link-up style boulder problems in Yorkshire and is guaranteed to work skin, muscles and technique in equal measure.

**Bouldering**: There are currently over 40 problems and link-ups at Whitehouses, some of which are classic testpieces for their grade. The real quality is reserved for climbers operating in the Font 7s and 8s though, for this is a tough arena with powerful and steep moves on marginal holds, often with subtle technical solutions.

**Conditions and Aspect:** The block takes the form of a large roof of near perfect grit, part natural and part quarried and almost 15m in length. It faces south and is exposed to all but northerly winds thus making it quick drying and reliable in winter. Best conditions can be found on breezy overcast days as many of the problems rely on good friction from sloping holds. The landings are grassy and flat and the largest problems reach approximately four metres in height.

**Parking, Approach and Access**: From lay-by parking, 1.5 miles east of Pateley Bridge on the B6265 Ripon to Glasshouses road (**Parking GPS: 54.08168, -1.71959**), go through the gate opposite Cliffe Farm, then head downhill over an exposed gritstone step and bear left beneath the dry-stone wall until the roof comes into view. The crag is reached along an unmarked public footpath. Care should be taken to park courteously, close the gate behind you and be thoughtful not to damage any dry-stone walls whilst at the crag. The approach takes less than a minute.

The climbing can be split into two areas, the West Wing and East Wing, separated by the wide *Central Crack*. For ease of identification problems have been described with a number and letter prefix. The **number** refers to a starting location and the **letter** defines the climbs finish. Use the line of least resistance to link these together. Where any specific rules exist they are explained in the descriptive text.

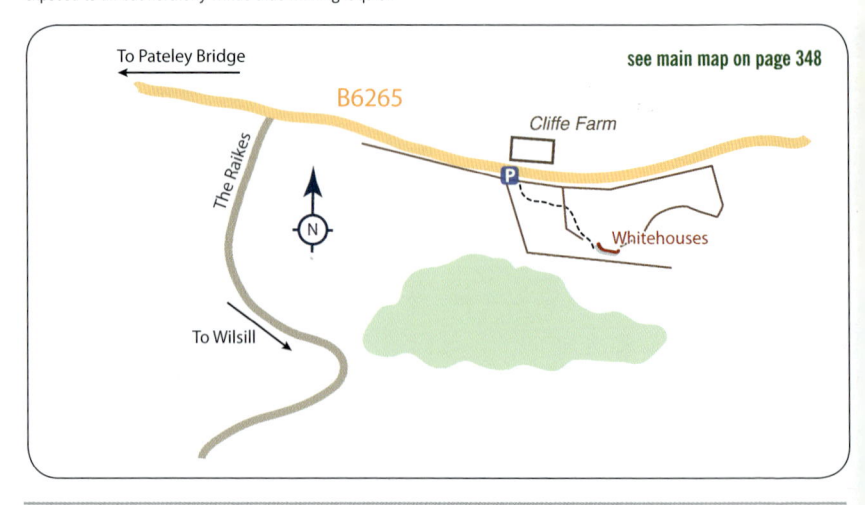

Neil Sugden delivers an outdoor broadcast on **Rageh Omaar** (Font 7a). Page 420.
Photo: Adi Gill

419

# WHITEHOUSES - West Wing

## West Wing

| Name | | | Grade | Description | Credit |
|---|---|---|---|---|---|
| Borderline | | | Font 6b+ | From a sit-down start just to the left of the slot, rock up and mantel leftwards with the help of a shallow dish and then a high pebble. | *Andy Crome, 2010* |
| Patterns in the Void | 1 | **A** | Font 7c | The sidewall, from sitting, hands in the slot via two small high crimps. | *Greg Chapman, 2008* |
| Conehead Bobstar | | | Font 7b | The stand-up version of *Patterns'*, starting from the high crimps. Possible with a static or dynamic method. | *Martin Parker, 2007* |
| Under Rumsfeld | 1 | **B** | Font 7b+ | The superb leaning arête from sitting, hands in the slot. | *Andy Crome, 2003* |
| Crazy Legs Crome | 1 | **C** | Font 7c+ | Continue *Under Rumsfeld* along the lip to the *Fat Punter* finish. 360 spin optional. More sustained now that a hold has deteriorated. | *Andy Crome, 2006* |
| Yes We Can | 1 | **E** | Font 8b | Link *The Trial* into *Whitefinger low*. Superb sustained climbing with no rests and with the crux coming right at the end. | *Mark Katz, 2011* |
| The Trial of Slinky Bobs Master | 1 | **F** | Font 8a | Continue *Crazy Legs* to *Central Crack* and finish stylishly up this. More sustained now that a hold has deteriorated. | *Martin Parker, 2006* |
| Rageh Omaar | 2 | **B** | Font 7a | The hanging arête from holds on the lip. Photo on page 419. | *Andy Crome, 2003* |
| Hercules | 3 | **B** | Font 7c+ | Start left-hand slot, right-hand shothole. Work out to and up the arête, finishing as for *Rageh*. | *Andy Swann, 2008* |
| Fat Punters' Roof | 4 | **C** | Font 6c+ | The central rib from the lip jug, passing the square cut chip. | *Fat punter, unknown* |
| Kenny Boy Lay | 5 | **B** | Font 7b+ | Start from the two shotholes. Out to the lip, then leftwards to the *Rageh* finish. Plinth allowed. | *Andy Crome, 2004* |
| Bush Bully | 5 | **C** | Font 7b | The short version of *Kenny Boy Lay* finishing up *Fat Punters' Roof*. Plinth allowed. | *Andy Crome, 2003* |
| Lazarus | 5 | **D** | Font 7c+ | From the twin shothole start, climb out to and over the lip to poor slopers in the scoop and a hard finish. Plinth allowed. | *Andy Swann, 2008* |
| Corporal Khan | 5 | **E** | Font 8a | By eliminating the plinth, link the *Bush Bully* start into *Whitefinger low*. | *Andy Crome, 2011* |
| Whitefinger | 6 | **E** | Font 7c | The rounded yet sharp arête. Plinth allowed. Very Fontesque. | *Gareth Parry, 2004* |
| Whitefinger low | 6 | **E** | Font 7c+ | Eliminate the plinth to make the arête better and harder. Even more Fontesque. | *Andy Swann, 2008* |

## East Wing

| Name | | | Grade | Description | Credit |
|---|---|---|---|---|---|
| First Tour of Duty | 7 | **B** | Font 7c | Sit-down start on the plinth by wedging your feet into the back of the crack. Cross the lip leftwards to the *Rageh* finish. | *Andy Crome, 2010* |
| Reflection Inspection | 7 | **C** | Font 7b+ | The short version of *First Tour*, finishing earlier up *Fat Punters' Roof*. | *Andy Crome, 2009* |
| Central Crack | 7 | **F** | Font 5 | From the sit-down start on the plinth, fight the fearsome feature. Several methods, all fun. | *Traditional* |
| Growled | 7 | **K** | Font 8a | From a crouched knee-bar start undercutting the right side of *Central Crack* undertake the rightwards lip excursion. Well named and a classic of its genre. Finish along *Only Half The Story*. | *Gareth Parry, 2004* |
| Baghdad Bunker | 8 | **G** | Font 4 | Use an undercut to stand on to the nose of the shelf, and then climb the wall rightwards finishing with the help of a short crack. | *Francis Holland, 2003* |

# East Wing - **WHITEHOUSES**

## East Wing (*continued*)

| Name | # | Letter | Grade | Description | FA |
|---|---|---|---|---|---|
| Aragoncillo | 9 | F | Font 7c+ | Sit-down start on the shelf. Use an undercut and the reinforced sidepull to throw over the roof to the largest lip holds. Join *Only Half The Glory* to finish up *Central Crack*. The high pointed footblock is allowed. | Andy Crome, 2011 |
| Hawala | 9 | G | Font 7c | Sit-down start on the shelf. As for *Aragoncillo* to the lip but then finish directly up *Pegleg*. | Andy Crome, 2011 |
| Hamidiya | 9 | H | Font 7b+ | Sit-down start on the shelf. As for *Aragoncillo* to the lip but then finish more easily to the right up *Peshmerga*. | Andy Crome, 2009 |
| People of the Book | 9 | K | Font 7c+ | Sit-down start on the shelf. As for *Aragoncillo* to the lip, linking into *Only Half the Story* to finish. | Andy Crome, 2011 |
| Only Half The Glory | 10 | F | Font 7c | From a kneeling start at the largest lip holds, shimmy leftwards along the lip to finish up *Central Crack*. It pays to pad underneath the nose carefully, without hindering clearance. | Andy Crome, 2010 |
| Pegleg | 10 | G | Font 7b | Kneeling start. Work up and leftwards and surmount the lip using a rough pebbled sloper and your best pirate technique. | Gareth Parry, 2004 |
| Peshmerga | 10 | H | Font 7a+ | Kneeling start. Work up to the flake passing a small sharp edge. A classic mantelshelf problem. | Jon Fullwood, 2003 |
| Only Half the Story | 10 | K | Font 7b+ | The second section of *Growled*. Kneeling start. Lip-traverse rightwards to the finish of *Dubya*. | Gareth Parry, 2004 |
| Spin Strategy | 11 | H | Font 8a | Combine *Spin Ghar* with *Exit Strategy*. A quality link. | Andy Crome, 2010 |
| Spin Ghar | 11 | K | Font 7c | Sit-down start on the shelf at the reinforced undercuts. Improvise to the lip and finish rightwards up *Dubya*. Technical dreamery. | Andy Crome, 2009 |
| Marjah Buzkashi | 12 | F | Font 8a | Combine *Exit Strategy* with *Only Half The Glory* to finish up *Central Crack*. | Andy Crome, 2010 |
| Exit Strategy | 12 | H | Font 7b+ | Sit-down start with hands on the shelf. Follow the lip leftwards to gain and finish up *Peshmerga*. | Andy Crome, 2010 |
| Dubya | 12 | K | Font 5 | Sit-down start with hands on the shelf and then follow the line of slopers over the roof and up the wall. | Francis Holland, 2003 |

Almscliff to Slipstones

# eavestone
by **Phillipe Osborne**

OS Ref: SE 223 680     Altitude: 190m

Eavestone is an enchanting and secluded anomaly; it is cloaked by trees, sports two lakes and is festooned by an assortment of 18 sheltered craglets. The place offers a unique climbing experience but it can get overgrown and green with vegetation and man-eating rhododendrons, so be prepared for some sympathetic gardening and/or vigorous bushwhacking on your visit, especially if some of the routes haven't had traffic for a while.

**The Climbing:** The rock is soft gritstone with 150 routes ranging from VD to E6, though the best quality is in the E1 to E5 range. That said, *Portcullis* and *Spinnaker* are arguably two of the best Severe routes in the county. In its heyday of active development, diligently cleaned by local activists, Eavestone offered scores of genuinely fine climbs. Since then the crag has fallen into neglect and is now a shadow of its former self. The routes are still there, waiting to reward those climbers with a sense of adventure and the wit to deal with a bit of jungle. All of the routes should be approached with a positive but open mind, and a preplaced belay would be wise for many of the top-outs. The small sector of The Crevasse is the exception to the rule with bullet-hard coarse gritstone and a newly discovered collection of bouldering testpieces up to Font 7c+.

**Conditions and Aspect:** The best time for a first visit is in Spring; the buttresses and approaches being easiest to identify before the trees come into full leaf. The northern buttresses (facing south) receive plenty of sunshine and these remain climbable throughout the year. In spring and summer the rock dries quickly, although the whole basin remains sheltered even on very windy days. The roofs and walls of The Crevasse seem to defy most weather and remain dry in all but the heaviest rain.

Try the Fort (upper lake) for a first visit, with everything from Severe to E3. The best of the long, hard routes are found on The Eavestone, Wedge and Tin Pan Alley (south bank of the large lower lake) and should be saved for spring or summer.

**Parking and Approach:** The crag lies halfway between Pateley Bridge and Ripon, half a mile north of the B6265 from which Eavestone is signposted down a gated road. Follow the road to the farm and bear right. Park in a lay-by on the hill adjacent to the woods (**GPS Lat Long 54.107534, -1.659601**). Follow a footpath (signposted to Ripon Rowel / Fishpond Wood) into the wood and downhill to the end of the upper lake in less than five minutes.

**Access:** The Drawbridge and Fort buttresses are on the upper lake and can be seen at the water's edge. Despite the public footpath much of the site is undoubtedly private woodland and shooting and fishing syndicates pay for their sport here. However climbers have never reported being challenged and the BMC has been unable to identify the landowner to discuss potential access issues. If fishermen, shooters or gamekeepers are present, be polite, and move on if requested.

Matt Kilner electing to lead over the DWS of **Portcullis** (S 4a). Page 424
Photo: Jamie Moss

# EAVESTONE - Fort Buttress

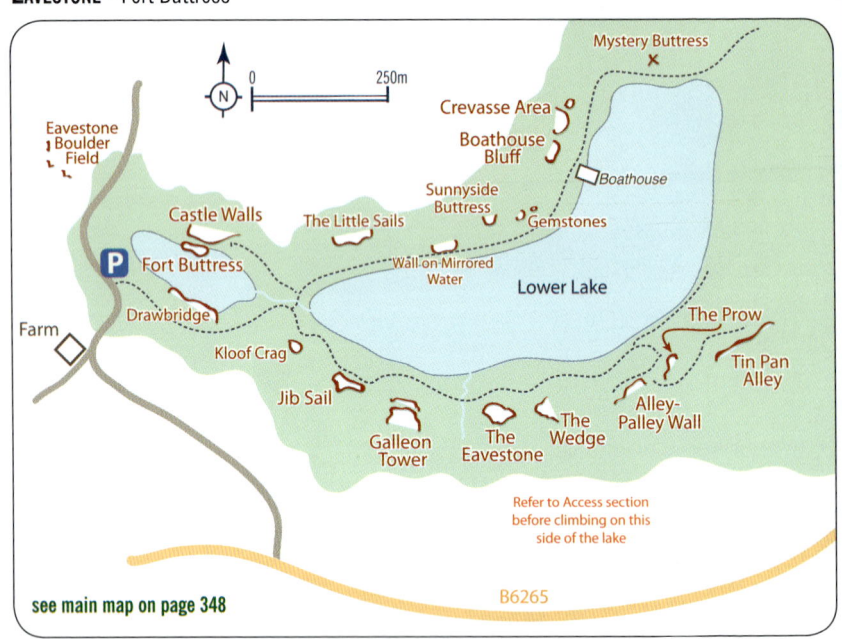

## The Upper Lake - Fort Buttress

This is the first buttress seen after entering the wood from the lay-by, standing proud on the north side of the small upper lake. Approach by bush whacking to a path that leads to the rift behind this buttress. The first climb is approached through the rift and from water level at the left side of the pinnacle (when looking from across the lake). Since the tree bridge collapsed, descent from the buttress requires a little forethought. An abseil and/or some down-climbing will be needed to return to the rift.

**1 Apache** E1 5c  9m  ☆
Climb the flake and step right to gain a short crack on the front. Step up and left from this to reach the shelf on the arête before a final move right and a precarious mantelshelf finish.
*Dave Musgrove, Tony Barley 1st May 1990*

**2 Wet Landing** S 4b  10m
Traverse right from the left arête to a crack, which is climbed to reach the block-filled chimney above.
*Robin Barley, Tony Barley  27th August 1965*

The next 3 climbs all start from water level below the right arête of the buttress when viewed from across the lake.

**3 Portcullis** S 4a  16m  ★★
Captures that sea cliff expedition feeling. Traverse left to a corner and then up to a ledge. Continue left, then up the chimney to finish up cracks on the right and onto the top of the buttress. Photo on previous page.
*Tony Barley (solo)  15th October 1989*

**4 Excalibur** E2 5c  17m  ★★
A spectacularly exposed trip across the buttress. Traverse left and, just short of the corner, climb the flake and then the slanting crack above to the break. Shake out well before launching onto the traverse. Finish just left of the blunt arête. The original finish (E1 5b) simply stepped left into the chimney at the start of the big traverse.
*Tony Barley, Dave Musgrove  15th October 1989*

**5 The Alamo** E2 5b  14m  ★★★
This photogenic line is well-protected but a fine battle; you earn the E points. Climb to the break and jam se-

Fort Buttress - **EAVESTONE**

curely up the hanging crack. Step left and boldly climb the right side of the slabby rib via a pocket to the top.
*Dave Musgrove, Tony Barley   15th October 1989*

**6 Oubliette**  E2 5b   13m   ★★
A worthy brother to its namesake at Almscliff. Start just left of the entrance to the tunnel and climb the pocketed wall to below the roof and then left to the top of the short crack of *Alamo*. Step up right to finish up dislocated cracks. Photo on page 430.
*Tony Barley, Chas Hird   April 1967*

**7 Hallmark**  E3 5c   11m   ★
This gymnastic but well-protected climb tackles the groove in the arête just left of the entrance to the tunnel.
*Tony Barley, Chas Hird   April 1967*

**8 Rearguard**  S 4a   10m
At the centre of the tunnel, bridge up to ledges on the pinnacle.
*Tony Barley (solo)   5th July 1990*

Almscliff to Slipstones    **425**

# Eavestone - Castle Walls

Further through the tunnel a short chimney provides a possible VD descent route off the pinnacle.

### 9 Scalp  HVS 5c  6m
At the far end of the tunnel climb the north-facing wall (i.e. the inside of the entrance) to a horizontal. Swing right to the arête and finish up the crack to the block.
*Tony Barley (solo)  28th June 1990*

The next climbs are on the edge behind the pinnacle starting at the end of the tunnel opposite *Scalp*. The first four are short and best treated as boulder problems. These are: **Portal Rib** (Font 5), the rib opposite *Scalp* climbed via a scoop and bulge on its left. The dirty wall just left of *Portal Rib* is Font 3+ when clean. The same rib keeping to the right gives **See the Light** (Font 4+). Finally **French Connection** (Font 4) climbs a short wall just right of the rib to finish up a good jamming crack.

### 10 Whistling in the Dark  HS 4b  10m
Start inside the tunnel, right of the jammed boulder, and climb the flake in the left-hand groove and a short steep crack. Traverse right and finish up the centre of the wall.
*Dave Musgrove (solo)  21st March 1991*

### 11 The Keep  S 4a  9m
A second shallow groove leads up the dark slabby wall from the centre of the tunnel. Take this, trending right on rather friable rock.
*Tony Barley  27th August 1965*

### 12 Look Out Below  VS 4c  12m
Follow *The Keep* to the traverse then move left along the friable ledge until a small tree is reached.
*Gareth Horton  23rd January 1999*

### 13 The Gatekeeper  E3 6b  8m  ☆
A subtle and technical little test. The blunt rib with two small prominent flakes immediately right of the entrance to the tunnel is climbed direct.
*Dave Musgrove, Nigel Baker, S. Webster, R. Ward  23rd June 1991*

### 14 For Keepsake  HVS 5b  9m  ☆
An interesting climb with a bold crux. Follow *Gatekeeper* to the two small flakes and step right to a ledge then boldly up the right arête.
*Dave Musgrove, Tony Barley  18th April 1990*

## Castle Walls
To the right is a neat accompaniment to Fort Buttress and a better choice for the landlubbers among us. Technical walls with a committing feel.

### 15 Castellan  HVS 5b  9m  ★
Start just right of the gully and take the slanting crack passing the overlap.
*Tony Barley, Anthony Roche  6th August 1971*

### 16 Battlement  E3 6a  9m  ★★
The fine rib direct. Small Friends on the left protect the crux – just.
*Dave Musgrove (solo)  16th Apr 1990*

## Castle Walls - EAVESTONE

**17 The Dirty Rascal**  E2 5c   10m
Climb to a hole and step up to the overlap, moving left to a short scoop just right of the blunt arête.
*Tony Barley, Dave Musgrove  5th October 1989*

**18 The King of the Castle**  E2 5c   9m   ★★
A superb steep slab with a balancey crux to surmount the small overlap.
*Dave Musgrove, Tony Barley  5th October 1989*

**19 Rampart**  E1 5b   10m   ★
Climb to the right rib of the slab to awkwardly gain a standing position. Trend right and swing round the rib to finish direct.
*Dave Musgrove (unseconded)  30th September 1989*

**20 Ditch**  HVS 5c   8m   ☆
The scoop gives a good direct start to *Rampart*.
*Tony Barley (solo)  23rd June 1991*

**21 Casement Crack**  HVD 4a   8m
The offwidth crack to the holly tree.
*Dave Musgrove (solo)  16th April 1990*

**22 Dungeon**  S 4a   9m
The dirty crack in the recess leading to a cave to finish up the chimney.
*Tony Barley (solo)  8th October 1989*

**23 Stockade**  VS 4c   9m
Climb to the break using the right edge of the crack of *Dungeon* and move right to finish.
*Tony Barley (solo)  8th October 1989*

**24 Merlon**  E1 6a   8m   ★
A technical start via layaways on the wall about 2m right of the crack leads to the horizontal break and an easier, but still interesting, direct finish.
*Robin Barley, Tony Barley  12th May 1990*

**25 Crenellation**  E1 6a   8m   ★
Climb the centre of the steep wall to the break and then make a long reach from an undercut to gain a good hold and a finish at a left-pointing horizontal spike and blocks.
*Tony Barley (solo)  8th October 1989*

**26 Machicolation**  VS 4c   7m
Climb the overhanging rib, trending rightwards to a long reach at the top.
*Tony Barley (solo)  8th October 1989*

**27 Arrow Slit**  HS 4b   6m
The cracks to the right of the rib. Just to the left, the reachy lower-wall to the handrail is **Boiling Oil** (Font 5+).
*Tony Barley (solo)  8th Oct 1989; BO:Paul Farrish  26th Feb 2012*

A useful warm-up is **Moat-ivation** (Font 4+), a strenuous fingery traverse along the handrail at the base of Castle Wall from the foot of *Stockade* to the foot of *Arrow Slit*.

**The Drawbridge** is the closest crag to the lay-by but lives very much in the shadow of Fort Buttress on the opposite side of the lake. An overgrown and unpopular area, which is a shame as the routes are good, particularly *Ripples* and *Dance on White Horses*, which are well worth the extra effort. Easy to clean by abseil from trees above. Reaching the start to all the climbs involves a steep scramble down, well to the right (looking out), with most routes requiring a traverse above the stagnant lake to get established. **Chain Mail** (VS 4b) takes the left rib of the buttress passing a block to start; **Sea of Tranquillity** (HVS 5b) tackles the first crack system with the crux near the top; **Dance on White Horses** (E2 5c) climbs direct from a huge undercut to the steep rippled wall above a bulge which leads to jugs on the protruding nose; **Ripples** (HVS 5a) starts as for '*White Horses*' then steps right to gain the crack; **Watery Grave** (E3 5c) starts below the hanging crack of *Ripples* and traverses right to a niche then gains the crack to finish out left; **Don't Pay the Ferryman** (HVS 5a) is a low-level left-to-right two-pitch traverse starting at *Ripples* and finishing on the beach.

# EAVESTONE - Wall on Mirrored Water

## The Lower Lake – Northern Bank

The first buttress encountered, high above the main path on the north side of the lower lake and 120m from the bridge is **The Little Sails**. It's a crag with loose rock and unpleasant landings. Whatever you do, don't fall off. **The Plunge** (S 4a) climbs the left end of the wall behind a holly tree; **Sea Dog** (VS 4c) starts below a curving flake to a ledge and follows the dangerously loose flake to the top; **Upper Sail** (VS 5a) takes the upper wall from a small protruding flake; **Lower Sail** (VS 5a) climbs past a sandy pocket in the lower wall, moves left and finishes direct; **Shiver Me Timbers** (VS 5a) gains a ledge to reach a steep upper wall, which is climbed by the right rib.

The remaining climbs on the ribs to the right are better tackled as boulder problems: **Cannon Fodder** (Font 5+) climbs the left rib of the overhanging prow; **Ready for Action** (Font 5) takes the overhang and right rib of the prow. On the narrow buttress to the right **Armada** (Font 4+) takes the short sharp arête then the left wall; **Finish the Bowls** (Font 4+) climbs the steep front of the narrow buttress via a sharp crack to a bold direct finish.

## Wall On Mirrored Water

A further 50m on, this excellent little buttress overhangs the path at the water's edge. Home to a clutch of great boulder problems that often save the crux for the top.

The left arête is (a) **Still Water** (Font 3+); (b) **Rough Water** (Font 5+) takes the scoop, the shelf and a precarious direct finish; (c) **Reflections** (Font 6b) uses a tiny pocket to gain the top edge. Step left to finish. The right arête gives (d) **Thin Ice** (Font 5), first on the left then the right with an awkward high step left to finish; (e) **Troubled Water** (Font 5+) takes the wall immediately right of the rib; The overhanging scooped wall just right holds (f) **Canada Dry** (Font 6c), climbed using a layaway pocket. The sandy bulge to the right is (g) **Murky Water** (Font 4+), trending right with a long reach to gain the top break. **Over the Looking Glass** (Font 6c) is an excellent traverse from the 'eyes' in the bulge near the start of *Rough Water*, reaching right then up to gain the central break, and followed to the finishing moves of *Canada Dry*. The low-level traverse is **Yorkshire Water** (Font 6b).

## Sunnyside Buttress

A further 40m right this tall buttress, higher up the slope, contains a prominent flake and is topped by a large tree. A neat area with some good climbs in the lower grades and a pleasant spot for evening soloing and for those getting acquainted with the crag's charms.

### 28 Sundown   D   6m   ★
The pleasant left arête, finishing right.
*Tony Barley (solo)   24th September 1989*

### 29 Sundial   S 4a   7m   ★
The scooped wall.
*Tony Barley (solo)   24th September 1989*

### 30 Sunstroke   VD   7m
The V-crack.
*Tony Barley (solo)   24th September 1989*

### 31 Winter Sunshine   MVS 4b   7m   ★
The blunt rib right of the V-crack to a ledge, finishing on the left or up right to the tree.
*Dave Musgrove (solo)   19th January 1991*

The Gemstones - **EAVESTONE**

### 32 Sun-Up  VS 4c  8m  ★
An excellent outing and well worth the star when clean. Enjoy the flake crack and step left to gain a ledge. Finish on the nose on the right or directly from the flake at 5a.
*Tony Barley (solo)  24th September 1989*

### 33 Sun Bird  HVS 5a  8m  ★
Climb the wall direct over two bulges to finish right of the tree.
*Tony Barley (solo)  24th September 1989*

### 34 Sun Bingo  S 4a  8m
Pushy at the grade. Climb to the overlap, move onto the right wall then up.
*Noel Curtis, Darren Wade, Jason Lister (all solo)  6th Aug 1994*

A mid-height right-to-left traverse of the buttress is possible, **Sunday Sun** (Font 4).

## The Gemstones
The next set of blocks to the right contain some excellent boulder problems. The scoop in the left wall of the first block is (h) **Bauble** (Font 4+). The left arête provides the best problem at the crag, (i) **Little Gem** (Font 6b) with the crux at the top; (j) **Too Much Too Young** (Font 7a) takes the wall between the arête and the obvious offwidth crack of (k) **The Flaw** (Font 5). The right arête of the first block, climbed on the right gives (l) **Flawless** (Font 5). Traversing the block is worth Font 5+. (m) **Rough Cut** (Font 5+) climbs the front face of the right-hand block finishing up the left arête; (n) **Little Sparkler** (Font 6b) takes the front face direct, moving right from the flake to a difficult finish.

The wall and scoop just right from a sitter is (o) **Pyrites** (Font 4+). Traversing the block is worth Font 4+. Another 60m to the right finds a collection of short rocks supporting a huge oak tree. The left block gives some problems, often dirty. The block to the right offers **I Need a Tree** (Font 5) up the diminutive but attractive arête on the left or right; (p) **Oakey Kokey** (Font 5) climbs the wall below the oak tree; (q) **Beech Peach** (Font 5+) climbs the overhanging block at its highest point just left of the beech tree. It's possible to climb just left of this, **Grove Hell** (Font 6c), to an unnerving grovel finish.

Follow the path to a wooden boathouse by the lake and thrash up the steep slope to seek out the following area.

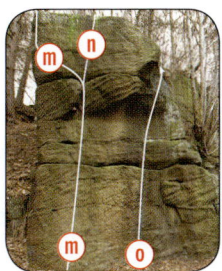

*Almscliff to Slipstones*

Jamie Moss mirrored high up on **Oubliette** (E2 5b). Page 425.
Photo: Jude Lane

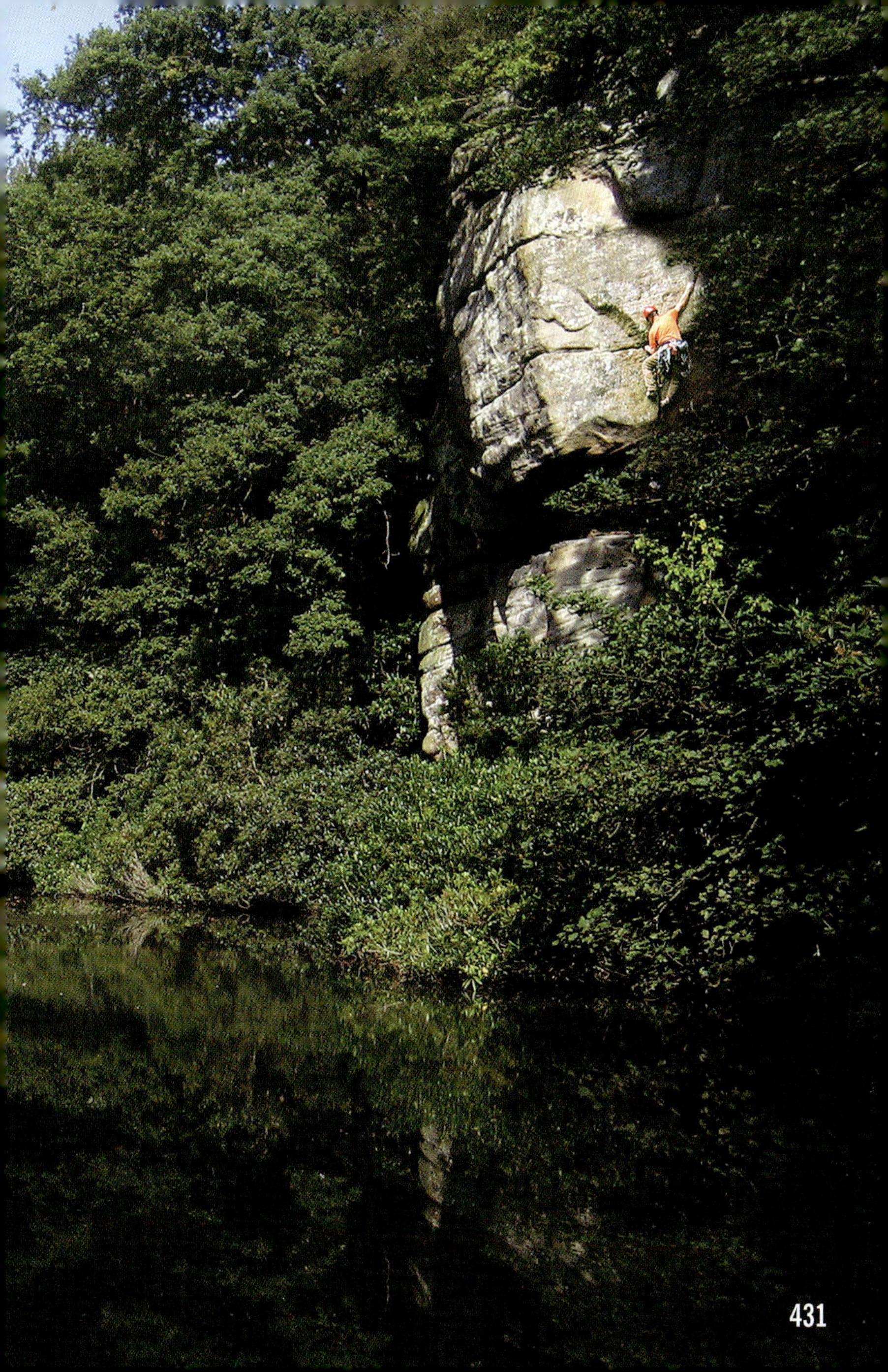

# EAVESTONE - Boathouse Bluff

## Boathouse Bluff
A solid chunk of clean gritstone with an alluring highball challenge.

**35 Strange Attractor** E3 6a  6m  ☆☆
Gaining the undercut flake is not easy, leaving it feels committing. Gain the high sidepull and finish on rounded ledges. Highball Font 6b.
*Kim Greenald  15th March 1990*

**36 Pebbledash** E4 6c  9m  ☆
A tendon-ripping pull on pebbles to the horizontal break. Traverse right to make a precarious mantel onto the nose.
*Kim Greenald  15th March 1990*

**37 Heave Ho** E2 5c  10m
Stretch for the handrail from the obvious pocket and traverse round the arête until it is possible to stand on the wall. Climb direct, passing a pocket, to a rounded finish. A direct and gymnastic start to reach the pocket is possible at around Font 6c.
*Tony Barley (solo)  20th March 1990*

**38 Pushing the Boat Out** E3 5c  10m
Starts around the arête. Follow the wide crack and then traverse left past the pocket to the nose and finish via a precarious mantelshelf.
*Dave Musgrove, Tony Barley  12th March 1990*

**39 Starboard Crack** S 4b  6m
The wide crack on the right.
*Tony Barley (solo)  19th November 1989*

A fight through the undergrowth to the right for a few metres reveals more clean and climbable rock.

## The Crevasse Area
On the low walls, to the left of, and abutting the routes is an old beech tree (used for ascents and descents) and a few boulder problems. **Middle Wall** (Font 3) is the wall just right of the tree descent. **Up to the Tree** (Font 2+) climbs the arête on its left to the little tree. The wall, **Right of Arête** is Font 3, and the featured wall between the arête and what is known as Sharp Corner, is **Side Wall** (Font 3). Other eliminates are possible here. The roof and walls to the right have seen a recent revival with some of the best hard problems in the area on superb rock that remains dry in all but the heaviest rain.

**40 The Fabulous Number 2**  Font 7c
Traverse the lip of the roof from left-to-right passing the large pocket to finish up the groove.
*Dave Sutcliffe  5th December 2011*

**41 Digital Delirium**  Font 7c+
Classic. Sit-down start at the slot in the back of the roof. Climb powerfully out to the lip and make a big move left to the large pocket. Use this, brute force and tiny crimps to gain a standing position on the lip. Reach the break then step left to finish in the big hole.
*Dave Sutcliffe  2nd January 2012*

**42 Sky Diamond**  Font 7c
A contender for the best line at the crag. Sit-down start from the slot in the back of the roof and climb out to the lip and the two finger pocket. From here style straight up the groove to the break. Photo on page 437.
*Dave Sutcliffe  12th November 2011*

**43 Good Friday** E3 5c  8m  ☆
Use the pockets to surmount the roof and traverse left to reach the gift of a pocket. Power up left to finish.
*Dave Musgrove (solo)  13th April 1990*

**44 Leaving the Bergschrund** HVS 5c  6m  ☆
Start as for *Good Friday* but continue up the groove and over the bulge to an easier, slabby finish.
*Tony Barley (solo)  19th November 1989*

Boathouse Bluff - **Eavestone**

### 45 Get a Grip  Font 7a
Sit-down start from the two good holds on the flake. Reach out right to the arête then climb straight out to the big pocket. Finish standing in the pocket or up *Das Kleiner Sprung*.
*Dave Sutcliffe  12th November 2011*

### 46 Das Kleiner Sprung  HVS 5c  6m
The hanging arête on its right. Jump from the ground using the big hold on the arête to the horizontal edge and campus/scrabble and hump embarrassingly up.
*John Hunt (solo)  2nd February 2011*

### 47 Glacier Apron  VS 5a  6m  ☆
Start right of the arête and climb slabby breaks to the top.
*Tony Barley (solo)  19th November 1989*

### 48 Dew Drop  Font 7a+
A direct and independent start to *Touching The Void*. Pull onto the tiny edge with your right hand then rock up left to a poor sloping hold. Pop right to the good slot then join and finish as for *Touching The Void*.
*Richard Mallinson  12th November 2011*

### 49 Touching The Void  E2 6a  7m  ★★
An excellent and stiff boulder problem just up to the sanctuary of the tree! Climb the centre of the crevasse wall to reach the dimples (tree runner only). For the E2 tick, move left to finish just right of another tree.
*Dave Musgrove, Tony Barley  24th April 1990,*

### 50 Diamond Lights  Font 7c
Another great problem. Master the centre of the steep slab on the left wall of the gully. Start at the large pocket and fathom out the sequence up the wall which appears easier than the grade suggests. Finish on the left side of the tree or drop.
*Steve Dunning  January 2012*

**Tree Slots** (Font 5+) climbs slots up the wall a few metres right.

# EAVESTONE - The Serac

Right of the Crevasse is a large block known as **The Serac**. The first problem lies on the slab opposite *Tree Slots*. **Dick Vierra** (Font 6c) takes the green font-like slab trending left without using the arête; **Daddies Source** (Font 6c+) climbs the same slab, finishing right without the use of the crack. The arête, cracks and chips give some good easier problems. **Glissade** (D) climbs the chimney, moves left along the ledge and around the rib to a slabby finish (a finish right of the rib is 5a); **Ice Dance** (HVS 5b) steps left from the top of the chimney to climb the wall in line with the left end of a small overhang; **Cracked Ice** (HVS 5a) is the bulging crack moving right from the chimney; **Iced Diamond** (E1 5b) starts up the crack then continues right to the arête; (a) **Cream** (E2 6a) takes the blunt central arête direct from the prominent pocket; (b) **Hanging Serac** (E1 5b) climbs the right arête via pockets and a shallow ramp on its left to an awkward finish.

### 51 The Traverse  Font 6c+
Stonking. Start in the pocket then make a big move to the sloping break and traverse left to finish in the big pocket.
*Jim Davies  January 2012*

**Mystery Buttress** is the most overgrown and least attractive buttress of the crag. Cross the dam at the foot of the lower lake and follow a path down the valley for about 150m to a scramble down the bank. Cross the stream and up the other side. **Narrow Slab** (VD) takes the cracked slab on the left; **Mystery Man** (VS 5a) climbs up right of the chimney-wide break in the top wall and moves left to finish up the chimney; **Central Chimney** (VD) starts left of the cave and climbs rightwards to finish up a chimney corner; **Tiptoe** (VD) climbs up to the right of the cave and overhang to bridge against a large detached block before moving left over some doubtful blocks to gain and finish up *Central Chimney*; **Checkmate** (HS 4b) takes the crack in the right wall. To the left of Mystery Buttress on an indistinct path which leads through some boggy ground back towards the lower lake you will pass a small block with E8 chiselled on its right side - **Microchip** (VS 4b) takes the obvious arête.

## The Lower Lake – Southern Bank
From the bottom of the upper lake a subsidiary path leads down on the right-hand side of the stream to gain the southern banks of the lower lake. *The buttresses are described from right-to-left.* See crag map on page 424. The small steep and very overgrown buttress on the right is **Kloof Crag**. **African Skies** (S 4a) climbs the gully wall just left of the arête; **Mhlabatini** (HVS 5c) uses the undercut left arête to climb the bulge direct to finish on the left; **Tonquani** (VS 5b) starts just right of the arête to surmount the bulge and climb the upper wall direct; **Umkomeni** (MVS 4c) climbs from the letter-box slot up the wall direct on widely-spaced breaks; **Sekorora** (HS 4b) takes the rectangular recess in the wall to finish adjacent to the rightward slanting ramp

## Jib Sail
After 150m struggle up the steep slope to reach the prominent plinth of **Jib Sail,** home to one of the finest Severes in Yorkshire town. Descent is usually down the route *Jib Sail* (Diff) and those climbing *Spinnaker* may wish to check this first.

### 52 Wildcat  VS 4b  9m  ☆
From the foot of *Spinnaker* climb the front of the pillar just left of the upper part of *Bowsprit*.
*David Roberts (solo)  27th July 1999*

### 53 Spinnaker  S 4a  18m  ★★★
When in condition this is a superb climb in an exposed position. Start on the extreme left end of the tower face and traverse right to a ledge above the overhang. Move up and step right to gain another ledge below a shallow corner and sail direct to the top. Much harder when damp.
*Tony Barley, Dave Musgrove  10th August 1989*

Jib Sail - **Eavestone**

#### 54 Bowsprit  VS 5a   12m  ☆
Start right of *Spinnaker* to gain the ledge on that route. Move up and left to follow the edge as closely as possible.
*Dave Musgrove, Tony Barley   10th August 1989*

#### 55 Atlantic Voyager  E2 5c   13m  ☆
Boldly climb the groove and finish direct.
*Dave Musgrove, Tony Barley   31st May 1990*

#### 56 Jigger Me Fingers  E3 5c   11m  ☆
Climbers with little stamina need not apply. Start as for *Spinnaker* then make bold moves across the scoop to gain and follow a thin break all the way to the arête.
*Phillipe Osborne, David Roberts   27th July 1999*

#### 57 Master Bates Left-Hand  E3 6a   12m  ☆
Gain the break beneath the right-angled triangular roof. Place good gear and reach the wall to move up left to ledges and an easier finish. (c) **Master Bates Right-Hand** (E3 6a) starts as for the *Left-Hand* but when established on the wall span immediately right to the arête and climb to the tree.
*Phillipe Osborne, David Roberts   27th July 1999 (both routes)*

#### 58 Up She Rises  E4 6b   10m  ★★
A stern line with a broad reach. Start from the far left on the back wall and make bold moves left to gain the overhanging arête which is climbed direct. One of the very few lines that stays clean. (d) **Seaman Staines** (E5 6b, ★) follow *Up She Rises* to the ledge and place a crucial Friend before shooting off diagonally left across the headwall to gain the top of a groove. Finish direct to an insecure top-out. Hanging belay advisable.
*Phillipe Osborne, David Roberts   3rd July 1999* ✦

#### 59 Yardarm  VD   9m
Start as for *Jib Sail* and climb diagonally to the left.
*Tony Barley (solo)   24th September 1989*

#### 60 Jib Sail  D   6m  ★
From the right end of the back wall meander left and back right to the top. The normal (but very tricky) descent route.
*Dave Musgrove, Tony Barley   10th August 1989*

*The Boathouse by the Lower Lake*

Almscliff to Slipstones

# EAVESTONE - Galleon Tower

## Galleon Tower

The overgrown Galleon Tower is in two distinct tiers with softer yellow rock at mid-height. The routes are described from left-to-right. Starting with the lower tier, **Captain Pugwash** (HVD) takes a short crack system in the lower left wall and then the upper wall just left of the capped corner of *Spanish Main*; (a) **Spanish Main** (E1 5b, 5a) is a 30m two-pitch route which starts below the left rib of the lower tier at a tiny shallow corner. It climbs the corner, rib and wall to the right on breaks to the terrace, just left of the stump (belay). From here it moves up to a capped corner at the left-end of the upper tier, swings right and pulls up onto the slab before moving right again to a steep crack to the tree; (b) **Galleon Tower** (HVS 5a, 5a) is another mighty ramble (32m) and climbs the corner below the left rib of the lower tier and exits left up the blunt rib to reach the terrace (and belay). It continues to the capped corner and swings right to the slab, crossing this to reach the top on the right-hand side; (c) **Treasure Island** (E2 5b, ☆☆), is one of the best E2s on the crag but needs a good digging out to return to its former glory. It climbs the prominent vertical crack to the horizontal break, steps left and then finishes straight up the centre of the wall; (d) **Jolly Roger** (VS 4b) goes from the lowest point of the buttress to follow a rounded ramp diagonally right, then back left; **Long John Sliver** (VS 5a) takes the short wall just left of the blunt rib to wide ledges before moving up and right from the top ledge to good finishing holds; **Banana Boat** (HVS 5b) tackles the blunt rib and scoop left of the easy groove and continues over ledges to finish up the rightward curving groove; **The Pirates Ear** (E1 5b) climbs just right of the large chockstone to the 'ear' in the undercut wall and a bold finish via a pocket and small holds; **Brave New World** (VS 4c) climbs the short flake to a ledge and continues above moving right to finish; **Savage** (Font 6a) climbs the right rib direct using a small finger flake and finishes on the front face; The scooped wall just right of the right rib of the lower tier is **Director** (Font 4+).

On the upper tier, **Swashbuckler** (HVS 5a) takes the yellow wall above the tree on the terrace to the roof just right of the capped corner and onto the upper slab to finish direct, left of the tree; **Roses of Picardy** (E4 5c) moves past the suspect flake in the roof on the right-hand side of the front face of the upper tier; (e) **Trapeze** (HVS 5a) tackles the left rib of the chimney to a niche just right of the upper arête then swings boldly round the nose and up into the short bottomless corner to finish direct; (f) **Keelhaul** (HVS 5b) goes up the undercut crack from a cave in the right wall to a corner then up and left, across the wall, to a wide ledge which is traversed to the exposed buttress front and direct to the top; (g) **Gangplank** (S 4a) gains and crosses a slab leftwards on suspect rock to finish up a chimney; (h) **Bilgewater** (VD) The short sharp corner high up towards the back of the tower.

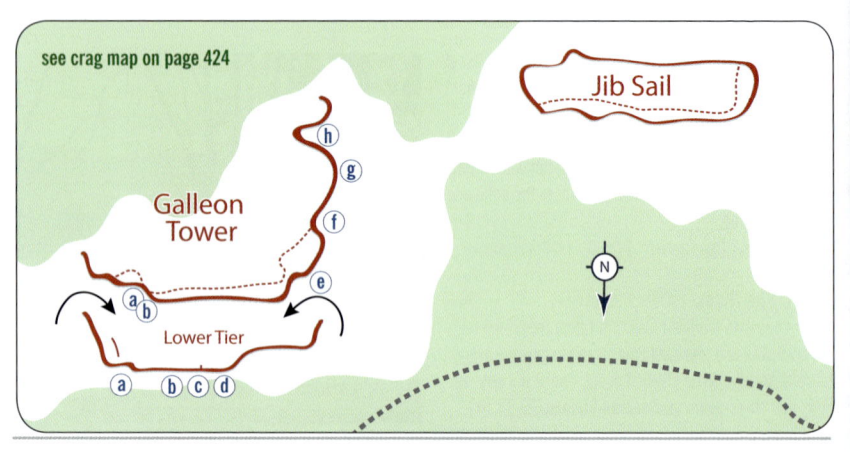

436     Yorkshire Gritstone

Dave Sutcliffe turning the lip of the awesome **Sky Diamond** (Font 7c). Page 432.
Photo: Mark Credie

# EAVESTONE - The Eavestone

### The Eavestone
An impressive, imposing hulk of rock, the scale of which is only appreciated from up close. This is the home of the biggest and baddest routes; here be monsters.

*The Eavestone has arguably the best concentration of quality routes at the crag - but only when in good condition. Many of the following routes warrant two to three stars when clean and all were thoroughly scrubbed-up in 2012. Get them done quick or be prepared to give some a dusting down at the start of each season.*

See map on page 440. The descent route begins at the top of *Evenso* and takes a diagonal line to the foot of *Stonerag*.

**61 Under the Eaves**  E2 5b  11m  ☆
Bold. Begin left of *Evenso*. Pull over the first overlap to reach two pockets. Move up and then right onto the slab under the overhang and gain the ledge above.
*Dave Musgrove (solo)  16th April 1990*

**62 The Garden of Eden**  HS 4b  14m
From *Evenso* move left across a groove and up and left via pockets to a slabby corner. Up this to exit direct to the tree.
*Dave Musgrove (solo)  30th May 1991*

**63 Evenso**  HVS 5a  10m  ☆
A quality pitch despite the lack of protection. Climb the rib boldly to a steep but positive finish.
*Tony Barley, John Williams  April 1967*

**64 Eavesdropper**  HVS 5b  10m  ☆☆
Very satisfying. The slabby rib just left of the left arête. Often green but a fine and well protected climb. The right side of the arête is **Lib Dem Arête** (E3 5c).
*Tony Barley, John Williams  April 1967* ✦

**65 Crazy Paver**  E2 5c  16m
A wonderfully meandering line. Climb just right of the arête to gain a hand-traverse line leading right to ledges just left of the hollow flake. Step up and left to climb the wall above the overlap, just right of the thin crack. From the start of *Eavestone Wall*, (a) **The Madcap Laughs** (E4 6c), climbs up and left to gain the handrail, hollow flake and resting place of *Crazy Paver*. It follows the blunt rib above on undercuts to a long reach to gain a good ledge before stepping left and finishing direct. A high side-runner in a crack that comes down from *Crazy Paver* is used at this grade.
*Tony Barley, Dave Musgrove (both led)  28th Sept 1989* ✦

**66 Eavestone Wall**  E3 6b  16m  ☆☆☆
Just brilliant. Boldly climb up the centre of the wall on rounded breaks to a ledge just right of a hollow flake. Place sound gear, you'll need it. Make very reachy/dynamic moves to the thin crackline up and right which leads to a rightwards finish. A three star classic which deserves more attention to return it to its rightful place.
*Tony Barley 20th May 1989; FFA. Kim Greenald, Paul Dawson 28th Apr 1990*

## The Eavestone - EAVESTONE

**67 Eavestone Crack** E4 6a 14m ☆☆
A cracker that separates the men from the boys. Mantel to the shelf and climb the wall to gain a good hold below the bulge. Move left to fight up the crack on strenuous jams.
*Dave Musgrove, Tony Barley 12th August 1989*

**68 Genesis** E5 6b 15m ☆☆☆
A brutal classic. Gain the sloping shelf from the right and move left to a flake. Climb up and right to gain the base of the crack. Place gear and go. Remain vigilant to the very top and whoop excessively if you have any strength left when you get there.
*Dave Musgrove, Tony Barley 8th June 1990* ✦

**69 Life Begins At Forty** E6 6c 22m
Another classic Eavestone big hitter which tackles the huge overhanging wall, to the right of *Genesis*, from left-to-right. Start up the crack in the hanging rib and move right, across the bulge, to a flake and traverse further to a smaller flake above the bulge which leads to a steep finish.
*Bob Smith (unseconded) 27th April 1991* ✦

**70 Stonechat Ramp** E3 5b 11m
Start round the back of The Eavestone. A bold, technical climb which stays close to the line of the ramp and avoids some of the long reaches of the original line of *Stonechat*.
*Robin Barley, Tony Barley 14th May 1990*

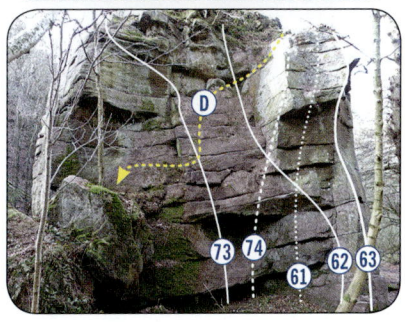

**71 Stonechat** E1 5c 10m
Climb directly up the wall just right of the slight ramp. Protection in the crack of *Stonerag* is allowed at this grade, as is minimal assistance from it for those with short arms.
*Dave Musgrove, Tony Barley, Dave Musgrove Jnr 10th May 1989*

**72 Stonerag** S 4a 10m
The south-east arête. Climb the wall just left of the rib and gain a short crack to the top of a pedestal to finish left.
*Tony Barley, John Williams April 1967*

**73 Forbidden Fruit** VS 4c 12m
From below the bulge move up left past a flake in the roof. Climb the slab direct to ledges and traverse left to finish on the rib.
*Dave Musgrove (solo) 30th May 1991*

**74 Eavestone Eliminate** E1 5c 12m
Start below the largest bulge on the back wall and move up right to cross the roof to gain the slabby groove. Step out right onto the hanging rib and 'barn door' for the top.
*Dave Musgrove (solo) 30th May 1991*

# EAVESTONE - The Wedge

## The Wedge
A prominent buttress with a sharp clean arête just 30m left of The Eavestone. Perpetually striped in woodland green but the good routes are on solid rock and tend to remain clean.

### 75 **Wedge Iron**  HVS 5a  9m
The left wall direct, just left of the cutaway scoop.
*Dave Musgrove, Tony Barley  19th September 1989*

### 76 **Gorilla**  VS 4c  12m
Climb the cutaway scoop to gain a handrail. Traverse right until it is possible to stand on the ledge and climb the cracks and blocks above, moving left.
*Tony Barley, Robin Barley, Dennis Gray  7th February 1966*

### 77 **The Thin End**  HVS 5a  10m  ★
The main arête climbed on the left. Escape directly over the perched blocks to finish on the nose at the very top.
*Tony Barley, Robin Barley  1965*

### 78 **Fat Chance**  E3 5c  11m  ★★
Superb, but the grade is inversely proportional to your reach. The main arête climbed on the right-hand side. Shorties really, really deserve the tick!
*Dave Musgrove Jnr, Dave Musgrove  18th April 1990*

### 79 **Wedgwood**  HVS 5a  12m  ★★
Solid and sustained. Climb the wall to the right of the wide green stripe to gain the ramp. Step right to the two thinner cracks in the upper wall and make haste for the top.
*Tony Barley, Robin Barley  21st April 1965*

### 80 **The Taper**  HS 4b  12m  ★
Climb the steep crack to the ramp on the left. Traverse this and gain the cracks just right of the arête.
*Tony Barley, John Williams  April 1967*

### 81 **The Heel**  S 4a  10m  ★
Climb leftwards out of the overhung bay to gain the main right-hand crackline and climb it direct by bridging.
*Robin Barley, Tony Barley  21st April 1965*

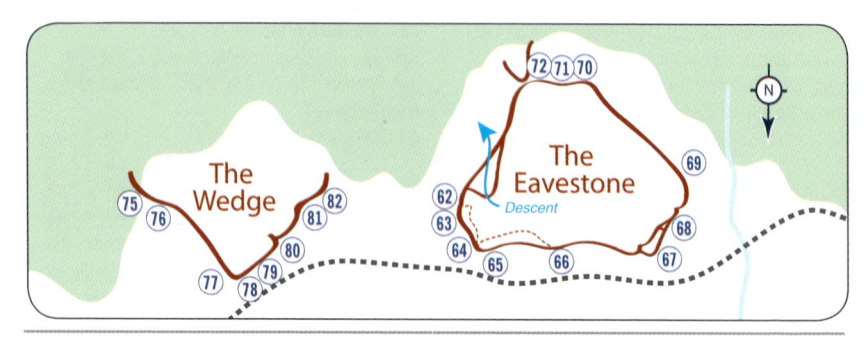

## The Prow - EAVESTONE

#### 82 Bunkered  E2 6a  9m  ★
From the overhung bay gain a corner above. Step left out of this and climb the rib to the tree.
*Tony Barley, Dave Musgrove  19th August 1989*

To the right of *Bunkered* past the tree-filled gully is a shorter wall containing two problems. **Rib Tickler** (Font 5) climbs the short stepped rib from the right. The steep wall just left of the rib, **Treebeard** (Font 6a), needs a long reach to start.

Right again a thin crack in a corner gives **Wellington Crack II** (S 4b) which tackles the thin crack with a long reach up left for a good hold; **Secret Obsession** (HVS 5a) climbs the impending groove in the centre of the wall from clean ledges down and right from the corner; **Purely Esoteric** (VS 5a) is the wall right of the groove to the beech tree on top; **The Fissure Barley** (HS 4b) slimes up the offwidth crack.

To locate the next buttress follow a narrow path from the foot of *The Wedge*, passing under Alley-Palley Wall to reach the impressive buttress of **The Prow**. See map on page 424.

#### 83 Hurricane  E1 5b  10m
A direct line up the slabby wall on the left of the buttress.
*Dave Musgrove (solo)  14th September 1990* ✦

#### 84 Prowler  HVS 5b  14m  ☆
Climb the left rib to the roof. Pull round left and via a long reach gain the ledge above the bulge.
*Tony Barley, Dave Musgrove  6th August 1989*

#### 85 Prow Crack  S 4c  11m
The oblique crack leading up right of the overhang is awkward at the start. It is easier to traverse in from the right (4a).
*Tony Barley  12th September 1990*

#### 86 Swinging Free  E2 5b  18m  ☆☆
Take the *Spitfire* crackline to the right of the overhangs then make an audaciously bold and wild right-to-left traverse under the roof to the relative 'Thank God' security of a narrow platform and an easier finish.
*Tony Barley, Robin Barley  27th August 1965*

#### 87 Spitfire  VS 5a  12m  ☆
Follow the crackline to a ledge. Traverse left above the main overhang to the arête and a slabby finish.
*Dave Musgrove (solo)  14th September 1990* ✦

#### 88 The Root to Success  E2 5c  12m  ☆
From the traverse ledge of *Swinging Free* climb the centre of the overhanging wall to a substantial tree root.
*Phillipe Osborne, David Roberts  27th July 1999*

Higher up the bank and 20m to the right is **Alley-Palley Wall**. The obvious chimney line is **Chiminalley** (S 4a).

#### 89 Officer Dibble  E1 5c  9m
The bulging wall between *Chiminalley* and *Alleycat* is climbed direct.
*Dave Musgrove, Steve Webster  3rd April 1991*

#### 90 Alleycat  HVS 5b  9m  ☆
The steep wide crackline with a difficult move right to finish.
*Tony Barley, K. Robson  6th August 1967*

#### 91 Alleycracker  HVS 5b  9m  ☆
The sustained right-hand, thinner crackline.
*Tony Barley, Dave Musgrove  6th August 1989*

# Eavestone - Alley-Palley Wall

## 95 Top Cat  HVS 5a   12m
Climb the left rib to the top and traverse the handrail rightwards until a step up can be made to ledges to finish.
*Dave Musgrove (solo)  20th September 1991*

## 96 Alligator  E3 6b   8m  ☆
Start at a two-finger pocket just left of a short corner and climb the wall to a projecting nose of rock. A serious Font 7a highball requiring several mats and dedicated spotters.
*Andy Moss (unseconded)  August 1997*

## 97 Crocodile  E4 6b   9m  ☆
Climb the short corner to a flake and the overlap. Pull right to a good flat hold and slap up to the break. Again, a serious Font 7a highball.
*Andy Moss (unseconded)  August 1997*

### Tin Pan Alley
Walk left up a ramp above **The Prow** for about 50m to find this large, severely undercut buttress. If the area looks clean and dry, take particular care to check the finishes before setting out on a ground-up attempt. On the extreme left is a bay from which a prominent traverse along a large smooth flake leads out right.

## 98 Jumping Jack  HVS 5b   8m
A direct line up the overhanging scoop left of the flake.
*Tony Barley (solo)  27th June 1991*

## 99 Dragonfly  HVS 5a   11m
Traverse the flake until just before the end and make a long reach up to reach a higher handrail leading back left to a superb jug and a direct finish to the tree.
*Tony Barley (solo)  15th June 1991*

## 100 Ride the Magic Dragon  HVS 5b   10m
Traverse right along the top of the flake to reach a good ledge. Step up to good holds and an easier finish.
*Tony Barley (solo)  15th June 1991*

## 101 Puff  E1 5b   11m
From the cave climb the strenuous crack then the wall above, just right of the curving overlap.
*Tony Barley, Dave Musgrove  15th June 1991*

## 92 Going Catatonic  E1 5c   9m  ☆
The wall right of *Alleycracker*.
*Steve Webster, Dave Musgrove  3rd April 1991*

## 93 Backalley  S 4b   8m
The front of the right arête, moving over or round the big block.
*Dave Musgrove (solo)  6th August 1989*

## 94 The Ginnel  HS 4b   7m
The side wall, just right of the arête, is climbed with a step right at half-height to finish at a slim ash tree.
*Dave Musgrove (solo)  20th September 1991*

Across a descent gully is a steep wall with a prominent horizontal crack at three-quarters height. This gives…

Yorkshire Gritstone

## Tin Pan Alley - EAVESTONE

**102 Where He Fell**  E2 5c  13m  ☆☆
A fine climb when clean. Bridge up out of the cave onto the traverse line of *Dragonslayer*. Climb the middle of the wall to the terminus of a left-to-right diagonal crack. Gain a short flake above with difficulty to an insecure finish.
*Phillipe Osborne, David Roberts  26th June 1999* ✦

**103 Dragonslayer**  E5 6a  14m  ☆☆☆
A technical and strenuous testpiece. Bridge up out of the cave and traverse right with feet just above the overhang to gain and climb the groove to the horizontal break. Follow the groove and then finish to the left of the tree.
*Dave Musgrove, Nigel Baker (both led)  4th August 1991*

**104 The Meaning of Life**  E2 5c  13m  ☆☆
Pull out from the niche and traverse left with feet just above the roof to a thin crack. Use this to gain the square ledge above and contemplate your fate before continuing boldly past a crucial pocket to the top. A gem when dirt-free.
*Dave Musgrove, Tony Barley  18th June 1991*

**105 Here There Be Dragons**  E3 5b  12m  ☆
A compelling line with great climbing but sparse protection. Move left from the niche and boldly climb the open groove on positive holds. The wet mulchy drop-zone is an advantage.
*Dave Musgrove (solo)  7th May 1991* ✦

**106 Tin**  VS 4c  11m
The left-hand of the twin cracks emerging from the top of the niche.
*Tony Barley, K. Robson  6th August 1967*

**107 Pan**  VS 5a  11m
The right-hand twin crack.
*Tony Barley, K. Robson  6th August 1967*

**108 Pendragon**  E2 6a  10m
Climb the wall, stepping left and up to gain the right side of the cave, and follow the final crack of *Pan*.
*Paul Clarke (solo)  16th March 2012*

**109 Don't Worry, I'm a Nurse**  E4 6b  10m  ☆
A thin crack in the wall leads desperately to slots and a step left to a ledge. Finish back right to the roots of the tree.
*Steve Webster, Pete Lawson  27th April 1991*

**110 Roots of All Evil**  E1 5b  11m
Haul over the cave roof to gain the diagonal crack and follow it to the big tree. Step left holding the substantial root and take the slotted wall to the top.
*Paul Clarke, Dave Musgrove  29th March 2012*

Almscliff to Slipstones   **443**

# EAVESTONE - First Ascent Information & Graded List

## Eavestone Boulder Field
The sheltered dry valley that runs north-west from below the Eavestone parking spot is home to a boulder field which was recorded by Tony Barley for the Wild Bouldering guide in 1997. It's a pleasant spot in rough pasture with easy access and good landings. The 28 recorded problems range from Font 2 to Font 5+. This is **not** on access land but climbers have not been challenged previously. If asked to leave, please do so politely.

---

## Further First Ascent Information (✦)
The boulder problems are largely the work of Tony Barley and Dave Musgrove c1989/91.

**African Skies:** *Dave Musgrove (solo) 13th June 1990*
**Banana Boat**: *Tony Barley (solo) 14th April 1991*
**Battlement**: *Tony Barley and Anthony Roche traversed in to the easier upper arête from Castellan in 1971. Barley named the line but Musgrove soloed the first ascent in 1990 as it is now described and most commonly climbed.*
**Bilgewater:** *Dave Musgrove 11th April 1981*
**Brave New World**: *Tony Barley and Tim Barley 20th April 1991*
**Captain Pugwash**: *Tony Barley, Barry Groves 16th April 1990*
**Central Chimney:** *Peter Checkland January 1962*
**Chain Mail:** *Tony Barley (solo) 23rd June 1990*
**Checkmate:** *Robin Barley, Tony Barley 27th August 1965 (but possibly the line of Chequers Crack (Peter Checkland, January 1962)).*
**Chiminalley**: *Dave Musgrove (solo) 6th August 1989*
**Cracked Ice:***Tony Barley (solo) 8th May 1991*
**Cream**: *Tony Barley (solo) 30th May 1991*
**Daddies Source:** *Mark Credie    January 2012*
**Dance on White Horses:** *Tony Barley (solo) 5th July 1990*
**Dick Vierra** : *Jim Davies   January 2012*
**Don't Pay the Ferryman:** *Tony Barley, Dave Musgrove (alt leads) 17th April 1990*
**Eavestone Wall:** *On the first ascent it was started from the left and a sling was used for aid.*
**Galleon Tower:** *Tony Barley, Robin Barley 21st May 1965 (P1), 15th March 1990 (P2).*
**Gangplank**: *Tony Barley, Nina Barley 10th September 1989*
**Genesis:** *A major prize - climbed at 6.30am before work on a Friday to beat an imagined weekend raid by an interested On The Edge team.*
**Glissade**: *Tony Barley (solo) 11th May 1991*
**Grove Hell**: *Phillipe Osborne Jan 2012*
**Hanging Serac**: *Tony Barley (solo) 8th April 1990*
**Here There Be Dragons:** *After cleaning the route Musgrove was unable to return to lead it for some days. So he boldly soloed it in fading light conditions.*
**Hurricane, Spitfire:** *Climbed on the 50th anniversary of the Battle of Britain. Bold solos above an unthinkable landing.*
**Ice Dance**: *Tony Barley, Robin Barley 18th May 1991*
**Iced Diamond:** *Tony Barley, Robin Barley 18th May 1991*
**Life Begins At Forty:** *The hardest route on the crag, completed only after two ground falls.*
**Jolly Roger:** *Tony Barley, Dave Musgrove, Dave Musgrove Jnr 31st May 1990*
**Keelhaul**: *Tony Barley, Steve Jenkins 13th September 1989*
**Lib Dem Arête**: *Paul Clarke, Ben Clarke, 28th March 2012*
**Long John Sliver**: *Tony Barley (solo) 30th April 1991*
**Lower Sail**: *Tony Barley 10th May 1989*
**(The) Madcap Laughs:** *Paul Clarke 13th April 2012*
**Mhlabatini**: *Tony Barley (solo) 13th June 1990*
**Microchip**: *Tony Barley, Robin Barley 27th August 1965*
**Moat-ivation**: *Dave Musgrove, Paul Farrish 26th Feb 2012 (FRA)*
**Mystery Man**: *Tony Barley, Steve Jenkins 6th August 1988*
**Narrow Slab:** *Peter Checkland January 1962*
**Purely Esoteric:** *Dave Musgrove (solo) 10th July 1991*
**Ripples**: *Tony Barley, Robin Barley 21st April 1965*
**Roses of Picardy**: *Steve Findlay, Chris Shorter 1992*
**Sea Dog**: *Johnny Cutliffe, Mick Darfield 19th April 1997*
**Sea of Tranquillity**: *Dave Musgrove, Andy Wild, Tony Barley 17th April 1990*
**Seaman Staines:** *Phillipe Osborne (unseconded) 23rd August 2009. 10 years on from 'Up She Rises', a 50th birthday E5 variation that just merits the grade.*
**Secret Obsession**: *Dave Musgrove (solo) 27th June 1991*
**Sekorora**: *Dave Musgrove (solo) 13th June 1990*
**Shiver Me Timbers**: *Tony Barley (solo) 16th June 1990*
**Spanish Main**: *Tony Barley (P1) 20th March 1990 (P2) Dave Musgrove Jnr 10th May 1989*
**Sunday Sun**: *John Hunt 26th February 2012*
**Swashbuckler**: *Dave Musgrove (solo) 11th April 1991*
**The Fissure Barley**: *Tony Barley (solo) 5th June 1991*
**The Pirates Ear**: *Tony Barley, Dave Musgrove 11th April 1991*
**The Plunge**: *Johnny Cutliffe, Mick Darfield 19th April 1997*
**Tiptoe** : *Peter Checkland January 1962*

# First Ascent Information & Graded List - EAVESTONE

**Tonquani**: *Tony Barley (solo) 13th June 1990*
**Too Much Too Young**: *by Tony Simpson solo 25th July 1993*
**Trapeze**: *Tony Barley, Steve Jenkins 13th September 1989*
**Treasure Island**: *Tony Barley, Dave Musgrove 1st May 1990*
**Tree Slots**: *John Hunt 2nd Feb 2011*
**Umkomeni**: *Tony Barley (solo) 13th June 1990*
**Upper Sail**: *Tony Barley 10th May 1989*

**Watery Grave:** *Tony Barley, Robin Barley 29th July 1965*
**Wellington Crack II**: *Dave Musgrove (solo - in wellies) 18th June 1991*
**Where He Fell**: *The name pays homage to Dragonslayer, but in reality due to a dirty top and a rather surprised belayer, Osborne fell the whole length of the route.*

## GRADED LIST

**Routes**

**E6**
Life Begins At Forty (6c)

**E5**
Seaman Staines (6b)
Genesis (6b)
Dragonslayer (6a)

**E4**
Pebbledash (6c)
The Madcap Laughs (6c)
Don't Worry I'm A Nurse (6b)
Up She Rises (6b)
Eavestone Crack (6a)
Crocodile (6b)
Roses of Picardy (5c)

**E3**
Eavestone Wall (6b)
Master Bates Left-Hand (6a)
Master Bates Right-Hand (6a)
Watery Grave (5c)
Pushing The Boat Out (5c)
Battlement (6a)
Strange Attractor (6a)
Hallmark (5c)
Jigger Me Fingers (5c)
Here There Be Dragons (5c)
Alligator (6b)
The Gatekeeper (6b)
Good Friday (5c)
Lib Dem Arête (5c)
Fat Chance (5c)
Stonechat Ramp (5b)

**E2**
Swinging Free (5b)
Cream (6a)
Touching The Void (6a)
Bunkered (6a)

Pendragon (6a)
Atlantic Voyager (5c)
Heave Ho (5c)
Where He Fell (5c)
Excalibur (5c)
The Meaning of Life (5c)
Crazy Paver (5c)
The Root to Success (5c)
Under The Eaves (5b)
Treasure Island (5b)
The Alamo (5b)
The King Of The Castle (5c)
Dance on White Horses (5c)
The Dirty Rascal (5c)
Oubliette (5b)

**E1**
Eavestone Eliminate (5c)
Officer Dibble (5c)
Going Catatonic (5c)
Stonechat (5c)
Spanish Main (5b)
Merlon (5a)
The Pirates Ear (5b)
Apache (5a)
Crenellation (5a)
Iced Diamond (5b)
Puff (5b)
Roots of All Evil (5b)
Hanging Serac (5b)
Hurricane (5b)
Rampart (5b)

**HVS**
Mhlabatini (5b)
Ditch (5c)
Das Kleiner Sprung (5c)
Prowler (5b)
Scalp (5c)
For Keepsake (5b)
Alleycracker (5b)
Ride The Magic Dragon (5b)
Banana Boat (5b)

Keelhaul (5b)
Alleycat (5b)
Castellan (5b)
Galleon Tower (5a)
Wedge Iron (5a)
The Thin End (5a)
Leaving The Bergschrund (5c)
Sea Of Tranquillity (5b)
Ripples (5a)
Ice Dance (5b)
Trapeze (5a)
Jumping Jack (5b)
Wedgewood (5a)
Eavesdropper (5a)
Cracked Ice (5a)
Don't Pay the Ferryman (5a)
Top Cat (5a)
Swashbuckler (5a)
Secret Obsession (5a)
Evenso (5a)
Sun Bird (5a)
Dragonfly (5a)

**VS**
Pan (5a)
Tonquani (5b)
Lower Sail (5a)
Upper Sail (5a)
Spitfire (5a)
Shiver Me Timbers (5a)
Brave New World (4c)
Tin (4c)
Long John Sliver (5a)
Microchip (4b)
Mystery Man (5a)
Bowsprit (5a)
Gorilla (5c)
Stockade (4c)
Forbidden Fruit (4c)
Purely Esoteric (4c)
Sea Dog (4c)
Glacier Apron (5a)
Machicolation (4c)
Sun-Up (4c)

Look Out Below (4c)
Jolly Roger (4b)
Wildcat (4b)
Chain Mail (4b)

**MVS**
Winter Sunshine (4b)
Umkomeni (4c)

**HS**
The Taper (4b)
The Fissure Barley (4b)
Whistling in the Dark (4b)
Sekorora (4b)
Checkmate (4b)
The Garden of Eden (4b)
The Ginnel (4b)
Arrow Slit (4b)

**S**
Prow Crack (4c)
Rearguard (4a)
The Heel (4a)
Spinnaker (4a)
Portcullis (4a)
Backalley (4b)
The Keep (4a)
Wellington Crack II (4b)
The Plunge (4a)
African Skies (4a)
Dungeon (4a)
Wet Landing (4b)
Chiminalley (4a)
Starboard Crack (4b)
Gangplank (4a)
Stonerag (4a)
Sundial (4b)
Sun Bingo (4a)

**HVD**
Casement Crack (4a)
Captain Pugwash

**VD**
Sunstroke
Bilgewater

Yardarm
Narrow Slab
Central Chimney
Tiptoe

**D**
Jib Sail
Glissade
Sundown

**Problems**
**Font 7c+**
Digital Delirium

**Font 7c**
The Fabulous Number 2
Diamond Lights
Sky Diamond

**Font 7a+**
Dew Drop

**Font 7a**
Too Much Too Young
Get A Grip

**Font 6c+**
Daddies Source
The Traverse

**Font 6c**
Dick Vierra
Canada Dry
Grove Hell
Over the Looking Glass

**Font 6b**
Reflections
Little Gem
Little Sparkler
Yorkshire Water

**Font 6a**
Savage
Treebeard

**Font 5+**
Beech Peach
Tree Slots
Troubled Water
Rough Cut
Cannon Fodder
Boiling Oil
Rough Water

**Font 5**
Portal Rib
Ready for Action
I Need a Tree
The Flaw
Thin Ice
Flawless
Oakey Kokey
Rib Tickler

**Font 4+**
Bauble
Pyrites
Director
Moat-ivation
See the Light
Armada
Finish the Bowls
Murky Water

**Font 4**
French Connection
Sunday Sun

**Font 3**
Still Water
Middle Wall
Right of Arête
Side Wall

**Font 2+**
Up to the Tree

Almscliff to Slipstones

445

# upper huller stones
by **John Hunt**

OS Ref: SE 197 687
Altitude: 250m

Yet another esoteric treasure and a Tony Barley find. This crag lies on the eastern bank of Skell Beck about a mile downstream of the Pateley Bridge to Kirby Malzeard Road.

**The Climbing:** From a routes point of view the mighty Skell Buttress is the real draw of this crag; *Too Gnarly For Barley* (E3 6a) should be an aspiration for any dedicated extreme climber. The climbs consist of short problems with decent landings or distinctly highball affairs, of which the challenges on Fountains Buttress really stand out.

**Conditions and Aspect:** A high moorland setting which feels more remote than it really is. While mostly north-facing, the buttresses are set down the hillside giving some protection from the weather. There is very sparse tree cover which keeps the buttresses clean and ensures that they catch all the sunlight going.

**Parking and Approach:** From the top of Pateley Bridge High Street, go east along Old Church Lane up onto the moor for three miles to a T-junction. Turn left (signed to Laverton and Kirkby Malzeard) and follow the sharp bend over Skell Gill bridge. Approximately 400m on the left is the large parking spot (**Parking GPS: 54.115882, -1.708574**). The crag can now be reached by heather bashing for half a mile south-eastwards across the moor and the stream.

An alternative is to turn right at the T-junction, park near the cattle-grid on the south side of the beck (**Parking GPS: 54.112047,-1.711649,** do not block the gate) and follow the ridge of the valley all the way to the crag. Do note that you will reach the last climbs first; Fountains Buttress then Skell Buttress, with its central birch tree

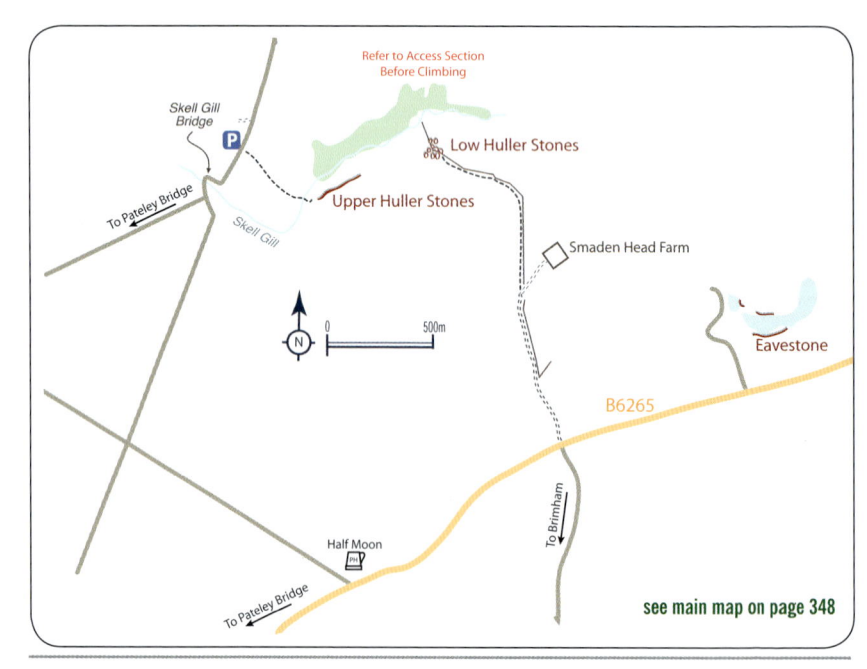

## Rievaulx Buttress - UPPER HULLER STONES

the most notable feature of the edge. Approach time: 15 minutes, but it depends on the height of the heather. A pleasant and easier, if longer, approach can be made from the Brimham crossroads via Lower Huller Stones.

**Access:** This crag is on CRoW access land. It is on a grouse moor so clearly needs to be avoided when a shoot is in progress. The first two approaches involve crossing walls or fences, so care and discretion are required. No dogs.

---

### Coverham Buttress
The climbable buttress on the left, identified by a huge slab leaning against its right wall.

**1 Evensong**  Font 4
The cracked wall and overhangs.
*Tony Barley   27th June 1991*

**2 Matins**  Font 4
Climb the nose to finish over the block on top. The sit-down start from the rusty wall to the left is quality (Font 4+).
*Tony Barley   27th June 1991*

### Jervaux Buttress
Just right is an undercut buttress with a small roof.

**3 Cardinal Wolsey**  HVS 5a   4m
Climb the overhang via a hold on the lip at the left-hand end. Move back right and finish direct.
*Tony & Tim Barley   28th June 1991*

**4 Henry the Eighth**  E1 5c   4m
Climb the overhang direct to a jug and continue to the top. A move right reduces the difficulty but avoids the main challenge. A four metre E1? Get it done, then scoff.
*Tony Barley (solo)   28th June 1991*

**5 Mother Superior**  HVS 5b   5m
The right rib, with a spectacular move over the bulge.
*Tony Barley (solo)   28th June 1991*

**6 Abyss**  S 3c   4m
The lovely sidewall. Great moves and ample gear.
*Tim Barley   28th June 1991*

**7 Abbot**  Font 4+
A subsidiary wall set back is climbed via a scoop.
*Tony Barley   15th July 1991*

### Rievaulx Buttress
The buttress with the monster roof.

**8 Mitre**  VS 5a   5m
Left of the roof is a pointed nose and a leaning slab. Climb these.
*Tony Barley   15th July 1991*

**9 Student Games**  E2 6a   6m   ★★
Cross the monster roof at its widest point using the creaky flakes. If you reach the lip, a move up and left gains good holds.
*Dave Musgrove (jnr) (solo)   28th June 1993*

**10 Chalice**  HVS 5b   5m
Start below the right side of the roof, reach round to good holds on the sidewall then swing back left onto the rib to finish.
*Tony Barley (solo)   28th July 1991*

**11 Missal**  Font 4
The sidewall, right of the roof.
*Tony Barley   27th July 1991*

**12 Rosary**  Font 3
The crack in the wall.
*Tim Barley   28th July 1991*

**Maux Wall** is a little wall between Rievaulx and the mighty Skell Buttress and contains **Evolution** (Font 4), which climbs the middle of the wall, and **Devolution** (Font 4) which takes the right-hand rib.

# Upper Huller Stones - Skell Buttress

## Skell Buttress
This is the largest buttress with four fine routes and a prominent birch tree growing out of its right face.

**13 Peace** VS 5a 9m ★
The centre of the wall is gained by moving left on good holds then up via a pocket to the break. Traverse this leftwards to the ledge on the arête. Climb delicately up the scooped rib and finish just on the right, or slightly more easily round to the left.
*Tony Barley, Anthony Roche 17th June 1970*

**14 Solitude** E3 6a 10m ★★
Gain the break as for *Peace*. A step right leads to a hard and committing move up to gain small but positive holds on the upper wall. Excellent climbing.
*Tony Barley (unseconded) 28th June 1991* ✦

**15 Too Gnarly For Barley** E3 6a 9m ★★
The right arête offers the best line on the crag with a reachy start and intimidating finish. Best taken at the gallop.
*Dave Musgrove (jnr & snr), Tony Barley 28th June 1993* ✦

**16 By the Birch** S 4a 7m
Climb the right wall past the tree and up cracks above.
*Tony Barley 27th June 1991*

## Fountains Buttress
The first buttress reached on the approach from the road. The height alone make these routes rather than boulder problems. Pure old school quality.

**17 Penitence** HVS 5a 6m
Straight up the left wall. Finish through a nick in the overhang.
*Tony Barley 15th July 1991*

**18 Abolition** VS 4c 7m
Strangely difficult. The left wall moving right to the ledge and back left to finish.
*Tony Barley, Robin Barley 1966*

**19 Retribution** E1 6a 7m ★★
The left-hand overhung arête. Vigorous moves on rounded holds.
*Tony Barley 15th July 1991*

**20 Hellfire** E1 5c 7m ★
The right arête. Similar to *Retribution* but on positive holds.
*Tony Barley 27th June 1991*

**21 Wonderbar** HVS 5b 6m ★
The wall on the right of the twin arêtes is climbed on superb holds after a reachy start.
*Tony & Tim Barley 28th June 1991*

**22 Cloisters** HVS 5a 7m
A traverse of the right wall to the ledge between the arêtes and then to a direct finish.
*Tony Barley 27th June 1991*

**23 Trust Ye** HVS 5a 5m
The last climbable wall on the far right has a block finish.
*Tony Barley 15th July 1991*

### Further First Ascent Information (✦)
**Solitude**: *Barley's masterpiece of the crag. As usual the one he could do seems harder than the one he couldn't.*
**Too Gnarly For Barley**: *After years of failing on it, Barley offered the lead to young Musgrove; he was pleased with the route, but less taken with the name.*
**Evolution and Devolution**: *Both climbed by Tony Barley 27th July 1991.*

# low huller stones

by **John Hunt**

---

OS Ref: SE 204 689
Altitude: 225m

---

An extensive collection of boulders. These have saved the day many times for teams who found conditions too cold or wet at Upper Huller Stones. The boulders divide between a southern bay and a northern area which is accessed by the gate.

**The Climbing:** Only one real route, but heaps of bouldering; 107 problems, some of which have a distinctly "old school" flavour (i.e. high, and you may well be scared). The landings are predominantly great. These are "proper" free-standing boulders with the lion's share of problems below Font 6a.

**Conditions and Aspect:** The boulders are high and exposed, although it is usually possible to find some shelter and have a good session here even in the depths of winter. It is also a nice place for children with flat ground and some exciting gullies to explore.

**Parking and Approach:** Either approach from Upper Huller Stones or park carefully on the B6265 near the Brimham turn and take the tarmac road (which is a footpath, although not signed as such) towards Smaden Head Farm. Continue past the farm, along the track by the wall, until this runs into another wall. At this point turn left (on access land by this point) and follow the wall to the rocks. 25 minutes. See map on page 446.

**Access:** The situation here is weird as the southern half of the boulders are on access land while the northern blocks are not. There have been trees planted around the boulders in the recent past which suggests that the landowner / user is not overly encouraging of climbing. This is also an active shooting moor; closures are posted at the parking for Upper Huller Stones. No dogs.

### The Southern Sector: Moorside Wall and Bird Blocks

Almost a ravine formed by boulders. The southern wall has lots of small problems with reasonable grades. Unfortunately, some of these tend to stay dank and some of the landings can be really mushy.

**1 End Wall** Font 1. Nice.
**2 Park 'n Ride** Font 5. Battle over the capping roof direct.
**3 Grotty Corner Wall** Easy. Yuck.
**4 WB 3** Font 3. **5 WB 4** Font 4. Wall centre.
**6 WB 5** Font 5+. The impending wall above the swamp.
**7 WB 6** Font 3. Left arête of the gully.
**8 Main Gully** Grade 1 (caving, but you don't need lights). The big gully provides an exciting expedition all the way through the crag.
**9 "Moor or Less"** Font 2.
**10 More or Even Less** Font 3. Use the in-cut holds in the break to reach to the top. Good – even when mucky.
**11 Lesser Gully** Font 1. Bridge up the smaller gully.
**12 Crater** Font 6b. Attach yourself to the lower arête and make a difficult slap for the sloping ledge. Keep it together to top-out.
**13 Little Toughie** Font 5+. The wall via the smooth flake.

The next sector is made up of the south facing sides of the **Bird Blocks.** They are linked to the northern sides by the drystone walls which run between the boulders. Nearly always in condition and an excellent circuit. This group starts on the ever clean, sun-catching Fourbee Wall of Cuckoo Crag (all the problems were '4b' in the cult guide, *Wild Bouldering*) beside the metal gate. This is also the first block reached if approaching from Upper Huller Stones.

**14 Arête, Arête** Font 6a. Left end of the wall taking advantage of all the arêtes on offer.
**15 Same Ground** Font 6a+. An eliminate just using the crack to gain a good edge. No arêtes.
**16 Again In This Golden Light** Font 6b. Another eliminate. Use only the crescent hold, a sloper and the top.
**17 Crescent & Break** Font 4+. A good problem based on these holds.
**18 4b Wall I** Font 4. Climb the wall from the break.
**19 4b Wall II** Font 4. From a sitter, climb the wall just right.

# Low Huller Stones - Map

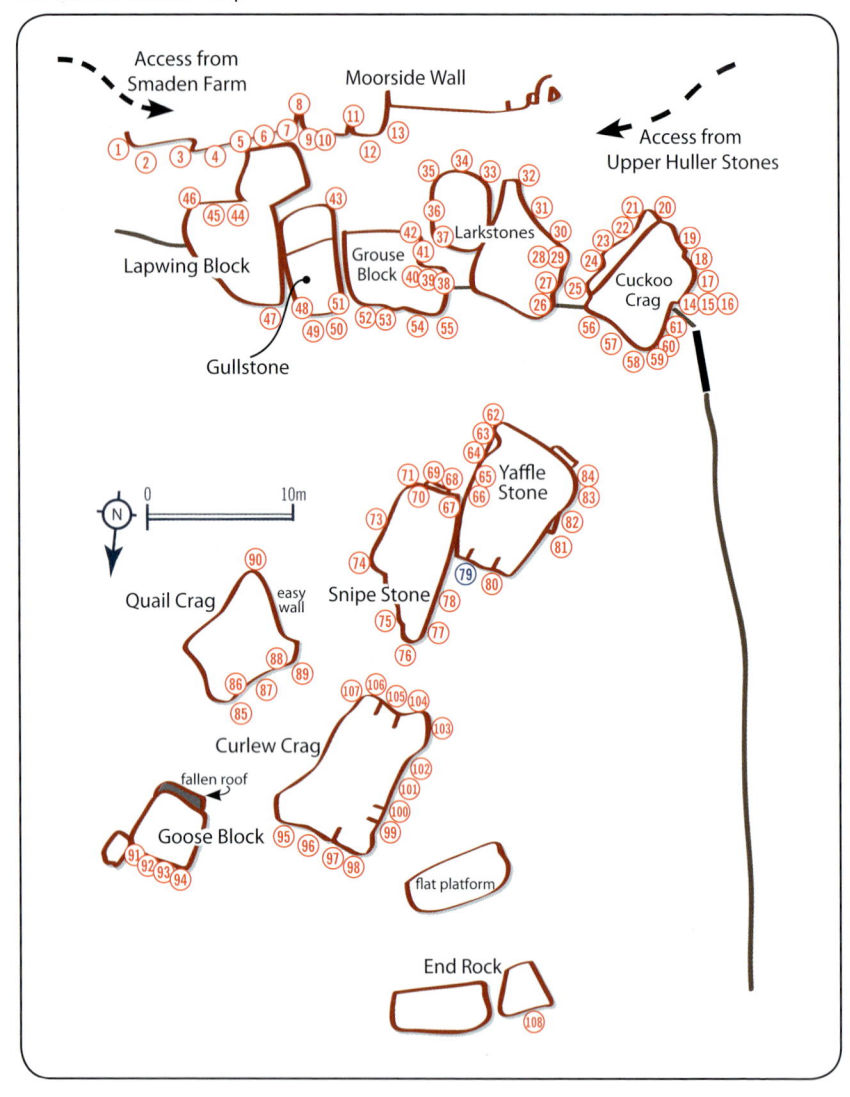

20 **End Wall** Easy. Even from a hanging start, but still fun. **I'm Shot** (Font 6b+) goes from a sit-down start on the little arête under the roof to span over.

Move to the back of the boulder. The flat platform just right makes a good stage just in case any of your team are feeling theatrical.

21 **WB 46** Easy. A good sliding off point.
22 **WB 47** Font 1.  23 **WB 48** Font 1.

450     Yorkshire Gritstone

## The Climbs - LOW HULLER STONES

**24 Wow! Big Number Jump**  Font 6a+. Span under the widest part of the roof and do battle with the headwall.
**25 Roof Right**  Font 5. The roof on the right.

The next problems are opposite the massive roof on the well-featured sidewall of **Larkstones**; easily overlooked but these are quality problems.

**26 Next T'wall**  Font 4+. Keep them hands off the flake system (and dry-stone wall) at this grade.
**27 No Larking**  Font 4. The impending, well-featured flake system.
**28 Stop Larkin' About**  Font 4+. From standing using the right edge. Using the deep holds around the arête is also a good exercise at Font 4.
**29 Stop Larkin' Eliminate**  Font 6b. From a sit-down start make technical moves without the aid of the right edge.
**30 WB 28**  Easy. Useful descent.
**31 WB 29**  Font 1. The wall centre.
**32 WB 30**  Font 3. Tackle the overhanging nose.
**33 WB31**  Font 2. The wall on the adjoining block.
**34 Not So Easy!**  Font 3. High and elegant. The fine open wall.
**35 Easy Arête**  Font 2. The arête with the big ledge. Superb.
**36 Side Wall 4c**  Font 4. The sidewall has just enough holds. Pure quality.
**37 Edge**  Font 3. The edge of the wall. Good.

The problems across the crevasse (on **Grouse Block**) can be a little green, but are still worth a go.

**38 Crevasse Wall Left**  Easy.
**39 Crevasse Wall Middle**  Font 1.
**40 Crevasse Wall Corner**  Font 2. The **Wall and Crack** is Font 4+ whilst **Clarke's Wall** (Font 6c) eliminates both the crack and arête.
**41 Son of Wild Bouldering**  Font 5+. The clean wall using the arête to the right. Commit to the toehold on the arête. Bliss.
**42 Layback Arête**  Font 4. Layback the arête on its right. Simply brilliant.
**43 Butch Hanging Arête**  Font 4+. Grab the hanging arête then dangle and campus like a maniac.

**Lapwing Block** catches the sun early and stays clean.

**44 New Wall 1**  Font 4. Gain the break using undercuts. The juggy roof is more awkward than it looks.
**45 Scamper**  Font 5+. Start on the high crimps with nothing for your feet. Go for the break. **46 Last Arête** Font 3.

### The Northern Sector
The next sector is through the gate in a big open bay. Some of the following problems are good but are north-facing and very slow to dry out.

**47 Big End**  Font 3.
**48 First Flank**  Font 2. The sidewall next to the huge roof.
**49 'Gulp'**  Font 6a. The lower wall is steady. Mantelling the overhanging roof (with the promise of being impaled on the underlying tree if you fail) isn't.
**50 Right Side of Roof**  Font 5. Mantel the roof on the right.
**51 WB 16 Right Flank**  Font 4.
**52 Left Arête**  Font 4. **53 WB 17**  Font 5.
**54 Don't Grouse WB 18**  Font 4.
**55 Grousy, Grousy WB 19**  Font 3.
**56 Get Tough**  Font 5.  **57 Cookie**  Font 4+.
**58 WB 38**  Font 4. Left of the arête.
**59 First Corner**  Font 1. The featured wall by the arête.
**60 Cuckoo**  Font 4. Climb the centre of the wall – blank at first, but soon leading to fantastic chicken-heads.
**61 Second Corner**  Font 1.

**Yaffle Stone & Snipe Stone**. The conjoined boulders. Some superb bouldering; the landings remain good, but some of the problems here get a little higher.

**62 Piffle Arête**  Font 4. The arête to the fluting at the top.
**63 Piffle**  Font 6a+. From a huge low undercut, climb the crimpy wall without the arête.
**64 Tony's 2**  Font 5+. Crimp up the wall above the right-side of the overlap.
**65 Tony's 3**  Font 3. Shoot the gap betwixt heather clumps.
**66 Another Traverse**  Font 3. Climb the slab to the right and traverse to *Piffle Arête*. The gully is a useful descent.
**67 Left Edge**  Font 4.
**68 Iron Stone**  Font 4. The iron-stone holds just right.
**69 Horns**  Font 4. **70 Beside Arête**  Font 4.
**71 Arête**  Font 3. The arête on both sides.

# Low Huller Stones - The Climbs

**72 Dave's Inevitable Traverse** Font 4+.
Traverse the wall from left-to-right (*Left Edge* to *Arête*) without using the big breaks.
**73 Tony's 7** Font 1.   **74 Tony's 8** Font 1. The arête.
**75 Left of Arête** Font 3. The wall just before the nose to welcoming jugs at the top.
**76 Crinkly Bit** Font 5+. The steep nose taken direct.
**77 Crinkle Cut** Font 5. Climb the crinkled wall with commitment. Beware exploding holds.   **78 Tony's 16** Font 5.
**79 Steep and Wrinkly** E2 5c   6m
The steep crack with a bold slopey finish; well-protectable with cams.
**80 Yaffle Not** Font 5.   **81 Woody** Font 4+.
The **Yaffle Stone Traverse** (Font 6c) goes from the huge flake to the right edge.
**82 Wood** Font 6a. A technical start just right of *Woody* to a rounded finish.
**83 Woodpecker** Font 4+. The wall via the ledge.
**84 Extra** Font 4+. The wall beside *Woodpecker*. The biggest challenge is not using the underlying boulder, followed by the fear of hitting it if you fall off.

**Quail Crag:** The isolated block to the east, opposite the sidewall of Snipe Stone. The overhanging end wall contains:

**85 Quail** Font 4.   **86 Quail II** Font 4.
**87 Quaker** Font 5+. The steep thin crack with a steeper finish.
**88 Oats** Font 5+. The scoop beside the arête is difficult.
**89 Ever Dry Arête** Font 4+. The arête without the underlying boulder to superb holds on top.

The wall facing the other boulders has 5-6 easy problems.

**90 WB9** Easy. The arête and end wall. There are other easy problems (and the best descent) just to the right.

**Goose Block.** A few new problems can be found around the back of the block with the massive roof with a fallen slab. They are overhanging and the grit is slightly snappy.

**91 Goose Arête** Font 5. Sit-Start.
**92 Wednesday Blues** Font 5+. Sit start. Climb to a dish just over the top without using the arête.

**93 Sandstone Times** Font 4+. Sit-start off the big hold behind the tree – climb direct.
**94 Rose Hold** Font 4+. Sit-start below a prominent hold with a broken top – climb direct.

**Curlew Crag.** The big block down the hill from the biggest cluster. The problems start on the overhanging wall around the back of the boulder:

**95 Got-Cha!** Font 4+. The overhung wall from the pointed boulder to a tough finish.
**96 Short and Curley** Font 5+. The hard overhanging crack.
**97 Bit Between** Font 4+. Tackle the bit between the crack and the arête.
**98 Nose Job** Font 4. Grope up the rounded end.
**99 Little Flake** Font 5. Harder than it looks.
**100 Flake Crack** Font 4+. Climb the prominent flake in the centre of the sidewall.
**101 The Real Thing** Font 5+. A good eliminate up the wall between the cracks.
**102 Impostor** Font 5. The crack just left of the arête's face.
**103 Mange Tout** Font 4+. The face of the arête using various cracks.
**104 Farish in the Parish** Font 5.
**105 Peapod** Font 4+. Making the butch pull into the feature is the crux.
**106 Wurley** Font 3. The wall just beside the arête.
**107 Curley** Font 2. The nice arête on either side.

Finally, on a block further down the valley, below the big flat boulder is **108 Too Far to Walk** Font 3.

### First Ascent Information

*Tony Barley climbed the majority of the problems, including Steep and Wrinkly between 1970 and 1993, occasionally joined by Anton Fatti. Barley found other chalk marks in the early 1990s. From 2009-11, John Hunt (alone and with combinations of Paul Farish, Dave Musgrove and Rachel Hunt) recorded: 2, 15, 16, 29, 41, 44-46, 62, 66, 72, 84, 89, 91-94, 104. Paul Clarke added 20a, 40a, 40b, 81a on 5th June 2011.*

Mike Hutton on **The Naked Edge** (E3 6a) at Simon's Seat. Page 475.
Photo: Robin Nicholson

# Barden Fell
# to Hunter's Stones

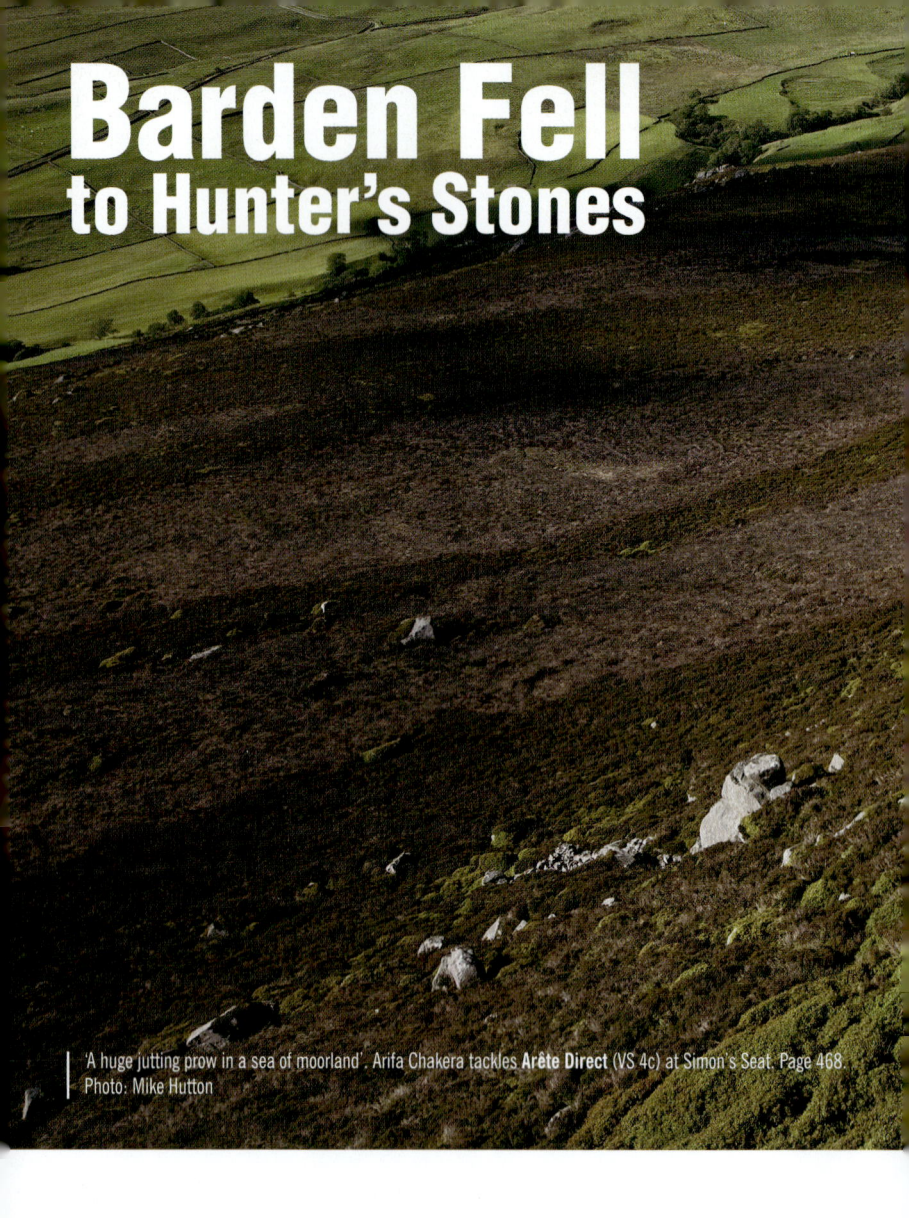

'A huge jutting prow in a sea of moorland'. Arifa Chakera tackles **Arête Direct** (VS 4c) at Simon's Seat. Page 468.
Photo: Mike Hutton

"Barden Fell is to remote moorland gritstone what Catalunya is to limestone 9a"

*Niall Grimes, Boulder Britain*

| | | |
|---|---|---|
| **Simon's Seat** 459 | **Brandrith** 510 | Little Almscliff 538 |
| Hen Stones 487 | **Dovestones** 518 | Norwood Edge 540 |
| **Lord's Seat** 488 | Cat Crags 524 | Hunter's Stones 544 |
| Earl's Seat 502 | Thruscross 528 | Birk Crag (Harlow Carr) 548 |
| North Nab 504 | Snowden 534 | Calf Crag 550 |

# Map

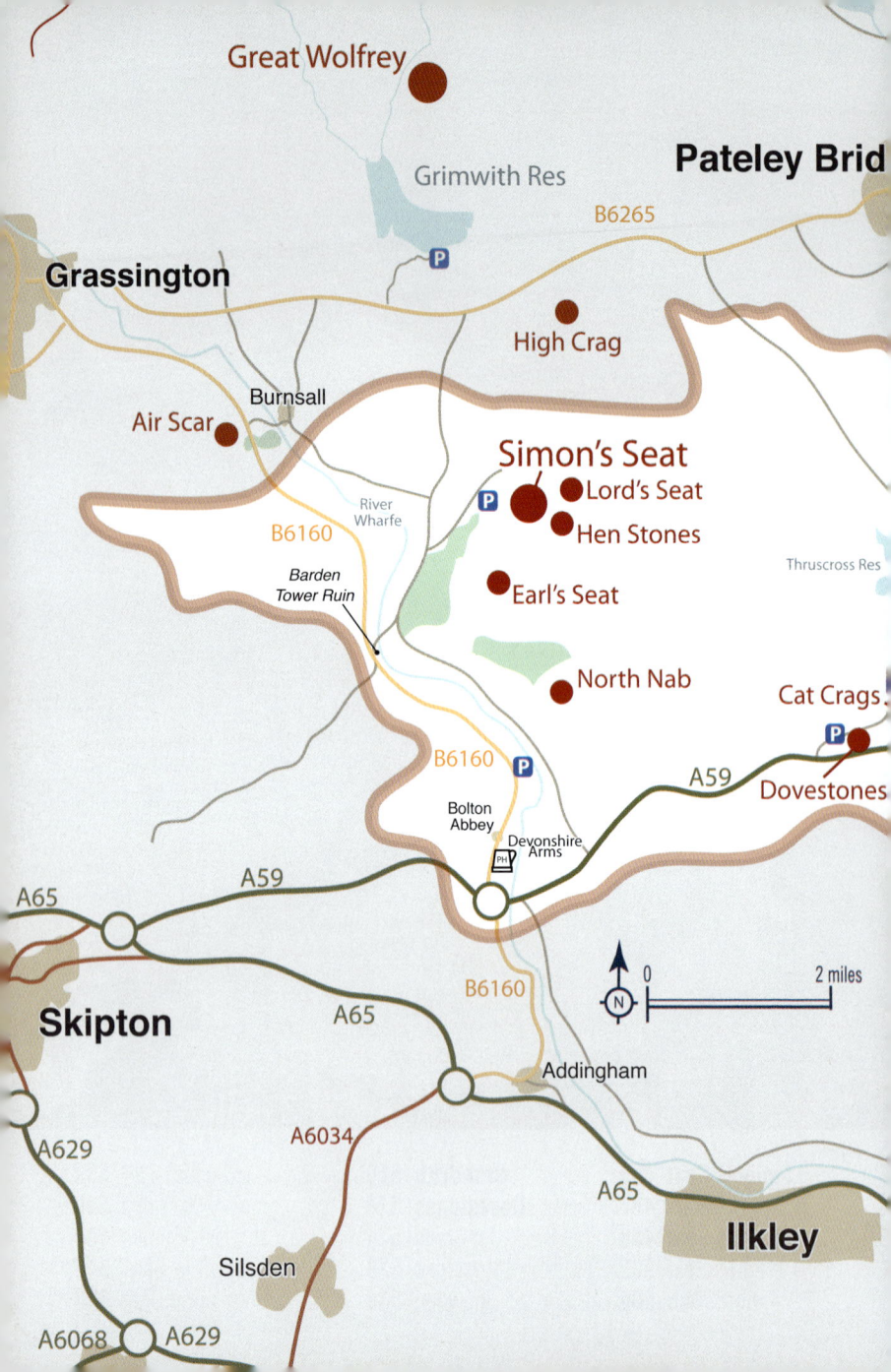

- Great Wolfrey
- Grimwith Res
- Pateley Brid
- B6265
- Grassington
- High Crag
- Burnsall
- Air Scar
- River Wharfe
- B6160
- Simon's Seat
- Lord's Seat
- Hen Stones
- Thruscross Res
- Barden Tower Ruin
- Earl's Seat
- North Nab
- Cat Crags
- A59
- Dovestones
- B6160
- Bolton Abbey
- Devonshire Arms
- A59
- A65
- B6160
- 0 — 2 miles
- N
- Skipton
- A65
- Addingham
- A629
- A6034
- A65
- Ilkley
- Silsden
- A6068 A629

457

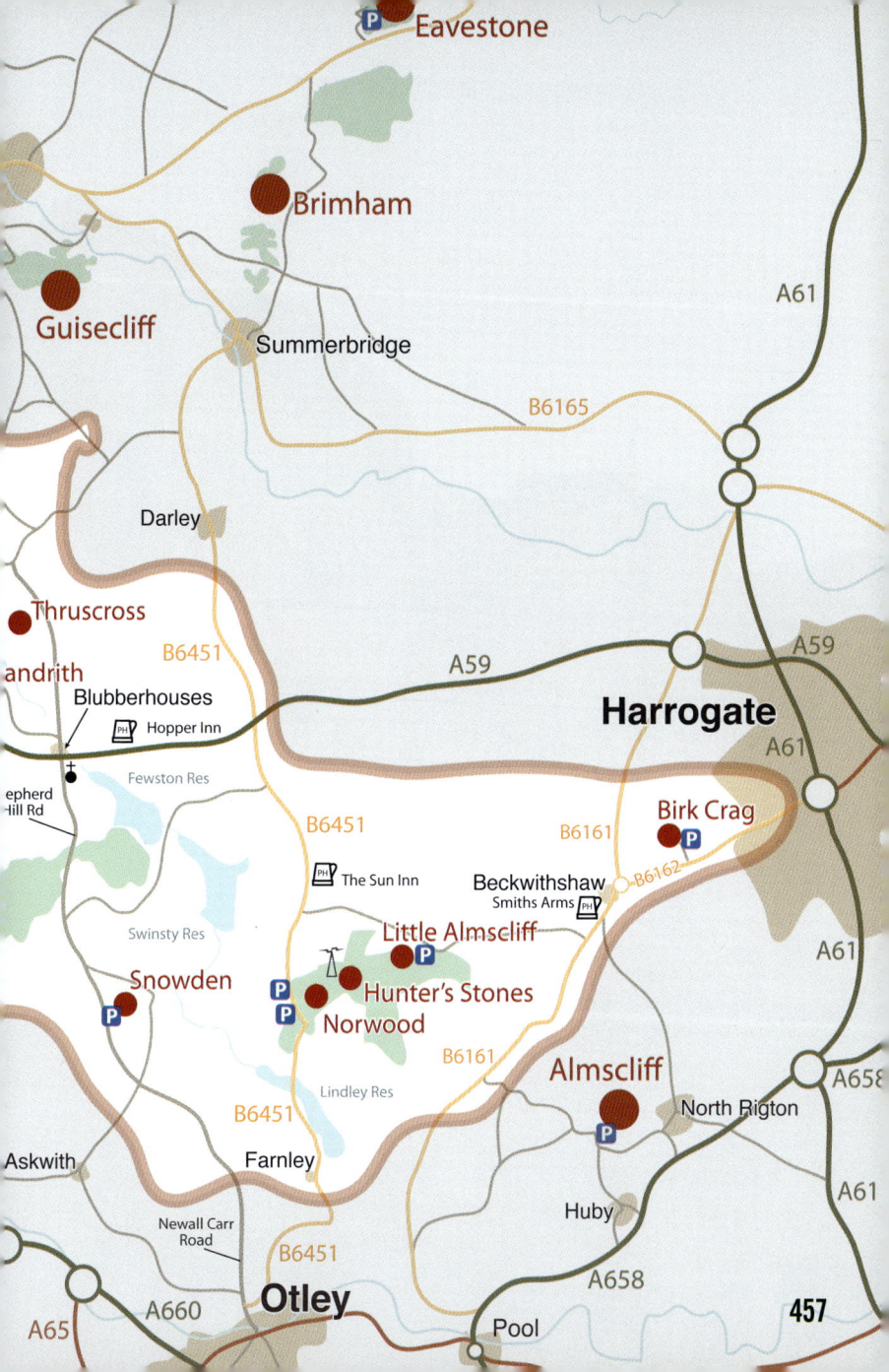

Dave Sutcliffe squeezing the blubber of **Whaleback** (Font 7a+). Page 478
Photo: Adi Gill

# simon's seat
## by Robin Nicholson

OS Ref: SE 079 598    Altitude: 485m

Amongst the wild and windy lunar plateau of Barden Fell sits a rough-cut diamond of Yorkshire Gritstone; Simon's Seat, a proud bastion of silver stone surrounded by a landscape that stirs the soul. As with many of the finer things in life, a spot of pain must be endured before the pleasure and this crag is no exception as the passage to the exposed summit is long and initially steep. The wide and lonely expanse of grouse moorland leads you to feel like you're the last climber in the world here. Yes, the solitude of Simon's Seat allows you to be a climbing legend in your own mind, where classic lines can be found throughout the grade range and give ample opportunity to demonstrate your new-found delusional rock domination.

This is an outstanding yet understated crag with routes to rival that of its lowland brothers in length, quality and climbing style. Isolated, peaceful and quiet may well characterise The Seat - but don't forget, it's the quiet ones you really have to worry about.

**The Climbing:** A bounty of excellent climbs, over 80 routes, ranging in challenge from Difficult to E6, with many a well-protected classic in the sub-extreme category. Fierce cracks, bold unrelenting pillars and lonely technical slabs that turn the smearability knob to eleven, all find a home here. Bosses, bumps and gargoyles of grit protrude from many a wall (especially the south face) adding to the charm and uniqueness of the climbing, not to mention the positive nature of the compact weathered rock.

There is one climbing feature that Simon's Seat has in spades - fantastic committing arêtes. *Arête Direct (VS 4c), And She Was (E3 6a), The Naked Edge (E3 6a)* and *A Life Less Ordinary (E6 6b)* set the yardstick for those looking to work their way through the theory and practical exams for bold grit arêtes. Pad enthusiasts however, won't want to miss *A Question of Balance (E2 5b)*, arguably the best E2 slab climb in the county.

**The Bouldering:** More recorded boulder problems exist now at Simon's than ever before and combined with the local neighbour, Lord's Seat, a great day out can be had with the mat. Not tons in the friendly grades here but Drift Wall area hosts some tip-top problems in the Font 4+ to Font 6b range. The classic ticks lie in, and above, the Font 7a mark with *Whaleback* (Font 7a+) leading the charge. Sufficient pads, a friendly wind and an agile ground support team mean the many highball extremes at the crag are more tempting than before...though this isn't a miracle cure for competency. Lots of problems continue to be unrecorded for the spirit of adventure and await rediscovery.

**Conditions and Aspect:** A crag of contrasts but with one constant – if it's windy there's limited shelter. There are two main areas, the south-west face and the north-facing main crag. The sparkling grey grit of the south face gets all the sun going, is rough as emery board, invariably clean and quick to dry. An all season candidate if you've wrapped up warm enough. The main crag is a different animal and the dark amphitheatre can fill the newcomer with a deep sense of foreboding. It is home to the longest routes but many sections can be green, slow to dry and can be particularly exposed. The climbs around the *Arête Direct* prow generally stay clean. Don't be dismayed; with spring evenings and summer days, the sun catches the main crag and the climbing here can be a special and memorable experience.

The Seat is often home to an extensive millipede population, typically in the shadier spots. However, occasionally the odd one will wrap itself round that crucial pebble...

# BARDEN FELL - Introduction

**Approach and Parking:** Heading north on the B6160 Bolton Abbey to Grassington road, take a sharp right signed to Appletreewick immediately after the Barden Tower ruin. Cross the narrow Barden bridge and follow the road uphill. After three-quarters of a mile, the road starts to descend and a gravel track (Howgill Lane) leads right (a red letter box and phone box are on the left of the track). The parking is on the right-hand side just past Howgill Farm and by the Barden Fell access information board (**GPS: 54.028206,-1.904673**). If parked considerately, 4 cars will fit in the lay-by. Please do not block access into the adjacent farmers field. From the parking, facing uphill, the path onto the moor is on the right through a wooden gate. Take this path as it meanders steeply around the plantation to a chained gate. The stile to the left allows you onward and around the next right bend the track opens out onto the moor (about 20 minutes so far). There are two access options now, both bring you out within yards of each other at Simon's Seat. The first takes the track which follows the dry stone wall on the left for approximately a hundred metres before it leaves the wall and forks right. Continue on this, rising steadily, and the track becomes a flagged path which leads to the south-west face of the crag. The second, and more scenic route, follows the dry stone wall only for a few metres before cutting right onto the moor. Earl's Seat can be seen up and to the right

## Approach & Access - BARDEN FELL

(south) as the path rises quickly to the plateau. Simon's Seat can be seen to the left (north) with the trig point on top. 25 more minutes on this track and you're at the top of the crag. The south-west face of the crag is reached by both of the routes mentioned above. 45-60 minutes car to crag.

**Access Issues:** Barden Fell is grouse moorland and owned by the Duke of Devonshire (Bolton Abbey Estate). No dogs or fires are permitted. The access information boards give closure dates due to grouse shooting which typically occur between 12th August and late December (never on Sundays). If there is a fire risk due to a particularly dry patch of hot weather the moor may be closed. The estate office can be contacted on 01756 718009 or check the website, www.boltonabbey.com. In the breeding season, disturbance to the ground nesting birds should be avoided by sticking to the main tracks.

# Barden Fell - Aerial Photograph

Lord's Seat - Wall Buttress

Trig Point

Simon's Seat
Main Edge (North Face)

Whaleback

Aerial Photograph - **BARDEN FELL**

# Simon's Seat - Aerial Photograph

To Lord's Seat

Trig Point

| # | Route | # | Route |
|---|---|---|---|
| 1 | Arête Direct p468 | 10 | Toe Fu / Trunk p476 |
| 2 | Turret Crack p469 | 11 | Fulvia p477 |
| 3 | A Question of Balance p470 | 12 | Trilogy p477 |
| 4 | Gymkhana p473 | 13 | Pinna p477 |
| 5 | Solipsism p474 | 14 | Simon Says Squeeze p477 |
| 6 | Spondonical p474 | 15 | Victorian Climb p477 |
| 7 | Simon Says p474 | 16 | A Life Less Ordinary p478 |
| 8 | Bashful p475 | 17 | Whaleback p478 |
| 9 | The Naked Edge p475 | | |

Aerial Photograph - **SIMON'S SEAT**

Simon's Seat - Main Edge (North Face)

465

# SIMON'S SEAT - The Main Edge

## The Main Edge

The showpiece of the crag. From the summit, pass to the right of the south face and follow the well-made path leftwards (north-west and downhill) with the trig point on your right. This stepped path drops steeply and as it levels out a minor track branches off to the right, passing The Naked Edge buttress and, on uneven ground, to the main crag. Alternatively, stay on the plateau, pass the trig point and descend the crag at the far end before cutting back into the *Arête Direct* area.

### 1 **Layback Crack** VD 10m
Hold on tight, could be a rough ride for the grade. Assume the position and romp up the lonely crack. Those not proficient in laybacking can shove the right arm and leg in and hump to victory.
*Arnold & Sidney Waterfall, Bill Bowler   Mid-1930s*

### 2 **North Gully Buttress** VS 5a 20m
A contrasting adventure on the slab left of *North Gully*. Ease onto the slab and make an awkward move to conquer the early overlap. Keep on the gas until the ledge and a breather. Once composed, tackle the wall and the finishing crack.
*Brian Evans, L. Howarth   July 1961*

### 3 **North Gully** D 22m
Meaty mileage at an amenable grade. Pull shapes up the obvious gully.
*Pre-1920*

### 4 **Flake Climb** VD 16m ★
Ascend *North Gully* for 6m, passing the conspicuous hanging flake then cut right onto the wall. Surmount the next flake on the wall and select from a couple of finishing options (a) the logical direct finish (b) the original, and best, traverse rightwards to the arête and up this for maximum exposure to the finishing platform.
*Arnold & Sidney Waterfall, Bill Bowler   Mid-1930s*

### 5 **High Nose Traverse** S 23m
A horizontal perambulation from one of grit's early pioneers, whereby you start and finish on the deck — by choice. Spurn the gully at the earliest opportunity and foot-traverse right to the arête. Step up to the next ledge and follow this around the nose of the buttress. Track this line across the main face until it's possible to 'step-off' at the entrance to *Window Chimney*. A good route for a link up with the plethora of lines hereabouts.
*Sidney Waterfall, W.J. Anderson   1949*

### 6 **Mosaic** VS 4c 20m ★
A recent addition that links up two of the old boys. Follow *High Nose Traverse* to the nose. Teeter up the left side of the arête until forced onto a short ramp/groove. From the ramp's uppermost part gain the good break on the right and finish straight up the left side of the arête to good finishing holds. (c) An easier finish can be made by stepping left at the top of the ramp to join the last few metres of *Flake Climb*.
*Tony Marr, Mike Tooke   3rd September 2010*

The Main Edge - **SIMON'S SEAT**

**7 Hair of the Dog** VS 5a 18m
Somewhat eliminate but takes in a modicum of untrodden territory and well worth a crack. Tackle the bulge on undercuts to a sloping ledge and pocket. Rock left (ledge) and cruise the slanting crack to join and finish as for *Arête Wall*. The direct finish up the slab is harder by a smidgen. (d) **Posh Spice and the Bend in Beckham's Set Piece** (VS 5a) goes from the boulder below then ascends the prow of the buttress for a couple of metres before following the cracks rightwards, across the face to the finish of *Y-Front*.

*John Cutcliffe, Mick Darfield, John Phoden   27th June 1998*

# Simon's seat - Arête Wall

### 8 Dog Lead  HVS 5a  17m  ★
A neat excursion up the wall and one which exposes any inadequacies in the climber's repertoire. From halfway along the *Arête Direct* traverse, yank hard up the crack and pockets in the overlap to reach the flake. Continue up the pocketed slab to the shallow vertical seam. A long reach, a helpful pocket out right and deft footwork brings the sanctuary of good jams and finishing flutings within reach. Daylight robbery for the tall at this grade.
*Johnny Cutcliffe, Mark Darfield  20th April 1997*

### 9 Arête Direct  VS 4c  20m  ★★★
An absolute corker of a climb with plenty of mileage, exceptional moves and in a fabulous position. Make a constricted traverse left to reach the arête (hold on for all you're worth if howling a gale) and make bold high steps to an exposed climax. Big gear helps. Photo on page 454.
*Allan Austin, Brian Evans, Frank Spence  30th August 1958* ✦

### 10 Arête Wall  S 4a  16m  ★
A cracking upward traverse line that takes the path of least resistance up the wall to the exposed finish on the arête. Start up the hill beneath the origins of the obvious leftward trending cracklines. Step up and follow these leftward to the arête and a spicy end.
*Arnold & Sidney Waterfall, Bill Bowler  Mid-1930s*

### 11 Y- Front  S 4a  12m  ★★
More crack-bashing entertainment. Make the initial moves of *Arête Wall* to the centre of the face. Scuttle up right and make taxing moves up the right-hand of the Y-shaped cracks to a crux exit. (e) A cheeky technical variation, **Gentleman's Support** (E1 5b) yards up the wall to the left. (f) **Brief Encounter** (VS 5a) tackles the wall direct with the aid of the two large pockets. Tiptoe up the left-hand crack to a rounded finish.
*Brian Evans, A. Evans  17th July 1960* ✦

## Turret Crack - SIMON'S SEAT

### 12 Chimney Wall  S 4b  12m
Pick-and-mix frivolities teasing the right flank of the buttress and chimney jaws. Climb to the ledge and inch-up to its topmost part. Hand jam the green crack-cum-flake and, for the purists, go as for the original method and back and foot it with the use of the chimney's right wall for a few metres before ending back on the left wall.
*Sidney Waterfall, W.J. Anderson   1949*

### 13 Window Chimney  D  13m
A troglodyte's delight! Answer the call of the beckoning abyss and follow any slight breeze that may indicate a way out (usually via the window above the chockstone). Finish direct or cut out left up the wall.

### 14 Clappers Crack  E1 5b  10m
Grunt, grimace and gurn the butch crack in the roof to the ledge. Not worth hanging about on. Finish as for *Turret Crack*.
*Allan Austin   30th August 1958*

### 15 Turret Crack  HVS 5a  20m  ★★
A game of two halves – prepare to lose if you underperformed at jam school. Front crawl up the green crack to the good ledge (optional stance). Step left and continue the jam-fest to the top. VS for jam masters.
*Allan Austin, Brian Evans, Frank Spence 30th August 1958* ✦

### 16 Panzer  E3 6a  15m  ★
A powerful and reachy affair straightening out *Turret Crack*. From the ledge, climb the wall and then fire the big guns to propel you over the bulge on pockets to the top.
*Nigel Baker, Dave Musgrove(snr)   11th July 1999*

### 17 Outside Finish  HVS 5b  20m  ★★
A variation on his original line, but an altogether bolder and electrifying affair from the wise owl of grit. Climb *Turret Crack* to the ledge then traverse the horizontal break to the right arête. Move up and weave back left under the overhang. Breathe deep, grab the big holds and pull for all your worth over the bulges to victory. (Only take one rope if you're in training for pulling trucks at the World's Strongest Man contest).
*Allan Austin   23rd July 1960*

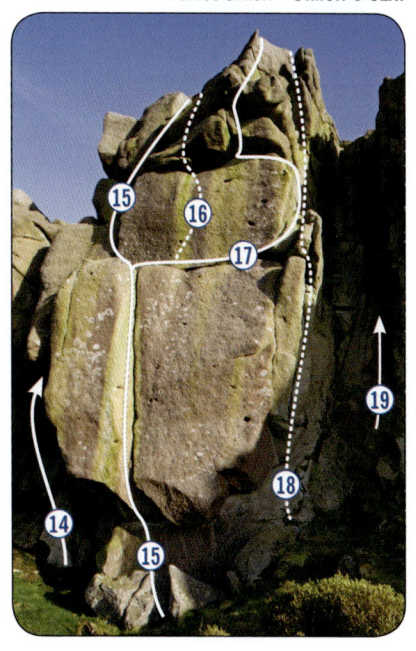

### 18 The Gunner  E1 5c  20m
Gain the hanging radioactive ramp with difficulty and continue up to meet *Outside Finish*. Truck right and up to the sloping ledge before finishing up the short steep corner.
*John Eastham, Geoff Myers, R. Pendleton   15th May 1988*

### 19 Square Chimney  VD  17m
An acquired taste. A pleasure for the traditionalist in a dry summer; a joy for the horticulturalist after a wet winter.
*Pre-1920*

### 20 Baggin's Variation  VS 4c  17m
Little new climbing but allows those with an appetite for destruction to reach their doom on the dodgy finish of *Azimuth* with less hassle. Ascend *Square Chimney* for a few metres until it's possible to trend rightwards to join and finish up the grooveline of *Azimuth*.
*Tony Barley, Robin Barley   June 1975*

# Simon's Seat - A Question of Balance

### 21 **Azimuth** E3 5b  16m
A real frightener with a top-out to (most likely) die for. Scamper up the shallow corner a metre right of *Square Chimney* to the roof. Rock right and launch over the overhang, up steep cracks and loose blocks to the relative safety of solid ground.
*Tony Barley, Robin Barley  June 1975* ✦

### 22 **Finesse** E4 6a  16m  ★★
The impressive hanging prow succumbs to a combative direct approach – a joy of a climb nonetheless. May need a spring clean before having a crack.
*Derek Hargreaves, Andrew Lindley  9th August 1988*

### 23 **Pothole Chimney** VD  20m
Good grief! Have you come all the way for this? Fair enough. Wriggle and writhe through the constriction behind the chockstone and to the summit. Now seek help.
*Pre-1920*

### 24 **Blind Alley** HVS 5b  18m
A tougher challenge which exchanges the spelunking mischief of *Pothole Chimney* for some honest open climbing. At the obelisk break out and tackle the hanging groove to the ledge. Scuttle right and finish up the crack.
*Tony Marr, K. Jackson, Paul Ingham  17th June 1984*

Immediately right, **Tartarus** (VS 5a), starts at the foot of the arête, climbs the shallow crackline into the square recess to then exit up the right-hand chimney.

### 25 **Chockstone Chimney** VS 4c  20m  ★
A tricky little number and not without its moments. The finale yields to a touch of imagination. Romp up the crack to the niche and then make perplexing moves to reach the top.
*Arnold & Sidney Waterfall, Bill Bowler  Mid-1930s*

### 26 **Shush Popeye** E3 5c  20m  ★★
Character building. A balancey and bold outing up the left arête with scarce opportunity to stop and take breath.
*Derek Hargreaves, Ian Farnsworth  July 1998*

### 27 **A Question of Balance** E2 5b  20m  ★★★
The aptly named and essential E2 of the crag - nay, nay and thrice nay – of Yorkshire? Tough pulls on awkward jams lead to a small ledge and an opportunity to compose oneself before the big push. Make delicate and lonely moves up the slab, tickling the arête on the right as you go before the break comes tantalisingly within reach. Romp home on slopers. An absolute must and one that will test all your grit arsenal. (*The initial crack and final break can be dirty and worth checking first*). Photo on page 472.
*John Eastham, Geoff Myers, John Myers  7th May 1978*

470  Yorkshire Gritstone

Simple Simon - **SIMON'S SEAT**

**28  Where's Grandma**  E4 6a   15m   ★
A bold line on the right arête, climbed on the right side. Warp speed required captain, although pausing to place a crucial Rock 4 in the thin seam may ease the nerves a tad.
*Matt Troilett, Mark Radtke   22nd August 1999*

**29  Griffiths Chimney**  D   20m
Gallop up the wide rock-strewn green gully.

**30  Winter Finish**  VD   23m
After sampling the gloomy delights of the chimney to its midpoint, shimmy rightwards along the ledge to the arête. Pad the slab on the right to the slanting crack and the top.
*Allan Austin, Jennifer Ruffe, Wilby Newton   1st March 1958*

**31  Another Question**  E2 5b   18m  †   ★
A sweeping line which calls for a sure steadiness in hand, foot and mind. From the foot of the buttress, climb cracks leftwards to the left of the arête and commence a precarious sequence of moves that allow the ledge to be reached. Climb directly and easily to the top.
*John Eastham, Geoff Myers   26th April 1987  ✦*

**32  Question Time**  E6 6b   20m   ★★
Delicate technical wizardry and a touch of daring is the order of the day for the serious slab. A critical RP3, placed blind in the seam, may calm the flight or fight in you.
*Mark Radtke, Matt Troilett   22nd Aug 1999*

**33  And Others**  HVS 5a   18m
A well protected expedition sampling most of the sights of the buttress. Start on the green sidewall left of *Real Chimney*. Fill the fissures with fingers and karate-chop up to the second break. Take a tricky traverse leftwards and summit via *Winter Finish*.
*John Eastham, Geoff Myers   26th April 1987*

**34  Real Chimney**  D   15m
Choices, choices. Either opt for cavernous contortions deep within the bowels of the chimney or throw caution to the wind and boldly skirmish the cleft's jaws. Dark and dingy or bright and airy.
*Pre-1920*

**35  Slant**  VS 5a   10m
More slope slithering shenanigans to the right of the 22nd Century arête. Launch up the lichenous ramp right of *Real Chimney* and tackle the short wall above.
*Tony Barley, Tony Roche   18th Sept 1971*

**36  Simple Simon**  S 4b   23m   ★★
A pleasurable weaving experience and quite high in the grade. Ascend the left edge of the slab until it's possible to move right to the deep crack and up to a satisfying ledge. Shuffle right again and attack the overlap with gusto to attain the steep finishing crack.
*Frank Spence   1958*

Robin Nicholson running it out on the eye-catching and celebrated E2 of the crag, **A Question of Balance** (E2 5b), Page 470
Photo: Adi Gill

Gymkhana - **SIMON'S SEAT**

**37 Paws for Thought** HVS 5b  8m  ★
The left-hand arête is short but packs a punch. Carefully launch from the boulder and commence a sequence of slopey mantels until difficulties ease.
*Johnny Cutcliffe   September 1997*

**38 Low Nose Traverse** VS 4c  17m  ★
A worthwhile well-protected meander that spirals up from beneath the *Beaky* spout to finish around the arête on the opposite wall. From the deck climb upward and outward on a ledge and continue around the nose of the buttress. With a taxing move, gain and finish up the deep crack.
*Allan Austin, Brian Evans, Frank Spence   30th August 1958* ✦

**39 Beaky** HVS 5a  10m  ★
Climb direct to the obscene green goo regurgitator. Use the spout to attain, and finish up, the curving crack above.
*John Eastham, Geoff Myers, John Myers   7th May 1978*

**40 Gymkhana** E1 5b  18m  ★★
A butch and bold classic from Barley. The initial roof crack can offer an early spanking for the weak, whilst the exposed rounded arête can leave the musclemen quivering. Surmount the crack and head left to the arête and round the corner. With insecure moves, ascend the arête on the left-hand side with pocket pulling and delicate padding.
*Tony Barley, Tony Roche   18th Sept 1971*

**41 Low Nose Crack** VS 5a  18m  ★
A top jam-fest with enough going on for the crack addict to get their fix. The strenuous start just about goes if you don't hide the good stuff with gear. Keep crankin', the difficulties are short lived.
*Allan Austin, Brian Evans, Frank Spence   30th August 1958*

**42 Flirtin' Cos I'm Hurtin'** E4 6a  10m  ★★
Bring it on! A cheeky test of nerve and technique up the unrelenting ground of the clean face of the buttress. From the boulder, launch up to the tadpole shaped shallow crater in the wall. Make a tough sequence of moves past shallow ramp-lines to the sanctuary of the left arête (thread runner). Top end for the grade.
*Derek Hargreaves, Matt Troilett   June 1998* ✦

**43 iPerbole** Font 7b
Tackle the thin vertical wall direct on pebbles and pebble scars to a vague ledge and escape off right. A spotter is worthwhile as it's a tad high with a fin of rock just behind you that could be problematic if you came off awkwardly.
*Greg Chapman   March 2011*

Just to the right, **Grumble and Grunt** (VS 5a), climbs the awkward tapering chimney to then follow a flake leftward across the wall to finish near the top of *Flirtin'*.

Almscliff to Slipstones

**473**

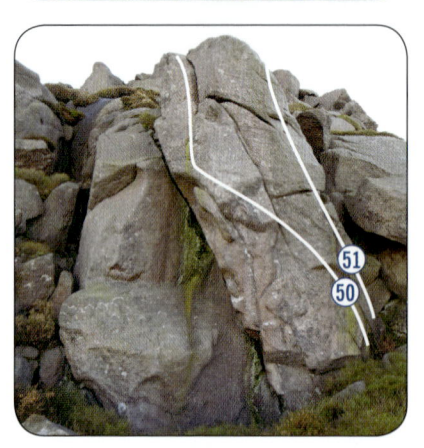

# Simon's seat - Solipsism

### 44 Solipsism  Font 7c
Mint crimp cranking. The wall on the right on crimps, a thin seam and a good pocket to reach the finish. Probably only ever achieved in your own mind. Try again in the real world.
*Greg Chapman    2008*

Back down to the track is the brutal hanging corner of *Amen* and a couple of top-notch problems.

### 45 Blood Brothers  Font 7b+
Class but not for the faint hearted. The highball wall on the left. Sitter crushes at Font 7c+.
*Greg Chapman    2008*

### 46 Amen  HVS 5b   12m
Old school thuggery at its best. Reaching the break via the green hanging corner is a struggle. Jamming leftward along the crack is a struggle. Leaving the break for the thin crack is a struggle. Doddle. At least you can fill the route with as much as it can eat gear-wise, safe in the knowledge that your second will appreciate you afterwards.
*Tony Barley, Robin Barley    April 1973*

### 47 The Pieman  E5 6a   9m   ★
Bold as brass with a touch of class. Start as for *Amen* but with technical trickery get established on the slab above. Shallow pockets and seams guide your path to the finish and although the crux is low down, don't underestimate the lob damage potential.
*David Musgrove (jnr), Dave Musgrove (snr)    1st August 1999*

### 48 Spondonical  Font 7b
The oft-chalked striking arête from a sit-down start.
*Tom Peckitt    2008*

### 49 Ouzo for Twozo  Font 5
Shimmy right-to-left around the fine arête.
*Greg Chapman    2008*

### 50 Simon Says  E2 5c   7m   ★
Ten metres right of *Amen* is a tall block with disconnected, left-leaning, cracks. Swing in from the bottom right and using poor jams and wide bridging gain good holds on the left arête and a fine, fingery finishing crack.
*David Musgrove (snr & jnr), Viv Durrant    1st August 1999*

Just up the hill is a quality sculpted boulder with a tough little number to go at. Surely there's room for more up here.

Yorkshire Gritstone

# The Naked Edge - SIMON'S SEAT

### 51 Touch your Toes  VS 4c  6m
The right arête of *Simon Says*, starting up the short chimney.
*Viv Durrant (solo)  1st August 1999*

### 52 Bashful  E1 5b  7m
The fine slabby arête of the boulder 20m right of *Simon Says*. If high on acid, when viewed from the right the lower section looks like one of The Seven Dwarves. Go to work onto his nose then up into the eye, and continue delicately up the right-hand side.
*David Musgrove (Jnr) (solo)  1st August 1999* ✦

## The Naked Edge Boulder
Further right again, and slightly lower down the hillside, is a large isolated boulder with a superb clean arête, home to three top quality hard micro-routes.

### 53 Fall from Grace  E6 6c  7m  ★★
A haunting exercise in technique and mind control. Answer the call of the compelling wall left of the arête. A big friend in the huge hole provides some cold comfort. The right arête wasn't used on the first ascent.
*Matt Troilett, Roy Healey  Sept 1998*

### 54 The Naked Edge  E3 6a  7m  ★★★
A technical classic where timidity will be justly punished. Solo the arête with a fabulous unrelenting sequence of moves. A buttock-clenching experience of the highest order. Highball Font 6b+. Photo on page 453.
*Jerry Peel  Autumn 1978*

### 55 Dino-Mania  E5 6b  7m  ★★
Premiership power play up the clean rough wall. Release the beast with a technically aerobatic start to conquer the groove and reach the good pocket (Font 6c if you bail now). From here a thin handrail and small pocket allows ascent leftwards. Now get a shift on to exit before the terror of it all really kicks in. Highball Font 6c+.
*David Musgrove (Jnr) (solo)  1st August 1993* ✦

### 56 The Scoop  Font 5
Cut into the scoop from the right. This can be used as an easier start to *Dino-Mania*.

# Simon's seat - Toe-Fu

Behind and uphill from the *Naked Edge* boulder is an impressive boulder with one of Yorkshire's hardest offerings.

### 57 **Toe-Fu**  Font 8a+
Monster moves that are size and reach-dependant. From a pinch on the rail, and with fingers in the large undercut pocket, throw a wild foot-dyno out to the arête. Match feet and, with the toe-hook still on, make a full-span lunge to the distant finger slot before a difficult dyno for the poor pocket in the underside of the roof. If you get that far don't go and blow it on the dropable topout. Photo on page 685.
*Tom Peckitt   July 2011* ✦

### 58 **Trunk**  Font 5+
Grapple with the prominent sculptured snout. The sit-down start is **Delta** (Font 7b), and launches from a low pocket to the ledge and up.

### 59 **Monte Carlo**  Font 7b
Tough moves from a sitter to grovel onto the slab.

Just slightly uphill and to the right is the **Fulvia** boulder. A few options exist here but the recorded problem gets the blood flowing.

Victorian Climb - **SIMON'S SEAT**

### 60 Fulvia   Font 6b+
From a sit-down start shuffle leftward on palm shredding slopers to the blunt arête. Chug on round or rock onto the slab and up.

### Victorian Climb Area
Up the hill and left, just before the summit plateau, is the prominent pillar containing the distinctive chimney-crack of *Victorian Climb*. Photographic evidence indicates this was soloed in 1895! To the left of this is a series of bays with many a good problem. The popular ones go at, and above, Font 7a and start from the third bay back and to the left past *Victorian Climb* and away from the track.

### 61 Triptych   Font 7a
Committing moves from a sitter up the crack and left arête. Maximum slopeyness to finish above a less than ideal drop zone.
*Tom Peckitt   2008*

### 62 Trilogy   Font 7a
The arête right of the crack rocking up to an equally rounded finish astride the blunt prow.
*Tom Peckitt   2008*

### 63 The Triad   Font 7a
Top pinch and slopers to the horror show finale you're now familiar with.
*Tom Peckitt   2008*

### 64 Pinna   Font 7a
The fine arête and wall with useful pockets in the next bay back towards the track. Bad landing. Font 7a+ from a sit-down start.
*Tom Peckitt   2008*

### 65 Simon Says Squeeze   Font 7b+
Stick it like a koala up the quality prow in the next bay toward the track. Originally climbed from a sit-down start at Font 7c.
*Tom Peckitt   2008*

### 66 Victorian Climb   HVS 5a   6m   ★
A 19th Century gem that can be a desperate vertical thrash for those that can't think laterally. Wrestle the pillar-splitting crack and be thankful for the solitude of Simon's Seat, as your humiliation is unlikely to be witnessed by too many onlookers. Shame it's not at Almscliff.
*c1895*

Almscliff to Slipstones

# Simon's seat - Whaleback

> Mountain magazine was the world climbing magazine at the time and there was an article about Harrison's Rock and about the local wizard down there. We arranged a Northern Counties versus Home Counties South. We had a minibus full of John Allen, Jerry Peel and his brother, Hank Pasquill, myself, Ron [Fawcett] wasn't but Chris Gibb, the lad he was climbing with was in it, Tom Procter and Geoff Birtles were in it for some reason. The cream. If that minibus had crashed that would have been the end of British climbing. We went "right let's go down to Harrison's see what it's all about". We just creamed them. It was embarrassing. We just obliterated them.
>
> Al Manson

## Whaleback
Onwards and upwards now to the plateau with either side of the track containing the greatest concentration of bouldering at The Seat. Clean highballs and the class of *Whaleback* to the left whilst the opposite wall, *Drift Wall*, is home to a neat line-up of problems on The Seat's characteristically rough protrusions.

### 67 Funky Jam  Font 4
Thrutch like a good un' up the short fissure.

### 68 A Life Less Ordinary  E6 6b  5m  ★★
A characteristic masterstroke by one of the modern day big hitters. Gird your loins, step from the boulder and levitate the left side of the unrelenting and immaculate arête. A serious outing that culminates in a rounded finish.
*Matt Troilett (solo)   July 1998*

### 69 Trigger Happy  Font 7b
Extreme highball swinging up the right side of the arête from the shallow flake.

### 70 The Shelf  Font 6b
Mantel the face.

### 71 Whaleback  Font 7a+
A beautiful line and true classic although sadly now showing detrimental signs of its own success. From a low start and good pocket make a long move for the obvious curving

Yorkshire Gritstone

# Drift Wall - SIMON'S SEAT

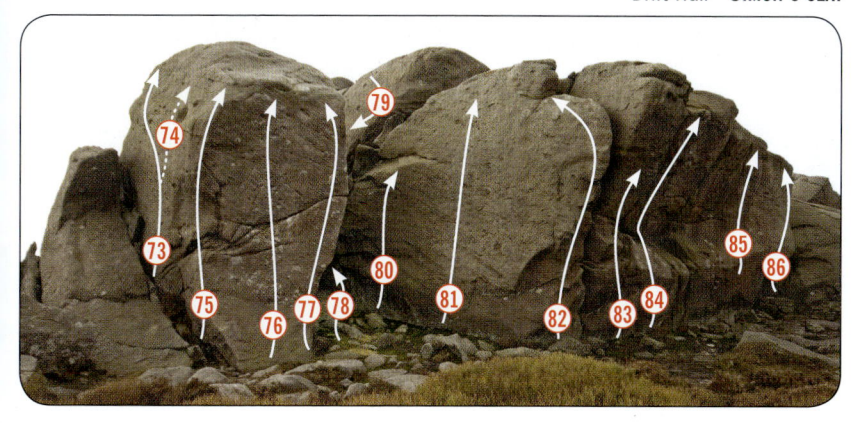

crack. Finish on easier ground. Leave the brush at home and protect the pocket for the future. Photo on page 458.
*Andy Swann   1990s*

### 72 Obsequious   E4 6a   7m
Delicately teeter up the prominent sculptured arête with the utmost confidence in success (for the landing doesn't bare thinking about).
*Derek Hargreaves, Matt Troilett   11th October 1999*

## Drift Wall
The brooding wall opposite is a sanctuary of class problems for us mortals that like to keep their ankles just the way they are.

### 73 Drift Wall   Font 5
The slab past the crater to a taxing top move.

### 74 In the Frame   Font 4
Shoot the gap between the arête and *Drift Wall*.

### 75 Canvas Arête   Font 6b
The rounded arête taken on its right. A tricky little number.

### 76 Masterpiece   Font 7a+
From good crimps in the break gurn for glory. Both arêtes are out-of-bounds.

### 77 Palette   Font 6b+
The sharp arête taken on the left.

### 78 Brushstroke   Font 6a+
The arête is a tad easier on the right.

### 79 Easel   Font 6a+
Cruise left from *Brushstroke* past the scoop.

### 80 Ledge-end   Font 6b
Give it some welly to the slopey ledge and on to glory.

### 81 Cock-a-Hoop   Font 4+
Brill slab using crimps and the hula-hoop.

### 82 Edge Udger   Font 6a
Seams guide your path for the balance lesson up the slab and arête.

### 83 Prowler   Font   6a+
Tough cookie. Commit to the steep prow. It's not over till it's over.

### 84 Splinter   Font 5
Attack the crack.

### 85 Mantel Upset   Font 5+
An oft frustrating exercise to get going but patience and imagination will pay dividends.

### 86 Wallender   Font 6a
Size isn't everything. The quality arête at the wall end.

Moorland grit summed up perfectly. Robin Nicholson on **And She Was** (E3 6a). Page 482.
Photo: Adi Gill

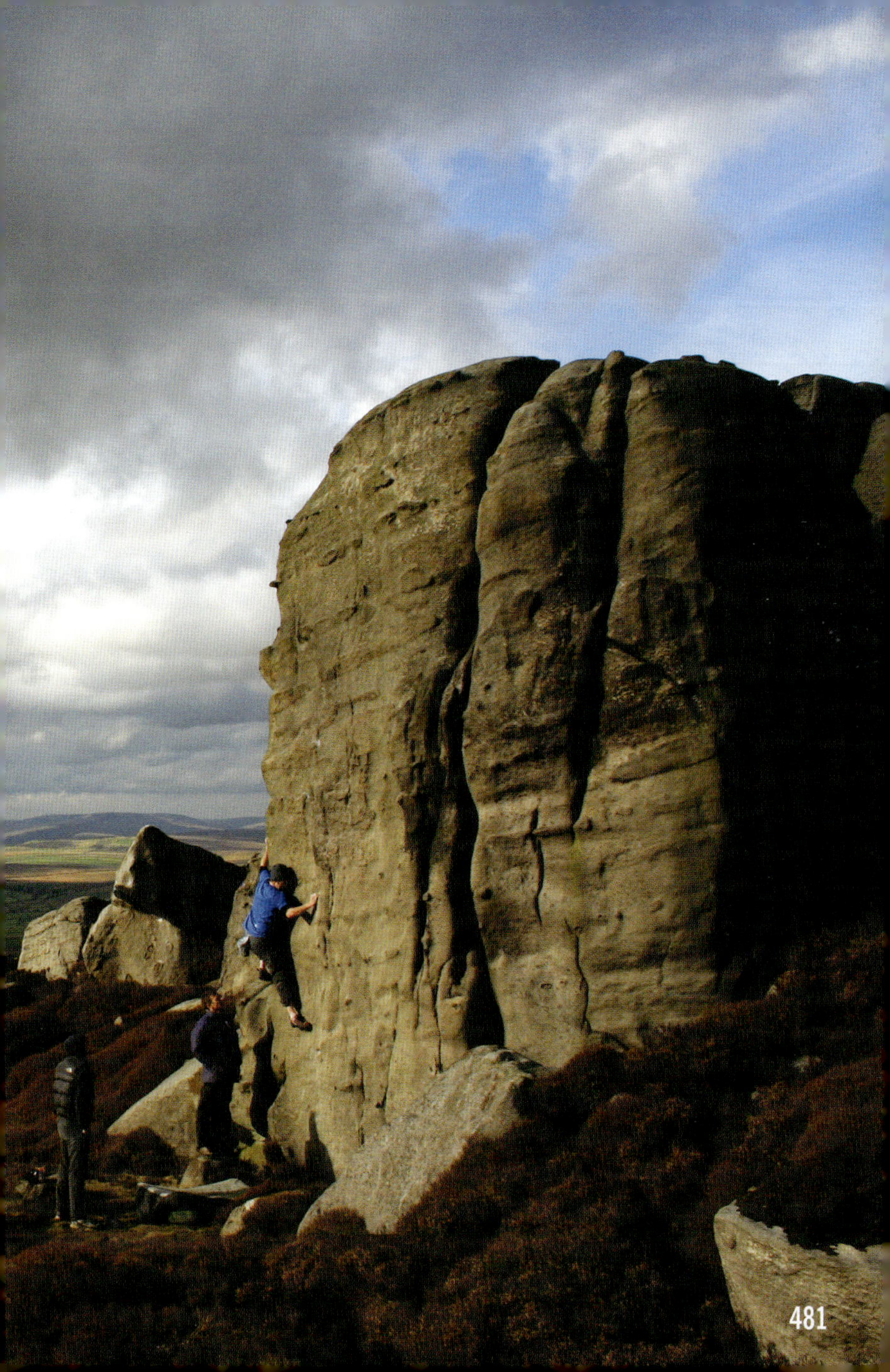

# Simon's seat - And She Was

## And She Was

From the left end of the Drift Wall Area follow the main track clockwise around to the sunlit south-west side of the crag. Walk past the main climbing area here to the far left-hand end. Here lies the jutting prow of the *Galaxy* boulder followed by the wonderful pillar of rock of the *And She Was* buttress, which is home to two utterly classic solos and an arm-shredding crack from bygone times.

### 87 Galaxy Left  Font 7c+
Classic reachy variation from two of the regions top bouldering protagonists. From the chamfered crimp, back-crawl into *Galaxy*.
*Dave Cowl / Andy Swann*

### 88 Galaxy  Font 7a
Sit-down start. Chips to prow to top. Neat.
*Andy Swann*

### 89 Red Hot Knob  VS 5a  6m
Tackle the overhanging prow to the sanctuary of the obscene protrusion (blistering in a hot summer apparently).
*Stuart Lancaster (solo)  10th July 1999*

### 90 Corner Crack  HVD 4a  7m
The easier of the routes hereabouts but still the site of a modicum of cursing. Tussle with the obvious steep corner.
*Arnold & Sidney Waterfall, Bill Bowler   Mid-1930s*

### 91 And She Was  E3 6a  8m  ★★
Another of the many immaculate natural lines of The Seat and one that requires unflinching commitment. Climb the left arête on its right side. Technical interest is maintained throughout. Photo on page 480.
*Derek Hargreaves (solo)   9th August 1988*

### 92 I'll Bet She Does  E3 6a  8m  ★★★
A bold beauty and the essence of climbing distilled into 6m of moorland grit. Unlock the initial puzzle and make urgent moves to easier ground. Climb it.
*David Musgrove (jnr) (solo)   23rd September 1995*

### 93 Straight Crack  VS 4c  8m  ★
Fine purveyors of crack climbing are in for a treat. Ascend the fissure on solid jams and the odd protrusions. From a time when men were men.
*Arnold & Sidney Waterfall, Bill Bowler   Mid-1930s*

### 94 Inaccessible Crack  VS 5a  8m  ★
Technical trickery gains the steep hanging crack from the right of the buttress.
*Allan Austin   1st March 1958*

The next climb takes the prominent crack on the right-hand side of the bay between *Inaccessible Crack* and *Left-Hand Arête*. **Big Ears and the Battle of the Millipedes** (S 4b), romps up the disappearing crack with the aid of the sharp ears of rock.

Central Cracks - **Simon's seat**

### Central Cracks
A few metres right in the next bay is a short clean wall with radiating cracks. Rough, with a multitude of rugosities and protrusions there's something for everyone here but the landings on the left-hand end leave a bit to be desired.

### 95 Left-Hand Arête  HVS 5a   6m
Scamper calmly up the arête, putting all plummeting possibilities to the back of your mind. (a) **Centipede** (HS 4c) ambles across the face via the horizontal break, across the cracks and to the prominent horn up and right.

### 96 Out With the Old  E1 5b   7m  ★
Thin moves up the wall lead to the sanctuary of good holds out right. Trend back left to a taxing top move.
*Andy Say (solo)   31st December 1989*

### 97 Central Cracks  S 4b   7m
A fun outing up the three hanging cracks and peculiar weathered knobs. (b) Using the prominent chickenheads from *Out With the Old*, **Gimp Left-Hand** (HVS 5a) squeezes an alternate finish up the shallow groove out left.

### 98 Right-Hand Crack  HS 4c   7m  ★
Battle merrily up the slanting crack. The 'baguette slice' out left allows momentum to be gained for the push to the top. Photo on next page.

### 99 Chunky Chicken  E1 5b   7m
The direct line up the rib and narrowing wall.
*David Musgrove (jnr)(solo)*

### 100 Rush Hour  HD   6m
The interesting corner-crack.
*Tony Marr, Mike Tooke   7th Oct 2010*

### 101 Bite Size  VD 4a   6m
The slanting crack from a hard start.
*Tony Marr, Mike Tooke   7th Oct 2010*

Right of *Bite Size* is a nice set of scrambly routes and easy boulder problems. Ideal for a family picnic spot.

### 102 Jug Arête  Font 4+
The prow tackled just on the left from a quality hold and pocket.

Arifa Chakera soaks up the evening light on **Right-Hand Crack** (HS 4c). Previous page.
Photo: Mike Hutton

## Open Face - SIMON'S SEAT

**Open Face Area:** From here more broken rocks lead to the right end of the outcrop, where the huge Magnolia boulder obscures the start of a few decent lines.

### 103 Magnolia   Font 7b+
From a super low start, heel hooking from the off (!), use marginal holds to gain the juggy flake. Follow this all the way to the top.
*Dave Cowl   2005*

### 104 Orchid   Font 6c
From sitting, gain the lip and traverse it left to finish via the dish. From standing it's Font 6b.
*James Kitson   2005*

### 105 Hidden Crack   S 4a   10m
Neat little combo of crack, mantel and slab climbing.

### 106 Hidden Chimney   S 4a   10m   ★
Pummel up the steep crack behind the *Magnolia* boulder with the occasional assistance from the small gargoyles.
*Pre-1920*

### 107 Open Face   HVS 5b   10m   ★
A pumpy and airy experience which can punish the shy. Step up and grapple with the arête's fluting until the break. Cut left and tread carefully, yet confidently, directly up the bumpy wall.
*Tony Barley, Tony Roche   18th Sept 1971*

### 108 The Egg of Course   E2 5b   10m   ★
A variation finish to *Open Face* which requires you to bravely battle the bulbous bulging rib out right. Not for the faint-hearted. A direct start goes at 5c.
*Julian Cooper, David Musgrove (snr & jnr)   23 Sept 1995*

### 109 Blinkers Rib   HVS 5c   8m
The rib immediately right of the easy gully around on the east face is tackled without deviation.
*David Musgrove (snr & jnr)   23 Sept 1995*

### 110 Grumpy's Crack   HS 4c   7m
Crimps and ripples lead to the steep diverging cracks. Only HVD 4a from the block behind.
*Dave Musgrove (solo)   23 Sept 1995*

# Simon's Seat - First Ascent Information & Graded List

## Further Information on First Ascents (✦)

Records show that Cecil Slingsby took his son-in-law to be, Geoffrey Winthrop Young, to the crag around 1910 but which new routes were achieved at this visit (or on previous visits) are unknown.

**Another Question:** Both the 1989 and 1998 topo illustrations for this route show the right arête of the buttress being climbed. The description and grade matches the left arête (the right being significantly harder than E2).

**Arête Direct:** This arête had been top-roped from pre-1923, but from a much higher traverse line. Originally known as Traverse and Arête.

**Azimuth:** A nut was used for aid to climb the overhang.

**Bashful:** Possibly climbed previously by Derek Hargreaves but unrecorded.

**Big Ears and the Battle of the Millipedes:** Climbed by Matt Kilner (solo) 8th June

**Beelzebub Crack** & several other routes: 7th August 1943 Recorded by the pioneering team of Arthur Dolphin and John Cook. Sadly, it is impossible to pinpoint these climbs.

**Centipede:** Traverse by John Hunt (solo) 27th July 2007.

**Dino-mania:** Top roped before a bold solo.

**Flirtin' Cos I'm Hurtin':** The start of a campaign by Hargreaves, Troilett and Radtke to bag a host of new classic hard routes (along with Fall from Grace, A Life Less Ordinary, Question Time, etc); many achieved with some 21st Century climbing just before time.

**Gimp Left-Hand:** First ascent by Dave Parton, Sven Rowan, John Buckley, Nige Hunt, Dave Ormerode on 14th Sept 2002.

**Grumble and Grunt** and **Tartarus:** Climbed by Tony Marr, Mike Tooke on 26th July 2011.

**Low Nose Traverse:** Top-roped in 1949 by Sydney Waterfall. "This is very difficult movement", He commented, "Rubbers recommended".

**Toe-Fu:** A cracking effort by Peckitt to put up one of Yorkshire's hardest problems on grit in the middle of a very hot summer.

**Turret Crack:** Originally called Antimacassar. Frank Spence fell down the hillside from the top of the crack while attempting the first ascent. He survived to lead the top pitch after Austin mastered the crack.

**Y- Front:** Variations to this route: Gentleman's Support by John Byrne, Peter Pozman in July 1988 and Brief Encounter by Tony Marr, Mike Tooke 3rd September 2010.

## Graded List

### Routes

**E6**
Fall from Grace (6c)
A Life Less Ordinary (6b)
Question Time (6b)

**E5**
Dino-Mania (6b)
The Pieman (6a)

**E4**
Finesse (6a)
Where's Grandma (6a)
Flirtin' Cos I'm Hurtin' (6a)
Obsequious (6a)

**E3**
Panzer (6a)
The Naked Edge (6a)
I'll Bet She Does (6a)
And She Was (6a)
Shush Popeye (5c)
Azimuth (5b)

**E2**
Simon Says (5c)
A Question of Balance (5b)
The Egg of Course (5b)
Another Question (5b)

**E1**
The Gunner (5c)
Gentleman's Support (5b)
Bashful (5b)
Gymkhana (5b)
Chunky Chicken (5b)
Out With The Old (5b)
Clappers Crack (5b)

**HVS**
Blinkers Rib (5c)
Outside Finish (5b)
Paws for Thought (5b)
Open Face (5b)
Amen (5b)
Blind Alley (5b)
Dog Lead (5a)
Turret Crack (5a)
Gimp Left Hand (5a)
Victorian Climb (5a)
Left-Hand Arête (5a)
Beaky (5a)
And Others (5a)

**VS**
North Gully Buttress (5a)
Brief Encounter (5a)
Low Nose Crack (5a)
Posh Spice and ' (5a)
Hair of the Dog (5a)

Tartarus (5a)
Grumble and Grunt (5a)
Red Hot Knob (5a)
Slant (5a)
Baggin's Variation (4c)
Touch your Toes (4c)
Low Nose Traverse (4c)
Mosaic (4c)
Straight Crack (4c)
Chockstone Chimney (4c)
Arête Direct (4c)

**HS**
Centipede (4c)
Right-Hand Crack (4c)
Grumpy's Crack (4b)

**S**
Chimney Wall (4b)
Central Cracks (4b)
Big Ears and the Battle of The Millipedes (4b)
Simple Simon (4b)
Y- Front (4a)
Hidden Chimney (4a)
Hidden Crack (4a)
Arête Wall (4a)
High Nose Traverse

**HVD**
Corner Crack (4a)

**VD**
Layback Crack
Flake Climb
Square Chimney
Pothole Chimney
Winter Finish
Bite Size (4a)

**HD**
Rush Hour

**D**
Griffiths Chimney
North Gully
Window Chimney
Real Chimney
Rush Hour

### Problems

**8a+**
Toe-Fu

**7c+**
Blood Brothers SDS
Galaxy Left

**7c**
Solipsism

**7b+**
Blood Brothers

Magnolia
Simon Says Squeeze

**7b**
iPerbole
Spondonical
Trigger Happy
Monte Carlo
Delta

**7a+**
Whaleback
Masterpiece

**7a**
Triptych
Trilogy
The Triad
Galaxy
Pinna

**6c**
Orchid

**6b+**
Fulvia
Palette

**6b**
The Shelf
Canvas Arête

Ledge-end

**6a+**
Brushstroke
Easel
Prowler

**6a**
Edge Udger
Wallender

**5+**
Trunk
Mantel Upset
In the Frame

**5**
Ouzo for Twozo
The Scoop
Splinter
Drift Wall

**4+**
Cock-a-Hoop
Jug Arête

**4**
Funky Jam
In the Frame

# HEN STONES

# hen stones

by **James Ibbertson**

OS Ref: SE 082 594
Altitude: 480m

This small annex to Simon's Seat is home to a clutch of high quality boulder problems and is well worth the five minute walk from the main crag. The situation and views here are second to none making it the perfect place to enjoy a couple of hours of solitary bouldering.

**Conditions and Aspect:** The boulders face south, are very exposed to the elements and dry very quickly. Be warned, the rock here is fragile. Any brushing could cause permanent damage. The holds can be sandy but the problems are graded to reflect this.

**Approach and Access:** Parking, approach and access restrictions are as for Simon's Seat (page 461). From the crossroads of the two main paths at Simon's Seat, head directly south-east across the open moor for 200m. A cluster of small boulders can be seen from the approach but Hen Stones lies immediately behind (north-east) of these. There is no path to follow and the bog is deep.

### 1 Chicken Run  Font 5
Climb the awkward crack to a tussle at the top.
*Naomi Buys, Jordan Buys & James Ibbertson   September 2004*

### 2 Hen Arête  Font 7a
The striking arête climbed on its left is undeniably the best problem hereabouts.
*James Ibbertson, Jordan Buys  September 2004*

### 3 Bird Flu  Font 7b
The blank looking right side can be surmounted using technical trickery. An ability to spatchcock oneself helps.
*James Ibbertson   October 2006*

### 4 Family Bucket  Font 3
Take the slabby face passing the large break.
*Naomi Buys, Jordan Buys & James Ibbertson   September 2004*

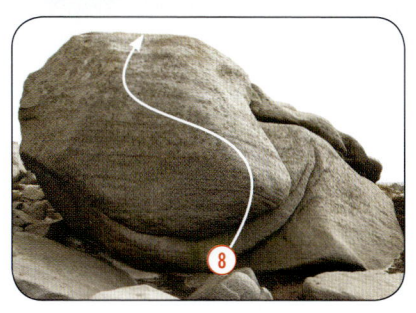

### 5 Chicken Tonight  Font 3+
Enjoyable moves up the obvious and pleasant groove.
*Naomi Buys, Jordan Buys & James Ibbertson   September 2004*

### 6 Hen Pecked  Font 6c
A barn door start and big move finish are required to tick the left arête.
*James Ibbertson   September 2005*

### 7 Free Range  Font 7b+
The tricky right arête certainly packs it in. From a tricky low start climb to a sloping top-out.
*James Ibbertson   September 2007*

### 8 Over Easy  Font 7a+
Deceptively pumpy. From the right side of the large undercut, a powerful sit-down start gains the leftward-trending ramp. Follow this on slopers to the highest point of the block.
*James Ibbertson   September 2004*

Almscliff to Slipstones

# lord's seat
## by Will Hunt

OS Ref: SE 085599　　　　　　　　　　　　　　Altitude: 470m

Lord's Seat is a particularly apt name for this wonderful little cluster of blue-grey gritstone buttresses. With its proud location on the edge of Barden Fell, it provides some superb, positive routes and problems and a noble vantage point for some of the best views in the area. The climbing is equally as charming as the situation; great for families, away from the crowds and plenty of soft, bouncy heather for ankle-friendly landings. The grit here is typical of that found on the fell in that it gives excellent friction but is a little grainy and extra care must be taken not to damage the fragile rock.

**The Climbing:** There are more than 60 climbs, mostly low or mid-grade with a healthy dose of hard, high-quality bouldering up to Font 7c+. Just a few of the many 'must-do' lines here include *Mantel Fantastic (HVS 5a)*, *Pure Gold (E1 5c)*, *McNab (Font 7b)* and *Pocket, Traverse and Arête (Font 5)*. In the previous guide all the routes here were given trad grades but, with its impeccable landings, Lord's Seat blurs the boundary between highballing and soloing on a regular basis and climbs generally fell as either VS or HVS. All the routes and problems are between 5m and 10m in height, though most don't exceed 8m. To improve accuracy here the routes are graded as boulder problems with the exception of those that can be led with trad gear, are too high or whose landing is poor.

**Conditions and Aspect:** Some parts of the crag take a little drainage and there are some breaks and cracks that take longer to dry through the colder months. However, the crag occupies a prominent position on the fell facing primarily south and south-west, catching all available sun and wind and so the majority of the climbs will dry quickly after rain in kind weather. In the wetter months, after the peatland water table has been recharged, the walk in may be a little 'spongy' but the ground around the crag is not badly affected.

**Parking and Approach:** The parking and approach are the same as for Simon's Seat (see page 461). When you reach Simon's Seat resist the temptation of this wonderful venue and continue east (on the path at the top of the crag) for 500m to reach Lord's Seat (6 minutes).

**Access:** The same access restrictions apply to Lord's Seat as that of Simon's Seat. Refer to page 461 for full details. No dogs.

The crag is split into three main sections: the Upper and Lower Tiers and the Wall Buttress which lies over the boundary wall.

'Watch me here'. Adi Gill getting his leg stuck on **Larkin's Right** (E1 5b). Page 496
Photo: Dave Sutcliffe

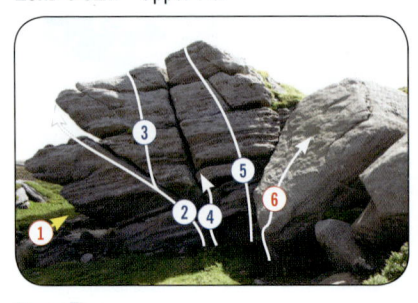

# Lord's Seat - Upper Tier

## Upper Tier
As the crag is approached, a distinctive cracked wall can be seen set back slightly from the main line of the Upper Tier. This small bay faces the path on the north side and kicks things off nicely.

### 1 Ironside  Font 7b+
Just around the corner from the main wall of the bay. Make a steep, low, left-to-right traverse on crimps to finish up the arête.

### 2 Harrogate Nights  HS 4b  5m
On the main wall of the bay, take the leftwards leading rising crack to the shelf. Top out directly above this.
*Will Hunt  23rd July 2010*

### 3 Harvey  S 4a  5m
The pleasant wall to the left of the main crack in the bay. The grade allows for doing the sensible thing and placing gear in *The Crack*.
*Bob Larkin  July 1998*

### 4 The Crack  S 4a  5m
Great fun. The obvious vertical crack.
*Bob Larkin  July 1998*

### 5 Wallbanger  VS 4c  6m
A neat route up the right wall.
*Bob Larkin  July 1998*

### 6 The Slab  Font 3 (HS 4a)
Step onto the delicate slab from the start of *Wallbanger*, or tackle it direct at Font 5+.
*Bob Larkin  July 1998*

Follow the crag around to the right and the south side of Upper Tier. Now the fun really starts with some of the classics and higher offerings of the crag. The climbing here starts with a slabby buttress.

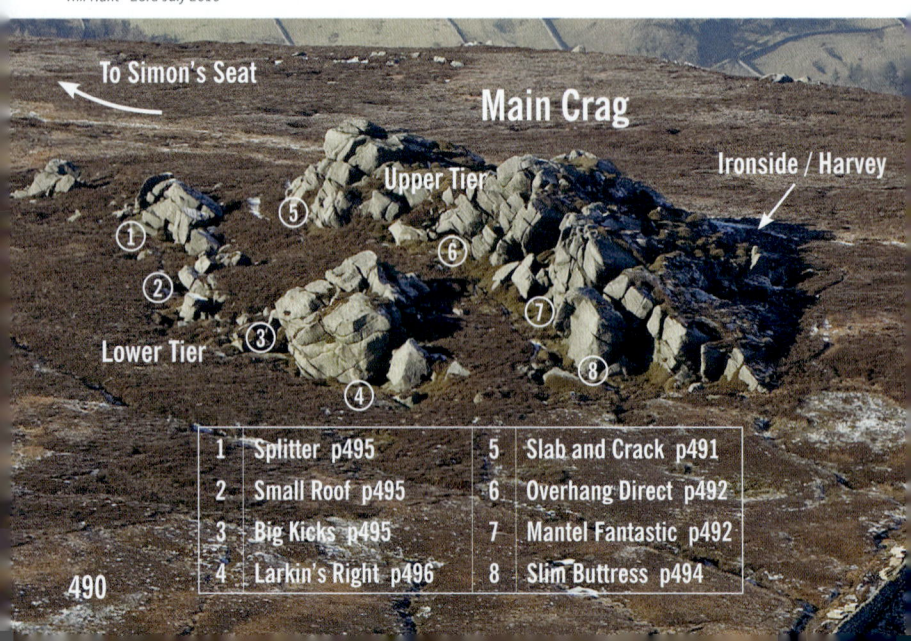

---

**To Simon's Seat**

**Main Crag**

**Upper Tier**

**Ironside / Harvey**

**Lower Tier**

| | | | |
|---|---|---|---|
| 1 | Splitter  p495 | 5 | Slab and Crack  p491 |
| 2 | Small Roof  p495 | 6 | Overhang Direct  p492 |
| 3 | Big Kicks  p495 | 7 | Mantel Fantastic  p492 |
| 4 | Larkin's Right  p496 | 8 | Slim Buttress  p494 |

Upper Tier - **LORD'S SEAT**

### 7 Slab and Crack  VD  6m
The far left of the buttress can be climbed by a variety of ways, all at about the same grade.
*Bob Larkin   July 1998*

### 8 Slab and Overlap  MVS 4b  7m
Follow the slab to the crack in the overlap. Pulling through this provides the well-protected crux.
*Bob Larkin   July 1998*

### 9 High Crack  VD  7m
The crack set high up on the wall can be gained by a scramble from the right and is very short-lived.

### 10 High Pebble Wall  HVD  6m
Approached the same way as the previous route, the pebble-stricken wall to the right provides a more continuous exercise.

### 11 Ladder Wall  Font 1
A lovely introduction to smearing.

### 12 Rail Mantel  Font 6a
From a sit-down start, with hands in the obvious scooped handrail, wrestle your way to a standing position on the rail using anything and everything that comes to hand.

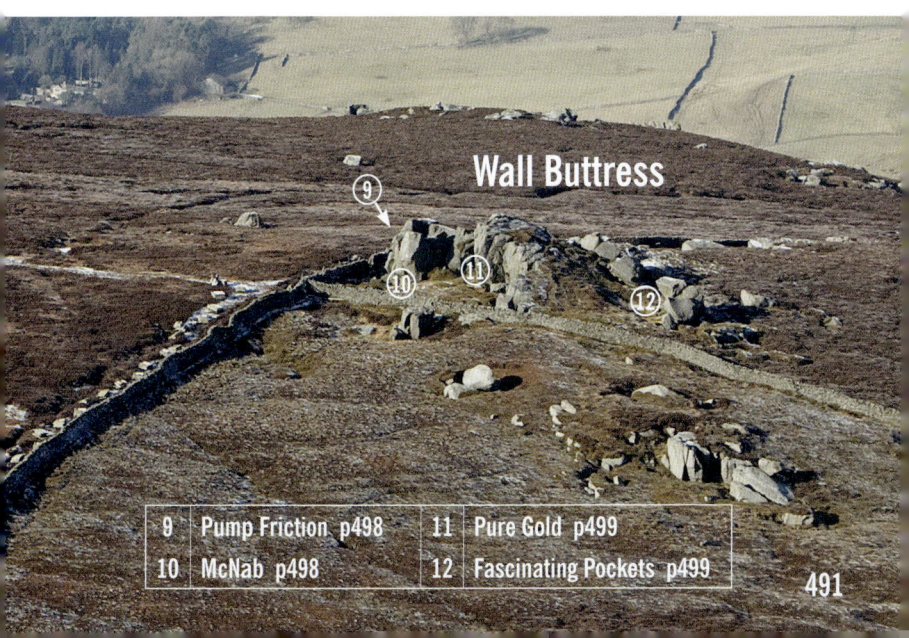

## Wall Buttress

| 9 | Pump Friction  p498 | 11 | Pure Gold  p499 |
| 10 | McNab  p498 | 12 | Fascinating Pockets  p499 |

491

# Lord's Seat - Mantel Fantastic

A little further to the right the steep prow provides the challenging **Gorgeous Geordies** (Font 7a). From a sit-down start on the front of the prow, follow the sloping lip leftwards to rock up and out at its terminus or, if you've left your biceps at home, take the easier rightwards exit at Font 6b+. A short way right again is a prominent overhang.

### 13  Overhang Direct  Font 5
There are a few different ways to tackle this superb line, the easiest being to follow the juggy right-hand lip to top-out up the central rib. A far better, more popular and slightly tougher variant is to make the (a) **Big Dyno** (Font 6b) from the flake in the centre of the roof to the jug on the lip. Go on, you know you want to. Photo on page 551.
*Nigel Baker, Andy Watts   18th July 1998*

### 14  Lagopus Laughter Indirect  MVS 4c  6m
Use the prominent flake crack and escape left onto the wide ledge. Finish direct on the slabs above.
*Will Hunt, Alec Smith   17th March 2011*

### 15  Hanging Groove  S 4a  7m
Exiting the small cave leftwards, gain the crack in the hanging groove and follow it to the top. The direct start to this groove, passing direct through the roof, is **Tranquility** (Font 5+).
*Bob Larkin (Tranquility)   15th August 1998*

### 16  Gritstone Special  HVS 5a  7m  ★
The hanging crack is reached by traversing rightwards from the cave. It's only trying to give your hands a big cuddle.
*Bob Larkin   July 1998*

Further to the right past a large boulder is a collection of excellent climbs.

### 17  Flake and Wall  VS 4c  8m  ★
Follow the flakes up the tall face moving slightly leftwards. From the small ledge, make a delicate move to gain the finish. Poorly-protected where it matters.
*Bob Larkin   July 1998*

### 18  Mantel Fantastic  HVS 5a  8m  ★★★
An excellent climb and the classic of the crag. Steady but bold climbing leads up the arête to the right and the wall above. If gripped, an easier exit can be found to the right.
*Bob Larkin   July 1998*

### 19  Reunion  VS 4c  8m
Squeezed between *Mantel Fantastic* and *Grit Crack* is a line that just about manages to be independent.
*Bob Larkin, Mick Haffner   14th June 2003*

### 20  Grit Crack  S 4a  8m
The easy crack in the centre of the wall is often climbed more as a layback.
*Bob Larkin   July 1998*

### 21  Bulging Wall  HVS 5a  8m  ★★
The superb wall to the right is boldly climbed through the bulge, finishing right of the crack.
*Bob Larkin   July 1998*

### 22  Spout Hangout  HVS 5a  8m  ★
Tackling the arête to the right via the large porthole and the wall above provides a bold test of courage.
*Robin Nicholson   23rd July 2010*

Dave Sutcliffe sampling **Crack Nose** (Font 6b). Page 498.
Photo: Adi Gill

# LORD'S SEAT - Lower Tier

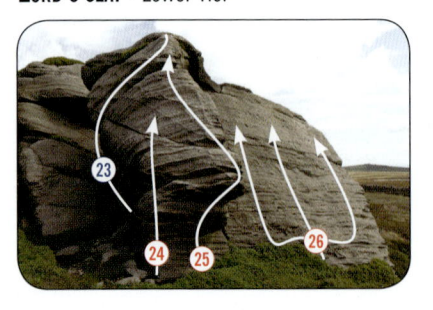

### 23 Widening Horizons  VS 4b  6m  ★
The large block to the right of *Spout Hangout* is split horizontally by a brutal rising, spiralling and widening break. Get ready to wedge yourself in the crack up to your armpits as you traverse this strenuously from the rear of the block where it can be reached from the ground until it is possible to finish up the front arête. Useful training for vets wanting to practise bovine rectal palpation.
*Andrew James, Conor Brown  15th March 2009*

The south face of this boulder is comprised of a clear arête, corner and slab containing the following climbs.

### 24 Slim Bay  Font 6a
Good holds from a sit-down start lead to a committing move right.

### 25 Slim Buttress  Font 5+
The arête climbed from a sit-down start.

### 26 Slim Buttress Slab  Font 3
The corner and slab can be climbed via multiple variations at the same grade.

To the right and set back a little from these routes is **Three Pocket Wall** (Font 4+). This climbs the obvious pocketed wall and is pleasing enough but the first ascensionist's arithmetic must be called into question. The obvious lone prow to the right can be climbed at Font 4 at various spots around its perimeter.

On the rear of the Upper Tier there are a couple of boulders that hold some harder climbs. These have a more northerly aspect and are surrounded by heather, so tend to stay a little green. The dedicated Lord's Seat connoisseur is advised to seek out the large boulder with a break and small roof near the top known as **Bottomless Arête**. This houses the excellent **Yorker** (Font 6c+), which romps up the steep wall starting from the edge and a mono, and **Maverick Mick** (Font 7c+), which goes from a sit-down start just to the right, off the low flake to an open pocket and ascends the steep prow above.

## Lower Tier
Less continuous than the Upper Tier and with a collection of thuggish problems that will doubtlessly make your skin beg for mercy. More care is required when walking along the vague path at the foot of this tier as in parts the heather conceals some unpleasant leg traps. The first boulder contains a number of taxing problems.

### 27 Clamper  Font 6b
The left-hand undercut arête is climbed from a sit-down start.

### 28 Right Arête  Font 6c
The right-hand arête is tackled on its left-hand side.

### 29 Pick Pocket  Font 6a
Gurn straight up for the obvious large pocket.

### 30 Slab and Crack  Font 4
Delicate moves up the middle of the slab to the crack.

### 31 Right Slab  Font 5
The right-hand side of the slab. It also has a fun sit-down start extension (Font 6a) to gain the arête.

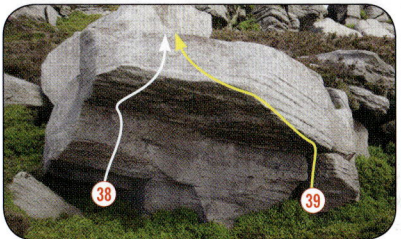

# Big Kicks - LORD'S SEAT

The next section of the Lower Tier is formed by a collection of short climbs surrounding a small cave and a block split by a large crack.

### 32 **The Nose**  Font 5+
The undercut nose is picked off from a sit-down start.

### 33 **Right of Way**  Font 6a+
The inside arête to the roof of the cave is climbed above a landing that leaves much to be desired.

### 34 **Traverse and Arête**  Font 4
Traverse from the back of the cave out right and finish up the arête more easily. The arête can be climbed direct at the same grade.
*Bob Larkin   July 1998*

### 35 **Ripple Wall**  Font 3
The rippled wall is straightforward enough but feels high.
*Bob Larkin   July 1998*

### 36 **Splitter**  Font 3
The obvious splitter crack can be laybacked or jammed according to whether you like the skin on your hands.

### 37 **Splitter Arête**  Font 5+
The arête to the right of the crack is great fun.

About 30m to the right is a small buttress with a steep mid-height roof. The roof may be climbed in many ways and discovering these for the first time with friends is a pleasure. Here are a couple of suggestions to break the ice.

### 38 **Small Roof Left**  Font 6a
Tough for the vertically challenged. From a sit-down start, use a handy layaway to reach the lip. Pass this with difficulty.

### 39 **Small Roof Right**  Font 6b
Sit-down start. From the right, traverse the lip of the roof and finish up the previous problem. *Another 30m to the right is a more imposing roof...*

### 40 **Serenity**  Font 6b+
From the left of the roof, traverse the pumpy break until below the soil filled pocket. Pull up bravely but perhaps not so 'serenely' through this.
*Bob Larkin   15th August 1998*

### 41 **Big Kicks**  Font 7c
One of the crag's testpiece problems to challenge the wads. Start on a small, oft-chalked, crimp in the roof then make a wild dyno to the break above. Awesome.
*Tom Peckitt   15th September 2007*

### 42 **Big Roof Traverse**  Font 6c
Back in the realm of the mortals the counter-line to *Serenity* goes from a sitter and traverses the lip from right–to-left to finish up the left arête.

### 43 **Right Rib**  Font 6b
The right rib of the buttress from a sit-down start.

*Almscliff to Slipstones*

# LORD'S SEAT - Larkin's Right

## Larkin's Right
The large buttress to the right contains some of the best climbs at Lord's Seat.

### 44 Pebble Wall  VS 4c  6m
The left-hand end of the large mid-height shelf is gained using pebbles.
*Bob Larkin   July 1998*

### 45 Layback Left  VS 4c  8m  ★
Great grunt value. Use the obvious left-slanting layback crack to gain height before concocting an awkward traverse leftwards to escape to the large shelf.
*Bob Larkin   July 1998*

### 46 Larkin's Right  E1 5b  8m  ★★
Precarious, high and worrying but great value and with endless variations. The crack leads to the meaner option of jamming rightwards to a small ledge and finishing slightly right before applying bandages. Photo on page 489. **No Larkin About** (E1 5b) turns left from the small ledge for a finish up the nose and **Larkin Goes Straight** (E1 6a) takes the whole affair direct.
*Nigel Baker, Dave Musgrove (and 'NLA' 17th July 1998)* ✦

### 47 Kermit  Font 7c
Delectably delicate. Make very tenuous moves on pebbles to climb the wall to the right of the layback crack..
*Tom Peckitt   June 2008*

To the right is a pocketed boulder that proves how much fun you really can have with such a small piece of rock.

### 48 Pocket Wall  Font 4+
Gain the obvious pocket and finish directly.
*Bob Larkin   July 1998*

### 49 Pocket, Traverse and Arête  Font 5
Pristine padding with every step worth a star. Gain the first large pocket and traverse to the right arête. Finish airily up this.
*Bob Larkin   July 1998*

### 50 Solitaire  Font 6a
More perfect padding up the centre of this slab with the help of a pebble. Eliminating all of the large pockets will push this up to Font 6b. Photo opposite.
*Bob Larkin   11th August 1998*

### 51 Lords a Leaping  Font 5+
The clue's in the name. The right arête direct.

### 52 Tough Cookie  Font 6a+
The short technical slab.

**Yorkshire Gritstone**

Perfect padding for Richard Mallinson on **Solitaire** (Font 6a). Opposite page.
Photo: Adi Gill

# Lord's Seat - McNab

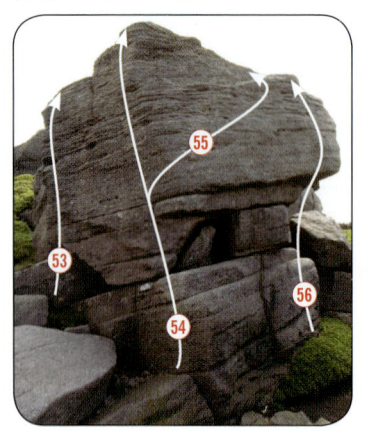

## Wall Buttress
Set away from the main crag a little are a great concentration of routes and problems. Follow the approach path to the boundary wall and cross this as sensitively as possible.

### 53 Munga  Font 4
Start on the juggy sidepull and romp the short arête.

### 54 Blunt Arête  Font 4+
Balance up the arête just above the ledge.

### 55 Wall of Pockets  Font 5
Diagonally up and across the pocketed wall from the arête.

### 56 Who Nose?  Font 5
The blunt nose above the right-hand end of the ledge.

### 57 Lay-Away  MVS 4b  5m
The fun crack is over far too soon.
*Nigel Baker, Andy Watts   18th July 1998*

### 58 Jammed Sandwich  S 4a  6m  ★★
Spread the word about this climb. Jam to the offwidth chimney and get sandwiched in. Very fulfilling.
*Nigel Baker, Andy Watts   18th July 1998*

### 59 Pump Friction  E2 6a  6m  ★★
A cool head and precise footwork is the key to this 'little-big' climb. The undercut slab is protected where it is needed by a Friend 4. One savagely hard and committing move then gains the slab above before the climbing eases dramatically.
*Nigel Baker, Andy Watts   18th July 1998*

### 60 Grit School  VS 4c  6m  ★
Ready for your exam? The crack in the corner epitomises 'awkward'. Finish up the wall to the right.
*Robin Nicholson, Will Hunt   23rd July 2010 (FRA)*

### 61 McNab  Font 7b
The main event for the boulderers. The blunt overhanging nose is touted by many as the best of its grade in Yorkshire. Given the signs of wear from over-brushing, that accolade might be a double-edged sword. Tackle the nose without using the tempting blocks for assistance. The sit-down start is Font 7c.
*Andy Swann (both starts)*

### 62 Deep Black  Font 7a
The prow just right of *McNab* is started on the arête and finishes up the left edge of the slab.

### 63 Crack Nose  Font 6b
Start on the ledge on the slabby side of the overhanging nose. Follow the cracks to swing around the arête and finish direct.

Yorkshire Gritstone

Steppin' Out - **LORD'S SEAT**

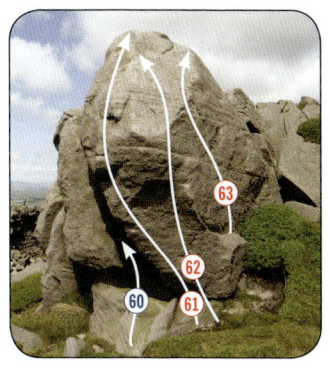

### 64 Pure Gold  E1 5c  6m  ★★
A 24-carat test of your jamming skills. Get digging up the fine overhanging crack.
*Nigel Baker, Andy Watts   18th July 1998*

### 65 Petrocelli  Font 6c
The bottomless crack and arête. High.

### 66 Steppin' Out  E1 5b  6m  ★★★
A brilliant route, or scary highball, with a ballsy and committing move on to the arête at half-height. Starting just right of the arête use good holds to step onto a hidden foothold and finish confidently above.
*Nigel Baker, Andy Watts   18th July 1998*

### 67 Into the Groove  Font 7a
Step off the block and teeter up the groove.

### 68 Groovy Baby  Font 5
Grapple with the corner-crack.
*Bob Larkin   July 1998*

Looking behind the wall, a pair of boulders contain the final quality offerings of Lord's Seat.

### 69 Fascinating Pockets  Font 5
The pockets may be fascinating but didn't curiosity kill the cat? Dramatic sentiments aside the final move is harder than it appears and the landing requires some padding.
*Nigel Baker, Andy Watts   18th July 1998*

### 70 Note to Comply  Font 6a
Fingery moves gain the pocket then the top. Photo page 501.

### 71 Ripping Roof  Font 6a
On the steep face of the boulder to the left, move from a sit-down start at the break to the lip. Move left to the arête to finish.

### 72 Ripping Traverse  Font 6b
From a low start, make a right-to-left traverse along the lip to finish up *Ripping Roof*.

Almscliff to Slipstones

# LORD'S SEAT - First Ascent Information & Graded List

## Further Information on First Ascents (✦)

Lord's Seat has been mentioned in Yorkshire Gritstone guides from time immemorial and it's almost certain many of these lines were climbed before but went unrecorded. In 1957 the guide simply said: "These rocks afford one or two 20 to 25 foot slab and crack climbs". Only recently the notes of Tony Barley were unearthed of his extensive and unrecorded exploits at the crag. Along with marked photo topos, he records climbing all the routes on the upper tier between **Overhanging Groove** and **Gritstone Special** back in 1963 and what appears to be (from his sketches) **Mantel Fantastic**, **Grit Attack** and **Bulging Wall** in 1996. What we now know as **Layback Left**, **Larkin's Right**, **Solitaire**, **Lords a Leaping** and **Big Roof Traverse** (all recorded in 1998), Barley claims he climbed in 1995/96 as **Kerfuffle**, **Shinannacking**, **Hook, Line** and **Sinker** respectively. He claims he climbed five 'problems' (all around UK 5b) on Wall Buttress with his brother, Robin, in 1973.

**Larkin Goes Straight:** Climbed by Phillipe Osborne, Andy Gudgeon 31st July 1999.

## Graded List

### Routes

**E2**
Pumped Friction (6a)

**E1**
Larkin Goes Straight (6a)
Pure Gold (5c)
Larkin's Right (5b)
No Larkin About (5b)
Steppin' Out (5b)

**HVS**
Bulging Wall (5a)
Gritstone Special (5a)
Mantel Fantastic (5a)
Spout Hangout (5a)

**VS**
Flake and Wall (4c)
Grit School (4c)
Layback Left (4c)
Pebble Wall (4c)
Reunion (4c)
Wallbanger (4c)
Widening Horizons (4b)

**MVS**
Lagopus Laughter Indirect (4c)
Lay-Away (4b)
Slab and Overlap (4b)

**HS**
Harrogate Nights (4b)

**S**
The Crack (4a)
Grit Crack (4a)
Hanging Groove (4a)
Harvey (4a)
Jammed Sandwich (4a)

**HVD**
High Pebble Wall

**VD**
High Crack
Slab and Crack

### Problems

**Font 7c+**
Maverick Mick

**Font 7c**
Big Kicks
Kermit
McNab (sit-down start)

**Font 7b+**
Ironside

**Font 7b**
McNab

**Font 7a**
Gorgeous Geordies
Into the Groove
Deep Black

**Font 6c+**
Yorker

**Font 6c**
Right Arête
Big Roof Traverse
Petrocelli

**Font 6b+**
Serenity

**Font 6b**
Big Dyno
Clamper
Small Roof Right
Solitaire (eliminate)
Right Rib
Crack Nose
Ripping Traverse

**Font 6a+**
Tough Cookie
Right of Way

**Font 6a**
Solitaire
Ripping Roof

Note to Comply
Rail Mantel
Slim Bay
Pick Pocket
Small Roof Left
Right Slab (sit-down start)

**Font 5+**
The Nose
Tranquility
Slim Buttress
The Slab (direct)
Splitter Arête
Lords a Leaping

**Font 5**
Overhang Direct
Right Slab
Groovy Baby
Fascinating Pockets
Who Nose?
Wall of Pockets
Pocket Traverse & Arête

**Font 4+**
Three Pocket Wall
Pocket Wall
Blunt Arête

**Font 4**
Munga
Traverse and Arête
Slab and Crack

**Font 3**
Slim Buttress Slab
Ripple Wall
The Slab
Splitter

**Font 1**
Ladder Wall

Richard Mallinson writing his **Note to Comply** (Font 6a). Page 499.
Photo: Adi Gill

# earl's seat
by **Will Hunt**

OS Ref: SE 071 584
Altitude: 425m

Earl's Seat is the dark horse of the Barden Fell family. Being protected on all sides by thick heather and a complete absence of paths, the crag has laughed heartily at many who scurried away to the easy comfort of Lord's and Simon's Seats. For the determined masochist, a small selection of some of the fiercest mid-grade jamming testpieces to be found on moorland Yorkshire grit lie in wait as well as a couple of overlooked 'last great problems'. As with all of Barden's lesser visited crags, great care must be taken with the delicate surface of the rock. In particular the expendable nature of many of the (often crucial) pebbles.

**The Climbing:** The main crag offers eight routes in the VS to E2 range, with the harder of these being very technical indeed. It's also home to one of Yorkshire gritstone's classic jamming crack climbs, *Jams to the Slaughter (HVS 5b)*, which is well worth the trek up Barden Fell for. The clue is in the name though; expect a battle if you want to earn this much-prized tick. The upper tier provides a selection of low-grade boulder problems.

**Conditions and Aspect:** The crag faces north-west but is less open than some of its neighbours and takes some drainage. Combined with the brittle nature of the pebbles, it is best to make sure this crag is thoroughly dry before a visit. If unfamiliar with the walk in it will become considerably more difficult in misty conditions.

**Parking and Approach:** The approach to the parking is the same as that used for Simon's Seat (see page 460). Follow the Simon's Seat approach track until past the plantation and the open moorland is reached. From here, look up the hill to your right (south-east) where a 'two-eyed' boulder can be made out on the skyline. Secure all valuables lest they become 'lost at sea' then make a beeline for this boulder for about 250m through the heather. Clambering on top of this boulder, Earl's Seat will become visible about another 150m ahead on the same bearing.

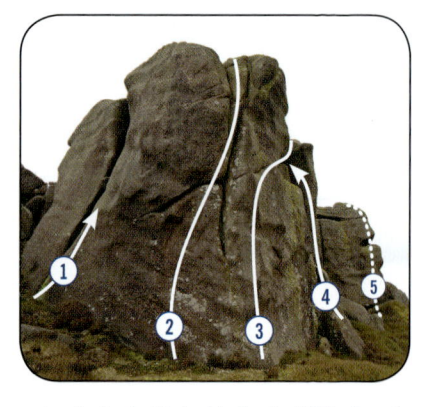

**Access:** The same access restrictions apply to Earl's Seat as that of Simon's Seat. Refer to page 461 for full details. No dogs.

## Lower Crag
The impressive blank wall on the left has yet to be led but has been top-roped with great use of a selection of very weak looking pebbles. A number of climbers have since been attempting this wall ground up. Back to reality though:

**1 Womb with a View** VD  6m  ★★
A classic of its type. The large crack is climbed past a chockstone. To the right lies another of Earl's Seat's unclimbed lines.
*N. Dalzell, Paul Clarke, T White  mid-1990s*

**2 Jams to the Slaughter** HVS 5b  7m  ★★★
Remember - you can't spell 'slaughter' without 'laughter'! The superb pebble-lined cracks gracing the angle of the crag make for a classic jamming testpiece and a rather thorough exfoliant. A mid-height ledge provides a welcome opportunity to prepare for the final fight at the top. Worth coming to the crag for this route alone.
*Paul Clarke, N. Dalzell, T. White  mid-1990s*

# EARL'S SEAT

**3 The Bold Ted Earl**  E2 6a   10m   ★
The wall and rib are climbed to the rest on the previous route. Traverse right to finish up *Crack with a View* or finish up *Jams to the Slaughter* if climbing it once wasn't enough.
*Paul Clarke, N. Dalzell, T. White   mid-1990s*

**4 Crack with a View**  S 4a   7m
The central crack-cum-chimney is charming and enjoys some of the best belay views in the Dales.
*T. White, N. Dalzell, Paul Clarke   mid-1990s*

**5 Offwidth His Head!**  VS 5a   7m   ★
VS going on E9! The offwidth is graded for the use of very large protection and a prowess in wide crack climbing.
*Paul Clarke, N. Dalzell, T. White   mid-1990s*

**6 Entrance Exam**  E1 6a   5m   ★
The bottomless crack in the right wall.
*Nigel Baker, Paul Kitchingman   28th July 1998*

**7 Pebble Pincher**  E2 6b   6m   ★★
The left arête is climbed mainly on the left via a long reach and with utmost care with the fragile and indispensable pebbles.
*N. Dalzell, Paul Clarke   mid-1990s*

**8 Gargling Crack**  E2 6b   6m
The obvious crack to the right is gained by a very technical set of moves and then followed to the top.
*Paul Clarke   Oct 2004*

**9 Knobbles In Toyland**  Font 5
This pleasant problem tackles the right wall using the rusty rugosities.

To the right is a boulder containing a few worthwhile problems. **John's Wall** (Font 4+) climbs the wall between the arêtes; **Broken Rib** (Font 4) takes the left rib at the back of this boulder on a wall in a corner and **Ribald** (Font 4), ascends the right rib in the corner.

## Upper Crag
From the top of the Lower Crag the diminutive Upper Crag can be clearly seen. All the most obvious problems here were climbed and recorded by Paul Clarke and John Hunt in October 2004 and the best few are described here.

**10 Lefty**  Font 6a
The left arête of the central crack.

**11 Low Traverse**  Font 6a+

**12 Central Crack**  Font 4

**13 The Wall**  Font 4+
The wall past the notch.

**14 Layback Flakes**  Font 4+
The flakes on the right-hand rib are pleasant.

## Carncliffe Top
About 150m east from the Upper Crag, below the crest of the hill above Earl's Seat, is the long, low, north-facing wall of Carncliffe Top. It has around 30 boulder problems in the Font 4-5 range, with a couple of harder ones at Font 6c.

# north nab
by **Simon Caldwell**

---

OS Ref: SE 080 564
Altitude: 260m

---

A little gem of a crag, situated above the Valley of Desolation with glorious views over Wharfedale. Despite being close to the honeypots of Bolton Abbey and a few hundred metres above the main walkers path to Simon's Seat, you're unlikely to meet another soul all day. The rock is superb, rough, unpolished gritstone, and though the routes are small the crag somehow manages to be greater than the sum of its parts.

**Conditions and Aspect:** The crag gets lots of sun and takes little or no drainage, so dries quickly after rain. The rocks face west to south-west and are in the sun from late morning until sunset. Sheltered from north through easterly winds, climbing is possible all year-round.

**Routes and Bouldering:** 20 routes, mainly in the lower grades, but with a fine selection of roof cracks in the low E grades. A similar number of boulder problems have been recently recorded and though there are few to tempt the committed boulderer there is plenty of sport here in the lower grades, and most problems are clean, on good rock, and with generally good landings.

**Parking and Approach:** There are very few free parking spaces near to the entrance to the Valley of Desolation, most of the older ones on the Storiths to Barden lane have recently been blocked with boulders. The lane is narrow so please don't park in passing places, they are there for a reason. The most reliable place to leave your car is in the main Cavendish Pavillion car park on the other side of the river (**GPS: 53.986415,-1.88692**), £6 per day in summer 2011 (sounds expensive but not too bad if you have a car full – the alternative is a much longer walk). To approach the crag, take the footpath to the Valley of Desolation until you reach the second fenced forestry plantation on the right, just after a marshy stream. The crag is clearly visible above the forest; follow a well-used (by sheep) track by the fence, a leisurely 25 minute walk from the main car park.

**Access Issues:** Part of the Bolton Abbey Estate with the normal access arrangements (See Simon's Seat access info on page 461). No Dogs.

The crag consists of four main areas. Overhang Buttress is the most impressive, with good routes on steep rock. Desolation Pinnacle has some longer but more discontinuous routes in the lower grades. The Lower Left Boulders have a varied range of 15 interesting problems whilst the Grouse Block has several problems in the lowest grades; suitable for warm-ups, beginners or children.

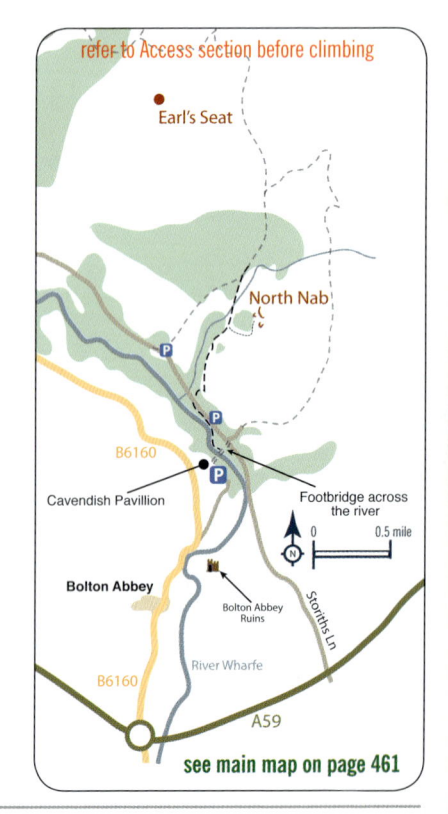

refer to Access section before climbing

see main map on page 461

Peri Stracchino pondering **Twisted Chick** (S 4a). Page 506.
Photo: Rob Stone

# North Nab - The Lower Left Boulders

## The Lower Left Boulders
These blocks form a mini-edge below the Overhang Buttress and are the closest to the main approach path.

**1 Wedge Traverse**  Font 6a

**2 The Wedge**  Font 4+
Small dinks to a rounded mantel.

**3 Thick End of the Wedge**  Font 6a+
Sit-down start. No jamming or bridging.

**4 Belly Hook**  Font 5
Sit-down start. Both arêtes to an amusing finish.

**5 Knees Up**  Font 4+

**6 Green Slab**  Font 2

**7 Full Frontal**  Font 4
Straight up the front face via the undercut ledge.

**8 Scoop**  Font 5+
Sit-down start. From the cave move up left to climb the upper slab via big dubious pebbles; Font 5 from standing.

**9 Cave Arête**  Font 6c
Three excellent problems for the price of one. Sit-down start at the back for the full tick. Good value from standing at Font 6b+. From the block on the right moving left, a bargain at Font 5+.

**10 Cave Wall**  Font 4+
From the block climb straight up.

**11 Arête and Traverse**  Font 4
Right arête then head leftward along the big break.

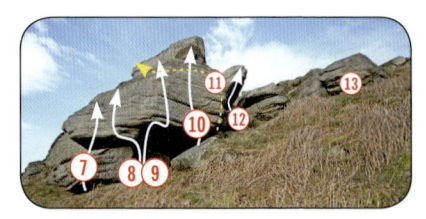

**12 Jagged Flake**  Font 5
Sit-down start. Follow the crack and top edge out right.

**13 Last and Least**  Font 4+
Small wall from a sit-down start.

## Overhang Buttress
A fine buttress offering an assortment of climbing styles.

**1 Chimney and Slab**  HD   7m
The outside of the chimney then the left side of the slab without using the left arête.
*Rob Stone, Simon Caldwell (both solo)  26th June 2010*

**2 Simon's Sat**  VS 4b   7m   ★
Climb the impending left wall on big holds via a nose at two-thirds height (good gear if you can hang on long enough to find it). Finish up the centre of the slab above.
*Rob Stone, Peri Stracchino   26th June 2010*

**3 Jojo la Perruque**  M   8m
Climb the broken corner and traverse left to a ledge and a finish up the crack. Pleasant.
*Stuart King, Karen King, Simon Reed  September 1998*

**4 Twisted Chick**  S 4a   8m   ★
Fingery climbing up the wall left of the main overhangs leads to the ledge. Traverse right with feet on the lowest break (the higher break is easier but not as good), and finish up the next crack. Photo on page 505.
*Stuart King, Karen King, Simon Reed  September 1998*

The next routes tackle the roof cracks in the main overhang. All use the crumbly plinth to start. Treat it with care.

**5 Twisted Twit**  E2 6a   7m   ★
A well-protected but highly contorted direct start to *Twisted Chick*. Climb the left-hand crack with great

Yorkshire Gritstone

Overhang Buttress - **NORTH NAB**

difficulty to gain an obvious foothold on the arête. Finish up the more sensibly-angled continuation of the crack. The E grade is notional and purely for effort.
*Richard Guest 2nd October 2010*

### 6 Cragrat Crack  E2 5c  7m ★
The left-leaning, central crack. Well-protected but sustained.
*Richard Guest 2nd October 2010* ✦

### 7 Inappropriate Behaviour  E2 5c  7m ★
The wider, right-hand crack. Start up *Cragrat Crack* before moving right at a horizontal flake to gain the offwidth above - which is then avoided with the help of some surprising but well-spaced holds on either side.
*Richard Guest 2nd October 2010*

### 8 Mangenon Groove  E1 5b  7m ★★
A neat and surprising pitch. Climb the steep groove and the overhanging rib on its left to reach a short crack in the wall above (which may provide a sting in the tail). Small cams provide better protection than is apparent from below.
*Stuart King, Karen King, Simon Reed September 1998*

### 9 Scunthorpe Traverse  S 3b  4m
Start at the foot of the sidewall to the right and make an increasingly exposed traverse out left to the nose, where you can step onto the slab. Unprotected and with a big drop from the start.
*Peri Stracchino (solo) 26th June 2010*

### 10 Wine Taster  D  4m
The short, wide corner-crack on the right of the grassy bay, with a tricky move to finish.
*Simon Caldwell (solo) 26th June 2010*

### 11 Frogslegs Slab  HS 4c  8m
Follow a broken slab to the ledge, then make a reachy move onto the upper slab. Lace the break with gear and finish with a stylish mantel or desperate belly flop according to taste.
*Stuart King, Karen King, Simon Reed September 1998*

### 12 Frogslegs Arête  S 4a  9m
Follow *Frogslegs Slab* to the top break. Hand-traverse left along this to finish up the left side of the arête.
*Simon Caldwell, Carmen Elphick 26th June 2010*

### 13 Time Waster  M  8m
Well named. Climb the wide crack to the right of the slab, and then meander up broken cracks above.
*Stuart King, Karen King, Simon Reed September 1998*

### 14 Slab Ledge Roof Ledge Roof  VS 5a  6m
Does as it says on the tin. Start up a black-streaked slab on the far right of the buttress and surmount the first overhang with relative ease. The easily escapable last move is the crux and may provide much amusement to onlookers if you are not used to getting your feet up level with your ears.
*Rob Stone, Peri Stracchino 26th June 2010*

# NORTH NAB - Desolation Pinnacle

## Desolation Pinnacle
This outcrop is down to the right and separated into two parts by a large ledge at two-thirds height. All routes start on the lower tier.

### 15 Formic Crack  D  8m
Follow the short arête and wide crack to the ledge. Climb the short wall on the left and mantel to the top.
*Stuart King, Karen King, Simon Reed  September 1998*

### 16 Peggy Babcock  VD  8m
Ascend diagonally right to a slot between the blocks. Climb this to the ledge and finish via a crack and steep broken wall above.
*Stuart King, Karen King, Simon Reed  September 1998*

### 17 Dungo Son of Dungo  HVD 4a  9m
Follow *Formic Crack* to the foot of the wide crack. Hand-traverse under the overhang to the slot and finish as for *Peggy Babcock*.
*Simon Caldwell (solo)  23rd October 2010* ✦

### 18 Desolation  S 4b  10m
Start at the foot of the right-hand side of the buttress and ascend a delicate slab to a heather ledge. Step right and climb the perched block to the large ledge. Finish up the steep wall behind, between the broken cracks on the left and the arête on the right. Good but disjointed.
*Stuart King, Karen King, Simon Reed  September 1998*

### 19 Inertia Arête  D  8m
The broken rib to the right, then take the juggy arête of the pinnacle with an exciting move to finish.
*Stuart King, Karen King, Simon Reed  September 1998*

## The Grouse
Higher up and 50m right is an isolated, slabby boulder.

### 1 I'm Famous  Font 5
The left arête has a rounded finish.

### 2 Red Grouse  Font 3+
The vague scoop right of the arête.

### 3 Lagopus Lagopus  Font 3
Straight up past the slot is nice and straightforward. From a sit-down start and avoiding the slot is **Lagopus Lagopus Scoticus** (Font 6a).

### 4 The Glorious 12th  Font 2
Just right of the blunt central rib.

### 5 No Butts  Font 1

### 6 Stop Grousing  Font 3
A rising traverse across the slab from *Game Pie* to the top of *I'm Famous* passing via the *Lagopus* slot.

### 7 Game Pie  Font 0
The easy arête is great for kids. Try it 'no hands'.

### 8 Twelve Bore  Font 6a
Sit-down start. Up the right-hand block.

# Ten of the Best Yorkshire Grit Pioneers
### By Dave Musgrove

## Further Information on First Ascent (✦)

**Cragrat Crack**: First climbed as "Lisa Rodent" by Mike Pike, 26 June 2010, using pre-placed gear and with one rest point.

**Dungo Son of Dungo**: The traverse was climbed from right to left by Simon Caldwell, Carmen Elphick, Rob Stone and Peri Straccino on 26 June 2010, but the direction described is both harder and more logical.

All boulder problems climbed by Paul Clarke, supported by Dave Musgrove and Paul Farrish, on 13th March 2012 though some must have been climbed before? **Stop Grousing** was a problem climbed by Stuart King et al. in 1998 and has been difficult to locate. It may in fact have been on the Lower Left Boulders, possibly what is now known as **Full Frontal**.

## GRADED LIST

**Routes**

**E2**
Twisted Twit (6a)
Cragrat Crack (5c)
Inappropriate Behaviour (5c)

**E1**
Mangenon Groove (5b)

**VS**
Slab Ledge Roof Ledge Roof (5c)
Simon's Sat (4b)

**HS**
Frogslegs Slab (4c)

**S**
Desolation (4b)
Frogslegs Arête (4a)
Twisted Chick (4a)
Scunthorpe Traverse (3b)

**HVD**
Dungo Son of Dungo (4a)

**VD**
Peggy Babcock

**HD**
Chimney and Slab

**D**
Formic Crack
Wine Taster

**M**
Jojo La Perruque
Time Waster

**Problems**

**Font 6c**
Cave Arête (SDS)

**Font 6b+**
Cave Arête (Standing)

**Font 6a+**
Thick End of the Wedge

**Font 6a**
Twelve Bore
Lagopus Lagopus Scoticus
Wedge Traverse

**Font 5+**
Scoop
Cave Arête (block start)

**Font 5**
I'm Famous
Jagged Flake
Belly Hook

**Font 4+**
Knees Up
The Wedge
Cave Wall
Last and Least

**Font 4**
Full Frontal
Arête and Traverse

**Font 3+**
Red Grouse

**Font 3**
Lagopus Lagopus
Stop Grousing

**Font 2**
The Glorious 12th
Green Slab

**Font 1**
No Butts

**Font 0**
Game Pie

- **Claude Dean Frankland** – Almscliff specialist in the 1920s. Green Crack still a formidable grit VS.
- **Arthur Dolphin** – Head and shoulders above the rest in the 1940s. Great Western, Demon Wall and Birdlime Traverse stand out as trademark routes.
- **Allan Austin** – Bold and prolific pioneer of the 1950s and 60s. The Wall of Horrors and Western Front at Almscliff, Pillar Front at Eastby and The Shelf at Crookrise just 4 of his best.
- **Tony Barley** – Nidderdale specialist from the early 60s. Barley Mow at Almscliff in 1966 probably Britain's first Font 7a boulder problem. Eavestone, Brimham, Guisecliffe and Sypeland all bear his stamp and style on the classic routes.
- **John Syrett** – Moved gritstone to a new level in the 1970s. He was one of the first to capitalise on the benefits of indoor training walls. The Big Greeny, Encore, and Joker's Wall bear witness to his skill.
- **Al Manson** – Contemporary of Syrett, but prolific for a longer period. The first to treat bouldering as an end in itself but routes like Adrenaline Rush, Marrowbone Jelly, Early Riser and High Noon proved he had the bottle to run it out.
- **Ron Fawcett** – Early apprentice of Pete Livesey (who just missed this list by a whisker). Ron's contributions were immense. Slip and Slide at Crookrise was probably the county's first E6 and was followed by Psycho at Caley. At Ilkley, of his many superb and bold leads, Milky Way and Desperate Dan stand out as true classics.
- **Jerry Peel** – The quiet Lancastrian crossed the border many times from the 1970s onwards. Giggling Crack at Brimham is still possibly the hardest climb of its type in the area whilst Galaxy at Ilkley rivalled the best that Fawcett had added. His contributions nearer to home at Widdop, Earl and Heptonstall are legendary with Desert Island Arête and Swift and Sure standing out as two of the best.
- **John Dunne** – Young Bradford hot-shot learnt his craft at Ilkley and added a stream of modern testpieces there during the 1980s and 90s several of which were of national importance. New Statesman at E8 was possibly the hardest route in the country in 1987. Ten years later his Widdop Wall became the new benchmark at E9.
- **Ben Bransby** – Around the turn of the millennium several contenders emerged but Ben gets my vote as, a) a true Yorkshireman brought up in the shadow of Almscliff; and b) for significant contributions up to E7 on Brimham, Almscliff, Caley, and Ilkley plus one of the best modern boulder problems in the county, Lanny Bassham (Font 8a+) at Rylstone.

Apologies to: Cecil Slingsby, Fred Botterill, Sydney Waterfall, Winston Farrar, Charlie Salisbury, Denys Fisher, Brian Evans, Robin Barley, Iain Edwards, Ken Wood, Pete Kitson, Mike Hammill, Pete Livesey, Rob Gawthorpe, Mark Radtke, Tony Marr, Bob Whittaker, Gordon Mason, Derek Hargreaves, Steve Rhodes, Dave Pegg, Brian Swales, Matt Troilett, Phillipe Osborne, Adi Gill, Dave Sutcliffe, Steve Dunning and Jordan Buys (and lots more who I've no doubt forgotten but who probably feel aggrieved not to be included - sorry).

# brandrith

by **Stuart Lancaster**

OS Ref: SE 153 564
Altitude: 270 m

Brandrith is a magnificent looking crag with a magnetic attraction on the eyes for the cragsman gazing south over Redshaw Gill. Pointy, jagged buttresses rise up out of the moor and beckon you to climb their dramatic features of fantastic arêtes, clean walls, roofs and grooves aplenty. Unsheltered from the ravages of the Yorkshire weather, the crag is sculptured with runnels and furnished with some superb finishing jugs. It's a stunning, peaceful spot to end a summer evening, catching the last of the sun's rays as you look out towards the Yorkshire Dales having had the crag to yourself.

**The Climbing:** With almost 50 routes from Diff to E3 and several boulder problems, the crag lends itself to the evening soloist, with much of the climbing falling into that fuzzy area of the micro-route. High enough to give you a moment or two but short enough to encourage you to have a go. Most of the longer lines are well protected, however, and there are a few genuine classics, which vary in style - just ticking off the best routes here will provide a great day's cragging. The buttresses are close together so you won't have to walk far to get between routes. *Cave Crack* (MS 4a) is the star turn but in *Battlecat* (E3 6b) Brandrith harbours a monster; a unique testpiece well worth waging war with, but come prepared for a proper fight!

**Conditions and Aspect:** The crag faces north-north-west, is remote and exposed to the elements. It can be a tad green and out of condition in the wintery months, but comes into its own given a bit of warmth, summer sun and a breeze (which you'll need to keep those pesky midges at bay). The rock is clean and ready to go on the whole but some of the more sheltered gems can hold a spot of moisture.

**Parking and Approach:** There are three different approaches for Brandrith. The quickest two are from the Kex Gill Road side. For these turn north off the A59 Skipton-Harrogate road onto Kex Gill Road (about two miles west of the Blubberhouses crossroads). Follow Kex Gill Road round to the right for about three-quarters of a mile and continue on it as it turns sharply left, heading north, for another quarter of a mile over the top of the moor.

**Option 1.** Just before the road bends left again there is limited space to park on the right before the wooden gate (park sensibly and be careful not to block access). Go through the gate and strike across (directly east) through the heather, which can be wet and boggy, to the crag for about a quarter of a mile. Head for the Menwith Hill 'golf balls' in the distance until you can see the crag. You will reach the western end of the crag first in about 10-15 minutes.

**Option 2.** (Recommended) For the second approach, continue driving past the parking spot mentioned above for about 400m to an obvious lay-by on the left of the road with space for a few cars. From here walk 50m further north along the road to the gate with the public footpath signpost for the Dales Way and Blubberhouses. You will see the crag on the moor top from here. Head diagonally across to the opposite corner of the field from this gate and go through the gap in the stone wall and then through a gap in the next stone wall after a few metres, walking down the hill to the wooden footbridge across the stream. On the other side go uphill and through the gate into the plantation, follow the path for about 50m and through the next gate out onto the open moor. From here go straight up towards the numbered grouse butts and then head directly for the crag, arriving at the western end first. About 20 minutes from the car.

**Option 3.** The third approach is from the opposite side of the crag. Turn north off the A59 Skipton-Harrogate main road at the Blubberhouses crossroads onto Hall Lane and signposted for West End. Follow this for half a mile to where the road turns sharply right (north) and a wooden-gated farm track leads west up Limekilns Hill. Just before this gate there is space on the left for a couple of cars to park on the grass by the trees (being careful not to block access through the metal gate for the farmer). Walk through the wooden gate up the farm track on Limekilns Hill for about 300m and then turn right onto a

## Introduction - BRANDRITH

public footpath before the first wall. Go north through four fields (the plantation and high dry stone wall will be on your left) to a gate in the top corner of the final field. Go through this and turn left (west) to go through the plantation and onto the open moor. You'll see the crag ahead and follow the rough track (or weave your own course through the heather) for about a quarter of a mile towards it, arriving at the western end. About 30 minutes from car to crag and be wary of curious cows as you go through the farmer's fields.

Please note that the West End Road approach described in the previous Yorkshire Gritstone guide (1998) now passes through a plantation used by the estate to raise grouse and is not on Open Access Land.

**Access:** The crag is on Open Access Land. The land is used for grouse shooting and dogs are banned so leave Rover at home. Respect any notifiable closures (re: the CRoW Act). Avoid the crag from 15th March to 30th June due to the possible disturbance of ground nesting birds. No dogs, no smoking and don't go in large groups any updates or grouse-shooting closures.

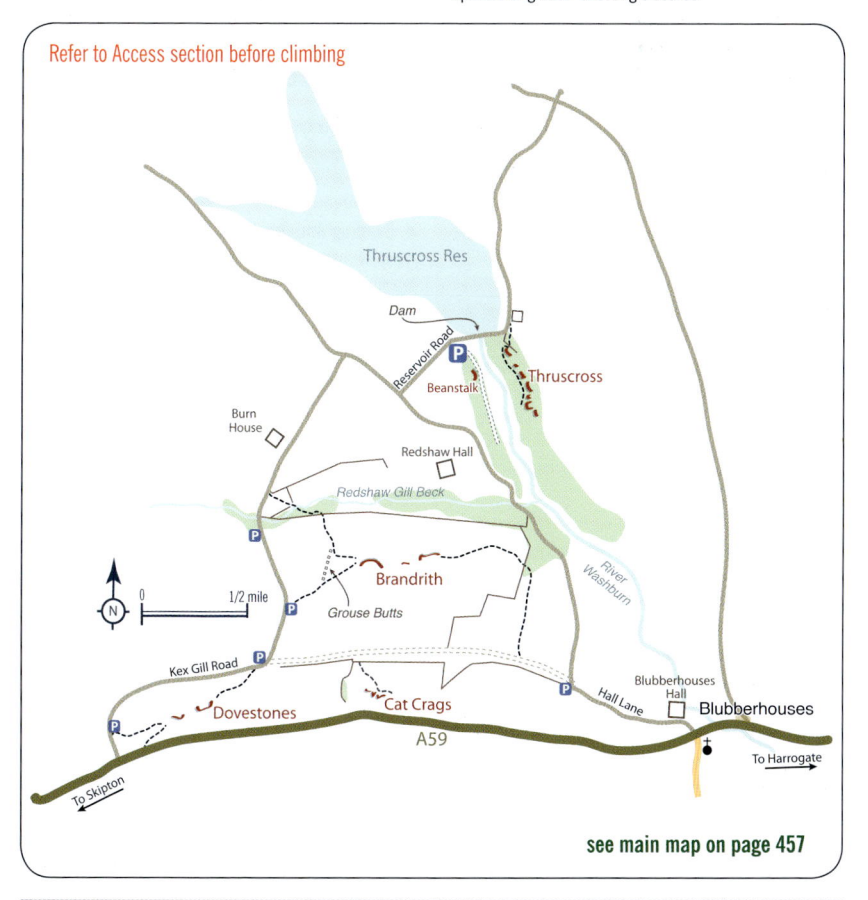

Refer to Access section before climbing

see main map on page 457

Almscliff to Slipstones

# BRANDRITH - The East Buttress

## The East Buttress

The first climbable boulder is slightly up from the east end of the main concentration of climbs and contains some decent low grade problems to warm up and get the blood flowing. The first proper routes start on the buttress to the left of the first prow – **The Indian's Fin**.

**Sunset Staircase** (D) takes the obvious steps 4m left of the prow; 2m right is the biological corner of **The Hoper** (VD) whilst **Left-hand Variant** (VS 4c) hand-traverses the crack on the prows left side to join *Indian's Fin*.

### 1 Little Bill  Font 7a
Gun up the arête on the left-hand side.

### 2 Indian's Fin  HS 4b  6m ★
From the ledge balance into the scoop, grab the crack and finish with a big grin up the prow (Font 4).
*Brian Evans  1953*

The corner in the bay to the right is the aptly named **Filthy Grovels** (S).

### 3 Battlecat  E3 6b  8m ★★
The mighty green monster of a roof crack. Some may profess to find it easy but it's definitely tough for its original HVS 5c grading. Most will have a right fight and end up in tatters. Steep, wide and a thorough test of the best forgotten art. Thankfully not too long, although you may think long enough. With enough pads and wicketkeepers in the ground support team it warrants Font 6c.
*Al Manson, Andy Wild (both led)  July 1984* ✦

### 4 Evening Ambler  VS 4c  10m ★★
A superb and varied climb. Climb up the wall to the lovely crack, which has great holds at the top. Swing round to the left to a thread then finish up the green slab. Great stuff.
*Brian Evans  1955* ✦

### 5 The Torso Twins  E2 5c  10m ★★
An impressive, direct line. Follow *Evening Ambler* to the roof, move slightly right and tackle the steep crack to reach magic holds in the break and hence the top. Don't be tempted by the other wall.
*Jeff Appleyard, Mike Gale  23rd July 1990*

### 6 Cave Crack  MS 4a  9m ★★★
The best lower grade route of the crag. Easier and much more pleasant than it looks, with brilliant climbing up the steady corner-crack. No horrible surprises, just great movement up fine open ground with big holds appearing just where you need them most.
*The Yorkshire Ramblers Club  c1952*

### 7 Butterfingers  E1 6a  9m ★
Well worth giving it some stick but don't let the initial holds slip through your hands. Once the lower, steep groove is solved the climbing eases. At the roof either

Yorkshire Gritstone

finish right and over on good holds or (a) left (harder) up to a flake then flaked groove.
*John Mackenzie, Mick Fowler (both solo) 17th June 1985*

**8 Rocking Chockstone Chimney** VD   8m
Disjointed. The broken crack is followed to the ledge. Finish up the crack in the left wall above.

**9 The Cheat** MVS 4c   10m
An exposed finish gives this route some merit. From the ledge on *Rocking Chockstone Chimney*, hand-traverse left and finish on the upper face of *Butterfingers*.

To the right is a moderate chimney and then:

**10 Upset Crack** HD   6m
The crack on the right-hand side of the split buttress.
*David Burnett  29th July 1997*

The pyramidal block on the right has a short, dirty left arête, **First Route** (Diff).

**11 Sharks Fin Crack** HS 4b   5m
Very enjoyable flaky crack climbing. A juggy romp up the crack in the ridge-like feature.
*David Burnett  29th July 1997*

**12 Pioneers Slab (Keep The Faith)** D 6m   ★
Independent and long enough to engage you. Head for the crack from the bottom of the slab.

Just below the crag is an odd shaped boulder.

**13 The Duck of Death**   Font 6a+
A big move up the south-east arête. Font 6b from a sitter.

**14 Brush me Down**   Font 5
Mantel onto the ramp.

**15 Diwaly** VS 5a   6m
Interesting. Start in the centre of the wall to the left of the prow and climb it using the left arête to gain the upper lip. Pull over onto the ledge and finish easily.
*David Burnett  29th July 1997*

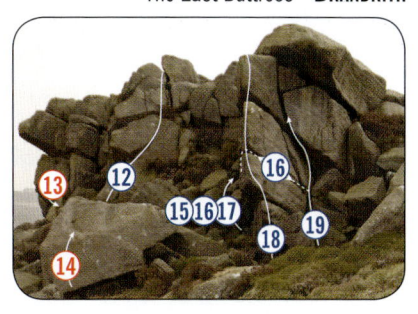

**16 Entertainment Traverse** VD   10m   ★
A good warm-up traverse moving left-to-right around the prow (and back) via the clean crack.

**17 Leader's Lament** HS 4c   9m   ★
Great jug-hauling, just go with the flow. Start along *Entertainment Traverse* and then forsake it for the greater excitement of the delicate moves straight up the arête.
*Brian Evans  1953*

**18 Leaders Lament Direct** HVS 5b   8m   ★★
Magnetic. Enjoy cutting loose, jug-pulling and laybacking up the prow direct. Quite unique and very photogenic. Can be done from a sit-down start for even more fun.
*Jeff Appleyard, Mike Gale  23rd July 1990*

**19 The Flakes** S 4a   6m
Attack the large flaked crack on the right side of the prow wall to a nose-grinding finish.

The last block has limited climbing entertainment. Walking a further 150m west leads to the central jumble of rocks which can provide some short, obvious challenges but the best bet is to keep on trekking for a further 150m to bring you to the mighty West Buttress.

# BRANDRITH - The West Buttress

## The West Buttress
Tall and impressive. Riddled with runnels and gorgeous finishing jugs, it contains some must-do classics. The first boulder on top contains a pumpy bum-scraping traverse, (a) **Lip Traverse** (Font 6a).

Down below is a neat boulder with an undercut slab and triangular face. The steep left wall of the former is (b) **Pit Bull** (Font 4) whilst the mantel onto the left end of the slab is (c) **Ecofriction** (Font 6b); (d) **Hoody** (Font 6b+) is a harder mantel just right again and (e) **ASBO** (Font 6c) struggles up the right-hand side of the slab from a sit-down start; Great laybacking can be had up (f) **Problem Child** (Font 6a) on the ridges steep side; (g) **Broken Home** (Font 6b) offers superb wall climbing direct up the wall to the apex, (h) **Block Crack** (Font 4) struggles out from the gully leftwards along the crack.

To the left of the huge roof is a jumbly bay. The right walls of this contain **Rocky Slab** (S) which starts just left of the cave then up the slab and awkward ledges to the rocking stone; **The Haven** (HVD) is the cave and square-cut chimney above.

## 20 Going Bald   HVS 5a   8m   ★
A good line requiring complete trust in rubber technology. Climb up the groovy rib to tackle the easy-angled slabby rib above. The step onto which requires a certain faith.
*John Mackenzie, Mick Fowler (both solo)   17th June 1985*

## 21 Sod's Law   VD   12m
A strange airwalk taking the easiest line up to the left side of the roof lip and along it. Oddly compelling.
*John Mackenzie, Mick Fowler (both solo)   17th June 1985*

There is an obvious challenge here for the human gibbon. An easier version being:

## 22 Edge Biter   Font 5
Swing through the crack on the right.
*Mick Fowler, John Mackenzie (both solo)   20th June 1985*

## 23 Bag of Snot   HS 4b   8m
Go right across the slabby boulder to finish up the bulge. Lacks any merit.
*David Burnett (solo)  9th August 1995*

## 24 West Buttress Route   S 4a   11m
Step over the overlap and climb the short vertical crack to the ledge. Move right up into a cleft and finish up the fluted rib (immediately right of the easy finish to *Discord*).
*Tony Marr, Alan Taylor, Mike Tooke, F. Fitzgerald.   30th July 2000*

## 25 Verdi Grease   VS 5a   8m
Follow the luminous green streak up the wall and bulge.
*John Mackenzie, Mick Fowler (both solo)   17th June 1985*

## The West Buttress - **BRANDRITH**

Now for the main event, **Brandrith Buttress**. Simply the bee's knees. The heavily-runnelled and grooved slab is quite magnificent and no trip to Brandrith is complete without sampling the many delights on offer here.

**26 New Broom Sweeps Green** HVS 6a    11m  ★
The first of a bunch of great challenges. Technical moves up the bulging wall lead to bold moves up the left-hand groove.
*Dave Musgrove (solo)   28th September 1990*

**27 Finger Dancer** HVS 5a    12m    ★★★
Pokey, but worth it up the 'heart in mouth' inducing runnel. The holds are small but positive and confidence is the key. This is why you're here! The final direct pull can be avoided by a marginally easier move to the right (i). Well worth doing both options for it's that good. Photo on page 517.
*John Mackenzie, Mick Fowler (both solo)   17th June 1985* ✦

**28 Intruding Fool** HVS 5b    12m
Once you've done the rest, have a go at the eliminate between *Finger Dancer* and *Harmony*. Use protection in *Harmony* (and blinkers).
*Stuart King   September 1996*

**29 Harmony** HVS 5a    12m    ★★
Good slab climbing up the horizontal rounded breaks and crack to the right. An awkward move gets you in a position to place a large (3.5) Friend in the top vertical crack. Now finish direct.
*Brian Evans   November 1953* ✦

**30 Discord** HVS 5a    10m    ★
A series of diagonal breaks from right-to-left across the buttress lead to a small ledge. Finish up the groove above as for *New Broom Sweeps Clean* or (more in keeping with the rest of the climb) move left, round the corner, and up into the short fluted groove to exit on good holds at HVD.
*Mick Fowler, John Mackenzie (both solo)   20th June 1985*

**31 Slab and Crack** MVS 4b    11m    ★★
Yosemite comes to the moors. Low in the grade. A short crack in the wall leads to a fantastic fist-sized fissure.
*Brian Evans   1953*

**32 Antlers Route** VS 4c    12m    ★
Wow – what the wind and rain can do. Get to the ledge (by the arête is the best way) then up the thin crack to reach the antlers. Try not to impale yourself pulling over them.
*Brian Evans   1953*

**33 Eastern Arête** VS 4c    11m    ★
Get the camera out for this one. Take the arête all the way to finish on the smaller antler on the right.
*Bob Larkin (solo)   26th July 1989*

**34 Nameless Chimney** D    11m
Nameless for a reason. It's there and has to be done. You choose your technique, but remember your mum'll kill you if you get too dirty.
*Brian Evans   1953*

**35 Summertime Solo** HS 4b    8m    ★
The pillar to the right using the front face only. No cracks allowed – you have been told.
*David Burnett (solo)   9th August 1995*

**36 Western Crack** S 4a    8m
The wide crack, right of the pillar, gets tough near the top.
*Brian Evans   1953*

**37 Western Bulge** HVS 5b    8m    ★
The buttress to the right explores many techniques. Pad the slab, pull the bulge and mantel the top. Finish easily.
*Paul Clough, Karl Zientek   22nd September 1996*

**38 The Opportunist** VD    7m
To the right of the bulge take a crack to a ledge. Traverse right along this to finish into the 'bucket' scoop above.
*Paul Kitchingman   9th August 1997*

**39 Crack and Wall** MS    7m
There is a small bay to the right. Follow a crack in the left wall to the ledge of *Opportunist* and finish just left of the 'bucket'.

**40 Flummox Arête** VS 5b    7m    ★
A good highball when clean. Style up the right arête of the gully (Font 5+).
*Kim Buck (solo)   2nd February 1989*

# BRANDRITH - Heaven in Your Hands

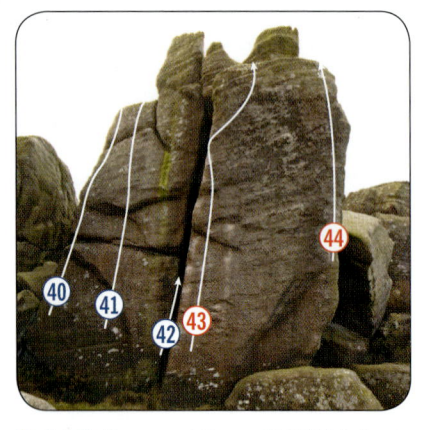

**41 Totally Flummoxed (for a while)** HVS 5c 7m ★
Powerful undercutting up the centre of the wall (Font 6a).
*Paul Bedford   11th May 2006*

**42 Flummox Crack** VS 4c   7m ★
Old school laybacking.(Font 4+).
*Mick Fowler , John Mackenzie (both solo)   20th June 1985*

**43 Heaven In Your Hands**   Font 7c+
The name says it all. Technical, bold and a beautiful line. The left arête reveals its charms to the brave and imaginitive wads amongst you.
*Dave Sutcliffe   20th April 2004*

**44 Ultimate Emotion**   Font 7a+
Spoilt (or enhanced) by the bad landing. Superb movement.
*Dave Sutcliffe   April 2004* ◆

**45 Why Not? (Do a Girdle)** S 4a   20m
All the way along the West Buttress. From *Bag Of Snot* follow the obvious breaks rightwards, reversing most of *Discord* and negotiating all the arêtes and chimneys, to *Flummox Crack* - keeping low towards the end. Finishing up *Flummox Crack* makes it 4c.
*David Burnett (solo)   9th August 1995*

---

### Further Information on First Ascents (◆)

*Brandrith has a chequered history, having been climbed on since 1952 or perhaps before. Many routes will not have been claimed by the original first ascentionists. In 1975 Ken Wood soloed 16 new routes. No doubt some done before and some claimed later.*

**Battlecat:** *Named after Andy Wild's son's favourite toy - the He-Man Masters of the Universe - Battle Cat.*
**Block Crack:** *By David Burnett  9th August 1997.*
**Butterfingers:** *Left-Hand finish Kim Buck (solo) 2nd Feb. 1989.*
**Evening Ambler:** *Mentioned as the 'fine vertical Very Severe crack' by Brian Evans in his guide in that year's YMC journal. Subsequently claimed by Robin Barley as 'The Twist' in 1961, and by Allan Austin in 1964.*
**Finger Dancer:** *Direct by Kim Buck  2nd Feb 1989.*
**Filthy Grovels**: *By David Burnett  29th July 1997.*
**Harmony**: *Originally named 'Brandrith Buttress' and done with a piton. Very bold for 1953 though.*
**(The) Haven:** *John Ward 7th  September 1997.*
**(The) Hoper**: *By David Burnett 29th July 1997.*
**Problem Child:** *By John Mackenzie, Mick Fowler, 17th June 1985.*
**Rocky Slab:** *David Burnett (solo)  9th August 1995.*
**Sunset Staricase**: *By Fiona Burnett  14th August 1997.*
**Ultimate Emotion:** *Was rumoured to have been done before by Tim Clifford or A.N. Otherdarkhorse.*

---

### GRADED LIST
**ROUTES**

**E3**
Battlecat (6b)

**E2**
The Torso Twins (5c)

**E1**
Butterfingers (6a)

**HVS**
New Broom ... (6a)
Problem Child (5c)
Western Bulge (5b)
Leaders Lament Direct (5b)
Intruding Fool (5b)
Finger Dancer (5a)
Going Bald (5a)
Discord (HVS 5a)
Harmony (5a)
Totally Flummoxed...(4c)

**VS**
Flummox Arête (5b)
Diwaly (5a)
Edge Biter (5a)
Verdi Grease (5a)
Evening Ambler (5a)
Eastern Arête (4c)
Antlers Route (4c)
Left-hand Variant (4c)
Flummox Crack (4c)

**MVS**
The Cheat (4c)

Slab and Crack (4b)

**HS**
Leaders Lament (4c)
Summertime Solo (4b)
Indian's Fin (4b)
Bag of Snot (HS 4b)
Shark's Fin Crack (4b)

**S**
Filthy Grovels
The Flakes (4a) West Buttress Route (4a)
Rocky Slab
Western Crack
Why Not ? (Do A Girdle) (4a)

**MS**
Cave Crack
Crack And Wall

**HVD / VD**
The Haven (HVD)
The Hoper
Rocking Chockstone
Chimney
Entertainment Trav.
Sod's Law
The Opportunist

**HD / D**
Upset Crack (HD)
Nameless Chimney
Sunset Staircase
First Route
Pioneers Slab

**PROBLEMS**
**Font 7c+**
Heaven in Your Hands

**Font 7a+**
Ultimate Emotion

**Font 7a**
Little Bill

**Font 6c**
ASBO

**Font 6b+**
Hoody

**Font 6b**
Ecofriction
Broken Home

**Font 6a+**
The Duck of Death

**Font 6a**
Lip Traverse
Problem Child

**Font 5**
Edge Biter
Brush Me Down

**Font 4**
Block Crack
Pit Bull

516   Yorkshire Gritstone

Andy McCue demonstrating a digit paso doble on the wondrous **Finger Dancer** (HVS 5a). Page 515.
Photo: Adi Gill

# dovestones
by **Stuart Lancaster**

OS Ref: SE 141 554
Altitude: 300m

Although fairly small, Dovestones (aka Raven's Peak) has good-quality, clean, weathered climbs and is a spot where there's a classic line waiting for you, whatever your grade. The entertaining short cracks provide fun for the fist-fighter but the main attraction is the large vertical wall (easily seen from the A59) which houses committing face climbs that rival most in the county. You won't be troubled by the crowds here, making this crag a great place to learn the art of gritstone jamming without upsetting too many people with your bad language. All in all, a top climbing venue with the added bonus of great views down the valley.

**The Climbing:** With 24 routes and some bouldering (and some blank walls with nothing on), Dovestones has a varied selection of routes with something to suit most climbers. Some of the routes are positive and short enough to provide a good solo circuit. It has fingery highballs, clean jamming cracks and superb well-protected wall climbs; *The Full Throttle (E4 6b)* is a true classic. The top-outs can be heathery or a little friable, so watch out.

**Conditions and Aspect:** The crag faces south-east and catches all sun going. The Main Wall takes little drainage and makes a cracking venue in the colder months providing the westerlies aren't too strong. It can be hot and midgy in summer. Please no brushing; the rock is already 'good to go'.

**Approaches and Access:** 5-10 mins and easy. Park on Kex Gill Road by the quarry entrance, two miles west of Blubberhouses, on the north side of the A59 (**GPS: 53.993503, -1.795844**). By the right of the quarry entrance is a gated gravel path leading to four telecom masts. Go up this a few yards then take the sheep track on the right which contours east and drops down to the left edge of Policeman's Buttress. Alternatively, walk down to the A59 and follow a marked footpath round the bank top to both buttresses. The crag is on access land. Respect any notifiable closures (re: the CRoW Act). Avoid the crag from 15th March to 30th June due to the possible disturbance of ground nesting birds. No dogs, no smoking and don't go in large groups.

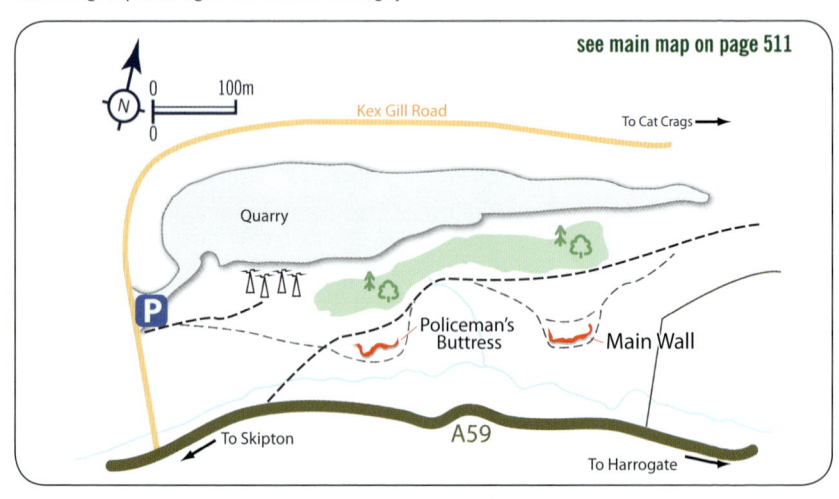

see main map on page 511

## Policeman's Buttress - DOVESTONES

### Policeman's Buttress
A handful of worthwhile routes feature on this clean and compact buttress, the first encountered on the approach paths. Heathery top-outs add to the spice.

### 1 The Filth  HVS 5c   6m
Climb (if you must) the dirty undercut left arête. After making strenuous pulls, heave over the heathered edge at the top. Perhaps a scary boulder Font 6a problem?
*Rob Weston (solo)  8 July 2000*

### 2 The Rozzario Syndrome  E2 5c   8m  ★
A series of varied and entertaining moves lead up the centre of the clean, solid wall to a pocket that takes gear. Execute long moves slightly leftwards to face a heathery mantel and nervy top-out. Good climbing.
*Stuart Lancaster, Rob Weston  8 July 2000*

### 3 Boy in Blue  HVS 5b   8m
No gear and a little spooky. Climb the right-hand wall by using the obvious small curving flake/groove.
*Rob Weston and Stuart Lancaster (both solo)  8 July 2000*

### 4 Waltzing Matilda  VD   7m
Go up to, and over, the overlap on the right side of the buttress. Finish up the obvious flaky right arête. Beware some loose rock.
*Jon Aylward  August 1997*

### 5 Class Warrior  VD   6m
The right edge of the wall to the top.
*Jon Aylward  August 1997*

# DOVESTONES - The Main Wall

## The Main Wall
The imposing buttress, 200m right and further downstream, which you rubbernecked from the road. There's great fun to be had on the 'crack'ing routes, and the sublime top-end lines make for a mint afternoon if operating at the E4 grade.

### 6 Winter Wall  S 4a   6m
The wall left of the crack gives some good moves. Not without interest, especially at the top.

### 7 Summer Crack  HS 4b   6m
The crack is the first of many and a good test of technique.

### 8 Rave On Wall  VS 4c   8m
'Ave it large' up the wall and crack to the right.

### 9 A Coin For A Beggar  E1 6a   8m  ★
Technical, reachy and committing. Style your way up the left side of the arête. Now check you still have some fingertips. A great problem on razor-edge holds. Highball Font 6b.
Photo on page 522.
*John Mackenzie  21 July 1983 (✦)*

### 10 Frogging Wall  E2 6b   8m
One for the hopping mad. Somehow get stood up in the wide break. Make a desperate rockover leftwards and spring up to a good hold and easier climbing.

### 11 The Fogger/Fog Crack  VS 4c   8m  ★
The left-hand crack. Great stuff, a shame it doesn't go on for another 42m.
*Allan Austin  17 December 1961*

### 12 Mist Crack/Autumn Fog  HVS 5c   8m
The wall between the two cracks requires some oomph. There are some small edges and a blind pocket high up. Use them.
*Tony and Robin Barley  1962*

### 13 Autumn Crack  VS 5a   6m  ★
Packs a punch. The right-hand crack is shorter and a little harder than the left.
*Probably Tony and Robin Barley  1962*

### 14 Gravity Brawl  Font 6c+
Undercut the break on the right-hand side of the blank wall to reach a positive crimp near the arête. Make a huge lock to the just-about-holdable top.
*Adi Gill  25th May 2011*

The next three routes start on the ledge and require you to ascend the wide flake crack.

### 15 Ravens Peak Wall  VS 4b   16m  ★
Step across the void and gain the ledge below the small overhang. Hand-traverse the ledge to reach a crack on the right before moving up. You then have a choice: **(a)** bite the bullet and head up and over the roof on the left (best - ups the grade to 4c but beware loose stuff) or **(b)** take the easy breaks and ledges to the top.
*Greg Tough and Miss A. Tough  29 July 1972*

### 16 Faithful Wall  HVS 5b   12m  ★
The obvious crack in the centre of the wall with good, varied climbing. Start from the ledge (or direct from the ground at the same grade). Dive into the crack for gear and make tricky moves up to gain a good hold. Finish as for either of the previous route options.
*Ken Wood, Gwyn Evans  22 May 1974*

### 17 The Great Santini  E4 6a   12m  ★★
A must. Exciting, well-protected climbing up the clean wall. Start as for *Faithful Wall* and traverse right into the centre of the face and good gear. Climb up the vague slopey groove via a technical sequence. Try for the onsight as the gear and holds are better than the blankness would suggest. Word to the wise, take a small cam. Photo on page 523.
*Mike Hammill, Paul Craven  Spring 1980*

Yorkshire Gritstone

## The Main Wall - DOVESTONES

**18 The Full Throttle** E4 6b  15m  ★★★
The classic of the crag and what a belter. Well-protected, sustained and technical. Climb the left side of the right arête by a bouldery sequence to good cams. Blast left to the gear on *The Great Santini* and finish up this. Brilliant.
*Phillipe Osborne, Andy Bunnage 16 March 2000*

**19 Knapper** E4 6b  14m  ★
Take the same start as *The Full Throttle* then continue up the arête desperately trying not to step into the next climb.
*Robin Warden, Chris Brockbank 26 February 2000*

**20 Pellet Climb** HS 4b  15m  ★★
An obvious line and challenge, a classic. Too technical for the old Severe grade but well-protected and worth a punt if trying to push into HS. Ascend the corner/groove on the right side of the buttress. Go up the broken, but solid, wall until you can step left into a steep, juggy corner to the top.
*Brian and Aileen Evans March 1960*

**21 Eliminate B** HVS 5b  12m
Start on the pedestal at the bottom of *Pellet Climb*. Leave the ground with difficulty and climb directly up the wall on sharp flakes and flat holds. A bit squeezed in.

**22 Fingers** VS 4c  10m  ★
A good solid climb and another aptly named crack. Take the crack direct until a move left, and then right and up lands you on the shelf.
*Tony and Robin Barley 1962*

**23 Eliminate A** VS 5a  10m
Climbs the right arête of the buttress on its left side. Using the arête, boulder up the undercut face and gain a standing position on the wall. Move up until level with the top of the crack of *Fingers* and step left onto the face proper and up to a horizontal break, a tricky move gets the top.

**24 Finale** S 4a  6m
A short route up the right wall of the buttress.

**25 Led Zeppelin** HVS 5b, 4c  35m
Now for the girdle to hold it all together.
**1**: Start up *Summer Crack* and move right at three metres to continue round the arête and across the sloping ramp to reach *Fog Crack*. Continue into *Autumn Crack* and up onto the ledge. Belay.
**2**: Follow *Ravens Peak Wall* then traverse right to the hole on *Faithful Wall* and continue round the arête passing a

Almscliff to Slipstones

DOVESTONES

natural thread into *Pellet Climb*. Descend a metre or so and continue traversing to the right arête. Move round the corner to finish as for *Finale*.

## Further Information on First Ascents (✦)

*All ascents as stated. All other first ascents are probably the work of Tony Burnell and pre-1989. He wrote up the crag for the 1989 guide but claimed nothing specific.*

**A Coin For A Beggar:** *possibly also climbed by Paul Craven around the same time and named August Arête.*

### GRADED LIST
**ROUTES**

**E4**
The Full Throttle (6b)
Knapper (6b)
The Great Santini (6a)

**E2**
Frogging Wall (6b)
The Rozzario Syndrome (5c)

**E1**
A Coin for a Beggar (6a)

**HVS**
The Filth (5c)
Mist Crack (5c)
The Boy in Blue (5b)
Faithful Wall (5b)
Led Zeppelin (5b)
Eliminate B (5b)

**VS**
Eliminate A (5a)
Autumn Crack (5a)
Fingers (4c)
The Fogger (4c)
Raven's Peak Wall (4b)
Rave On Wall (4c)

**HS**
Summer Crack (4b)
Pellet Climb (4b)

**S**
Winter Wall (4a)
Finale (4a)

**VD**
Waltzing Matilda
Class warrior

**PROBLEMS**
Gravity Brawl   Font 6c+

Richard Mallinson demonstrates
**A Coin for a Beggar** (E1 6a). Page 520.
Photo: Mike Hutton.

Andy Hall thankfully reaches easy street on **The Great Santini** (E4 6a). Page 520.
Photo: Mike Hutton

# cat crags
by **John Hunt**

OS Ref: SE 148 556
Altitude: 250m

A quaint venue set high on a hillside between Blubberhouses and Bolton Abbey on the Harrogate-Skipton road. The rock is solid and stays clean year-round. The climbing is split between true boulder problems, short solos and a couple of much wilder challenges.

**Routes and Bouldering:** Something of a classic highball venue with 38 named routes and problems. The routes on the front of the main buttress are short, but the overhanging nature of the rock and the huge spans between some of the holds makes them feel hard for the grade.

**Conditions and Aspect:** The crag is south facing above the busy A59 and it's best to visit before the bracken gets too tall. The rocks are sheltered as they sit below the brow of the hill and the place can be lovely on a summer evening once the rush hour has died away.

**Parking and Approach:** The best approach is to turn off the A59 onto Kex Gill Road towards Blubberhouses Quarry (parking for Dovestones crag on the right) and follow this until a sharp leftward bend. Park here (**GPS: 53.996904,-1.782182**) and follow the "Roman Road" (a well-made bridal track) until the wall beside it kinks and there is a wooden gate on the right. Follow the obvious track downhill until the top of the crag is reached. Under 10 mins (bracken allowing). See map on page 511.

**Access:** Cat Crags is **not** on Open Access land. Contact the Head Ranger of Blubberhouses Estate on 01943 880905 before going climbing to ascertain permission. Respect any notifiable closures (re: the CRoW Act). Avoid the crag from 15th March to 30th June due to the possible disturbance of ground nesting birds. No dogs, no smoking and don't go in large groups. Do not park on the A59 or block the farmers access.

### Wobble Block
**1 Wobble Block** Font 4. Climb the arête from a low start. Watch your fingers in the wobbly block.
**2 Thin Breaks** Font 3. Cruise the centre of the wall.
**3 Cave Rider** Font 3. Trend right over the little cave.

The next problems are on the prominent pinnacle just before the Main Buttress.:

**4 Pinnacle Climb** Font 2. A nice climb just left of the big overhang. Also useful as the descent.
**5 Pussy Galore** Font 6a+. A strict direct over the main overhang.
**6 Felix** Font 6b. A full circumnavigation of the block.
**7 Pinnacle Arête** Font 4+. The superb arête.
**8 Pinnacle Wall** Font 5+. The centre of the wall. Variations are possible on this wall.
**9 Steal Yourself** Font 6a (E1 5c). The gritty right edge of the wall. Difficult to pad out, but satisfying.
**10 Pussy** Font 6a (E1 5c). The wall facing the road. Gird yer loins for this one.

Yorkshire Gritstone

Dave Sutcliffe milking the rest on **Ginger Tom** (E4 6b), Page 526.
Photo: Mike Hutton

# CAT CRAGS

## Rear Buttress
The next routes are on the big undercut buttress set into the hillside. **Route One** (VD) takes the open crack splitting the short wall left of the undercut buttress; **Route Two** (HS 4c) climbs the fingery wall immediately right of the open crack to good finishing holds; **Route Three** (VS 4c,★) is just left of the undercut arête at a shallow groove, undercut at its base. Pull over and climb the groove direct.

## 11 Route Four  E1 5c  5m
Start just right of the undercut arête. With difficulty gain a standing position on the lip, reach the top.

## 12 Supermodel  Font 7a+
From the back of the cave, strut your stuff over the middle of the roof to reach slopers on the second lip. Traverse left to easy ground and jump off, or finish up the arête. Only size zeros need apply.
*Dave Sutcliffe  March 2005* ✦

## 13 Route Five  VS 5a  6m
Start as low as you can under the roof on the right. Climb out and up onto the wall via a crack and hollow sounding flake system.

## 14 Getting Groovy  VS 4c  6m
Climb the short vertical crack and stretch left to flakes. Finish up the shallow groove.

## 15 The Red Wall  HVS 5b  5m
From the top of the short crack move up to the overlap and step precariously up right to finish.

## 16 Rear Traverse  Font 6b
A right-to-left traverse of the rear buttress exiting around the nose.

The wall to the right provides various problems whilst the next routes are on The Main Buttress, the big overhanging lump standing proud in front of the previous routes.

## Main Buttress
**There Is No Route Seven** (S 4a) climbs the slabby arête at the rear of the buttress to a ledge. Finish by springing off the heather "caterpillar" to a classic mantelshelf. **The Yak's Progress** (HS 4b) is a mixture of the start of the previous route and the finishing crack of the next.

## 17 Caterpillar Crack  HVS 5a  6m
Mantelshelf onto the ledge left of the prow-like arête. A second mantelshelf leads over the dirty undercut ledge to the bilberry caterpillar below a short crack. Climb the crack to finish.

Traversing the whole block via the middle break is **Lord Hunt's Jig** (Font 6b). A high version has also been done.

## 18 Ginger Tom  E4 6b  6m  ★
Mantel onto the ledge directly below the prow. Gain the undercut arête with difficulty before reaching the 'thank-god' hold and welcome protection. Continue up the left side of the arête to finish. Photo on page 525.

## 19 Cat Baloo  E3 6b  6m  ★★
Climb the centre of the wall using horizontal breaks and then pockets, (not so much a pocket, more a hope). Move left and up to the top.

Yorkshire Gritstone

# CAT CRAGS

### 20 Cats Eyes  E3 6a  6m  ★
A taxing little number. Start just left of the obvious shallow corner. Using vague flakes attain a standing position in the break. Move left to the suspect block, continue straight up the wall to finish in a rightward-trending crack.

### 21 Bonington's Made It  E2 6a  6m  ★★
The stepped corner which splits the face looks steady, but requires power and dynamism. Save yourself repeated trips to just below the top and back down again by placing some gear.
*Tony & Robin Barley 1960s*

### 22 Catastrophe  E3 6a  6m  ★
Start just right of the shallow corner. Climb the steep wall using horizontal breaks to the roof and make a jump to gain the top of the crag....hopefully.

## Plantation Rocks
A short walk along the edge takes you to the right-hand crag. The main areas of interest are the buttress behind the plantation and a smaller buttress about 10m left.

The small square buttress on the left has four vertical problems on its front face and the obligatory traverse (grades Font 3-5), plus a Font 4 on its right wall between the arête and the sapling.

A narrow gully runs behind the right-hand buttress. Up the centre of the back wall is **The Rack** (Font 5), a good problem with a long stretch for the top; the brilliant **Prow** (Font 3), climbs the blunt arête passing two spikes (worth savouring again from a sitter); **Fine Time** (VS 4c) tackles the 'spiky' arête from the right from a reachy start; **Jet Propulsion** (E2 6b) starts two metres right of the arête and thrusts directly up to gain the small hole in the wall and on to easier ground; the excellent **Double Stretch** (HVS 5a) climbs the flake system in the centre of the buttress; **Longer Stretch** (E1 5c) climbs the wall between the flake system and the undercut arête which bounds the right-hand end of the buttress; **The Shelf** (HVS 5b) cruises the undercut arête somewhat dynamically if starting direct; **God** (HVS 5b) is two metres right and moves up the wall using good horizontal flakes to a poor ramp, moving right to finish; three metres right of the arête is

**Faith** (E1 5c), which mantels, then precariously balances upon, the high perch to reach the top; round the corner is a narrow wall where **Friction** (VS 4c) uses horizontal breaks and long reaches to top-out.

## Further First Ascent Information (◆)
*First ascent information for the crag is hazy. John McKenzie wrote an article for Climber in August 1985. He felt that all the routes mentioned had been done before with the exception of Bonington's Made It, which he named. Tony Barley retro-claimed this. The harder Cat routes seem to have been done by Tony Burnell, Chris Sowden and their team just before the 1989 guide. However, records were not kept. The hardest problem here, Supermodel, was repeated by Sutcliffe later the same year after the loss of a crucial hold.*

**GRADED LIST**
**ROUTES**
**E4**
Ginger Tom (6b)

**E3**
Cat Baloo (6b)
Cats Eyes (6a)
Catastrophe (6a)

**E2**
Jet Propulsion (6b)
Bonington's Made It (6a)

**E1**
Longer Stretch (5c)
Route Four (5c)
Faith (5c)

**HVS**
The Shelf (5b)
God (5b)
The Red Wall (5b)
Double Stretch (5a)
Caterpillar Crack (5a)

**VS**
Route Five (5a)
Getting Groovy (4c)
Fine Time (4c)
Route Three (4c)
Friction (4c)

**HS**
Route Two (4c)
The Yak's Progress (4b)

**S**
There Is No Route Seven (4a)

**VD**
Route One

**PROBLEMS**
**Font 7a+**
Supermodel

**Font 6b**
Felix
Rear Traverse

**Font 6a+**
Pussy Galore

**Font 6a**
Steal Yourself (E1 5c).
Pussy (E1 5c)

**Font 5+**
Pinnacle Wall

**Font 5**
The Rack

**Font 4+.**
Pinnacle Arête

**Font 4**
Wobble Block

**Font 3**
Thin Breaks
Cave Rider
Prow

**Font 2**
Pinnacle Climb

Almscliff to Slipstones

# thruscross

by **Andy McCue**

OS Ref: SE 157 574
Altitude: 250 m

This jumble of short buttresses and boulders, scattered among the heavily wooded hillsides above the River Washburn is one of Yorkshire grit's more esoteric venues. Hidden among the trees and man-eating bracken are a mixture of micro-routes and bouldering, much of it highball and of varying quality, but there are a few superb harder lines worth seeking out that have been added since the last guide.

**The Climbing:** The climbing is limited, with 28 problems and routes detailed here. The best of the action is centred on the Thruscross Boulder, which features several highball problems, and Beanstalk Buttress, which has some hard extreme routes. Fresh traffic to both of these will help to keep some brilliant lines clean and prevent the better parts of Thruscross falling back into the lichen-coated clutches of the reservoir hobbits. Some of the 'must-do' ticks that make a visit worthwhile include *Cracklin' Crease*, *Cotton Reel*, *Heart of Oak*, *Stir Frenzy*, *Doe Traverse*, *Ratlin' Row* and *The Atom Smasher*. Although not covered here, Tony Barley and friends have also documented more than a hundred problems in the *Wild Bouldering in Yorkshire* guide (1998 - now out of print), for those with a fetish for green, esoteric bum-scraping Lost World-style exploration.

**Conditions and Aspect:** The main bunch of craglets and boulders, including the Thruscross Boulder, lie on the east of the river and face west. Beanstalk Buttress sits on its own, facing east, on the opposite bank. For all areas the heavy tree cover and bracken mean a certain amount of bush-whacking is needed to locate the boulders and buttresses, although sunny days from late autumn through to early spring after a sustained dry spell are the best time to visit.

**Parking and Approach:** See map on page 511. From the A59 Skipton-Harrogate road turn north onto Hall Lane at the Blubberhouses crossroads by the church (signposted 'West End 2½ miles' on the approach from both the east and west). Follow this road for 1¾ miles and turn right onto Reservoir Road (signposted Dacre, Greenhow Hill and Pateley Bridge). Follow this for just under a quarter of a mile to the large, free Yorkshire Water Thruscross Reservoir car park on the right. (**Parking GPS: 54.012267, -1.766949**)

**Access:** Access has never previously been challenged but the high deer fence suggests care should be taken on your choice of approach.

Made to measure gritstone. Dave Sutcliffe tries **The Atom Smasher** (E6 6c) for size. Next Page.
Photo: Mark Credie

# THRUSCROSS - Beanstalk Buttress

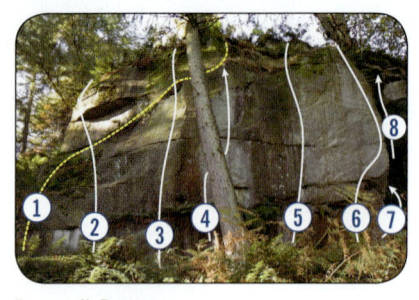

## Beanstalk Buttress
This is the nearest climbing to the car park and contains some of the best lines at Thruscross. Most are in the higher grades and require a cool head but are good when clean and dry. Follow the steps down from the east corner of the car park to pick up a path that goes due south (parallel with the reservoir water outlet river for about 150m). The buttress is deep in the wooded hillside to the right.

**1 Wet, Wet, Wet** HVS 5a  14m  ☆
From the left rib head for the prominent horizontal crackline where solid jams aid a traverse past a drainage streak to a steep finish behind the tree.
*Tony Barley (solo)  20th May 1993*

**2 Chloride Attack** HVS 5b  10m
A tricky start gains the sloping shelf, which leads up left to an awkward finish out on the arête.
*Tony Barley (solo)  March 1995*

**3 Stir Frenzy** E4 6b  10m  ☆
A great line up the wall just left of the tree with decent gear in the big pocket in the horizontal break.
*Ben Bransby  October 1999*

**4 The Atom Smasher** E6 6c  ☆
One of the two hardest Thruscross testpieces requiring gymnastic moves up the wall just right of the tree.
Photo on previous page.
*Dave Sutcliffe  May 2011*

**5 Barnes Wallace** E5 6b  10m  ☆
Hard moves straight up the centre of the wall between the tree and the right arête.
*Matt Troilett, Neil Herbert  Spring 2004*

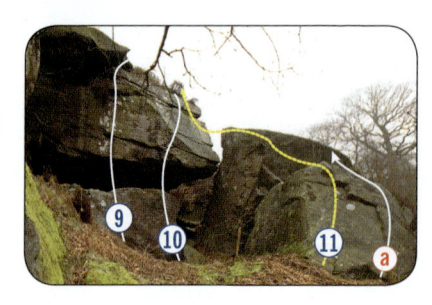

**6 Word to Your Mother** E5 6a  7m  ☆
The big, bold, blunt overhanging arête to the right of the tree.
*Ben Bransby  October 1999*

**7 Jack's Grotto** VS 5a  9m
The overhanging corner to the right of the main buttress is climbed until the left wall can be gained for a finish.
*Tony Barley (solo)  March 1995*

**8 Lurker at the Threshold** E4 6b  6m  ☆
Start up the wall in the gully immediately right of the arête. Use slopers and crimps to gain a small ledge then make a nasty mantel to gain the top and an easier finish.
*Paul Clough, Karl Zientek  8th July 2010*

## Main Area
The rest of the climbing at Thruscross is on the opposite hillside to the Beanstalk Buttress. Walk across the dam wall and continue on the road up the hill to a driveway/turning on the right. Keeping to the dam side, follow the fence back for 100m to a ladder crossing the large deer fence. Descend the mossy rocky gully into the woodland where **Landside Buttress** is back right down towards the dam.

**9 Holland, Hannen & Cubbitts** E1 5b  6m
Start direct up the centre of the wall on the main buttress, trending right above the overhang to finish.
*Tony Barley (solo)  July 1965*

**10 Dam It All** E2 5c  6m  ☆
A good little route tackling the tough undercut main buttress and with a precarious step.
*Tony Barley (solo)  7th June 1994*

Yorkshire Gritstone

# Heart of Oak - THRUSCROSS

Around the right-hand side of the main buttress are three problems **No left block** (Font 5+), **No right block** (Font 4+) and **Anyway** (Font 4). **Dambuster** (Font 5) gains a horizontal slot to climb the left side block next to the right arête at the front of the main buttress.

On the subsidiary block at the right of the main buttress:

### 11  Stenislag  S 4a  9m  ☆
Size isn't everything and this mini-adventure is superb value for the grade. Start up the lower subsidiary slab to gain a hand-traverse across the left edge of the next block before transferring to the rib of the main buttress for an airy finish up the slabby arête. (a) **Compulsory Purchase** (Font 5) climbs the two lower blocks to the right.
*Tony Barley (solo)   July 1965*

A short wall (**Wild Walls**) and large, undercut slabby boulder in front of it (**Cuckoo Slab**) lie 80m right along the hillside from Landslide Buttress. Between them are 15 problems from Easy up to Font 6b+, with the pick of the bunch being **Wilderbeast** (Font 6b), a tough little monster just right of a tiny scoop. Just down the hill from Cuckoo Slab is a low boulder with **Doe Traverse** (Font 6c+), a brilliant pumpy traverse of the crack from the far right end. A further 80m right of Wild Walls and Cuckoo Slab, at roughly the same level on the hillside, is **Nothing Rocks** and **Flatfish Slab** with 11 short, and generally poor quality, problems from Easy up to Font 6a.

### Under Oakwood
Another 80m right and slightly down the hillside is this little treat of a buttress with one of the best problems of the crag, *Heart of Oak*.

### 12  Rising of the Sap  E3 5c  7m  ☆
Don't be put off by the colour. Brilliant and rather committing moves taking the diagonal rising traverse from the green slab to the green flakes to a green rounded finish.
*Tony Barley (solo)   1st June 1995*

### 13  Strong as an Oak  Font 6a+
You'll need all your strength for this cool low-level left-to-right traverse of the break - all the way.
*Jerry Peel (solo)   7th June 1994*

### 14  Heart of Oak  Font 6a+
A genuine hidden gem; the big green arête behind the tree is simply brilliant. After unlocking the tricky initial moves (the finger bowl helps), climb the front face with full use of the arête. Photo on page 533.
*Tony Barley (solo)   28th April 1994*

(b) **Heycorn** (Font 5) takes the arête on the right side while (c) **Barking up the Wrong Tree** (Font 4+) takes the pleasant ramp with a tricky and thoughtful finish in the gully just right of the tree. On the rocks left and right of this main buttress and on boulders about 20m down the hill are another 15 problems up to Font 5.

Containing around 20 short routes/highballs, the little edge of the **Washburn Walls** lies at the far right end of the crag, about 150m right of *Under Oakwood*. Poor landings and vegetation abound here. The climbs start below the obvious large overhanging block with the best ones as follows. **Green Syke** (Font 5) starts up the wall below the overhanging boulder, moving left to a shelf before finishing up a scoop in its left side; **High Lair** (Font 5) follows the cracked wall up to the roof below the overhanging boulder, moves out right to the rib and then finishes boldly up the wall of the perched block; **Ratlin' Row** (Font 6a) is the best climb hereabouts, just a shame about the drop zone. It tackles the thin vertical crack up the crimpy wall, traverses right and then swings out for a satisfying jug over the lip of the overlap to a strenuous finish: **Capelshaw Beck** (Font 4+) takes the stepped corner to the right whilst **Laughter Lines** (Font 6c) takes the vicious overhanging chimney crack.

Almscliff to Slipstones        **531**

# THRUSCROSS - The Thruscross Boulder

## The Thruscross Boulder
One of the main events of the crag, with some of the finest climbing that Thruscross has to offer. The large free-standing block is a few metres down the hill on the right from Washburn Walls. There are two problems that make use of the horizontal slot halfway up the left side of the block; (a) **Flax Trade** (Font 5) on the left and (b) **Right Eye** (Font 5+) on the right.

### 15 Yarn Spinner  E2 6a  6m  ★
A difficult start allows the left arête to be climbed direct. Highball Font 6b.
*Tony Barley (solo)  July 1965*

### 16 Cotton Reel  E2 5c  8m  ★
A delicate test of nerve. Start up the right arête of the front face of the block to a scoop and traverse precariously to the front of the left-hand arête. Better holds and a step right lead to a finish over the centre of the wall.
*Tony Barley (solo)  June 1973*

### 17 Rewind  E6 6c  8m  ★
Takes the right arête on the front face on its right-hand side. May now be better as a highball Font 7b since the landing area has improved.
*John Dunne  February 2001*

### 18 Cracklin' Crease  Font 6c
A highball classic with a scary landing. Start from a ledge on the right wall and follow the very slim groove.
*Jerry Peel (solo)  7th June 1994*

### 19 Winkling Wall  Font 6b
A serious problem up the horizontal creases in the upper wall on the right-hand side of the block. Poor landing.

### 20 Holy Trinity  HVS 5b  8m  ☆
A good line up the truncated arête to the right of the main boulder. The technical crux is at the start but, even with a wire in the slot, the upper edge feels quite precarious. Easier starts can be made from either side.
*Tony Barley (solo)  26th March 1994*

Another 20m further along the hillside, heading towards the dam, is a collection of blocks (the **Blondin Boulders**) with 20 problems ranging from Font 3 to Font 6b. The best two are detailed here. **Walk the Blondin** (highball Font 5) climbs the large trapezoid boulder, gained from the left wall, and balances along the ridge crest; on the block up and to the right **Toughwood (Font 6b)**, makes strenuous moves through the overhang and left over the sharp edge.

### Further First Ascent Information (✦)
*Tony Barley discovered the crag in 1965 and developed more than 100 problems here over 30 years. Jerry Peel added the crunching **Laughter Lines** in June 1994. Beanstalk Buttress saw a flurry of activity in 1999. It then fell into neglect before being cleaned, reclimbed and a new testpiece added by Dave Sutcliffe and his crew in early 2011. Sutcliffe proclaimed the routes on this buttress as being 'of the highest quality' when clean and dry. Tom Peckitt added the excellent **Doe Traverse** in June 2011.*

### GRADED LIST
**ROUTES**

**E6**
The Atom Smasher (6c)
Rewind (6c)

**E5**
Barnes Wallace (6b)
Word to Your Mother (6a)

**E4**
Lurker at the Threshold (6b)
Stir Frenzy (6b)

**E3**
Rising of the Sap (5c)

**E2**
Yarn Spinner (6a)
Cotton Reel (5c)
Dam It All (5c)

**E1**
Holland, Hannen & Cubbitts (5b)

**HVS**
Holy Trinity (5b)
Chloride Attack (5b)
Wet, Wet, Wet (5a)

**VS**
Jack's Grotto (5a)

**S**
Stenislag (4a)

**PROBLEMS**
**Font 7b**
Rewind (highball)

**Font 6c+**
Doe Traverse

**Font 6c**
Laughter Lines
Cracklin' Crease (highball)

**Font 6b**
Yarn Spinner (highball)
Winkling Wall
Wilderbeast
Toughwood

**Font 6a+**
Heart of Oak
Strong as an Oak

**Font 6a**
Ratlin' Row

**Font 5+**
Right Eye
No left block

**Font 5**
Heycorn
Green Syke
High Lair
Flax Trade
Dambuster
Walk the Blondin (highball)

**Font 4+**
Barking up the Wrong Tree
Capelshaw Beck
No right block

**Font 4**
Anyway

Yorkshire Gritstone

Andy McCue well and truly feeling the beat of **Heart of Oak** (Font 6a+). Page 531.
Photo: Adi Gill

# snowden

by **Nigel Poustie**

OS Ref: SE 176 514
Altitude: 250 m

A number of low slung blocks, proud prows and strength-sapping sidewalls combine to give a bouldering venue that's well worth seeking out. Beautiful scenery, generally good landings and a short walk-in. What more could you want?

**The Climbing:** Nearly 30 problems with the prize plums gathering in the Font 6b+ to Font 7c+ range. The rock is excellent grit though sadly often lichenous. The majority of problems are sit-down starts and traverses so if this is your bag then you're in for a treat.

**Conditions and Aspect:** Snowden lends itself to being a possible year-round venue. It's north facing but don't let that put you off as there's shelter to be had for the majority of problems.

**Parking and Approach:** The crag is between Otley and Blubberhouses. From the bridge over the River Wharfe in Otley take Newall Carr Road north (later becoming Asquith Moor Road) for 4.3 miles as it meanders uphill and onto the moor. Parking can be found on the right in a dry-stone wall enclosure with room for 2 cars (**GPS: 53.957889, -1.736973**). Carefully cross the wall and head northeast (in the direction of Swinsty reservoir visible in the distance) for 200m to the crag.

**Access:** Snowden is on CRoW access land but is also grouse moorland and subject to the usual shooting restrictions. Respect any notifiable closures, try to avoid the crag during May and June due to the disturbance of ground nesting birds, do not take dogs at all and avoid large groups.

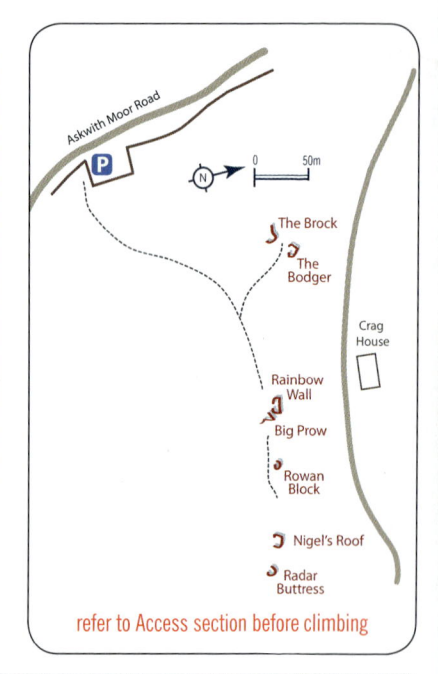

refer to Access section before climbing

**Yorkshire Gritstone**

Nigel Poustie squeezing his way up **The Brock** (Font 7c). Next page
Photo Paul Clough

# SNOWDEN - The Brock

## The Brock
This undercut block is home to probably the best problem at Snowden. It has brilliant lip/roof climbing making Snowden worth a visit for this alone.

**1 '99'** Font 7a. Sit-down start to the blind thin flake line. Difficult to get stood up. *Nigel Poustie*
**2 That's the Badger** Font 7a. Sit-down start to the short groove. *Andy Swann*
**3 The Brock** Font 7c. One of the main attractions of Snowden. Photo on previous page. From a sit-down start, as far right as possible, on slopers traverse the lip of the roof to finish around the arête. Quality. *Nigel Poustie*

## The Bodger
The free standing square block, 10 metres below The Brock. A good place to start and home to some technical wall climbing. *Skull Wall* is a must do problem.

**4 JCB** Font 6b+. Use small crimps to gain a sloping top. *James Kitson*
**5 Bodger** Font 5+. Sit-down start. The bulging flaked wall leads to an interesting top-out. *Nigel Poustie*
**6 Madame la Blaireau** Font 4+. SDS. *Tom Crane*
**7 Skull Wall** Font 6b. Take the wall just around the nose to the right using thin slopey crimps. Would be a classic anywhere. *Paul Clough*

There are a few ways of climbing the wall further right of the nose, all around Font 4+ and useful for warming up.

## Rainbow Wall
Approximately 200m right (east) is this beautifully rippled, low gritstone face, with some excellent problems.

**8 Naked Yoga** Font 6c. Sit-down start at the large pocket on the left arête. Move up to a sloping shelf then right and up to pockets and a big move to a good hold over the top. (a) **The Bridge** (Font 7a) continues traversing right on pockets below the top to finish as for *Rainbow*. *Andy Swann; (The Bridge – Nigel Poustie).*

It is possible to finish direct to *Naked Yoga* via **No Chemistry** (Font 5a+).

**9 Tantric Traverse** Font 7b+. A great line that requires long arms. From a sit-down start, climb the obvious diagonal line up and left. *Andy Swann*

Yorkshire Gritstone

# Nigel's Roof - SNOWDEN

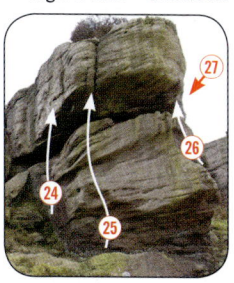

**10 Rainbow** Font 6a. Superb climbing up the steep groove. The sit-down start (Font 6c) adds flavour. *Paul Clough. (SDS: Nigel Poustie)*

**11 Pot of Gold** Font 6c+. Sit-down start. Make a big move to a sloping pocket, a boss and a sloping top-out. A nice little problem. *Nigel Poustie*

The problem on the short steep block behind is a Font 5+ one-move wonder (sit-down start). Directly above Rainbow Wall is a hanging prow.

**12 Optical Illusion** Font 6c. A short but serious problem. From the grassy ledge pull onto the prow where you're immediately committed. *James Kitson*

### Rowan Block

More top quality gritstone. Due to the top-outs these problems are much more involving than their size would imply.

**13 Shrub Arête** Font 6a. Sit-down start. The left arête, taken on its right. Good holds lead to a much easier finish. *Nigel Poustie*

**14 Rowan** Font 7b. Dynamic climbing leads to a disproportionately involved top. From a sit-down start climb the steep arête on its left. Hard. *Nigel Poustie*

**15 Sorbus** Font 5. From the arête, step on and climb diagonally right on pockets to a slopey top. *Nigel Poustie*

### Nigel's Roof

This low roof, split by a horizontal crack, is home to some tough problems and one serious prow.

**16 Snowball** Font 6b. From the good pocket make a tricky move to the break and up to an extremely sloping top-out. *Nigel Poustie*

**17 Fore!** Font 7a+. The short prow has a serious feel to it with some ankle snapping boulders below. The undercut nose, taken on the left, is (b) **Snowflake** (Font 6c). *Nigel Poustie*

**18 Nigel's Roof Left-Hand** Font 7a. From holds at the back of the roof, cross it to finish left of the blunt rib via a delicate mantel. *Nigel Poustie*

**19 Nigel's Roof Right-Hand** Font 7b+. From the same start as 'NRL-H', cross the roof to a good hold right of the blunt rib. Finish with difficulty up the thin and thrutchy wall. *Nigel Poustie*

**20 Energy Crisis** Font 7c+. Start from the good hold and as far right as possible. Traverse the lip of the roof to finish up the wall around the left arête. As the name suggests, quite an undertaking. *Nigel Poustie*

**21 Girl Next Door** Font 4. Delicate moves up the wall on rounded holds. *Becky Cumberworth*

**22 Blonde Be Brave** Font 4. Up the crack from the boulder. *Becky Cumberworth*

**23 Short and Sweet** Font 4. The wall past the big pocket. *Becky Cumberworth*

### Radar Buttress

The final boulder with the crack in its stumpy nose.

**24 Getting Warmer** Font 5
**25 Tested On Animals** Font 5. The nose and crack to a taxing finish.
**26 Welly Wall** Font 4. Just right of the nose.
**27 The 19th Hole** Font 4. The wall to the right.

Almscliff to Slipstones  537

# little almscliff

by **Rachel Hunt**

OS Ref: SE 232 523
Altitude: 245m

The little brother of its more famous sibling sits a few miles north-west of its larger namesake and is a brilliant bouldering venue, especially for those operating in the low and fun grades. Documented here for the first time, but please don't imagine that any hold has been left unfondled. The crag made The Climbers' Club Journal in 1901 and you'll probably agree with H.V. Reade's verdict that "the climbing is varied and amusing, two or three problems being more than I could solve alone."

**The Climbing:** Mostly enjoyable boulder problems with excellent landings, the hardest being Font 6a, plus a couple of stiffer highball offerings thrown in for good measure. Only the most obvious problems are described here; numerous sit-down starts and 'trick' climbs can be contrived.

**Conditions and Aspect:** A mini 'tor' with problems facing most directions. Often a good bet in the depths of winter, but it really comes into its own as a family venue in spring and summer.

**Parking and Approach:** Just over a mile away from Hunter's Stones as the crow flies, but most will arrive by car. Continue north on the B6451 for a further mile past the Hunter's Stones parking until a turning on the right (Broad Dubb Road). Take this road and follow it for 1.8 miles. Clearly visible on the right, Little Almscliff has its own lay-by and footpath (on the flat) leading right to the crag in less than two minutes. (**Parking GPS: 53.966914,-1.644924**).

**Access:** The crag is not on access land, but the well used footpath runs directly through the boulders. No issues have ever been reported.

**1 Twin Pockets** Font 3. A dinky problem using the pockets for the starting holds.
**2 Green Runnel** Font 3+. Only short, but harder than it looks.
**3 Wall Between** Font 4+. Use pockets to climb the wall between the runnels. Loads of eliminates are possible.
**4 Higher Runnel** Font 4
**5 Rail & Arête** Font 4. Use the big polished hold to gain the ramp. The crux is the top-out. The rail traverse can be continued to finish up *Plaque Wall* giving a superb Font 4 stamina-fest.
**6 Shiny Arête** Font 4. Climb the well buffed arête on the right-hand side.
**7 Echo Wall** Font 3+. Classic. Follow the pockets straight up the wall. Shout towards the plantation for the eponymous experience
**8 Echo Edge** Font 3. Climb the right edge via the sandy break. No harder from a sit-down start off the polished rail.
**9 Mantel** Font 5+. Butch moves conquer the stepped wall between the gullies. Amazing flutings and bowls provide the high, but easy, finish.

# LITTLE ALMSCLIFF

**10 The Prince** Font 6a+. Bag this one and you'll leave happy. The steady lower wall leads to an obvious slot in the overhanging headwall. Lay off this to grope for the finishing holds.

**11 Almais** Font 4+ (HVS 5a). The big arête on its right – gritty and gripping at the top.

**12 Plaque Wall** Font 4 (HS 4c). Climb past the site of the missing plaque. Awkward landing.

**13 Big Polished Pockets** Font 4. Use the big artificial pockets. Harder than it looks and a bit reachy at the top. Go again with **Eliminate 'em** (Font 5+), but you're only allowed the little stuff. Brilliant.

**14 Crack** Font 3+. Fight up the crack with a bit of jamming and pulling. It's all good for you.

**15 Twin Pockets II** Font 3. Another mini-problem. Avoid the crack for the finish for the Font 4 tick.

The other side of the gully yields no problems apart from a good Font 4 undercut jamming crack from a sit-start above mud. The undercut block down and right has the following problems. **Community Hall** (Font 2) climbs the left side of the bulging wall on good holds; **Meeting Place** (Font 2) takes the right side on more good holds whilst the hanging groove just right gives a good, but frustrating, Font 4+ problem. From a sit-down start, **Jutish Overmantel** (Font 6a) gains the nose and surmounts it by pressing like hell.

The biggest boulder in the field towards the plantation is inscribed with '1968 EM CM' and it provides a few easy, but interesting, problems ranging from about Font 2 to Font 4+.

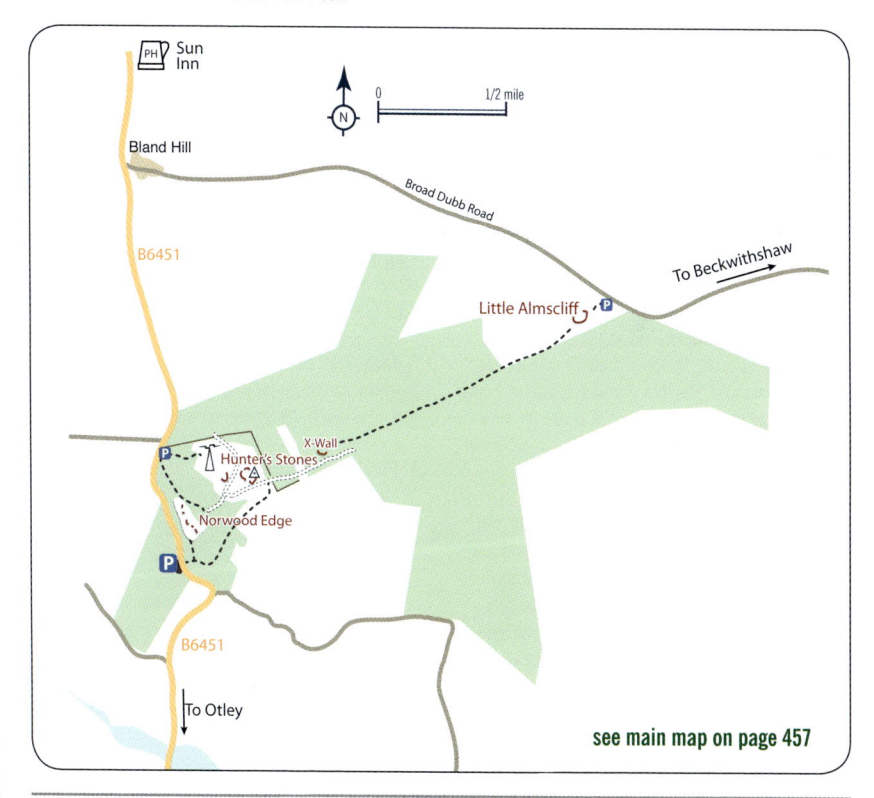

see main map on page 457

Almscliff to Slipstones     539

# norwood edge
### by **Robin Warden**

OS Ref: SE 209 513
Altitude: 230m

On the wooded hillside of Stainburn Forest, beneath the nearby crag of Hunter's Stones, sit the charming boulders of Norwood Edge. A venue which offers fantastic vistas, afternoon sun and some brilliant climbing across the grades; all just a five-minute walk from the car.

**The Climbing:** Over 30 problems for all abilities providing you don't mind sit-down starts. A wide variety of bouldering styles are on offer, from technical slabs, steep walls and highball classics to sustained lips and butch caves. The brilliant flake of *Larchbow* (Font 6b) is a must for the ticklist, while Tom Peckitt's *Archimedes* (Font 7c+) is the crag testpiece. We have only included a selection of the best problems here - a more definitive list can be found on **www.yorkshiregrit.com**. Well worth combining with a trip to the neighbouring Hunter's Stones further up the hillside.

**Conditions and Aspect:** A jumble of peculiar, yet endearing, west-facing boulders located on the hillside above the main road. The rock is predominantly of a raspy disposition but some boulders consist of smooth, pure grit. Shelter from the wind can be found in the nooks and crannies on the more tempestuous days.

**Parking and Approach:** See map on page 539. The edge lies on the east side of the B6451 about four miles north of Otley in Stainburn Forest, or three miles south from the A59 Skipton-Harrogate road (taking the signposted Otley B6451 turn-off at the Pately Bridge/Menwith Hill junction). Park at the Stainburn Forest Norwood Edge car park (on your left if approaching from Otley). (**GPS: 53.953967,-1.681677**). From the car park walk across the road and through a gate into the forest. Take the path immediately to your left, which runs parallel to the road, heading up the hillside towards a clearing where you will see the boulders as you approach (five minutes).

**Access:** At present there are no restrictions regarding access. To keep it this way, please ensure all vehicle track entrances are left clear. The area is frequented by mountain bikers so take care.

---

The boulders are described from left to right.

### Bankside Block
A compact boulder with good problems that pack a punch. It offers good warm-ups and a few tough nuts.

**1 Night Raiders**  Font 7a+
Painful. From the bottom left, traverse up diagonally on crimps to twin pockets and a mono. Climb through to the pocket above to then finish top right.

**2 Lumber**  Font 6b
Sit-down start on the rail to the left hole and small finger pocket. Go up left to the large hole (Font 5+ if you drop here) then move for the top.

**3 Jack**  Font 6a
Sit-down start to the rail on the lip then up left to the large hole. Finishing to the right from the lip is the same grade.

**4 Pinchy**  Font 6b
Sit-down start to small pinch then lurch direct to edges.

**5 Banksy**  Font 6a
Sit-down start to the lip, then to small pockets, right to jug and then the top. Font 5+ from standing.

Larch Cave - **NORWOOD** EDGE

### The Bat
A small perched block with a hole to the sky and good landings.

### 6 Head Plant  Font 6a
Named for the third ascentionist's stylish dismount. Through the roof to the set-back pocket and a stylish rockover (or grind) round the lip.

### 7 Sky Hole  Font 4
Up past an unusual hole through which you can see the sky. (a) is a neat Font 3 problem.

### 8 Stomp  Font 5
Sit-down start to the rail with feet initially on the left plinth and without the right arête. Sustained moves to the top.

From a sit-down start, a right-to-left traverse of the boulder, below the lip, around the corner with a rockover onto the face is Font 6b.

### Larchbow Wall
A deceptively high boulder offering some classic lines, the obvious being the flake of *Larchbow*. Take the pads for this one, as they add to the bounce factor.

### 9 Lust and Caution  Font 6a+
The left arête, without standing on the boulder.

### 10 Pie r Squared  Font 7c
Start at the obvious undercut flake left of *Larchbow*. Move up via the perfect circular hold in the centre of the wall.

### 11 Larchbow  Font 6b
Superb. Follow the flake to its end, swinging left to finish.

### 12 Larch Slab  Font 6a
Start as for *Larchbow* but move onto the slab via good holds above the flake.

### 13 Archimedes  Font 7c+
The testpiece of the crag, with excellent moves on good rock. Take the sit-down start to *Larchbow* from low in the pit then traverse up and across the undercut flake to join *Pie r Squared*. The landing is awkward but it is possible to wedge a pad in the gap and not hinder the climbing.

### Larch Cave
A collection of steep powerful problems with committing top-outs and tricky landings.

### 14 Robin's Nest  Font 6c+
A superb sit-down start with hands in the bucket. Go up to the crack then continue left for an exciting top-out. A lower start to this, starting further left is **Caspar's Start** (Font 7b+).

Almscliff to Slipstones

# NORWOOD EDGE - Diamond Block

### 15 Larch Link  Font 7a
Start at *Robin's Nest* and finish over *Bulge Head*.

### 16 Backbite  Font 7a+
From a sit-down start on the loose hold and deep flake, go up right to the sharp break then finish left of the runnel with a big move off crimps. Using the runnel for the right-hand is Font 7a. Brilliant either way.

### 17 Bulge Head  Font 7a
As for *Backbite*, but go right of the runnel using a sloper on the bulge head. Finish direct on crimps and sidepulls.

## Twitcher's Hide
Further up the hill lies a large undercut buttress with a couple of quality problems.

### 18 Ruff Traverse  Font 6c
Super-sustained traverse along the lip. Sit-down start from left-to-right (arête not in), finishing up the high wall.

### 19 Falcon  Font 7a+
Tight and powerful. From a sit-down start in the cave go from the low rail to the lip.

## Diamond Block
An isolated boulder perched on the hillside with a host of powerful, sustained lines on Gaudi-esque rock. Tree stump landings.

### 20 Blood Diamond  Font 6a
Sit-down start beneath the undercut arête and power up to the leftward rail, avoiding the plinth at halfway for feet. The left edge (a) goes at Font 3.

### 21 Ross's Rockover  Font 6a
Sit-down start beneath the undercut arête, up to the nose and gain the large flake out right. Then cock your leg over, take a deep breath, grunt and repeat until complete.

### 22 Can Can  Font 5+
Sit-down start with hands and heels in sockets of *Squat* and join the finish of that problem.

### 23 Squat  Font 5+
Sit-down start from under the right nose. Swing left into sockets and gain the top via a small finger dish.

## A n' R Wall
Some classic challenges on clean rock with good landings.

### 24 Squitter  Font 5
Good moves. Sit-down start with hands in the break. Using edges, cruise up the centre of wall direct. Classic.

### 25 Mono  Font 6a
Sit-down start, gain the mono direct from the break.

⚠️
**DANGER**
Poisonous snakes
in the compound

# hunter's stones
by **Tom Peckitt**

OS Ref: SE 213 514
Altitude: 290m

Marked by the towering antenna on the summit of Stainburn Forest, the small bouldering venue of Hunter's Stones offers climbing of surprising quality and variety in a picturesque environment. This hidden gem actually managed to remain concealed for decades by dense forest in one of the region's most explored areas until recent tree felling exposed its secrets and unearthed a delightful collection of boulder problems; some of which deserve to stand shoulder-to-shoulder with Yorkshire's finest.

**The Climbing:** There are just over 20 problems in a mid grade circuit offering fun and varied climbing, welcoming the grit-newcomer with open arms. The more stunning lines, however, mainly lie in the harder grades especially on the steep and powerful X-Wall. The main areas encompass all of the bouldering features an enthusiast would wish to find with slabs, walls, arêtes, overhangs and roofs aplenty lying in wait. The landings are generally flat, instilling confidence and concentration for all levels of ability. There is enough climbing for a full day out, with an abundance of challenges to leave you wanting more, especially if combined with a visit to Norwood Edge. The climbing can vary from the technical and delicate to the thuggy, slopey and crimpy. Tussles with some of the problems will inflict an impressive grit rash to flaunt to your friends in the pub afterwards.

**Conditions and Aspect:** The coarse and exposed hilltop boulders are quick to dry, much like their near neighbour Almscliff. Deeper into the shelter of the forest, a finer grained grit is present and cool conditions are preferred on the X-Wall, primarily due to the deficit of features that pass as holds. The natural protection of the trees means that you can seek solace from the wind on the most blustery of days without your pad making a break for it.

**Parking and Approach:** See map on page 539. Hunter's Stones lies on the eastern sides of the B6451 about four miles north of Otley in Stainburn Forest, or three miles south from the A59 Skipton-Harrogate road (taking the signposted Otley B6451 turn-off at the Pately Bridge/Menwith Hill junction). If approaching from Otley the easiest parking for Hunter's Stones is on the brow of the hill on the B6451 on the right (east) side of the road (**GPS: 53.959403, -1.683443**), which is about 100-200m further on past the main Stainburn Forest Norwood Edge car park (**GPS: 53.953967,-1.681677**). There are currently no restrictions for parking here but take care not to block the gate or vehicle access tracks. Alternatively you can park at the Norwood Edge car park, which only adds a few minutes onto the already short walk.

Walk up the obvious vehicle track into the forest, bearing left at the fork junction after 200m. A short distance uphill after this turning, the Antenna boulders are visible underneath the huge transmitter. The Trig Point boulders can be found on the summit to the right of the Antenna boulders and can be reached by walking a little further along the main path and taking the track to the hilltop or heading directly from the Antenna boulders. The X-Wall boulder in the forest can be reached by continuing along the main path, becoming visible on your left-hand side in less than five minutes.

**Access Issues:** At present there are no restrictions regarding access. To keep it this way, please ensure all vehicle track entrances are left clear.

### The Antenna
This first area sits directly below the huge antenna.

**1 Resonance**   Font 6b
A sit-down start from the low break, making a couple of tricky moves through the roof trending rightwards.

**2 Wavelength**   Font 6c+
Sit-down start from the lowest break with sustained and burly moves leading to the sloping break.

## Trig Point - HUNTER'S STONES

**3 Frequency**   Font 5+
A big move from the break to a good sloping hold.

### Trig Point
The large boulder with the impressive prow and the white trig point on top.

**4 Kai's Wall**   Font 4
The left-hand side of the boulder is a good warm up.

There are three decent un-named problems either side of *Kai's Wall*. On the left (a), taking the right-hand side of the rounded arête is Font 5 and, to the right (b), straight up the centre of the face is Font 4. Further right just before the prow/roof go direct up the wall (c) at Font 5.

**5 Hunter's Roof**   Font 7c
Starting on a good hold at the back of the roof, traverse rightwards on slopers. Thrutch round the nose to a short crack and huge jug. The left-hand side of the nose (d) is shorter, but just as brutal at Font 7b+/7c. Another fun variation is to start as for the main problem but traverse slightly right and climb the hanging wall on the left-hand side of the prow at Font 6a.

**6 Orion**   Font 7a+
Start sitting on the block and use an undercut to gain a crimp and shallow pocket then a big jug. Top-out direct or trend leftwards to the crack.

**7 Mnemonic**   Font 6c+
The right-hand rounded arête requires a tactile approach. The sit-down start adds a good deal more at Font 7b.

The wall to the left of *Mnemonic*, from the pit (e), goes at Font 6b, while to the right (f) you can start on slopey crimps and make a dynamic move to a diagonal crimp at Font 7b.

**8 Sohcahtoa**   Font 6c+
The wall to the left of the arête via sloping breaks to a sloping top.

*Almscliff to Slipstones*   **545**

# Hunter's Stones - X-Wall

The tricky slab (g) right of the arête is a neat Font 5+.

## Gav's Block
The mossy green boulder a few metres right of Twin Arêtes hides a couple of surprisingly good problems.

**12 Gav's Mantel**   Font 6b
Sit-down start from the flake/crack past the sloping break to a mantel.

**13 Press Problem**   Font 6c
Sit-down start from the large hole to climb direct.

To the right (h), climb the arête and groove from a sitter at the break on sharp holds at Font 6b.

## X-Wall
For the wads, the X-Wall boulder is hidden deep in the woods and has several good but very hard problems that require thick skin and steel fingers. Head east from Trig Point boulder to follow the path towards the woods. Drop down the hill until a main track is reached. Follow this for about 350m, passing a break in the forest, to a jumble of boulders on the left-hand side. The X-Wall is directly to the right in the wooded area.

**14 Hook or by Crook**   Font 7a+
The fine, technical left arête from a sit-down start. From standing it is Font 6c+.

**15 Hunter's Wall**   Font 7c
The thin crimpy wall, avoiding the left arête.

**16 X-Calibre**   Font 8a+
Sit-down start in the low crimpy break and move for the 'X-Hold' then up. The 'jumping start' goes at Font 7b.

**17 X-Calibre Direct**   Font 8b
Start as for *X-Calibre* but get the 'X-Hold' with your left hand and commit to an all-out dyno for the top.

**18 Lock Down**   Font 8a
Sit-down start from the large hole. Climb direct past a sharp crimp and small pocket to a dynamic finale. Font 7c from standing.

## Twin Arêtes
There are two brilliant arête problems on this small block, which sits 50m west of the Trig Point boulder.

**9 Left Arête**   Font 6c
Sit-down start from the scoop and follow the tricky left-hand side of the arête using a series of slopers.

**10 Twin Arêtes**   Font 6a
Fantastic. Use both arêtes to gain the top. Photo opposite.

**11 Right Arête**   Font 6b
Sit-down start. Use the crack and thrutch a series of slopers up the right-hand arête. Avoid the crack at Font 6c.

Yorkshire Gritstone

# X-Wall - HUNTER'S STONES

**19 Shot-hole Wall**  Font 7c+
Sit-down start from the large hole, trend right past an undercut flake and small pockets to micro crimps near the top. Font 7c from standing.

**20 Shot-hole Arête**  Font 6b
The right arête.

**21 Curlicue**  Font 3
The easiest problem here by some way! A short mantel on the far right of the boulder.

### First Ascent Information

At Norwood Edge, once the trees were down the race was on to clean and climb the lines. So, in 2008 the strong team of Robin Warden, Ross Williams and Amanda Philips laid siege in a four week period. Plenty of tree debris was removed and the lines began to tumble, with the majority sent by Warden including *Larchbow*, *Backbite* and *Bulge Head*. Matt Wilcox and Simon Marson snook in to climb the excellent *Falcon* and *Night Raiders*; the latter, as the name suggests, done by torchlight. The big guns in the shape of Tom Peckitt were sent in to mop up the remaining hard lines of *Pie r Squared* and *Archimedes*.

Hunter's Stones were well and truly hunted down by Peckitt, also in 2008 after the tree clearances, with the biggest prizes all falling his way. *Wavelength*, *Resonance*, *Orion* and *Hunter's Roof* to name a few, but in terms of difficulty the problem at the top of the pile is the dynamic *X-Calibre Direct*. Rob Fenton turned his hand to *Shothole Arête*, *Curlicue* and *By Hook or by Crook* and a visiting Lakes boulder master in the shape of Greg Chapman nipped in to claim the stiff *Hunter's Wall*.

Menwith Hill eavesdrops in on Jamie Moss climbing **Twin Arêtes** (Font 6a). Opposite page.
Photo: Matt Kilner

**BIRK CRAG**

# birk crag (harlow carr)

OS Ref: SE 278 547
Altitude: 120m

A quaint woodland crag with a series of buttresses situated two miles from the centre of Harrogate and a stone's throw away from RHS Harlow Carr Gardens.

**The Climbing:** Around 25 climbs with the majority between Diff and HS. Almost all are covered in moss, heather and typical woodland verdure which means a quick hit is rarely possible. That said, the two best routes, *Ilex Wall Direct* (HS) and the fine *Armpit* (HVS) are often clean and warrant an afternoon visit one day. The *Interflora Slabs* area could, with a little effort, become a useful training ground for school and beginners groups. The 1998 guide stated there is little room for future development and with regards to routes this is true. It may be a good time for the woodland esoteric boulderer to step forward though, as the hillside has a smattering of boulders that may warrant closer inspection. **Conditions and Aspect:** The crag faces generally north-west and even in summer gets very little sunshine due to the thick woodland setting. The buttresses vary in height from 6m to 15m and are of generally good quality gritstone. They are, unfortunately, heavily vegetated and will require constant traffic to keep them in a climbable condition. Possibly the best time to visit is late spring before the woodland canopy becomes all-enveloping.

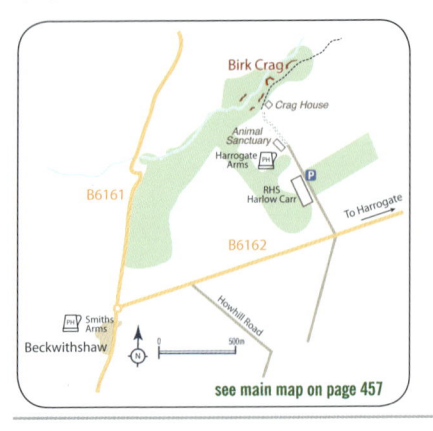

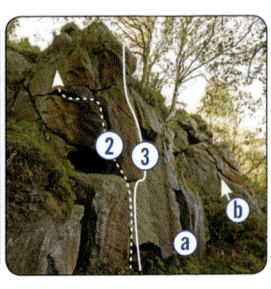

see main map on page 457

**Parking and Approach:** From Harrogate take the B6162 Harrogate-Beckwithshaw road turning right on a minor road well signed towards Harlow Carr Gardens. Several parking options are available on this road, including the Harlow Carr overflow car park on the right, and the coach park further down on the left. Probably the best spot is the lay-by opposite the Gardens' iron gates and by a wood a quarter mile down the road on the right (**Parking GPS: 53.982833, -1.572708**). Walk down the road (past the sign for the Harrogate Arms) until the road becomes a track (animal sanctuary on the left). Continue for 300m until the track bends round to the right to Crag House. Continue straight on, into the wood and the marked footpath. The easy *House Slabs* are immediately below the entrance to the woods. Turn right (east) and follow the top path (parallel to the drive for Crag House and the stone wall) for 75m. The main *House Buttress* is directly below here. Continuing for a further 150m and the *Interflora Slabs* are below on the left whilst Woodpecker Crag lies in the jungle 500m left (west) and upstream of Crag House on the opposite bank of Oak Beck. **The wood is a SSSI so treat the place with respect. Any crag cleaning must be very judicious indeed.**

**Interflora Slab:** An easy-angled 12m quarried slab suitable for novices. Tree belays or top ropes can be arranged. **Wendy** (VD) starts on the ledge 6m above the base of the crag on the left, adjacent to a small silver birch, and climbs straight up to mantel over a small overhang; **Fiona** (D) goes from the ledge above and left of the toe of the buttress to take the slab direct; **Moira** (M) start at the toe of the slab, climbs directly to the birch tree at 10m and finishes up the upper slab to the rowan tree; **Hilary** (VD) starts at the narrow gangway 6m up and right of the toe of the buttress, goes straight up for 3m, moves left to mantelshelf by a twin tree and finishes directly just right of the rowan; **Tom**

Yorkshire Gritstone

## BIRK CRAG

(VD) starts 6m left of *Hilary* below a short groove. Climb up obvious holds to a heather ledge (the heather now almost reaches the ground) and trend left on good holds to finish right of the rowan; **Jerry** (D) is as for *Tom* to the ledge, steps left and goes up just right of the overgrown rib.

**House Buttress:** The first four routes climbed the easy angled, but now heavily vegetated, slabs to the left of the prominent slender pinnacle of *Ilex Wall*. They would require a mammoth cleaning effort to restore them to their former glory. For the record they were, **Fox Trot** (M); **Reptile** (VD); **Grapolite** (VD) and **Trilobite** (VD). To the right of the slabs, on the downhill side of the slender pinnacle is the best line on the crag:

**1 Ilex Wall Direct**  HS 4b  8m  ☆
Climb the slabby rib on the left.

The green wall behind the holly tree, finishing with a mantelshelf at the top, is **Ilex Wall** (VD). Just to the right and uphill is a buttress which is split into a steep and slabby section by a gully.

**2 Rosla**  S  15m
The obvious crack just left of the eastern most rib. Ascend the crack and mantelshelf left at 3m. Pull into the crack above and ascend this moving left to finish with an interesting move up the front of the left-hand pinnacle.

**3 Armpit**  HVS 5b  11m  ☆
A fine route if the bulge above the overhang is clean. Move up to reach undercut holds beneath the prominent hanging inverted rock finger. Layback up to the right and, with difficulty, attain a bridging position beneath the overhang. Surmount this strenuously with the aid of two pocket holes. Go directly up the front of the remaining wall to the top of the pinnacle.

The next crack to the right is (a) **Birk Crack** (S) which climbs a chimney to a ledge at 5m and continues up the crack to a dirty finish. The crack 3m right is **Surprise Crack** (S) and climbs just left of the rib to a large ledge at 3m and ascends the crack to a heathery finish; across the easy gully on the left wall is an obvious diagonal crack, (b) **Lilac Crack** (HS 4a). Climb this to the ledge at 10m and move with difficulty into the wide crack slanting up leftwards and finish by mantelshelfing; **Lilac Slab** (MS) starts just right of the rib to the right and tackles the wall directly to the undercut then climbs slabs above to a ledge below the final crack of *Lilac Crack*. Finish up just to the right of this. The **Girdle Traverse** (MS), when clean, was described as an extremely enjoyable route. It started 5m right of the start of *Lilac Slab* and finished by crossing *Armpit* above the crux bulge to reach the final moves of *Rosla*. If you can find any rock in between consider it a bonus.

Further to the right, below the entrance to the woods are the easy *House Slabs*, suitable for absolute beginners. Below these and to the left is a slab which has at its base a peculiar spider-like tree. This is **Joan's Climb** (VD) which ascends the slab (without the help of the tree) and eases towards the top. Walking rightwards (east) by 10m is a small chipped slab. **Epilobium** (HD) climbs the chips. Above this is a loaf-shaped boulder with (c) **Generalissimo** (Font 4+) grappling with the fine layback crack on the right (originally climbed as a route by starting up the chipped slab below the path, but far better as a problem); **Trotter** (M) climbs the grim, moss-covered narrow slab below *Epilobium* to finish with a move up onto the sharp horizontal arête.

**Woodpecker Crag:** A steep buttress, 10m in height, heavily disguised as a mound of moss and half a kilometre further right on the opposite side of Oak Beck. **Woody Woodpecker** (S) climbs a line 2m left of the right-hand rib with the hard move on the steep section 3m from the top; **Woodpecker Crack** (VD) is the obvious crack in the centre of the buttress; **Firefly** (D) ascends the obvious holds 1m left of *Woodpecker Crack*; **Brush-Off** (D) climbs the obvious line on an isolated vegetated buttress 18m to the left of *Firefly*.

**First Ascent Information:** *The majority of climbs were recorded by Greg Tough, R. Kinnaird and C. Stuttard in 1972.*

# calf crag
## by Adi Gill

OS Ref: SE 165 588
Altitude: 270m

Sat like two crashed UFO's in an Area 51/Menwith Hill scenario, Calf Crag is a surprising find that warrants just one visit for the captivating roof problem alone. The seven problems spread between the two boulders are in close proximity to Thruscross so a combined visit would lengthen your day. **Approach**: From the A59 at Blubberhouses take Hardisty Hill towards Pateley Bridge for 3.5km where a right turn after the Stone House Inn leads to a sharp right and left bend after 800m. Park conservatively on your right and take the track south-east which becomes a footpath and the boulders emerge up to the right (5 mins from the car). **The Climbs**: On the Upper Roof Boulder, **Cookie Monster** (Font 6b, and the reason you came), breaches the roof leftwards to an old school thrutch; **Dr MG** (Font 6c) crosses the roof on the right to a sloping finish with **Who Took the Cookie** (Font 4) to the right again. The lower sloping boulder starts with **Bald Eagle** (Font 5) over the nose on the front face. **Rob's Problem** (Font 7a) is the sloping horror show from the big undercut; **Foocalf** (Font 6b) is the right arête to the big pockets and finally, **The Traverse** (Font 7a), travels the obvious break from left to right. The general condition of all problems are sandy but don't let that put you off; you really need to try that roof.

# havarah park
OS Ref: SE 250 534  Altitude: 185m

A small outcrop close to Ten Acre Reservoir in Havarah Park near Beckwithshaw. Approach by a 20 minute walk along a pleasant track from directly opposite the cricket ground in Beckwithshaw village towards Springhill Farm. There are small boulders close to the path but the main attraction is a larger block towards the left of the dam easily approached along a subsidiary path. Several boulder problems and a handful of micro routes are on offer. Currently the crag isn't accessed by a public footpath and the tennant of the land isn't happy about access for climbing.

Andrew Emery getting swallowed up by the **Cookie Monster** (Font 6b). This page.
Photo: Tom Peckitt

Richard Mallinson standing out on the outstanding **Overhang Direct** (Font 5), Lord's Seat. Page 492.
Photo: Adi Gill

# Slipstones Area

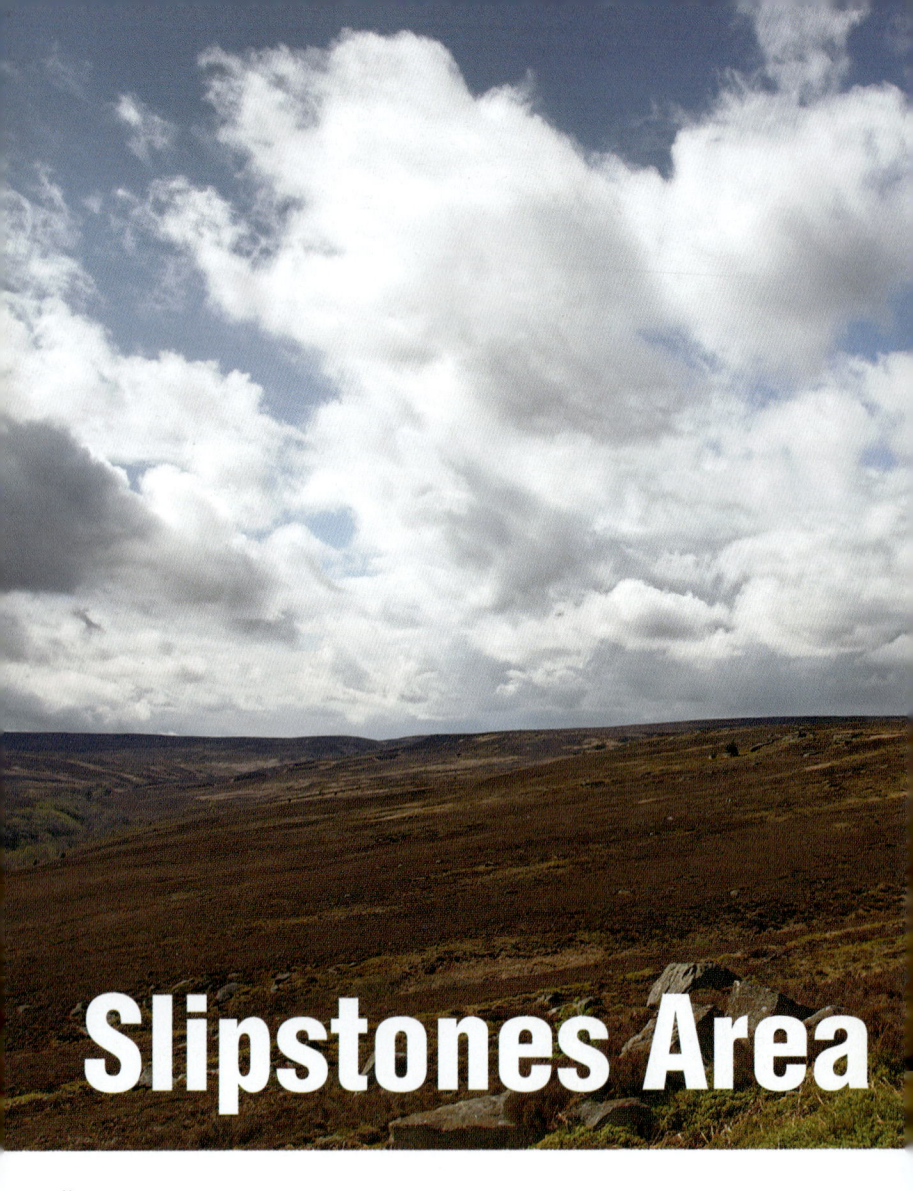

"Quality wise it is world class and there isn't much better than feeling strong on the pinch and the undercling as you arc your leg back getting ready to "boot it." Then the catch takes a moment to sink in as you swirl about a bit, arguing with gravity."

*Dan Varian on his repeat of Cypher (Font 8b)*

Andi Turner elegantly poised for the finish of **Original Route** (HVS 5a) at Slipstones. Page 564
Photo: Jonathan Read

| | | |
|---|---|---|
| **Slipstones** 556 | **Sypeland** 604 | Roundhill 624 |
| **Brown Beck** 586 | Lulbeck 619 | Clint Crags 631 |
| Birk Gill 596 | Ash Head Crag 620 | Arnagill 633 |
| Roova 600 | | |

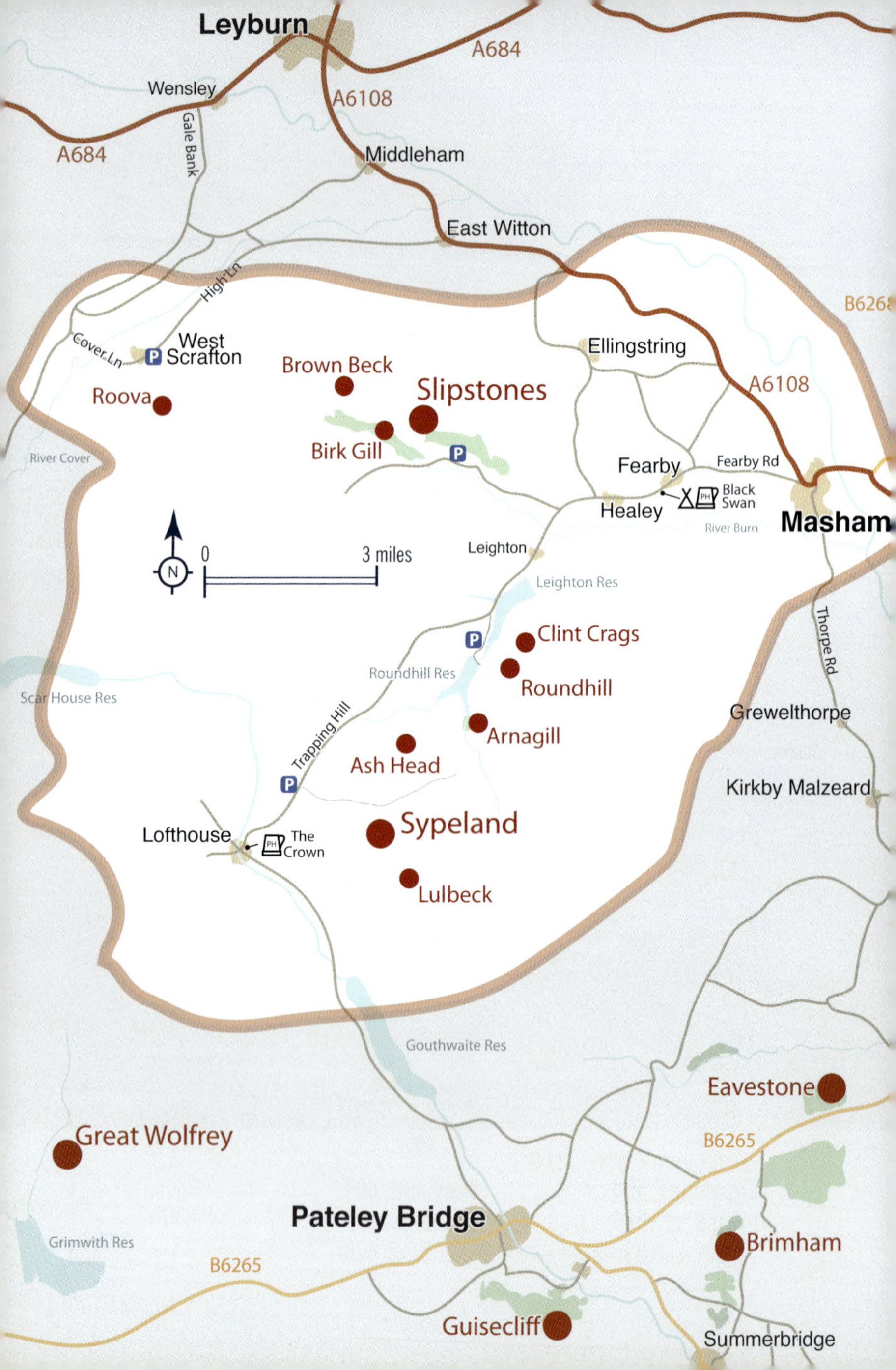

Leyburn
A684
Wensley
A6108
Gale Bank
A684
Middleham
East Witton
High Ln
B6268
West Scrafton
Cover Ln
Ellingstring
Brown Beck
Slipstones
A6108
Roova
Birk Gill
River Cover
Fearby
Fearby Rd
Black Swan
Healey
Masham
River Burn
Leighton
0
3 miles
N
Leighton Res
Clint Crags
Thorpe Rd
Roundhill Res
Roundhill
Scar House Res
Grewelthorpe
Trapping Hill
Arnagill
Ash Head
Kirkby Malzeard
Sypeland
Lofthouse
The Crown
PH
Lulbeck
Gouthwaite Res
Eavestone
Great Wolfrey
B6265
Pateley Bridge
Brimham
Grimwith Res
B6265
Guisecliff
Summerbridge

# Introduction - SLIPSTONES

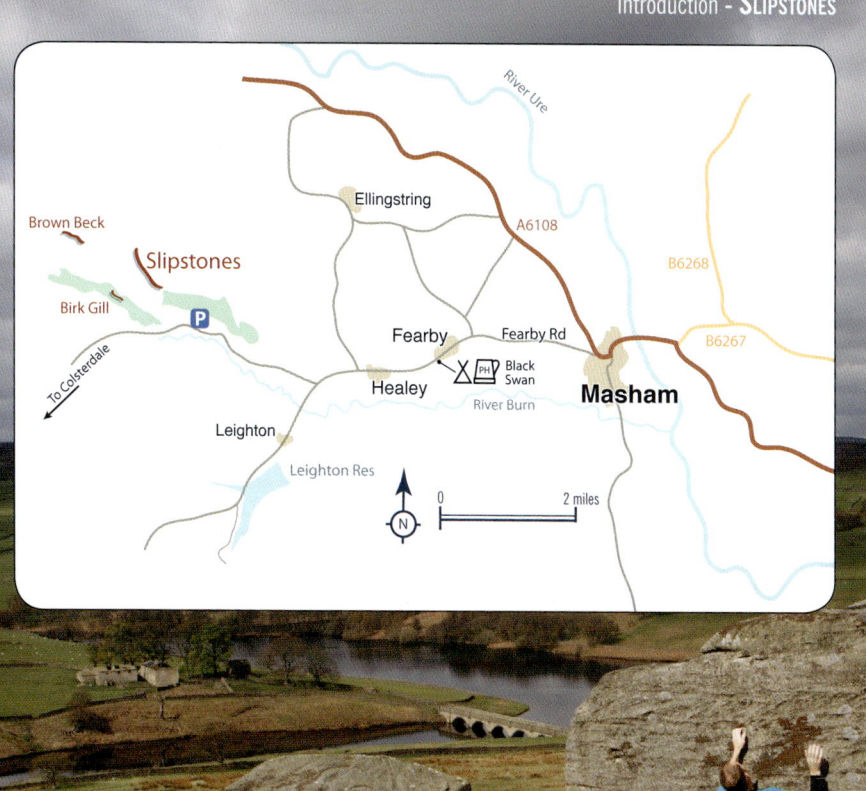

Adi Gill on the superb **Top Pocket Finish** (Font 5+) at Roundhill. Page 626
Photo: Michelle Gill

555

# slipstones
by **Ryan Plews**

OS Ref: SE 138 821                    Altitude: 310m

The single malt of gritstone, distilled to perfection, leaving only the finest routes on perfect rock in a truly serene moorland setting. This remote northern outpost of Yorkshire never fails to make an impression whatever your grade, making the longest journeys irrelevant.

**The Climbing:** Line after line of quality. Plum cracklines, formidable wall climbs and every conceivable shape of arête can be found here to baffle even the most technically astute. For the three-star route bagger, the steep front face of the *Beldin Buttress* should not be missed; particularly *Original Route* (HVS 5a) and *Zoom* (HVS 5b), whilst *Atomic* (E3 6a) and *Agra* (HVS 5b) on the adjacent buttress fulfill every gritstone wish. As the crag gently relents in height the boulderer becomes king, flocking to sample the delights of *Paul's Arête, Ripper, Lay-by Arête* and *Micro Corner*.

The crag's development was a slow and secretive one and due to its location the majority of the lines are the work of the great and good from Teesside. Martin Berry and Geoff Milburn kicked it off, the Marr brothers picked up the pace and by the 1980s the full force of the North-East's strong was felt with Ian Cummins, Alan Taylor, Paul Ingham and Ian Dunn realising the cream routes of the crag. By the turn of the century Yorkshire's "long term loaned" Teessider, Steve Dunning, finally brought the crag into Font 8 territory with *Super Furry Animal* and *Exocet*, but it was the offcomedun from the Peak, Ben Moon, who stole the holy grail of arêtes with his outstanding *Cypher* in 2002.

The 200+ lines along the crag lie in that seamless juncture between route and problem with numerous highballs marrying the two. As a result, the bouldering pad is most people's weapon of choice but with many hazardous landings, roped climbing should be considered, especially where route grades are given.

**Conditions and Aspect:** Gently sweeping the crest of the moorland the crag's south-west aspect is a sunny and quick drying one making this a year-round venue, though a visit on a still winters day can be a euphoric experience. Due to the crag's remote location the road conditions after periods of snow and ice can be tricky so be prepared.

The ground erosion around the first area upon approach (from *Sulky Little Boys* to *Super Furry Animal*) is becoming unsightly so do what you can to minimise this (go exploring; there's quality to be had in each area). The use of excessive brushing is now, sadly, very evident. Just don't do it. It's so unnecessary here and Slipstones is particularly vulnerable as the grit is more fragile than its cousins in deeper Yorkshire. Once the outer skin is broken or worn through, it exposes the softer sandstone underneath and that's when the problems escalate. A rag or beer towel is far more appropriate for this venue.

**Access:** On open access land. Respect any notifiable closures with regard to the CRoW Act and avoid the crag during May and June to minimise disturbance to ground nesting birds. No dogs.

Desperate for most, a mere walk in the park for Sam Whittaker on **Lay-by Arête** (Font 7b+). Page 576.
Photo: Keith Sharples

# SLIPSTONES - Aerial Photo

**Parking and Approach:** When heading north from Masham on the A6108 Leyburn Road, turn left onto Fearby Road signed to Fearby, Healey and Leighton (and the *Black Swan* — a good pub and campsite). After 3 miles and after passing through the villages of Fearby and Healey the road bends left to Leighton but on this bend is a single road on the right (dead-end sign) signed to Colsterdale. Take this. Follow this single road for 1.5 miles. Shortly after a red postbox and a red phonebox on the left the road takes a right-to-left hairpin and the parking is just after this on the right (**GPS: 54.228103,-1.77685**). Park considerately to maximise the number of cars for the lay-by and **do not block the access road to the farm.** (Alternatively there is further off-road parking a few min-

| 1 | Far Left Buttress | 8 | Lean Buttress | 14 | Buttress 17 |
| 2 | Escalator Buttress | 9 | Marr's Buttress | 15 | Lay-by Buttress |
| 3 | Beldin Block | 10 | Siamese Blocks | 16 | Twenty Something |
| 4 | Agra Buttress | 11 | The Deck / Aces High | 17 | The Middle Tier |
| 5 | Bait & Squark's Buttress | 12 | Ellingstring Buttress | 18 | The Lower Tier |
| 6 | Sevens & Eights Buttress | 13 | Stainthorpe's Buttress | 19 | Sulky Little Boys |
| 7 | Sowden Buttress | | | | |

## Approach Map - SLIPSTONES

utes up the road (maximum 2-3 vehicles) or you can park back down the road, where the phone box is situated, if the main parking is full). Follow the track for 600m towards the farm but continue with the wall to the gate accessing the open moorland. To reach the far left of the crag follow the track and trench north-east for a further 700m where a faint path leads right for 100m through the heather up to the edge and *Far Left Buttress*. Alternatively the right-hand side of the crag can be reached by turning right at the gate and following the wall. Both approaches are 20 and 15 minutes respectively from the lay-by.

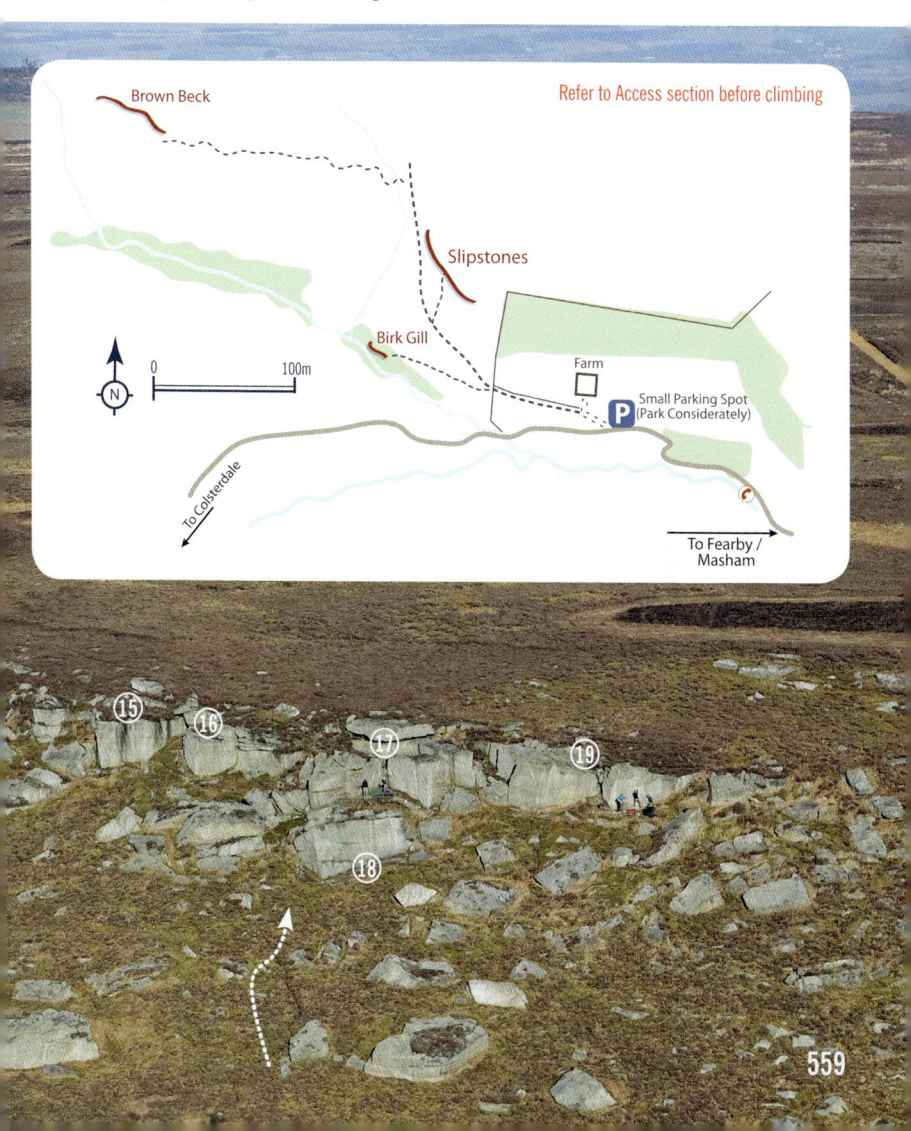

# SLIPSTONES - Far Left Buttress

## Far Left Buttress
The featureless and bold buttress located at the extreme left-hand side of the crag.

**1 Extremities** Font 6a (E1 5c)
Starting left of the arête, climb the centre of the wall using small sloping crimps. A left-hand variation is also possible, but lacks the quality due to the fragile weathered holds.
*Tony Marr   14th February 1982*

**2 Paul's Arête Left-Hand** Font 6b (E1 6a)
Starting from the ground! The impressive left-hand side of the arête with intricate moves and a horrible landing.
*Paul Ingham   14th February 1982*

**3 Paul's Arête Right-Hand** Font 5 (E1 5b)
The stunning right-hand side of the arête is approached with a highball in mind. Use the rounded arête and positive holds for your right hand. The large flake at half-height has slightly improved but does not effect the quality of the climb. Just be extra cautious upon approach.
*Paul Ingham   14th February 1982*

**4 Steve's Wall** Font 5 (E1 5b)
Start between *Paul's Arête Right-Hand* and the centre of the wall. Climb direct on good but spaced holds with a long move out right to finish.
*Steve Brown   14th February 1982*

**5 Heather Crack** D   5m
The large crack.
*Martyn Berry with lads from Pollington Borstal   1957*

**6 Heather Wall** Font 4
The short wall right of *Heather Crack* using the right arête.

**7 Heather Wall Right-Hand** Font 2+ (VD)
The short juggy wall right of the arête.

## Escalator Buttress
A further 25m to the right is the start of the main edge.

**8 Roofed Corner** Font 2+ (VD)
A short corner climb in a half-pint recess.
*Martyn Berry with lads from Pollington Borstal   1957*

**9 Little Arête** Font 4
The right-hand side of the arête from the break.

**10 Little Corner** Font 2 (D)
The right-hand corner with a large hanging block above.
*Martyn Berry with lads from Pollington Borstal   1958*

**11 Overhanging Crack** Font 2+ (VD)
The small prow with the wide crack on the right.
*Martyn Berry with lads from Pollington Borstal   1958*

**12 Undercut Double Crack** HS 4b   6m   ★
The steep and thuggish crackline stepping right at the top.
*Cleveland Mountaineering Club   April 1964*

**13 Ginger Badger** HVS 5b   6m
Climb the wall between the wide crack and the large chimney. Good protection in the first break prepares you for crimpy moves, then a big reach for the mammoth break.
*James Karran and Grant Brewer   12th March 2002*

**14 Not So Tight Chimney** VD   6m   ★
This stupendous and very satisfying chimney will certainly give you a sweat. Old skool classic!
*Geoff Milburn and Peter Martin   October 1960*

**15 Breakwind Arête** HVS 5b   8m   ★
The arête on its right-hand side just slightly right of *Not So Tight Chimney*. The quality diminishes towards the top as soon as you realise you can easily escape the final strenuous moves. Hang on in there.
*Phillipe Osborne and David Maudley   15th January 1995*

## Escalator Buttress - SLIPSTONES

**16 Space Truckin'** E1 5b  8m  ★
The blunt arête starting 2m right of *Breakwind Arête*. A small foot ledge leads you to a fragile flake. Continue up the blunt arête via the big breaks.
*Ian Dunn, Steve Brown and Paul Ingham  14th February 1982*

**17 Escalator** HVS 5b  8m  ★★
A wonderful climb that takes you directly up the centre of the buttress on good holds to a crux finish.
*Tony Marr and Eric Marr  July 1964*

**18 Diminuendo** HVS 5c  8m  ★
Start with a big move to the first break. Gain a sidepull pocket out left with a strenuous move to a good hold in the break on the right arête. Gain the ledge and finish up the left-hand side of the arête above. Sustained, feeling a little contrived in places.
*Alan Taylor and Tony Marr  13th September 1999*

An optional extra once you have ticked the buttress, (a) **Rogue's Gallery** (VS 5a), starts up *Mantelshelf Crack*, meanders into *Escalator* and finishes round the arête up *Not So Tight Chimney*.

The following climbs start immediately right of *Diminuendo* on Escalator Buttress and are situated in the large gully behind Beldin Block.

**19 Mantelshelf Crack** VD  6m
The large problematic crack into the recess with a finish of your choice.
*Geoff Milburn and Peter Martin  October 1960*

**20 Staircase** M  6m
The leftward gangway into the recess.
*Martyn Berry with lads from Pollington Borstal  1957*

**21 Mantelshelf Wall** VS 4c  5m
The thin wall right of *Staircase*. From a problematic move, gain the ledge to comfortably finish up the rightward slanting ramp. A variation (b) is also possible by climbing direct to the top of the ramp.
*Cleveland Mountaineering Club  April 1964*

**22 Cold Wall** VS 4c  4m
Start 2m right of *Mantelshelf Wall*. Gain the break via a tricky move then finish on good holds.
*Ken Jackson and Tony Marr  1968*

**23 Hole in The Wall** HS 4b  4m
From the large hole, gain the break. Escape via a tricky finish up the leftwards sloping ramp.
*Tony Marr and Eric Marr  Easter 1964*

Almscliff to Slipstones  561

# Slipstones - Beldin Block

## Beldin Block
The very large tilting block, right of Escalator Buttress. Beldin Block boasts climbing on all four sides with the premier climbing on its slightly overhanging south face. The east face is home to possibly one of the best E3s in Yorkshire town, whilst the slabby north side's quality is not to be underestimated. Classics all around.

The next eight climbs are situated in the large gully, on the north side of Beldin Block, opposite *Mantelshelf Wall*. The slabby wall can be very deceiving with its green appearance, but the routes prove very worthwhile.

### 24 Left Edge  Font 2+ (D)
The short slab on the far left of the face has a tricky start.
*Martyn Berry with lads from Pollington Borstal  1958*

### 25 Inside Left  S 4a  4m
Start slightly right of *Left Edge* to finish directly up the slab.
*1960s*

### 26 Old Corner  VD  4m  ★
A wispy, shallow, right-facing corner.
*Geoff Milburn and Peter Martin  October 1960*

### 27 Petch's Groove  S 4a  5m
The curved groove above the cave provides some interesting moves.
*Geoff Milburn and Peter Martin  October 1960*

### 28 Groove Eliminate  HS 4b  5m
The slabby wall right of the groove using the pockets. Try not to let your feet wander into the groove.
*1960s*

### 29 Twenty Foot Crack  HVD 4a  6m
The hanging crackline is hard to get established on. Holds on the left are allowed at the grade (more like S 4b direct).
*Ernie Shield, Dave Staton and Malcom Farrow  1962*

### 30 North Wall  HVS 5b  6m
Starting a metre right, climb the slabby wall direct.
*Alan Taylor  1977*

### 31 Offspring  HVS 5c  6m
Climb to a finger pocket then make a long reach to the break.
*Alan Taylor, Tony Marr and Chris Taylor (aged 9) 10th Sept 2006*

### 32 Tranmire Arête  MS 4a  6m  ★★
The right arête of the north wall is simply brilliant. The right side of the arête is a bold and harder variation.
*Cleveland Mountaineering Club  April 1964*

The following eight climbs are situated on the west face of Beldin Block, which start to gain more height.

### 33 Tranmire Crack  VS 4c  6m
Start by stepping off the large block underneath the arête. Climb the short crack with the large pocket, which eases

562  Yorkshire Gritstone

towards the top. A 5b direct start (c) to the left is also possible by avoiding the boulder.
*Tony Marr 1978*

**34 Girdle Buttress**  E1 5b   50m  ★★
A classic left-to-right girdle of Beldin Block, which was originally soloed. Starting up *Tranmire Crack*, traverse the first main break rightwards to the nose of *West Face Eliminate*. Follow the upper break all the way along the south face to finish up *Zoom* on the east face. Feeling pumped? Extend this to finish up *Wise Crack*.
*Paul Ingham and Ian Dunn  14 February 1982*

**35 Jenny Binks Wall**  VS 5a   7m  ★
Start in the left side of the large slot. Finish direct with long reaches between the breaks.
*Many claims from back in the day  1968ish*

**36 Twixt**  HVS 5a   7m
A similar route to its neighbour. Start on the right side of the slot with an even longer reach between the breaks.
*Alan Taylor, Tony Marr and Mike Tooke  13 September 1999*

**37 Easy Pickings**  VS 4c   7m  ★★
Start from the large block and the smaller right-hand slot. Climb up and right to another smaller slot then step left to finish direct.
*Alan Taylor, Tony Marr and Paul Ingham  1978*

**38 The Handrail**  HVS 5a   20m
Starting as for *Easy Pickings* from the sloping boulder, traverse around the arête along the mid-height break across the south face of the Beldin Block and join the classic route of *Zoom*. Escape here or finish up *Zoom* for the full experience (at E1 5b). A whole manner of variations are possible: traversing leftwards to finish up *Easy Pickings* is HVS 5a; joining the *Low Level Traverse* below *Zoom* and reversing it leftwards to the start is Font 6b.
*Tony Marr and Mike Tooke  22nd April 2009*

**39 West Face Eliminate**  E2 6a   8m
A strenuous route that climbs the left side of the blunt arête starting from its lowest point. Finish over the double nose.
*Steve Brown and Dave Paul  1986*

Jon Stewart high on the glorious finish of **Sowden** (HVS 5a). Page 570
Photo: Jamie Moss

## SLIPSTONES - Beldin Block

**40 Beldin Direct** E1 5b  8m  ★
The imposing blunt arête up its right-hand side with a long reach to the second break via a sloping slot. Finish right up the large crack.
*Alan Tylor, Tony Marr and Ken Jackson   April 1975*

**41 Low Level Traverse**  WTF  100m  ★★★
A brilliant low-level left-to-right traverse that stretches over six buttresses, rarely climbing more than a metre above the ground. Paul Ingham had successfully climbed the full traverse after climbing various sections with Tony Marr as individual winter training exercises, which started life in 1983. Paul thought he was quite generous giving the grade of HVS 5c. Truly satisfying, very strenuous and totally deserves the recognition. Also possible from right to left. There are two variations. The first (Font 7a+) is impressive and a difficult one to grade. Starting low on the left arête of *West Face Eliminate*, traverse the low break rightwards all the way across six buttresses to finish up *Dennis In Darlo*. The second, an easier variation, finishes earlier at the base of *Atomic* (Font 6b+).

**42 Beldin Variation** E1 5b  8m  ★
A funky climb with adequate protection although originally soloed on the first ascent. From a large pocket, gain the first break. From a small undercut, make a strenuous reach for a large break. Finish leftwards up the large crack.
*Paul Ingham   15th March 1981*

**43 Beldin** HVS 5b  10m  ★★
A forearm-busting classic that follows the natural ramp line leftwards up the striking front face. Gain the break and finish leftwards up the large crack. Hang on in there.
*Ken Jackson and Tony Marr   1968*

**44 Original Route** HVS 5a  10m  ★★★
Another fantastic pump fest with a real sting in the tail. Follow the ramp line to its end then climb out right to finish via the large flake. Photo on page 552.
*Tony Marr and Eric Marr   July 1964*

**45 Gollinglith** E1 5b  8m  ★★
A strenuous test of crack climbing which was soloed on the first ascent. Finish through the imposing flake.
*Steve Wilson   1969* ✦

564                    Yorkshire Gritstone

### 46 Tachyon  E2 5c  8m  ★
A difficult climb that takes the left-hand side of the arête. Once the last large break is reached, move right to finish up *Zoom*.
*Alan Taylor and Tony Marr  9th May 1999*

The follow climbs are located in the **East Alcove** of the Beldin Block.

### 47 Zoom  HVS 5b  7m  ★★★
An absolute must if you're visiting the crag. This classic climb starts right of the arête using the large undercut flake to your right. Gain the break from the small overlap and finish by laybacking the large flake crack leaving you in an awesome position.
*Tony Marr, Eric Marr and Ken Jackson  June 1966*

### 48 Atomic  E3 6a  7m  ★★★
Your grit logbook is not complete without bagging this beauty. Technical but well-protected (some say E2...) and climbed easily enough with hot aches. Climb the centre of the wall to a tricky move to gain the break. Continue to a committing crux move way above.
*Ian Dunn and Paul Ingham  17th April 1982*

### 49 Atomic Right-Hand  E3 6b  7m  ★
Start as for *Atomic*. After halfway, move out right up the awkward, and very reachy, bold wall.
*Hugh Harris and Ian Cummins  1994*

### 50 Barnley Crack  S 4a  7m  ★
The satisfying and awkward left-hand corner-crack with a reachy mid-height move.
*Geoff Milburn and Peter Martin  October 1960*

### 51 Barnley Wall  HS 4b  7m  ★
A fun climb that takes the centre of the wall from a problematic start.
*Steve Wilson  June 1966*

### 52 Ulfer's Crack  HVD 4a  7m  ★★
A fabulous corner-crack; almost as good as anything of its height on gritstone.
*Geoff Milburn and Peter Martin  October 1960*

### 53 Forever Onward  E1 5c  7m
The centre of the right wall in the East Alcove using the large pockets. Tackle the thin section to gain the large break. Finish direct up the blank wall.
*Paul Ingham  1988*

### 54 Timeless Divide  Font 6a+  (E2 6a)
The blunt arête is climbed direct with a difficult start to gain the first break. Finish up the striking fin.
*Paul Ingham  20th November 1983*

Karin Magog embracing **Right Wall** (Font 6a+ / HVS 5c). Page 572
Photo: Steve Crowe

Almscliff to Slipstones

# Slipstones - Agra Buttress

## Agra Buttress
The next large buttress with its capping roof at the top boasts a quality selection of thin and technical climbs with adequate protection at three-quarter height.

### 55 Variation Start  Font 6c (E2 6c)
A technical monster using super thin holds up the right-hand side of the arête. Finish up the fin.
*Ian Cummins 1980s*

### 56 Agrete  Font 6b  (HVS 5c)
Starting a metre or so from the left arête, gnarly moves lead you to a hollow undercut flake. Bear leftward to finish up the fin. A variation finale (a) that adds spice climbs rightwards through the roof on sloping holds.
*Tony Marr (start) 1965; Paul Ingham Mike Davidson 5th Oct 1980*

### 57 Agra Direct Start  HVS 5c   7m
Start 3m right of the arête. Make a thin move from a sidepull to stretch for crimps. Gain the ledge and finish directly through the roof.
*Tony Marr  15th March 1980*

### 58 Agra  HVS 5b   7m    ★★★
A pure natural line. Start from the good ledges at the centre of the buttress and make a delicate move to gain the reasonable pockets. Move leftwards to join the gangway then the ledge. Finish directly through the cracked roof. A marginally easier alternative, (b) **Agra Right-Hand** (HVS 5b), climbs through the pockets directly to the top with a strenuous finish over the roof.
*Tony Marr and Eric Marr  1965*  ◆

### 59 Agra Variation  VS 4b   14m
Follow the same line as *Agra*. Once the ledge is surmounted, traverse leftwards following the break all the way into the East Alcove and finish up *Ulfer's Crack*. Aka: **Wimp's Finish.**
*Tony Marr and Eric Marr  1965*

### 60 Narrow Margin  E2 6a   8m
Start right of *Agra*, passing through a small overlap to start. Gain the pockets at mid-height and climb directly to the broken rock underneath the roof. Take care on the fragile holds. Climb boldly rightwards through the roof to finish.
*Tony Marr and Linda Marr  26th July 1992*

### 61 Wisecrack Direct Start  Font 6c (HVS 6b)
An exceptional problem that climbs directly into the thin crack on very slopey holds.
*Ian Cummins 1980s*

Yorkshire Gritstone

## Agra Buttress - SLIPSTONES

**62 Wisecrack**  HVS 5c   6m   ★★★
An outstanding teaser. Start below and right from the large slot. Gain the thin hanging crack with a demanding move. Highball Font 5+.
*Paul Ingham   4th December 1982*

**63 Wisecrack Super Direct**  Font 7b
From the large slot of *Wisecrack*, climb the technical wall directly above and finish at the ledge.

**64 Alan's Arête**  VS 5b   5m
The bold right arête is climbed on its left-hand side. The right-hand side is an easier variation (VS 4c).
*Alan Taylor   7th September 1980*

**65 Mark Turner's Rockover**  VS 5a   4m
Climb the problematic wall right of the arête.
*Mark Turner   1990s*

**66 Shine On**  VD   5m
An entertaining problem laybacking the large corner-crack.
*Martyn Berry and the lads from Pollington Borstal   1958*

**67 Mantel On**  Font 4 (S 4c)
A gut busting mantel or technical trickery into the leaning groove.
*Cleveland Mountaineering Club   April 1964*

**68 Groove On**  Font 3 (VD 4a)
The boulder problem groove has a hard start.
*Cleveland Mountaineering Club   April 1964*

Danny Towers enjoying magical conditions on **Flakey Wall** (VS 4c). Page 578.
Photo: Graham Derbyshire

## SLIPSTONES - Bait Buttress

### Bait Buttress
Across the gully is this large undercut block with a hole in its front face.

### 69 Block Arête   Font 3+   (S 4b)
The wall left of the arête. The wall just left again is Diff.
*Steve Wilson 1967*

### 70 Beta Blocker   E1 5b   6m
A great problem up the arête but medication may be necessary to slow the heart above that landing.
*Paul Ingham   14th February 1982*

### 71 Impregnable   E2 6a   8m   ★★
The stand-out central line of the buttress using the hole.
*Paul Ingham   14th February 1982*

### 72 Get Nervous   E2 5c   8m
Stay true to the right arête with every reason to have a knee trembler in its upper reaches.
*Ian Dunn and Paul Ingham   14th February 1982*

### 73 Chockstone Overhang   HS 4b   7m
Delve deep inside and relish some traditional techniques.
*Geoff Milburn   Oct 1960*

### Squawk's Buttress
The continuing block with the class namesake arête and the extremely popular *Undercut Flake*.

### 74 Squawk's Arête   HVS 5b   8m   ★
March boldly on up the fine arête and keep that positive self-talk going towards the top to calm the nerves.
*Ian Dunn   7th September 1980*

### 75 Undercut Flake Variations   HS 4c   8m   ★
A fine climb. Either climb *Squark's Arête* and step right or jam and stretch up the middle to reach the main line.
*Cleveland Mountaineering Club   April 1964*

### 76 Self Suicide   Font 7b
Much butch. From sat deep in the pit, breach the roof out to the good hold on the lip. A summit bid is optional.
*Dave Cowl 2006*

### 77 Undercut Flake   HS 4b   8m   ★★
An 'A-star' outing using the obvious feature up the arête to lay siege to the rising groove to the left. Cracking stuff. To continue directly up the arête is (a) Tilt (HVS 5a).
*Malcolm Farrow, Ernie Shield, Dave Staton 1962* ✦

### 78 Flakeout Arête   HVS 5a   8m   ★
A tricky line up the wall and, you've guessed it, the flake on the arête is out of bounds.
*Phillipe Osborne   15th January 1995*

### 79 Dark Cleft   VD 4a
If you fit, chimney up through the darkness. A superior alternative, **Face to Face** (HS 4b) climbs the chimney's wide entrance.
*Martyn Berry/Pollington Borstal 1958; Tony Marr 1998 (FtF)*

### Sevens and Eights Buttress
A continuation of four joined buttresses full of quality low-grade extremes.

### 80 Forever Young   E2 6a   7m
A challenge with a landing to make you weep. Take the thin crack with increasing difficulty.
*Steve Brown, Dave Paul   June 1983*

Yorkshire Gritstone

## Sevens and Eights Buttress - SLIPSTONES

**81 Seven Up** E2 5c   6m   ★★
Small but mighty. Starting on the left arête, launch into the centre of the face heading for the huge flake above the horizontal slot on your right.
*Paul Ingham   15th March 1981*

**82 Direct Finish** E3 6a   6m
Start as for *Seven Up*. Once you reach the horizontal slot, finish direct up the left arête. Bold with a committing finish.
*Tony Marr and Peter Martin   October 1960*

**83 Variation Starts** E3 6a   6m
A direct variation climbing the front face via a rockover from underneath the roof.
*Paul Ingham 1983*

**84 Fuser** HVD 4a   4m
The corner-crack is a bit of a layback brute. Highball Font 3.
*Geoff Milburn   1960*

**85 Tony's Torment** HVS 6a   4m
Climb the centre of the wall avoiding both cracks. Make a committing move for the good ledge.
*Tony Marr 1983*

**86 Wedge Down Crack** HS 4c   5m
The wide crack is very awkward to get started on and all too easy to fall out of. One for the specialists. Originally down-climbed on the first ascent.
*Martyn Berry & Borstal 1958 (descent): Tony Marr 1964 (ascent)*

**87 Thingumy In Thirsk** E3 6a   6m
The arête right of the wide crack climbed on its right-hand side. Finish with difficulty gaining the large obvious pocket on the left side of the arête, but still finish on the right.
*Andy Moss   2000*

**88 Dennis In Darlo** E1 5c   6m   ★
Quality and not to be underestimated. Climb directly up the centre of the buttress, finishing on a blind flake and pocket. Awful landing.
*Steve Brown   1981*

**89 Barren Waste** E2 5c   6m
The wall left of the arête with interesting moves to reach the slot. A long reach from here to finish. An alternative finish
(b) **Little Willy** (E1 5c) gains the top via the large undercut.
*Steve Brown 1984; John Hunt 5th March 2006 (Little Willy)*

**90 Easy Groove** D   5m
A pleasant climb up the groove and wide crack.
*Martyn Berry and the lads from Pollington Borstal   1957*

**91 Edge Route** M   5m
Scramble up the large stepped blocks.
*Martyn Berry and the lads from Pollington Borstal   1957*

From *Dark Cleft*, a supercool, sustained, low-level traverse should not be missed. Finish up *Dennis In Darlo* (Font 6a).

Katherine Schirrmacher poised for the rockover on **Sulky Little Boys** (Font 7a+). Page 583
Photo: Simon Panton

# SLIPSTONES - Sowden Buttress

### Inconsequential Wall
Located 6m right of *Edge Route*, in the large gully, is a handful of small routes that can be accessed by scrambling up the boulders. **Little Arête** (Font 3) takes the minuscule buttress left of the chimney; **Roofed Chimney** (M) is the tiny chimney; **Awkward Finish** (Font 3) takes the well named short wall via the pocket; **Staircase Mantel** (Font 4) takes the wall passing another pocket. Thin for the feet.
*All by Martyn Berry and the lads from Pollington Borstal 1957*

An **Inconsequential Traverse** (Font 6a) is possible moving left-to-right at a low level to finish up the right-hand arête.

### Sowden Buttress
The large detached block opposite hosts some fabulous routes on its front face. The climbs start in the gully. The descent requires care and is via *Right Arête*.

### 92 **Left Arête**  Font 3 (HVD 4a)
The gritty right-hand side of the left arête with a tricky start.
*Martyn Berry and the lads from Pollington Borstal 1958*

### 93 **Frank's Wall**  Font 2+ (HD)
Start off the block, climb the centre of the wall. Thin.
*Frank Fitzgerald, Mike Tooke 26th January 1997*

### 94 **Scratch and Go**  Font 3+ (HVD 4b)
Start left of the curving undercut and pull on and right to step over it. A direct start on the right of the undercling is a reachy Font 4 (S 4c).
*Tony Marr, Frank Fitzgerald, Mike Tooke 26th January 1997*

### 95 **Right Arête**  VD   4m
The right arête above a poor landing. Also the main descent.
*Tony Marr 7th September 1980*

### 96 **Problem Wall**  HVS 5b   5m   ★
From the horizontal slot, climb the wall on small edges.
*Paul Ingham 1982*

### 97 **Left Wall**  HVD   5m   ★★
The shallow corner and pockets give a unique, bold and brilliant test. A blinkered direct start from the ground is Font 4.
*Geoff Milburn, Peter Martin October 1960*

### 98 **Low-level Traverse**  HVS 5b   12m
Starting left of the arête, traverse the break to join and finish up *Sowden*. Continuing the traverse to finish up *Dixon's Dilemma* is (a) **Chris Cross** (E1 5c).
*Paul Ingham 28th June 1984*

### 99 **Sowden Left-Hand**  E1 5b   6m
Starting on the front face, climb the wall to join and finish up the blunt arête.
*Paul Ingham 1982*

### 100 **Sowden**  HVS 5a   6m   ★★
Climb the thin flake in the shallow groove. Gets better towards the top. Stunning. Photo on page 563.
*Malcolm Farrow 1962 or Mike Railton 1964*

### 101 **Sinbad**  E3 6b   6m   ★★
A bold route which follows the thin flake to a pocket on the upper wall. A blind finish over the top.
*Dave Paul 1983*

### 102 **Space Plucks**  E3 6a   6m   ★★
Launch up the wall to the slot and gun for the break above.
*Paul Ingham 1983*

### 103 **Forthright**  E2 5c   5m
The right arête on its left-hand side.
*Steve Crowe 2000*

### 104 **Dixon's Dilemma**  VS 4c   5m
Start in the gully by the large boulder. Follow the line of ramps. The boulder is out of bounds.
*Nick Dixon 1984*

# Lean Buttress - SLIPSTONES

**105 Witton Wall**  S 4b  4m
The flake and crack on the left-hand side of the gully.
*Mike Railton  1964*

## Lean Buttress
The buttress right of *Sowden* separated by the gully.

**106 Halfway Chockstone**  VD  4m  ★
Great fun for such a short route. Tackle the dark chimney escaping left around the chockstone.
*Martyn Berry and the lads from Pollington Borstal  1958*

**107 Central Bay Route**  HVD  4m
The bold, teetering and gritty groove requires care (spotter useful).
*Martyn Berry and the lads from Pollington Borstal  1958*

**108 Psyche**  E1 5c  4m
Starting left of *Leany Meany*, use the adequate pocket and climb the thin groove above.
*Tony Marr  25th January 1998*

**109 Leany Meany**  E2 5c  8m  ★
Start at the base of the left arête. Climb to the good slot on the arête then head rightwards to the horizontal slot. The pockets above lead to a reachy finish. A direct finish, **Old Peculiar**, climbs at the same grade.
*Paul Ingham  1980; Tony Marr  2003 (Old Peculiar)*

**110 Twilight Session**  Font 7c+
Sit-down-start. A monster dyno to the break.
*Steve Dunning  2000s*

**111 Ripper Traverse**  Font 4
Traverse the lower break to *Ripper*. Either finish here (Font 4) or finish thugging up *Ripper* (E1 5c).
*Paul Ingham  23rd January 1983*

**112 Killer**  E3 6b  7m
Starting left of *Ripper*, a technical start in the shallow corner leads you leftwards to pockets on the wall. Bold finish.
*Dave Paul  1983*

**113 Ripper**  E1 5c  7m  ★★★
The grooved arête. A superb climb with a heart stopping finish if approached nervously. Highball Font 6a.
*Paul Ingham  1980*  ✦

**114 Ripper Right-Hand**  E3 6c  7m
Thin climbing on the right-hand side of the *Ripper* arête.

**115 Cyclops**  E2 5c  7m
Starting from the boulder, somehow, gain the large hole to a big move for the small niche.
*Alan Taylor, Tony Marr  9th May 1999*

Below Lean Buttress is a jumble of boulders with various small problems including a large slabby face where a multitude of easy climbs can be worked out.

Almscliff to Slipstones

# Slipstones - Marr's Buttress

## Marr's Buttress
A sheltered buttress just to the right.

### 116 Picnic Wall  D  4m
A blocky chimney on the left-hand side of the buttress.
*Martyn Berry and the lads from Pollington Borstal  1957*

### 117 Cummin's Route  Font 5+  (HVS 5c)
The centre of the wall left of the wide crack. Tricky moves to gain the ledge.
*Paul Ingham  1982*

### 118 Christopher Robin  VS 4c  6m  ★
The wide crack is climbed awkwardly. Highball Font 4.
*Geoff Milburn  1960*

### 119 Right Wall  Font 6a+  (HVS 5c)
The technical wall right of the crack. Photo on page 565.
*Tony Marr  1983*

### 120 Marr's Route  VS 5a  6m  ★
Follow the thin flake line to the break, climb rightwards to finish over the roof.
*Eric Marr, Tony Marr  1964*

### 121 Da's Route  VS 5a  6m
The thin groove left of the chimney. Either escape right of the roof, or carry on straight through.
*Steve Crowe  1994*

### 122 Moderator  M  4m
Tight, so don't get stuck! The chimney. Font 3 on its outside.
*Martyn Berry and the lads from Pollington Borstal  1958*

### 123 Pa's Route  Font 3 (VD 4a)
The centre of the thin buttress is a nice enough problem.

### 124 Gully Wall  S 4b  4m
The left-hand wall in the recess, straight over the top block. The gully at the back of the recess is (a) **Little Gully** (Mod).

## Siamese Blocks
Two protruding buttresses with a variety of excellent problems.

### 125 Friday the 13th  Font 6a+  (HVS 6a)
The left-hand side of the blunt arête. Scary.
*Steve Brown  1982*

### 126 Sunday the 20th  Font 6b (HVS 6a)
The blunt arête on its right-hand side starting from the good slot.
*Paul Ingham  1983*

### 127 Slipway  Font 6b (HVS 6a)
The right-hand side of the buttress following the blunt arête. Finish over the small overlap. High.
*Richard Davies  1990s*

### 128 Siamese Bridge  D  4m
The wide broken chimney.
*Martyn Berry and the lads from Pollington Borstal  1958*

### 129 Right-Hand Twin  HVS 5c  5m  ★
The left-hand side of the arête is superb technical climbing. Highball Font 6a.
*Tony Marr  1980*

572  Yorkshire Gritstone

Siamese Blocks - **SLIPSTONES**

**130 Leaning Wall**   Font 6c+ (HVS 6b)
Another superb addition climbing the right-hand side of the arête.
*Alan Taylor   1980*

**131 Strictly Personal**   Font 6b+ (HVS 6a)
An absolute stunner. The left-hand side of the right arête.
*Paul Ingham   1983*

**132 Brush Up**   Font 5 (VS 5b)
A technical wall right of the arête.
*Paul Ingham   1983*

## BEN MOON ON CYPHER

On his return from injury and making his first ever visit to Slipstones, British bouldering maestro Ben Moon spotted the prize arête of Cypher (Page 583), which he succeeded in unlocking the moves and making the first ascent of at the grade of Font 8b in 2002.

I'd just moved back from America at the end of the summer and I'd been injured. I'd separated my shoulder in a snowboarding accident and I'd just got over that was climbing hard again.

I went to Slipstones for the first time and that arête just stood out like a sore thumb, it looked amazing. I started trying it. I think I spent about five days trying it with Malcolm Smith and Steve Dunning. I was just very focused on doing it.

I thought it was possible straight away but I thought it would be hard. You need strong fingers because the initial move off the flake is quite fingery and then you've got a small edge with your right hand to get to the little pocket. I wouldn't say it's too technical.

The main thing was the initial pull off the undercut flake to get that pocket and then the next move which is kind of a slap for a little edge which I just sussed out this little sort of kick that you do with your foot to get you swinging in the right direction.

I was really impressed by Slipstones, definitely one of my favourite gritstone crags in a great location and obviously to get such a proud line is brilliant.

Ben Moon on **Cypher** (Font 8b). Page 583.
Photo: Simon Panton

*Almscliff to Slipstones*

# Slipstones - Aces High

## The Deck/Aces High Block
A large buttress with enjoyable routes that can be on the committing side. The very small chimney on the left of the block is (a) **Pothole Chimney** (Diff).

**133 Jack the Lad**  VS 4c   6m
Starting off the boulder, climb the left arête.

**134 String Vest**  HVS 6a   6m   ★
The shallow groove right of the arête. Continue through the small overlap to finish on the wall above.
*Steve Brown 1982*

**135 Withering Heights**  HVS 5c   6m
Start slightly left of centre from a small ledge. Climb the wall on positive holds to a small ramp. Gain the break and commit to a long reach to finish.
*Steve Brown 1982*

**136 Aces High**  VS 4c   6m   ★★
The Big Blind! Go all in and tackle the wall to a finish that really ups the ante. Starting just right of *Withering Heights*, climb the wall and gain the break below the top. Depending on if you'd rather go all in, or fold, a choice of finishes are available to suit.
*early 1970s*

**137 Trumps**  VS 4c   6m   ★
The blunt right arête.
*Ken Jackson 1968*

**138 Trumps Right-Hand**  HS 4b   5m
The slabby wall right of the arête to finish up a black streak.
*Ken Jackson 1968*

## Ellingstring Buttress
**139 Heather Wall**  Font 2 (D)
The short stepped wall.
*Martyn Berry and the lads from Pollington Borstal 1958*

**140 Itchy And Scratchy**  Font 3+ (S 4b)
The awkward and reachy wall.
*Kevin Mercer 1999*

**141 Pinnacle Chimney**  M   4m
The wide enjoyable chimney.
*Martyn Berry and the lads from Pollington Borstal 1958*

**142 Two Startled Sheep**  VS 5b   5m
The wall right of the chimney trending rightwards to finish.

**143 Yaud Wall**  VS 5a   5m
Gain the hanging corner. Awkward.
*Geoff Milburn 1960*

**144 Ellingstring**  VS 4c   5m   ★★
Marvellous moves breach the centre of the wall. Start below the small overlap then move right to good holds. Pull up and use a pocket to finish.
*Ron Kenyon 1968*

**145 Diagonal**  VS 4b   5m   ★
Starting right of *Ellingstring*, climb directly to the start of the hanging flake. Follow this rightwards to finish.
*Steve Wilson 1966*

**146 Gymnast**  VS 5c   5m
The undercut right arête with an awkward start.
*Tony Marr 1980*

574    Yorkshire Gritstone

## Stainthorpe's Buttress - SLIPSTONES

**147 Fiddlesticks** VS 5b   4m
The deceiving wall right of the arête.
*Tony Marr  1997*

A traverse of the lower break either way is Font 3.

### Stainthorpe's Buttress
**148 Sweet Sixteen** VD   4m
The unsatisfying left arête on its left; an exposed S 4a finishing on the right side.

**149 Fearby** VS 4b   6m
The wall right of the arête starting on the block.
*Geoff Milburn  1960*

**150 Alan's Wall** HVS 5a   6m
Climb the system of flakes directly to the top.
*Alan Taylor  1999*

**151 Stainthorpe's Wall** E1 5b   6m   ★★
The first of a pair of unmissable wall climbs which rank highly in the E1 zone. Start as for *Alan's Wall* then pull right for the break. Gain the pocket then the groove.
*Dave Stainthorpe  1980*

**152 Variation Start** E1 5c   6m   ★★
The second is comparable in quality though a shade more awkward to start. Begin slightly right of the groove and pull through the overlaps and gain the break. Finish as for *Stainthorpe's Wall*.
*Tony Marr  1965* ✦

**153 Only Sixteen** E1 6a   6m
Start below the overhangs at a very thin crack. Pull through the overlap and gain the break. Trend leftwards to finish up *Stainthorpe's Wall*.
*Paul Ingham  1982*

**154 Fascinationby** E2 5c   6m
The hanging groove is a stiff little number.
*Paul Ingham  1983*

### Buttress 17
**155 Jug Handle Pull Up** HVD 4a   5m
From the boulder, climb the left arête on big holds that could be more juggy. Avoiding the boulder notches the grade up to Font 3 + (S 4b).
*Geoff Milburn  1960*

**156 Wall Centre** VS 4b   5m
The centre of the fine wall with a committing reach to finish.

**157 Happy Daze** VS 4c   5m
Start below the arête and ledge. Trend leftwards on pockets.
*Alan Taylor  1979*

**158 Double Mantelshelf** VD   5m
The large stepped groove eases once on the ledge. Font 2+.
*Geoff Milburn  1960*

**159 Out On Bail** HVS 5b   5m
Bridge up the groove below a broken flake. Use a finger pocket to finish.
*Ian Henderson  2000*

**160 Right Edge** HVS 5c   4m
The tricky right arête.
*Tony Marr  1980*

# Slipstones - Lay-by Buttress

## Lay-by Buttress
This is where things really start warming up for the boulderer. Line after line of quality climbing can be found here with the echoes of foul language coming predominantly from *Lay-by Arête*.

Just before the main *Lay-by* block, a small buttress is found and is home to two minor routes **Easy Mantelshelf** (Diff) on the front face and **Right Arête** (Font 3+).

### 161 Hand Traverse  HD   6m
Starting on the far left of the upper break, shuffle rightwards quickly to improving holds and a wonder-jug finish.
*Geoff Milburn   1960*

On the approach path to the crag is this memorial to the crew of a Halifax bomber which crashed here in 1943. All crew were lost.

### 162 Rock Over  Font 4
From the large break/ledge, climb up the shallow groove left of the arête.
*Steve Crowe   1995*

### 163 Lay-by Arête  Font 7b+ (E2 6c)
A technical master that requires a delicate approach and a little patience. You could be the strongest boulderer around and this problem will shut you down - guaranteed. Photo on page 557.
*Paul Ingham   1985*

### 164 Lay-by Arête Direct  Font 7c (E3 7a)
A direct finish to this classic arête completes the chapter.
*Ian Cummins   2001*

### 165 Lay-by  Font 6a
Superb. The often damp flake/crack is harder than it looks.
*Alan Taylor   1976* ✦

### 166 Little Baldy  Font 6c
Avoiding the flake to your left, this beauty follows very thin crimps with delicate footwork to the obvious bullet scar.
*Ian Cummins   1985*

### 167 Rock On Left-Hand Variation  Font 6b+
Reach the obvious slot and traverse leftwards to reach the bullet scar of *Little Baldy*.
*Paul Ingham   1981*

### 168 Rock On  Font 6a
Gain the obvious slot of this entertaining problem and commit to a tricky move to a good edge.
*Paul Ingham   1980*

### 169 Rock Off  Font 5+
The small hanging arête is a tricky number.
*Paul Ingham   1980*

### 170 All Off  Font 4+ (HVS 5a)
From the good low slot, gain the good hold at the top of the flake. Make a long move to finish.
*Paul Ingham   1980*

A young Rob Brown showing the elders how it's done on **Slanting Flake** (Foot 4). Page 583.
Photo: Claire Graham

# SLIPSTONES - Twenty Something Buttress

## Twenty Something Buttress
Located a few metres right, after the gully. This little wall has good problems which can often be unkind to your fingers. It's host to a few good warm-ups.

### 171 Ten Foot Moderate  M   3m
The crack left of the arête.
*Martyn Berry and the lads from Pollington Borstal  1958*

### 172 Ten Foot Arête  Font 4
The enjoyable right-hand side of the arête.

### 173 Twenty Something  Font 5
The centre of the wall with a long reach.
*Steve Crowe  1994*

### 174 Overhanging Arête  Font 5
A great problem finishing in an impressive position.
*Steve Wilson  1966*

### 175 Reason and Rowan  Font 6a+
From the slot in the middle of the wall, dyno to the top.
*Andy Banks  2001*

### 176 Flakey Wall  VS 4c   4m
The centre of the wall on good holds to a dubious finish.
Photo on page 567.
*Tony Marr  1970*

### 177 Problem Traverse  Font 6c
Traverse leftwards along the faint break using sharp but positive holds. Tricky for your feet near the end.

### 178 Left Wall  HVD   4m
The blunt arête on jugs.
*Geoff Milburn, Peter Martin  October 1960*

### 179 Two Chockstones  D   4m
The awful looking crack on jugs.
*Martyn Berry and the lads from Pollington Borstal  1958*

### 180 Right Overhang  Font 3 (HVD 4a)
The wall right of *Two Chockstones* with a midway crux and some dodgy looking blocks.
*Martyn Berry and the lads from Pollington Borstal  1958*

## The Middle Tier
The next section lies in the jumble of blocks that form in three tiers. The two large blocks known as **The Son** and **Steptoe** are host to some of the crag's biggest bouldering numbers.

### 181 Son of a Bitch  HVS 5c   7m
A real pump fest from left-to-right along the 'Son's' top.
*Steve Crowe  1994*

### 182 Super Furry Animal  Font 8b
Sit-down start. Unleash the big guns for this one. From the edge and ear-shaped hold, take the sidepull and launch skywards to the distant top. Photo on page 581.
*Steve Dunning  2001*

### 183 Sidewinder  Font 7b+
Sit-down start. Wind sideways up the crimpy wall from the double undercuts to reach the left of the capping roof.
*Steve Crowe  2002*

### 184 Exocet  Font 8a
Sit-down start. Use the undercuts to gain the sidepulls and slap for the sloper. Turn the roof on its right.
*Steve Dunning  2002*

### 185 Stipule  Font 7c
Sit-down start. More dynamic delicacies. From the undercuts reach right to a layaway and unfurl one to the top.
*Steve Dunning  2002*

Yorkshire Gritstone

# The Middle Tier - SLIPSTONES

### 186 Curving Crack Arête  Font 6a
Sit-down start. This neat little arête is a real class act giving untold pleasures.

### 187 Curving Crack  Font 4
Climb the overhanging crack hidden in the corner.
*Geoff Milburn, Peter Martin   October 1960*

### 188 Bert Wells  Font 6a
The thin wall right of the corner needs a bit of a grunt to get going.
*Paul Ingham   20th November 1983*

### 189 Centre Left  Font 6a
Breach the wall with the useful slot but can you reach the top?
*Tony Marr   13th November 1983*

### 190 Steptoe  Font 6a+
The problem of the wall. A steadily increasing challenge.
*Steve Brown   September 1982*

### 191 Tiptoe  Font 5+
Tiptoe indeed, especially when the arête climaxes in an on-off sequence.
*Tony Marr, Eric Marr, Ken Jackson   May 1965*

Hidden behind Steptoe block is *Micro Corner*, the smallest problem with the biggest reputation.

### 192 Micro Wall  Font 6c
Sit-down start. The left wall of the recess beginning at the slot. The superceded stand-up is **Shorty's Dilemma** (Font 5).
*Tony Marr   19th January 1997 (Shorty's Dilemma)*

### 193 Micro Machine  Font 7a
A taxing little number up the arête left of *Micro Corner*.

### 194 Micro Corner  Font 6c
Good things come in small packages. No amount of strength will bring success on this one. A pure technical joy.
*Paul Ingham   28th November 1982*

### 195 Problem Arête  Font 4
Honest climbing up the arête on its left side.
*Tony Marr   28th November 1982*

There are a short selection of routes starting in the crevasse formed by the Upper and Middle Tier including; **(a) Stomach Traverse** (Easy), a belly grovel for the whole family to enjoy along the shelf beneath the overhang; **(b) Bratt Pack** (VS 4c), the wall in its centre is passed just left of the arête; **(c) Play-A-Long** (HVS 5b), where either side of the main arête is possible at the same grade; **(d) Wild Thing** (VS 4b, ✦), the easiest route up the block.

Almscliff to Slipstones

# PROFILE

**Darlington's ginger invader** spotted the untapped potential for new hard bouldering on Yorkshire grit after moving to the white rose county in 2000 and threw himself into a rigorous regime of training and climbing. That focus, dedication and vision paid off with some plumb hard Font 8b first ascents (see list). Away from Yorkshire grit Dunning also put up some equally impressive hard sport routes at Kilnsey and Raven Tor up to F8c+. Aiming to return from a series of injuries he is now also managing director of one of the UK's best dedicated indoor bouldering facilities, The Depot Climbing Centre in Leeds.

### Which is the favourite of your Yorkshire first ascents?
High Fidelity is probably the best line but it's not the hardest and nor is it the one that took the greatest effort. My favourite is probably Rhythm on Flasby Fell. Visually it's a stunning line and in its original state was utterly desperate – unfortunately the rock is a little soft and traffic has changed the nature of the holds and it's climbed in a different way now as a result. However, it's still hard and only had two repeats. When I first spotted the line I was blown away - it's a seriously impressive boulder. It was clear that it was going to require some effort so I concentrated on training for it and started walking up on an evening after work with petrol lamps to catch the best temperatures. It was ultimately the effort that I put in that made it so rewarding. The difference this time was that I knew it would be my last major contribution for some time as I felt (for the first time) my motivation start to slide.

### What was your training regime when you were climbing at your best?
Training was something that I took very seriously almost immediately. My preference has always been to train on my own and do it in my own way. When I was climbing at my best I trained twice a day, six days a week; basic strength in the gym or cellar before work and board sessions in the evening after work. The simple things made the biggest differences and I was very methodical and completely dedicated. However, I did put a huge amount of miles in on the grit at the start of every season, mixing up crags and getting in tune with the climbing style.

### What does the future hold for you in climbing terms?
Injuries have taken their toll for the last four years and as a result I've not been anywhere near my 'A' game. However, during this time I have enjoyed climbing at any level and certainly it's made me realise that I can get something out of climbing regardless of the grade. Ultimately I want to get back in the game and push things on again and I don't think that's unfeasible. The thing you need more than anything is intensity and that's something that once it goes is very difficult to recapture and for me I need that more than anything to climb hard.

### A word on Yorkshire grit ethics and style?
My feeling is that when it comes to grit routes and highballs we have all taken the wrong approach. Developing these routes with a ground up ethic would have preserved something for future climbers to aspire to. Although new lines can still be unearthed the bumper years have been and gone and not much real quality remains. For sure a ground up ethic would have preserved something and it's a real shame it didn't happen.

**Interview by Adi Gill**

---

## STEVE DUNNING

*Grit era: Early 2000s*
*Top grit first ascents: High Fidelity (Font 8b) and Ullola (Font 8b) at Caley, Rhythm (Font 8b) at Flasby Fell and Super Furry Animal (Font 8b) at Slipstones.*
*What they say about him: "Steve is a distinctly average winter climber." - from his Scarpa bio.*

Steve Dunning on **Super Furry Animal** (Font 8b). Page 578.
Photo: Dalvinda Sodhi (with kind permission from www.total-climbing.com)

# SLIPSTONES - The Lower Tier

## The Lower Tier
The fine concave slab is home to some pleasant warm-ups/downs and smeary dilemmas.

### 196 Welcome Wall  Font 4+
The left-hand wall of the block.
*Paul Ingham   October 1982*

### 197 Steroid Android  Font 4+
Bound up the arête on its left.
*Paul Ingham   October 1982*

### 198 Tommy's Dilemma  Font 4
A popular problem that you'll come back to again and again. Pad the narrow slab.
*Geoff Milburn, Peter Martin   October 1960*

### 199 Gypsy Wham  Font 3
The centre of the slab via the obvious large ledge.

### 200 Tea Party Slab  Font 4+
To claim the slab you must avoid the ledge.
*Tony Marr, Eric Marr, Ken Jackson   May 1965*

### 201 Question of Balance  Font 5
The slab left of the small pocket.
*Tony Marr, Eric Marr, Ken Jackson   May 1965*

### 202 Right Edge  Font 5+
The right most line of the slab.
*Tony Marr, Eric Marr, Ken Jackson   May 1965*

## Sulky Little Boys/ The Arch
The final section of the main edge with its big numbers is slowly becoming a victim of its own quality. Please be aware of the erosion that is being caused and act responsibly.

### 203 Left Arête  Font 2
Short and easy rib.
*Martyn Berry with lads from Pollington Borstal   1958*

### 204 Goblin's Ear  Font 3+
The miniature curving flake has a reachy start and a tricky top-out.

### 205 3.3 Metre Slab  Font 4
The reachy wall via curving lips. Much harder than it looks and no bridging allowed.
*Steve Crowe   Mid 1990s*

### 206 Ten Foot Slab  Font 2
The easy slab passage.
*Martyn Berry with lads from Pollington Borstal   1958*

### 207 Davies Ramp  Font 6b+
The original line of the wall that began to unlock the possibilities of the buttress. Tackle the arête which leads to the deceptive rampline.
*Richard Davies   1985*

### 208 Simple Sally  Font 7a+
A straightened version of *Davies Ramp* avoiding the block and by using edges on the wall to get established on the arête.
*Dave Slater   28th August 1994*

# Sulky Little Boys - SLIPSTONES

### 209 Holeshot  Font 7b+
Make a start on *Simple Sally* then forge a line rightwards on edges to the arête.
*Ian Cummins  2000*

### 210 Anniemutt  Font 7c+
From the middle of the wall utilise two edges to launch for a good crimp on *Holeshot* then press on directly above. An unforgettable dog of a problem.
*Steve Dunning  2001*

### 211 Cypher  Font 8b
One of the crag's "last greats" finally realised by the Peaks bouldering maestro. A desperate series of moves unlock the arête in its entirety. Only the tall and strong need apply. Photo on page 573.
*Ben Moon  2002*

Pass the last great project of the crag into the short corner.

### 212 All the Twos  E2 6a   10m
A forearm burning traverse along the top edge all the way to *Ten Foot Slab*.
*Steve Crowe  23rd April 1995*

### 213 Chockstone Pull Up  Font 2+  (HD)
Fight the block in the corner cleft.
*Martyn Berry with lads from Pollington Borstal  1958*

### 214 Supple Wall  Font 6c
Hang the obvious sloper and progress to the good flake. Suppleness in rockovers may be an advantage.
*Ian Cummins  1985*

### 215 Sulky Little Boys  Font 7a+
Perhaps the best addition from the crag's stalwart and a real tussle for many. Begin on the right and rockover to reach the pocket on the left of the arête. Photo on page 569.
*Ian Cummins  1985*

### 216 Slanting Flake  Font 4
The feature climbs beautifully, enjoy. The direct finish rocking out left to join the small flake is **(a)** Font 6c. Photo on page 577.
*Geoff Milburn  July 1959, Paul Ingham  1983*

### 217 Everything Counts  Font 7c+
Sit-down start. The extremely problematic arête avoids the flake and finishes right on slopers.

# SLIPSTONES - First Ascent Information

## Further First Ascent Information (✦)

**Agra Right Hand:** *Paul Ingham's first visit to the crag was unplanned because of rain at Brimham. The team detoured to Slipstones on the way home. Ingham was not impressed as the crag came into view, "poxy little thing" he said, but on closer inspection and a guided tour his views were changed. In fact, it was difficult to get him to leave, and the team returned on several consecutive weekends. The crag would never be the same again.*

**Bratt Pack, Play-a-Long, Wild Thing:** *By Andrew Webb mid 1970s*

**Gollinglith:** *A typical "Wilson" problem, steep and strenuous. Unfortunately we will never know how talented Steve would be as an abseiling accident a few months later cruelly ended his climbing career.*

**Lay-by:** *Taylor produces the hardest problem on the crag at that time.*

**Ripper:** *Taylor solved the start but Ingham claimed the prize.*

**Stainthorpe's Wall Variation Start:** *Climbed as a problem before the "wall" was ascended in 1980.*

**Stomach Traverse:** *By Martyn Berry, Pollington Borstal lads 1958*

**Tilt:** *Climbed by Tony Marr, Ken Jackson, Alan Taylor 23rd Apr 1979*

**Wisecrack:** *also claimed by Steve Crowe as* **Shadows of the Night** *on 14th Feb 1982.*

## GRADED LIST
### ROUTES

**E3**
Ripper Right-Hand (6c)
Killer (6b)
Sinbad (6b)
Atomic Right-Hand (6b)
Space Plucks (6a)
Atomic (6a)
Thingumy In Thirsk (6a)
Direct Finish (6a)
Variation Starts (6a)

**E2**
West Face Elim' (6a)
Forever Young (6a)
Narrow Margin (6a)
All the Twos (6a)
Impregnable (6a)
Get Nervous (5c)
Forthright (5c)
Cyclops (5c)
Fascinationby (5c)
Seven Up (5c)
Barren Waste (5c)
Tachyon (5c)
Old Peculiar (5c)
Leany Meany (5c)

**E1**
Only Sixteen (6a)
Psyche (5c)
Chris Cross (5c)
Ripper (5c)
Variation Start (5c)
Dennis In Darlo (5c)
Forever Onward (5c)
Little Willy (5c)
Beldin Direct (5b)
Stainthorpe's Wall (5b)
Beldin Variation (5b)
Girdle Buttress (5b)
Sowden Left-Hand (5b)
Gollinglith (5b)
Space Truckin' (5b)
Beta Blocker (5b)

**HVS**
String Vest (6a)
Tony's Torment (6a)
Rock On (6a)
Agra Direct Start (5c)
Son of a Bitch (5c)
Diminuendo (5c)
Right-Hand Twin (5c)
Withering Heights (5c)
Right Edge (5c)
Wisecrack (5c)
Offspring (5c)
Beldin (5b)
Breakwind Arête (5b)
Squawk's Arête (5b)
Out On Bail (5b)
Rock Off (5b)
Problem Wall (5b)
Ginger Badger (5b)
Play-A-Long (5b)
Agra (5b)
Escalator (5b)
North Wall (5b)
Agra Right-Hand (5b)
Zoom (5b)
Low-level Traverse (5b)
Twixt (5a)
Flakeout Arête (5a)
Tilt (5a)
Original Route (5a)
Sowden (5a)
The Handrail (5a)
Alan's Wall (5a)

**VS**
Gymnast (5c)
Alan's Arête (5b)
Two Startled Sheep (5b)
Fiddlesticks (5b)
Jenny Binks Wall (5a)
Marr's Route (5a)
Yaud Wall (5a)
Mark Turner's Rockover (5a)
Da's Route (5a)
Rogues Gallery (5a)
Trumps (4c)

# Graded List - SLIPSTONES

Cold Wall (4c)
Happy Daze (4c)
Ellingstring (4c)
Jack The Lad (4c)
Flakey Wall (4c)
Aces High (4c)
Easy Pickings (4c)
Bratt Pack (4c)
Face to Face (4c)
Dixon's Dilemma (4c)
Tranmire Crack (4c)
Wild Thing (4b)
Mantelshelf Wall (4c)
Wall Centre (4b)
Diagonal (4b)
Christopher Robin (4c)
Fearby (4b)
Agra Variation aka
  Wimps Variation (4b)
Agra Variation (4b)

**HS**
Wedge Down Crack (4c)
Hole In The Wall (4b)
Barnley Wall (4b)
Trumps Right-Hand (4b)
Chockstone Overhang (4b)
Undercut Flake (4b)
Undercut Flake-
  Variation's (4c)
Undercut Double Crack (4b)
Groove Eliminate (4b)

**MS**
Tranmire Arête (4a)

**S**
Gully Wall (4b)
Witton Wall (4b)
Inside Left (4a)
Petch's Groove (4a)
Barnley Crack (4a)

**HVD**
Fuser (4a)
Ulfers Crack (4a)

Twenty Foot Crack (4a)
Central Bay Route
Jug Handle Pull Up
Left Wall

**VD**
Shine On
Right Arête
Left Wall
Double Mantelshelf
Sweet Sixteen
Not So Tight Chimney
Pinnacle Chimney
Dark Cleft
Halfway Chockstone
Mantelshelf Crack
Old Corner

**HD**
Hand-Traverse

**D**
Picnic Wall
Two Chockstones
Heather Crack
Easy Mantelshelf
Siamese Bridge
Easy Groove
Pothole Chimney

**M**
Edge Route
Moderator
Roofed Chimney
Ten Foot Moderate
Staircase
Little Gully

**Easy**
Stomach Traverse

**PROBLEMS**
**8b**
Super Furry Animal
Cypher

**8a**
Exocet

**7c+**
Twilight Session
Everything Counts
Anniemutt

**7c**
Lay-by Arête - Direct (E3 7a)
Stipule

**7b+**
Lay-by Arête (E2 6c)
Holeshot
Sidewinder

**7b**
Wisecrack Super Direct
Self Suicide

**7a+**
Simple Sally
Sulky Little Boys

**7a**
Micro Machine

**6c+**
Leaning Wall (HVS 6b)

**6c**
Micro Corner
Supple Wall
Micro Wall
Little Baldy
Variation Start (E2 6c)
Problem Traverse
Wisecrack Direct -
  Start (HVS 6b)

**6b+**
Davies Ramp
Strictly Personal (HVS 6a)
Rock On Left-
  Hand Variation

**6b**
Paul's Arête Left Hand (E1 6a)
Sunday the 20th (HVS 6a)
Slipway (HVS 6a)
Agrete (HVS 5c)

**6a+**
Steptoe
Reason And Rowan
Right Wall (HVS 5c)
Friday the 13th (HVS 6a)
Timeless Divide (E2 6a)

**6a**
Extremities (E1 5c)
Curving Crack Arête
Bert Wells
Rock On
Lay-by
Centre Left
Inconsequential Traverse

**5+**
Cummin's Route (HVS 5c)
Right Edge
Tiptoe
Rock Off

**5**
Twenty Something
Paul's Arête Right-
  Hand (E1 5b)
Question of Balance
Shorty's Dilemma
Steve's Wall (E1 5b)
Overhanging Arête
Brush Up (VS 5b)

**4+**
All Off (HVS 5a)
Welcome Wall
Tea Party Slab
Steroid Android

**4**
Heather Wall
Rock Over
Tommy's Dilemma
Slanting Flake
Staircase Mantel
Curving Crack
Problem Arête
Mantel On (S 4b)
Ten Foot Arête
3.3 Metre Slab
Ripper Traverse
Little Arête

**3+**
Itchy And Scratchy (S 4b)
Scratch and Go (HVD 4b)
Block Arête (S 4b)
Right Arête
Goblin's Ear

**3**
Groove On (VD 4a)
Right Overhang (HVD 4a)
Pa's Route (VD 4a)
Little Arête
Awkward Finish
Left Arête
Gypsy Wham

**2+**
Roofed Corner
Heather Wall
  Right-Hand (VD)
Chockstone Pull Up
Left Edge (D)
Overhanging Crack (VD)
Frank's Wall (HD)

**2**
Left Arête (HVD 4a)
Little Corner
Ten Foot Slab
Heather Wall (D)

## BROWN BECK - Introduction

# brown beck
by **Kim Buck**

OS Ref: SE 125 827
Altitude: 350 m

One of the forgotten jewels of Yorkshire's moorland grit crags; Brown Beck lies in a sheltered, secluded position on the southern flanks of Agra Moor. An arduous walk-in, plus the difficulty of resisting the obvious distractions of the easily accessed Slipstones, deter all but the most resolute visitors, lending the crag an unspoilt air. Despite the lack of traffic, the rock remains relatively clean, though it is slightly softer and can be sandier than its more illustrious neighbour.

For those yearning some solitude and a real sense of adventure, a day's highball bouldering or soloing here is hard to beat. It is worth mentioning the complete lack of mobile phone signal in the valley, because any accident here would be very serious, given the length of the walk-in and the confusion over the location (it is referred to as Lobley Crags on some maps). In fact, if you're planning anything untoward, you might want to invite an international standard fell-runner or a suitably equipped helicopter pilot along for the ride…

**The Climbing:** Never more than eight metres high, this crag is the home of the micro-route. By and large, only some of the climbs on the Main Wall and adjacent buttresses are protectable, the rest of the routes are best treated as solos or boulder problems. Of course the distinction between the two comes down to some very subjective decisions (mostly revolving around how brave you feel on the day). The best way to get the most out of the crag would involve bringing full trad gear for the protectable leads, and double mats for the highballs; but I guarantee you won't agree with me when you have to lug that lot all the way in. In reality, most visitors will be better making the choice just to bring pads and boulder; or just to bring a rope and rack to route climb. Of course, the especially adventurous/bold/mildly insane will have no such qualms and will solo everything without bothering with any such trivial distinctions.

**Conditions and Aspect:** Facing south-south-west, the crag is a sun-trap for most of the day, though also tends to catch any prevailing winds. It takes no seepage from the moor above and dries almost instantly. Don't be deterred by the green lichen – it's the grippy type encountered on Northumberland sandstone, to which the climbing style is arguably more akin than most traditional Yorkshire gritstone fare.

**Parking and Approach:** See map on page 559. Follow the general approach to the same parking for Slipstones and Birk Gill. Follow the farm track and bridleway, past Sliptones and up the hill towards the open moor. Once the track starts to flatten out towards the crest, bear left to the west across a patch of burnt heather and find a track leading down towards a ravine. Cross the beck at a natural ford and head up the gully (faint quad track) onto the heather bog beyond. Head across the heather, bearing west - following the edge of the escarpment is easiest. Don't bother looking for a track, there isn't one! A solitary pine tree below the edge is a useful landmark, the crag becomes visible from here. Allow 45 minutes from the car. Note that once the bracken is up, any approach to the crag becomes considerably harder.

**Access:** Access land. Respect any notifiable closures with regard to the CRoW Act (especially during shooting season) and avoid the crag during May and June to minimise disturbance to ground nesting birds. Late winter or early spring is best, although heather burning can affect this time of year too. No dogs.

---

The crag consists of a broken escarpment of square-cut buttresses, with smaller blocks and boulders in front of them at a lower level. The first area described (appropriately called **Last Buttress**), is the leftmost end of the main edge. It has a large, slabby boulder slanting down the hillside in front of it. The climbs start at the small edge behind the boulder.

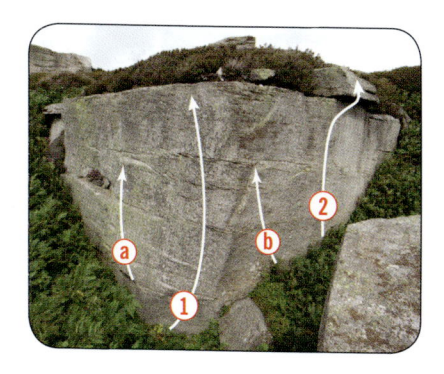

## Sunken Block - **Brown beck**

### 1 **Bedlam**  Font 3+
Aptly named. The arête on its left. Even easier warm-ups tackle (a) the ledges to the left, while the wall just right (b) of the arête is **Bonzer**, a good Font 6a.

### 2 **Foolproof Zip**  Font 4+
The centre of the wall using a layaway to attain the break. Now mantel straight over the capping overhang.

### Sunken Block
The slabby block with an overhanging south face.

### 3 **Heatsink**  Font 6a+
Tackle the overhanging left arête of the front face, then hand-traverse the slopey top all the way to the end of the block. Breathe in going through the boulder gap. A boulder problem that's longer than most of the routes.
*Steve Crowe   9th August 2002*

### 4 **Drop Zone**  Font 6b  (E1 5c)
The right side of the steep, scooped front face. Great moves up the rounded breaks gain crimps in the scoop and an interesting finish. Beware the frictionless, brown lichen.
*Tony Marr, Geoff Vaughan   May 1989*

### 5 **Big Easy**  Font 6a  (HVS 5b)
Climb easily up breaks a metre right of the left edge of the slab, to a crux top-out.
*Tony Marr, Geoff Vaughan   May 1989*

### 6 **Slant**  Font 5  (HVS 5b)
Climb diagonally leftwards to obvious holds below the top. The name describes both the line and the landing!
*Paul Ingham, Tony Marr   June/July 1984*

### 7 **Dungud**  Font 6b+  (HVS 6a)
Gain finger edges just to the right. An entertaining high step onto them leads to a stretch for the top.
*Will Buck   20th March 2011*

### 8 **Undun**  Font 5  (VS 5a)
Climb directly up the slab a metre left of its right arête.
*Paul Ingham, Tony Marr   June/July 1984*

# Brown beck - Leaning Buttress

Just to the right of the steep, front face of Sunken Block, is the square, bullet scarred boulder of **Target Block**.

**9 Cross Fire**  Font 3+. The left arête.

**10 Target Wall**  Font 4+. Centre of the valley side.

Just below is the slabby, east-facing **Triangular Block**.

**12 Art Flakey**  Font 3+
Ape the flake at the left side of the slab, then hand-traverse the top of the boulder to rock round onto the right side. The slab right again is a tenuous, perplexing Font 6b.

**11 South Face Route**  Font 4+
Quality moves using the slanting seam to ascend the slabby face.

Returning to the top edge, directly above Target Block is the appropriately named **Little Buttress.** Climb it anywhere on well-weathered gritstone, never harder than Font 3, but always worthwhile, especially the slabby nose. Right again is the more impressive, detached block of **Leaning Buttress**.

**13 The Crevasse**  VD   4m   ★
Back and foot the wide chimney on the left of the buttress and pirouette round to mantel onto the top of the block. Fun.

**14 Clueless**  Font 4+  (VS 5a)
The right arête of the chimney on its right side has some fine holds and a rare finishing jug.
*Paul Ingham, Tony Marr   June/July 1984*

**15 Lunar Perigee**  Font 6b  (HVS 5c)
Climb the wall to the right via a slanting crimp.
*Will Buck  20th March 2011*

**16 Last Gasp**  Font 6b+  (E2 5c)
The centre of the wall starting at the capped groove. Climb direct to an 'interesting' rounded finish.
*Paul Ingham, Tony Marr   June/July 1984*

**17 Controlled Burning**  Font 7a  (E1 6c)
A very dynamic solution to the wall. Gain two crimps above the break and throw to the distant top and a thankfully easier finish.
*Will Buck  20th March 2011*

**18 L'unacy**  Font 6c+  (E2 6a)
The overhanging arête that dominates the block. Hard moves gain the top. Now do the crux.
*Paul Ingham, Tony Marr   June/July 1984*

**19 Next of Kin**  Font 6b+  (E2 6a)
The left arête of the chimney – crafty footwork gains lovely pinches on the upper arête, but the top is still a long stretch away.
*Tony Marr, Geoff Vaughan   May 1989*

**20 Fire Brigade**  VD   5m. The wide chimney.
*Tony Marr  23rd February 1997*

**21 Smiley Dog Arête**  Font 6b  (E1 6a)
Undercling the base of the arête and use a slopey horizontal to gain the big break. Mantel it to gain the upper arête and another tricky finish.
*Matt Henderson   January 2000*

**22 Heart Ache**  Font 6a  (HVS 5b)
The next arête to the right. Easy moves lead to a b-i-g stretch to the top and yet another mantel.....are your triceps knackered yet?
*Matt Henderson   January 2000*

**23 Heartbeat**  VD   4m
Thrutch up the wide crack to the right. Try not to get irretrievably wedged.
*Tony Marr  23rd February 1997*

Yorkshire Gritstone

# Owl Buttress - BROWN BECK

The crag now turns through a right-angle, the next buttress increasing in height towards an undercut arête. This is **Owl Buttress**.

### 24 Owl Corner  D  3m
The short corner at the back of the bay.
*Tony Marr, Mike Tooke, Peter Shawcross  9th March 1997*

### 25 Go Within  Font 4+  (VS 4c)
The blank-looking wall. On closer inspection, a line of good hidden edges materialises, although with no gear, you might need a cool head to use them.
*Dave Paul, Steve Brown  spring/summer 1983*

### 26 High Adventure  HVS 5a  8m  ★
Start under the roof, climb up to the chimney then traverse out to the arête. Gain the ledge and finish up the left side of the arête.
*Dave Paul, Steve Brown  spring/summer 1983*

### 27 Pussy Cat  VS 5a  7m
Start just right of the cut-out roof. Climb to the break, traverse left to gain the weakness in the upper wall.
*Tony Burnell, Chris Sowden  January 1988*

### 28 Owl Wall  HS 4b  5m
The right side of the wall on more flat holds.
*Tony Burnell, Chris Sowden  January 1988*

### 29 Square Corner  VD  4m
Struggle up the corner behind the block.
*Tony Marr  23rd February 1997*

**Narrow Buttress** is the proud rectangular face to the right.

### 30 Cave Chimney  D  5m. The short chimney.
*Tony Marr  23rd February 1997*

### 31 Eric  Font 6a  (HVS 5b)
Swing into the centre of the wall from the left. Pull (gently) up the sandy edges.
*Dave Paul, Steve Brown  spring/summer 1983*

### 32 Derrick  Font 6b  (HVS 6a)
Just right of centre, layaway off a rounded flake to stretch up to a left-hand crimp. Rock up to good holds and glory.
*Matt Henderson  28th December 2000*

### 33 Den  Font 5+  (VS 5a)
Nice moves up the left side of the arête. Photo on page 594.
*Paul Ingham, Tony Marr  June/July 1984*

The edge now deteriorates into a jumble of blocks, but a small, flat-capped pinnacle gives a couple of Font 3s up either face.

Almscliff to Slipstones  589

# BROWN BECK - Letterbox Wall

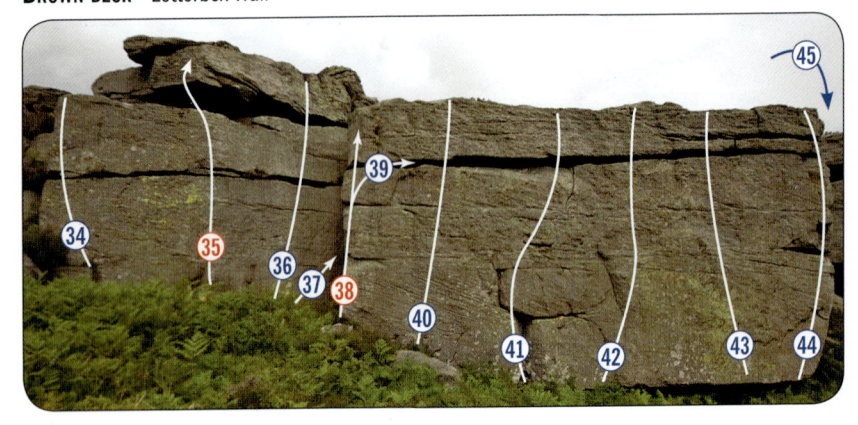

A further 15m right of *Den*, the edge re-appears as the impressive **Letterbox Wall**. To the left of the wall is a short chimney, with a two-tier wall to its left. This is home to:

### 34 Sweep's Arête   S 4a   4m. The left arête.
*Jamie Moss, Jussi Juutinen   20th April 2002*

### 35 Clean Sweep   Font 3   (MS 4a)
Ascend the vague arête in the centre of the wall. Nice moves. Escape at the ledge or top-out for the MS tick.
*Tony Burnell, Chris Sowden   January 1988*

The flakes in between these last two climbs are also climbable at a similar grade.

### 36 Chimney Wall   MS 4a   4m   ★
Starting with an obvious pocket, climb direct up the wall.
*Tony Burnell, Chris Sowden   January 1988*

### 37 Curving Chimney   D   4m
The short chimney in the right angled corner.
*Tony Marr   June/July 1984*

### 38 Dawn   Font 3   (S 4a)
The left arête of the main wall.
*Dave Paul, Steve Brown   spring/summer 1983*

### 39 The Other Arête   VS 4c   10m
Climb *Dawn* to the break. Follow this – the route name tells you where the finish is.
*Tony Burnell, Chris Sowden   January 1988*

### 40 Big Boots   VS 4c   5m. The wall just right.
*Dave Paul, Steve Brown   spring/summer 1983*

### 41 Brown Boots   HVS 5b   6m   ★
Climb the wall via the letterbox, direct.
*Dave Paul, Steve Brown   spring/summer 1983*

### 42 The Wobbler   E1 5b   6m   ★
Fine, technical climbing up the wall on a faint, right-trending diagonal, starting a metre right of the niche. Finish direct from the break. Photo on page 595.
*Tony Burnell, Chris Sowden   January 1988*

### 43 Brigand   E1 5c   6m
Boulder out the wall right of the ramp.
*John-Paul Hotham   11th March 2000*

### 44 Bahia   HVS 5b   6m   ★
Climb the wall just left of the arête, until forced onto it near a rock scar.
*Dave Paul, Steve Brown   spring/summer 1983*

### 45 Dealer   VS 4c   6m
Climb the narrow face forming the left side of the wide gully and don't fall off!
*Dave Paul, Steve Brown   spring/summer 1983*

Main Wall - **BROWN BECK**

The wide gully is the easiest descent for routes on both Letterbox and **Main Wall**, which follows.

### 46 Mouth to Mouth  Font 5  (VS 5a)
At the right side of the gully, climb the wall two metres left of a heathery, hanging ledge.
*Tony Burnell, Chris Sowden   January 1988*

### 47 Browned Off  VS 5a   17m
Starting up *Mouth to Mouth* and gain the break. Follow it across the entire wall to finish (appropriately enough) up *Escape*.
*Tony Burnell, Chris Sowden   January 1988*

### 48 Cadbury's Flake  HVS 5a   6m
The flake proves just as crumbly but not as tasty as its name, however it might enable you to gain the ledge and an awkward finish up the top wall.
*Tony Burnell, Chris Sowden   January 1988*

### 49 Child's Play  HVS 5c   6m  ★
The wall to the right of the hanging ledge to a tasty finish.
*Dave Paul, Steve Brown   spring/summer 1983*

### 50 Let the Children Play  VS 4c   6m  ★
Straight up to the compelling hand jam crack.
*Dave Paul, Steve Brown   spring/summer 1983*

### 51 Nuttalls Mintoe  HVS 5a   6m
Squeezes up the gap between the crack and the obvious groove, direct.
*Tony Burnell, Chris Sowden   January 1988*

### 52 Pella  VS 4c   7m  ★★
The high, left-facing capped corner is the dominant feature of Main Wall, and one of the classics of the crag. High step up the initial wall to Friend protection in the break. Laybacking into the groove and round the roof gives a fine finish.
*Dave Paul, Steve Brown   spring/summer 1983*

### 53 Phenomenonlogy  E2 6a   7m  ★
Go direct up the impressive wall just right of *Pella*.
*Dave Paul, Steve Brown   spring/summer 1983*

### 54 Transcendance  E1 5c   8m  ★
Another fine route, heading up the wall to a flake in the break. Go over the overhang and gain a rightward-trending ramp line. Teeter delicately up this to finish.
*Dave Paul, Steve Brown   spring/summer 1983*

### 55 Ingham's Route  E3 5c   8m  ★
Attain the ledge below and right of the striking upper arête. Swing round onto the left side of the prow for a gripping finale.
*Paul Ingham, Tony Marr   June/July 1984*

### 56 Escape  VS 5a   8m  ★
Onto the ledge and head up and right towards the hanging flake, which proves easier to leave than to gain.
*Dave Paul, Steve Brown   spring/summer 1983*

### 57 Big Mig  E3 5c   5m
Link tiny pockets in the thin wall right of *Escape*.
*John-Paul Hotham   March 2000*

Almscliff to Slipstones

# BROWN BECK - Main Wall

### 58 Clangers  E1 6a  5m ★
The centre of the wall to the break and good protection. Use an undercut pocket to make a big reach to the top.
*Ian Cummins, Ryan Plews  31st October 2004*

### 59 The Fly  E1 6a  5m ★
A similar line climbing the wall just left of the arête. Tricky moves to the break and gear, then a big crux reach to finish.
*Ryan Plews, Ian Cummins  31st October 2004*

### 60 Cutting Edge  E1 6a  5m ★
The arête goes mainly on the front face. Thought provoking.
*Tony Marr, Geoff Vaughan  May 1989*

### 61 Dab Hand  VS 4c  4m
Start in the chimney but swing out onto the right arête. Climb it without bridging.
*Tony Marr, Mike Tooke, Peter Shawcross  9th March 1997*

### 62 Talespin  VS 4b  4m
The wall to the right leads past a shallow pocket to an awkward top-out.
*Tony Marr, Mike Tooke, Peter Shawcross  9th March 1997*

### 63 Gully Wall  S 4b  3m
The slabby scoop in the far end of the wall.
*Tony Marr, Mike Tooke, Peter Shawcross  9th March 1997*

Across the gully lies **Holly Buttress**, really two distinct blocks with undercut starts and some dodgy landings.

### 64 Fists of Fury  E2 5c  5m ★
The frowning, bald-headed front face; stepping off the block. Bring a a cool head for this one.
*John-Paul Hotham  March 2000*

### 65 Witchita Linesman  HVS 5b  6m ★★
The other protectable crag classic. Launch positively over the roof and layback the hanging corner-crack.
*Dave Paul, Steve Brown  spring/summer 1983*

### 66 Holly Hover  VS 4c  5m ★
Start in the pit. Climb the right arête to the ledge, up to the break and follow this leftwards. Reach up for the finishing flake with some trepidation.
*Tony Burnell, Chris Sowden  January 1988*

Yorkshire Gritstone

# Tilting Buttress - **Brown beck**

### 67 **Top Man**  S 4b   5m
The arête behind the holly tree on its right side is really only one move (and not that wonderful either).
*Dave Paul, Steve Brown   spring/summer 1983*

### 68 **Big Boss**  VS 4c   5m   ★
The right arête of the gully is much better. Climb on its left side to the break and over the bulging finish on good holds.
*Dave Paul, Steve Brown   spring/summer 1983*

### 69 **Staircase**  HD   5m   ★
Step off the boulder onto stepped ledges. Up these, trending leftwards for maximum exposure.
*Tony Marr   9th March 1997*

This marks the end of the main edge. However, numerous smaller pinnacles and boulders further right and at a slightly lower level keep the climbing coming. Below Holly Buttress lies **Tilting Buttress**, consisting of a low bouldering wall flanked on either side by taller walls.

### 70 **Rugrats**  Font 4+ (VS 5a)
The steep, west-facing wall passing a recess in the break. Good moves.
*Tony Marr   23rd February 1997*

Both arêtes of this section of wall are worthwhile at S 4b/Font 4. To the right, the wall drops in height towards an arête, then turns through 90 degrees to give a fine south-facing wall.

### 71 **Beat It**  Font 3+
The slabby arête of the lower wall.

The 'routes' previously written up right of the arête, have all now been extended with sit-down starts and are still only tiny boulder problems.

### 72 **Off Beat**  Font 5. Sit-down start into the curving flake.

### 73 **The Crack**  Font 5+. From a sit-down start.

### 74 **Giddy Up**  Font 6b
Sit-down start the bulge right of (and avoiding) the crack. A tad morpho.

### 75 **Mantel Madness**  Font 5
Standing start. From both hands in the low pod, with a pop for the ledge is Font 6b+.

### 76 **Cheap Trick**  S 4b   6m   ★
From the sloping ledge, attack the hanging crack on the left of the tower. A grim grovel may attain the upper ledge and finishing slab.
*Tony Marr   23rd February 1997*

### 77 **Tyto**  S 4b   6m   ★
The right arête of the tower. Steep moves up the breaks to an awkward exit on the top block. The wall to the right is a poor problem.
*Tony Marr   23rd February 1997*

# BROWN BECK - The Watch Tower

A 10m bash through the bracken to the right gains the obvious pinnacle of **The Watch Tower**, commanding fine views back down the valley.

### 78 The Watchman  VD  5m  ★
The left side of the front face. Solo over the overlap and up the short wall to a lichenous top-out.
*Frank Fitzgerald, Tony Marr  9th March 1997*

### 79 Watchman's Neb  VS 4c  5m
Pull over the roof on creaking juggy flakes to gain the right arête.
*Matt Henderson  January 2000*

Will Buck on **Den** (Font 5+ / VS 5a). Page 589
Photo: Kim Buck

Further down the hill to the south, two obvious large boulders can be seen. The first, **Flat Topped Block**, lies 30m below Tilting Buttress.

### 80 Splat  Font 4+
The centre of the west face.

### 81 Free Fall  Font 5+
Good value. Climb the left side of the overhang and follow the vague upper arête.

### 82 Problemina  Font 6c  (HVS 6b)
A solution to the massive roof. Low start just left of *Hanging Crack*; make a huge move to an edge and the good break. Follow this left to a difficult pull over the roof on rounded, sandy flakes.
*Geoff Vaughan  May 1989*

### 83 Hanging Crack  HVS 5c  4m
Urrgghh! No Font grade; they don't do this sort of thing there.
*Tony Marr, Geoff Vaughan  August 1988*

### 84 Bandyido  Font 5+
Gain the ledge and obvious pocket. Good eliminates to the right range from Font 5 to Font 6c.
*Tony Marr, Geoff Vaughan  August 1988*

### 85 Hombre  Font 5+. The left side of the arête.
*Tony Marr, Geoff Vaughan  August 1988*

### 86 The Bravados  Font 6c
The right side of the arête from a sit-down start. Technical, balancey, slopey....good.

### 87 El Mariachi  Font 7a
Left-hand in the eye, then dynamically to the top. Now harder due to the demise of the chicken-head. The most sought-after piece of climbing on the crag?

The lowest block is **Easy Block**. The problems here are left for rediscovery.

The final problem of note lies some 200m west of the main crag in a jumble of small, undocumented boulders. The proud arête is **The Outlaw** (Font 5+).

# Graded List - BROWN BECK

## Graded List

### Routes

**E3**
Ingham's Route (5c)
Big Mig (5c)

**E2**
Phenomenonlogy (6a)
Fists of Fury (5c)

**E1**
Clangers (6a)
Cutting Edge (6a)
The Fly (6a)
Brigand (5c)
Transcendance (5c)
The Wobbler (5b)

**HVS**
Child's Play (5c)
Hanging Crack (5c)
Brown Boots (5b)
Witchita Linesman (5b)
Bahia (5b)
High Adventure (5a)
Nuttalls Mintoe (5a)
Cadbury's Flake (5a)

**VS**
Pussy Cat (5a)
Browned Off (5a)
Escape (5a)
The Other Arête (4c)
Dab Hand (4c)
Big Boots (4c)
Watchman's Neb (4c)
Holly Hover (4c)
Dealer (4c)
Let the Children Play (4c)
Big Boss (4c)
Pella (4c)
Talespin (4b)

**HS**
Owl Wall (4b)

**MS**
Chimney Wall (4a)

**S**
Top Man (4b)
Cheap Trick (4b)
Tyto (4b)
Sweep's Arête (4a)
Gully Wall (4b)

**VD**
The Crevasse
The Watchman
Fire Brigade
Heartbeat
Square Corner

**HD**
Staircase

**D**
Owl Corner
Cave Chimney
Curving Chimney

### Problems

**Font 7a**
Controlled
  Burning (E1 6c)
El Mariachi

**Font 6c+**
L'unacy (E2 6a)

**Font 6c**
Problemina (HVS 6b)
The Bravados

**Font 6b+**
Last Gasp (E2 5c)
Dungud (HVS 6a)
Next of Kin (E2 6a)

**Font 6b**
Drop Zone (E1 5c)
Lunar Perigee (HVS 5c)
Smiley Dog Arête (E1 6a)
Derrick (HVS 6a)
Giddy Up

**Font 6a+**
Heatsink

**Font 6a**
Big Easy (HVS 5b)
Heart Ache (HVS 6b)
Bonzer
Eric (HVS 5b)

**Font 5+**
Den (VS 5a)
Bandyido
Hombre
The Crack
Free Fall
The Outlaw

**Font 5**
Undun (VS 5a)
Slant (VS 5a)
Mouth to Mouth (VS 5a)
Off Beat
Mantle Madness

**Font 4+**
Foolproof Zip
Target Wall
South Face Route
Splat
Rugrats
Go Within (VS 4c)
Clueless (VS 5a)

**Font 3+**
Bedlam
Cross Fire
Art Flakey
Beat It

**Font 3**
Clean Sweep (MS 4a)
Dawn (S 4a)

Mark Credie soaking up the isolation on **The Wobbler** (E1 5b), Page 590.
Photo Dave Sutcliffe

# BIRK GILL - Introduction

# birk gill
### by Kim Buck and Will Buck

OS Ref: SE 136 817
Altitude: 230 m

Nestled in ancient woodland (a SSSI) on the north side of the ravine of Birk Gill, this compact little edge of course grit offers a handful of pleasant low grade outings and some testing E2s. If you're seeking isolation then look no further, whilst its close neighbour has the traffic you are sure to have the crag to yourself.

**The Climbing:** The angular nature of the crag offers routes that follow arêtes and slabs with a couple of blocks beneath the edge holding a handful of boulder problems.

**Routes and Bouldering:** There are 28 routes up to E2 and half a dozen boulder problems, though a keen explorer could quite possibly unearth more. *Class Action* (E2 5b) and *Narrow Margin* (E2 5c) are sure to grab your attention.

**Conditions and Aspect:** Facing south, it is a picturesque and sheltered sun-trap in winter. However, once the spring arrives, the leaves are on the trees and the bracken is out; be sure to pack your machete, paraquat and loin cloth – you're heading for the jungle! Entomologists will also have a field day with the numerous ants nests and swarms of flies in summer.

**Parking and Approach:** See map on page 559. Park as for Slipstones. Once through the gate and onto the open moor, leave the bridleway for a faint track on the left starting immediately after the gate, going diagonally down through the heather. Once this flattens out (250m from the gate), it leads north-east for 300m along the edge of the wooded embankment until the first boulders become visible. 15 minutes from the car.

**Access:** Access land but the crag is a SSSI and you can see why when you visit the place; unspoilt ancient woodland with amazing lichens, wildlife, flowers, etc. Respect the place; no large groups, no dogs. Respect any notifiable closures with regard to the CRoW Act. Please take care to stick to established paths, especially from April to July when the birds are nesting; not just grouse but other ground nesting species such as curlew and redshank, which inhabit the area.

The climbs are described from left-to-right, so you'll have a sneak preview as you walk to the far end of the crag.

After a prominent square block with a tree to its left, is a smaller buttress containing a pleasant, clean wall, with a descent gully and a small pinnacle to the left. The two obvious arêtes of the pinnacle can be climbed at HVS 4c (the left is **Poolysses**, the right, **Shite Wand**), but they hardly seem worth disturbing the lichen/tree to top-out. Moving back to the start of the main edge the routes begin with a fine little challenge.

**1 Madagascar** HVS 5b 5m ★
Climb the left arête of the prominent square-cut buttress on its right side throughout.
*William Buck 2nd May 2010* ✦

Watch where you put your feet on the walk leftwards across to the top of the descent gully.

**2 Tough Enough** HVS 5b 5m ★
From just right of *Madagascar*, follow the thin crack.
*Tony Marr, Mike Tooke 18th September 1994*

596      Yorkshire Gritstone

Narrow Margin - **BIRK GILL**

### 3  Party Piece  HS 4b   5m   ★
A pleasant warm-up. Various methods gain jugs in the heathery break. Climb direct to finish.
*Tony Marr, Mike Tooke   18th September 1994*

### 4  Fast Track  HS 4b   5m
The right side of the wall to a square recess below the heather cornice. Probably best to move left to the mantel finish of *Party Piece*.
*Tony Marr, Mike Tooke, Frank Fitzgerald   5th February 1995*

### 5  Sorrento  HS 4b   7m   ★★
A super solo; stretchy moves lead to surprising holds but you'll need a steady head. The fun doesn't end when you top-out either…
*Frank Fitzgerald, Peter Shawcross   20th March 1994*

### 6  Little Midget  HVS 5b   7m   ★
The right arête, initially on its left, up to good holds and a small wire placement on the right side. Now, go straight up to the slopey, crux finish. Packs quite a big feel, despite its name.
*Alasdair Kennedy   6th December 2003*

### 7  Weany Meany  E1 5b   7m   ★
Direct up the wall to the shelf on small crimps and finish as for the next route. Good moves.
*William Buck   2nd May 2010*

### 8  Little Wonder  HVS 5a   7m   ★
Another solo with a big feel. Climb the leftward-trending flakes to good holds, then pull out right to gain a shelf. A small crimp above aids the awkward mantel finish.
*Tony Marr, Mike Tooke, Peter Shawcross   20th March 1994*

### 9  Narrow Margin  E2 5c   8m   ★★
Quality. Start from the lowest point of the buttress, small holds on the left of the arête gain a good shoulder and the shelf.
*Tony Marr, Mike Tooke   20th March 1994*

### 10  Black Groove  HS 4b   7m
Tricky moves gain the groove and improving holds. Pull out onto the right wall at the top for an exposed finish which avoids the heather.
*Tony Marr, Mike Tooke, F. Fitzgerald, P. Shawcross   20th Mar 1994*

### 11  Façade  E1 5b   7m   ★
The impressive arête on its right-hand side. Equally fine, although easier (and more escapable) on its left side.
*Tony Marr, Mike Tooke, Frank Fitzgerald   9th October 1994*

### 12  Cutting Edge  HVS 5c   5m
The steep and technical arête of the pillar before the descent gully.
*Tony Marr   9th October 1994*

Almscliff to Slipstones

# BIRK GILL - Class Action

Beyond the gully, the edge deteriorates into a blocky buttress, before a final, impressive bay behind the huge oak tree.

### 13 Downbeat  VD   5m
Route number 13 - unlucky for some. The centre of the stepped wall. Three stars for lichen lovers, a 'bag of' for everyone else.
*Frank Fitzgerald, Mike Tooke   13th March 1994*

The next two routes lie in the left wall of the bay behind the tree and rarely if ever lose their mantel of greenness. If you must…

### 14 Heartbeat  S 4b   8m
The awkward chimney in the left wall of the bay.
*Frank Fitzgerald, Tony Marr, Mike Tooke   9th October 1994*

### 15 Birk Gill Crack  HS 4b   8m
The amenable corner-crack.
*Tony Marr, Frank Fitzgerald, Mike Tooke   13th March 1994*

The main wall is cleaner, but is more akin to quarried sandstone and runs to small edges and cracks which tend to be quite friable.

### 16 Something to do in the Rain  HVS 5a   8m
Training for Millstone / Yosemite? Climb the obvious, disappearing finger crack in the right wall of *Birk Gill Crack*, which is out of bounds. Eliminate but fun.
*Malcolm Townsley   26th November 2005*

### 17 Class Action Left-Hand  E2 5b   9m
Start as for the previous route but trend diagonally right to join *Class Action* at mid-height. Finish up the upper section of this.
*Tony Marr, Mike Tooke   18th September 1994*

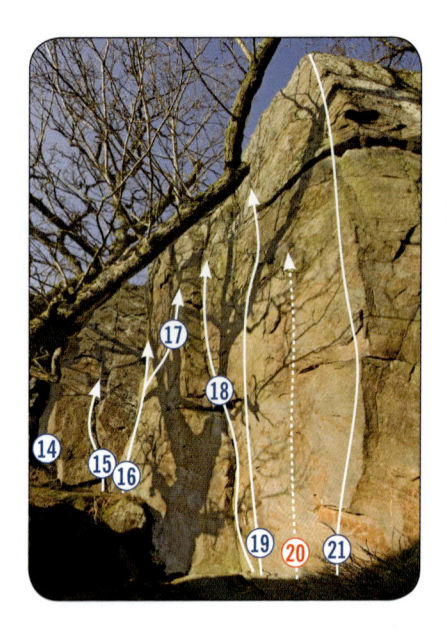

### 18 Class Action  E2 5b   10m   ★★
The obvious slim corner in the impressive back wall forms a classic of the crag. A steep start passing various small, blown-out wire placements leads with some excitement to improving holds and a rightwards exit.
*Tony Marr, Mike Tooke   18th September 1994*

### 19 Fifteen Million Plastic Bags  E1 6a   10m   ★
Start just right of *Class Action*. Climb the wall rightwards to gain the left end of a juggy ledge (side-runner at the right side of this). Go up and left on friable flakes to the good break. Finish up the short wall just right of the wide crack.
*Malcolm Townsley   12th February 2005*

### 20 Birk Gill Wall  Font 6b+
A superb, direct ascent of the wall to the juggy break starting from small crimps and sidepulls. From a sit-down start it's Font 7a. Fragile edges so no brushing please.
*Will Buck   2nd May 2010*

### 21 Quantum Leap  E2 5c   10m   ★★
The last major line climbs the right arête of the wall on its left side throughout. Great moves and good gear in the break, but cock-up your sequence at the top and your 'leap' will be more Quantas than Quantum!
*Tony Marr, Mike Tooke   18th September 1994*

The short crack on the right side of the buttress is **Bygones** (VD) whilst **Cat Walk** (HS 4b), starts just right of the arête to gain the right-hand crack and follows it left-

# Frank's Slab - BIRK GILL

wards to finish up a short chimney. The next worthwhile routes lie on the jumble of boulders that run downhill from the main edge.

### 22 Jolly Jeffery  HVS 5a   6m
The arête at the left-hand side of the undercut front face of the buttress overlooking the beck. Boulder out a tricky sequence on its left side.
*Tony Marr, Alan Taylor, Frank Fitzgerald, M. Tooke   9th Jan 2002*

### 23 Oliver's Overhang  VS 4c   7m
Grapple straight over the overhang.
*Vic Scott   1998*

### 24 Corvus  VS 4c   9m
Follow *Mary Archer* then traverse left above the overhangs to finish on the left arête. Impressive situations.
*Frank Fitzgerald, Tony Marr, Mike Tooke   5th February 1995*

### 25 Mary Archer  VD   8m
The crack between the overhangs and the slab.
*Mike Tooke, Frank Fitzgerald   13th March 1994*

### 26 Frank's Slab  VD   9m   ★
Jump onto the slab and follow the easiest line. Just made to be soloed in trainers.
*Frank Fitzgerald, Peter Shawcross   20th March 1994*

### 27 Scott's Corner  HS 4b   9m
To the right of *Frank's Slab* up the right-hand corner direct.
*Vic Scott   1998*

### 28 Frank's Slab - Variation Start  VS 5a   9m
Start up the shallow groove in the steeper, right-hand sidewall for four metres before pulling onto the slab and finishing up its edge.
*Tony Marr, Alan Taylor   9th January 2002*

The next boulder to the right, up the hill towards the main crag, contains an obvious challenge:

### 29 Cave Crack  S 4a   5m
Thrutch up the overhanging crack to escape the confines of the cave. The hardest Severe in the world?
*Tony Marr, Frank Fitzgerald   9th January 2000*

A couple of boulder problems take the 'boiler plate' slab to the right: **Tony's Slab** takes the centre of the slab, while **Frank's Arête** takes the right edge of the block from its lowest point, both at around Font 3.

For the dedicated, a number of other problems can be found up on the remaining boulders, but the lichen clinging to most of the holds will deter all but the keenest. The promising boulder right down by the river, next to the wall, contains one worthwhile problem: **Pit Pull** (Font 5), the arête from the pit taken on its left (Font 6b+ from a sitter).

---

### Further Information on First Ascents (✦)
**Madagascar:** *An alternative start,* **Pod Racer** *by Matt Henderson (October 1999) started on the blind crack left of the arête at VS 5a.*
**Pit Pull:** *climbed by Kim Buck 25th April 2010*
**Poolysses:** *by Ali Kennedy, Jamie Moss 6th December 2003*
**Shite Wand:** *by Jamie Moss, Ali Kennedy 6th December 2003*

# roova

by **Adi Gill**

OS Ref: SE 083 824 (Great Roova)
SE 081 818 (Little Roova)
Altitude: 230 m

This small but perfectly formed edge comprises a selection of high quality highball challenges that rival some of the best in the county. Its enviable location, hugging the ridge above the quaint village of West Scrafton, presents you with stunning views into Coverdale and beyond. It has slept beneath the radar for many years to all but a few connoisseurs of wild remote bouldering and goes to show there is still rock to be discovered in them thar hills.

**The Climbing:** The majority of the problems follow striking arêtes and walls with minimal holds though there is the odd roof at the northern end of the main crag and at Little Roova. The landings are generally good though a bouldering mat would be an asset where the base is uneven and rock strewn. If you are operating in the Font 7a territory then the lines of *Aurora* and *Icicle* will make the uphill slog a distant memory.

**Routes and Bouldering:** There are 31 problems at Great Roova and a further seven at Little Roova which lies 500m to the south. Most of the lines are approaching highball territory with four warranting route status though only *Great Roova Roof* and *Great Roova Wall* yield any protection.

**Conditions and Aspect:** The compact edge gracefully sweeps from north to west along the ridge of the hill with the main central section having the sunniest aspect from noon onwards. The angular nature of the arête problems means their north sides are slow to dry in winter. Its lofty elevation makes it a windy venue which threatens to snatch away an unguarded bouldering mat. The rock is a similar grain to Slipstones but much less trodden so can be scrittly in places.

**Parking, Approach and Access:** The village of West Scrafton in Coverdale can be approached from Kettlewell (8 miles) or Leyburn (6 miles). Park just outside the village to the east on the grass verge **(GPS: 54.249033, -1.887284)** and walk back west to reach the bridleway

Adi Gill electing to go dymanic on **Aurora** (Font 7a). Opposite page.
Photo: Dave Sutcliffe

# Great Roova - Roova

marked Nidderdale/Colsterdale. Follow this uphill for approximately 1 mile and where it bends to the right make a beeline up the steep slope direct to the crag (30 mins). Pass in front of the crag, crossing the fence with care, to reach the shooting hut and the start of the Northern end. Little Roova is clearly visible to the south of the main crag. The crag lies on open access moorland though restrictions will apply during the shooting season. No dogs.

## Great Roova - The Northern End

Travelling left-to-right from the shooting hut you encounter two obvious undercut blocks.

### 1 Summer Bed Linen  Font 5+
Make an assault on the hanging prow topping out to the left of the small roof.
*Phillipe Osborne  27th April 2011*

### 2 Campus  Font 6a
Ape your way up the angular stepped roof from the right or the left.
*Phillipe Osborne  27th April 2011*

### 3 Mmmmm  Font 5+
The wall to the right of the roof is breached with comparative ease.
*Phillipe Osborne  27th April 2011*

The short walls to the right host several warm-up problems in the Font 4 region.

## The Central Section
Cross the fence with care to reach the main event.

### 4 Double Cap  Font 4+
A steep but juggy line over the stepped roof.

### 5 Great Roova Roof  VS 4c   7m  ★
The left-hand side of the big nose of perfect rock is diminutive for a route but nonetheless an enticing line. Meander up left and over the small roof with good protection where required.
*Phillipe Osborne, Elisabeth Osborne  1st May 2011*

### 6 Great Roova Wall  VS 5a   7m  ★
A well-protected VS leaders gem. Climb the right side of the arête directly to the short left-to-right crack (avoid the roof to the left), and finish on the right wall.
*Phillipe Osborne, Elisabeth Osborne  1st May 2011*

### 7 Moorland Bow  Font 5+
The small neat crescent arête using holds on the right wall.

### 8 Wild Roova  Font 6b
From in the big break launch onto the arête and grapple your way over the top with the correct choice of holds.
*Adi Gill, Dave Sutcliffe  11th May 2011*

### 9 Aurora  Font 7a
Atmospheric. Starting on the rail on the lip reach a sharp crimp out right and gain the hanging flake. Composure may bring the top within reach dynamically, or statically for the technically astute. The direct, climbed from the left of the arête, is an all too obvious challenge. Photo opposite.
*Jon Pearson  2005*

### 10 Dean Martin  Font 6a
The wall just right of the corner succumbs by way of a big reach or a little jump.
*Phillipe Osborne  27th April 2011*

# Roova - The Pinnacle Walls

### 11 **The Forbidden Corner**  Font 4
The unappealing corner is a classic layback when dry.

### 12 **Icicle**  Font 7a
The undisputed line of the crag. The perfect hanging ships-prow has just the right amount of holds to enable the top break to be reached, but not without a fight.
*Jon Pearson  2005*

### 13 **Fifth Arête**  Font 6a+
The two layaways to the left are key but mind that landing.
*Jon Pearson  2005*

### 14 **Easy Passage**  Font 3
The steady corner above the cave.

### 15 **Mattie's Mantel**  Font 3
The nice line to the left of the nose.
*Phillipe Osborne, Matilda Osborne  1st May 2011*

### 16 **Smooth**  Font 3+
The smooth wall is trivial for tall people.

## The Pinnacle Walls
The three distinct buttresses behind the pinnacle are host to a fine selection of problems.

### 17 **The Only Remaining Question**  Font 7a+
The centre of the narrow wall appears to be straightforward but lo and behold...
*Jon Pearson  2005*

### 18 **Dry Stone Base Line**  Font 5
The arête on its right-hand side above a work of art landing zone.
*Jon Pearson  2005*

### 19 **The Endless Dog**  Font 6a+
The arête right of the hold-less wall has hidden holds on the right to aid progress.
*Jon Pearson  2005*

### 20 **The Appliance of Science**  Font 6c
A classic fridge hugging venture with a dynamic finish thrown in.
*Adi Gill  11th May 2011*

### 21 **Spring Haze**  Font 6b+
Mantel onto the ramp left of the arête and reach high crimps which allow a throw for the top.
*Jon Pearson  2005*

### 22 **Roova Riser**  Font 4
Rock onto the ramp and and relish it to its end.

Next up is **Green Corner** (Font 3+), where appearances can be deceiving. On the boulder just right again, **Bullnose** (Font 5), takes the smooth slabby arête and **Last Wall** (Font 3+) is an easier alternative to its neighbour.

## The Pinnacle
The problems on this striking feature are described in an anticlockwise direction starting at the inner arête. Descent can be made with care by reversing *Litchfield Wall* or by jumping onto a pile of mats in the back of the gully.

### 23 **The Blazing Apostle**  Font 7a  (E2 6b)
Blaze a trail up the tall dark arête passing the big hold of unusability.
*Dave Sutcliffe, Jim Davies  10th May 2011*

# Little Roova - ROOVA

**24 Shoot to Kill** Font 6b+ (E2 6a)
A one mat route or a multiple mat highball with an exciting final move to a good edge.
*Phillipe Osborne 1st May 2011*

**25 Short Arête** Font 3+.
Climbed on the front face.

**26 Litchfield Wall** Font 3+
The short face above the carvings.

**27 Cat Piano** Font 6b
Step off the perched block on the back wall and gain the top by various methods. The longer start up the scoop on the right still requires mastering.
*Jim Davies 10th May 2011*

**28 Apostle Left-Hand** Font 6c+
The shorter and slightly easier way up the arête. Making the mantelshelf on the shoulder is still thought provoking at that height.
*Dave Sutcliffe, Jim Davies 10th May 2011*

## Little Roova

This small collection of problems on the long roof are all of a similar grade and nature.

**1 Sammi** Font 5+
Tackle the hanging rib from standing, though a sit-down start adds spice.
*Phillipe Osborne 27th April 2011*

**2 The Director of the Board** Font 5+
A splitter crack that just begs to be climbed.
*Phillipe Osborne 27th April 2011*

**3 Austin Roova** Font 6a
The central line over the roof. Choose your crimps on the lip and lock to better holds above.
*Adi Gill 11th May 2011*

**4 Frank** Font 5
Romp up the shallow rib in the front face.
*Phillipe Osborne 27th April 2011*

**5 Dino** Font 6a
The right arête of the buttress.
*Phillipe Osborne 27th April 2011*

**6 The Voice** Font 6a
Nip over the roof and take the wall direct.
*Phillipe Osborne 27th April 2011*

**7 The Sands** Font 5
The short wall climb starting at the edge of the roof.
*Phillipe Osborne 27th April 2011*

## Further Information

*Thanks to Fran Holland, Jon Pearson and Phillipe Osborne for bringing this new kid on the block into the open.*

# sypeland
## by Malcolm Townsley

OS Ref: SE 132 738      Altitude: 390m

A crag that's about as far removed from the scene as you can get. Sypeland offers beautiful isolation and some of the best low to middle grade wild bouldering in the county. The edge sits high up on the moors with a commanding view of the dale and surrounding hills and has the ever-changing hum of moorland wildlife to accompany your visit. It comprises a series of small crags and boulders that extend for about half a mile from the isolated pinnacles of Jenny Twig and her daughter Tib at the western end, to an unusual tent-shaped boulder named Tib's Tent in the east. Most of the routes are fairly short with good landings and virtually all have been soloed. If you want more of the same, then Lulbeck Crag lies about a mile further south, beyond the track, and offers some of the roughest grit you are ever likely to come across.

**The Climbing:** There are 56 routes and highballs (rarely exceeding 6m in height) across the HVD to E3 grade range and over 50 boulder problems between Font 3 and Font 7c+. Many striking features and lines can be found here as well as more slopers than you can comfortably handle in one sitting. *Caught in an Eddy (E2 6a)*, *A Little Trouble (E2 6a)* and *Striding Edge (E1 5b)* are three classic tasters which will only will fuel your appetite for more.

**Conditions and Aspect:** The edge faces south-west, has a pleasant sunny aspect and dries quickly after rain. The crag is worth a visit at most times of the year except the grouse shooting season where crossing open moorland should be avoided. The rock is generally good-quality, softish coarse gritstone, which takes on a pale grey colour due to an extensive covering of lichen. Some lines can be sandy if they've not been climbed on for a while. Taping the back of your hands may prove beneficial on the rough cracklines. It is worth noting that many of the descriptions could have ended with the words "to a sandy, rounded finish" (the typical Sypeland top-out), so bear this in mind when going for the highball.

**Parking and Approach:** See map on page 554. If travelling from the Masham direction, from Healey village go west for half a mile until the fork in the road (the right fork goes to Slipstones). Take the left fork downhill and follow this road (Healey-to-Lofthouse road) passing Leighton reservoir as you go. After 5½ miles a rough road is reached on the left, signposted 'Unsuitable for Motor Vehicles'. This track leads to Sypeland but continue down the road for 100m and park considerately at the wide track entrance on the right of the road. (**Parking GPS: 54.170072, -1.827507**) If approaching from Lofthouse, travel north-east up and along Trapping Hill (the Lofthouse-to-Healey road) for 1½ miles and the parking is on the left-hand side.

Walk back up the road to the track and follow it east for just over a mile through two gates (always keeping left) until a shooting lodge is reached on the right. It is possible, but not recommended (both for your car and for relations with other users of the moor), to drive up the rough track from the main road to park at this point. Climb over the locked gate by the lodge with care and follow a line of grouse butts south and downhill passing the prominent pinnacles of Jenny Twig and her Daughter Tib on the left (a rough track leads off to them). Unless you plan to climb on Jenny, the least heathery approach is to continue following the butts until you come to another gate and fence line. Turn left before the gate and follow the fence until you come to the western end of the main crag on your left. This approach can be wet in winter, in which case pass between the 3rd and 4th grouse butt and head directly towards Jenny and then directly south to the right end of the main crag skirting around a large marshy area on your right.

Nigel Poustie shows us how it's done on his **Piglet Arête** (Font 7a). Page 610
Photo: Paul Clough

# SYPELAND - Introduction

**Access:** The crag is on CRoW access land. Allow 20 minutes to the shooting cabin and a further 20 minutes to the eastern edge of the crag. Dogs are **not** permitted and there are usually access restrictions during the grouse shooting season from August to December. These restrictions are well-posted at the start of the access track and rarely affect weekends. Avoid the crag during May and June to minimise disturbance to ground nesting birds.

The two prominent pinnacles of Jenny Twig and her daughter Tib offer five named problems with grades between Font 3 and 5 and the obvious unmissable jump between the two is worthy of Font 7a alone. The steep west face of the higher pinnacle, Jenny, remains unclimbed.

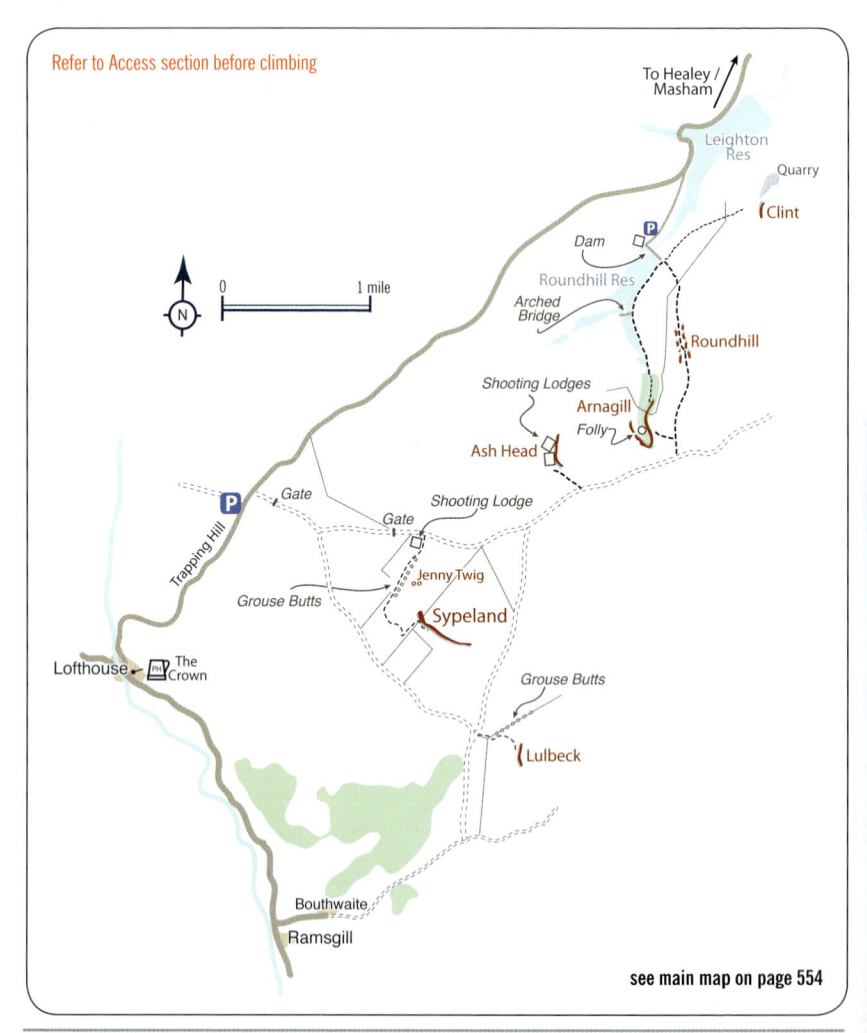

*Refer to Access section before climbing*

see main map on page 554

606      Yorkshire Gritstone

# The Towel Horse - SYPELAND

The first boulders and buttresses on the main edge lie about 150m to the south of the Jenny pinnacles, immediately left of a dry stone wall. The largest of these is The Towel Horse and immediately left of this are:

**1 North End of Pooh** Font 5
The right-hand side of the left arête is far better than its name suggests.

**2 Slenderer** Font 5
Meaty moves up the right arête and blind cracks.

### The Towel Horse
A larger, and oddly-shaped tiered buttress with two prominent overhangs, directly abutting the dry stone wall. It offers three short routes and the potential for some much harder problems.

**3 All Pull Together** S 4a   6m
Climb the short slab on the detached block and the sidewall above on positive holds.
*Tony Barley (solo)*

**4 Round in Circles** VS 5a   10m
Two boulder problems linked by an easy traverse. From the short slab gain the left-hand ledge between the two overhangs. Follow this round to the right and climb the top roof via a nick and blind crack to a difficult exit.
*Tony Barley (solo)*

**5 What Happens Now?** E3 6b   7m   ★
One of the best harder lines at the crag. From right of centre, tackle the first roof with difficulty and trend left to an awkward position onto the ledge. Continue over the second overhang to finish. Climbing to the first ledge is Font 6c+.
*Jerry Peel (solo)   1996*

Tom Griffin takes flight between Jenny Twig and her Daughter Tib.
Photo: Tom Peckitt

# SYPELAND - Rabbit Rock

The dry stone wall is best crossed using a stile over a gate 40m below the edge. About 30m right of the wall is a prominent clean square buttress known as **Tracking Tor** which offers three enjoyable micro routes.

### 6 **Foolish and Deluded**  Font 5  (HVS 5b)
After puzzling out the awkward shallow groove, finish direct via the crease.

### 7 **Sweat It Out**  Font 5  (HVS 5b)
A semi-independent line starting immediately left of the flake and climbing directly up the wall on small positive holds and pockets, finishing left of *Hot and Anxious*.
*Malcolm Townsley, 2010*

### 8 **Hot and Anxious**  Font 4+  (HVS 5a)
Enjoyable pocket pulling on clean rock gives an excellent micro-route. Start at the prominent short flake and follow the ripples above, trending slightly right.

## Rabbit Rock
Approximately 10m to the right is a severely undercut and slightly creaky buttress. It offers a good selection of overhanging problems with that unique Sypeland flavour.

### 9 **Alexander Beetle**  Font 6a
Great for practicing your Sypeland top-out technique. Start just right of the two big low holes on small incuts and trend left to the lip of the overhang and a spike hold, which is used to exit the overlap. A slightly harder version can be taken from a sit-down start at the left end of the overhang and traversing right (Font 6a+).
*Tony Barley; (sit-down start Malcolm Townsley 2010)*

### 10 **Bother**  Font 4  (VS 5a)
Place your faith in the creaky flake and exit the left-hand side of the central recess, trending left.

### 11 **Henry Rush**  HVS 5a   6m
A committing line taking the nose above the big thread before traversing left to a bold finish.
*Tony Barley (solo)*

### 12 **Condensed Milk**  Font 5
The overhang on the right-hand side of the buttress is climbed via a poor problem with a hard exit and a bad landing. Finishing at the right-hand end of the overhang is safer and easier (Font 4).

The next boulder to the left contains two small problems in the Font 3 to 4 range. To the right, a larger rounded boulder has a prominent walled cave at its right-hand end. A good place to shelter from the rain providing you do not mind nettles and sheep. This offers a further three problems.

### 13 **Bell Pull**  Font 3
The prow, from a sit-down start, just right of the arête.

## Pounds and Shillings Boulders - Sypeland

### 14 A Campanologists Tale  Font 5
The wall with some attractive moves.

### 15 Tails Get in the Way  Font 5
The attractive overhanging scoop direct to a slopey finish.

### The Sixpence
About 30m to the right of the walled cave a larger rounded block is reached. This pinnacle has a small stream to its right feeding an in-situ pool below its southern bulges.

### 16 Crustimoney Proceedcake  Font 6a+
The enjoyable short corner in the centre of the south face on tricky slopers.

### 17 One Hundred Inches Long  E1 5c   7m
Not really deep water soloing but you won't want to splash out. Start up the steep scoop at the left end of the north face and traverse left on rounded holds over the water to finish at the upper weakness.
*Tony Barley (solo)*

### 18 Dates  Font 5
The wall in the centre of the north face is best from a sit-down start at a jug on the right.

### 19 Whispering  Font 3
The short wall on the right-hand side of the north face.

Approximately 10m south, off the main edge, is a rectangular undercut boulder with a prominent leering crack splitting its west face. From a sit-down start **The Woozle**, (Font 6a), crawls as far back as possible into the recess and climbs the compelling crack.

### Pounds and Shillings Boulders
Back on the main edge, a few metres right of The Sixpence, are two more adjoining rounded boulders. Lovers of Brimham-esque roundedness should go no further as these offer some of the best concentrations of boulder problems and micro-routes on the crag. The east (back) face offers a good selection of slopey highballs, all of which are escapable at the obvious break.

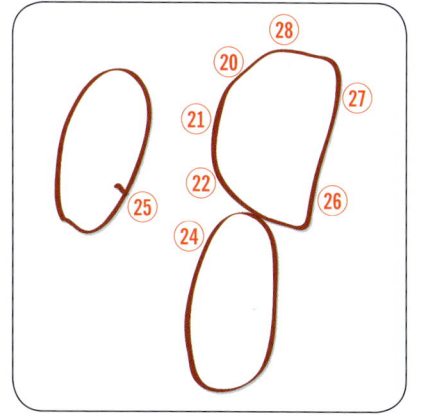

### 20 Peaceful Smile  Font 5  (HVS 5b)
The water-worn scoop to the far left gives interesting moves and a bulging finish on the right.

### 21 Boughed  Font 5+  (HVS 5c)
Another technical gem. From the left of the arête, step off the grass using an obvious flake and finish up the technical wall above. Even better from a hanging start with the big pocket and low footholds at Font 6a.

### 22 Bounces  Font 5+  (E1 5c)
The classy slanting scoop is more positive than it first appears. The sit-down start from the low scoop to the right is also a gem and gives a more sustained sequence at Font 6a.

### 23 The Boss aka Loose Change  Font 6c+
A refugee from Almscliff and a worthwhile problem. Use the *Bounces* sit-down start to gain the low break and follow this powerfully left to finish up *Boughed*.

# SYPELAND - Piglet Pinnacle Area

## 24 Malt Extract  Font 4+
The short impending crack on the next block, finishing up the rounded nose to the left. Much better than it first appears. Font 5 from a sit-down start.

## 25 Stones Too Much  Font 3  (VS 4b)
Across the way, take the crack, or the wall just to the right, leading to the standard bulgy exit tussle.

A short walk around to the sunnier west face offers a selection of shorter but equally powerful problems.

## 26 Strengthening Medicine  Font 5+
Appropriately named. The short steep corner, right of the prominent nose, to a tricky finish.

## 27 Large Gollolup  Font 6a
More balancey roundedness. The scooped face using the hole.

## 28 Pence  Font 5+
The bulging rib on the right is more awkward than it looks.

The nose of the more isolated pinnacle a few metres south is **Droopy Drawers** (MVS 4b).

### Piglet Pinnacle Area
The next boulder marks the start of one of the higher parts of the edge. These pinnacles offer several longer routes with the fairly soft gritstone forming distinct cracks, arêtes and rounded bulges giving technical, and often bold, climbing. The surrounding boulder field offers a good selection of problems.

## 29 Henry Pootel  Font 5
The awkward wall just to the right of the left arête on flakes and sloping incuts. Using the left arête is slightly easier, but better, at Font 4.

## 30 Piglet Arête  Font 7a  (E3 6a)
The striking central arête of the pinnacle on its left-hand side. High, but with a good landing. Photo on page 605.
*Nigel Poustie, 2007*

## 31 A Very Grand Thing  Font 5  (HVS 5b)
A tricky customer. Gain the hanging crack from the adjacent block and exit this with interest.

## 32 Blunt Arête  Font 6a
Delicate. The blunt arête up the middle of the low block.

## 33 In As Much As  Font 4
The straightforward wall.

### Heffalump Tor
The highest buttress on the edge and clearly identifiable by a prominent S-shaped crack splitting its west face and a slabby boulder leaning against its central arête. The impressive left-hand side of this arête remains unclimbed.

## 34 On The Other Hand  VS 5a  7m
The thin blind crack hiding behind the boulder has a good finish to the left.
*Tony Barley (solo)*

## 35 Heffalump Wall  Font 7a  (E3 6c)
Impressive, thin and technical, with a wall that is just a bit too high to bail out with comfort from. Follow the blank-looking wall to the half-height break. Escape.
*Nigel Poustie, 2007*

## Heffalump Tor - SYPELAND

### 36 Twiggy  E1 5b  8m  ★★
A committing route with a serious feel. Climb the prominent S-shaped crack then take the upper rounded bulges direct.
*Tony Barley, Dave Musgrove  8th June 1991*

### 37 Lumping Along  VS 5a  10m  ★
A worthwhile, if slightly disjointed, route. Climb the triangular slab on the detached block to a difficult mantel from its apex onto the half-height ledge. Finish by traversing into, and up, the easier chimney.
*Tony Barley (solo)*

### 38 Ramble On  Font 6a+
Unless your technique is flawless you will want to be wearing a long-sleeved top for this. The square arête gives excellent balancey moves to a difficult finish in the half-height break. Finish up *Cracking Up*.
*Malcolm Townsley, 2010*

### 39 Cracking Up  HVD  8m  ★
The prominent crack and chimney splitting the south face of the tor has an awkward start.
*Tony Barley (solo)*

### 40 Long Time Coming  Font 6a+  (E1 6a)
A good, technical arête. Climb the short overhanging rib at the entrance to the gully to the break and finish up the chimney of *Cracking Up*.

### 41 A Deep Pit  HVS 5a  8m
Bold. Start in the back of the gully. Traverse up and left out of the gloom following the straightforward rising ramp and then tackle the capping roof.
*Tony Barley (solo)*

### 42 Got Any String  VS 5a  5m
The rib and capping bulge at the right end of the gully is well worth a crack. Best started from inside the gap.
*Tony Barley (solo)*

### 43 Sinking Feeling  Font 4+
The dirty rounded rib on the opposite side of the gully.

### 44 A Cunning Trap  E3 5c  6m
A real buttock clencher. From the right end of the shelf, climb the pillar, trending left, and tackle the rounded roof.
*Tony Barley (solo)*

### 45 Like Nothing  E1 5b  5m
A more amenable affair than its neighbour. Climb the easy pillar and finish through the eyes in the capping roof.
*Tony Barley (solo)*

Five metres down to the left, at a lower level, is a short attractive wall where **Nothing in Particular** (Font 5) ascends the centre, past two thin pockets. The small triangular boulder with a slabby south face just in front of this buttress offers four good problems including **Fond of Pigs** (Font 3), which follows the flakes up the left edge of the slabby boulder (a good problem whether or not you're a piggy lover); **Nothing Slab** (Font 4) pads up the slab; **Found Nothing** (Font 3), cruises the right arête and **Almost Nothing** (Font 5+), takes the leaning right arête, above the hole, of the next boulder.

# Sypeland - The Tablecloth

## The Tablecloth
In front of Heffalump Tor is a prominent rectangular block with a flat top which offers a good collection of short arête and wall problems with tricky finishes.

### 46 Agog  Font 5
Start just to the right of the left arête on positive holds and climb directly to the highest point on the face.

### 47 Agroan  Font 6a+
Much more fun for the short. The south-west wall using a small low ledge.
*Dave Musgrove, 1996*

### 48 Aghast  Font 5
Powerful and balancey. The arête, taken on the left-hand side, to an interesting exit.

### 49 Why  Font 4+
Another challenging exit mantel. The arête taken on its right-hand side.

### 50 Wherefore  Font 4+
The centre of the face.

### 51 Whenever  Font 4
The right arête of the short scooped face.

### 52 What  Font 5
Thin, with another taxing finalé. Start 2m left of *Agog*. Slap up the blunt arête on its right-hand side and then mantel onto the narrow ledge in the scoop.

Down the slope are two further boulders offering six short rounded problems in the Font 4 and 5 grade range. These can be worth exploring, especially if you apply a bit of imagination. About 40m right of the Tablecloth is another triangular boulder with one problem, **Quite At Ease** (Font 3), which climbs the slabby corner and left edge of the undercut slab.

## Woozle Tor
Another 30m right is a fine monolithic block. A sound buttress offering the best concentrations of routes on the edge. It has a clean, wide, west face, providing good wall problems and a fine overhung south face offering excellent technical lines. The first few metres to several of the routes on the south face can be done as boulder problems by finishing at the break.

### 53 The Blue Bomber  HVS 5a  5m
The blocky landing concentrates the mind. The left-hand side of the blunt arête, finishing rightwards.
*Malcolm Townsley (solo)  October 2010*

### 54 Thoughtful Way  HVS 5b  5m
The wall immediately right of the arête has good moves above a poor landing. Careful pad-craft will pay dividends.
*Tony Barley (solo)*

### 55 Tracking Something  HVS 5b  6m  ★★
The standout wall. The centre of the clean face passing the obvious lenticular pocket to an unsecure finish.
*Tony Barley (solo)*

### 56 Funnything Accidents  E1 5c  7m  ★
The narrow corner is an enjoyable technical line. With the difficulties low down and a positive finish, what have you got to worry about?
*Tony Barley (solo)*

### 57 Breaking Out  E3 6b  7m  ★★
A real teaser; the memory of which will stay with you for days to come. Taxing moves following the left-hand side of the right arête of the west wall.
*Dave Musgrove Jnr (solo)  31st July 1996*

Woozle Tor - **SYPELAND**

**58 Caught in an Eddy**  E2 6a  8m  ★★★
A superb line surfing its way up the arête in a tremendous position. Take off on the right-hand side of the arête and break right, following the sloping rail to good holds and a solid finish. A direct start **(a) Lacking In Smack** (E2 6b ★★) starts below and right of the rib and climbs direct to the bulge. An excellent sequence.
*Tony Barley (solo)*

**59 Eeyore**  E2 6a  8m  ★★
Good with puzzles? The attractive corner beckons to be climbed but unlocking the sequence is another thing. Start in the shallow corner and make thin moves up and right to the handrail then head left to finish as for *Caught in an Eddy*. Alternatively, boldly tackle the bulge to the right.
*Dave Musgrove Jnr (solo)  31st July 1996*

**60 Horse Gone Wonky**  E2 6a  9m  ★★★
A great variation and perhaps the line of the buttress if the going's good. Gallop up the centre of the west wall to the handrail then trot left to join *Caught in an Eddy*.
*Tony Barley (solo)*

**61 Trained Bloodhound**  HVS 5b  9m  ★
Follow the start of *Horse Gone Wonky* to the roof then bypass this by traversing the rail right to the arête before moving back left to finish up the centre of the buttress. It is also possible to start independently via the right arête.
*Tony Barley (solo)*

**62 Drop the Dead Donkey**  E3 6c  11m  ★
A painful, and bafflingly thin, low right-to-left traverse across the wall finishing up *Eeyore* or *Lacking in Smack*. Font 7a if you finish at the break.
*Dave Musgrove Jnr (solo)  31st July 1996*

Five metres to the right is the lower pinnacle of **The Spinney** which offers two problems. **Make Waves** (Font 4) cruises the left arête from good holds whilst **Lazy River** (Font 4), climbs the blunt right-hand arête and is another of those innocuous-looking Sypeland problems that provides a rewarding tussle. Right again is the low rounded block of **The Copse** where **Ice Box** (Font 4), eases up the left-hand blunt rib and **In a Cooling Manner** (Font 4+) shuffles up the interesting undercut wall past the slanting pocket.

Almscliff to Slipstones

# SYPELAND - Tigger's Tor

### 63 A Little Something  Font 5
The bulging front face of the pinnacle behind Tigger's Tor, starting in the short corner.

### 64 Bounced  Font 5  (HVS 5a)
The slabby north face provides a good varied line past the water-worn groove.

### 65 Tiggers Can Fly  Font 6a  (E1 6a)
Another classic rounded arête. The gently impending western nose has a highball rounded finish.

Right again and after a short gap, is a larger undercut boulder called **Pooh Profile** with the prominent capping roof.

### 66 Pooh Sticks  S 4a  6m
The sidewall starting in the scoop and finishing at the crack.
*Tony Barley (solo)*

### 67 A Little Anxious  E1 5b  7m  ★
Gain the shelf from the left, traverse right and then finish up the centre of the overhang via the crack and nick.
*Tony Barley (solo)*

### 68 Of Little Brain  Font 4
The rounded right arête of the lower block.

The slabby boulder to the right offers two easy lines. A further 30m to the right the aptly named leaning square cut block of **The Honey Pot** offers a fine selection of problems with a subtly different and more positive style.

### 69 Another Winters Edge  Font 4  (VS 5a)
The left arête on its right-hand side.
*Malcolm Townsley (solo)   May 2010*

### 70 Twitchy Sort of Way  Font 5  (HVS 5b)
Enjoyable wall climbing with a positive top-out. Start just left of centre and head for the highest point on the wall.
*Tony Barley (solo)*

### 71 Adulterated Bliss  Font 4  (VS 5a)
Another good line and not a sloper in sight. The scoop and short crack at the right-hand side of the wall.
*Tony Barley (solo)*

### Tigger's Tor
This excellent, compact, rounded pinnacle stands forward from the line of the edge. It offers two highball problems and scope for much harder fare on its south face. The descent for both of these problems is via the left-hand edge of the north face.

## Tib's Tent - SYPELAND

### 72 Gales  E1 5c  6m
Well worth the effort. Start on the right of the arête but slap around onto its left side above the bulging nose. The direct slopey right-hand finish is much harder.
*Dave Musgrove (solo)  1st June 1996*

### 73 A Little Trouble  E2 6a  6m  ★★★
An excellent and sustained offering with the crux being the rounded top-out. Commit to the centre of the impending wall on positive, spaced holds to the break, then finish rightwards. It is at least protectable.
*Tony Barley (solo)*

### 74 Twice 19  Font 5
The east wall starting right of the arête and trending right to a finish with a poor landing. A sit-down start at the hole is Font 5+.

### 75 Say Nothing  Font 6a+
Start at the right end of the next block. From a sit-down start at the undercut, gain the slopey lip and slap right to the right arête then follow this on its left-hand side.
*Tony Barley, (sit-down start Malcolm Townsley 2010)*

### 76 Heap of Everybody  HVS 5c  5m
The undercut wall to the right is powerful, technical and more worthwhile than its appearance would suggest.
*Tony Barley (solo)*

The last block of this group is the **The Honey Comb.** Recognisable by an obvious nose, it has three problems.

### 77 The Jagular  Font 3  (VS 4b)
The wall and steep scoop on the left.

### 78 Sparkling Along  Font 4+  (HVS 5b)
At last, some welcome jamming practice. An excellent problem up the flake in the centre of the buttress and up the crack splitting the right side of the nose.

### 79 What If  Font 3  (VS 4c)
The slabby right wall is better and harder than it looks.

### Tib's Tent
The surreal triangular block stands alone on the moor about 100m east of the Honey Comb and must be one of the county's most recognisable boulders. It offers a superb collection of highball problems/routes and no visit to Sypeland is complete without sampling some of its delights. The sandy nature of the rock can take both the uninitiated or happy-go-lucky climber by surprise. Descent is via chips on the slabby south face.

### 80 Testicle  VS 5a  8m  ★
An interesting slab problem with an improbable starting move. Stand on the boulder and use the flake to get established on the slab then follow the left edge to the top.
*Dave Musgrove (solo)  1st June 1996*

### 81 Tentacle  VS 4c  8m  ★
A good, smeary slab problem. Mantel onto the slab using the embedded block then pad up the slab between the edge and the chipped holds.
*Dave Musgrove (solo)  1st June 1996*

### 82 Just Pad Dad  S  10m  ★
The path of least resistance up the Tent and a good route for getting your eye in. Gain the slab using the first chips of the descent route then move right and pad to the top.
*Tony Barley (solo)*

## SYPELAND - Tib's Tent

### 83 Itchy Chin  E3 6c  9m  ★
A fond favourite. Tackle the undercut slab direct between the chipped descent and *Swirral Edge*, with a desperate start leading to an easier finish. The lower part can be bouldered out at Font 7a.
*Dave Musgrove Jnr (solo)  31st July 1996*

### 84 Swirral Edge  E3 6b  9m  ★★
A rewarding challenge up the perplexing right arête. Make best use of the edge and slopers to balance gracefully onto the slab and pad elegantly up the edge. Quitting at the slab is Font 6b+.
*Jerry Peel (solo)  1996*

### 85 Striding Edge  E1 5b  7m  ★★★
Barley's grand addition to the crag and a fitting reward for those that make the trek in. Take the left-hand side of the arête via two obvious pockets to the flutings. It's not seen as many rescues as its Cumbrian counterpart but the ill-prepared may be in for a shock.
*Tony Barley (solo)*

### 86 Jaw Crawler  Font 7c+
An impressive right-to-left low traverse along the lip of the bulging lower part of the north face. Link into *Flying Colours* to finish.
*Ben Meeks  2005*

### 87 Flying Colours  HVS 5b  7m  ★★
The first of three atmospheric lines on the daunting north face of the boulder. Follow the scoop in the arête to finish on flutings. Sustained climbing in a fine position.
*Tony Barley (solo)*

### 88 Under the Awning  E3 6a  7m  ★
The centre of the excellent face draws you in to a difficult and committing finish. After an awkward start follow the flake to a taxing finalé.
*Robin Barley (solo)  26th May 1991*

### 89 Burglary Within Tent  E2 5c  7m  ★
The right-hand side of the overhung face is awkward to start and has a thin reachy crux near the top.
*Dave Musgrove (solo)  8th June 1991*

Yorkshire Gritstone

# Graded List - SYPELAND

### 90 No Loitering  E2 5c  6m
Make a series of powerful moves up the rounded, slanting crack to an awkward finish.
*Tony Barley (solo)*

### Puff Pastry
The last boulder on the edge lies 50m south of Tib's Tent and comprises a rounded block, undercut on three sides. Powerful problems on rounded holds is the order of the day here. The landings are generally good although some of the rock is not above suspicion.

### 91 Cissy Greens  Font 6a
From the ground boulder, go through a nick in the middle of the overhang using a creaky hold. Traversing left (a) from *Flakey Pastry* is Font 6b.
*Jerry Peel, 1996*

### 92 Flakey Pastry  Font 6a
Mantel the overhanging west face direct.

### 93 Sausage Roll  Font 4+
Another good problem up the scoop.

### 94 Tasty Pastry  Font 6a
Tantalisingly technical. Bust some moves up the rounded wall.
*Jerry Peel, 1996*

### 95 Chip Butty  Font 5
More slopey shenanigans.
*Jerry Peel, 1996*

### 96 Crumbli  Font 5+
Sit-down start. The overhanging north-east face, tackled at its widest point, gives a good sequence.

### 97 Apfel Strudel  Font 5
From a sit-down start at the left edge of the north face, exit leftwards onto the heathery slab.

### 98 Vol au Vont  Font 5+
The centre of the overhung scooped north face from a sit-down start.

### 99 Cheese Straw  Font 5
From the sit-down start to *Vol au Vont* follow the obvious low ramp leftwards to finish up the big jugs left of *Crumbli*. Finishing up that problem is Font 6a.

### 100 Vanilla Slice  Font 6a
The right side of the undercut north face left of the ground boulder from a sit-down start.

### Further Information on First Ascents (✦)
*All named routes and boulder problems credited to Tony Barley were climbed between 1988 and 1996 during his development of the crag.* **The Woozle** *was climbed by Malcolm Townsley in 2010.*

---

**GRADED LIST**

**ROUTES**

**E3**
Itchy Chin
Drop the Dead Donkey
What Happens Now?
Swirral Edge
Under the Awning
A Cunning Trap
Breaking Out

**E2**
Lacking in Smack
Eeyore
A Little Trouble
Caught in an Eddy
Horse Gone Wonky
Burglary Within Tent
No Loitering

**E1**
One Hundred Inches Long
Gales
Funnythong Accidents
Twiggy
A little Anxious

Striding Edge
Like Nothing

**HVS**
Heap of Everybody
Flying Colours
Trained Bloodhound
Tracking Something
Thoughtful Way
The Blue Bomber
Bounced
A Deep Pit
Henry Rush

**VS**
Testicle
Got Any String
Lumping Along
Round in Circles
On the Other Hand
Bother
Tentacle

**MVS**
Droopy Draws

**S**
Just Pad Dad
All Pull Together
Pooh Sticks
Cracking Up (HVD)

**PROBLEMS**

**Font 7c+**
Jaw Crawler

**Font 7a**
Heffalump Wall
Piglet Arête

**Font 6c+**
The Boss aka Loose Change

**Font 6a+**
Long Time Coming
Agroan
Ramble On
Crustimoney Pancake
Say Nothing

**Font 6a**
Alexander Beetle
Blunt Arete
The Woozle
Large Gollolup
Cissy Greens
Tiggers Can Fly
Flakey Pastry
Tasty Pastry
Vanilla Slice

**Font 5+**
Almost Nothing
Crumbli
Boughed
Bounces
Strengthening Medicine
Pence
Vol au Vont

**Font 5**
North End of Pooh
Slenderer
Foolish and Deluded
Sweat it Out

Condensed Milk
A Campanologists Tale
Tails Get in the Way
Nothing in Particular
Dates
Peaceful Smile
A Very Grand Thing
Henry Pootel
Agog
Aghast
What
A Little Something
Bounced
Twitchy Sort of Way
Twice 19
Chip Butty
Apfel Strudel
Cheese Straw

**Font 4+**
Hot and Anxious
Sinking Feeling
Why
Malt Extract
Wherefore

Sparkling Along
In a Cooling Manner
Sausage Roll

**Font 4**
Bother
Whenever
Of Little Brain
Another Winters Edge
In As Much As
Adulterated Bliss
Nothing Slab
Make Waves
Lazy River
Ice Box

**Font 3**
Bell Pull
Fond of Pigs
Found Nothing
Quite At Ease
The Jangular
What If
Whispering
Stones Too Much

*Almscliff to Slipstones* **617**

SYPELAND - Bouldering Circuit

# THE SYPELAND WILD GREY CIRCUIT

Unsurprisingly for an edge that mainly offers boulder problems and micro-routes, the crag offers an excellent circuit in the Font 5 and 6 grade range; a real test of stamina and skin. If you have not perfected the Sypeland top-out by the time you finish then you never will.

| Problem | Name | Grade | Problem No. | Problem | Name | Grade | Problem No. |
|---|---|---|---|---|---|---|---|
| 1 | North End of Pooh | Font 5 | 1 | 17 | Ramble On | Font 6a+ | 38 |
| 2 | Slenderer | Font 5 | 2 | 18 | Long Time Coming | Font 6a+ | 40 |
| 3 | Foolish and Deluded | Font 5 | 6 | 19 | Aghast | Font 5 | 48 |
| 4 | Hot and Anxious | Font 4+ | 8 | 20 | Agroan | Font 6a+ | 47 |
| 5 | Sweat It Out | Font 5 | 7 | 21 | Agog | Font 5 | 46 |
| 6 | Alexander Beetle | Font 6a | 9 | 22 | Caught in an Eddy* | Font 6b | 58 |
| 7 | Crustimoney Proceedcake | Font 6a+ | 16 | 23 | Horse Gone Wonky* | Font 6b | 60 |
| 8 | The Woozle | Font 6a | 19+ | 24 | Bounced | Font 5 | 64 |
| 9 | Bounces | Font 5+ | 22 | 24 | Tiggers Can Fly | Font 6a | 65 |
| 10 | Boughed | Font 5+ | 21 | 26 | Twice 19 | Font 5 | 74 |
| 11 | Peaceful Smile | Font 5 | 20 | 27 | Say Nothing | Font 6a+ | 75 |
| 12 | Pence | Font 5+ | 28 | 28 | Sparkling Along | Font 4+ | 78 |
| 13 | Large Gollolup | Font 6a | 27 | 29 | Vanilla Slice | Font 6a | 100 |
| 14 | Strengthening Medicine | Font 5+ | 26 | 30 | Crumbli | Font 5+ | 96 |
| 15 | Henry Pootel | Font 5 | 29 | 31 | Tasty Pastry | Font 6a | 94 |
| 16 | Blunt Arête | Font 6a | 32 | 32 | Sausage Roll | Font 4+ | 93 |

The last climb is optional as it's a route, however it provides a fitting ending. **Striding Edge** (E1 5b, Route 85)
Top out on the magnificent boulder and survey your moorland kingdom.
*Escape at the break.*

# LULBECK

# lulbeck

by Chris Sowden

OS Ref: SE 139 727
Altitude: 370 m

This superb little buttress is located on Corvill House Moor overlooking the picturesque valley of Upper Nidderdale. **The Climbing:** Although originally recorded as routes, the shortness, total lack of runners and the use of a bouldering mat mean that all lines can be climbed without resorting to a rope. Not having to carry a rope and runners also makes the walk-in much easier.

**Conditions and Aspect:** The aspect is west and the crag receives any available afternoon sun. The natural gritstone buttress is undercut at its base, and although the rock is generally excellent, it's worth checking the top-outs beforehand for the 'scrittle' to ensure a pleasant visit is had by all. There is a smaller and rather friable buttress 100m to the left which contains four unsatisfactory problems that are best avoided. **Parking and Approach:** (See map on page 606) The most direct approach to the crag is via Bouthwaite Lane which, when approaching from Pateley Bridge, is the first turning on the right after passing through the village of Ramsgill. Immediately after turning right, park at the side of the road. Walk along the road to Bouthwaite go straight ahead at the crossroads and continue up the hill on the dirt track passing through four gates. Turn left at the first junction and continue until a double-gated y-branch is reached. Go through the right-hand gate, up the side of the wall to some grouse butts through yet another gate and the crag is facing you. It takes about 40 minutes but is well worth the effort. Approach is also possible as for Sypeland. From the moorland track (heading east from the Healey-to-Lofthouse road) turn right at the second junction (1.75 miles from the road) and follow this track for 1.25 miles south. The crag is then a 10-minute walk up to the left. **Access**: Please no dogs, no fires and no large parties. The crag should be avoided during the shooting season; details showing dates on which the moor is closed to the public are posted at the moorland access points. Avoid the crag during May and June to minimise disturbance to ground nesting birds.

**1 Face the Enemy** Font 4. The wall just right of the arête.
**2 Confrontation** Font 4+. Sit-down start.
**3 Cat Balloo** Font 5. Sit-down start. Climb the wall directly to the hanging crack and an interesting finish.
**4 Lullaby** Font 5+. Sit-down start to the crack then finish rightwards over the bulge.
**5 Pocket Puller** Font 6a+. Awkward to both start and finish. After a sit-down start, use the two finger pockets to climb the blunt rib and bulge.
**6 Hullaballoo** Font 5+. Sit-down start to the pocket. Finish leftwards.
**7 Ready Brek** Font 5. The pocket and top bulge direct.
**8 Butt Nine** Font 5. The slot and wall above.
**9 Force Ten** Font 6a. Sit-down start. Gain the slot then reach rightwards to the upper pocket to finish.
**10 Support the Allies** Font 5. The small undercut scoop and wall.
**11 Beckon** Font 5. The bulging rib and wall.
**12 Lulbeck** Font 5+. Sit-down start to the right of the arête. Pull over the upper bulge using pockets. The dirty wall at the right end of the crag is **Beck and Call** (Font 4+).

**13 Short Arse Traverse** Font 6c. Traverse the wall from *Face the Enemy* to *Lulbeck*. Can be climbed in either direction.

### First Ascent Information

Beck and Call, Beckon, Butt Nine, Cat Balloo, Face the Enemy, Hullaballo, Lullaby, Ready Brek, Support the Allies *were climbed by either Nigel Baker or Tony Barley between June 1993 and July 1995.* **Confrontation, Force Ten, Lulbeck, Pocket Puller, Short Arse Traverse** *were climbed by Chris Sowden in 2008.*

# ASH HEAD - Introduction

# ash head crag

### by Chris Sowden

OS Ref: SE 143 754
Altitude: 370 m

Masham Moor can be a desolate place, and not somewhere you would necessarily choose to locate a crag. Approximately three miles north-east of Lofthouse near the top of the moor, however, such a place exists. The feeling of remoteness has been somewhat shattered by the land owner who, in his wisdom, chose to build two shooting lodges just in front of the crag. This unique feature certainly doesn't impact on the quality of the climbing, with a compact collection of buttresses and boulders that are well worth visiting, especially on a fine summer's day.

**The Climbing:** There are 26 routes and several boulder problems with flat user-friendly landings helping to make this a fine little crag. The classic lines of *Thunder Crack (VS 4c)* and *Lightning Variation (HVS 6a)* are both well worth the walk.

**Conditions and Aspect:** The aspect is generally north-west. The crag is fairly quick-drying and the rock is well-weathered natural grit with an abundance of chicken heads which can be quite friable, especially after rain. During the winter months parts of the crag remain wet and uninviting.

**Parking and Approach:** The best approach to the parking is as for Sypeland crag (see map on page 606). Walk up the same approach track as for Sypeland and follow it east for two miles through two gates and past two turnings always keeping left. Leave the main track and follow the path on the left (north-west) for 500m where the crag and shooting lodges come clearly into view. 45 minutes.

A shorter way (25 mins), but often muddier, is to head back towards Masham on the main road for 1.7 miles and park on the roadside 100m before West Summer Side Farm, the first farm on the right, where a public footpath leads through the wall and down to the right of the farm buildings. Shown on the OS map as Combs Crags, it can be clearly seen behind the two shooting lodges from both the rough road and the farm.

**Access:** Climbing access, as always with grouse moor-land, is dependant on considerate behaviour; please no dogs, no fires, no large parties and, of prime importance, don't damage or burn down either of the shooting lodges. The crag should be avoided during the shooting season; details showing dates on which the moor is closed to the public are normally posted at the moorland access points.

Photo: Jamie Moss

# Thunder Crack - ASH HEAD

Behind the centre of the left-hand building is the first route.

**1 The Horn** HVS 5a 8m
Climb directly to the obvious line of knobs. A good lasso technique helps with the protection.
*Robin and Tony Barley 27th September 1965*

**2 Barnstorm** HS 4b 9m
Climb up to the thin crack. Traverse right and finish up the corner above.
*Tony and Robin Barley 27th September 1965*

**3 Flake Crack** S 6m
The obvious flake right of the arête between the buildings.
*Tony Barley 13th July 1974*

**4 Dust Off** E2 5c 11m
Located on the wall behind the right-hand building. Climb a short crack then go straight up the blank wall above to the horizontal break. Move right to finish direct.
*Tony Barley, Ken Wood 13th July 1974*

**5 Tip Off** VS 4c 9m
Start left of the arête behind the middle of the right-hand building. Climb directly past the break and up the wall to the top break. Finish direct.
*Martin Hannan 30th November 1988*

**6 Windy Wall** S 10m
Climb the arête to the top break then move left and finish up *Tip Off*.
*Jack Wilson early-1950s*

**7 Headstand** HS 4a 10m
Climb the chimney to the overhang and move right to finish.
*Robin and Tony Barley 27th September 1965*

An easier variation combining parts of *Windy Wall* and *Headstand* was originally recorded as **Fluted Rib** (VD).

**8 Last Rites** VS 4c 9m
Climb the crack system in the wall to the top break. Move right under the overhang and finish direct.
*Greg Tough, R. Kinnard 18th July 1972*

**9 Thunder Crack** VS 4c 12m ★★
A belting route that is a tough challenge if you can't move like lightning when the going gets tough. Climb the arête to the break. Hand traverse right to the base of the overhanging curving crack. Climb this and move left under the overhangs and onto the slab to finish.
*Tony and Robin Barley 27th September 1965* ✦

**10 Lightning Variation** HVS 6a 11m ★★
Storms a comin'. Another tough offering requiring a positive charge of energy to overcome the difficulties. Climb the blunt rib to gain the crack and follow this to the overhang. Move right and finish up the slab. Bouldering out the start to the crack is Font 6a.
*Tony and Robin Barley 27th September 1965*

**11 The Storm** Font 6c
Climb the delicate wall right of *Lightning Variation*.

**12 Right to Roam** VS 5a 8m
The wall right of *Thunder Crack* contains a vegetated crack. Climb the slab to its right to a bilberry ledge and v-chimney, then exit left.
*Malcolm Townsley 28th May 2005*

**13 Up and Under** VS 4c 9m
Climb the arête just to the right to the bilberry ledge. Move left and up the v-chimney to finish on the right.
*The Barley Brothers 27th September 1965* ✦

**14 Over Easy** Font 6a
From a sit-down start underneath the small roof, traverse left under the arête and finish up the wall on chicken heads.

## Ash head - Rhombic Block

#### 15 Easy Over  Font 5+
From the same start as *Over Easy* reach and climb the slanting crack to the break.

#### 16 Alien Kiss  E1 5c   9m  ★
Climb right of the arête to the break of *Wanderlust*. The hanging arête (long reach) is used to gain the upper break. Finish between the horns of the 'alien head'.
*Malcolm Townsley   11th July 2005*

#### 17 Chicken Eddy  Font 6a+
Traverse the bottom break in either direction, the hard part being at the right-hand side.

#### 18 Chicken Scoop  Font 5+
Climb the shallow scoop at the right end of the wall.

#### 19 Wanderlust  S   17m
A journey of adventure along the wide horizontal break that crosses the wall from right-to-left. Yep that's leftwards along the very big ledge to finish as for *Up and Under*.
*The Barley Brothers   27th September 1965 ✦*

#### 20 A Climb  S   6m
The A-shaped crack system via the left-hand crack.
*Roger Sutcliffe, Chris Amber, Ernie Hodgson   May 1962*

#### 21 Ledge and Scoop  S   6m
Tackle the right-hand side of the A-shaped crack system via a mantel onto the ledge. Finish up the leftward-trending scoop.
*Malcolm Townsley   11th June 2005*

Opposite *A Climb* and *Wanderlust* is a large detached boulder known as the **Rhombic Block**. Originally graded Severe, the block can be traversed in its entirety at varying grades dependent upon ones personal altitude ceiling.

Rocking around the block anti-clockwise starting on the north side (this is the rather dirty green wall facing *Wanderlust*, best left to the heather and lichen) are:

#### 22 The American Girl  VS 4b   8m
The wall right of the arête on small chicken heads.
*Jamie Moss   16th July 2005*

#### 23 The Actress  VS 4c   8m
The dirty green wall finishing up the short shallow corner.
*The Barley Brothers   27th September 1965 ✦*

#### 24 Gangreen  HS 4b   8m
Climb a different bit of green wall this time to reach a shallow, sloping groove full of heather. This leads to the top or, better still, don't bother.
*Roger Sutcliffe, Chris Amber, Ernie Hodgson   May 1962*

On the west side of the Rhombic Block is:

#### 25 Cockerel Wall  Font 6b
Sit-down start. The wall just right of the arête, climbed on chicken heads.

#### 26 The Result  HS 4b   8m
Climb the diagonal crack, move left and finish up the slab.
*Robin Barley, Tony Barley   27th September 1965*

#### 27 The True Knobbler  E1 6a   8m
The wall to the left of the wide, bulging crack.
*Al Manson, Ken Wood   25th June 1976*

#### 28 The Tea Party  HVS 5c   8m
The bulging crack in the middle of the south face.
*Tony Barley, Robin Barley   27th September 1965*

#### 29 Rhyme  S   7m
The blunt south-east arête of the block.
*The Barley Brothers   27th September 1965 ✦*

#### 30 Rhythm  VD   8m
The central crack on the east face of the block leads directly to a huge perched block. Finish to its left or risk riding it down.
*The Barley Brothers   27th September 1965*

Yorkshire Gritstone

## Ash head

**31 21st Birthday Wall** VS 4b  8m
Climb directly up the wall to the huge perched block, finish to its right this time.
*Jamie Moss  16th July 2005*

**32 Easy Ridge**  M  7m
The north-east arête of the block.
*Roger Sutcliffe, Chris Amber, Ernie Hodgson  May 1962*

Opposite the west face of the Rhombic Block is a large boulder that acts as the southern support for an enormous block. There are five problems on this boulder all of which have heather finishes.

**33 Gordon's Slab**  Font 5. The right side of the slab moving left at the top to finish.
**34 Eric's Wall**  Font 6a. The wall left of the undercut arête. A pocket just right of the arête proves to be a useful finishing hold.
**35 Eric's Arête**  Font 4. The undercut arête started on the left.
**36 Ain't no Yoke**  Font 5. The wall just left of the wide crack.
**37 Steve's Arête**  Font 5. The arête on the right of the wide crack. Opposite *Steve's Arête* is:
**38 Chicken Shit**  Font 6a. The shallow scoop in the middle of the wall. Photo this page.

On the boulder to the left of the boulder containing *Gordon's Slab* there are a further five problems.

**39 Big Scoop**  Font 5+. The vague crack and wall left of the hanging groove.
**40 Hanging Groove**  Font 5
**41 Blunt Nose**  Font 6a. The rounded nose just right.
**42 Hole Arête**  Font 5+. Climb the undercut arête past the badly created hole.
**43 Easy Wall**  Font 4. Climb the wall/slab on the right of the undercut arête.

There are two problems on the stand-alone boulder that is in front of the left-hand building. **Barn Door** (Font 6a) climbs the shallow sccop on the front face whilst **Rock On** (Font 4+) climbs the arête to the left from a sit-down start.

### Further First Ascent Information (✦)
**The Actress, Rhythm, Wanderlust, Up and Under:** *First recorded ascents but probably climbed earlier. Most of these climbs were included in an interim guide published in various journals.*
**Thunder Crack**: *Top-roped in 1962 by Roger Sutcliffe, Chris Ambler and Ernie Hodgson.*

Jamie Moss soaks up the sun on **Chicken Shit** (Font 6a). This Page. Photo: Jamie Moss collection.

*Almscliff to Slipstones*

**623**

# roundhill

by **John Hunt**

OS Ref: SE 155 765
Altitude: 300 m

An extensive boulder field high on Ilton Moor and a wonderful contrast to the neighbouring Slipstones. Great for families; all bilberries and no ferns. Nice and flat. Yorkshire's answer to the child-friendly bouldering in Derbyshire's Burbage Valley.

**Routes and Bouldering:** All bouldering. Four circuits with a total of 114 problems. There are many excellent lower grade problems in addition to some real testpieces, particularly on the Roman Walls. An excellent place for a mixed team.

**Conditions and Aspect:** Very pleasant on a summer's day, but can feel very exposed in rough weather. The boulders face in all directions.

**Parking and Approach:** See map on page 606. If approaching from Lofthouse, travel north-east along Trapping Hill (the Lofthouse-to-Healey road) for 4¾ miles at which point the road drops downhill and the reservoirs are in view on the right. Take the sharp right up the single track road for half a mile to the dam. Park considerately just before the big gate, away from the house and the dam **(Parking GPS: 54.194091, -1.767135)**. Please do not park in the small space directly at the end of the dam where signs state 'for emergency vehicles only'.
If travelling from the Masham direction, from Healey village go west for half a mile until the fork in the road (the right fork goes to Slipstones). Take the left fork downhill for a further mile until Leighton reservoir is reached. Follow the road around the reservoir and across the inlet bridge. After 450m the single track road, mentioned above, appears on the left.

Once parked up, as you cross the dam and look left you can see Clint Crags on the near skyline to the north-east with the track that heads across to it. From the dam, Roundhill is ahead and to the right (almost south), hidden behind a brow. You can see the track which heads up then right to this. There is also a collection of boulders midway between the two on the scarp edge ('Halfway Boulders'). This is not as good as it looks from the dam but has 10ish good-looking problems mainly on the highest right section from the south-east end (furthest from the approach).
15 minutes.

**Access:** Temporary access restrictions are posted on a sign at the head of the dam. The boulders are on access land under current CRoW arrangements, but you have to cross some non-access land, so please stick to the footpath which runs through the rocks. No dogs.

Adi Gill receives vital beta from Lily on **Senator** (Font 5+). Page 628.
Photo: Michelle Gill

# Roundhill - The Cobble

### Circuit 1 - Below The Track Circuit
The Cobble and the Pebble boulders. All the recorded problems are downhill from the track.

### The Cobble
The first boulder reached after approaching from the dam, immediately beside the track. There are a few awkward problems mounting the overlap to reach the heathery shelf.

1 **Scrabble** Font 5. Pass the slot.
2 **Scribble** Font 6a. Left of the arête.
3 **Right of Rib** Font 5
4 **Top Pocket Finish** Font 5+. Excellent. Jam the break, then use the pocket to finish. A crimpy sit-down start is possible. Photo on page 555.
5 **Head Banger** Font 6a. Beware the boulder behind.
6 **Backbreaker** Font 6a
7 **Little Step Start** Font 6a
8 **Two Pocket Wall** Font 3
9 **Left of Rib** Font 5
10 **Hewn Pocket** Font 2+
11 **Twin Scoop** Font 3
12 **Flutings** Font 2

### The Pebble
Downhill from the Cobble, the Pebble provides low grade problems. Four pockets above the bulge provide the targets for the first four problems:

13 **Wall Pocket** Font 3
14 **Little Top Pocket** Font 3
15 **Bigger Top Pocket** Font 2+

## The Ramps - ROUNDHILL

**16 Left of Arête Pocket** Font 4+
**17 Arête Pocket** Font 5+. Avoid pockets on either face. Brilliant. (**The True Bum Start** (Font 6a) starts from small pocks below the ledge).
**18 Right Arête Pocket** Font 4. (Better without the big central pocket at Font 5+).
**19 Ripples** Font 3

A left-to-right traverse, finishing up the arête is **All Pockets** (Font 5). Low feet help.

### Circuit 2 - The Slab Area Circuit
Move back across the track for the next circuit based around the prominent slab. The Slab is situated on the best picnic spot and in front of The Ramps. Brilliant bouldering.

**20 Grasp** Font 5. The narrow wall between the arête and the big slot.
**21 Grip** Font 3. Use the wide slot.
**22 Billy-No-Mats** Font 5+. A Font 4+, **Guts**, is just to the right.
**23 Gnat** Font 4. The slight scoop to the pocket above.
**24 Knott** Font 4. Move right from a waist high scoop.
**25 Knit** Font 5. (Font 6a from a sit-down start).
**26 Nose Span** Font 6a
**27 Knotty** Font 4
**28 Team Sowden Traverse** Font 6a. The discontinuous break. Finish up the final arête on the right.

Just up and left is **The Easy (!) Angled Slab.**

**29 Kings of Northumbria Overmantel** Font 6b
A full body pump and tough to grade. Hang the lip, heel-hook and press like mad. *John Hunt 23rd November 2010.*
**30 Middle Lip** Font 6c. Sit / hang the start. Make a rounded traverse left into the arête. *Bob & Steve Blake*
**31 Right End** Font 6c. Sit / hang the end lip to climb the right edge. *Bob & Steve Blake*

### The Ramps
Behind the brilliant slab is a split upper tier which looks disappointing, but turns out to house a collection of excellent problems. The first problems are on the low roof left of the main twin blocks. **Roof Central** (Font 4+) takes the middle of the roof from a sit-down start and **Roof Arête** (Font 4+) grinds over the rounded break, again from a sitter. Moving right there are two obvious flake systems.

**32 Left Flakes** Font 4+. Sit-down start.
**33 Major Flakes** Font 5. The shallower flake just right, from a sitter.
**34 Jacob** Font 3+. The crack and the side wall left of the left buttress. The sit-down start is Font 5.
**35 Rameses** Font 4+. Above the cut out.
**36 Abdullah** Font 5. Use the left end of the slot.
**37 Tribal Wars** Font 6b+. Sit-down start. Hang the centre of big low slot. Fight hard to reach and use the shallow pockets. Font 5+ from standing. *Chris Sowden.*
**38 Jonah** Font 5. The shallow flake in the headwall. The top isn't allowed as a starting hold.

The right-hand boulder looks more impressive, but doesn't match the quality of its left-hand neighbour.

**39 Jugs** Font 3. Anywhere up this wall. Exciting.
**40 Pair of Eyes** Font 3. Harder if the eyes aren't used.
**41 High Jug** Font 3. Gun to the huge bucket.
**42 Right Face** Font 3

A traverse is possible, **Prepare For Pump** (Font 5), which moves left along the big break to *Jugs* then returns via the holds above. The two edges of the little pyramid boulder just in front of the last group have been climbed from sit-down starts.

*Almscliff to Slipstones*

# ROUNDHILL - Roman Wall

## Circuit 3 - The Roman Empire Circuit
A circuit based on Roman Wall, The Ramparts and The Villa.

## Roman Wall
30m right of The Ramps is a roofed left-hand section and a main wall. Home to the hardest testpieces. Hard problems aside, doing *Senator*, *Gladiator* and *Arête Eliminate* on their own make the long drive worth it. A sit-down start from the big flake on the left has been done.

**43 Musgrovel**  Font 5+
**44 Rollerball**  Font 6a+. Wild stuff. The roof and wall left of the cave. Expect some heart-flutter.
**45 Little Grunt**  Font 4+. A butch struggle out of the cave.
**46 Roof 1**  Font 6a. Sit-down start. *Chris Sowden*
**47 Roof 2**  Font 6a. Sit-down start. *Chris Sowden*
**48 Little Arête**  Font 6a. Sit-down start. The arête on the seperate block facing the next problem. *Chris Sowden*
**49 Fangy Mouth**  Font 6b. Risk your hands in the mouth to gain a rounded finish. *Chris Sowden*
**50 Crack**  Font 3
**51 Shekels**  Font 6a. Reachy. The crack is out.
**52 Left O'Rib**  Font 6c. Sit-down start. *Steve Rhodes* From a standing start, traversing left to join *Shekels* is **Sinistra** (Font 5+).
**53 Right O'Rib**  Font 6b. Sit-down start *Steve Rhodes*
**54 Good Enough**  Font 3. Layback the big crack.
**55 Tiny Corner**  Font 7b. Levitate up the feature. Font 7b+ from a sit-down start. *Andy Swann*
**56 Jumping Left**  Font 7a. Dyno leftwards to the big pocket. *Robin Ward or Jon Pearson*
**57 Trend Rights**  Font 7a. Use little crimps to move right. *Jon Pearson*
**58 Senator**  Font 5+. Superb. Up the crack, left to a jug and finish right. Font 6a from sitting. Photo on page 625.
**59 Gladiator's Arête**  Project. Wrestle with the elephant's bum arête direct.
**60 Gladiator**  Font 5+. A great expedition from the left arête moving right onto the top wall. Font 6a from a sit-down start and slopers.
**61 Ahenobarbus**  Font 6b. Lunge from the break to the high hold. *John Hunt*
**62 Wall Direct**  Font 6c. Excellent. From the break to the high sloper.
**63 Slave**  Font 5+. Reachy.
**64 Arête**  Font 5
**65 Top Traverse**  Project..
**66 Middle Traverse**  Font 7a. A classic. *Andy Swann*

## The Ramparts
Immediately right of Roman Wall, this block is just separated from the escarpment. There is a good cave for shelter or for playing dens.

**67 Arête**  Font 5. **Arête Eliminate** starts from a sitter and eliminates the big break at Font 6a.
**68 Wall**  Font 4+
**69 Overhang**  Font 4+
**70 Scoop Wall**  Font 4+

628  Yorkshire Gritstone

## The Villa - ROUNDHILL

There are three tiny problems on the little wall just to the right. Further right, around and behind the boulder, is a blunt rib. The problems are short and steep. **Wall and Rib** (Font 5) climbs the left side of the rib and **Scoop Direct** (Font 4+) takes the right-hand side.

Rightwards and back towards the track is a small cracked pinnacle.

**71 South Arête** Font 5. Sit-down start. A fun problem with a trapped wobble stone.
**72 East Finger Wall** Font 5. Sit-down start. Possible with or without the arête. Both are worthwhile.
**73 Lower Wall** Font 5. Sit-down start.
**74 Tiny Wall** Font 5. Sit-down start.
**75 Finger Holds Traverse** Font 6a.

There is the potential for some other problems on the left of the front face.

### The Villa
The boulder opposite the face of Roman Wall has a wide crack the west face. Start on the sharp arête facing the dam moving anti-clockwise. Graded for standing starts; but *Arête* to *Right Step* have all been done from a sit-down start.

**76 Arête** Font 3+
**77 Right of Scoop** Font 3
**78 Top Pocket** Font 3
**79 Left of Crack** Font 4. Layback the left edge. The crack is Font 3.
**80 Tiny Pocket** Font 5
**81 Large Pocket Finish** Font 5
**82 Blunt Arête** Font 5
**83 Right Step** Font 5
**84 Scoop it Left** Font 5
**85 Scoop it Right** Font 5

**86 Wall Arête** Font 4. The arête on the left-hand side.
**87 Steve Rhodes' Warm Up (!)** Font 4+. Great warm up. Traverse the whole block with hands on top.

### The Back Of The Villa
A good bet in poor weather.

**88 Genuinely Easy** Font 3. (Font 5 from a SDS).

The next three problems all start hanging the break:

**89 Weather Window** Font 5. Grope for the huge undercut in the break and use pockets on the head wall.
**90 Use the Corner** Font 5. The wall using the corner at the top. Eliminating the corner is Font 5+.
**91 Corner Climb** Font 3
**92 Dyno** Font 5+
**93 Very Squeezed In** Font 5+. Claw up the slopers and crimps.
**94 Looks Harder** Font 5. From under the little roof, gain the bigger sloper and go for the top.

### Circuit 4 - The Bonus Boulders Sit-Down Circuit
All problems are graded from sit-down starts but most are fun from standing.

### Bonus Boulder 1
Hidden away 10m right of The Ramparts, this boulder has a fine horizontal seam full of holds and some neat problems.

**95 Opening Wall** Font 4. Hang the seam, grab the lip and go.
**96 Severus** Font 5. A great gymnastic problem.
**97 Snake Flake** Font 4. Up the prominent flake.
**98 Boulder 1 Traverse** Font 5+

# ROUNDHILL - Bonus Boulders

## Bonus Boulder 2
40m right is a well featured boulder with an undercut prow.

**99 Mega Traverse** Font 5+. Shimmy along the principal ledge in either direction.
**100 Converger I** Font 5+. Rounded.
**101 Converger II** Font 6a
**102 Bulbous** Font 5+
**103 Many Holds** Font 5+

## Bonus Boulder 3
Move right again for 20m for this block.
**104 Bonus Traverse** Font 7a+. Descending left-to-right traverse.
**105 To Horn** Font 5+. A hard start off the lowest seam holds.
**106 Pompey Moon** Font 6a. Follow the crescent of improving holds from a poor sloper. Hands start below the lip-holds at this grade.
**107 Tough's Arête** Font 3

## Bonus Boulder 4
The last boulder in this group, 20m right, is the one with the mighty line of roofs. Recorded as being taken in at least four places from sit-down starts (from Font 4 to Font 6b).

Following the track further and **White Lodge Crags** are reached. These have been climbed on and are left for the really adventurous to rediscover for themselves.

### First Ascent Information & A Brief History
*Tony Barley first climbed here in 1991 prior to his extensive explorations at Sypeland. The Romans beat him to it and the boulders sit astride what could be on an offshoot of one of their military roads. Barley took this as inspiration for many of the names. The vast majority of the problems with unattributed first ascents above belong to him.*

*Chris Sowden, Robin Barley, Nick Barley, Dave Musgrove, Steve Blake, John Earl, Mike Gray, Steve Rhodes, Bob Smith, Andy Swann, Jon Pearson and Francis Holland have all been active in the area over the years, with some of the problems formally recorded, others not.*

*Barley passed his secret notes over to John Hunt in 2008 and Chris Sowden generously posted his notes and amendments to support the compilation of the above crag description. These notes also detail three other boulders with at least twelve more problems to the right of the main group. The Bonus Boulders are the work of Chris Sowden and friends whilst the problems on The Back of the Villa were first recorded by John Hunt.*

# The Wall Boulders - CLINT CRAGS

# clint crags
by **John Hunt**

OS Ref: SE 161 778
Altitude: 300 m

A collection of boulders and a massive dirty quarry above Leighton Reservoir. The following covers two of the natural bouldering sectors.

The Wall Boulders are a nice safe venue for teams with small children in tow as the surrounding area is grassy and flat. The Optical Illusion Boulders are unsuitable for kids due to the concealed drops and jumbled blocks, though there are some quality easier lines.

**Routes and Bouldering:** A circuit of 26 problems is described here. More have been done on the moor above and on the little edge to the south.

**Parking and Approach:** As for Roundhill. Once through the gate on the left at the end of the dam, follow the obvious wide track in a north-easterly direction. Pass several gates and stiles until The Wall Boulders come into view. About 0.6 miles. See map on page 606.

**Access:** Restrictions as for Roundhill boulders. Please do not approach from the dam of Leighton Reservoir. The warden is very friendly, but Yorkshire Water have had to close this approach due to public liability concerns.

### The Wall Boulders
The first boulder set into the wall has **Woodlice Manor** (Font 3) which climbs the blasted flakes left of the rear arête; (**1**) **Over Wall Arête** (Font 4) is, well, the arête over the wall (the wall without the arête is Font 5). The arête and centre wall with the shallow pockets have been climbed.

**The Main Boulder** has **Boot Jam** (Font 3) up the crack between the boulders; (**2**) **Scooped Arête** (Font 5) up the tricky dusty arête; (**3**) **Centre of Slab** (Font 5) is excellent and goes from the good pocket; (**4**) **Arête** (Font 6a) up the wall using the arête; (**5**) **Right of Arête** (Font 6b) uses tiny holds, no footholds, and the arête; (**6**) **Backward J** (Font 6c) The best problem hereabouts (photo on page 632). From the shallow flake grab the large sloper on the right. Deft footwork is required for success; (**7**) **Long Lob** (Font 7a) apes from a low layback in the arête to better holds. Don't evolve too much; (**8**) **End Wall** (Font 5) where everything's in, but it's still thought provoking.

There is a fun boulder down and left of the main group which contains **Crusty slab** (Font 2). Climb it or go for a fun run up it.

**The School House** is the boulder in the wall to the left of the main boulder. The left side of the front face (**9**) is Font 3. Use the (**10**) **Two Chicken Heads** (Font 4) to climb the centre of the wall and don't be fooled by the gentle angle; (**11**) **Grooves** (Font 3) the highball groove system to the right; (**12**) **School Me** (Font 6a) is the intricate wall and arête to the right (beware the wall). Over the wall and starting with the lowest level exam first: (**13**) **A2** (Font 6a) hangs the middle chicken head and the crimp beside it. Move right to the upper rail and go for the top; (**14**) **AS** (Font 5+) goes straight from the upper rail to the top whilst a better problem is **GCSE** (Font 5) which uses holds to the right and the upper rail; next is (**15**) **Easy Crack** (Font 3).

Almscliff to Slipstones

# CLINT CRAGS - The Optical Illusion Boulders

It looks magnificent as you approach it, but proximity brings it down to size. **The Optical Illusion Boulders** however, have some classic problems.

Clearly visible from the parking; the easiest approach is to go to the Wall boulders, cross the wall where it is broken down and go rightward around the spoil heap. From left-to-right on the small left hand block is **Left Edge** (Font 4) the (16) **Centre Wall** (Font 4) and the (17) **Right Edge** (Font 3) taking the right side, using the arête at the top. (18) **Ladder** (Font 2) climbs the easy wall.

The next three problems all finish magnificently over the capping roof on good holds. (19) **Wacky Death-trap** (Font 6b) boldly takes the arête above the hole; (20) **Princeps** (Font 6a) has super moves up the centre of the wall whilst (21) **Right Arête** (Font 5+) is a good introduction to the previous two routes. The block to the right has the fun (22) **Break, Slopers, Top** (Font 5+) and (23) **Pull** (Font 4) from a sitter and the big incut hold. Three brilliant easier problems remain on the slab, (24) **Sublime Slab Left** (Font 2+). Just left of the slab, the facet is the best problem on the boulder...a lovely Font 3+; (25) **Sublime Slab Middle** (Font 2+); (26) **Sublime Slab Right** (Font 2).

Tony Barley climbed eleven routes in the extensive quarry in the early 1990s (from HS 4a through to E1 5b) though it is difficult to pinpoint exactly which from his sketches; there is the potential for hundreds of others although the large clay-slope top-outs leave much to be desired, with very few belay opportunities. Above the quarry and a few hundred metres to the east are several problems behind a tabletop block, again, a Barley find, and graded between Font 3 and Font 5+.

### First Ascent Information
*This is fairly unclear. Tony Barley pointed this craglet out to John Hunt who produced the first mini guide. On The Wall Boulders, Francis Holland did* **Centre of Slab**, **Arête** *and* **End Wall** *in April 2006; Jon Pearson accounted for* **Long Lob***. Other teams have been active in the area with little recorded. The huge quarry has evidence of climbing.*

John Hunt on **Backward J** (Font 6c+). Page 631
Photo: John Hunt collection

# arnagill

by **Tony Barley**

OS Ref: SE 152 757
Altitude: 280 m

The connoisseur's connoisseur crag. If the routes were at Brimham they'd be classics. The Arnagill valley buttresses stretch extensively across the partly wooded, partly moorland area in the magic of the upper valley. Gushing streams, waterfalls, diverging valleys, unspoilt oak wood, complete with a prominent stone built tower all contribute to the area's magnificent beauty.

**Routes and Bouldering:** A dozen routes although the routes on Folly crag by the waterfall see little traffic and are generally out of condition. All Black Buttress and Sandhurst Walls have excellent steep climbing and are generally clean. There are various boulders scattered in and above the valley with around 20 problems in total and the cleanest, and best bouldering to be had is on Arnagill Slab.

**Parking and Approach:** Parking as for Roundhill. See map on page 606. Two approaches are then possible:

**1:** Follow the approach as for the Roundhill boulders. Go beyond the boulders on the track for half a mile until a distinct path on the right cuts back north-west, past grouse butts in the direction of the castellated folly. Follow this path for 150m and carefully scramble down into the wood on a line adjacent to the waterfall. Folly Crag is to the left and Sandhurst Wall to the right.

**2:** From the far end of the dam, go through the gate on the right and follow the track along the south-east bank of Roundhill reservoir. The track will cut right over the six-arched masonry bridge but continue straight on, over the fence and for a further half a mile on the faint path adjacent to the reservoir left spur. Cross the small Arnagill dam, go 10m left to a 'pipe' stile over the stone wall. Walk across the field with All Black Buttress and Sandhurst Walls first encountered on the left.

Both options take around 30 minutes. The folly is a good landmark to aim for once in the area as all climbing sectors can be easily reached from it but beware the bottom of the valley as this can be particularly boggy.

**Access:** This crag is on access land under the current CRoW arrangements. It is on a grouse moor so clearly needs to be avoided when a shoot is in progress. Whichever approach taken involves crossing walls or fences, so care and discretion are required. No dogs.

# ARNAGILL - All Black Buttress

## All Black Buttress
The imposing undercut buttress. An extremely technical left arête and front wall show evidence of climbing but, as yet, no one's come forward to claim.

### 1 Think on Tha' Nose  E3 6a   8m   ★
An excellent line with a committing and technical finish. Tackle the right arête of the buttress on the left side until all but the final move. Tough for the short.
*Stuart Lancaster, Robin Nicholson   12th May 2011*

## Sandhurst Wall
The steep flat wall high on the bank 40m right of All Black Buttress and 30m left of the waterfall. The first route is on a clean wall in the bay just before the main wall.

### 2 Swerve To Leave  HVS 5a   8m
From the right arête, move into the centre of the wall and continue traversing to finish up the left arête.
*John Hunt, Scott Walker   10th May 2008*

### 3 Mosside  VS 4c   6m
On the little tower abutting the main wall, climb the overhanging face to a mossy finish.
*John Hunt (solo)   10th May 2008*

### 4 In the Nick of Time  E3 5c   9m   ★★
A clean and exciting route. Tackle the crackline and pockets in the middle of the wall.
*Nick Barley, Robin Barley, Tony Barley   21st September 1997*

### 5 In the Reach of Nick  E3 6a   9m   ★
The demanding right arête gained from the front face.
*Nick Barley, Robin Barley, Tony Barley   21st September 1997*

## Folly Crag
Continue to the right for 60m, across the waterfall, to the wide undercut buttress directly below the tower folly. Sadly an area that has been reclaimed by mother nature and will need some work before climbing. All climbs are between 10 and 12m high; the first starts just left of the pointed basal boulder in the undercut cave. **Break for Cover** (HVS 5b) climbs pockets and good holds to the rail then cuts right to the shallow leftward slanting line before moving up and awkwardly rightwards to the horizontal break. Traverse left and up past the protruding birch; **Nightflight** (HVS 5a) takes the short curving crack passed the slanting line crack and up to gain a ledge below the slab. Climb the slab, moving leftwards to a bulge which is past with difficulty to finish past the tree.

On the right is an overhanging undercut buttress above the wall. **Heart Breaker** (E3 6a) starts in the niche on the left side and moves up and rightwards to a horizontal crack in the front of the face. It continues left to an essential 'friend' pocket in the next rail and traverses left to the edge. Straddle the arête, move up and gain the finishing slab with difficulty; **Brave Heart** (E1 5c) goes from the niche to gain the front face and up left to the friend pocket. Traverse right then steeply up the middle on incut holds to a scoop. Move left to a steep finish; **Early Warning** (E2 5c) The blunt extreme right arête of the buttress, finishing with the most difficult move on the right

## Arnagill Slab - ARNAGILL

wall; **Mitral** (VS 5a) takes the right wall and steep arête on the narrow buttress to the right.

Two boulders (**Buzzard and Squirrel Block**) below the crag were cleaned off back in the 1990s giving three problems each between Font 4 and Font 5+. There are some more boulders in the upper depression behind the folly. A clean arête is worth seeking out.

Prominent high on the far side of the valley is **Arnagill Slab**; quite disappointing in itself but the impressive walls around it may yet yield testpieces. The climbs are opposite Sandhurst Wall and can be reached directly across the marsh. Possibly the best approach is to come in from the Roundhill Boulders path and curve round the folly tower to drop into the rocks from above. The approach is difficult whichever way you choose. The rock is variable so care is needed. **Cut the Crap** (Font 6a/E2 6a) takes the slabby wall and shallow rightward leaning scoop; **Arna Arête** (Font 5+/E2 5c) is the steep wall and then arête, finishing on its right; **Slippery Jim** (Font 4+) the short vertical finger crack; **Gym Slip** (Font 4) from the grooved base and up right; **Peasy** (Font 3) from the flat boulder and up; **Weasy** (Font 2) straight up 1.5m left of the edge; **Easy** (Font 1) from the same start take the easiest line rightwards; **Edgy** (Font 2) the right edge; **Slant** (Font 4+) layback strenuously up the slanting crack and climb the wall direct to the apex; **Pyramid** (Font 4) goes rightwards up the lower pyramid and layback onto the upper slab.

To the right of *Arna Arête* are four problems on short steep walls. There are also a couple of problems on a lower level slab in the corrie. Nothing has been formally recorded in the amphitheatre of buttresses up behind.

**Further First Ascent Information.**
*All climbs on Folly Crag were lead or soloed by Tony Barley between July 1994 and May 1999. His second for **Break for Cover**, **Heartbreaker** and **Braveheart** was Robin Brown. All Arnagill Slab problems were the work of Tony and Robin Barley between April 1995 and September 1997. This crag write up is based on a previously unseen text from Tony Barley, revamped by John Hunt.*

---

## flaystones
OS Ref: SE 063 725   Alt: 439m

We have covered some fairly remote crags in this volume of the guide and perhaps this place wins the prize for most "out there". Nestled high above Backstean Gill, (Stean Moor, Upper Nidderdale) lies this north-facing outpost which mainly consists of one big wet green roof. The best approach is by mountain bike departing northwest from Middlesmoor up the moor lane and then on the left fork after 700m. After 2km take a left turn downhill passing a beck then a cattle grid after 500m. Continue a further 2.75km, high above How Stean Beck, where a left turn crosses it, staying left on the track to reach the rain gauge in Backstean Gill (leave bikes here). The crag is high on the hillside to the left (map essential for a visit). The only recorded route is **Far from the Madding Crowd** (HS 4b) by Mick Darfield and Andrew Lawrence (29th August 2008) which takes the left-hand corner of the rippled wall just right of the overhangs. Perhaps one for the walkers and mountain bikers amongst you. Or does that huge roof yield anything ?

Photo: John Hunt

Midway on our life's journey, I found myself
In **dark woods**, the right road lost. To tell
About those woods is hard-so tangled and rough
*From The Divine Comedy (Inferno) by Dante Alighieri*

# Hetchell
## & Outlying Crags

Adi Gill flying high on **Crutch** (HVS 5b). Page 649. One of the great prizes of the wooded wonderland that is Hetchell.
Photo: Mike Hutton

| | |
|---|---|
| **Hetchell** | **641** |
| Spofforth Pinnacles | 652 |
| Plompton Rocks | 660 |
| Henry Price | 662 |
| Adel Crag | 664 |

# Hetchell & outlying crags - Chapter Map

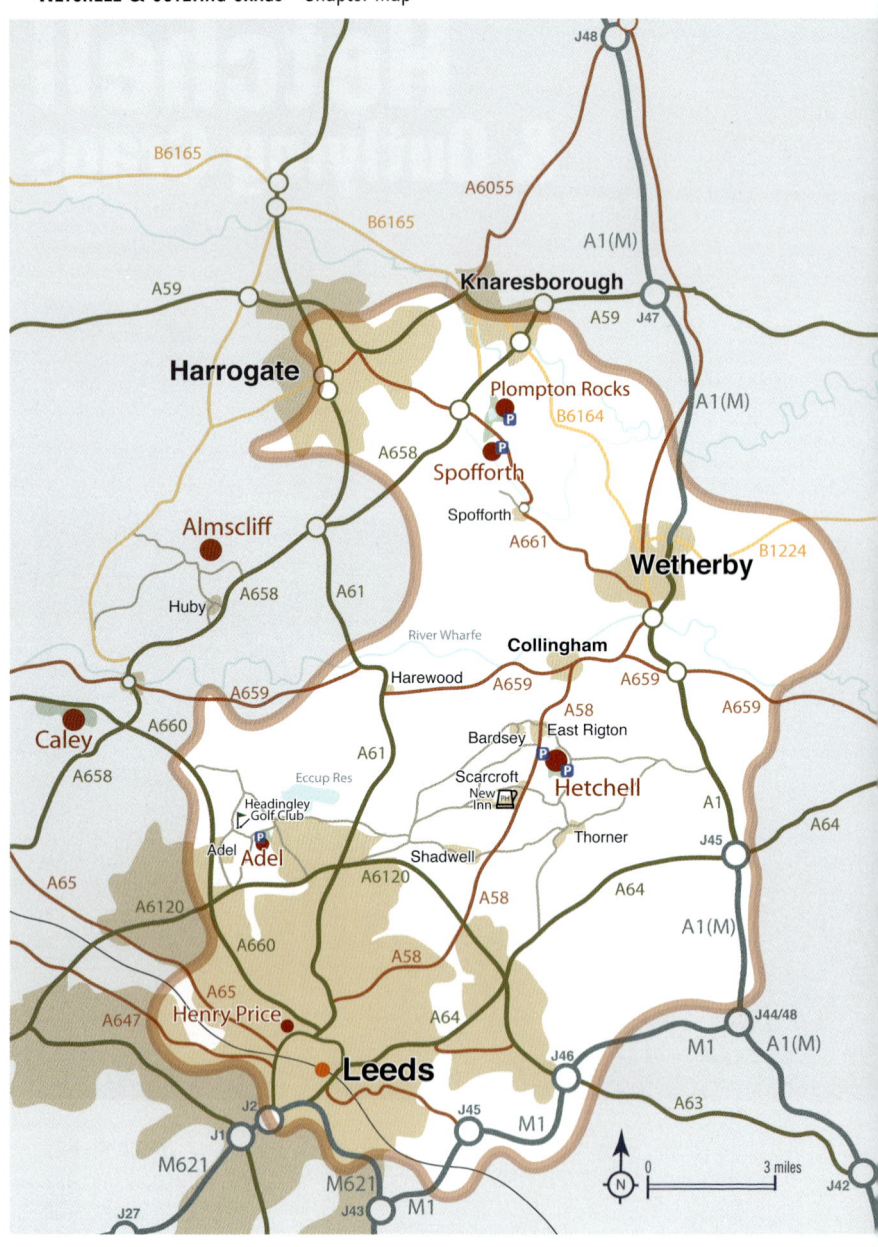

638 — Yorkshire Gritstone

## Crag Map - HETCHELL

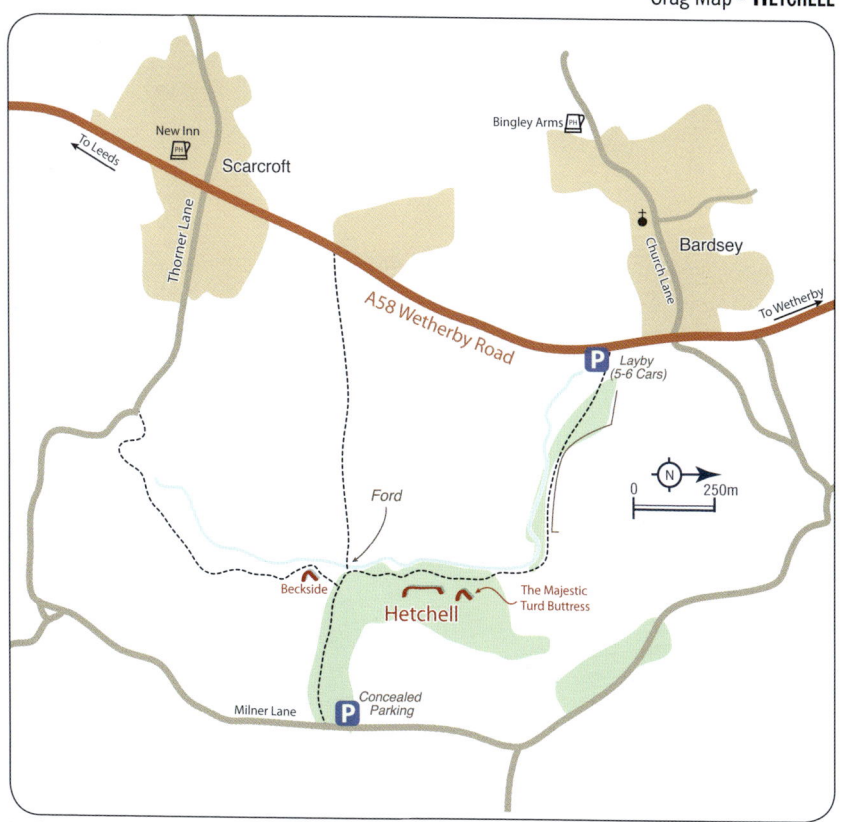

Hetchell Crag

Almscliff to Slipstones

639

Arifa Chakera excellently spotted by Ethan and Adi on **Cassius Crawl** (HS 4b). Page 649.
Photo: Mike Hutton

# hetchell
by **Matt Kilner**

OS Ref: SE 376 424  Altitude: 90m

Out on the eastern front, Hetchell stands as the last bastion of the mighty Yorkshire gritstone empire. It guards a sylvan hillside near the village of Bardsey and the earthworks of an old Roman settlement named Pompocali, the inspiration for many of the crag's imperial-themed route names. It is a unique crag to Yorkshire as it climbs something more akin to sandstone. This means there are holds and rock features to get you salivating at the thought of pulling on - jugs, pockets, droopy flutings and its main feature, slopers galore. It also means occasional holds breaking, and sandy rock, but come to Hetchell with a positive outlook and you will not be disappointed.

**The Climbing:** 60 routes and lots of bouldering with a couple of three-star HVS classics in *Wailing Wall* and *Crutch*, plus slightly more serious E-grade fun on the likes of *Livia* and *Dead Angst*. Fans of sideways climbing will be in traverse heaven and are guaranteed a workout on what was local climbing legend Al Manson's grit training playground back in the day. Be prepared for bold climbing, little in the way of gear, but good landings. Solo the route or bring a pad and treat it as a highball, either way you will have fun. Most of the routes can be started as boulder problems, the classics are mentioned in the text and highballers will get plenty of kicks. Some choose to top rope – if this is the case please ensure you protect the top of the route from wear.

**Conditions and Aspect:** The crag faces west-south-west and really comes into its own in the spring and the autumn, when light can reach all of the buttresses. The main buttress can be climbed on all year-round but needs a few days of dry weather to be at its best. Avoid climbing on Hetchell after rain as the rock softens and risks being worn away. Holds can also snap so take care (take heed of this - it doesn't make Hetchell your wisest choice for pushing into the next grade). Make sure you bring something to clean your shoes to protect the soft rock - a little consideration will ensure the classics remain for the next generation.

**Parking and Approach:** The nearest parking to the crag is in a set of lay-bys by the main entrance to Hetchell Wood on Milner Lane (**Parking GPS: 53.875278,-1.423601**). This is very secluded and suffers from more than its fair share of car crime. Approaching on the A58 from Leeds (towards Wetherby) take the right turn into Thorner Lane at the Scarcroft crossroads (New Inn pub on your left). Just under a mile along this road is a triangular intersection. Turn left here (signposted East Rigton and Collingham) onto Milner Lane and follow it for half a mile to reach the lay-by on the left, just after the bridleway entrance to Hetchell Wood. The bridleway heads west, then north, for 500m before the main crag is reached.

Alternatively, safer parking can be found on the opposite side of the woods (**Parking GPS: 53.882166, -1.439727**). From the New Inn crossroads, continue for a further three-quarters of a mile towards Wetherby on the A58 until the lay-by with space for a few cars can be seen on the right (by the entrance to the bridleway). The best option is to U-turn at the wide entrance to Bardsey village, just a few hundred yards up the road, then park up. Don't block the gated entrance. Follow the bridleway east, taking the minor track on the left after 100m (through the broken stile). Continue through the wood for 520m until you reach open fields. Head due south for a further 400m, back into the wood, and the crag appears up on the hillside to the left. It is also possible to get a bus from Leeds that will drop you near this parking. Walking time from road to crag: 15 mins.

**Access:** No problems. This is an SSSI so treat the place with respect.

# HETCHELL - Turd Buttress

## The Majestic Turd Buttress
About as esoteric as it gets at Hetchell. Despite its less than inspiring name there are a few routes of worth here, including a classic hard traverse. The top of most of the routes is very overgrown and care should be taken when topping out (many choose to treat the area as highball territory and drop off early). There are two buttresses split by a deep gully and the climbs begin on the left-hand buttress.

**Bronco** (E3 5c), takes the left arête, finishing on the left-hand side, if the ivy allows; **Tear Across the Dotted Line** (E1 6a), climbs the wall using big pockets and a giant's reach to a serious finish, swinging rightwards on suspect holds; **Adamant** (E2 6b), goes up the centre of the wall, just left of the tree, using small finger pockets; the gully to the right, **Proctologist's Delight** (Mod), is normally climbed in its depths and is exceedingly well named. It's a nice bridging problem and a useful descent nearer the entrance.

### 1 Turd  E1 5c   8m
Named after the ancient (Roman?) rock carving that adorns the rock below the problem. Using large holds monkey out right until an exit can be made at the left end of the main roof, level with an old bolt. Highball Font 5+ if you drop off early. (a) **Turd Direct** (E1 5b), climbs direct using a shallow pocket, slopers and whatever brambles you happen upon.
*Al Manson  1976 (both routes)*

### 2 S for B  E2 6b   6m
Difficult moves using undercuts and pockets lead through the left end of the roof. Highball Font 6c+ to the roof.
*Al Manson (solo)  June 1984*

### 3 Preparation H  Font 7b+
Traverse right using an old skyhook chip under the roof until you get to the end. If you're feeling strong, finish back along *Superturd Traverse*.
*Kim Buck, Dave Sarkar  1997*

### 4 Superturd Traverse  Font 6c+
A right-to-left traverse using the crack on the lip of the roof until it's possible to escape through a depression.
*Al Manson (solo)  June 1976*

## Reach For A Peach
Moving 30m to the right (south), this area has its fair share of interesting climbing, a few classic micro-routes and some hard problems. Most can be bouldered out as highballs thanks to the flat landings. Check the topouts first though.

### 5 The Green Wall  Font 3+  (HS 4b)
If you can see past the green you'll find some great holds and moves. A handy tree or Grade II moss climbing complete the adventure.
*Brian Evans  1962*

### 6 Smokeless Zone  Font 4+  (VS 5a)
Climb the difficult wall and rib on small holds with no bridging and definitely no recourse to the chimney.
*Dave Musgrove (solo)  23rd November 1990*

### 7 Hanging Chimney  HS 4b   6m
Really awkward. Don't underestimate the challenge.
*Harold Barraclough, Bill Todd, Ron Tyler  11th February 1962*

### 8 Mitchell's Wall  HVS 5b   7m   ★★
Brilliant. Crimpy moves lead to the crux, stepping right at the top. A quality highball at Font 5. A harder start is (a) **Lunging for Melons**, which joins the route from the base of *Reach for a Peach* and increases it technically to 6c (or Font 6c+ if treated as a boulder problem).
*Chris Mitchell, Allan Austin  17th April 1968*

### 9 Reach for a Peach  Font 7b+  (E4 6c)
Desperate. A route for technical wizards and incorrigible perverts alike! Rockover for the obscene orifice. One finger undercut this and go for the two nipples miles above.

Yorkshire Gritstone

# Reach For A Peach - HETCHELL

Pinch these, think of England and execute the horrendous final moves. The crux is now even harder since the better nipple suffered an unfortunate mastectomy.
*Al Manson Summer 1968* ✦

### 10 Corbel Variation  E3 6b   6m
A poor man's *Lurcio's Lip*. Mantel onto the left protrusion using any trick that you can muster. Then, with some difficulty, use small holds to reach the top.
*Al Manson, Stuart Lindsey   September 1978*

### 11 The Corbel  HVS 5b   6m   ★★
One of the best routes on this part of the crag, requiring flexibility, ingenuity and a stiff pull to make the tricky move from the protrusions at half-height to more positive holds on the upper wall. Finish direct.
*Allan Austin 1962*

### 12 Lend Me Your Ears  E3 6a   15m
From the top of *The Corbel* wander left keeping below the top on reasonable handholds and non-existent footholds to finish in the delightful *Hanging Chimney*.
*Al Manson 1977* ✦

### 13 Low Peach Traverse  Font 7b
A difficult right-to-left traverse keeping low on predominantly good footholds and seriously slopey handholds.
*Al Manson, Rob Gawthorpe   1979*

### 14 Dutch Elm  VS 5a   5m
Tackle the bulging, wrinkled wall without recourse to either *The Corbel* or *Oak Scoop*. Font 4+ for the brave.
*John Harwood   pre-1975*

### 15 Oak Scoop  HS 4b   5m
The moss-filled runnel has some good climbing on finger locks, crimps and anything else you can find beneath the greenery (Font 3+). Sadly the tree is long forgotten.
*John Johnson, Bill Todd   27th January 1962* ✦

### 16 Twin Cracks  HS 4b   5m   ★★
Surprisingly pleasant climbing up the twin cracks. One crack is a lot more useful than the other. Font 3+.
*Harold Barraclough, Ron Tyler, Bill Todd   11th February 1962*

# HETCHELL - Reach For A Peach

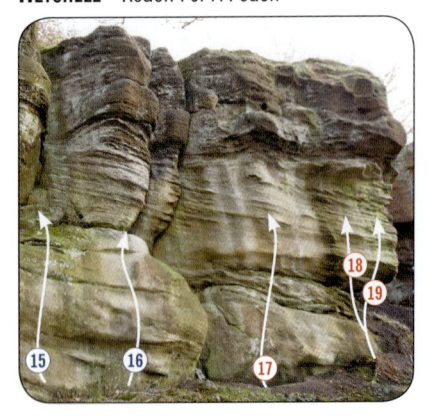

### 17 End Wall Direct  Font 5+
A satisfying, but very escapable, eliminate problem on small holds, avoiding the cracks.

### 18 End Wall  Font 4
Move up and left from the arête.
*Probably Brian Evans or Allan Austin  1962*

### 19 Layback Rib  Font 4+
A neat little problem laybacking the rib. Feels tricky at the top. The eliminate sidewall to the right is Font 6a.

To get back to terra firma you have a choice, either scrabble down the tree at the back of the gully or complete **The End Dismount** onto the next buttress for a jump grade of **J1**.

### Dave's Wall
Across the gap you will find a number of quality roof problems/routes that really blur the distinction between highball bouldering and trad climbing. A mat won't do a lot to soften your fall when you are high up on some of these beauties.

### 20 The Undercut  Font 5
A one-brilliant-move wonder from the undercut 1m left of the arête. **Not the Undercut** (Font 6b), eliminates the undercut and follows the same line.

### 21 The Arête  Font 5
Pinch and high step your way up the left-hand side of the arête.

### 22 Dave's Wall  Font 4+  (HVS 5a)
The undercut wall right of the arête on flat holds, provided the overhanging crab apple tree is not insitu.
*Dave Musgrove  c1975*  ◆

### 23 Soothsayer  E1 6a  6m
Use a pocket on the lip, a two-finger pocket and then a long reach for a small hold and the top.
*Craig Hannah  June 1990*  ◆

### 24 Daniel's Den  HVS 5b  5m  ★★
Three metres right of the arête, campus your way up the steep roof on great holds. You only really need your feet at the end. Higball Font 5.
*Mike Butler (solo)  July 1975*

### 25 Et Tu Brute  E1 5c  6m
Starting at the chockstone under the roof, make a big stretch for holds in the break and then power through the hanging bulge to the top.
*Nigel Baker (solo)  19th February 1998*

### 26 Squirm  Font 2 (to 5)
Squeeze yourself, your child, or your dog up or down the constriction to get the easiest tick on the crag (if you fit).

### 27 Julius Caesar  E1 5c  6m
The hanging arête right of the cleft. No escaping into the gully at this grade.
*Pete Brown (solo)  26th June 2001*

### 28 Augustus  E1 5c  7m  ★★
High and bold but great fun. A superb position. Climb the blank lower wall then, using the undercut, launch out onto the upper wall on big holds.
*John Syrett (solo)  28th March 1972*

### 29 Hadrian's Wall  E4 6b  8m
Power up the gritstone campus board until it runs out and then up the blank wall, avoiding the temptation of the holds on adjacent routes.
*Al Manson (solo)  1983*

### 30 Livia  E2 5c  8m  ★★★
Incredibly rewarding. Commit to an exciting rockover to

## Dave's Wall - HETCHELL

enter the runnel. As your pulse quickens follow small but good holds to a finish just to the left. A low down thread might just protect the rockover, but that isn't very sporting of you is it?
*John Syrett (solo)   28th March 1972* ✦

### 31  Newton John   E3 6a   7m   ★
Tackle the wall using an undercut slot to reach a small ledge on the slab. Now fully committed, teeter up the slab.
*Al Manson   Spring 1978*

### 32  Grease   E4 6c   7m
The bold, blank scoop rewards you with a good pocket near the top. But how will you get there?
*Al Manson   October 1979*

### 33  The Empire Strikes Back   E2 6a   12m   ★
A bizarre line climbing the wall to the right of *Grease* and then pretty much all of the buttress. Climb up to an obvious finger pocket, then gain with difficulty some rounded holds up and left, just shy of the top. Whatever you do, don't top out. Instead, traverse the wall without touching the top to a fitting finale at *Augustus*.
*Dave Musgrove (solo)   21st August 1989*

> **❝ ❞**
>
> I thought I was alone at the crag and was attempting the crux wall solo when Al Manson wandered around the corner. I came down for a chat but we didn't specifically discuss the line I was trying but I knew he'd seen me on it. I asked him if he was climbing but he said no, he was just taking his dogs for a walk, and he wandered off. I made several more attempts before finally committing to the moves and completing the route. When I saw Al a few days later I told him I had done it. He said, "Yes I know. I was watching you from the bushes. I had my boots with me ready to have a go if you'd given up"
>
> Dave Musgrove, on his FA of **The Empire Strikes Back**

### Wailing Wall
Congratulations on persevering. You will now be rewarded with some of the best that the crag has to offer. In general the walls are high, beyond what could be called a highball, and most routes are soloed and are serious.

### 34  Narrow Chimney   VD 3c   7m   ★
For fans of back-and-foot, Hetchell delivers.
*Bill Todd, John Johnson   27th January 1962*

### 35  Veni Veci Oblivisci   HS 4b   8m   ★
"I came I conquered and then I forgot." But you'll not forget whaling the top of this gem.
*Dave Musgrove, Mike Butler   c1975*

### 36  Roman Crack   S 4a   8m   ★
The brilliant crack succumbs to a confident approach. Well-protected and very worthwhile.
*Harold Barraclough, Ron Tyler, Bill Todd   11th February 1962*

### 37  Bob's Traverse   VS 5b   15m   ★
A satisfying left-to-right traverse. From the base of *Roman Crack,* shuffle right along the horizontal break until you reach *Centurion* and finishing holds just when it's getting high (crux). Finish up the crack.
*Bob Knapton (solo)   5th November 1966*

### 38  Tarquin's Terrace   VS 4b   13m   ★
Overshadowed by its big brother next door, to some it's a cop-out, to others it's more than worthy on its own. Beauty is in the eye of the beerholder. If your hands aren't on a huge hold then you're probably off-route.
*Dave Musgrove, Bob Thornton   Easter 1966*

# HETCHELL - Wailing Wall

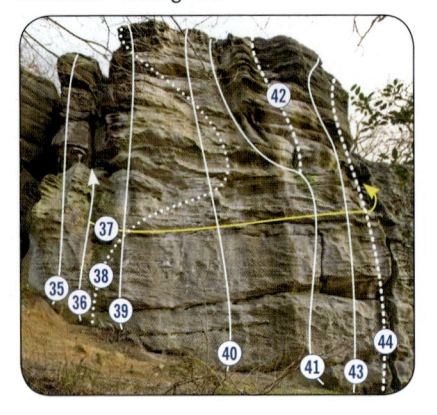

## 39 Caligula  E1 5b  10m  ★
A direct line up the left of the face, crossing *Tarquin's Terrace* twice but avoiding it for much upwards progress as far as you can.
*Dave Musgrove  3rd April 1990*

## 40 Wailing Wall  HVS 5a  10m  ★★★
The route of the crag and worth every one of its three stars. A tricky start (particularly for the short) leads to fantastic jug-hauling and exciting moves up the steep wall. A comforting ledge at half-height allows possibly the only worthwhile protection on the route to be placed and an opportunity to compose yourself for the finish, which takes the wall left of the corner.
*Dave Musgrove (solo)  July 1966*

## 41 Tiberius  E2 5c  11m  ★
A climb of two halves. A tricky boulder start leads into the green hole. Launch out left to reach cracks, holds, gear and the shallow left-facing corner that leads to the top. Originally graded VS 5a, you decide who's right.
*John Syrett (solo)  1972*

## 42 The Fall of the Roman Empire  E4 6a  10m
Follow *Tiberius* to the green hole but ignore the temptation to continue on this line. Instead, climb up and left to ascend the exciting sandy bulges in the groove above. For a more sane Font 5+, escape right at the green hole.
*Justin Vogler (solo)  Spring 1988*

## 43 Dead Angst  E4 5c  10m  ★★
A serious proposition taking the impressive wall with little protection. Use positive edges to gain a large hold and rest at the break, then press on up and diagonally left through the bulging headwall to a sharp handrail. Using a crucial hold on your left, make a long move up and right to finish. If you're not feeling brave you can escape right at the lower break for Font 6a.
*Kim Buck (solo)  10th July 1988*

## 44 When in Rome  E3 5b  9m  ★
Another serious line. Start up the strange scoop and fluting and then continue up the left-hand side of the arête to an exciting finish.
*Dave Musgrove (solo)  1st November 1990*

### The Main Wall
The main event, with traverses that turn your forearms to concrete and bold routes that make mice or men. Superbly sculpted and with class climbs throughout the grades, this is where most earn their Hetchell medals.

## 45 Centurion  S 4a  8m  ★★
Choose your weapon – perfect holds or perfect jams guard the way on this steep crack. Either way, savour every minute. A micro-eliminate, **If Owls Could Talk** (HVS 5b), climbs the narrow wall just right. Holds on routes either side are out; blinkers essential.
*Bill Todd, J. Johnson 27th Jan 1962; Danny Fleming 1998 (Owls)*

## 46 Ripple Arête  VS 5a  9m  ★
Photogenic moves up the front of the arête. Stay away from *Centurion* for the full tick.
*Possibly Paul Exley  pre-1969*

## 47 The Scoop  HVS 5a  9m  ★
A variation to *Ripple Arête*, climbing the scoop to the right.

## 48 Pompeii Chimney  HVD 3c  10m  ★★
A justifiably popular route, welcoming you in with precise bridging and leading to a fairly awkward move at the top.
*Bill Todd, John Johnson  27th January 1962*

Yorkshire Gritstone

**Robin Nicholson** caressing the slopers of **The Standard Traverse** (Font 6a). Page 648
Photo: Mike Hutton

### 49 The Standard Traverse  Font 6a
Top-notch forearm burning horizontal action. A left-to-right traverse starting at the foot of *Pompeii Chimney*, with hands in the break level with *Lurcio's Lip*. Finish up any of the problems on the far right. Photo on page 647.

### 50 The High Traverse  Font 6b+
As for the standard traverse but with feet generally at the level of *Lurcio's Lip*.

### 51 Up Pompeii  E2 6a  10m
Not as easy as it looks, with difficult climbing up the slopers to the right of the chimney. Carry on to the top or escape from the good break at Font 6b.
*Al Manson (solo)  1974*

### 52 Lurcio's Lip  E3 6c  10m  ★
A doddle for those of you with double-joints. For the rest of us, specialist training is needed. Three months of yoga should do. Once warmed up, surmount the lip and carry on up for the full tick, or jump off at a more realistic Font 7a.
*Al Manson (solo)  1974*

### 53 Bell End  E2 5c  11m  ★★
Crimps and promising nodules entice you into the groove. Once there, provided the ivy allows, awkward and serious moves lead through the depression. Holes below the finishing moves allow some protection to be arranged.
*LUUMC  pre-1975*

### 54 Bell Left-Hand  E1 5c  13m
An easier, but less satisfying, alternative to the next route. Escape left from the base of the thin crack, crossing *Bell End* and traversing into *Pompeii Chimney*.
*Dave Musgrove, Mike Butler  7th August 1973*

### 55 Bell  E3 5c  11m  ★★
A superb line following the bottomless diagonal crackline in the centre of the main face. Boulder out the wall and reach the thin vertical crack. Climb this with some difficulty to the sanctuary of the niche. Finish up the cracks out right or, if you are brave, straight up, which is worth at least a grade more.
*Allan Austin, C. Mitchell 17th Apr 1968; Rob Gawthorpe 1980 Direct*

### 56 Hunchback  E4 6b  10m
Climb up to the shallow horseshoe-shaped depression and undercut like crazy until you can reach a poor hold above. Finish direct. At this grade side-runners are allowed at either side, level with the depression. To the first break, via slopers, makes a good Font 6b problem.
*Rob Gawthorpe, Pete Jackson  1979*

### 57 Crutch Direct  E1 5c  10m  ★
A more direct finish to the original, which climbs the scoop above where *Crutch* moves right. Some gardening of the ivy may be required to reveal gear placements and holds but a worthwhile adventure nonetheless.
*Al Manson (solo)  1975*

### 58 Crutch  HVS 5b  11m  ★★★
One of the best here. Climb the groove with some difficulty and when you get to the large boss, reach across right into bucket holds. Swing across, savour the view and sprint to the top. The start itself is Font 4+. Photo on page 636.
*Dave Musgrove (solo)  5th November 1966* ✦

### 59 Rainbow  E1 6a  10m
Tricky moves lead through the left-hand side of the bulge to reach a good break. Step up into the scoop on the right, where you can drop off for Font 6a or, more satisfying, carry on for the full tick.
*Pete Kitson, Al Manson  May 1974*

### 60 Arc En Ceil  E2 6b  10m
A colourful route gaining the break using small but positive holds on the right-hand end of the roof. Jump off at the break for Font 6c or continue directly through the scoop between *Rainbow* and *Cassius* without recourse to either for the full experience.
*Kim Buck (solo)  6th March 1989*

### 61 Cassius Crawl  HS 4b  15m  ★★★
A satisfying route requiring a little commitment to launch out of the groove and along the sideways adventure. Good holds lead the way. Escaping at the scoop is possible at Font 3+. Photo on page 640.
*Brian Evans, Aileen Evans  1962*

### 62 Cassius Direct  VS 4c  10m  ★
Feels bold. A direct mantel finish to the previous route.
*Dave Musgrove, Bob Thornton  Easter 1966*

### 63 The Main Wall Girdle  HVS 5a  36m  ★★★
A brilliant adventure and a great introduction to Hetchell, taking you on a tour of the main crag. If you only do one route here, make sure it's this one.
**1.** Follow *Cassius Crawl* all the way to its final crack but instead of topping out step down into the green niche of *Bell*. Easy but airy moves left bring you to a large platform above *Centurion* and a comfortable belay.
**2.** Descend *Centurion* until you reach a traverse line, which can be followed across to the green hole of *Tiberius*. Move across this hole, stretching leftwards with difficulty to reach the line of *Wailing Wall*. Climb from here diagonally up and left to finish on the last few moves of *Tarquin's Terrace*.
*Dave Musgrove, Bob Knapton (alt leads)  5th November 1966*

### 64 Zig-Zag  VD 3c  7m
Climb the obvious wide cracks.
*Bill Todd, John Johnson  27th January 1962*

### 65 Jim's Wall  Font 4+
Small but positive holds lead the way.
*Jim Worthington (solo)  1968*

### 66 The Right Arête  Font 6a
The technical arête requires a tough pull off the small pocket to get established.

### 67 The Low-Level Traverse  Font 7a
Awesome. Shimmy from right-to-left, keeping hands below the standard traverse, continuing below *Lurcio's Lip* and finishing on the slopers of *Up Pompeii*. Drop off, and take your Font 6c+ tick or allow yourself a couple of minutes to de-pump before pressing on, keeping low all the way to *Caligula*. When you've mastered that lot, try going back along *Bob's Traverse* and the *Standard Traverse* to complete the circuit. The short section from *Up Pompeii* to *Caligula* is Font 6b+.

### 68 The Super Low-Level Traverse  Font 7c
As for the low-level traverse but nothing above a metre and a half allowed. If you do this then you deserve a medal for your dedication to Hetchell. Make sure a friend and tape measure are around to validate your ascent.

### 69 The Right Wall  Font 4+
The wall right of the arête. Topping out is the crux.

### 70 The First Crack  Font 3
The last crack at Hetchell to another fun topout.

# HETCHELL - Beckside Buttress

## Beckside Buttress
Shallow water soloing comes to Yorkshire. From the main crag, drop down to the main path until you get to the stream with the bridge on the right over the ford, which is on the edge of the Pompocali Roman earthworks. Don't cross the bridge but instead, follow the bridleway left up the hill to a gate with a public bridleway marked on the right. Go through the gate and follow the path for about 100m to Beckside Buttress on the left. A number of problems and variations are possible. The best are:

### 71 Tide Mark  Font 6b   7m
Traverse the buttress left-to-right keeping low.

### 72 Tadpole Traverse  VS 4c   10m
Start on the left of the buttress. Pull up below the roof and traverse diagonally right to finish up the right-hand corner.

### 73 Beckside Buttress  VS 5b   6m
From a very tricky start, climb through the undercut wall in the centre of the main face.
*Brian Evans  1962*

## Further First Ascent Information (✦)
**Adamant:** *Climbed by Kim Buck (solo) 4th March 1989*
**Bronco:** *Climbed by Al Manson (solo) 1974/75*
**Cassius Direct:** *The first of Musgrove's additions to the crag uses chipped holds at the top, suggesting it was probably climbed earlier.*
**Crutch:** *Also climbed by Paul Exley at the same time and the name Crutch was carved into the rock below the route, though this has long gone.*
**Dave's Wall:** *All the problems round the descent gully were worked out around 1975 by Dave Musgrove and Mike Butler though they could well have been pre-dated by the other local activists.*
**Mitchell's Wall:** *The hard start Lunging for Melons was added by Kim Buck in October 1989 during his exploration of what was possible on some of the blank walls of Hetchell.*
**Lend Me Your Ears:** *Al "accidentally" wandered across this while checking out the line of Reach for a Peach.*
**Oak Scoop:** *Graded VD with the tree insitu, the demise of the tree to Dutch Elm is well documented through previous Yorkshire Gritstone guides. Its first treeless ascent was recorded by Craig Hannah on 2nd February 1990. It is awaiting its first moss-filled ascent, however.*
**Proctologist's Delight:** *Climbed by Matt Kilner, Andy Hobson 29th October 2010*
**Reach for a Peach:** *Named after a problem in Tuolumne Meadows in the US where Al honed his skills prior to clutching the route from the many who had tried. The crucial nipple parted company not long after and the route once again became a battleground for the first re-ascent sans nipple. Andy Swann was pipped to the post by Kim Buck in October 1990. Kim's excellent description from the 1989 guide is repeated here for posterity.*
**Soothsayer:** *Retro claimed and named by Pete Brown (solo) on 26th July 2001*
**Tear Across the Dotted Line:** *Climbed by Al Manson (solo) 1974/75*
**The Green Wall:** *Formerly known as "The Wall", following a nuclear winter during the cold war it had to be renamed.*
**Wailing Wall:** *Also climbed around the same time by Paul Exley who wrote the crag up and named it for the 1969 guide.*
**Zig Zag:** *Known previously as Cassius Chimney with a left-hand start.*

Yorkshire Gritstone

# Graded List - Hetchell

## Graded List

### ROUTES

**E4**
- Grease (6c)
- Hadrian's Wall (6b)
- Hunchback (6b)
- The Fall of the Roman Empire (6a)
- Dead Angst (5c)

**E3**
- Lurcio's Lip (6c)
- Corbel Variation (6b)
- Lend Me Your Ears (6a)
- Newton John (6a)
- Bell (5c)
- Bronco (5c)
- When in Rome (5b)

**E2**
- Adamant (6b)
- Arc En Ceil (6b)
- S for B (6b)
- The Empire Strikes
- Back (6a)
- Up Pompeii (6a)
- Bell End (5c)
- Livia (5c)
- Tiberius (5c)

**E1**
- Rainbow (6a)
- Soothsayer (6a)
- Tear Across the Dotted Line (6a)
- Augustus (5c)
- Bell Left Hand (5c)
- Et Tu Brute (5c)
- Julius Caesar (5c)
- Turd (5c)
- Caligula (5b)
- Crutch Direct (5b)
- Turd Direct (5b)

**HVS**
- The Corbel (5b)
- Crutch (5b)
- Daniel's Den (5b)
- If Owls Could Talk (5b)
- Mitchell's Wall (5b)
- The Main Wall Girdle (5a)
- The Scoop (5a)
- Wailing Wall (5a)

**VS**
- Beckside Buttress (5b)
- Bob's Traverse (5b)
- Dutch Elm (5a)
- Ripple Arête (5a)
- Cassius Direct (4c)
- Tadpole Traverse (4c)
- Tarquin's Terrace (4b)

**HS**
- Cassius Crawl (4b)
- Hanging Chimney (4b)
- Oak Scoop (4b)
- Twin Cracks (4b)
- Veni Veci Oblivisci (4b)

**S**
- Centurion (4a)
- Roman Crack (4a)

**HVD**
- Pompeii Chimney (3c)

**VD**
- Narrow Chimney (3c)
- Zig-Zag (3c)

**M**
- Proctologists's Delight

### PROBLEMS

**7c**
- The Super Low-Level Traverse

**7b+**
- Preparation H
- Reach for a Peach (E4 6c)

**7b**
- Low Peach Traverse

**7a**
- The Low Level Traverse
- Lurcio's Lip Start

**6c+**
- Superturd Traverse
- Lunging for Melons

**6c**
- Arc En Ceil Start

**6b+**
- The High Traverse

**6b**
- Not the Undercut
- Up Pompeii Start
- Tide Mark

**6a**
- The Standard Traverse
- Rainbow Start
- Dead Angst Start
- The Right Arête

**5+**
- End Wall Direct
- The Fall of the Roman Empire Start

**5**
- The Undercut
- The Arête

**4+**
- Layback Rib
- Smokeless Zone (VS 5a)
- Dave's Wall (HVS 5a)
- Crutch start
- Jim's Wall
- The Right Wall

**4**
- End Wall

**3+**
- The Green Wall (HS 4b)
- Cassius Crawl start

**3**
- The First Crack

**2**
- Boulder Squirm

651

# spofforth pinnacles

by **Simon Kimber & Jack Colbeck**

OS Ref: SE 357 531
Altitude: 48m

A collection of boulders set in a delightful little meadow just off the A661 Harrogate-Wetherby road. Well worth a visit, whether you're a boulderer that's looking for an altogether different scene, an experienced highballer looking to escape the crowds, or a connoisseur of scrittle.

**The Climbing:** Soft sandy rock. Mostly vertical problems with predominantly slopey and scary finishes (novices take note). Low to medium grade bouldering, often rather highball in nature, with good flat landings. Ropes are somewhat superfluous but sticking one in the bag to facilitate rescues is recommended! A stack of pads and a good spotter is the best way to protect the gnarly topouts (often the crux of the problems). Nearly 90 problems, almost all below Font 6c. Do not brush, or the boulders will disappear...

**Conditions and Aspect:** The boulders face in all directions so sun, shade, breeze and shelter can usually be found. The soft rock can be extremely fragile when damp, so give it time to dry out after wet weather.

**Parking and Approach:** Leave Spofforth heading north-east on the A661. After 1.8 miles, park in a small layby on the left-hand side, next to the wooded area opposite Plompton Rocks (**Parking GPS: 53.973316, -1.456802**). If you hit the roundabout (crossing the A658) you've gone about a mile too far north. Space for 3 cars (just) but please don't block the gate and take care when pulling out. Go over the stile and walk along the edge of the field to a second stile. Cross this into the meadow where the main boulders are to be found. (4 mins)

**Access Issues:** All the boulders are situated on private farm land and access issues have been reported in the past. Cow Block and the Hell Hole both lie in the grounds of the farm itself, are currently surrounded by electric fences, and should be considered out of bounds for the time being.

# Introduction - SPOFFORTH

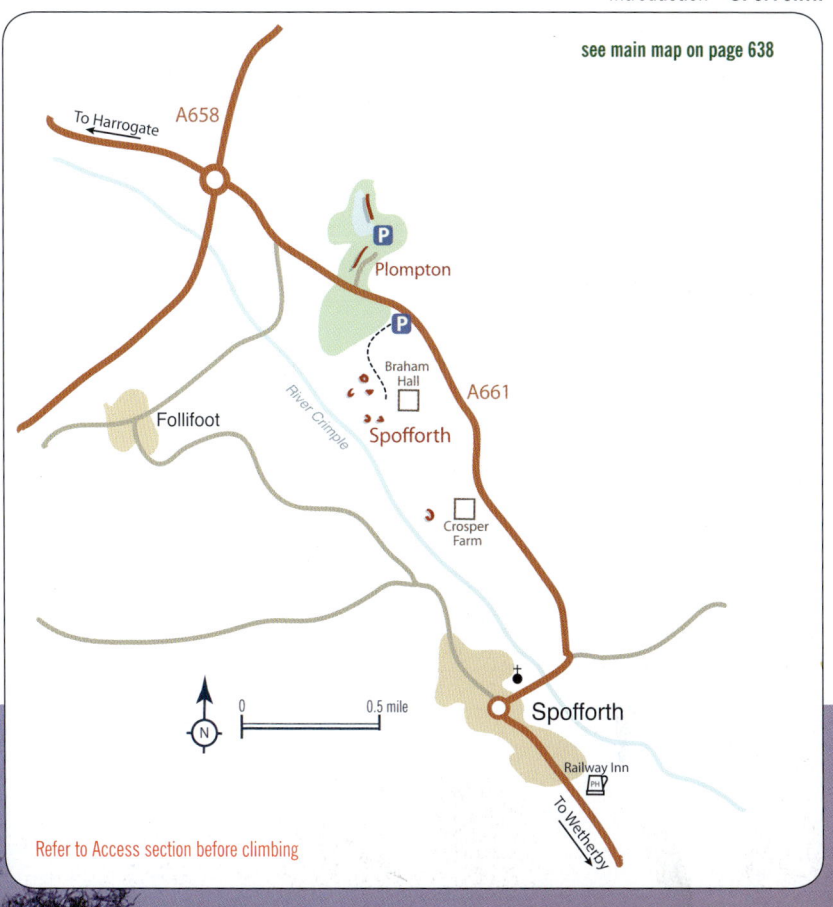

see main map on page 638

*Refer to Access section before climbing*

A coveted problem seen here in a different light. Jamie Moss on **Rock Around The Block** (Font 6b). Page 657.
Photo: Jamie Moss collection.

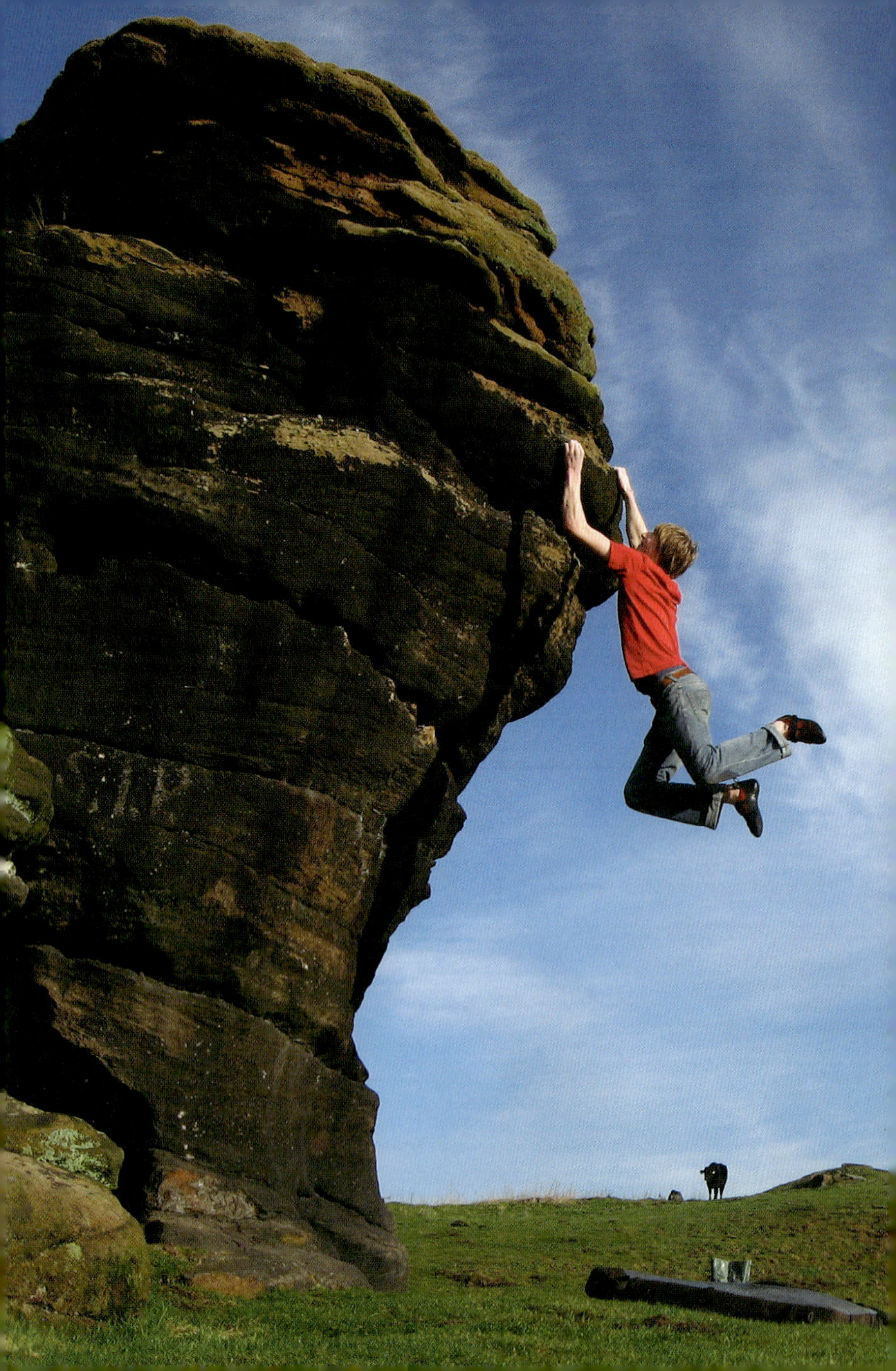

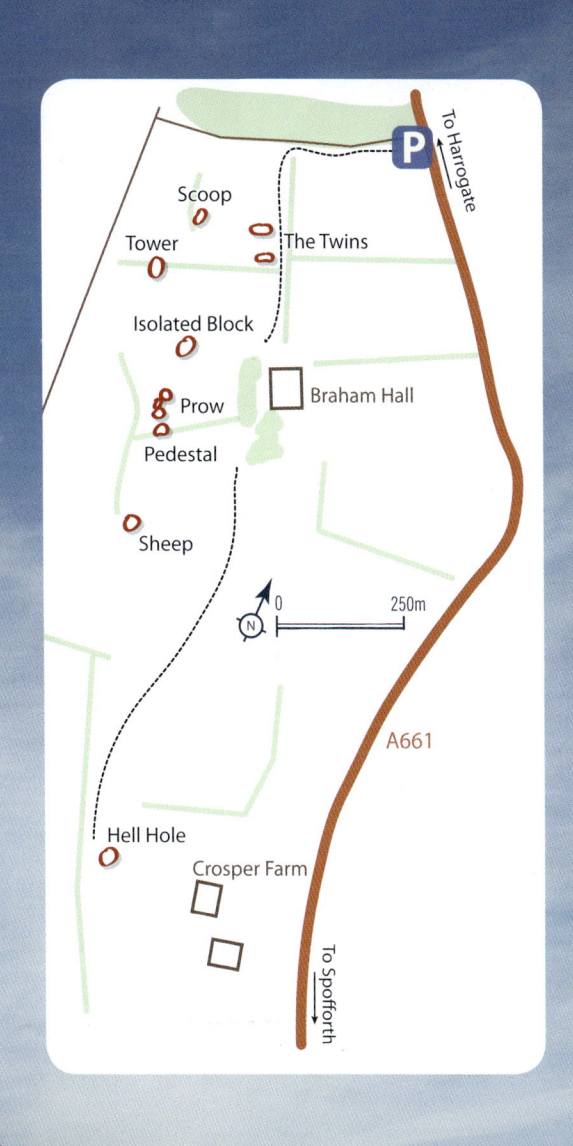

Jack Colbeck sticks the lip on **Pockets Wall** (Font 6a+). Page 658
Photo: Jack Colbeck collection

655

# SPOFFORTH - The Twins

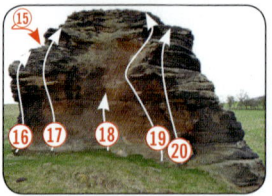

### Left Twin
**1 The Slab** Font 2. The stepped slab. Also started by mantelling over the little roof to the right (Font 3+).
**2 Jamline** Font 4. Romp past the bulge at the notch. The painful jam over the roof is optional, but scary without!
**3 Hang Up** Font 4. Highball. Mantel over the overhang on the south-west corner.
**4 Birds Lavatory** Font 3+. Direct into and out of the limey scoop.
**5 Let Loose** Font 4. Up and over the small bulge then straight up the wall. Sit-down start is Font 5.
**6 Little Cleft** Font 3.

### Right Twin
**7 The Manatee** Font 4+. Grapple with the obvious protrusion on the left of the boulder.
**8 The Whale** Font 3+
**9 Tricky Dicky** Font 3+
**10 South Face Crack** Font 4. Not really a crack, more of a small notch up high.
**11 Whalerider** Font 4. Over the hanging shelf.

### Scoop Block
A big sandy boulder with a little hole through it. The scooped side is exceptionally soft and crumbly. Climb with care.

**12 Scoop Block Arête** Font 1+. The stepped arête on the left edge with the crux at the top. Superb.
**13 Limboist** Font 4+. The overhang above the hole.
**14 South Face** Font 1. Also the way down but best if scoped first.
**15 Green Wall** Font 4. Climb directly up the centre of the north face.
**16 Crumbling Edge** Font 4+. The right side of the north-west arête. Surprisingly solid.
**17 Light Muscovado** Font 5
**18 Where's the Beach?** Font 6a+. The sandy scoop has been climbed with some delicate bridging and an escape left, probably not on the holds that remain though.
**19 Shell Shocked** Font 5+. The bulge on the right of the scoop.
**20 PTSD** Font 5. The smaller bulge above the hole.

### Baby Scoop
The little scoop next to the big one.

**21 The Embalmer** Font 6b. From a sit-down start on crimps under the roof, mantel the lip above an awkward landing.
**22 Deadbeat** Font 5. Mantel the lip.

Fifty metres east of Scoop Block is a small nose with a good warm-up problem (Font 3); useful as an introduction to both the rock type and the committing finishes here at Spofforth.

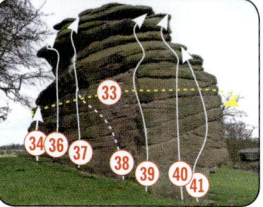

Tower Block - **SPOFFORTH**

## Tower Block
The biggest and best block in the field. Top outs are high and scrittly, best attempted with either a large stack of pads, a reliable spotting team or large cojones. Only the main problems are listed, there's plenty of scope for eliminates and link-ups.

**23 North West Arête** Font 3+. Brilliant. One of the best problems at this grade. Climb the arête, starting just left of the undercut. A sit-down start is Font 5+.

**24 Sandman** Font 6a
Climb the crumbly wall just right of the arête. The sit-down start from the pocket & crimp on the nose just right is excellent (Font 6b+).

**25 Sandman Right** Font 6c+. From a sit-down start on the blunt nose move up and right to an undercut on the face and power up (or crimp through) to the break.

**26 West Face** Font 4+. Another gem. Climb the short steep central rift to finish over bulges.

**27 Rising Traverse** Font 6b. A sit-down start to the right of the crack and traverse the break rightwards. The full traverse starting low from *North West Arête* is a little harder.

**28 Western Edges** Font 6a+. Sit-down start. Muscle over the initial bulge before the harrowing top-out up and right.

**29 Prow** Font 6c. Scary, slopey and scrittly. Mantel directly over the two prows.

**30 Doobie** Font 5+. Sit-down start at a pinch, crank straight up to the ledge. Continue to a scary finish using the slanting crack (or, more sensibly, jump off).

**31 Stone Me** Font 5+. Start by a pebbly hole at head height and climb straight up the wall to finish via the slanting crack.

**32 South West Corner** Font 4+. Sit-down start. Climb the overhanging nose to a tricky finish up a crack.

**33 Rock Around The Block** Font 6b. One of the best problems here. From the ledge on the south face, traverse the block at mid level. Photo on page 652.

**34 Reefer** Font 5. Romp up the wall on slopers.

**35 East South East Route** Font 5+. Climb a shallow groove to a good hole and exit left across the slab.

**36 East South East Direct** Font 6c. Start as before but make two progressively harder mantels to reach the top.

**37 Crimple** Font 6b. Small undercut crimp to sloper. Finish at the pocket up left, or top-out for the full tick.

**38 Curlew** Font 5+. Start near *North East Corner* by a crack. Climb the wall to a horizontal break and move left to a pocket. Go up and left over a bulge to more bird limed holes. Finish over the final overhang which, alarmingly, is detached.

**39 North East Corner** Font 5. The fine arête on its left side. Move right at the top to finish up a slanting crack.

**40 Left Side Story** Font 5. Climb the wall left of centre via a wee hole.

**41 North Face** Font 5. Straight up the centre of the face. Easier variants meander from the true line.

# SPOFFORTH - Isolated Block

**Small Block** is the little boulder next to Tower Block.
**42 Mini** Font 5. Sit-down start from obvious holds on the left of the block. Follow the holds rightwards and over the overhang.
**43 Me** Font 6a+

## Isolated Block
About 200m right of Tower Block. The top layer of this boulder consists of barely held together coarse pebbles coated with thick flaky lichen. Topping out can be frightening, but at least the landing is good.
**44 Graffiti Arête** Font 4+
**45 Pockets Wall** Font 6a+. Climb the steep wall right of the graffiti using obvious pockets. Photo on page 654.
**46 Isolated Crack** Font 5
**47 Isolated Wall** Font 5+. Climb boldly up the wall on green and sometimes friable holds.
**48 Side-show** Font 4. Take the left edge of the bulging north face, finishing on grassy holds.
**49 Isolation Ward** Font 6a. Climb the bulging wall on dubious holds.
**50 North Face Groove** Font 5.
**51 Sideline** Font 3. Climb the short wall.

## Prow Blocks
These are small overhung blocks amongst the gorse south of Isolated Block. **How** (Font 2+) goes straight up the left wall; **Now** (Font 2+) starts up the faint groove and exits through the protruding roof; **Brown** (Font 4+) starts at a rounded flake, climbs direct onto the ledge and tops out above the triangular niche; **The Prow** (Font 4) heaves over the overhanging west nose.

**52 Pot Scoop** Font 3+. The central scoop.
**53 Shelfelmount** Font 4+
**54 Stepped Arête** Font 4+
**55 Set Square** Font 4+

## Pedestal Block
The round block next to the fence has a few nice problems. Scope the descent on the back first.
**56 Pedestal Arête** Font 4. Delicious. Climb the blunt arête directly above the pedestal. A sit-down start from the right (a) is excellent (Font 6a+).
**57 The Scoop** Font 5+. A quality problem crimping diagonally leftwards through the scoop.
**58 Exclusive** Font 3
**59 Lime Hole** Font 3+

Yorkshire Gritstone

Sheep Block - **SPOFFORTH**

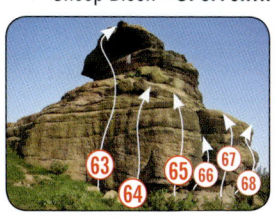

### Sheep Block
Follow the fence up the hill, over the stile and 230m into the next field to find this rough pebbly prow-on-a-plinth.

**60 Lanolin** Font 2+
**61 Nose Direct** Font 5+. Press and reach. Lovely.
**62 Off the Wall** Font 3+

### Cow Block
This sandy lump lies 400m south of Pedestal Block. Very close to the farm, and currently behind an electric fence.

**63 Green Lining** Font 6a. Climb direct from the short vertical crack onto the ledge. Top out via a niche in the roof.
**64 Dewlap** Font 6a+. From a sit-down start at the flake, ascend sandy slopers.
**65 Bull Nose** Font 4. The blunt arête to finish easily up ledges. A sit-down start from the little flake is nasty (Font 6c).
**66 Heifers Cleft** Font 3. Layback the obvious short, wide crack. May as well sit it for an extra couple of moves.
**67 Cattle Prod** Font 6b
**68 Cow Poke** Font 6c+

The cleft on the south face is **The Inquisitive Bullock** (Easy); exit either left or right. The slabby arête right of the cleft is even easier whilst the wall and overhang on the east face goes at Font 4 and is known as **The Gathering**.

The block in the next field is known as **Horse Block**. **Ben** (Font 4) climbs the slabby front face onto the ledge and up the wall above and left of two small rock horns; **Billy** (Font 3+) tackles the very blunt right arête to a tricky move onto the ledge. Top out straight up; **Rosie** (Font 3) climbs past the big hole just right of the arête then the wall above directly and **Diva** (Font 3) starts on the ledge on the right and makes an awkward mantel on to the top.

**Hell Hole Block** lies on the grounds of Crosper Farm surrounded by an electric fence. There's the potential for some pumpy traverses along the low overhang that curves around half the boulder but the recorded problems are as follows. **The Nose** (Font 6b) mantels the nose at the north end of the block with difficulty; **Hell's Bells** (Font 4+) climbs the overhanging crack right of the nose, finishing delicately up the wall above; **Wee Nick** (Font 5) takes the face on the right to a scoop hold in the wall above; **Devil Make Care** (Font 4+) takes the wall right again and is climbed via undercuts, finishing boldly up the wall or sneaking into the hole on the right; **The Trunk** (Font 4) climbs the 'trunk' on the south face and finishes up the shallow crack; **Leftward Ho!** (Font 4+) is on the north east face, left of the crack, and climbs the bulge to an escape along the grassy finish as for *Hell Crack*; **Hell Crack** (Font 5) takes the brutal crack to a grassy finish; **Poisson Rouge** (Font 4) is the next crack to the right.

# PLOMPTON ROCKS - Introduction

# plompton rocks

OS Ref: SE 356 537
Altitude: 55 m

A collection of steep, rough and predominantly green buttresses lurking in the bluebell woodland and ornamental gardens of Plompton Rocks. A beautiful spot, with most of the climbing hidden within the trees south of the lake. Just a shame you can't climb here. 'Covert Ops' climbers need only apply.

**The Climbing:** Over 20 routes, between VD and E4 recorded on 5 buttresses and no bouldering. The majority of routes are on the north-west faces of the blocks and although the climbs carry the luminous look well, they tend to be in good nick for all but the top-outs, where great care is required. All climbs are less than 15m in height.

**Approach and Parking:** Located on the A661 Wetherby-to-Harrogate road, 2 miles north of Spofforth and clearly signed. Turn into the wide entrance and, if the grounds are open, turn left immediately after the main gate. A shed kiosk is on the right where you can pay to look at the rocks but not to touch. Parking is 100m further into the grounds (**GPS: 53.976225,-1.458683**).

**Access:** **Climbing is actively discouraged by the landowners**. The grounds are only open to the public on weekends and bank holidays, 11am to 6pm, March to October for £2.50 (*in 2011*). The gates are locked outside of this and hopping the wall from the A661 side may seem a good idea until you're stopped by a man and a rifle. A shooting club use the grounds midweek evenings and probably pose more threat to the climber than angry fishermen, who also have licence to use the lake. The following climbs have been recorded in case access arrangements improve.

Over the last century multitudes have climbed, named and reclaimed routes at this crag. By all means continue this process but let it be your little secret.

## The Climbs - PLOMPTON ROCKS

The island pinnacle at the lake edge has been climbed and involves a spectacular rope pendulum to gain the foot, and U-boats to escape if the fishermen see you.

From the nearside of the dam, when approaching from the official parking, is **Cannonball Block**, a squat buttress on the right with a large circular hole through the centre. Climbs start through the hole on the left side of the north face. The left arête is VD while the wall just to the right is **Far Left** (VS 4c); the short wall above the hole is VS 4c and the prominent open crack is **Spider Crack** (VS 4c). The wall to the right of the crack is **E!** (E2 5b). Trending right from the blunt left arête to the undercut right arête is a project, as is the taxing deep water solo option of the right arête direct.

Through the hole on the south side is the obvious groove of **Contortionist Crack** (VS 4c).

To the right (i.e. back towards the main A661 road), past the dam and into the wood are two clean craglets separated by a tree. **Roof Block** to the north and **Pothole Crag** to the south. On the former, **The Roof** (VS 5a) goes direct up through the jam crack in the roof to finish right; **Jugglers Groove** (VS 4c) tackles the arête and groove to the right. On the short east face at the back of Pothole Crag, near the tree, is **Swine Groove** (HVS 5b) taken direct; up to the pothole and through the bulge at the left end of the north face is **Pothole Wall** (HVS 5a); right again is **Evening Temptation** (E2 5b) whilst **Cyprinidae** (E2 5b) climbs the arête to the right of the slab to join the hanging wall; **Catwalk** (VD) trends up and right on the north-side slab, over the small roof, to finish round the front face in the chimney (a variation starts up **The Nose** (HVS 5b) of the front slab to finish right up the chimney whilst the direct start to the chimney is 5b); **Gritwalk** (VD) takes a good line up the diagonal crack from the right toe of the buttress up left to the chimney whilst a finish direct up the wall to the right is **The Great Carp Hunt** (E2 5b): around to the south side of the buttress is the obvious chimney (Mod) and the route which climbs past the large nostril is **Nasal Passage** (HVS 5a).

Just to the right is **Log Block** with a bulging front and fine crack. The mossy short ramp left of the crack is **One Pebble Mantel** (VS 5b); next is **Pleasant Crack** (HS 4c); **The Shield** (HVS 5c) grapples the bulges just before the chimney to a difficult mantel; **Briar and Log Chimney** (D) culminates with the briars.

There are several blocks further south including one with a fine crack on its east face. All have seen some goings-on in the past but the main climb of note is on **The Matterhorn Block** on the southern extremity of the grounds before the road. **Militant Tendency** (HVS 5c) takes the north-west arête to gain the short crack and cave on the north face before surmounting the top bulge.

Further climbing can be had at an extremely green and overgrown area with an overhanging face and roof some 90m north of Cannonball Block on the east of the lake. If you must climb here, you might as well know what's gone on before. Counselling is available. **Fissure de Chaussure** (HS 4b) the left corner of the slab; **L'Escalier** (S 4a) the slabs right corner; **La Crepe** (HVS 5b) takes the big roof to the right via a central scoop between the 'pancakes'; **Malemort** (XS 6c) climbs the oppressive central chimney through the roof using thigh jams; **Mange-Tout** (E2 6a) is the offwidth to the right and **La Botte** (HVS 5c) takes the next short groove.

#### Information on First Ascents

*The above named routes were the work of John MacKenzie and Glenn Gorner who climbed these routes in the autumn of 1981 but some bore signs of earlier traffic. In the summer of 2011, The Great Carp Hunt and E! were recorded by Robin Warden whilst Evening Temptation and Cyprinidae were recorded by Rob Weston. The illustrious team of Brian Fuller, Allan Austin and Doug Verity recorded 36 routes in the 1962 YMC journal, some of which possibly overlap with the MacKenzie records but it is difficult to say for definite. You'll know where to look if the place ever becomes in-vogue.*

**HENRY PRICE** - Introduction

# henry price

### by **Will Hunt**

OS Ref: SE 291 347
Altitude: 90m

Henry Price is unlike any other 'crag' in this guidebook. This wall, nearly 140m long, constructed of gritstone blocks used to mark the boundary of Leeds General Cemetery. The cemetery was closed in 1969 and incorporated into the Leeds University campus, being renamed St George's Fields. When the Henry Price hall of residence was constructed, it was balanced just above the gritstone wall, which was preserved. Both structures are now Grade II listed.

Time invested in long traverses along this wall have turned many weedy 'nobodies' into stamina-imbued wads. Being a man-made structure, its presence in the venerable YMC Yorkshire Grit guidebook will doubtlessly be questioned. However, its significance as a historic training venue for local climbers since the 1960s makes it worthy of inclusion. Dennis Gray's excellent book, "Slack - the fun of climbing", provides some history to the Henry Price wall. Nowadays, the wall continues to be used by students of Leeds University and also gets attention from other locals who pop in during their lunch hour or after work.

**The Climbing:** Long traverses are the order of the day. There are some pleasing 'up' problems to be had on the main wall, but more entertainingly on an antiquated stone arch situated next to the wall. Bouldering mats are not required.

**Conditions and Aspect:** The wall can be accessed 24 hours a day at all times of year and is lit at night to enable inebriated freshers to find their way home safely. The wall is comprehensively overhung by the Henry Price hall building at all points so is permanently dry.

Richard Connors teaching the undergrads a lesson in the old side shuffle.
Photo: Andy McCue

# The Climbs - HENRY PRICE

**Parking and Approach:** The Henry Price hall of residence is located on Clarendon Road opposite Woodhouse Moor (known as Hyde Park colloquially). Parking can be found on this road (**GPS: 53.80862, -1.558861**) or at any number of locations in the surrounding streets. Leave no valuables on display and head to the rear of the building. From Clarendon Road head to the far right of the Henry Price building and turn left onto University Road. Just past the car barrier giving access to the University of Leeds campus, turn left and walk across a small car park to find the wall looking out onto St George's Park.

**Access:** Climbing on the wall is neither formally recognised by the University, nor is it prevented. Keeping a low profile and being courteous and polite to all residents of the building will help to keep this happy arrangement. Besides from those on the main wall and the nearby stone archway there are a number of climbs that have been completed on the surrounding buildings. These are not advised and, from personal experience, persons attempting to snatch a quick repeat will be apprehended by Campus Security.

## The Main Wall

The wall is divided by doors into four panels (plus a tiny one). Climbing these left-to-right is de rigeur, but extra pump can be obtained by reversing them. The rules are simple: the top of the wall is not in, all footholds are in, even the lowest ones, but not the thin rim of the paving. **The traverses have been given sport climbing grades**. This wall has recently seen a great deal of damage from dry tooling by persons unknown. This practice is unacceptable and risks access to the wall.

### 1 Beyond Far Left Panel  6b+
Pull onto the arête and begin your crab-like shuffling traverse-athon with this very short panel.

### 2 Far Left Panel  7a+
Fiercely technical to start. Things become easier but more sustained.

### 3 Middle Left Panel  6a
The 'easy panel' makes a pleasant warm-up with some good rests.

### 4 Middle Right Panel  6b
Can be linked with the *Middle Left Panel* to provide a stamina test without any major technicalities.

### 5 Far Right Panel  6c
Sustained climbing but without the technical nature of the *Far Left Panel*, but some tough bunched up moves.

### 6 The Big Traverse  7b
The obvious challenge is to link all panels without stepping off the wall, climbing across the doors on route. Cheeky rests can be engineered via the door furniture but you might surprise a resident trying to leave! Added difficulty can be gained via the *Campus Extensions* which requires slapping footless around the stairwells that overhang each door.

## The Arch
The arch adjacent to the *Far Right Panel* has a number of problems. The most obvious are described here.

### 7 Arch Arête  Font 4+
Either of the 'legs' of the arch climbed on the outside using the arêtes. This is also the easiest descent from the *Arch*. The arêtes can be eliminated for a harder, better problem.

### 8 Undercling  Font 5
On the side of the *Arch* facing the *Far Right Panel*, use the old gate hook found on the right-hand leg and a long reach to find a concrete blob on the top of the arch. Use this to top-out.

### 9 Overcling  Font 5+
On the side of the *Arch* facing away from the *Main Wall* and on the same leg as *Undercling* grab the old gate hook and make a monstrous reach to the top of the arch.

### 10 The Pocket  Font 6a
Climb the *Arch* as for *Overcling* but do not use the gate hook. A crumbling pocket allows a reach through to the top. Tricky!

# adel crag

by **Will Hunt**

OS Ref: SE 281 402
Altitude: 140 m

Adel Crag consists of a pair of large boulders situated in a peri-urban setting in Adel Woods, to the north of Leeds. The crag is of minor historical note for its inclusion in the 1960 book, *Where to Climb in the British Isles*, by Edward C. Pyatt and may also be of some interest to locals who are taking their first steps in climbing.

**The Climbing:** The climbing is somewhat underwhelming, especially as much of it takes place on large, chipped holds. It primarily consists of easy bouldering though there is the odd opportunity to tie on. The following climbs are some of the better offerings but many variations are possible.

**Conditions and Aspect:** The boulders are situated in a shaded clearing the woods and can take a little time to dry. Some of the walls are dirty through lack of traffic and require an exploratory mindset.

**Parking and Approach:** As the A660 (Otley Road) passes north through Adel it meets one set of traffic lights. At these turn right onto Church Lane and turn left at the T-junction shortly afterwards. After approximately half a mile turn right at the church onto Back Church Lane before turning left onto Stair Foot Lane at the next T-junction. There is a small car park 300m further on the right (**GPS: 53.857807, -1.574865**). From the rear left corner of this car park the boulders can be reached after a walk of a minute or so along a vague path through the woods.

**1 Swastika Rib**  VS 4c   5m
The top tier features a large scoop which is commonly used to access the 'summit' of Adel Crag. The rib on the left of this scoop can be led with low gear and is sapped of its seriousness by the opportunity of an easy escape rightwards. The route takes its name from the rather unsavoury graffiti gracing the top-out.

**2 Wandering Chips**  Font 4+
The face of the next boulder is split by a small overlap. Starting at the lowest point on this wall follow chips up and rightwards before they lead you back leftwards to the slabby west side of the boulder. Surprisingly satisfying, if only the holds were natural.

**3 Narrow Wall**  Font 5
The narrow, steep face can be climbed with a left or right finish.

**4 Tricky Arête**  Font 5
The worthwhile arête of the west wall feels high at the top.

**5 High Arête**  Font 4+
The short-lived arête of the boulder facing the approach.

Between the two boulders is a space commonly used as a fire pit. **Firestarter** (Font 6b+) takes the steep and uncompromising roof out of the pit. Climbed from a sit-down start without using the right arête.

# woolley edge quarry

by **Anthony Matthews**

OS Ref: SE 307 137
Altitude: 160m

Once a mighty face that could have easily rivalled that of Millstone in the Peak District, however the fate of this quarry was to be back-filled. This created two quite different sections either side of Common Lane. As climbing came to the masses in the 1980s, some of what we now call boulder problems were climbed using pegs, and the crag was even used for outdoor education by Woolley School. Nowadays it is more popular with fly-tippers and occasional illicit after dark activities. The subsequent lack of traffic and extensive tree cover mean the crag is often green and damp in places and so is best enjoyed during the winter months after a dry spell. This small crag still contains a handful of worthy problems and, if you can see through the imperfect scenery, is an invaluable training venue for local climbers or passing commuters when the conditions are right. The routes have not been recorded by the first ascensionists but almost all lines here have been climbed at some point.

**Approach**: Situated close to a picnic area approximately 4 kilometres from Junction 38 on the M1 Motorway. Leave the motorway at junction 38 and drive towards the village of Woolley. At the first cross-roads after the village turn left, at the next, turn right.

**Access:** A small, hard to find section of the lower quarry is on private property in peoples back gardens. Barbed wire and walls give this away. The rest of the quarry has no known access issues, but please don't use the farmers fence as belay stakes.

**Lower Quarry:** This is the larger and more broken section with a scattering of spread-out small bays, and a 50m section of wall at the far right-hand end reaching almost 10m in height. Containing around 30 or so problems and micro-routes, it also suffers the most from fly-tipping.

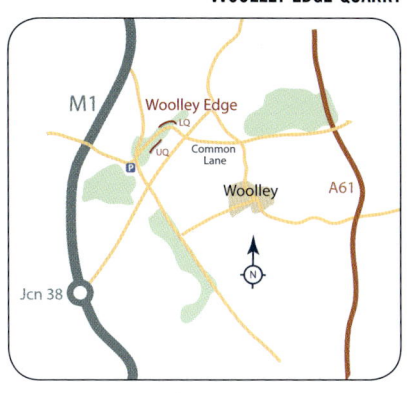

**Upper Quarry:** Smaller than its other half, the upper quarry contains a bigger selection of boulder problems. Starting with a small 3m slab on its left-hand edge, a long main wall in the middle, and the impressive 5m overhanging wall at its far right. Interspersed with several smaller sections there are problems from Font 4+ to Font 7a and beyond. With the left-hand arête of the overhanging wall (climbed on the right) been the best problem hereabouts at Font 6b+. The low-level traverse of the central wall provides good sport for the shorter climber. Some sections look undeveloped and unloved due to lack of traffic but give them a closer inspection and you will see evidence of pegs and chipping on almost all the decent rock. All they need is a bit of a clean.

## rein road quarry (morley)

OS Ref: SE 269 265

A truly esoteric spot, Rein Road Quarry is disused and full of water but has one clean wall which rises 10m above the usual water line. In 1995 the following description appeared in the Centresport new routes book accompanied by map and confirmatory photographs compliments of Mike Hibbert and Keith Tilley. **Splash Dance** (HVS 5a): below a hawthorn bush on top of the north-east wall, abseil in to the water line. Take a hanging belay and climb back out again up a widening crack. Step left to a mantel at the top.

Al Manson on the first ascent of **High Noon (E4 6a)**. Page 144
Photo: Manson Collection

# history / volume 1

## by Dave Musgrove

As far as we know it all began during the second half of the 19th century. The early days are a bit of a mystery but anecdotal accounts suggest that during this golden age of alpinism, the first routes on grit genuinely were 'training for the greater ranges'. Victorian mountaineers cut their teeth close to home on the gritstone outcrops of the Pennines then progressed, via the gullies and ridges of the Lake District and North Wales, to the snowy peaks of France, Switzerland and Norway.

The Yorkshire Ramblers Club was formed in 1892; the first mountaineering club in the county. Several of its early members were veterans of the Alpine Club and the early recorded history of the YRC mostly deals with overseas expeditions. The first elected president of the YRC was Cecil Slingsby from Skipton. Slingsby was reputed to have climbed several chimneys and gullies at Almscliff and on the crags around Barden Moor in the 1860s and 70s, but the recorded history begins with a pencil written guide by Thomas Gray dated 1894 that included 10 climbs at Almscliff. It appears Gray climbed regularly at Almscliff, partnered by Herbert Ingle, Edward Calvert and C.T. Dent. Undoubtedly these characters pioneered many more climbs here and further afield than they deemed notable.

The next clue that rock climbing in Yorkshire was alive and well before the turn of the century was unearthed in a small paperback book written around 1900 by Edmund Bogg. This contains a photograph dated 1895 of an unknown climber in nailed boots soloing a crack on one of the large boulders on Simon's Seat. This crack had never previously been recorded as a route but 100 years later, guided by the photograph it was re-discovered, re-climbed and found to be HVS 5a. Our Victorian ancestors were clearly more capable than we had previously believed.

In 1906 Claude Benson wrote an article for Fry's *The Outdoor Magazine* which described in detail, accompanied by photographs, some of the more popular climbs at Almscliff and Ilkley. These included Birds Nest Crack (then known as The Beehive) at Almscliff, and Flake Climb and Blasphemy Crack at Ilkley. By this time the Botterill brothers, Fred and Matthew, were cycling regularly from their home in Leeds to climb at The Cow and Calf. Fred in particular was said to have been keen on bouldering at Almscliff. In 1911, an article by Walter Greenwood listed 22 climbs at Ilkley. John Laycock's 1913 guidebook explicitly recorded only 26 routes at Almscliff, but suggested there were upwards of 170. Benson remarked "One meets nail marks everywhere. I should think that almost every yard of cliff and boulder has been tried at one time or another".

It is strongly suspected that the YRC visited most of the gritstone outcrops in the county around the turn of the century. Another article by Benson featured the relatively innocuous Spofforth Pinnacles in some detail. Can it be true that this group never climbed on the nearby and nationally famous Brimham Rocks?

We turn to Bradford in 1922; The Gritstone Club was formed and set about preparing the 1923 guidebook 'Recent Developments'. Claude Dean Frankland started the tradition of putting up a new route at Almscliff for the guide. His ascent of The Green Crack stood out as the major testpiece of the era. Frankland was regarded as one of the best rock climbers of his generation. A letter from Geoffrey Winthrop Young states "I wish to be allowed to thank you for giving me one more - and that perhaps the best - demonstration of how beautiful climbing movements on difficult rock can be".

Frankland was killed in 1927, on the relatively simple Chantry Buttress on Great Gable, and his untimely death left a void. Standards of technical difficulty didn't progress for over a decade. Nevertheless, activists of the 1930s kept busy with the Craven Pothole Club (led by its best known member Sydney Waterfall, his brother Arnold and friend Bill Bowler) continuing development of the Barden Moor and Barden Fell crags with their most notable find being the 'unearthing' of Dental Slab in 1933. They also visited Great Wolfrey and climbed extensively at Sharphaw but recorded nothing at either.

# Volume 1 - History

Guisecliff first attracted attention in 1910, when Erics Addyman and Roberts braved its dank and forbidding gullies. Their findings didn't attract many followers until brothers Harry and Fred Stembridge pioneered several routes between 1930 and 1950, only a couple of which can still be identified. Guisecliff even drew in Lancashire raiders, with Arthur Birtwhistle adding the first significant line, Roc's Nest Chimney, in 1937.

The first record of any activity at Brimham dates from the 1930s with Cubic Corner, Notice Board Crack and Lover's Leap Chimney being mentioned by Sydney Thompson. He witnessed some indications of previous activity but considered the crag relatively unexplored. This is surprising given the area's geological interest unless, because of this, climbing was actively discouraged? Thompson also, around this time, made a significant contribution at Almscliff with his technical and bold traverse of the South West Face.

As the 1930s ended Denys Fisher became an influential figure at Almscliff and Caley. He led Pothole Direct, Jacob's Ladder and his eponymous Traverse and Stride and became an early mentor and close friend of the next great Yorkshire pioneer Arthur Dolphin.

Like Frankland before him, Dolphin met a tragic end when he slipped during the descent of the Dent du Géant in 1953. He was 28. But the Dolphin era, from 1940 until his death, produced some of the all-time classics of British outcrop climbing. Virtually every one of his climbs shows true simplicity of line. He top-roped The Wall of Horrors, years ahead of its time, and but for his untimely death, may well have led it. The ethics and attitude of the day involving new routes were simple. According to Dolphin's friend, John Cook, the sequence was: top rope in rubbers, top rope in boots, and then lead in rubbers. The climb was only considered fully developed after a lead in nailed boots! Demon Wall, Z Climb, Overhanging Groove, Black Wall, Birdlime Traverse and the superb Great Western are all products of Dolphin's craftsmanship. His crossing of the North-West Girdle, with John Cook and John 'Pug' Ball, is a remarkable exploit, particularly as Ball, totally unprotected as the last man, had no inkling as to where he was being taken.

Al Manson and Pete Kitson at Almscliff
Photo: Bernard Newman

# History - Volume 1

Rivalry and competition has doubtless always been a feature of climbing. Cook remembers the team holding perhaps the first-ever speed climbing competition at Almscliff (just for fun, mind you). Cook recalled his time to do Bird's Nest Variation: 16 seconds.

In the early 1950s, after Dolphin's death, Brian Evans and friends from the newly formed Yorkshire Mountaineering Club took up the reins and systematically charted several edges including Brimham, Hebden Gill, and Guisecliff. The most active club members as 'new routers' in these early days were Ronnie Hields (who added Comet Wall to Guisecliff), Charlie Salisbury, Ron Hirst and Harold Barraclough. Evans himself developed the outlying Brandrith and Great Wolfrey, before teaming up with the area's new star, Allan Austin, in 1955.

Allan Austin typifies the classic Yorkshire stereotype, stubborn, determined, rooted in the county's woollen district heritage and, allegedly, not too keen on 'wasting' money. He had a reputation for always wearing several layers of jumpers and of insisting in climbing in all weathers. It was under his leadership that the YMC guidebook style took shape and he, perhaps more than any other, kept meticulous records of new climbs. In the mid-50s the Austin / Evans partnership was the dominant force in new route development. At Brimham alone their tally includes Rough Wall, Allan's Crack, Lancet Crack and Frensis Direct, finally establishing this crag as a major climbing venue.

Austin's team didn't have it all their own way however, as Dennis Gray kept importing the Rock and Ice stars to snatch several plums. The best of these in this guidebook area were Joe Brown's Charming Crack and White Wash at Brimham. Brown also nearly succeeded on Gigglin' Crack, slithering back down from close to the top in a fit of hysterics brought about by the jocular comments of his companions. This route today merits E6 - it is interesting to speculate what Brown would have given it had he succeeded.

It was back at Almscliff that Austin really pushed standards. In the late 1950s he was undisputedly the leading climber of his generation in Yorkshire and dominated the local scene for the next decade. His ascent of Western Front in 1958, after a miraculous escape from a ground fall on the first attempt, brought a new standard of difficulty to the crag that could only be bettered by his lead of The Wall of Horrors three years later. Both routes were horrendously bold undertakings without the assurance of modern protection, and it took the introduction of wired nuts and Friends in the 1970s before they saw regular repeats.

During the following decade Austin became less prolific on grit, though still produced a steady stream of hard climbs: Noonday Ridge at Caley, The Waster on Chevin Buttress, Monument Crack at Rylstone, Fishladder at Earl, Bell at Hetchell and Pillar Front at Eastby. While none surpassed the big two at Almscliff for steepness and sheer technical difficulty they were all bold and the hardest routes on their respective crags at the time. Pillar Front must have given Austin a particular fright because he told friends at the time he thought it the most serious first ascent he had ever done. All these routes now rate 3 stars and, though trade routes by today's standards, still command respect.

During the 1960s two young brothers from Summerbridge emerged as a fresh dominant force on the grit. Robin and Tony Barley initially concentrated their attentions on the Nidderdale crags closest to home, re-vitalising Guisecliff with the addition of around 50 routes during the decade including Creation and Dingbat. At the same time they were scouring Brimham adding another 30 or so there, including the famous testpiece Beatnik on the Cubic Block. The brothers were still teenagers during this period and were equally prolific on limestone, writing the Malham section for the first Yorkshire Limestone guide during 1967.

The Barleys opened up new crags as well during the 1960s being the first to report routes at Ash Head, Panorama, and Cat Crag. At Eavestone they climbed many fine lines, including the futuristic and gymnastic Swinging Free. Tony's best known work is the spectacular crowd pleaser of Black Wall Eliminate at Almscliff, and only yards away is perhaps his most ground breaking: the scary highball Barley Mow, soloed onsight long before bouldering mats had been dreamed off. This is now recognised as possibly the first Font 7a boulder problem in the country.

*Almscliff to Slipstones* **669**

# VOLUME 1 - History

Slipstones was becoming a popular venue for Teesside based climbers. Geoff Milburn and Peter Martin added a dozen routes in 1959 but serious development only commenced in the mid-60s when Eric and Tony Marr turned up at the crag. The brothers soon worked through all the established routes and noted the gaps. A few weeks later they returned for Tony to lead the then unprotected Escalator and the strenuous Original Route. They ended their visit with Eric adding Marr's Route. Returning in 1965 the brothers worked on solving the slab start to Buttress 4 and eventually produced the excellent Agra, along with a variation start to the left which eventually became Agrete. The following year, accompanied by Ken Jackson, Tony took the lead and won the first ascent of the superb Zoom.

Hetchell, or Pompeii Caley as it used to be known, had probably been frequented by locals for many years and John Temple recalls that he climbed there in 1955, having been introduced to the crag by his Scoutmaster J.A. (Rex) Fairbrother who'd climbed there in the early war years with Arthur Dolphin and Bill Brigham. In 1962 John Johnson and Bill Todd climbed and named seven of the most obvious crack and chimney lines including the excellent and still popular Centurion and Pompeii Chimney. They then introduced other friends, including Brian Evans, to the crag. Evans added a few harder climbs including the superb Cassius Crawl with his wife Aileen. However, the hardest climb of the year, The Corbel, required the importation of the club's 'top gun', Allan Austin, to ensure success. By the end of the 1960s Dave Musgrove had led (or soloed) several new routes including Wailing Wall, Crutch and, with Bob Knapton, added a girdle (with a ground fall from the second pitch when a hold broke). Allan Austin returned with Chris Mitchell climbing Mitchell's Wall and the previously pegged Bell.

The late 1960s saw a general lull in major developments on grit as most of the established activists were lured away by the chance for fame and glory on the limestone. It wasn't until 1970 that the focus was rightly restored to the grit, by a group of highly talented students from the Leeds University Union Climbing Club. The notion of training in order to climb harder had been around for decades, but you could say the appearance of the Leeds University Wall started the modern era. Healthy competition at the climbing wall pushed training standards, and when this fitness was taken to the crag the rewards were immediately clear.

John Syrett became the best known, but with co-stars like Pete Kitson, Geoff Hankinson, Brian Hall, Tim Jepson, Mike Hammill and John Stainforth, and a full supporting cast including journal writer, log keeper and bouldering king, Bernard Newman, their place in climbing folklore soon became assured. The club was not exclusive and several non-university members such as Al Manson, Ken Wood and Andy Wild, became almost indistinguishable from the students because of associations struck up at The Wall. The 70s group sparked a gritstone revolution of spectacular proportions. The first new route was Ken Wood's True Grit at Brimham in June 1970 then in November 1970 John Syrett opened his account on The Brutaliser at the same crag. The following day he made what was then thought to be the second ascent of The Wall of Horrors at Almscliff.

Over the next four years there was an avalanche of hard new routes: The Big Greeny, Encore, Rectum Rift, The Virgin and The Gypsy at Almscliff; Jokers Wall, Picnic, and Red Tape at Brimham; Fingernacker Crack and Dypso at Caley; Gronff and Backslider on the Chevin; Earl Buttress and Early Riser at Earl Crag, After Eight at Rylstone; Guillotine at Guisecliff; Brown Sugar and Heatwave at Heptonstall; Augustus and Livia at Hetchell and Propeller Wall at Ilkley. A list that stands proud next to those of previous generations including Dolphin's and Austin's. In the LUUCC logbook, where most of this record of achievement is chronicled, descriptions are recorded in a modest and matter-of-fact way. The boys just didn't appreciate how good they were. Most of these climbs were ridiculously undergraded, a typical example was Propeller Wall at Ilkley which Syrett soloed and graded VS. It was repeated in similar fashion by several others in this group and someone added an H to the grade; there was no recognition that it was significantly harder and bolder than most of what had gone before. The grade eventually peaked at E5 and even now sees very few onsight repeats. Syrett's dominance faded in the mid-70s following a succession of tendon injuries but the momentum was maintained by Mike Hammill and Al Manson. High Noon

## History - VOLUME 1

was a route typical of this pair and born out of a friendly, but serious, rivalry. Manson won in this case but some of Hammill's later efforts such as Opus, The Ems Telegram and Yellow Peril at Almscliff; Swan Arcade and Left Wall at Brimham and Quark at Caley put him firmly in the 'top flight' of contemporary pioneers. Al Manson continued developments throughout the 70s and 80s, climbing the perfectly named Grit Expectations at Brimham and much sought after Adrenaline Rush at Caley. The latter, Manson felt, was by far the hardest route he had ever climbed and gave it Hard Extremely Severe (7b) in the 1982 guide, adding to the venerable catalogue of great climbers who have no clue about grading. Manson went on to even greater things at Caley during the 80s, which we'll return to. Meanwhile, his long 'affair' with Hetchell that started in 1974 produced technical gems such as Lucio's Lip, Up Pompeii, and Reach For A Peach.

The Leeds University boys didn't have it all their own way during the mid-70s. The partnership of Pete Livesey and Ron Fawcett became instantly famous, not least because of monthly publicity in a news hungry new magazine called *Crags*. A full page advertising picture of Fawcett soloing Western Front at Almscliff was particularly memorable, and highly inspiring. Most of this pair's achievements on Yorkshire Grit came on crags featured in volume two of this guide so we won't dwell on them all here. However at Almscliff Livesey teamed up with Manson to create All Quiet traversing the most impressive wall on the crag whilst, with Fawcett in tow, he made the first complete lead of 'Arries 'Ook, although Hammill and Manson had climbed the upper crux a few days earlier.

Among Fawcett's best efforts on the eastern crags is the iconic chicken-headed Psycho at Caley, a crag that has become synonymous with serious highballing now the landings can be padded out. Andy Brown added to Caley's collection of superb highball problems through the 70s. His best known being the wall left of The Great Flake but he vied with Manson for the first ascents of several others. In the same period, over at Almscliff, Martin Berzins was adding micro-routes to the Virgin boulder.

While the Leeds University teams plus Livesey and Fawcett dominated the 1970s, others were also keeping busy. Tony Barley continued his passion for green and vegetated Guisecliff producing two of its best climbs yet, Aftermath and Mastermind amid a host of less memorable excavations. At Brimham he 'imported' Jerry Peel to triumph where Brown had failed 20 years earlier on Gigglin' Crack. Jerry's Naked Edge climbed in 1978 at Simon's Seat is still one of the finest 'micro-routes' on Yorkshire grit.

The early 1980s saw new teams emerge at Almscliff. First off the mark were Charles Cook and, up and coming guidebook editor, Graham Desroy who produced three hard climbs including the intimidating Grand Illusion. Even harder, however, and not repeated for many years were Rob Gawthorpe's Forgotten Wall and China Syndrome,

Mike Hammill on the first ascent of **Opus** (E4 6b). Page 41.
Photo: Al Manson

## Volume 1 - History

which sports probably the first 7a move on a grit route in Yorkshire. Al Manson and Pete Kitson re-formed their old partnership to celebrate All Our Yesterdays on the crag that made them famous a decade earlier. Gawthorpe also climbed Hetchell's last great problem, Hunchback, during this period.

At Slipstones, Ron Kenyon and Stew Wilson recorded the first ascent of the excellent Ellingstring in 1980. The very strong Teesside team of Paul Ingham, Ian (Squawk) Dunn, Steve Brown and Dave Paul were introduced to the crag by Tony Marr and Alan Taylor later the same year and impressive results followed. Over several consecutive weekends Taylor added Alan's Arête and Easy Pickings, Ingham climbed Agra Right-Hand, Leany Meany, Rock On and the superb Ripper, whilst Marr added Agrete and Right-Hand Twin. Squawk's Arête was the work of Ian Dunn and finally Dave Stainthorpe climbed 'his' wall to end a very productive years work.

Returning early in 1982 Ingham produced the bold, Paul's Arête and the testing Impregnable, and later added two popular testpieces - Wisecrack and Micro Corner. The highlight of the year came from Ian Dunn with his three star gem Atomic. In February 1983 an article in a new magazine, *Rock Action One*, updated the developments at Slipstones and one of Yorkshire's best kept secrets was finally open to all. The crag became increasingly popular but it was the Teesside regulars who maintained the developmental momentum well into the 80s.

Visitors to Great Wolfrey were infrequent until, in the mid-70s, Ken Wood climbed Walter's Rib, the prominent arête above the plaque and John Eastham recorded Werewolf in 1980. The crag became relatively popular for a time with regular forays by John Mackenzie who on one of his visits made the unfortunate mistake of letting go, the penalty was a slow and painful retreat. Martin Berzins, Chris Sowden and Tony Burnell visited the crag in 1988 and climbed several routes including, Little Red Riding Hood, A Company of Wolves and Sheep's Clothing. This crag is on a jealously keepered grouse moor and access was always a problem for the masses, hence it never gained the popularity it deserved. Only since the CRoW Act of 2005 have things changed, but more of that later.

During the mid-80s, activity on the mainstream crags involved both old and new pioneers. Caley witnessed some early breakthroughs in 1984 with the ascent of two last great problems. The Great Flake by Craig Smith was closely followed by Al Manson's bold push on Marrowbone Jelly creating the county's second true E7. At Chevin Quarry in 1983 a young Don Barr beat the opposition to the major line of Jenny Tulls but fate cruelly robbed us of an outstanding young climber later the same year when he was killed by lightning in the Verdon Gorge.

A lot of the activity on Yorkshire grit in the 1980s centred on Ilkley, and in particular the exploits of John Dunne. In this volume of the guide, perhaps John's most significant contribution is Nothing's Safe at Caley. Originally considered a bold route at E5 6c and rarely, if ever, repeated until the boulder mat revolution of the 21st century turned it into a classic and much coveted Font 7c.

Work on the 1989 edition of this guide prompted a surge of activity. Several crags, such as Hebden Gill and Great Wolfrey, received a complete overhaul to bring them up to date following periods of developmental decline. At Brimham a frenzy of activity was on-going under the 'captaincy' of Steve Rhodes. His team, including Martin Berzins, Chris Sowden, and local guru Al Manson accounted for around 30 hard new climbs almost all in the E2 to E5 category. Rhodes led Steady VS Arête and Berzins Michael, Michael Superman. Berzins and Manson inspired each other to some excellent finds, the best being Sow's That and Reach for the Sty and Berzins got Rat Arsed with the help of Nic Kidd. The old notice boards and their bolts were put to use on a unique trio of routes, Cocoa Club Board Meeting, Take No Notice and Board to Tears by Rhodes who then shared leads with Greg Rimmer on Mae West's Rib and House Points Tomorrow. Peak activist John Allen stole a march on the locals in September by sneaking in like a Morose Mongoose – possibly still unrepeated onsight?

1988 was also another important year at Caley. Following John Dunne's ascent of Nothing's Safe, Al Manson got worried that his long-term projects on the far left of the Roadside Group may be under threat so he pulled out the stops to finalise matters on Death Drop 2000 and To Be

Is Not To Bolt. Quark at last got its scientific bedfellows when Graham Desroy added Charm and Steve Rhodes led Strangeness.

At Hebden Gill a young YMC team including Adam Wainwright, Fraser Hardie and John Paul Hotham almost doubled the number of routes in this sleepy valley. Finally, just before that edition of the guide came out, Dave Pegg emerged on the scene with a series of bold, bald leads rivalling the best of Dunne's Ilkley testpieces. Two of these, Resurrection and The Bottom Line at Brimham were probably as hard if not harder, than anything that had gone before.

The 1989 guidebook, edited by Graham Desroy, was the first in Yorkshire to attempt to fully document the history of the region and certainly the first to contain first-ascent lists. It was a mighty and very successful modern volume containing 650 pages and needing a hard back cover for the first time. Perhaps inspired in some way by this guide, developments continued apace after publication and the 1990s were just as productive as the previous decade.

It almost seems impossible to imagine that such a relatively small and continuously popular crag as Almscliff could go on producing a steady flow of new routes through yet another decade but the 1990s saw no change in the pace of development. The title of 'Almscliff Obsessive Of the Decade', however, went to Pete Brown from York who, over a period of eight years produced over a dozen new climbs or variations as well as repeats of every then-existing route, including the second ascent of China Syndrome. Brown's final contribution of 1997, and perhaps his most impressive was Megadoom, the direct finish up the magnificently exposed headwall above Impending Doom.

Al Manson and Ken Wood look on as John Syrett attempts the first ascent of **The Big Greeny** (E3 6a).Page 70.
Photo: John Harwood

One of the iconic images from that age: John Syrett's onsight ascent of **The Wall of Horrors (E3 6a)**. Page 78
Photo: John Stainforth

# History - Volume 1

Developments continued apace elsewhere and at Brimham Nick Dixon broke into E8 territory in 1990 but almost also broke some bones during a ground fall from Tender Homecoming. This fine arête lost a crucial pebble soon afterwards and resisted all repeat attempts for a long time until Tom De Gay worked out a left-hand sequence many years later.

Tony Marr with friends from Teesside, notably Mike Tooke, Frank Fitzgerald, Peter and Pam Shawcross, then began to seriously apply themselves to route development. Few major climbs were added by this most enthusiastic team but around 50 very worthwhile variants and fillers in were added in that decade. They also added ten routes on the previously undeveloped Hare's Head rocks in the north-eastern corner of the Brimham estate, bringing to attention the huge, sheltered bouldering potential of these isolated blocks.

Late in 1989 Tony Barley co-opted Dave Musgrove to try a couple of lines at Eavestone. Three years, two pruning saws, a machete, a yard broom and several brushes later the pair emerged with a fully developed crag containing around 160 routes. Musgrove's best efforts included The Alamo, Battlement, Touching The Void, Here There Be Dragons and the crag's first two E5s, Genesis and Dragonslayer, whilst amongst Barley's leads, Crazy Paver, Treasure Island, Little Gem, Canada Dry, Cream and Over The Looking Glass were outstanding.

Several others became enchanted with this idyllic location for a while, but few were prepared to put in the required cleaning time. Kim Greenald led Strange Attractor and the highly technical Pebbledash before making the first free ascent of Eavestone Wall. Steve Webster made a comeback to lead Don't Worry I'm A Nurse, and Going Catatonic whilst Dave Mugrove Jnr snatched Fat Chance from under dad's nose. The hardest route, only completed after two ground falls, was Life Begins At Forty, an E6 'birthday present' for Bob Smith.

Guisecliff had slipped from popularity during the 80s but in 1990 Paul Jenkinson and Steve Earnshaw climbed the striking arête of On the Edge to provide a superb and committing adventure which, at E6, became that crag's hardest route. Mark Radtke made an early repeat and on this visit made a mental note of several other possibilities. In 1997, keen for something new, Mark discovered the high quality Scryking and Over The Top, both climbed with Dave Barton who was enticed onto the sharp end for the latter. On Slot Buttress Radtke and Jerry Peel both led the superb Warriors of Hanuman which ascends an improbable but irresistible feature. Greg Rimmer concentrated on the boulders near the folly and produced about fifteen good problems although it was Andy Cave who pulled out the stops and climbed the obvious but bold overhanging nose.

At Simon's Seat the 1993 film Jurassic Park inspired Dave Musgrove Jnr to add the short but serious Dino-Mania. He returned in 1995, with dad and Julian Cooper in tow, to clean up various lines on the south-west buttress, though many of these had probably been done before. In 1998/99 Derek Hargreaves headed onto the moor with Matt Troilett and led Flirtin' Cos I'm Hurtin', a fine clean E4 before Matt soloed the crag's first E6, the bold arête he named A Life Less Ordinary.

This Lancashire team really got cranking around the turn of the century. In 2000, Troilett, this time joined by Mick Johnston and Neil Herbert, sneaked into Brimham and added the bold E7 arête of Walk in Silence. Troilett returned in 2005 to climb a hard eliminate on Grit Expectations and again in 2008 with Neil McCallum to add the classic lines Stone the Crows and Scarecrow, along with a couple of hard boulder problems, to the outlying Brimham crags.

Inspired by the 1998 guide, Ben Bransby and Gareth Parry engaged in a campaign to make it out of date as soon as possible. In 1999 they added around 10 hard routes and several easier ones to the Brimham pinnacles including The Chisel and Rod's Roof, and Ben accompanied Chris Savage on The Green Giant all at the same grade of E7. At Almscliff Ben led Right Cheeky, still apparently unrepeated, which he described as E6 so long as you don't fall off but probably E7 if you do! At Caley, Gareth added a very improbable looking direct start, Saying Grace, to the undercut arête of Amazing Grace. Ben also made the first lead of Fred Zinnerman without the bolt runner at E6, only to be upstaged when Ben Tetler made the first lead of Charm without side-runners at E8.

Almscliff to Slipstones  **675**

# VOLUME 1 - History

Despite the long history of bouldering, there is no doubt that through the 1990s and into the early 21st century a significant change in climbing attitudes was taking place. Big names in the climbing media were seen focussing on bouldering, adding legitimacy to this climbing discipline as an end in its own right and, not coincidentally, effective pads started to become commercially available. The beer towel landing pad days were gone for good.

As with the very early days of route climbing, the first ascent details of many boulder problems were not deemed sufficiently worthwhile to record. The conviviality of bouldering with friends and the competition that inevitably ensues, has naturally lead to a profusion of eliminates and variants. The only way to locate the best problems at an unfamiliar venue was to seek out a local aficionado who could point out the lines and explain the eliminates. Tradition has it that the visitor would pay for this service by failing in a humiliating fashion on the most outrageous sandbags that the local could effortlessly cruise. The demand for a specialised bouldering guide grew.

Steve Rhodes obliged us first in 1993 when his *Bouldering on Yorkshire Grit* was published providing details of several hundred problems on selected crags. The main activists involved in developing many of the new power problems were recorded in that guide. This was updated by the exhaustive Alan Cameron-Duff guide published by Rockfax in 2000 that covered all the main crags. Tony Barley and Nigel Baker's *Wild Bouldering* guide from 1997 dealt with the less frequented Nidderdale crags and introduced the moorland bouldering playground of Sypeland. Their unveiling of Thruscross sparked interest and John Dunne added the highball Rewind (E6/Font 7b) in 2001. Others came for a look and eventually found the more significant Beanstalk Buttress on the other side of the valley and before we knew it a handful of quality hard extremes had fallen into the hands of Messrs Bransby, Troilett and Sutcliffe.

As the bouldering revolution gathered pace, mats were getting bigger and some lines previously recorded as routes with big E numbers were now considered fair game by teams of boulderers padding out hitherto dangerous landing zones. At the time of the 1998 YMC guide a debate was underway to define the borderline between a route and a highball problem, and which of several available grading systems should be used. While general understanding of bouldering grades has undoubtedly consolidated, there is no definitive categorisation of routes, micro-routes and highball boulder problems. Should you pile up the pads or tie on for the Great Flake? The choice is yours.

Many of the now-classic boulder problems were first put up in the 1970s and 1980s by the likes of Al Manson, Pete Kitson, John Syrett, Mike Hammill, Ron Fawcett, Bob Berzins and later Graham Desroy, John Dunne and Steve Rhodes. Exactly who did what before whom is never now likely to be unravelled with any certainty.

In the last decade, before the turn of the old millennium, things certainly started to hot up on the bouldering front. In 1990 Ben Moon nipped up from the Peak to climb the fabulous Font 7c+ highball Terry, only to discover Andy Swann had done it the week before. At Almscliff, Oliver Wright discovered the pumpy Jess's Roof in 1994. Later the same year John Gaskins breached the 8th grade when he climbed a problem on the back of the Virgin at Almscliff. This historically significant problem has been a source of great confusion, which we will attempt to clear up once and for all in this guide. John visited Almscliff to climb what appeared to be the hardest line in Steve Rhodes' guide at V12, and thought he was just making a repeat so didn't claim or report it. It later transpired this was a project at the time the guide was published, and John had in fact made the first ascent of a line that was significantly harder than anything done before. Things then became really confused. The line most people mistakenly assumed John had climbed became known as The Gaskins Problem. This desperate line was actually first climbed by Tim Clifford in 2002 and has now been renamed Identity Crisis. The much sought after line of Cherry Falls, a few metres to the right of Identity Crisis, also fell to Tim in 2002. The line actually climbed by John Gaskins in 1994 is now known as Cherry Falls Right and, despite the name, is a separate problem sharing only one hold with Cherry Falls.

Steve Dunning's serious bouldering campaign got going in 2000 with his ascents of Exocet and Annimut at

Steve Dunning on his stunning **High Fidelity** (Font 8b) at Caley. Page 118.
Photo: Pete Chadwick

677

# Volume 1 - History

Slipstones, and he followed these up with the dyno-tastic Super Furry Animal (8a+). It was Ben Moon who took home the real prize from this glorious northern outpost with his ascent of the stunning arête of Cypher (8b) in 2002. A year later, Steve headed up the tallest line on the Great Flake boulder to bring Font 8b to Caley with High Fidelity. This didn't dent Ben Moon's interest in Caley though, and in 2004 he succeeded on the obvious and tantalising traverse of Ranieri's Reach, following this up with the second ascent of High Fidelity in 2005.

In 2002 a new player, Dave Sutcliffe, emerged on the scene. On the Chevin he claimed several tough new lines in and around the old quarry. Clarence Tenthumbs, Stonequest and Primate raised the standards significantly at this oft neglected venue. In 2004 Sutcliffe paid a visit to Brandrith to investigate the two obvious and oft tried arêtes at the far right of the crag. After a repeat of the left-hand one he made the first ascent of the other to establish Heaven in Your Hands at Font 7c+, by far the hardest line on the crag.

People were still climbing with ropes, and back at Almscliff Pete Brown continued his new routing campaign; 2002's Few Tomorrows (E6) perhaps being the best of his latest crop. Steve Dunning outstretched all previous aspirants when in 2005 he claimed the right-hand finish to The Big Greeny as The Ginger Whinger (E7 7a). Also around this time James Ibbertson was on a ground-up first ascent quest, creating the bold line of Hokum (above Magnum Opus), 'Arries Left Ook on Black Wall, and Jack Be Nimble on the Virgin, only to find Ben Bransby had already done it. Ben Meeks, Mike Gray and Ian Bitcom have also left their marks here. All the major players seem to have been involved in a friendly rivalry to eliminate every hold yet climb every inch - from sitting starts - at Almscliff, yet this all-weather, all year-round venue, probably the most popular and intensively climbed lump of grit in Britain for well over 100 years, still keeps revealing new secrets and challenges.

During the 00's the love of bouldering unearthed smaller venues that, though known to a few, were never documented. Roundhill, Clint Crags and Bolton Haw were introduced to the wider public; Nigel Poustie unlocked the hard possibilities of Snowden; Andy Crome laid siege to the Whitehouses roof and Jon Pearson mopped up the lines of Roova. The Forestry Commission's extensive tree clearing revealed Norwood and Hunter's Stones where Robin Warden and team developed a mass of problems on the former and Tom Peckitt was awarded the prize of Hunter's Roof (Font 7c) and the incredible X-Calibre Direct (Font 8b) at the latter.

Grade 8's were falling county-wide into the capable hands of Andy Swann (To You Too, Mr C and Ironside at Brimham to mention a few) and Tom Peckitt (Fluide Dynamics (West Chevin), Toe-Fu (Simon's Seat) topped by the monster link up at Almscliff with Bulbhaul Font 8b+).

As the production of this guide came to a close the pace quickened by the keen to unearth the glaring lines on the county's less frequented venues. The Crevasse Area of Eavestone yielded an intense collection of hard problems with Sky Diamond (Font 7c) and Digital Delirium (Font 7c+) falling into the hands of Dave Sutcliffe whilst Steve Dunning produced Diamond Lights (Font 7c). The Upper Tier of Crow Crag gave Robin Nicholson and Adi Gill the lines of Tetelestai (E4 6a) and Jericho Falls (E4 6b) respectively, whilst Sutcliffe nailed his Chevin Quarry project, From the Shadow (E7 6c) before he turned his attention to Guisecliff. The team of Ric Mallinson, Gill and Sutcliffe seiged four neighbouring routes, Doomed Oasis (E6 6b), Low Downs (E6 6b) and Wild Abandon (E5 6b) and culminated in one of this volume's hardest lines, The Climb That Time Forgot (E8 6c), dispatched by Sutcliffe whilst aggressively confronted by the landowner from the crag top during the crux dyno; probably adding another E point alone.

So these keen activists have proved, if proof were needed, that class lines and problems are still out there. Maybe seeing some of the more remote Yorkshire crags (and even some of the local popular ones) in full-colour topo format for the first time in this guide will entice the great and the good to look hard at those gaps between the thin white lines and ask the enduring question, 'I wonder if that'll go?'

Jim Davies on a true old school classic, **Parson's Chimney** (HS 4b) at Almscliff. Page 70.
Photo: Adi Gill

# graded list
the best routes, the best problems

**Crag Key:** Air Scar (As), Almscliff (A), Arnagill (Ag), Ash Head (Ah), Bat Buttress (Bat), Birk Crag (Bc), Birk Gill (Bg), Bolton Haw (Bh), Brandrith (Bd), Brimham (B), Brown Beck (Bb), Caley (C), Calf Crag (Cc), Cat Crags (Cat), The Chevin (Ch), Crocodile Crag (Cr), Crow Crag (Cw), Dovestones (Dv), Earl's Seat (Es), Eavestone (E), Great Wolfrey (Gw), Guisecliff (G), Hare's Head (Hh), Hebden Gill (Hg), Hen Stones (Hn), Henstone Band (Hb), Hetchell (H), High Crag (Hc), Hunter's Stones (Hs), Little Almscliff (La), Little Brimham (Lb), Lord's Seat (Ls), Low Huller Stones (Lh), Lulbeck (Lk), North Nab (Nn), Norwood Edge (Ne), Nought Bank (Nb), Panorama Crag (Pa), Plantation Crack (Pc), Roova (Rv), Roundhill (Rh), Simon's Seat (Ss), Slipstones (S), Snowden (Sw), Spofforth Pinnacles (Sp), Sypeland (Sy), Thruscross (Th), Upper Huller Stones (Uh), Whitehouses (Wh).

## the routes

### E8
Tender Homecoming (7a) (B)
The Climb That Time Forgot (6c) (G)
Charm (6c) (Ch)

### E7
Saying Grace (6c) (C)
The Bottom Line (6c) (B)
The Chisel (6c) (B)
Strangeness (6c) (C)
Walk in Silence (6c) (B)
Bellyporker's Progress (6c) (B)
From the Shadow (6c) (Ch)
Right Cheeky (6c) (A)
Marrow Bone Jelly (6b) (C)
Clarence Tenthumbs (6b) (Ch)

### E6
China Syndrome (7a) (A)
Ginger Whinger (7a) (A)
On the Edge (6c) (G)
Fall from Grace (6c) (Ss)
Gigglin' Crack (6c) (B)
Life Begins at Forty (6c) (E)
The Great Flake (6b) (C)
Fred Zinnerman (6b) (C)
Resurrection (6b) (B)
Little Red Riding Hood (6b) (G)
Ancient (6b) (Lb)
Doomed Oasis (6b) (G)
Primate (6b) (Ch)
Question Time (6b) (Ss)
A Company of Wolves (6b) (Gw)
Stonequest (6b) (Ch)
A Life Less Ordinary (6b) (Ss)

### E5
Inner State (6c) (B)
Orchrist (6b) (A)
Magnum Opus (6b) (A)
Megadoom (6b) (A)
Dino-Mania (6b) (Ss)
Genesis (6b) (E)
One Man And His Dogmas (6b) (C)
Wild Abandon (6b) (G)
The Warriors of Hanuman (6b) (G)
The Fourth Dimension (6b) (Hg)
Sow's That (6b) (B)
Three Day Rave (6b) (Hg)
Troubled with Lycans (6b) (Gw)
Nipscrew (6b) (G)
The EMS Telegram (6b) (A)
Psycho (6b) (C)
Adrenaline Rush (6b) (C)
Stone the Crows (6b) (Cw)
Quark (6a) (C)
Charlie's Dilemma (6a) (B)
Skryking (6a) (G)
Dragonslayer (6a) (G)
In Memoriam (6a) (Gw)
Left Wall (6a) (B)
Wolf at the Door (6a) (Gw)
Retribution Rib Direct (5c) (A)

### E4
The Lady (6c) (A)
Blackhead (6c) (A)
Rat Arsed (6c) (B)
Successor State (6b) (B)
Up She Rises (6b) (E)
True Grit (6b) (B)
Jericho Falls (6b) (Cw)
The Full Throttle (6b) (Dv)
Wolverine (6b) (Gw)
Opus (6b) (A)
Stone Age Reveller (6b) (B)
'Arries 'Ook (6a) (A)
Joker's Wall (6a) (B)
Eavestone Crack (6a) (G)
World in Action (6a) (Pa)
The Great Santini (6a) (Dv)
Diethard, Slim With Avengence (6a) (Hg)
Scarecrow (6a) (Cw)
High Noon (6a) (C)
Spring Roll (6a) (B)
Werewolf (6a) (Gw)
Tetelestai (6a) (Cw)
Amadeus (6a) (Cw)

A route where there's never a dull moment. Climbers on **Frankland's Green Crack** (VS 4c) at Almscliff. Page 70.
Photo: Richard Nolan

# GRADED LIST - The Best Routes, The Best Problems

The Wilderness Years (6a) (Gw)
Grit Expectations (6a) (B)
Over the Top (6a) (G)
Performance Management (6a) (Hg)
Finesse (6a) (Ss)
Flirtin' Cos I'm Hurtin' (6a) (Ss)
All Quiet (6a) (A)
Mastermind (5c) (G)
Cutting the Cord (5c) (G)
Dead Angst (5c) (H)

## E3
Battlecat (6b) (Bd)
Eavestone Wall (6b) (E)
Sinbad (6b) (S)
The Virgin (6b) (A)
What Happens Now? (6b) (Sy)
Swirral Edge (6b) (Sy)
Happy Days (6b) (B)
Cat Baloo (6b) (Cat)
Breaking Out (6b) (Sy)
Strange Attractor (6a) (E)
The Naked Edge (6a) (Ss)
The Big Greeny (6a) (A)
The Wall of Horrors (6a) (A)
Finger Knacker Crack (6a) (C)
The Mighty Oak (6a) (Bat)
Think on Tha' Nose (6a) (Ag)
And She Was (6a) (Ss)
Rotifer (6a) (B)
The Riddler (6a) (Bat)
Too Knarly for Barley (6a) (Uh)
Board to Tears (6a) (B)
Midway (6a) (Hg)
Solitude (6a) (Uh)
I'll Bet She Does (6a) (Ss)
Under the Awning (6a) (Sy)
Not the Nine O'clock News (6a) (Pa)
Space Plucks (6a) (S)
Grand Illusion (6a) (A)
Battlement (6a) (E)
Pathos (6a) (B)
Atomic (6a) (S)
Western Front (5c) (A)
Who Needs Friends (5c) (B)
Croc Bloc (5c) (Cr)

Acme Wall (5c) (B)
In the Nick of Time (5c) (Ag)
Fryer's Front (5c) (As)
Bell (5c) (H)
Shush Popeye (5c) (Ss)
Cowell's Rib (5c) (Gw)
Fat Chance (5c) (E)
Whisky Wall (5b) (A)

## E2
Pebble Pincher (6b) (Es)
Caught in an Eddy (6a) (Sy)
Bonington's Made It (6a) (Cat)
Eeyore (6a) (Sy)
Horse Gone Wonky (6a) (Sy)
Touching the Void (6a) (E)
Impregnable (6a) (S)
Habberdashery (6a) (G)
The Arch (6a) (B)
Crock Around the Block (6a) (Gw)
Student Games (6a) (Uh)
A Little Trouble (6a) (Sy)
Pump Friction (6a) (Ls)
Yorkshire Puddin' (5c) (A)
Skyjacker (5c) (G)
The Creation (5c) (E)
The Torso Twins (5c) (Bd)
Ruscator (5c) (G)
Where He Fell (5c) (E)
The King of the Castle (5c) (E)
Black Wall Eliminate (5c) (A)
Picnic (5c) (A)
Livia (5c) (H)
Walter's Rib (5c) (Gw)
Jehu's Chariot (5c) (G)
Narrow Margin (5c) (Bg)
Gronff (5c) (Ch)
Bell End (5c) (H)
Quantum Leap (5c) (Bg)
Seven Up (5c) (S)
Halcyon Daze (5c) (B)
Tip Off (5c) (C)
Scales (5c) (Cr)
Autobahn (5c) (G)
Hobgoblin (5c) (A)
Clematis (5c) (A)

No Mans Land (5b) (A)
Class Action (5b) (Bg)
Yesterday's News (5b) (Pa)
Red Tape (5b) (B)
Swinging Free (5b) (E)
The Black Chipper (5b) (B)
A Question of Balance (5b) (Ss)
Treasure Island (5b) (E)
Crevasse Wall (5b) (Hg)
The Alamo (5b) (E)
Ichthys (5b) (Ch)
Oubliette (5b) (E)

## E1
Charming Crack (5c) (B)
Retribution (6a) (Uh)
Permutation Rib (5c) (C)
Ripper (5c) (S)
Variation Start (5c) (S)
Pure Gold (5c) (Ls)
Augustus (5c) (H)
Right-Hand Twin (5c) (S)
Dennis In Darlo (5c) (S)
North West Girdle (5b) (A)
Stone Wall (5b) (B)
Gymkhana (5b) (Ss)
Blackpool Promenade (5b) (A)
Tippling Crack (5b) (C)
Striding Edge (5b) (Sy)
Enigma (5b) (B)
Girdle Buttress (5b) (S)
Love Bug (5b) (B)
Gollinglith (5b) (S)
Stainthorpe's Wall (5b) (S)
The Wobbler (5b) (Bb)
Ritornal (5b) (B)
Hook Route (5b) (G)
The Waster (5b) (Ch)
Holly Tree Hover (5b) (Gw)
Noonday Ridge (5b) (Ch)
Steppin' Out (5b) (Ss)
The Way (5b) (Hg)
No Prisoners (5b) (Ch)
Bad Company (5b) (Gw)
Larkin's Right (5b) (Ss)
Z Climb Eliminate (5b) (A)

## The Best Routes, The Best Problems - GRADED LIST

Frensis Direct (5b) (B)

### HVS
V Crack (6a) (A)
Lightning Variation (6a) (Ah)
Wisecrack (5c) (S)
Desperation Crack (5b) (B)
Jams to the Slaughter (5b) (Es)
Castellan (5b) (E)
Crutch (5c) (H)
Plantation Wall (5b) (C)
Rabbit's Paw Wall (5b) (C)
Escalator (5b) (S)
Zoom (5b) (S)
Weasel (5b) (Ch)
Eavesdropper (5b) (E)
Daniel's Den (5b) (H)
Mitchell's Wall (5b) (H)
Lithos (5b) (B)
Birdlime Traverse (5b) (A)
Thompson's Traverse (5b) (A)
Squawk's Arête (5b) (S)
Woodbine (5b) (B)
Breakwind Arête (5b (S)
Flying Colours (5b) (Sy)
The Corbel (5b) (H)
Leaders Lament Direct (5b) (Bd)
Agra (5b) (S)
Beldin (5b) (S)
Witchita Linesman (5b) (Bb)
Tracking Something (5b) (Sy)
Minion's Way (5b) (B)
Outside Finish (5b) (Ss)
Wedgwood (5a) (E)
Great Western (5a) (A)
The Hattery (5a) (B)
Finger Dancer (5a) (Bd)
Red & White Traverse (5a) (Hg)
Magnificat (5a) (G)
The Main Wall Girdle (5a) (H)
Hatter's Groove (5a) (B)
Prosecutor (5a) (Hg)
Comet Wall (5a) (E)
Bulging Wall (5a) (Ls)
North Wall Eliminate (5a) (G)
Mantel Fantastic (5a) (Ls)

Trio Wall (5a) (Bat)
Auternative Arête (5a) (Gw)
Wailing Wall (5a) (H)
Harmony (5a) (Bd)
Demon Wall (5a) (A)
Original Route (5a) (S)
The Horn (5a) (Ah)
Sowden (5a) (S)
Double Top (5a) (G)
Plantation Crack (5a) (Pc)
Turret Crack (5a) (Ss)
Angel's Wall (5a) (C)
Overhanging Groove (5a) (A)
The Hattery Arête (4c) (B)

### VS
Pothole Direct (5b) (A)
Black Wall (5b) (A)
Fisher's Stride (5a) (A)
Rough Wall (5a) (B)
Route 2 (5a) (C)
Pram Pusher's Paradise (5a) (A)
Central Crack (5a) (B)
Great Roova Wall (5a) (Rv)
White Rose Flake (5a) (B)
The Girdle Traverse (5a) (Ch)
Lancet Crack (5a) (B)
Central Route (5a) (C)
Jabberwok Variation (4c) (B)
Parallel Cracks (4c) (B)
Easy Pickings (4c) (S)
Piggott's Stride (4c) (A)
Right Wall (4c) (B)
Birch Tree Wall (4c) (B)
Aces High (4c) (S)
Fag Slab Variant (4c) (B)
Pella (4c) (Bb)
Evening Ambler (4c) (Bd)
Frankland's Green Crack (4c) (A)
Maloja (4c) (B)
Thunder Crack (4c) (Ah)
Chevin Buttress (4c) (Ch)
Moss Side (4c) (B)
South Wall Traverse (4c) (A)
Allan's Crack (4c) (B)
Right of Way (4c) (Hg)

Sun-Up (4c) (E)
Crack of Doom (4c) (A)
Central Climb (4c) (A)
Lad's Corner (4c) (C)
Arête Direct (4c) (Ss)
High Level Traverse (4c) (A)
The Scoop (4c) (C)
Unfinished Crack (4c) (C)
The Traditional Climb (4c) (A)
Zig Zag Direct (4c) (A)
Z Climb (4c) (A)
Ellingstring (4c) (S)
Jabberwok (4b) (B)
Central Route Direct (4b) (Ch)
Notice Board Crack (4b) (B)
Right-Hand Crack (4b) (B)
Tarquin's Terrace (4b) (H)
Boot Crack (4b) (C)

### MVS
Bird's Nest Variation (4c) (A)
Square Chimney & Whisky
  Crack (4b) (A)
Cubic Corner (4b) (B)
Slab And Crack (4b) (Bd)
West Face (4b) (Gw)

### HS
Undercut Flake Variation's (4c) (S)
Parson's Chimney (4b) (A)
Pellet Climb (4b) (Dv)
Bird's Nest Crack (4b) (A)
Pig Traverse (4b) (B)
Druid's Chimney (4b) (B)
Undercut Flake (4b) (S)
Cassius Crawl (4b) (H)
Keystone Chimney (4b) (B)
Hawk Traverse (4b) (B)
Sorrento (4b) (Bg)
Twin Cracks (4b) (H)
Roc's Nest Chimney (4b) (G)
The Goblin (4b) (A)
Jezebel (4b) (G)
Alternative Arête (4a) (Gw)

# GRADED LIST - The Best Routes, The Best Problems

## MS
Cave Crack (4a) (Bd)
Tranmire Arête (4a) (S)

## S
Shorty's Dilemma (4c) (B)
Central Route (4b) (Ch)
Zig Zag (4b) (C)
Pedestal Wall (4b) (C)
Cheap Trick (4b) (Bb)
Simple Simon (4b) (Ss)
South Chimney Layback (4b) (A)
Tyto (4b) (Bb)
Peerless (4b) (B)
Loyalty Crack (4b) (Gw)
Heather Wall (4b) (B)
Portcullis (4a) (E)
Fag Slab (4a) (B)
Kiernan's Traverse & Rough Crack (4a) (A)
Spinnaker (4a) (E)
Jammed Sandwich (4a) (Ls)
The Belfry (4a) (B)
Centurion (4a) (H)
Pinnacle Flake Climb (4a) (A)
Sack Race (4a) (As)
Safe As (4a) (A)
V Chimney and Traverse (4a) (A)
The Virgin Climb (4a) (A)
Stenislag (4a) (Th)
Branch Line (4a) (Bat)
Jumbo Jam (4a) (B)
Arête Wall (4a) (Ss)
Barnley Crack (4a) (S)
Cave Chimney (4a) (B)
Hidden Chimney (4a) (Ss)
Roman Crack (4a) (H)
The Heel (4a) (E)
North Chimney (4a) (Gw)
Twisted Chick (4a) (Nn)
Thin Veneer (4a) (Bat)
Old Corner (4a) (B)
Wolfrey Crack Indirect (4a) (Gw)
Fag End (4a) (B)
Fluted Crack (4a) (A)
Ladder Climb (4a) (Ch)

Long John's Rib (4a) (B)
Corner Crack (4a) (B)
Just Pad Dad (Sy)

## HVD
Long Chimney (4a) (A)
President's Progress (4a) (B)
Ulfer's Crack (4a) (S)
Lover's Leap Chimney (4a) (B)
Cup and Saucer (4a) (A)
Great Slab (4a) (B)
Oak Tree Crack (4a) (Bat)
Square Chimney (4a) (C)
Dancing Bear Variant (4a) (B)
Grit Corner (4a) (B)
Argy Bargy (4a) (B)
Cyclops (3c) (B)
Long Funnel (3c) (B)
Pompeii Chimney (3c) (H)
Lichen Slab (3b) (B)
Fluted Columns (A)
Wall And Nose (Hg)
Cracking Up (Sy)
Sundial (E)
Left Wall (S)
Stew Pot (A)

## VD
South Chimney (4a) (A)
Difficult Crack (3c) (B)
The Turtle Rocks Chimney (3c) (B)
Slab Arête (3c) (B)
Cracked Corner (3c) (B)
Narrow Chimney (3c) (H)
Dancing Bear (3b) (B)
Problem Wall (3b) (B)
Leapfrogger (3a) (Gw)
Heather Groove (Gw)
Womb with a View (Es)
Halfway Chockstone (S)
Frank's Slab (Bb)
Bisexual Bratwurst (Hg)
Sunstroke (E)
Buttress Route (G)
Old Corner (S)

Entertainment Traverse (Bd)
The Crevasse (Bb)
Not So Tight Chimney (S)
The Watchman (Bb)
Flake Climb (Ss)

## HD
Chockstone Chimney (3b) (B)
Vamoose (3b) (B)
Bat Buttress Original (3b) (Bat)
Slab Central (2c) (B)
Staircase (Bb)

## D
Castle Corner (3b) (B)
Tight Chimney (3b) (B)
Cannon Route (3a) (B)
Low Man Easy Way (A)
West Chimney Variation (A)
Holly Bush Crack (Gw)
Sundown (E)
Pioneers Slab (Bd)
Arvel Chimney (Gw)
Holly Tree Scoop (C)
Groove Time (Gw)

## M
Idle Slabs (2b) (B)
Chockstone Crack (Gw)

# the problems

## Font 8b+
Bulbhaul (A)

## Font 8b
Ulloha (C)
High Fidelity (C)
Yes We Can (Wh)
Super Furry Animal (S)
X-Calibre Direct (Hs)
Cypher (S)
The Real Keelhaul (A)

Yorkshire Gritstone

## The Best Routes, The Best Problems - GRADED LIST

### Font 8a+
Brownian Motion (Ch)
Keelhaul (A)
Ironside (B)
Toe-Fu (Ss)
X-Calibre (Hs)
The Cherry Falls (A)
Fluid Dynamics (Ch)
Mr C (B)

### Font 8a
Harvest (Ch)
The Full Virgin Traverse (A)
Ranieri's Reach (C)
Lock Down (Hs)
Omega (Ch)
Identity Crisis (A)
Vogue (Bat)
Mistaken Identity (C)
Canine (A)
Growled (Wh)
New Blood (C)
To You Too (Hh)
Zoo York (C)
Chiasmata (A)
All Natural (A)

The Trial of Slinky Bob's Master (Wh)
Zen (A)
The Fonze (B)
Banana Republic (C)
Vicious Streak (C)
Exocet (S)

### Font 7c+
Heaven in Your Hands (Bd)
Ben's Groove sit-down-start (C)
Anniemutt (S)
Digital Delirium (E)
Like a Hurricane (Ch)
Underhand Super Extension (A)
Archimedes (Ne)
Ponce (B)
No More Mr Next Try (C)
Mike's Problem (B)
Hercules (Wh)
Blood Brothers Sit-Down Start (Ss)
Galaxy Left (Ss)
Hussefelt (B)
Salsa Start (C)
Super G aka Pinch Perfect (Nb)
Northern Soul (C)
Energy Crisis (Sw)

The Fridge (B)
Ralph (C)
Stu's Roof (A)
Twilight Session (S)
To me to you (Hh)
Everything Counts (S)
Magnum Opus (start) (A)
The Real Keel (A)
Crazy Legs Crome (Wh)
The Bulb (A)
Big Fish (Pc)
Three Squirrels (C)

### Font 7c
Terry (E5 7a) (C)
Juha's Arête (C)
Diamond Lights (E)
Jess's Roof (A)
Big Kicks (Ls)
Fluide (Cw)
Sky Diamond (E)
The Brock (Sw)
The Archer (B)
Whitefinger (Wh)
The U-Tube (B)
Hunter's Roof (Hs)

Tom Peckitt showing the way on his **Toe-Fu** (Font 8a+) at Simon's Seat. Page 476.
Photo: Will Buck

# GRADED LIST - The Best Routes, The Best Problems

Pot Black (Lb)
The Fabulous Number 2 (E)
Waite (C)
Kermit (Ls)
Agrippa (C)
Pedestal Arête (C)
5p 10p (B)
Nothings Safe (E6 6c) (C)
Guacamole (C)
Jumper's Dyno (B)
Pencil Problem (C)
Stipule (S)
Andy's Route Sit-Down-Start (C)
The Keel (A)
Solipsism (Ss)
Blockbuster (C)
Pounce (B)

## Font 7b+
Lay-by Arête (E2 6c) (S)
The True Pebble Wall (E5 6c) (C)
Syrett's Saunter (C)
Underhand (A)
Reach for a Peach (E4 6c) (H)
One Love (B)
Crystal Method (C)
Magnolia (Ss)
Streaky's Traverse (A)
No Pebble Arête (C)
I'm Chief Kamanawanalaya (Pc)
The Dark Side of Chi (A)
Phoenix Wall (Pa)
Stu's Roof Left-hand (A)
Holeshot (S)
Sewer Rat Connection (A)
Wainwright's Wobble (C)
Jaws (Pc)
Blood Brothers (Ss)
Ju Ju Club (C)
Pieces of Eight (B)
Bad Etiquette (C)
Eclipse (Nb)
Psycho Direct Start (E5 6c) (C)
Two Squirrels (C)
E.S.P (B)
Scary Canary (C)

Tantric Traverse (Sw)
Freak Technique (C)
Secret Seventh (C)
The Titfield Thunderbolt (S)

## Font 7b
Toboggan Wall (Nb)
To Be Is Not To Bolt (E6 6c) (C)
McNab (Ls)
Pinky Traverse (B)
Crucis (A)
The Longhaul (B)
Millionaire (Gw)
Pistol Whip (A)
iPerbole (Ss)
Trust (Nb)
Wisecrack Super Direct (S)
Self Suicide (S)
Smooth Wall Dyno (C)
Chocolate Orange (E5 6c) (C)
The Good News (Lb)
So Pussy (Lb)
Half A Drainpipe (Cw)
Crimpy Roof (B)
The Prow (C)
Ben's Groove (C)
Mystical Powers (Bh)
Particle Collision (Ch)
Low Pressure (Ch)
Monsoon Monsoon (C)
Benchmark (B)
Kindergarten Wall (E5 6b) (C)
Andy's Route (C)
Ian's Traverse (B)
Sirpicco (B)
Short Wall Dyno (C)
Ripper Arête (C)
Fieldside Traverse (A)
The Grouch (B)

## Font 7a+
Sulky Little Boys (S)
Wongy (Bat)
Pinky (B)
Fantasy League (B)
Whaleback (Ss)

Hook or by Crook (Hs)
Demon Wall Roof (A)
Simple Sally (S)
Supermodel (Cc)
Backbite (Ne)
Eat the Light (Ch)
Dew Drop (E)
Dreamland (A)
'Arries 'Ook Direct Start (A)
Ahab (C)
Pocket Knife (C)
Peshmerga (Wh)
Slapstick Arête (C)
Rachael's Box (B)
Over Easy (C)
Falcon (Ne)
Jumpin' Jack Flash (Gw)
Finches Fuel (C)
Flapjack Traverse (C)
Ultimate Emotion (Bd)
Chipper Traverse (A)
Black Chipper Arête (B)
Longbow (B)
The Governor (B)
Si's Arête (A)
The Rack (B)
Horn Rib (C)
Joker's Wall Traverse (B)
Brown's Roof (A)
The Anchor (B)

## Font 7a
Pair in a Cubicle (B)
Morrel's Wall Traverse (A)
Whisky Galore (B)
Rageh Omaar (Wh)
Barley Mow (A)
Icicle (Rv)
Hen Arête (Hn)
Low Level Traverse (H)
Suckerpunch (Nb)
Piglet Arête (E3 6a) (Sy)
Hammill's Rib (A)
Slideshow (Nb)
Patta's Arête (A)
The Blazing Apostle (E4 6b) (Rv)

## The Best Routes, The Best Problems - GRADED LIST

Aurora (Rv)
C and A Traverse (A)
Controlled Burning (Bb)
Middle Traverse (Rh)
Pocket Wall (C)
Little Bill (Bd)
The Cream Egg Eliminate (C)
Pok-A-Tok (Nb)
Galaxy (Ss)
Pinna (Ss)
Yuletide Wall (C)
New Jerusalem (C)
Think Pink (Lb)
Rodeo Rider (Lb)
Death Drop 2000 (E4 6b) (C)
Crucifix Traverse (A)
Too Much Too Young (E)
Get a Grip (E)
Pussy Galore (B)
Cleft Dyno (B)
Elwood P Dowd (Hh)
Dolphin's Nose (Hh)

### Font 6c+
Pebble Wall (A)
Green Fingers (Nb)
Gypsus (A)
Not My Stile (C)
Sloper Patrol (A)
Doe Traverse (Th)
Robin's Nest (Ne)
Pancake Scoop (C)
The Boss (Sy)
Pine Tree Arête (C)
Pot of Gold (Sw)
I am Walrus (A)
Flapjack Groove (C)
Ed's Dyno (A)
Wall of Horrors Traverse (A)
Syrett's Roof (A)
Dolphin Belly Slap (A)
Joker's Flake (B)
Pommel (B)
Heart Shaped Slab (B)

### Font 6c
The Virgin Traverse (A)
Boris or Bust (Lb)
Lichen Grope (E4 6b) (Gw)
Clingon (A)
Petrocelli (Ls)
Optical Illusion (Sw)
Micro Corner (S)
Rick's Rock (E3 6a) (C)
Cracklin' Crease (Th)
Cowboy Daze (Lb)
Supple Wall (S)
Horn Dyno (C)
Hump Bump (Nb)
Looking Glass (E)
Wall Direct (Rh)
Green Wall (C)
Cave Arête (Nn)
Rocking Groove (C)
Pocket Wall (C)
The Hanging Nose (C)
The Money Shot (C)
The Pinch (C)
Dead Point Dyno (C)
MBKC Arête (C)
The Palm Press (C)
Micro Wall (S)
Little Baldy (S)
The Traverse (E)
Murky Rib (B)
Lost World (B)
Black Dog Arête (B)
Niche Arête (B)

### Font 6b+
Davies Ramp (S)
Lightning Crack (C)
Ripper Trav/Ron's Reach (E3 6a) (C)
Fat Punter's Roof (Wh)
Bancrofts Roof (A)
Last Gasp (A)
Dungud (A)
The Gypsy (A)
Birk Gill Wall (Bg)
Shoot to Kill (E2 6a) (Rv)
Mantel Illness (C)

Pocket Rock (C)
Strictly Personal (HVS 6a) (S)
Anniversary Arête (B)
Saffner Arête (Nb)
Plum Prow (Ch)
Murky Way Kid (B)
Moss Arête (B)
Bellyflop (B)
Perky (B)
Niche Corner (B)

### Font 6b
Mr Smooth Sit-Down-Start (C)
The Cookie Monster (Cc)
Cold Crack (A)
Rock Around the Block (Sp)
Flying Arête (A)
Glitterbug (Nb)
Crack Nose (Ls)
The Right Wing (A)
Skull Wall (Sw)
Maurice Chevalier (C)
Fiddlesticks (Bat)
The Bat (C)
Larchbow (Ne)
Roof of the World Left Arête (C)
License to Thrill (Lb)
The Horn (C)
Big Dyno (Ls)
Little Gem (E)
The Glass Chipper (C)
Hanging Flake (C)
Broken Home (Bd)
Otley Wall Right-Hand (C)
Otley Wall Traverse (C)
Flake Wall (C)
The Great Flake Sit-Down Start (C)
Smooth Wall (C)
Joker's Reach (B)
Dugout (B)
Backward J (Rh)
Flipper (B)
Niche Roof (B)
Drop Zone (Bb)
Smiley Dog Arête (Bb)

Almscliff to Slipstones          **687**

## GRADED LIST - The Best Routes, The Best Problems

### Font 6a+
Teeter Totter (A)
Heart of Oak (Th)
Backhander (A)
Teaspoon Variation (A)
Strong as an Oak (Th)
The Crucifix Warm-up (A)
Crucifix Arête (A)
Stretcher (C)
Back Wall (C)
Corvus Arête (Cw)
The Phat Traverse (C)
Otley Wall (C)
Thin Slab Direct (C)
Back Stabber (C)
The Scone (C)
Our Fathers Arête (C)
Steptoe (S)
Reason And Rowan (S)
Green Roof (B)
Cubic (B)
Pockets Wall (Sp)
Joker's Wall Left (B)
The Prince (La)
Trench Left (B)
Love Scoop (B)
The Doomed Dromedary (Hc)
Striding Edge (B)
Gwyneth Left (B)

### Font 6a
Bert Wells (S)
Raynman (E2 6a) (Ch)
Solitaire (Ls)
Hanging Rib (A)
Wallender (Ss)
Morrell's Wall (A)
The South West Face (A)
Shadows of Forgotten Ancestors (Hb)
Trackside Arête (A)
Note to Comply (Ls)
Princeps (Rh)
Twin Arêtes (Hs)
All Buns Blazing (Bat)
Bun Fight at the OK Coral (Bat)
Rainbow (Sw)

Fingers Rib (Bat)
Rock On (S)
Lay-by (S)
For Queen and Country (Lb)
Centre Left (S)
Low Pebble Wall (C)
Cavity (C)
Overhanging Nose (A)
The Halo (C)
Wolfsbane (Gw)
Twin Pockets (C)
Smear Arête (C)
Mr Smooth (C)
The Flakes (Gw)
Time After Time (E1 6a) (Ch)
Third Lucky Friend (E2 5c) (Ch)
Supergreen (Ch)
Mantel Arête (C)
Fingers Crack (C)
Gray's Wall (A)
Cream Egg Arête (C)
Pockets or Drop (C)
The Standard Traverse (H)
Bob's Bastard (C)
Breakfest (C)
Chicken Scoop (C)
Stretch (B)
Heart Ache (B)
Roofer (B)
Sharkbait (B)
Minidigit (B)
Capsize (B)
King Worm (B)
Gwyneth Right (B)

### Font 5+
Morris Dance (HVS 5b) (C)
Heart Shaped Arête (A)
End Wall Direct (H)
The North Ridge (A)
Super Central (Ch)
Eliminate Em' (La)
The Niche (A)
Tree Slots (E)
Right Edge (S)
Pork Chop Slab (A)

Splitter Arête (Ls)
Tiptoe (S)
Rock Of (S)
Gripping Groove (C)
Scone Centre (C)
Fairy Cake (C)
The Neat Wall (C)
Couser Edge (C)
Pinnacle Arête (Gw)
Rough Rib (C)
ROTW (C)
Lippy Luvin' (C)
Cruel Crack (C)
The Thin Slab (C)
Neat Wall Arête (C)
Gladiator (Rh)
MBKC Groove (C)
Jam Pot (A)
Den (Bb)
Three Swings Traverse (A)
Arête Pocket (Rh)
Hombre (Bb)
The Outlaw (Bb)
Senator (Rh)
Rib Tickler (E)
Cannon Fodder (B)
Cleft Butty (B)
Top Pocket Finish (Rh)
Green Arête (B)
Murky Way (B)
Trench (B)
Fisherman's Friend (B)
Yoke of Oxen (B)

### Font 5
Matterhorn Ridge (A)
Fascinating Pockets (Ls)
North Top Boulder (A)
Dry Stone Base Line (Rv)
Squitter (Ne)
Central Crack (Wh)
The Chimney Flake (A)
Mick Dundee (Nb)
Undun (Bb)
Twitchy Sort of Way (HVS 5b) (Sy)
Mantle Madness (Bb)

Andy McCue on **Pick Pocket** (Font 3+) at Almscliff, Page 54
Photo: Adi Gill

The Undercut (H)
Chicken Arête (C)
North East Corner (Sp)
Overhang Direct (Ls)
Chicken Heads (C)
Recorder (Bh)
Little Red-Haired Girl (Gw)
Scone Slab Left (C)
The Barn Door (Ch)
Pocket Traverse and Arête (Ls)
Thin Ice (E)
Neat Arête (C)
Suckers Rib (C)
Question of Balance (S)
Shorty's Dilemma (S)
The Hillary Step (A)
Portal Rib (E)
Ready for Action (E)
I Need Tree (E)
MK Original (A)
The Nose Direct (A)
The Crucifix (A)
Orange Crush (B)
Trackside Right (B)
Huey (B)
Facade (B)
Pod Wall (B)
Moat Rib (B)

### Font 4+
Rocking Stone Roof (VS 5b) (C)
The Nose (VS 5b) (A)
Point 'n' Shoot (C)
Matterhorn Ridge (Right Side) (A)
South Face Route (A)
Rugrats (Bb)
How Green Was My Valley (Ch)
All Off (S)
Hot and Anxious (HVS 5a) (Sy)
The Gatekeeper (C)
Fried Green Tomatos (VS 4c) (C)
Epitaph (C)
Flaky Groove (C)
Classic Traverse (A)
Pinnacle Arete (Cc)
West Face (Sp)

Missile Attack (Lb)
Field Mouse (A)
Welcome Wall (S)
Tea Party Slab (S)
Steroid Android (S)
See the Light (E)
Go Within (Bb)
Murky Water (E)
Sideline (B)
Pantomine (B)

### Font 4
Ripper Traverse (S)
The Lhotse Face (A)
The East Face (A)
By The Fin (Nb)
Shadow Face (A)
Rail and Arête (La)
The Nose (A)
Heather Wall (S)
The Postman (A)
Tommy's Dilemma (S)
Morris Crack (HS 4b) (C)
Suckers Wall (C)
Roova Rise (Rv)
Pedestal Arête (Sp)
Pancake Arête (C)
Slanting Flake (S)
Nought Corner (Nb)
Curving Crack (S)
Micro Arête (B)
Heart Arête (B)
Duey (B)
Sunbeam (B)
Raspberry Ripple (B)
Piglet Wall (B)

### Font 3+
Sunshine (B)
Pick Pocket (A)
Right Arête (S)
Goblin's Ear (S)
Rippled Corner (C)
Gun Barrel (Gw)
Pot Scoop (Sp)
Scone Arête (C)

Echo Wall (La)
Hamble's Arête (A)
North West Arête (Sp)
Flapjack Arête (B)
Fairy Slab (C)
Bedlam (Bb)
Art Flakey (Bb)
Barnacle Bill (B)

### Font 3
The South Col (A)
Still Water (E)
Flapjack Pockets (C)
Morris Minor (MS 4b) (C)
Fairy Arête (C)
Mini Wall (C)
Little Arête (S)
West Cave wall (A)
Jugs (Rh)
Awkward Finish (S)
Little Acorns Grow (Bat)
Left Arête (S)
Gypsy Wham (S)
Clean Sweep ( Bb)
Wall Bar Buttress (B)
Dark Deed (B)

### Font 2+
Roofed Corner (S)
Chockstone Pull Up (S)
Overhanging Crack (S)
Sublime Slab Left (Rh)
Slab (C)
Yule Slab 3 (C)
Frank's Wall (HD) (S)

### Font 2
Little Corner (S)
Squirm (H)
Ten Foot Slab (S)
Chipped Slab (A)
Heather Wall (S)
Playground Crack (C)

Janine Kavanagh on **Cubic** (Font 6a+) at Brimham. Page 285.
Photo: David Simmonite

# Index

3.3 Metre Slab 582
3'10 207
5p 10p 305
21st Birthday Wall 623
99' 536

## A

Above Average Age 359
Abrasion 315
Abolition 448
A Campanologists Tale 609
Aces High 574
Acetabulum 86
A Climb 622
Acme Error 277
Acme Wall 282
A Coin For A Beggar 520
A Comedy Moment 151
A Company of Wolves 357
A-Corner 335
A Cunning Trap 611
Adamant 371
Adam's Ale 326
Adam's Apple 326
A Deep Pit 611
Adrenaline Rush 124
Adulterated Bliss 614
After Thought 345
Aftermath 393
Aghast 612
Agog 612
Agra 566
Agrete 566
Agroan 612
Ahab 108
Alan's Arête 567
Alan's Wall 575
Alcove Chimney 263
Alcove Wall 256

Alexander Beetle 608
Alien Kiss 622
Alien Nation 199
A Life Less Ordinary 478
A Little Anxious 614
A Little Something 614
A Little Trouble 615
Allan's Crack 240
All Bark and No Bite 365
All Buns Blazing 332
Alleycat 441
Alleycracker 441
All Off 576
All Our Yesterdays 64
All Pull Together 607
All Quiet 78
All the Twos 583
Almanac 380
Al Says 6a 71
Alternative Arête 355
Amadeus 341
Amazing Grace 147
Ambidexter 261
Amen 474
Ancient 323
And Others 471
And She Was 482
Andy's Route 118
Andy's Traverse 207
Angelic Upstart 48
Angel's Wall 134
Angel's Wing 134
Angle Crack 398
Angua 357
Annie Oakley 333
Anniemutt 583
Anniversary Arête 262
Another Question 471
Another Winters Edge 614
Antlers Route 515
Apache 424

Apfel Strudel 617
Apostle Left-Hand 603
Apparition 396
Appiewand 282
A Question of Balance 470
Arc En Ceil 649
Archimedes 541
Arête Direct 360, 468
Arête Pocket 627
Arête Wall 468
Argy Bargy 232
Armpit 549
Arna Arête 635
'Arries Left 'Ook 88
'Arries 'Ook 89
Arrow Slit 427
Art Flakey 588
Arthur 257
Arvel Chimney 357
A Sign for the
  Dynosaurs 256
A Step in the Right
  Direction 48
Askance 54
Atlantic Voyager 435
Atomic 565
Augustus 644
Aurora 601
Austin Roova 603
Auternative Arête 354
Autobahn 396
Autumn Crack 520
Autumn Gold 354
Avatar 181
A Very Grand Thing 610
A Wolf in the Wild 356
Azimuth 470

## B

Bacchus 373
Backalley 442
Backbite 542

Back Breaker 220
Back Crack 139
Backhander 57
Back In The U.S.S.R 324
Back Stabber 139
Back Wall 139
Backward J 631
Bad Company 357
Bag End 382
Baggin's Variation 469
Bag Of Snot 514
Bahia 590
Banana Republic 142
Bancroft's Roof 81
Bandyido 594
Bare Back Side 206
Barleycorn 392
Barley Mow 36
Barnacle Bill 231
Barnes Wallace 530
Barney Rubbles 2
Bookcase 399
Barnley Crack 565
Barnley Wall 565
Barnstorm 621
Barren Waste 569
Bashful 475
Bat Buttress Direct 333
Bat Buttress Original 333
Bat Crack 330
Batman 332
Battlecat 512
Battlement 426
Beached Whale
  Traverse 112
Beaky 473
Beat It 593
Beatnik 291
Beckside Buttress 650
Bedlam 587
Beef Crisis 319
Beldin 564

Beldin Direct 564
Bell 648
Bell End 648
Bellow 171
Bellyflop 297
Bellyporker's Progress 237
Benchmark 298
Ben's Groove 116
Bert Wells 579
Beta Blocker 568
Big Boots 590
Big Boss 593
Big Easy 587
Big Fish 316
Big Kicks 495
Big Mig 591
Big Roof Traverse 495
Bilberry Groove 211
Bilberry Jam 262
Bilge Crack 281
Bilge Pump 281
Bill & Ben 214
Birch Climb 263
Birch Tree Wall 260
Bird Flu 487
Birdlime Traverse 88
Bird's Nest Crack 85
Bird's Nest Variation 85
Birk Gill Crack 598
Birk Gill Wall 598
Bisexual Bratwurst 372
Bit of a Jerk 54
Bite Size 483
Black Bob 258
Black Chipper Arête 253
Black Dog Arête 298
Black Groove 597
Blackhead 89
Black Jumper 139
Blackpool Promenade 89
Black Tower Face 209
Black Wall 89

**692**   **Yorkshire Gritstone**

| | | | | |
|---|---|---|---|---|
| Black Wall Direct 90 | Brigand 590 | Cannon Route 199 | Charlie Sheen 47 | Cissy Greens 617 |
| Black Wall Eliminate 89 | Bring Out The Funk 109 | Cantilever Pinnacle 226 | Charm 151 | Clamper 494 |
| Blind Alley 470 | Britt 236 | Canvas Arête 479 | Charming Chimney 245 | Clangers 592 |
| Blinkers Rib 485 | Britt Right-Hand 236 | Caped Crack 332 | Charming Crack 245 | Clappers Crack 469 |
| Blobby 181 | Brown Boots 590 | Capsize 231 | Chastity 41 | Clarence Tenthumbs 170 |
| Block Arête 568 | Browned Off 591 | Capstan Full Strength 241 | Cheap Trick 593 | Claret 306 |
| Blockbuster 115 | Brownian Motion 182 | Captain Hook 413 | Cheese Straw 617 | Class Action 598 |
| Block Chimney 147, 282 | Brown's Roof 80 | Captive Conscience 341 | Cherry Falls 41 | Classic Bagger 245 |
| Blood Brothers 474 | Brush Stroke 479 | Cardinal Wolsey 447 | Chevin Buttress 175 | Classic Traverse 84 |
| Blunt Arête 610 | Brush Up 573 | Casement Crack 427 | Chewing the Cud 320 | Class Warrior 519 |
| Bluster Arse Vessel 354 | Brutaliser 245 | Cassius Crawl 649 | Chiasmata 50 | Clean Sweep 590 |
| Boa Cracks 247 | Bucking Broncos 319 | Cassius Direct 649 | Chicken 253 | Cleft Arête 273 |
| Board to Tears 232 | Buena Ventura 275 | Cassock Slap 71 | Chicken Arête 122 | Cleft Buttress 274 |
| Bob's Bastard 118 | Buffalo 322 | Castellan 426 | Chicken Eddy 622 | Cleft Dyno 273 |
| Bob's Traverse 645 | Bulbhaul 46 | Castle Corner 218 | Chicken Heads 121 | Cleft Pinnacle 273 |
| Bog Crack 215 | Bulge Head 542 | Castle Crack 220 | Chicken Run 158 | Clematis 82 |
| Bold Finger 324 | Bulging Wall 492 | Castle Traverse 218 | Chicken Scoop 622 | Clingon 273 |
| Bomber Command 322 | Bungle Traverse 36 | Catastrophe 527 | Child's Play 591 | Clodhopper 394 |
| Bonington's Made It 527 | Bunkered 441 | Cat Baloo 526 | Chimney and Slab 506 | Cloisters 448 |
| Bonjoy's Wall 409 | Buns to Batman 332 | Caterpillar Crack 526 | Chimney Arête 282 | Closet Crack 202 |
| Bonus Traverse 630 | Bureaucrat 279 | Cat Piano 603 | Chimney Wall 469, 590 | Close to Critical 261 |
| Boomerang 283 | Burglary Within Tent 616 | Cats Eyes 527 | China Syndrome 88 | Close to the Hedge 249 |
| Boot Crack 139 | Burnsall Ham 383 | Caught in an Eddy 613 | Chinese Crack 236 | Clueless 588 |
| Boris or Bust 324 | Burnsall Sports 382 | Cave Arête 506 | Chin's Prow 365 | Cockerel Wall 622 |
| Born Slopey 304 | Butterfingers 512 | Cave and Slab 148 | Chip Butty 617 | Cocoa Club Board |
| Botany Bay 210 | Buttie 159 | Cave Chimney 291, 589 | Chipped Edges 136 | Meeting 206 |
| Bother 608 | Buttress Route 393 | Cave Crack 512, 599 | Chipped Slab 71 | Cocoa Runnel 206 |
| Bottom's Up 218 | By-Pass 396 | Caveman 214 | Chipped Slab 1 121 | Coldfinger 325 |
| Boughed 609 | By the Birch 448 | Caveman's Corner 402 | Chipper Traverse 253 | Colditz 330 |
| Bounced 614 | | Cavity 134 | Chips 121 | Cold Turkey 158 |
| Bounces 609 | **C** | Central Bay Route 571 | Chloride Attack 530 | Cold Wall 561 |
| Boundary Chimney 396 | Cadbury's Flake 591 | Central Climb 68 | Chockstone Chimney | Collyhirst 285 |
| Bowsprit 435 | Cakewalk 219 | Central Crack 86, 268 | 280, 470 | Combination Cracks 256 |
| Boy in Blue 519 | Caligula 646 | Central Cracks 483 | Chockstone Crack 355 | Comet Wall 398 |
| Braised Steak 320 | Calvinistic 121 | Central Eliminate 68 | Chockstone Overhang 568 | Compulsion Crack 147 |
| Branch Line 335 | Camel and Fish Slab 369 | Central Route 42, 134, 177 | Chockstone Pull Up 583 | Compulsive Viewing 147 |
| Breakfest 112 | Camel's Crack 368 | Central Route Direct 177 | Chockstone Wall 355 | Concave Slab 210 |
| Breaking Out 612 | Campanile 403 | Centre Left 579 | Chocolate Orange 117 | Condensed Milk 608 |
| Break Out 330 | Campus 601 | Centre Point 277 | Choked Chimney 247 | Connoisseurs Corner 247 |
| Breakwind Arête 560 | C and A Traverse 46 | Centurion 646 | Chox Away 263 | Constipation Crack 82 |
| Brian's Climb 397 | Canine 42 | Chalk Scratchings 48 | Christopher Robin 572 | Constrictor Chimney 247 |
| Brief Crack 249 | Cannon Fodder 199 | Charlie's Dilemma 247 | Chunky Chicken 483 | Controlled Burning 588 |

Almscliff to Slipstones

| | | | |
|---|---|---|---|
| Cool for Cats 170 | Crucifix Arête 87 | Dead Man's | Diwaly 513 |
| Cool Runnings 409 | Crucifix Traverse 87 |   Crankshaft 372 | Dixon's Dilemma 570 |
| Corbel Variation 643 | Crucis 41 | Dead Man Walking 211 | Doberman Pincher 205 |
| Cock-a-Hoop 479 | Crumbli 617 | Dead Point Dyno 124 | Dog Lead 468 |
| Corkage 343 | Crustimoney | Dealer 590 | Dogleg Crack 254 |
| Corkscrew 343 |   Proceedcake 609 | Dean Martin 601 | Dolphin Belly Slap 87 |
| Corner and Traverse 360 | Crutch 649 | Death Drop 2000 108 | Dolphinian 86 |
| Corner Crack 62, 247, 482 | Cuban Blockade 323 | Deception 169, 358 | Dolphin's Nose 306 |
| Corvus 599 | Cubic 285 | Deep Black 498 | Donald 281 |
| Corvus Arête 345 | Cubic Corner 286 | Deepfry 253 | Don't Step Back Crack 203 |
| Cotton Reel 532 | Cuddles 161 | Defence System 181 | Don't Worry, I'm a |
| Count Duckula 330 | Cummin's Route 572 | Delphinus 87 |   Nurse 443 |
| Counting Crows 345 | Cup and Saucer 65 | Delta 476 | Doomed Oasis 392 |
| Courser Edge 121 | Curious Motion 341 | Demon Wall 85 | Do or Diet 373 |
| Cowboy Daze 320 | Curver 112 | Demon Wall Roof 86 | Dots and Dabs 84 |
| Cowell's Rib 357 | Curving Chimney 590 | Den 589 | Double Back 263 |
| Crack and Wall 86, 515 | Curving Crack 579 | Dennis In Darlo 569 | Double Cap 601 |
| Crack Attack 333 | Curving Crack Arête 579 | Dennis the Menace 235 | Double Mantelshelf 575 |
| Crack Nose 498 | Curving Overlap 324 | Depth Charger & | Double Ridge 152 |
| Crack of Bof 227 | Cuticula 57 |   Up Periscope 49 | Double Top 401 |
| Crackaroo 210 | Cutie 285 | Derrick 589 | Down Under 409 |
| Cracked Corner 268 | Cutting Edge 592, 597 | Desolation 508 | Downbeat 598 |
| Cracked Rib 249 | Cutting the Cord 401 | Desperation Crack 218 | Dragnet 333 |
| Cracked Slab 160 | Cyclops 277, 304, 571 | Detour 235 | Dragonfly 442 |
| Cracking Up 611 | Cypher 583 | Devious Dave's | Dragonslayer 443 |
| Cracking Yarn 54 | |   Dubious Direct 360 | Dreamcast 207 |
| Cracklin' Crease 532 | **D** | Dew Drop 433 | Dreamland 88 |
| Crack Nose 498 | Dab Hand 592 | Diablo 331 | Dr Green Thumb 153 |
| Crack of Bof 227 | Daisy Chain 82 | Diagonal 574 | Drift Wall 479 |
| Crack of Doom 80 | Dali 409 | Dialectics 87 | Drop the Dead Donkey 613 |
| Crack with a View 503 | Dame Edna 210 | Diamond Lights 433 | Drop Zone 587 |
| Cragrat Crack 507 | Dam It All 530 | Dick 331 | Druid's Chimney 263 |
| Crazy Paver 438 | Dancing Bear 229 | Diethard, Slim with a | Druid's Reality 272 |
| Cream Egg Arête 160 | Dancing Bear Variant 229 |   Vengence 373 | Drumstick 158 |
| Crenellation 427 | Dan Dare 374 | Difficult Crack 258 | Dry Stone Base Line 602 |
| Crevasse Wall 376 | Daniel's Den 644 | Digital Delirium 432 | Dry Stone Wall Traverse 87 |
| Crimpy Roof 305 | Dark Cleft 568 | Dimbleby's Crack 416 | Duey 281 |
| Crimpy Wall 106 | Darkside 270 | Diminuendo 561 | Duggie's Dilemma 252 |
| Crinkle Cut 71 | Das Kleiner Sprung 433 | Dingbat 393 | Dungeon 427 |
| Croc Bloc 412 | Da's Route 572 | Dino 603 | Dungo Son of Dungo 508 |
| Crock Around the | Daubenton's Wall 330 | Dino-Mania 475 | Dungud 587 |
|   Block 355 | Dave's Saunter 117 | Direct Finish 569 | Dusk 152 |
| Crocodile 393, 442 | Dave's Wall 644 | Discord 515 | Dust Off 621 |
| Crocodile Gully 412 | Davies Ramp 582 | Dispatches 415 | Dutch Elm 643 |
| Cross Fire 588 | Dawn 590 | Disreali Gears 383 | Dypso 148 |
| Crossover 263 | Dead Angst 646 | Ditch 427 | |

| | |
|---|---|
| **E** | |
| Easel 479 | |
| Easter Egg Crack 314 | |
| Easter Egg Ridge 314 | |
| Eastern Arête 515 | |
| Eastern Block 322 | |
| East Ridge of the | |
|   Eccles Cake 200 | |
| Easy Groove 569 | |
| Easy Over 622 | |
| Easy Pickings 563 | |
| Easy Ridge 623 | |
| Easy Way 335 | |
| Eat the Light 181 | |
| Eavesdropper 438 | |
| Eavestone Crack 439 | |
| Eavestone Eliminate 439 | |
| Eavestone Wall 438 | |
| Echo Wall 538 | |
| Eclipse 411 | |
| Edge Biter 514 | |
| Edge Route 569 | |
| Edge Udger 479 | |
| Edge Wall 122 | |
| Ed's Dyno 47 | |
| Eeyore 613 | |
| Eliminate A 521 | |
| Eliminate B 521 | |
| Ellingstring 574 | |
| El Mariachi 594 | |
| Elwood P. Dowd 304 | |
| Emmaus Road 82 | |
| Encore 65 | |
| End Slab 343 | |
| End Wall 34, 644 | |
| Energy Crisis 537 | |
| Enigma 260 | |
| Entertainment Traverse 513 | |
| Entrance Exam 503 | |
| Envy of Angels 48 | |
| Ephedrine 125 | |
| Eric 589 | |
| Escalator 561 | |
| Escape 591 | |
| Escape Route 330 | |

E.S.P. 257
Ethel 201
Et Tu Brute 644
Evening Ambler 512
Evenso 438
Evergreen Cracks 315
Every Man Has His
 Niche 78
Everything Counts 583
Excalibur 424
Exit Stage Left 64
Exocet 578
Exorcist 87
Exorcist Green 181
Extremities 560
Eyes Left 230
Eyes Right 230

# F

Façade 297, 597
Fag End 241
Fag Slab 240
Fairy Cake 161
Faithful Wall 520
Falcon 542
Fall from Grace 475
Fall In 34
Fallout 323
Famous 45 410
Fantasy League 206
Fascinating Pockets 499
Fascinationby 575
Fast Track 597
Fat Chance 440
Fat Crack 374
Fat Man's Misery 71
Fat Man's Slab 373
Fearby 575
Feel The Noise 108
Feeling Gravity's Pull 365
Felicity 202
Fell Race 382
Fence Buttress 86
Few Tomorrows 64
Fiddlesticks 331, 575
Field Fair 34

Fieldside Traverse 34
Fifteen Million
 Plastic Bags 598
Fifth Arête 602
Filter Tip 241
Finale 521
Finale Slab 64
Finesse 470
Finger Dancer 515
Finger Knacker Crack 143
Fingers 521
Fingers Rib 331
Finite Field 34
Fire Brigade 588
First Night 65
First Strike 323
Fisherman's Friend 306
Fisher's Stride 41
Fisher's Traverse 62
Fist Fight 232
Fists of Fury 592
Flake Ache 298
Flake and Wall 492
Flake Arête 109
Flake Climb 466
Flake Crack 621
Flakeout Arête 568
Flake Wall 109
Flakey Pastry 617
Flakey Wall 578
Flapjack Arête 158
Flatline 211
Flibbetigibbet 244
Flipper 306
Flirtin' Cos I'm Hurtin' 473
Flobbalobba 214
Flow Arête 358
Flue Crack 149
Fluid Dynamics 183
Fluide 345
Flummox Arête 515
Flummox Crack 516
Fluted Columns 50
Fluted Crack 50
Flying Arête 38
Flying Colours 616

Fook Nose 235
Foolish and Deluded 608
Foolproof Zip 587
Foot in Mouth 182
Footpatter 394
Footprints in the Butter 227
Forbidden Fruit 439
For Crying Out Loud 254
Forced Entry 306
Fore! 537
Forecourt Crawler 147
Forecourt Traverse 147
Foreign Bodies 394
Forever Man 283
Forever Onward 565
Forever Young 568
Forgotten Buttress 262
Forgotten Rib 374
Forgotten Wall 85
For Keepsake 426
For My Next Trick 305
Formic Crack 508
For Queen and Country 325
Forthright 570
Foxy 359
Fractal 50
Frank 603
Frankland's Green
 Crack 70
Frank Miller 144
Frank's Slab 599
Freak Technique 116
Fred Zinnerman 144
Free and Breezy 330
Free Fall 594
Free Range 487
Free Stile 106
Freestyle 170
French Fancy 374
Frensis 199
Frensis Direct 198
Friday the 13th 572
Fried Green Tomatoes 142
Friendly Fun 375
Friends and Enemies 258
Fright Arête 297

Frogging Wall 520
From The Shadow 170
Front Traverse 136
Frost in the Shadows 268
Fruit Of The Vine 373
Fryer's Front 383
Fug Dup 108
Full Traverse of
 High Man 90
Fulvia 477
Fungus the Bogeyman 70
Funky Jam 478
Funny Friends 375
Funnything Accidents 612
Fun with Friends 375
Fuser 569

# G

Galaxy 482
Gales 615
Galleon Tower 436
Games with the
 Nephfesch 247
Gamma Goblins 199
Gangreen 622
Gardening at Night 365
Gargling Crack 503
Gary Cooper 144
Gaskins' Problem 40
Gav's Mantel 546
Gecko Arête 415
Genesis 439
George II 257
Get a Grip 433
Get Nervous 568
Getting Groovy 526
Giddy Up 593
Gigglin' Crack 242
Ginger Badger 560
Ginger Tom 526
Ginger Whinger 70
Girdle Buttress 563
Glacier Apron 433
Glasshouse Groove 416
Glitterbug 411
Gluon 275

Gnome's Arête 251
Goanna Arête 415
Goblin's Ear 582
Going Bald 514
Going Catatonic 442
Go Joe 198
Gollinglith 564
Good Friday 432
Good Friends 358
Goof Aydee and the
 Mango 198
Goose Bumps 158
Gordon's Proffer 277
Gordon's Wall 272
Gorilla 440
Got Any String 611
Got It in One 359
Governor 274
Go Within 589
Graft Crack 249
Grand Defiance 357
Grand Illusion 78
Grape Strain 36
Grasshopper 340
Gravedigger 152
Gravity Brawl 520
Gray's Wall 65
Grease 645
Great Roova Roof 601
Great Roova Wall 601
Great Slab 286
Great Western 78
Great Wolfrey Buttress 359
Green Arête 274
Green Crack 292
Green Fingers 411
Greenfingers 315
Green Gully Rib 62
Green Gully Wall 62
Green Nose 283
Green Prioress 245
Green Roof 279
Green Traverse 159
Green Wall 62, 153
Green Wing 182
Griffiths Chimney 471

Almscliff to Slipstones **695**

Grimace 411
Grimwith Bridge 365
Gripping Groove 117
Grit Attack 268
Grit Bit 251
Grit Corner 251
Grit Crack 492
Grit Escape 250
Grit Expectations 250
Grit School 498
Gritstone Special 492
Grizzly 251
Gronff 176
Gronff Left-Hand 176
Groove Eliminate 562
Groove On 48, 567
Groove Time 354
Groovy Baby 499
Grotto Wall 332
Ground Up 181
Grow Up 409
Growler 177
Grumpy's Crack 485
Guacamole 115
Guillotine 398
Gully Arête 251
Gully Wall 592
Guy's Traverse 214
Gwyneth 201
Gymkhana 473
Gymnast 574
Gypsy Wham 582
Gypus 41

## H

Haberdashery 399
Hadrian's Wall 644
Hair of the Dog 467
Halcyon Chimney 226
Halcyon Daze 226
Half A Drainpipe 345
Halfway Chockstone 571
Hallmark 425
Hamble's Arête 36
Hammill's Rib 36
Hand Traverse 576

Hang 'em Low 319
Hanging Arête 280
Hanging Chimney 642
Hanging Crack 594, 280
Hanging Groove 125, 244, 492
Hanging Nose 108
Hanging Rib 37
Hanging Wall 121
Hangover Chimney 356
Hangover Crack 356
Happy Days 281
Happy Daze 575
Hare's Head Crack 306
Harmony 515
Harobics 304
Harrogate Nights 490
Harry 331
Harry's Crack 232
Harry's Heap/The Knobbler 117
Harum–Scarum 152
Harvest 169
Harvey 490
Hats Off to Andy 199
Hatter's Groove 250
Hat Trick 248
Hawk Traverse 218
Headstand 621
Heap of Everybody 615
Heart Ache 588
Heart Arête 270
Heartbeat 588, 598
Heart of Oak 335, 531
Heart Shaped Slab Arête 211
Heather Crack 560
Heather Groove 360
Heather Wall 286
Heather Wall Variant 286
Heat Seeker 323
Heatsink 587
Heave Ho 432
Heaven In Your Hands 516
Hedgeup 249
Heffalump Wall 610

Hellfire 448
Hen Arête 487
Hen Pecked 487
Henry Pootel 610
Henry Rush 608
Here There Be Dragons 443
Hidden Chimney 485
Hidden Crack 209, 485
Hidden Roof Traverse 207
Hidden Wall 209
Hideaway 283
Hieronymouse 372
High Adventure 589
High Crack 491
High Fidelity 118
High Level Traverse 84
High Noon 144
High Nose Traverse 466
High Pebble Wall 491
High Steppa 274
Hippo 413
H.K.T. 280
Hobgoblin 82
Hokum 41
Hole In The Sky 372
Hole In The Wall 561
Holeshot 583
Holland, Hannen & Cubbitts 530
Holly Bush Crack 359
Holly Hover 592
Holly Tree Hover 359
Holly Tree Scoop 144
Holy Trinity 532
Hombre 594
Homefront 306
Homeland 181
Home on the Range 319
Honey Comb 84
Hook Or By Crook 546
Hook Route 393
Hop Scotch 48
Horizontal Memories 345
Horse Gone Wonky 613
Hot and Anxious 608
Hot Green Chillies 142

Hourglass Chimney 237
House Points
 Tomorrow 203
Huey 281
Huff-Puff Chimney 356
Hump Bump 409
Humper 373
Humus 398
Hunchback 648
Hunter's Roof 545
Hunter's Wall 546
Hurricane 441
Hussefelt 214

## I

I am a Walrus 36
I Can't Believe It's A
 Girdle, Girdle 149
Ian's Traverse 281
Ichthys 169
Icicle 602
Icing on the Cake 200
Identity Crisis 40
Idle Slabs 292
Ilex Wall Direct 549
I'll Bet She Does 482
Illusion 392
I'm Chief
 Kamanawanalaya 316
Impending Doom 78
Impregnable 568
Inaccessible Crack 482
Inappropriate
 Behaviour 507
In As Much As 610
In Cahoots 382
Indecent Postures 147
Indian's Arête 231
Indian's Fin 512
Indian's Turban Route 232
Indian's Turban West 231
Inertia Arête 508
Ingham's Route 591
In Limbo 46
In Memoriam 357
Inner State 256

Innominate 375
In Retrospect 263
Inside Left 562
Inside Out 305
In the Frame 479
In the Nick of Time 634
In the Reach of Nick 634
Into the Groove 499
Intreegued 344
Intruding Fool 515
iPerbole 473
Ironside 291, 490
Itchy Chin 616

## J

Jabberwok 219
Jackabu 201
Jack Be Nimble 40
Jack On Fire 40
Jack's Grotto 530
Jack The Lad 574
Jacob's Ladder 86
Jam Hard 108
Jammed Sandwich 498
Jam Pot 84
Jams to the Slaughter 502
Jaw Crawler 616
Jaws 316, 413
JCB 536
Jehu's Chariot 396
Jelly Baby Wall 243
Jemima 36
Jenny Binks Wall 563
Jenny Tulls 170
Jericho Falls 341
Jerry and Ben 374
Jess's Roof 80
Jezebel 395
Jibber 232
Jib Sail 435
Jigger Me Fingers 435
Jimmy's Crack 227
Jim's Mantel 207
Jim's Problem 274
Jim's Wall 649
Jojo La Perruque 506

Joker's Flake 291
Joker's Reach 290
Joker's Wall 290
Joker's Wall Arête 290
Joker's Wall Crack 290
Joker's Wall Traverse 290
Jolly Jeffery 599
JP's Problem 54
Jug Arête 483
Jug Handle Pull Up 575
Juha's Arête 148
Ju Ju Club 115
Julius Caesar 644
Jumbo Jam 227
Jumper's Dyno 215
Jumper's Traverse 273
Jumping Jack 442
Jumpin' Jack Flash 362
Jumping Left 628
Just Another Saturday 334
Just Do It 211
Just Grazing 319
Just Pad Dad 615
Just the One 109

# K

Kangaroo Wall 210
Keeper Crack 235
Kermit 496
Kestrel on a String 371
Keyhole Cops 201
Keystone Chimney 226
Kiernan's Traverse & Rough
 Crack 51
Killer 571
Kindergarten Wall 116
King Cobra 200
King of the Snakes 226
King Snake 226
Kings of Northumbria
 Overmantel 627
Kiosk Crack 220
Kitson Did It First 88
Knapper 521
Knee Biter 71
Kneewrecker 219

Knobbles In Toyland 503
Knobbly Wall 305
KOYLI 396
Kruschev's Chimney 323

# L

Lacking In Smack 613
Ladder Climb 171
Ladder Wall 491
Lad's Corner 144
Lagopus Laughter
 Indirect 492
Laid to Rest 376
Lancet Crack 272
Larch Link 542
Larchbow 541
Lardies Route 373
Large Gollolup 610
Lariat 320
Larkin's Right 496
Last Crack 249
Last Gasp 588
Lasting Satisfaction 36
Last Regret 169
Last Rites 621
Lay-Away 498
Lay Back and Think 203
Layback Corner 172
Layback Crack 281, 466
Layback Left 496
Lay-by 576
Lay-by Arête 576
Lay-by Arête Direct 576
Leader's Lament 513
Leaders Lament Direct 513
Leaf Climb 78
Leaning Wall 573
Leany Meany 571
Leap Frog 261
Leapfrogger 354
Learn 'n' Groove 276
Leaving the
 Bergschrund 432
Ledge and Scoop 622
Ledge-End 479
Led Zeppelin 521

Leech's Wall 175
Left Cheek 86
Left Edge 262
Left Flake 215
Left-Hand Arête 314, 483
Left-Hand Bias 200
Left Wall 261, 570
Left-Wall Girdle 260
Left Wolfrey Crack 359
Lend Me Your Ears 643
Let the Children Play 591
Leverage 54
Leveretation 306
Licence to Kill 325
License to Thrill 324
Lichen Grope 362
Lichen Slab 262
Lichen Wall 245
Life and How to Live It 365
Life Begins At Forty 439
Life in the Old Dog Yet 365
Lightning Crack 126
Lightning Variation 621
Like a Hurricane 180
Like Nothing 611
Limited Company 358
Lipstick Wall 358
Lip Traverse 122, 159
Lithos 243
Little Acorns Grow 333
Little Baldy 576
Little Bill 512
Little Cenotaph 124
Little Funnel 240
Little Midget 597
Little People 172
Little Red Riding Hood 357
Little Wonder 305, 597
Livia 644
Lizard Wall 415
Lobo 304
Lock Down 546
Longbow 270
Long Chimney 71
Long Funnel 242
Long John's Rib 277

Long Time Coming 611
Look No Hands 235
Look Out Below 426
Lookout Wall 207
Lords a Leaping 496
Lost Corner 262
Lost Crack 344
Lost World 283
Love Bite 262
Love Bug 261
Love Handle 262
Lover's Leap Chimney 261
Lover's Leap Chimney
 Right-Hand Variation 261
Love Scoop 211
Low and Mighty 334
Low Arête 140
Lowdowns 393
Low Impact 334
Lowlander 334
Low Level
 Traverse 564, 570
Low Man Easy Way 51
Low Nose Crack 473
Low Nose Traverse 473
Low Peach Traverse 643
Low Pebble Wall 126
Low Season 334
Low Spirits 334
Low Rib 107
Low Tide 334
Low Traverse 140
Loyalty Crack 358
LSG 172
Luey 281
Lumping Along 611
Luna 157
L'unacy 588
Lunar Perigee 588
Lunatic Rib 251
Lurcio's Lip 648
Lurker at the Threshold 530

# M

M 325
Machicolation 427

Madagascar 596
Mae West's Rib 237
Magnetic Heels 137
Magnificat 390
Magnificrack 378
Magnolia 485
Magnum Opus 41
Making Shapes 54
Maloja 198
Malt Extract 610
Mammoth 229
Mangenon Groove 507
Mantel Arête 140
Mantel Fantastic 492
Mantel Illness 111
Mantel Madness 593
Mantel On 567
Mantel Upset 479
Mantelshelf Blues 274
Mantelshelf Crack 561
Mantelshelf Corner 245
Mantelshelf Wall 561
Man with a Golden
 Bun 332
Man With the Golden
 Gun 325
Mark Turner's
 Rockover 567
Marrow Bone Jelly 124
Marr's Route 572
Martin's Muff 109
Mary Archer 599
Master Bates
 Left-Hand 435
Mastermind 397
Masterpiece 479
Mastodon 229
Matterhorn Ridge 50
Mattie's Mantel 602
Matt's Roof 57
Maurice Chevalier 126
Maverick Mick 494
Max Crax 273
Max Wall 171
MBKC Arête 117
MBKC Groove 117

Almscliff to Slipstones **697**

McNab 498
Megadoom 78
Ménage a Trois 261
Merle 280
Merlin 71
Merlon 280, 427
Michael Michael
  Superman 218
Mick Dundee 413
Micro Corner 579
Micro Machine 579
Microscopic Wall 68
Micro Wall 579
Middle Lip 627
Middle Traverse 628
Midsummer Night's
  Dream 402
Midway 374
Mike's Problem 233
Mild Steel 276
Millionaire 362
Minidigit 234
Mini Mati 109
Minion's Way 291
Minnow 316
Mirky Way Kid 273
Misshape 159
Missile Attack 323
Missile Crisis 322
Miss Monypenny 324
Mistaken Identity 136
Mist Crack/Autumn
  Fog 520
Mitchell's Wall 642
MK Original 54
Mmmmm 601
Mnemonic 545
Moat Rib 218
Moderator 572
Mohole 244
Monostate 262
Mons Meg 198
Monsoon Monsoon 118
Monte Carlo 476
Moon Madness 354
Moorland Bow 601

Morose Mongoose 200
Morrell's Wall 34
Morrell's Wall Traverse 34
Morris Crack 125
Morris Dance 125
Morris Minor 125
Mortal Wall 172
Mosaic 466
Moss Alley 284
Moss Arête 279
Mosside 634
Moss Side 286, 364
Mouth to Mouth 591
Mr. C 281
Mr Smooth 155
Muck & Brass 412
Mumbojumbo 220
Munga 498
Murky Crack 273
Murky Rib 274
Myopia 136
Mystery 169
Mystical Powers 381

## N

Naked Yoga 536
Nameless Chimney
  262, 515
Narrow Buttress
  Chimney 344
Narrow Chimney 645
Narrowing Chimney 241
Narrow Margin 566, 597
Natasha's Just
  Desserts 324
Natural Grit 253
Neat 117
Neat Arête 111
Neat Crack 111
Neat Wall Arête 117
New Blood 126
New Broom Sweeps
  Green 515
New Jerusalem 126
News Night 416
Newton John 645

Next of Kin 588
Niche Arête 215
Niche Corner 215
Niche Dyno 215
Niche Roof 215
Niche Wall 215
Nidderdale Wall 416
Nigel's Roof Left-Hand 537
Nigel's Roof
  Right-Hand 537
Night Raiders 540
Nipscrew 399
No Doubt 251
No Loitering 617
No Mans Land 78
No More Mr Next Try 143
Nonawin 343
No News is Good News 415
Noonday Ridge 144
No Pebble Arête 126
No Prisoners 171
No Rest for the
  Whippet 365
North Buttress Crack 402
North Buttress Direct 402
North Buttress
  Ordinary 402
North Chimney 355
North End of Pooh 607
Northern Shuffle 71
Northern Soul 115
North Gully 466
North Gully Buttress 466
North/South Divide 355
North Top Corner 42
North Wall 562
North Wall Eliminate 397
North-West Arête 209, 657
North West Girdle 66
Nosebag 46
Note to Comply 499
Nothing's Safe 118
Notice Board Crack 275
Notice Board Wall 275
Not My Stile 106
Not So Army Barmy 281

Not So Tight Chimney 560
Not the Nine O'clock
  News 416
No Way Out 291
Nuttalls Mintoe 591

## O

Oak A Arête 333
Oak Scoop 643
Oak Tree Crack 201, 335
Obsequious 479
Octopus 413
Off Beat 593
Off Campus 42
Officer Dibble 441
Offspring 562
Off The Wall 88
Offwidth His Head! 503
Of Little Brain 614
Old Corner 285, 562
Old Pals 292
Oliver's Overhang 599
Omega 180
One Flew Over the Eccles
  Cake 200
One Hundred Inches
  Long 609
One Love 257
One Man And His
  Dogmas 153
On Her Majesty's Secret
  Service 325
Only Sixteen 575
On the Edge 392
On The Fence 57
On The Other Hand 610
Opeless 41
Open Face 485
Optical Illusion 537
Opus 41
Orange Crush 262
Orchid 485
Orchrist 81
Original Route 564
Orion 545
Otley Wall 121

Otzi 140
Oubliette 82, 425
Our Father's Arête 106
Out of Pocket 71
Out On Bail 575
Outside Finish 469
Out With The Old 483
Ouzo for Twozo 474
Overdo 297
Over Easy 160, 487, 621
Overhang Direct 492
Overhanging Arête 578
Overhanging Groove 68
Overhanging Nose 36
Overhung Buttress 314
Overlapping Wall 251
Over the Top 402
Owl Chimney 340
Owl Corner 589
Owl Wall 589

## P

Pablo 274
Padded Arête 416
Pair in A Cubicle 274
Pair in a Cubicle
  Traverse 274
Palette 479
Pan 443
Pancake Arête 155
Pancake Day 155
Pancake Scoop 155
Pancake Sloper 155
Panorama 416
Panzer 469
Parallel Cracks 268
Parallel Universe 372
Parson's Chimney 70
Particle Collision 182
Party Piece 597
Pa's Route 572
Pateley Show 416
Pathos 243
Patta's Arête 57
Paul's Arête Left-Hand 560
Paul's Arête Right-

**698**          **Yorkshire Gritstone**

Hand 560
Paws for Thought 473
Peace 448
Peaceful Smile 609
Pebbledash 251, 432
Pebble Frog 46
Pebble Pincher 503
Pebble Wall 87, 496
Pedestal Arête 147, 354, 658
Pedestal Wall 148
Peekabu 201
Peerless 283
Peggy Babcock 508
Pella 591
Pellet Climb 521
Pence 610
Pencil's Problem 118
Pendragon 443
Pendulum 394
Penitence 448
Penny Pip 64
Perfect Day 219
Perfect Jam 183
Perfectly Gasless 358
Performance Management 376
Perky 233
Permutation Rib 125
Perverted Crack 274
Petch's Groove 562
Petrocelli 499
Phenomenonlogy 591
Phillipa's Ridge 396
Phoenix Wall 415
Pick and Nick 220
Pick Pocket 54, 494
Picnic 219
Picnic Alternative Start 219
Picnic Variation 219
Pieces of Eight 300
Pie r Squared 541
Piggott's Stride 50
Piglet Arête 234, 610
Piglet Wall 233
Pig's Ear 242

Pig Slip Cow Punk 242
Pig Traverse 242
Pine Tree Arête 157
Pinky 233
Pinky Traverse Flake Finish 233
Pinna 477
Pinnacle Direct 50
Pinnacle Flake Climb 50
Pioneers Slab 513
Pipe Dreams 169
Pipestrelle 330
Pipping Arête 57
Pistol Whip 54
Plantation Crack 315
Plantation Ridge 134
Plantation Wall 134
Playground Crack 121
Playground Traverse 121
Pocket, Traverse and Arête 496
Pocket Drop Traverse 284
Pocket Rock 139
Pockets Wall 658
Pocket Wall 107, 123, 496
Pocket Watch 46
Pod Wall 306
Point Blank 199
Point Break 139
Pok-A-Tok 409
Pommel 298
Pompeii Chimney 646
Ponce 231
Pond Life 48
Pony Express 320
Pooh Sticks 169, 614
Pork Chop Slab 37
Porky 172
Porno Crack 172
Pot Black 319
Portcullis 424
Pothole Chimney 470
Pothole Direct 84
Pot Of Gold 537
Pounce 231
Power Pull 416

Powered by Gaz 280
Pram Pusher's Paradise 48
Predator 413
Preparation H 642
President's Progress 262
Press Problem 546
Primate 171
Problem Arête 579
Problemina 594
Problem Traverse 578
Problem Wall 292, 570
Problem Wall Arête 296
Problem Wall Direct 296
Promises More 372
Prosecutor 374
Prow Crack 441
Prowler 441, 479
Prows That 183
Psyche 571
Psycho 124
Puff 442
Pulpit Chimney 390
Pulpit Corner 71
Pulpit Friction 71
Pulse Rate 211
Pump Friction 498
Puncture Repair 54
Pure Gold 499
Pushing the Boat Out 432
Pussy Cat 589
Pussy Galore 252
Pygmy Traverse 172
Pygmy Wall 172

## Q

Quantum Leap 598
Quark 151
Quark Quack 151
Quark Walk 151
Que Fastidio 54
Question of Balance 582
Question Time 471

## R

Rabbit's Paw Wall 125
Rachael's Box 270

Rachael's Box Variation 270
Rail Mantel 491
Rainbow 537, 649
Rainy Day 219
Raj 232
Ralph 136
Ramble On 611
Ram Jam 252
Rampant Hippo 171
Rampart 427
Ranieri's Reach 148
Raspberry Ripple 234
Ratanoee 205
Rat Arsed 204
Ratatwoee 205
Ratbag 204
Rat Catcher 204
Ratfink 204
Ratlin' 205
Rattler 204
Rattlesnake 205
Rat Trap 204
Ravens Peak Wall 520
Raven Arête 345
Rave On Wall 520
Rawhead Rex 172
Rawhide 319
Raynman 182
Reach for a Peach 642
Reach for the Sty 242
Real Chimney 471
Rear Entry 175
Rearguard 425
Rear Traverse 526
Reason And Rowan 578
Recess Arête 358
Rectum Rift 86
Red Alert 323
Red Hot Knob 482
Red or Dead 279
Red Square 324
Red Tape 279
Red Tape Traverse 279
Redundancy Rib 143
Red & White Traverse 373

ResErection 261
Resonance 544
Restless Natives 304
Resurrection 261
Retribution 448
Retribution Rib 80
Reunion 492
Revision Revolt 170
Rewind 532
Rhyme 622
Rhythm 622
Rib and Slab 148
Rib Right 37
Rick's Rock 139
Ride The Magic Dragon 442
Riding Bareback 319
Rift Crack 82
Right Arête 494
Right Cheeky 86
Right Edge 575, 582
Right End 627
Right Flake 215
Right-Hand Arête 250
Right-Hand Bias 201
Right-Hand Crack 268, 483
Right-Hand Twin 572
Right of Way 374
Right to Roam 621
Right Wall 112, 262, 572
Rigsby 263
Ripley Bank 416
Rip Off 149
Ripper 571
Ripper Arête 116
Ripper Traverse 571
Ripper Traverse/Ron's Reach 116
Ripping Roof 499
Ripping Traverse 499
Ripple Arête 646
Ripple Traverse 234
Rising of the Sap 531
Ritornal 254
Roadside Crack 200
Roadside Mantel 107
Roaring Boys 200

Almscliff to Slipstones **699**

Roast Beef 51
Robin 333
Robin's Nest 541
Rock Around The Block 657
Rocking Arête 116
Rocking Chockstone
  Chimney 513
Rocking Stone Traverse 116
Rock 'n' Roll 354
Rock Off 576
Rock On 576
Rock Over 576
Roc's Nest Chimney 394
Rodeo Rider 319
Rod's Roof 220
Rogue Trader 254
Rollerball 628
Roll Over 136
Rolo 140
Romancing The Stone 413
Roman Crack 645
Roofer 304
Roof Layback 137
Roof Of The World 142
Roof Traverse 109
Roots of All Evil 443
Rosla 549
Rotifer 254
ROTW Left Arête 142
ROTW Right Arête 142
Rough Neck 286
Rough Rib 107
Rough Stuff 286
Rough Wall 286
Round in Circles 607
Route 1 136
Route 2 136
Route 3 134
Route Five 526
Route Four 526
Route Three 526
Rowan 537
R.P.T. 280
Rubic 290
Rubicon 345
Ruff Traverse 542

Rugrats 593
Runnel Trilogy No 1 226
Runnel Wall 107
Running on Red 248
Ruscator 395
Rush Hour 483
Rustler 320
Ryvita 409

# S
Sack Race 383
Saddle Sore 320
Safe As 48
Saffner Arête 409
Salieri 340
Salsa Start 115
Salubrious Navaho
  Indians 315
Salvador 409
Sameness 341
Sammi 603
Sand Crab 169
Sandwich Slopers 159
Sarnie 159
Saunter 371
Sausage Roll 617
Savage Sentence 398
Saying Grace 147
Say Nothing 615
Scales 413
Scalp 426
Scarecrow 344
Scary Canary 136
Scone Arête 160
Scone Centre 160
Scone Slab Left 160
Scott's Corner 599
Scrambled Egg 160
Scuff 47
Sculptured Wall 220
Scunthorpe Traverse 507
Seaman Staines 435
Secret Crack 262
Secret Seventh 116
Self Suicide 568
Senator 628

Serendipity 249
Serenity 495
Seven Up 569
Sewer Rat Connection 42
S for B 642
Shades of Green 356
Shadow Face 71
Shadows of Forgotten
  Ancestors 367
Shake, Cattle and Roll 320
Shaken Not Stirred 325
Shark Attack 413
Sharkbait 306
Shark Nose 412
Sharks Fin Crack 513
Shed Ahoy! 372
Sheep's Clothing 358
Shine On 567
Shoe Shine 140
Shoot to Kill 603
Short Arête 106
Short Arse 54
Short Arse Traverse 619
Short Slab 107
Short Wall 109
Shorty's Dilemma 285
Shot-hole Wall 547
Shuffle Crack 88
Shush Popeye 470
Siamese Bridge 572
Sideliner 181
Side-show 398
Sidestep 270
Side Track 315
Sidewinder 578
Silent Memory 372
Silkcut 241
Silver Trout 57
Simon Says 474
Simon Says Squeeze 477
Simon's Sat 506
Simple Sally 582
Simple Simon 471
Sinbad 570
Sinking Feeling 611
Sir Les 210

Sirpicco 298
Si's Arête 82
Si's Cheese Slice 243
Six Inch Stare 344
Sky Diamond 432
Skyjacker 397
Slab and Crack 491
Slab And Crack 515
Slab and Overlap 491
Slab Arête 277
Slab Central 292
Slab Ledge Roof Ledge
  Roof 507
Slab Right 292
Slant 471, 587
Slanting Flake 583
Slap and Traction 36
Slapstick 290
Slapstick Arête 143
Slenderer 607
Slide In 177
Slideshow 409
Slim Bay 494
Slim Buttress 494
Slippery Crack 249
Slipway 572
Sloper Patrol 46
Sloper Traverse 139
Slopey Traverse 34
Small Roof 122
Small Roof Left 495
Small Roof Right 495
Smear Arête 137
Smiley Dog Arête 588
Smokeless Zone 642
Smoke Ring 241
Smooth and Groovy 182
Smooth Arête 107
Smooth Wall 107
Smooth Wall Dyno 107
Smooth Wall Traverse 107
Snappy Roof 42
Sneakers 140
Snowball 537
Sod's Law 514
Soft Shoe Shuffle 140

Sohcahtoa 545
Sola Fide 340
Solipsism 474
Solitaire 496
Solitude 448
Solo Slab 169
Some Holds are Bigger than
  Others 365
Something's Cooking 51
Something to do in the
  Rain 598
Somnolent Jack 360
Son of a Bitch 578
Soothsayer 644
So Pussy 325
Sorrento 597
South Cave Traverse 57
South Chimney 88
South Chimney Layback 88
Southern Belle 315
Southern Shuffle 57
South Face Arête 126
South Face Climb 88
South Face Direct 126
South Face Route 588
South Wall
  Traverse 88, 126
Sowden 570
Sow's That 242
Space Plucks 570
Space Truckin' 561
Spare Rib 252
Sparkling Along 615
Sparrow Wall 335
Speedway 401
Spinnaker 434
Spirit Level 50
Spitfire 441
Splat 594
Splinter 479
Split Ends 180
Split Second 180
Splitting Heirs 180
Spoiler 343
Spondonical 474
Spout Hangout 492

Spring Fever  402
Spring Haze  602
Spring Roll  252
Spring Steal  276
Sprite  411
Square Chimney  148, 469
Square Chimney & Whisky Crack  50
Square Corner  589
Square Root  286
Squat Rocket  241
Squawk's Arête  568
Squeeze Crack  220
Squirm  644
Stainthorpe's Wall  575
Staircase  593
Staircase Chimney  344
Starboard Crack  432
State of the Union  315
Steady Arête  107
Steady VS Arête  202
Steep and Wrinkly  452
Steer  322
Stenislag  531
Stepoffable  90
Stepped Buttress  262
Steppin' Out  499
Steptoe  579
Steroid Android  582
Steve Rhodes' Warm Up (!)  629
Steve's Wall  560
Stew Pot  51
Stile Council  106
Stipule  578
Stir Frenzy  530
Stirk  322
Stockade  427
Stomach Traverse  86
Stone Age Reveller  272
Stonechat  439
Stonechat Ramp  439
Stone Cold  305
Stonequest  169
Stonerag  439
Stones Too Much  610

Stone the Crows  344
Stone Wall  286
Stop Motion  341
Storm In A Tea Cup  143
Straight Crack  172, 482
Strange Attractor  432
Strangeness  151
Streaky's Traverse  57
Strengthening Medicine  610
Stretch  283
Stretch Armstrong  42
Stretcher  121, 394
Stretching Hekate  280
Strictly Personal  573
Striding Edge  206, 616
String Vest  574
Stroll  48
Strong as an Oak  531
Strongbow  340
Stubby Arête  71
Student Games  447
Stu's Roof  86
Successor State  256
Suckerpunch  411
Suckers Rib  136
Suckers Wall  136
Sulky Little Boys  583
Summer Bed Linen  601
Summer Crack  520
Summer Dreams  343
Summer of 76  354
Summertime Solo  515
Sunbeam  297
Sun Bingo  429
Sun Bird  429
Sunday the 20th  572
Sundial  428
Sundown  428
Sunny Scoop  71
Sunshine  297
Sunstroke  297, 428
Sun-Up  429
Super Central  181
Super Furry Animal  578
Supermodel  526

Superturd Traverse  642
Supple Wall  583
Supreme Soviet  323
Swampy Arête  34
Swan Arcade  219
Swastika Rib  664
Sweat it Out  608
Sweep's Arête  590
Sweet Sixteen  575
Sweet Tooth  134
Swerve To Leave  634
Swing Arête  206
Swinging Free  441
Swirral Edge  616
Synchromesh  396
Syrett's Rib  272
Syrett's Roof  80
Syrett's Saunter  117

# T

Tachyon  565
Tadpole Traverse  650
Taggart  304
Tail Swipe  412
Tails Get in the Way  609
Take a Bough  229
Take No Notice  275
Talespin  592
Tall Man in the Bidet  372
Tan Your Hide  319
Tantric Traverse  536
Tao  137
Target Wall  588
Tarquin's Terrace  645
Tasty Pastry  617
Tea-Cake Wall  354
Tea Party Slab  582
Tears  412
Teaspoon Variation  65
Teflon Traverse  47
Ten Bears  251
Tender Homecoming  230
Ten Foot Moderate  578
Ten Foot Slab  582
Tensile Strength  276
Tentacle  615

Ten Traverse  305
Terry  117
Testicle  615
Tetelestai  341
Tetrapak Crack  57
That's the Badger  536
The Actress  622
The Afghan Whigs  365
The Alamo  424
The American Girl  622
The Anchor  300
The Anthill Mob  365
The Appliance of Science  602
The Arch  254
The Archer  270
The Arête  112
The Atom Smasher  530
The Backslider  177
The Barn Door  181
The Belfry  280, 390
The Big Greeny  70
The Bitch  42
The Black Chipper  253
The Blazing Apostle  602
The Blue Bomber  612
The Bold Ted Earl  503
The Boss aka Loose Change  609
The Bottom Line  291
The Bravados  594
The Breath of a Camel  369
The Brock  536
The Brute  235
The Bulb  46
The Buneater  375
The Buns of Navarone  332
The Can  134
The Cheat  513
The Chicken Scoop  122
The Chimney Flake  37
The Chisel  227
The Climb That Time Forgot  392
The Cooler King  330
The Corbel  643

The Crack  46, 490, 593
The Cream Egg Eliminate  160
The Creation  392
The Crenellated Ridge  142
The Crevasse  588
The Crucifix  87
The Crucifix Warm-up  87
The Cruel Crack  126
The Crystal Method  123
The Dark Side of Chi  68
The Director of the Board  603
The Dirty Rascal  427
The Drey  161
The Duke  354
The Ear  36
The East Face  38
The Easy Way  71
The Egg of Course  485
The Elf  81
The Empire Strikes Back  645
The Ems Telegram  78
The Endless Dog  602
The Fabulous Number 2  432
The Fall of the Roman Empire  646
The Fang  358
The Filth  519
The Final Finale  62
The Flakes  362
The Fly  592
The Fogger/Fog Crack  520
The Fonze  281
The Forbidden Corner  602
The Fourth Dimension  373
The Fridge  284
The Full Throttle  521
The Full Virgin Traverse  42
The Garden of Eden  438
The Gatekeeper  142, 426
The Ginnel  442
The Girdle Traverse  177
The Glass Chipper  139

| | | | | |
|---|---|---|---|---|
| The Goblin 81 | The Main Wall Girdle 649 | 475, 646 | Hanuman 399 | Tiptoe 579 |
| The Good News 323 | The Mantelshelf 202 | The Scryking 398 | The Waster 176 | Toad's Nose 68 |
| The Greasy Pole 383 | The Meaning of Life 443 | The Sentry Box 143 | The Watchman 594 | To Be Is Not To Bolt 109 |
| The Great Escape 331 | The Mighty Oak 334 | The Shelf 478 | The Watering Hole 320 | Toboggan Wall 409 |
| The Great Flake 118 | The Money Shot 106 | The Shim 402 | The Way 374 | Toe-Fu 476 |
| The Great Santini 520 | The Mutant Midge 374 | The Shootist 241 | The Wilderness Years 357 | Toe Poke 48 |
| The Green Giant 227 | The Naked Edge 475 | The Slab 490 | The Wishing Chair 373 | Tom 331 |
| The Green Room 124 | The Neat Wall 117 | The Snuffer 242 | The Wobbler 590 | Tombstone 395 |
| The Green Streak 140 | The North Ridge 37 | The South Col 38 | The Wood Cutter 335 | To Me To You 305 |
| The Green Wall 642 | The Nose 80, 88 | The South-West Face 38 | The Yoke of Oxen 231 | Tommy's Dilemma 582 |
| The Groove 107, 116 | The Nose Direct 80 | The Spy Who Loved Me 324 | The Zig Zag 80 | Tony's Torment 569 |
| The Grouch 231 | The Now Show 416 | The Standard Traverse 648 | Thick As Thieves 382 | Too Gnarly For Barley 448 |
| The Gunner 469 | The Only Remaining | The Storm 621 | Thick Skin 412 | Top Cat 442 |
| The Gypsy 41 | Question 602 | The Super Low-Level | Thin Crack 374 | Top Cat Traverse 42 |
| The Halo 106 | The Opportunist 515 | Traverse 649 | Thingumy In Thirsk 569 | Top Dead Centre 200 |
| The Handrail 563 | The Other Arête 590 | The Taper 440 | Think on Tha' Nose 634 | Top Man 593 |
| The Hattery 248 | The Palm Press 108 | The Tea Party 622 | Think Pink 320 | Top Pocket finish 626 |
| The Hattery Arête 248 | The Periwocky 209 | The Tear Jerker Finish 412 | Thin Line 286 | Tortoises and Hares 68 |
| The Hattery Chimney 248 | The Pieman 474 | The Thin Crack 170 | Thin Veneer 335 | Totally Flummoxed (for a |
| The Heel 440 | The Pinch 136 | The Thin End 440 | Third Friend Lucky 182 | while) 516 |
| The High Scary Groove 152 | The Plat Traverse 112 | The Thin Slab 112 | Thompson's Route 42 | Touching the Void 433 |
| The High Step 34 | The Postman 37 | The Titfield | Thompson's Traverse 85 | Touch your Toes 475 |
| The High Traverse 648 | The Pothole 84 | Thunderbolt 253 | Thoughtful Way 612 | Tough Enough 596 |
| The Hillary Step 38 | The Prayers of a Fish 369 | The Tombstone 152 | Three Chockstones | To You Too 305 |
| The Horn 157, 621 | The Prince 539 | The Torso Twins 512 | Chimney 86 | Tracking Something 612 |
| The Horror 71 | The Prow 137, 161 | The Traditional Climb 84 | Three Day Rave 376 | Trackside Arête 270 |
| The Imp 81 | The Rack 283 | The Tramp 42 | Three Squirrels 161 | Traditional Eliminate 84 |
| The Indirect Start 139 | The Red Squirrel 161 | The Traverse 434 | Three Swings Traverse 36 | Tradnasty 413 |
| The Jagular 615 | The Red Wall 526 | The Triad 477 | Three Trees Crack 244 | Trailblazer 320 |
| The Jewel in the Crown 231 | The Result 622 | The True Knobbler 622 | Thriller 263 | Trained Bloodhound 613 |
| The Keel 46 | The Riddler 333 | The True Pebble Wall 109 | Thug Arête 123 | Tranmire Arête 562 |
| The Keep 426 | The Rifles 396 | The True Two Ton | Thunderball 325 | Tranmire Crack 562 |
| The King of the Castle 427 | The Rift Traverse 84 | Sardine 64 | Thunder Crack 621 | Transcendance 591 |
| The Kraken 396 | The Right Wing 38 | The Turtle Rocks | Tiberius 646 | Transmission 411 |
| The Lady 40 | The Ripple Effect 283 | Chimney 226 | Tide Mark 650 | Treasure Island 436 |
| The Left Arête Of | The Road Rage | The Undercut 644 | Tigga, the Bagpipe Dog 374 | Tree Climb 374 |
| Psycho 124 | Experience 210 | The Unpaid Chauffeur 371 | Tiggers Can Fly 614 | Trench 298 |
| The Lhotse Face 38 | The Rocking Groove 116 | The U Tube 292 | Tight Chimney 82, 252 | Trench Foot 298 |
| Thelma 274 | The Rocking Stone | The Verger 390 | Time After Time 182 | Trends Right 628 |
| The Long Haul 215 | Roof 116 | The Virgin 40 | Timeless Divide 565 | Triangular Roof 270 |
| The Long Slab 54 | The Root to Success 441 | The Virgin Climb 41 | Time Waster 507 | Tribal Wars 627 |
| The Loser 360 | The Rose 109 | The Virgin Traverse 40 | Tin 443 | Tricky Wall 160 |
| The Lowdown 334 | The Rozzario Syndrome 519 | The Voice 603 | Tiny Corner 628 | Trident 49 |
| The Low-Level | The Sands 603 | The Wall 88 | Tip Off 149, 621 | Trigger Happy 478 |
| Traverse 649 | The Scone 160 | The Wall of Horrors 78 | Tippling Crack 148 | Trilogy 477 |
| The Low Man Girdle 51 | The Scoop 42, 151, | The Warriors of | Tipster 149 | Trio Wall 332 |

Triple 'A' 148
Triptych 477
Troilett Wall 250
Troubled with Lycans 355
True Brit 304
True Grit 241
Trumps 574
Trunk 476
Trust 409
Trust Ye 448
Tube Break 202
Tumbledown 36
Turd 642
Turn Me Loose 333
Turret Crack 469
Turtleneck Crack 220
Tusk Chimney 229
Twelfth Night 62
Twenty Foot Crack 562
Twice 19 615
Twiggy 611
Twilight Session 571
Twin Arêtes 546
Twin Cracks 172, 375, 643
Twin Finish 181
Twin Pockets 136
Twisted Chick 506
Twisted Twit 506
Twitchy Sort of Way 614
Twixt 563
Two Squirrels 161
Two Startled Sheep 574
Two Tier Crack 201
Tyto 593

## U

Ugly 285
Ulfer's Crack 565
Ullola 106
Ultimate Emotion 516
Undercut Double Crack 560
Undercut Flake 568
Undercut Wall 107
Underhand 42
Under the Awning 616
Under the Eaves 438

Undun 587
Unfinished Crack 124, 280
Unit of Power 181
Unwanted Gift 324
Up and Under 621
Up Pompeii 648
Upset Crack 513
Up She Rises 435

## V

Vam 202
Vamoose 201
Vampire Rib 331
Vampire's Ledge 176
Vanilla Slice 617
Variation Start 575
Variation Starts 569
V Chimney 151
V Chimney and Traverse 48
V Chimney Direct 48
V Crack 50
Veni Veci Oblivisci 645
Verdi Grease 514
Vicious Streak 123
Victorian Climb 477
Viper 247
Virtual Reality 340
Vision On 211
Visual Deception 175
Vlad Von Carsen 330
Vogue 333
Vol au Vont 617
Vomer 340
Vomerite 340
Vomit 340

## W

Wacko Saco 376
Wailing Wall 646
Wainright's Wobble 116
Waite 125
Walking the Plank 181
Walk in Silence 248
Wall And Nose 374
Wallbanger 490
Wallender 479

Walleroo 210
Wall of Horrors Traverse 71
Wally 297
Walter's Rib 357
Waltzing Matilda 519
Wanderlust 622
WASC 68
Wasted Years 291
Waster Wall 176
Watchman's Neb 594
Wavelength 544
Weany Meany 597
Weasel 171
Webster's Whinge 109
Wedge Crack 247
Wedge Down Crack 569
Wedge Iron 440
Wedgwood 440
Welcome To The
  Neighbourhood 144
Welcome Wall 582
Well Worn 48
Werewolf 356
West Buttress Route 514
West Cave Wall 36
West Chimney Variation 80
Western Alliance 323
Western Bulge 515
Western Crack 515
Western Front 78
West Face 360, 657
West Face Eliminate 563
West Face Variant 360
West Indian's Turban
  Route 232
Wet Landing 424
Wet, Wet, Wet 530
Whaleback 478
Wharfedale Wall 50
What 612
What!!! 371
What a State 256
What Happens Now? 607
What If 615
Whenever 612
When in Rome 646

Wherefore 612
Where He Fell 443
Where's Grandma 471
Whip and Top 331
Whisky Galore 252
Whisky Wall 50
Whisky Wall Direct 50
Whistling in the Dark 426
White Flag 257
Whitehall 324
White Rose Flake 257
White Wash 245
Whiz-Bang 199
Who Needs Friends 258
Why 612
Why Climb 65
Why Not? (Do a Girdle) 516
Widening Horizons 494
Wielding the Branding
  Iron 319
Wigged Out 365
Wild Abandon 393
Wildcat 434
Wild Roova 601
Window Chimney 469
Wind Rider 373
Windy Day Flop 219
Windy Miller 219
Windy Wall 621
Wine Taster 507
Winkling Wall 532
Winter Finish 471
Winter of Discontent 354
Winter Sunshine 428
Winter Wall 520
Wisecrack 291, 567
Wisecrack Direct Start 566
Witchita Linesman 592
Withering Heights 574
Witton Wall 571
Wobble Block 524
Wolf at the Door 356
Wolfrey Crack Direct 359
Wolfrey Crack Indirect 359
Wolfschmidt 355
Wolverine 359

Womb with a
  View 273, 502
Wonderbar 448
Wongy 333
Woodbine 240
Wooden Heart 333
Word to Your Mother 530
World in Action 415
Worn Down 54

## X

X-Calibre 546
X-Calibre Direct 546
X-Factor 65

## Y

Yankee Beau 315
Yardarm 435
Yarn Spinner 532
Yaud Wall 574
Yellow Peril 88
Yellow Wall 88
Yesterday's News 416
Y-Front 468
Yipycaye 320
YMC Revisited 372
Yorkshire Puddin' 51
Yorkshire Relish 82
You Only Live Twice 325
Yo-Yo 331
Yule Slab 157
Yuletide 157

## Z

Zakely Syndrome 306
Z Climb 65
Z Climb Eliminate 68
Zen 57
Zero Option 233
Zig-Zag 151, 649
Zig-Zag Bear 229
Zig Zag Direct 81
Zoom 565
Zoo York 115

# In Volume 2:
**Ilkley**
**Rylstone**
**Crookrise**
**Widdop**
**Heptonstall**
**Earl Crag**
**Hawkcliffe**
**Shipley Glen**
**Baildon Bank**
**Woodhouse Scar**
**and many more...**

Matt Troilett bouldering at Scout Crag with the glorious Widdop in the background.
Photo: Mike Hutton